Beyond Disney

THE *unofficial* **GUIDE**®

ᵀᴼ SeaWorld,®
Universal Orlando,®
& the Best of
Central Florida

9TH EDITION

COME CHECK US OUT!

Supplement your valuable guidebook with tips, news, and deals by visiting our website:

theunofficialguides.com

Also, while there, sign up for The Unofficial Guide newsletter for even more travel tips and special offers.

Join the conversation on social media:

 @theUGSeries

 theUnofficialGuides

 theUGSeries

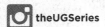 theUGSeries

#theUGseries

Other Unofficial Guides

The Disneyland Story: The Unofficial Guide to the Evolution of Walt Disney's Dream

Mini-Mickey: The Pocket-Sized Unofficial Guide to Walt Disney World

Universal vs. Disney: The Unofficial Guide to American Theme Parks' Greatest Rivalry

The Unofficial Guide Color Companion to Walt Disney World

The Unofficial Guide to Disney Cruise Line

The Unofficial Guide to Disneyland

The Unofficial Guide to Las Vegas

The Unofficial Guide to Universal Orlando

The Unofficial Guide to Walt Disney World

The Unofficial Guide to Walt Disney World with Kids

The Unofficial Guide to Washington, D.C.

Beyond Disney

THE *unofficial* GUIDE®

to SeaWorld,® Universal Orlando,® & the Best of Central Florida

9TH EDITION

BOB SEHLINGER *with*
SETH KUBERSKY

keen
communications

Please note that prices fluctuate over the course of time and that travel information changes under the impact of many factors that influence the travel industry. We therefore suggest that you write or call ahead for confirmation when making your travel plans. Every effort has been made to ensure the accuracy of information throughout this book, and the contents of this publication are believed to be correct at the time of printing. Nevertheless, the publishers cannot accept responsibility for errors or omissions, for changes in details given in this guide, or for the consequences of any reliance on the information provided by the same. Assessments of attractions and so forth are based upon the author's own experience; therefore, descriptions given in this guide necessarily contain an element of subjective opinion, which may not reflect the publisher's opinion or dictate a reader's own experience on another occasion. Readers are invited to write the publisher with ideas, comments, and suggestions for future editions.

Published by:
Keen Communications, LLC
2204 First Ave. S, Ste. 102
Birmingham, AL 35233

Cover design by Scott McGrew

Text design by Vertigo Design with updates by Annie Long

For information on our other products and services or to obtain technical support, please contact us from within the United States at ☎ 888-604-4537 or by fax at ☎ 205-326-1012.

Keen Communications, LLC, also publishes its books in a variety of electronic formats. Some content that appears in print may not be available in electronic formats.

ISBN: 978-1-62809-044-4; eISBN: 978-1-62809-045-1

Manufactured in the United States of America

CONTENTS

LIST OF MAPS

ABOUT *the* AUTHORS

BOB SEHLINGER is the author of *The Unofficial Guide to Walt Disney World* and *The Unofficial Guide to Las Vegas* and is also the publisher of The Unofficial Guide series.

SETH KUBERSKY is the author of The *Unofficial Guide to Universal Orlando,* the coauthor of *The Unofficial Guide to Disneyland,* and a contributor to *The Unofficial Guide to Walt Disney World* and *The Unofficial Guide to Las Vegas.* A resident of Orlando since 1996, Seth is a former employee of Universal Orlando's entertainment department. He covers arts and attractions for the *Orlando Weekly* newspaper, *Orlando Attractions Magazine,* and other publications. You can find Seth online at **sethkubersky.com** or on Twitter **@skubersky.**

INTRODUCTION

WHY "UNOFFICIAL"?

THE AUTHORS AND RESEARCHERS of this guide specifically and categorically declare that they are and always have been totally independent. The material in this guide originated with the authors and has not been reviewed, edited, or in any way approved by the companies whose travel products are discussed. The purpose of this guide is to provide you with the information necessary to tour Central Florida with the greatest efficiency and economy and with the least hassle and stress. In this guide we represent and serve you, the consumer. If a restaurant serves bad food, or a gift item is overpriced, or a certain ride isn't worth the wait, we can say so, and in the process we hope to make your visit more fun, efficient, and economical.

THERE'S ANOTHER WORLD OUT THERE

IF YOU THINK THAT CENTRAL FLORIDA consists only of Walt Disney World, you're wrong. What's more, you're passing up some great fun and amazing sights. Admittedly, it's taken a while, but Walt Disney World now has plenty of competition that measures up toe to toe. And though it may sound blasphemous to suggest a whole vacation in Central Florida without setting foot on Disney property, it's not only possible but also in many ways a fresh and appealing idea.

The big five non-Disney theme parks are Universal Studios Florida, Universal's Islands of Adventure, SeaWorld, Legoland, and Busch Gardens. Each is unique. Universal Studios Florida, a longtime rival of Disney's Hollywood Studios, draws its inspiration from movies and television and is every bit the equal of the Disney movie-themed park. Universal's Islands of Adventure is arguably the most modern, high-tech theme park in the United States, featuring an all-star lineup of thrill rides that makes it the best park in Florida for older kids and young-at-heart adults. For the under-11 crowd, nobody does it better than Legoland. If your primary mission is to delight your pre-tweens, Legoland is the place to go. SeaWorld provides an incomparable glimpse into the world of marine mammals and fish, served up in a way that (for the most part) eliminates those never-ending lines. Finally, Busch Gardens, with its shows, zoological exhibits, and knockout coasters, offers the most eclectic entertainment mix of any theme park we know. All five parks approximate, equal, or exceed the Disney standard without imitating Disney, successfully blending distinctive presentations and personalities into every attraction.

In addition to the big five, there are several specialty parks that are also worthy of your attention. The Kennedy Space Center Visitor Complex at Cape Canaveral provides an inside look at the past, present, and future of America's space program, and Gatorland showcases the alligator, one of the most ancient creatures on Earth. SeaWorld's Discovery Cove offers Central Florida's first-ever dolphin swim, and The Holy Land Experience is the first Christian theme park in the state and quite likely the most elaborate one in the world. All of these places offer an experience that is different from a day at one of the big theme parks, including a respite from standing in line, all of the walking, and the frenetic pace.

But these are just for starters. In Central Florida, you'll also find a vibrant dinner theater scene, three excellent non-Disney water parks, hundreds of holes of mini-golf, nightlife, and great shopping, all surrounded by some of the best hiking, biking, fishing, and canoeing available anywhere.

The **ATTRACTION** *That* **ATE FLORIDA**

BEFORE WALT DISNEY WORLD, Florida was a happy peninsula of many more or less equal tourist attractions. Distributed around the state in great profusion, these attractions constituted the nation's most perennially appealing vacation opportunity. There were the Monkey Jungle, the Orchid Jungle, venerable Marineland, the St. Augustine Alligator Farm, Silver Springs, the Miami Wax Museum, the Sunken Gardens, the Coral Castle, and the Conch Tour Train. These, along with the now-defunct Cypress Gardens, Busch Gardens, and others, were the attractions that ruled Florida. Now, like so many dinosaurs, those remaining survive precariously on the leavings of the greatest beast of them all, Walt Disney World. Old standbys continue to welcome tourists, but when was the last time you planned your vacation around a visit to Jungle Larry's African Safari?

When Walt Disney World arrived on the scene, Florida tourism changed forever. Before Disney (BD), southern Florida was the state's and the nation's foremost tourist destination. Throngs sunned on the beaches of Miami, Hollywood, and Fort Lauderdale and patronized such nearby attractions as the Miami Serpentarium and the Parrot Jungle. Attractions in the Ocala and St. Augustine areas upstate hosted road travelers in great waves as they journeyed to and from southern Florida. At the time, Orlando was a sleepy Central Florida town an hour's drive from Cypress Gardens, with practically no tourist appeal whatsoever.

Then came Disney, snapping up acres of farm- and swampland before anyone even knew who the purchaser was. Bargaining hard, Walt demanded improved highways, tax concessions, bargain financing, and community support. His California Disneyland had been so successful, that whatever he requested, he received.

Generally approving, and hoping for a larger aggregate market, the existing Florida attractions failed to discern the cloud on the horizon. Walt had tipped his hand early, however, and all the cards were on the table. When Disney bought 27,500 Central Florida acres, it was evident that he didn't intend to raise cattle.

The Magic Kingdom opened on October 1, 1971, and was immediately successful. Hotel construction boomed in Orlando, Kissimmee, and around Walt Disney World. Major new attractions popped up along recently completed I-4 to cash in on the tide of tourists arriving at Disney's latest wonder. Walt Disney World became a destination, and suddenly nobody cared as much about going to the beach. The Magic Kingdom was good for two days, and then you could enjoy the rest of the week at SeaWorld, Cypress Gardens, Circus World, Gatorland, Busch Gardens, the Stars Hall of Fame Wax Museum, and the Kennedy Space Center.

These attractions, all practically new and stretching from Florida's east to west coasts, formed what would come to be called the Orlando Wall. Tourists no longer poured into Miami and Fort Lauderdale. Instead they stopped at the Orlando Wall and exhausted themselves and their dollars in the shiny attractions arrayed between Cape Canaveral and St. Petersburg. In southern Florida, venerable attractions held on by a parrot feather, and more than a few closed their doors. Flagship hotels on the fabled Gold Coast went bust or were converted into condominiums.

When Walt Disney World opened, the very definition of a tourist attraction changed. Setting new standards for cleanliness, size, scope, grandeur, variety, and attention to detail, Walt Disney World relegated the majority of Florida's headliner attractions to comparative insignificance almost overnight. Newer attractions such as SeaWorld and the vastly enlarged Busch Gardens successfully matched the standard Disney set. Cypress Gardens, Weeki Wachee, and Silver Springs expanded and modernized. Most other attractions, however, slipped into a limbo of diminished status. Far from being headliners or tourist destinations, they plugged along as local diversions, pulling in the curious, the bored, and the sunburned for mere 2-hour excursions.

Many of the affected attractions were and are wonderful places to spend a day, but even collectively they don't command sufficient appeal to lure many tourists beyond the Orlando Wall. We recommend them, however, not only for a variety of high-quality offerings but also as a glimpse of Florida's golden age, a time of less sophisticated, less plastic pleasures before the Mouse. Take a day or two and drive 3½ hours south of Orlando. Visit the Miami Seaquarium, Vizcaya Museum and Gardens, Fairchild Tropical Botanic Garden, and Lion Country Safari. Drive Collins Avenue along the Gold Coast. You'll be glad you did.

When Epcot (then EPCOT Center) opened in Walt Disney World on October 1, 1982, another seismic shock reverberated throughout the Florida attractions industry. This time it wasn't only the smaller and more vulnerable attractions that were affected but also the newer large-scale attractions along the Orlando Wall. Suddenly, Disney World swallowed up another one or two days of each tourist's vacation week. When the Magic Kingdom stood alone, most visitors had three or four days remaining to sample other attractions. With the addition of Epcot, that time was cut to one or two days.

Disney ensured its market share by creating multiday admission passes, which allowed unlimited access to both the Magic Kingdom and Epcot. More cost-efficient than a one-day pass to a single park, these passes kept the guest on Disney turf for three to five days.

Kennedy Space Center and SeaWorld, by virtue of their very specialized products, continued to prosper after Epcot opened. Most other attractions were forced to focus on local markets. Some, such as Busch Gardens, did very well, with increased local support replacing the decreased numbers of Disney World tourists coming over for the day. Others, such as Circus World and the Stars Hall of Fame Wax Museum, passed into history.

Though long an innovator, Disney in the mid-1980s turned to copying existing successful competitors. Except *copying* is not exactly the right word. What Disney did was take a competitor's concept, improve it, and reproduce it in Disney style and on a grand scale.

The first competitor to feel the heat was SeaWorld, when Disney added the Living Seas Pavilion to the Future World section of Epcot. SeaWorld, however, had killer whales, the Shark Encounter, and sufficient corporate resources to remain preeminent among marine exhibits. Still, many Disney patrons willingly substituted a visit to the Living Seas for a visit to SeaWorld.

One of Disney's own products was threatened when the Wet 'n Wild water park took aim at the older and smaller but more aesthetically pleasing River Country. Never one to take a challenge sitting down, Disney responded in 1989 with the opening of Typhoon Lagoon, then the world's largest swimming theme park.

Also in 1989, Disney opened Pleasure Island, a single-cover multinightclub entertainment complex patterned on Orlando's successful

Church Street Station. Tourist traffic around the theme parks started gravitating to Pleasure Island for nightlife rather than traveling to Church Street.

The third big Disney opening occurred in 1989 with Disney-MGM Studios (now Disney's Hollywood Studios), a combination working motion picture and TV-production complex and theme park. Copying the long-lauded Universal Studios tour in Southern California, Disney-MGM Studios was rushed into operation after Universal announced its plans for a Central Florida park.

Disney-MGM Studios, however, affected much more than Universal's plans. With the opening of Disney-MGM, the Three-Day World Passport was discontinued. Instead, Disney patrons were offered a single-day pass or the more economical multiday passports, good for either four or five days. With three theme parks on a multiday pass, plus two swimming parks, several golf courses, various lakes, and a nighttime entertainment complex, Disney effectively swallowed up the average family's entire vacation. Break away to SeaWorld or the Kennedy Space Center for the day? How about a day at the ocean (remember the ocean)? Fat chance.

In 1995, Disney opened Blizzard Beach, a third swimming theme park, and began plans for a fourth major theme park, the Animal Kingdom, designed to compete directly with Busch Gardens. During the same year, the first phase of Disney's All-Star Resorts came online, featuring (by Disney standards) budget accommodations. The location and rates of the All-Star Resorts were intended to capture the market of the smaller independent and chain hotels along US 192 (Irlo Bronson Memorial Highway). Disney even discussed constructing a monorail to the airport so that visitors wouldn't have to set foot in Orlando. Though this proved impractical, Disney eventually accomplished the same thing by launching Disney's Magical Express, free bus transportation to and from the airport.

As time passed, Disney continued to consolidate its hold. With the openings in 1996 of Disney's BoardWalk, Fantasia Gardens miniature golf, and the Walt Disney World Speedway; in 1997 of Disney's Wide World of Sports, Disney's West Side shopping and entertainment district, and a new convention center; and in 1998 of the Animal Kingdom, Disney attracted armies of Central Floridians to compensate for decreased tourist traffic during off-season. For people who can never get enough, there is the town of Celebration, a Disney residential land-development project where home buyers can live in Disney-designed houses in Disney-designed neighborhoods, protected by Disney-designed security.

In 1999, however, for the first time in many years, the initiative passed to Disney's competitors. Universal Studios Florida became a bona fide destination with the opening of its second major theme park (Islands of Adventure), on-property hotels, and the CityWalk dining and entertainment complex that directly competed with Pleasure Island (and Church Street Station). SeaWorld announced the 2000 debut of its Discovery Cove park, and Busch Gardens turned up the heat with the addition of new roller coasters. The latest additions bring Busch Gardens's total to seven (soon to be eight) coasters, making them the roller-coaster capital of Florida. Giving Disney some of its own medicine, Busch Gardens, SeaWorld, and Universal combined with Wet 'n Wild to offer multiday passes good at any of the parks. In 2010 the opening of The Wizarding World of Harry Potter at Islands of Adventure dealt yet another blow to Walt Disney World, as did the opening of Diagon Alley at Universal Studios Florida in 2014. Though it may be too early to say that Disney's hegemony is at an end, one thing's for sure: Disney's not the only 800-pound gorilla on the block anymore.

The tourism slump caused by the Great Recession is just now running its course. While the big boys are tightening their belts and cutting corners where they can, some have had to call it quits. Splendid China—a vast, landscaped garden filled with miniature re-creations of Chinese buildings, monuments, palaces, cities, temples, and landmarks—closed its doors in 2003; Water Mania, a swimming park, followed in 2005; and Cypress Gardens said good-bye in 2009 after a valiant attempt at staying open only to reemerge in 2011 as Legoland Florida. On September 30, 2013, Silver Springs, Florida's oldest tourist attraction, dating from the 1870s, ceased operations and turned the property over to the state.

Even with these recent bad patches, most attractions and theme parks in Central Florida are just learning how to become more adaptive and creative. Those that survive will be leaner, cleaner, and even more competitive than ever before. All this competition, of course, is good for Central Florida, and it's good for you. The time, money, and energy invested in developing ever-better parks and attractions boggle the mind. Nobody, including Disney, can rest on their laurels in this market. And as for you, you're certain to find something new and amazing on every visit.

TRYING *to* REASON *with* *the* TOURIST SEASON

CENTRAL FLORIDA THEME PARKS and attractions are busiest December 25 through the first few days of January. Next busiest is the spring break period from mid-March through the week of Easter, then Thanksgiving week. Following those are the first few weeks of June, when summer vacation starts, and the week of Presidents' Day.

The least-busy time is from Labor Day in September through the beginning of October. Next slowest are the weeks in mid-January after the Martin Luther King Jr. holiday weekend up to Presidents' Day in February. The weeks after Thanksgiving and before December 25 are less crowded than average, as is mid-April–mid-May, after spring break and before Memorial Day.

Late February, March, and early April are dicey. Crowds ebb and flow according to spring break schedules and the timing of Presidents' Day weekend. Besides being asphalt-melting hot, July brings throngs of South American tourists on their winter holiday.

WE'VE GOT WEATHER!

Tourists visit Florida year-round to enjoy the temperate tropical and subtropical climates. The best weather months generally are October, November, March, and April (see table below). Fall is usually dry, whereas spring is wetter. December, January, and February vary, with average highs of 72°–73°F intermixed with highs in the 50°–65°F range. May is hot but tolerable. June, July, August, and September are the warmest months. Rain is possible anytime, usually in the form of scattered thunderstorms. An entire day of rain is unusual.

ORLANDO CLIMATE

JAN	FEB	MAR	APR	MAY	JUN	JUL	AUG	SEP	OCT	NOV	DEC
AVERAGE DAILY LOW (°F)											
47	50	54	59	65	71	73	73	72	66	58	51
AVERAGE DAILY HIGH (°F)											
71	73	78	83	89	91	92	92	90	84	78	72
AVERAGE DAILY TEMPERATURE (°F)											
60	61	67	71	77	81	82	83	81	75	68	62
AVERAGE DAILY HUMIDITY PERCENTAGE											
62	73	71	70	71	70	74	76	76	75	74	73
AVERAGE RAINFALL PER MONTH (INCHES)											
2.9	2.7	4.0	2.3	3.1	8.3	7.0	7.7	5.1	2.5	2.1	2.9
NUMBER OF DAYS OF RAIN PER MONTH											
6	7	8	6	8	14	17	16	14	9	6	6

IT TAKES MORE THAN ONE BOOK *to* DO *the* JOB RIGHT

WE'VE BEEN COVERING CENTRAL FLORIDA tourism for almost 30 years. We began by lumping everything into one guidebook, but that was when the Magic Kingdom was the only theme park at Walt Disney World, at the very beginning of the boom that has made Central Florida the most visited tourist destination on Earth. As Central Florida grew, so did our guide, until eventually we needed to split the tome into smaller, more in-depth (and more portable) volumes. The result is a small library of titles, designed to work both individually and together. All provide specialized information tailored to very specific Central Florida and Walt

Disney World visitors. Though some tips (such as arriving at the theme parks early) are echoed or elaborated in all the guides, most of the information in each book is unique.

- *The Unofficial Guide to Walt Disney World* is the centerpiece of our Central Florida coverage because, well, Walt Disney World is the centerpiece of most Central Florida vacations. *The Unofficial Guide to Walt Disney World* is evaluative, comprehensive, and instructive—the ultimate planning tool for a successful Walt Disney World vacation. The Unofficial Guide to Walt Disney World is supplemented by six additional titles, including this guide:

- *Mini-Mickey: The Pocket-Sized Unofficial Guide to Walt Disney World,* by Bob Sehlinger, Len Testa, and Ritchey Halphen

- *The Unofficial Guide Color Companion to Walt Disney World,* by Bob Sehlinger and Len Testa

- *The Unofficial Guide to Universal Orlando,* by Seth Kubersky with Bob Sehlinger and Len Testa

- *The Unofficial Guide to Walt Disney World with Kids,* by Bob Sehlinger and Liliane J. Opsomer with Len Testa

- *The Unofficial Guide to Disney Cruise Line,* by Len Testa with Laurel Stewart, Erin Foster, and Ritchey Halphen

Mini-Mickey is a nifty, portable, CliffsNotes-style version of *The Unofficial Guide to Walt Disney World.* Updated semiannually, it distills information from this comprehensive guide to help short-stay or last-minute visitors decide quickly how to plan their limited hours at Disney World. **The Unofficial Guide Color Companion to Walt Disney World** is a visual feast that proves a picture is worth 1,000 words. **The Unofficial Guide to Universal Orlando** is our first in-depth guide devoted to Disney's fastest-growing competitor, featuring a greatly expanded version of the Universal information found in this volume. **The Unofficial Guide to Walt Disney World with Kids** presents a wealth of planning and touring tips for a successful Disney family vacation. **The Unofficial Guide to Disney Cruise Line** presents advice for first-time cruisers; money-saving tips for booking your cruise; and detailed profiles for restaurants, shows, and nightclubs, along with deck plans and thorough coverage of the ports visited by DCL. Finally, this guide, **Beyond Disney,** is a complete consumer guide to the non-Disney attractions, hotels, restaurants, and nightlife in Orlando and Central Florida. All of the guides are available at most bookstores.

LETTERS *and* COMMENTS *from* READERS

MANY OF THOSE WHO USE The Unofficial Guides write us to make comments or share their own strategies for visiting Central Florida. We appreciate all such input, both positive and critical, and encourage our readers to continue writing. Readers' comments and observations are frequently incorporated into revised editions of The Unofficial Guides and have contributed immeasurably to their improvement. If you write us, you can rest assured that we won't release your name and address to any mailing lists, direct-mail advertisers, or other third party.

HOW TO WRITE THE AUTHORS

Bob Sehlinger and Seth Kubersky
The Unofficial Guides
2204 First Ave. S, Ste. 102
Birmingham, AL 35233
UnofficialGuides@menasharidge.com
Or visit us online at **unofficialguides.com**.

When you write by mail, put your address on both your letter and envelope, because sometimes the two get separated. It is also a good idea to include your phone number. If you e-mail us, let us know where you're from. And remember, as travel writers, we're often out of the office for long periods of time, so forgive us if our response is slow.

PART ONE

ACCOMMODATIONS

■■ ORLANDO LODGING OPTIONS

SELECTING AND BOOKING A HOTEL

LODGING COSTS IN ORLANDO vary incredibly. If you shop around, you can find a clean motel with a pool for as low as $40 a night. Because of hot competition, discounts abound, particularly for AAA and AARP members. There are four primary areas to consider:

1. INTERNATIONAL DRIVE AREA This area, about 5 minutes from Universal, parallels I-4 on its eastern side and offers a wide selection of hotels and restaurants. Prices range from $56 to $400 per night. The chief drawbacks are terribly congested roads, countless traffic signals, and inadequate access to westbound I-4. While International Drive's biggest bottleneck is its intersection with Sand Lake Road, the mile between Kirkman and Sand Lake Roads is almost always gridlocked.

Regarding traffic on International Drive (known locally as I-Drive), a convention-goer from Islip, New York, weighed in with this:

> When I visited Orlando with my family last summer, we wasted huge chunks of time in traffic on International Drive. Our hotel was in the section between the big McDonald's [at Sand Lake Road] and Wet 'n Wild [at Universal Boulevard]. There are practically no left-turn lanes in this section, so anyone turning left can hold up traffic for a long time.

Traffic aside, a man from Ottawa, Ontario, sings the praises of his I-Drive experience:

> International Drive is the place to stay in Orlando. Your description of this location failed to point out that there are several discount stores, boutiques, restaurants, mini-putts, and other entertainment facilities, all within walking distance of remarkably inexpensive accommodations and a short drive away from the attractions.

I-Drive hotels are listed in the *Orlando Official Visitors Guide,* published by Visit Orlando. To obtain a copy, call ☎ 800-972-3304 or 407-363-5872, or check **visitorlando.com.**

2. LAKE BUENA VISTA AND THE I-4 CORRIDOR A number of hotels are along FL 535 and west of I-4 between Walt Disney World and I-4's intersection with Florida's Turnpike. They're easily reached from the interstate and are near many restaurants, including those on International Drive. The *Orlando Official Visitors Guide* (see above) lists most of them. This area includes Disney's new Flamingo Crossings Value-priced resort area (see page 31).

3. US 192 (IRLO BRONSON MEMORIAL HIGHWAY) This is the highway to Kissimmee, to the southeast of Disney World. In addition to large full-service hotels, many small, privately owned motels often offer a good value. The number and variety of restaurants on US 192 has increased markedly, compensating for the area's primary shortcoming. Locally, US 192 is called Irlo Bronson Memorial Highway. The section to the west of I-4 and the Disney Maingate is designated Irlo Bronson Memorial Highway West, while the section from I-4 running southeast toward Kissimmee is Irlo Bronson Memorial Highway East.

The combined east and west sections have numbered mile markers that simplify navigation if you know which marker is closest to your destination. Though traffic is heavy on Irlo Bronson west of the Maingate, it doesn't compare to the congestion east of the Maingate and I-4 between mile markers 8 and 13. This section can—and should—be avoided by using **Osceola Parkway,** a toll road that parallels Irlo Bronson to the north and terminates in Walt Disney World at the entrance to Animal Kingdom.

Hotels on US 192 and in Kissimmee are listed in the *Kissimmee Visitor's Guide.* Order a copy by calling ☎ 800-327-9159, or view it online at **experiencekissimmee.com.**

4. UNIVERSAL STUDIOS AREA In the triangular area bordered by I-4 on the southeast, Vineland Road on the north, and Turkey Lake Road on the west are Universal Orlando and the hotels most convenient to it. Running north–south through the middle of the triangle is Kirkman Road, which connects to I-4. On the east side of Kirkman are a number of independent hotels and restaurants. Universal hotels, theme parks, and CityWalk are west of Kirkman. Traffic in this area is not nearly as congested as on nearby International Drive, and there are good interstate connections in both directions.

HOTEL SHOPPING ON THE INTERNET: WELCOME TO THE WILD WEST

UNMATCHED AS AN EFFICIENT and timely distributor of information, the Internet has become the primary resource for travelers seeking to shop for and book their own air travel, hotels, rental cars,

Continued on page 18

South Orlando

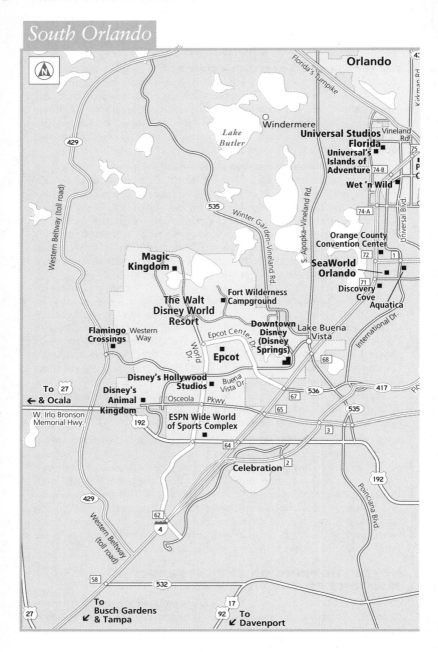

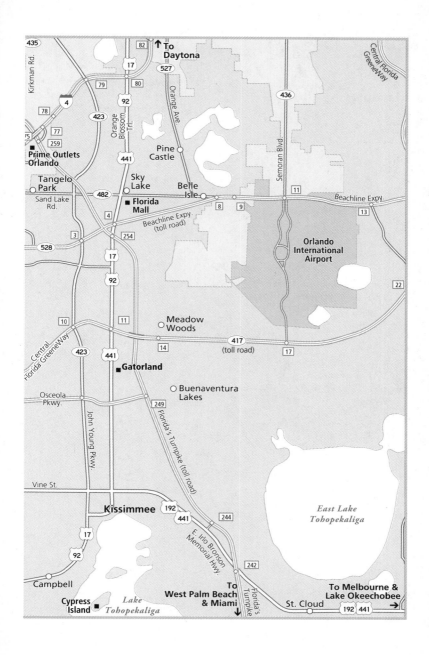

Hotel Concentrations Around Orlando-Area Attractions

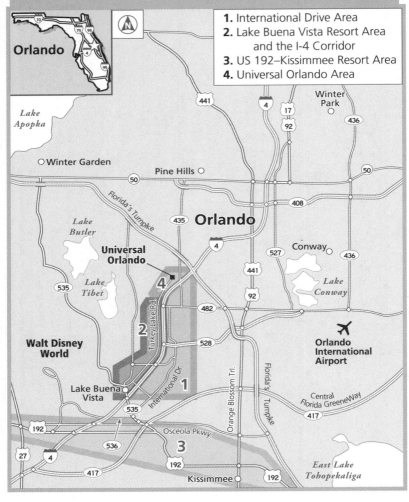

1. International Drive Area
2. Lake Buena Vista Resort Area and the I-4 Corridor
3. US 192–Kissimmee Resort Area
4. Universal Orlando Area

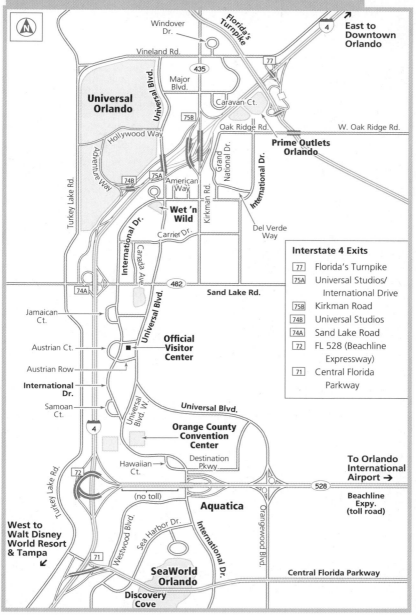

International Drive & Universal Areas

Interstate 4 Exits

77	Florida's Turnpike
75A	Universal Studios/International Drive
75B	Kirkman Road
74B	Universal Studios
74A	Sand Lake Road
72	FL 528 (Beachline Expressway)
71	Central Florida Parkway

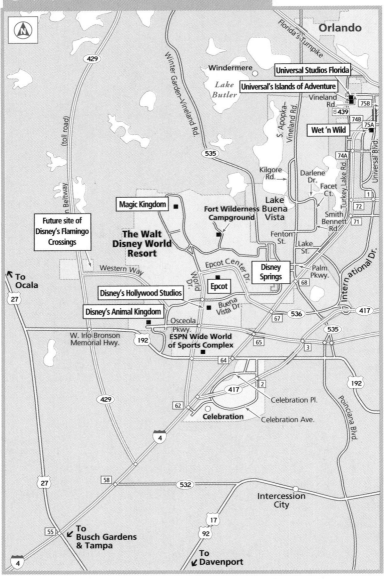

Lake Buena Vista Resort Area & the I-4 Corridor

US 192–Kissimmee Resort Area

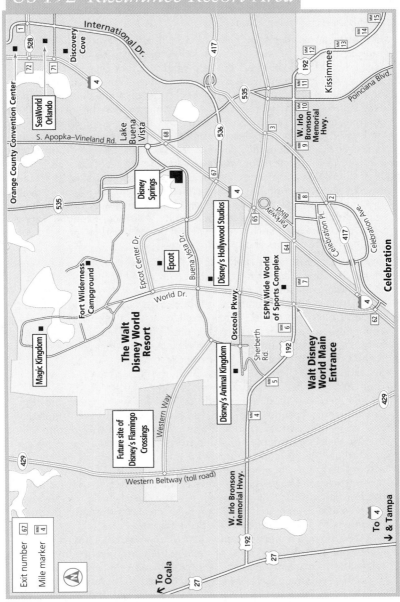

Continued from page 11

entertainment, and travel packages. It's by far the best direct-to-consumer distribution channel in history.

INTERNET ECONOMICS 101 The evolution of selling travel on the web has radically altered the way airlines, hotels, cruise lines, rental-car companies, and the like do business. Before the Internet, they depended on travel agents or direct contact with customers by phone. Transaction costs were high because companies were obligated to pay commissions and fund labor-intensive in-house reservations departments. With the advent of the Internet, inexpensive e-commerce transactions became possible: Airlines and rental-car companies began using their own websites to effectively cut travel agents out of the sales process. Hotels also developed websites but continued to depend on wholesalers and travel agents as well.

It didn't take long before independent websites sprang up that sold travel products from a wide assortment of suppliers, often at deep discounts. These sites, called **online travel agencies (OTAs),** include such familiar names as **Travelocity, Orbitz, Priceline, Expedia, Hotels .com,** and **Hotwire.** Those mentioned and others like them attract huge numbers of customers shopping for hotels.

OTAS AND THE MERCHANT MODEL In the beginning, hotels paid OTAs about the same commission that they paid travel agents, but then the OTAs began applying the thumbscrews, forcing hotels to make the transition from a simple commission model to what's called a merchant model. Under this model, hotels provide an OTA with a deeply discounted room rate that the OTA then marks up and sells. The difference between the marked-up price and the discounted rate paid to the hotel is the OTA's gross profit. If, for example, a hotel makes $120 rooms available to an OTA at a 33% discount, or $80, and the OTA sells the room at $110, the OTA's gross profit is $30 ($110 − $80).

The merchant model, originally devised for wholesalers and tour operators, has been around since long before the Internet. Wholesalers and tour operators, then and now, must commit to a certain volume of business, commit to guaranteed room allotments, pay deposits, and bundle the discounted rates with other travel services so that the actual hotel rate remains hidden within the bundle. This is known as opaque pricing. The merchant model costs the hotel two to three times the normal travel-agent commission—considered justifiable because the wholesalers and tour operators also promote the hotel through brochures, websites, trade shows, print ads, and events.

OTAs now demand the equivalent of a wholesale commission or higher but are subject to none of the requirements imposed on wholesalers and tour operators. For instance, they don't have to commit to a specified volume of sales or keep discounted room rates opaque. In return, hotels give up 20–50% of gross profit and are rewarded by having their rock-bottom rates plastered all over the Internet, with corresponding damage to their image and brand.

What's more, doing business with OTAs is very expensive for hotels. The cost for a hotel to sell a multiday booking on its own website is $10–$12, including site hosting and analytics, marketing costs, and management fees. This is 10–20 times cheaper than the cost of the same booking through an OTA. Let's say a hotel sells a $100 room for six nights on its own website. Again, the booking would cost the hotel around $12, or $2 per night. If an OTA books the same room having secured it from the hotel at a 30% discount, the hotel receives $70 per night from the OTA. Thus the hotel's cost for the OTA booking is $30 per night, or $180 for six nights—15 times as costly as selling the room online with no middleman.

In the hotel industry, occupancy rates are important, but simply getting bodies into beds doesn't guarantee a profit. A more critical metric is *revenue per available room* (RevPAR). For a hotel full of guests booked through an OTA, RevPAR will be 20–50% lower than for the same number of guests who booked the hotel directly, either through the hotel's website or by phone.

It's no wonder, then, that hotels and OTAs have a love–hate relationship. Likewise, it's perfectly understandable that hotels want to maximize direct bookings through their own websites and minimize OTA bookings. Problem is, the better-known OTAs draw a lot more web traffic than a given hotel's (or even hotel chain's) website. So the challenge for the hotel becomes how to shift room-shoppers away from the OTAs and channel them to its website. A number of hotel corporations, including Choice, Hilton, Hyatt, InterContinental, Marriott, and Wyndham, have risen to that challenge by forming their own OTA called **Room Key** (**roomkey.com**). The participating chains hope that working together will generate enough visitor traffic to make Room Key competitive with the Expedias and Travelocities of the world.

MORE POWER TO THE SHOPPER Understanding the market dynamics we've described gives you a powerful tool for obtaining the best rates for the hotel of your choice. It's why we tell you to shop the web for the lowest price available and then call your travel agent or the hotel itself to ask if they can beat it. Any savvy reservationist knows that selling you the room directly will both cut the hotel's cost and improve gross margin. If the reservationist can't help you, ask to speak to his or her supervisor. (We've actually had to explain hotel economics to more than a few clueless reservation agents.)

As for travel agents, they have clout based on the volume of business they send to a particular hotel or chain and can usually negotiate a rate even lower than what you've found on the Internet. Even if the agent can't beat the price, he or she can often obtain upgrades, preferred views, free breakfasts, and other deal sweeteners. When we bump into a great deal on the web, we call our agent. Often she can beat the deal or improve on it, perhaps with an upgrade. *Reminder:* Except for special arrangements agreed to by you, the fee or commission due to your travel agent will be paid by the hotel.

THE SECRET The key to shopping on the Internet is, well, shopping. When we're really hungry for a deal, there are a number of sites that we always check out:

OUR FAVORITE ONLINE HOTEL RESOURCES
mousesavers.com Best site for hotels in Disney World
hotelcoupons.com Self-explanatory
experiencekissimmee.com Primarily US 192–Kissimmee area hotels
orlandovacation.com Great rates for condos and home rentals
visitorlando.com Good info; not user-friendly for booking

We scour these sites for unusually juicy hotel deals that meet our criteria (location, quality, price, amenities). If we find a hotel that fills the bill, we check it out at other websites and comparative travel search engines such as **Kayak** (**kayak.com**) and **Mobissimo** (**mobissimo.com**) to see who has the best rate. (As an aside, Kayak used to be purely a search engine but now sells travel products, raising the issue of whether products not sold by Kayak are equally likely to come up in a search. Mobissimo, on the other hand, only links potential buyers to provider websites.) Your initial shopping effort should take about 15–20 minutes, faster if you can zero in quickly on a particular hotel.

*un*official **TIP**
Request a renovated room at your hotel—these can be much nicer than the older rooms.

Next, armed with your insider knowledge of hotel economics, call the hotel or have your travel agent call. Start by asking about specials. If there are none, or if the hotel can't beat the best price you've found on the Internet, share your findings and ask if the hotel can do better. Sometimes you'll be asked for proof of the rate you've discovered online—to be prepared for this, go to the site and enter the dates of your stay, plus the rate you've found to make sure it's available. If it is, print the page with this information and have it handy for your travel agent or for when you call the hotel. (*Note:* Always call the hotel's local number, not its national reservations number.)

INDEPENDENT AND BOUTIQUE HOTEL DEALS While chain hotels worry about sales costs and profit margins, independent and so-called boutique hotels are concerned about discoverability—making themselves known to the traveling public. The market is huge and it's increasingly hard for these hotels to get noticed, especially when they're competing with major chains. Independent and boutique hotels work on the premise that if they can get you through the front door, you'll become a loyal customer. For these hotels, substantially discounting rates is part of their marketing plan to build a client base. Because such hotels get lost on the big OTA sites and on search engines like Kayak and Google, they've jumped on the flash-sale bandwagon. Offering almost irresistible rates on daily-coupon sites like **Groupon** and **LivingSocial,** the independents can get their product in front of thousands of potential guests.

These offers are very generous but also time-limited. If you're in the market, though, you'll be hard-pressed to find better deals. While an OTA such as Expedia generally obtains rooms at a 20–35% discount off the hotel's published rate, flash sites cut deals at an extra-deep discount. This allows their subscribers to bid on or secure coupons for rooms that are often as much as 50% lower than the hotel's standard rate, and that frequently include perks such as meals, free parking, waived resort fees, shopping vouchers, spa services, and entertainment. On Groupon's home page, click "Get-aways" or just wait for Getaway coupons by e-mail as part of your free subscription. On LivingSocial you have to specifically subscribe to "Adventures" and "Escapes"; otherwise, you'll receive only non-travel-related offers.

ANOTHER WRINKLE Finally, a quick word about a recent trend: bidding sites. On these sites you enter the type of accommodation you desire and your travel dates, and hotels will bid for your reservation. Some sites require that you already have a confirmed booking from a hotel before you can bid. A variation is that you reserve a room at a particular hotel for a set rate. If the rate drops subsequently, you get money back; if the rate goes up, your original rate is locked in.

Late 2011 and early 2012 saw the launch of TripAdvisor's **Tingo** (**tingo.com**) and Montreal-based **BackBid** (**backbid.com**), each claiming to be able to beat rates offered by hotel websites and OTAs.

Slamming the lodging industry in full-frontal assault is **Airbnb** (**airbnb.com**), a site that hooks up travelers with owner-hosted alternative options all over the world: bedrooms in people's homes, private apartments, vacation homes, and even live-on boats. The hotel industry is up in arms because Airbnb is not subject to most of the regulation and taxes that dedicated hotels must observe. Though an Airbnb reservation is a little dicier than one with a chain hotel, it's also considerably cheaper. Most reports on Airbnb have been positive, and we've had good experiences with them ourselves.

IS IT WORTH IT? You might be asking yourself if it's worth all this effort to save a few bucks. Saving $10 on a room doesn't sound like a big deal, but if you're staying six nights, that adds up to $60. Earlier we referred to unusually juicy deals, deep discounts predicated by who-knows-what circumstances that add up to big money. They're available every day, and with a little perseverance you'll find them. Good hunting!

New Is Better—and Sometimes Cheaper

New hotels rarely burst on the scene at 100% occupancy. During a hotel's first year, when it strives to generate buzz and attract clientele, it often offers deeply discounted rooms. This is true even of prestigious brands. One thing's for sure: A new hotel will charge less the first few months that it's open than subsequently, and a hotel that opens during low season will discount more than hotels that come on line during high season.

Two Other Discount Sources Worth Mentioning

1. ORLANDO MAGICARD This discount program is sponsored by Visit Orlando. Cardholders are eligible for discounts of 12–50% at about 50 hotels. The Magicard is also good for discounts at some area attractions, three dinner theaters, museums, performing-arts venues, restaurants, shops, and more. Valid for up to six persons, the card isn't available for larger groups or conventions.

To obtain a free Magicard and a list of participating hotels and attractions, call ☎ 800-643-9492 or 407-363-5872. On the web, go to **visitorlando.com/magicard;** the Magicard and accompanying brochure can be printed from a personal computer. If you miss getting one before you leave home, obtain one at the Visit Orlando Official Visitors Center at 8723 International Dr. When you call for your Magicard, also request the *Orlando Official Visitors Guide.*

2. HOTELCOUPONS.COM *FLORIDA GUIDE* This book of coupons for lodging statewide is free in many restaurants and motels on main highways leading to Florida. Because most travelers make reservations before leaving home, picking up the book en route doesn't help much. To view it online or sign up for a free monthly guide sent by e-mail, visit **hotel coupons.com.** For a hard copy ($3 for handling, $5 if shipped to Canada), call ☎ 800-222-3948 Monday–Friday, 8 a.m.–5 p.m. Eastern time.

Scratch That Itch . . . for Information

Granted, it won't help you find good deals on hotels, but **The Bedbug Registry** (**bedbugregistry.com**) is nonetheless a useful resource, allowing you to peruse reports of bedbug and other insect infestations at any hotel in the United States. Simply enter the name, city, and state of the property in question; you can also submit a report of your own. Understand that bedbug outbreaks are usually confined to particular rooms and that the creepy-crawlies were probably brought in by previous guests.

CONDOMINIUMS AND VACATION HOMES

VACATION HOMES ARE FREESTANDING, while condominiums are essentially one- to three-bedroom accommodations in a larger building housing a number of similar units. Because condos tend to be part of large developments (frequently time-shares), amenities such as swimming pools, playgrounds, game arcades, and fitness centers often rival those found in the best hotels. Generally speaking, condo developments don't have restaurants, lounges, or spas.

With a condo, if something goes wrong, someone will be on hand to fix the problem. Vacation homes rented from a property-management company likewise will have someone to come to the rescue, though responsiveness varies from company to company. If you rent directly from an owner, correcting problems is often more difficult, particularly when the owner doesn't live in the same area as the rental home.

In a vacation home, all the amenities are contained in the home. Depending on the specific home, you might find a small swimming pool, hot tub, two-car garage, family room, game room, and even a home theater. Features found in both condos and vacation homes include full kitchens, laundry rooms, TVs, DVD players, and frequently stereos. Interestingly, though almost all freestanding vacation homes have private pools, very few have backyards. This means that, except for swimming, the kids are pretty much relegated to playing in the house.

Time-share condos are clones when it comes to furniture and decor, but single-owner condos and vacation homes are furnished and decorated in a style that reflects the taste of the owner. Vacation homes, usually one- to two-story houses in a subdivision, very rarely afford interesting views (though some overlook lakes or natural areas), while condos, especially the high-rise variety, sometimes offer exceptional ones.

The Price Is Nice

The best deals in lodging in the Orlando area are vacation homes and single-owner condos. Prices range from about $65 a night for two-bedroom condos and town homes to $200–$500 a night for three- to seven-bedroom homes. Forgetting about taxes to keep the comparison simple, let's compare renting a vacation home to staying at the Cabana Bay Beach Resort, a Universal value resort. A family of two parents, two teens, and two grandparents would need two hotel rooms at Cabana Bay. At the lowest rate obtainable, that would run you $119 per night, per room, or $238 total. Rooms are 300 square feet each, so you'd have a total of 600 square feet. Each room has a private bath and a television.

Renting at the same time of year from **All Star Vacation Homes** (no relation to Disney's All-Star Resorts), you can stay at a 2,001-square-foot, three-bedroom, two-bath condo 3.5 miles from Universal Orlando for $159 per night.

The condo comes with the following features and amenities: a big-screen TV with surround sound, a computer, three additional TVs (one in each bedroom, all with DVD players and one with a PlayStation 2), a fully equipped kitchen, a full-size washer and dryer, and a fully furnished private patio.

The condo is in a community with a 24-hour gated entrance. At the community center are a large swimming pool, a kiddie pool, a hot tub, a poolside refreshments bar, a fitness center, a theater, a game room, a basketball court, a business center, and a convenience store.

One thing we like about All Star Vacation Homes is that its website, **allstarvacationhomes.com,** offers detailed information, including a dozen or more photos of each specific home. When you book, the home you've been looking at is the actual one you're reserving. If you want to see how the condo previously described is furnished, for instance, go to the home page, scroll down to "Select Code" and look for a small search window in the upper-right side of the photograph that reads "Search a Property Code." Enter **5-5024 SL-VC #305** in the search window. You'll be taken to another page with a description of the condo, a slide show, a floor plan, and additional information.

Continued on page 26

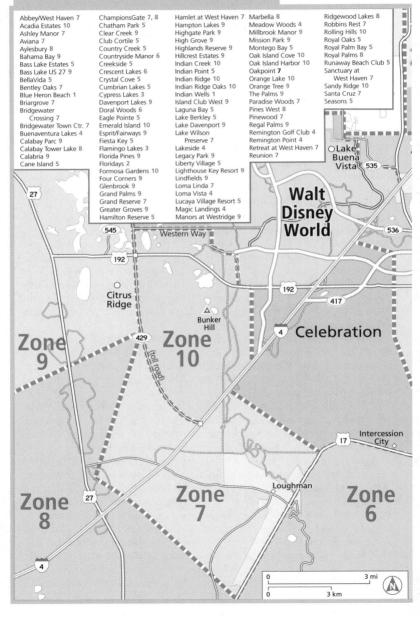

Rental-Home Developments in South Orlando

Abbey/West Haven 7
Acadia Estates 10
Ashley Manor 7
Aviana 7
Aylesbury 8
Bahama Bay 9
Bass Lake Estates 5
Bass Lake US 27 9
BellaVida 5
Bentley Oaks 7
Blue Heron Beach 1
Briargrove 7
Bridgewater
   Crossing 7
Bridgewater Town Ctr. 7
Buenaventura Lakes 4
Calabay Parc 9
Calabay Tower Lake 8
Calabria 9
Cane Island 5

ChampionsGate 7, 8
Chatham Park 5
Clear Creek 9
Club Cortile 5
Country Creek 5
Countryside Manor 6
Creekside 5
Crescent Lakes 6
Crystal Cove 5
Cumbrian Lakes 5
Cypress Lakes 3
Davenport Lakes 9
Doral Woods 6
Eagle Pointe 5
Emerald Island 10
Esprit/Fairways 9
Fiesta Key 5
Flamingo Lakes 3
Florida Pines 9
Floridays 2
Formosa Gardens 10
Four Corners 9
Glenbrook 9
Grand Reserve 7
Greater Groves 9
Hamilton Reserve 5

Hamlet at West Haven 7
Hampton Lakes 9
Highgate Park 9
High Grove 9
Highlands Reserve 9
Hillcrest Estates 9
Indian Creek 10
Indian Point 5
Indian Ridge 10
Indian Ridge Oaks 10
Indian Wells 1
Island Club West 9
Laguna Bay 5
Lake Berkley 5
Lake Davenport 9
Lake Wilson
   Preserve 7
Lakeside 4
Legacy Park 9
Liberty Village 5
Lighthouse Key Resort 9
Lindfields 9
Loma Linda 7
Loma Vista 4
Lucaya Village Resort 5
Magic Landings 4
Manors at Westridge 9

Marbella 8
Meadow Woods 4
Millbrook Manor 9
Mission Park 9
Montego Bay 5
Oak Island Cove 10
Oak Island Harbor 10
Oakpoint 7
Orange Lake 10
Orange Tree 9
The Palms 9
Paradise Woods 7
Pines West 8
Pinewood 7
Regal Palms 9
Remington Golf Club 4
Remington Point 4
Retreat at West Haven 7
Reunion 7

Ridgewood Lakes 8
Robbins Rest 7
Rolling Hills 10
Royal Oaks 5
Royal Palm Bay 5
Royal Palms 8
Runaway Beach Club 5
Sanctuary at
   West Haven 7
Sandy Ridge 10
Santa Cruz 7
Seasons 5

○ Lake Buena Vista 535

27

545

Western Way

192

○ Citrus Ridge

Bunker Hill

Walt Disney World

536

192

417

Zone 9

429 (toll road)

Zone 10

4 Celebration

Zone 8

27

Zone 7

Loughman

17 Intercession City ◇

Zone 6

4

0   3 mi
0   3 km

N

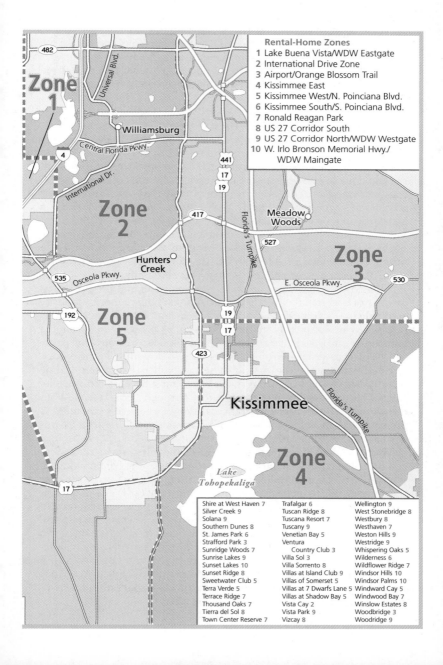

Rental-Home Zones
1 Lake Buena Vista/WDW Eastgate
2 International Drive Zone
3 Airport/Orange Blossom Trail
4 Kissimmee East
5 Kissimmee West/N. Poinciana Blvd.
6 Kissimmee South/S. Poinciana Blvd.
7 Ronald Reagan Park
8 US 27 Corridor South
9 US 27 Corridor North/WDW Westgate
10 W. Irlo Bronson Memorial Hwy./
     WDW Maingate

Shire at West Haven 7
Silver Creek 9
Solana 9
Southern Dunes 8
St. James Park 6
Strafford Park 3
Sunridge Woods 7
Sunrise Lakes 9
Sunset Lakes 10
Sunset Ridge 8
Sweetwater Club 5
Terra Verde 5
Terrace Ridge 7
Thousand Oaks 7
Tierra del Sol 8
Town Center Reserve 7

Trafalgar 6
Tuscan Ridge 8
Tuscana Resort 7
Tuscany 9
Venetian Bay 5
Ventura
  Country Club 3
Villa Sol 3
Villa Sorrento 8
Villas at Island Club 9
Villas of Somerset 5
Villas at 7 Dwarfs Lane 5
Villas at Shadow Bay 5
Vista Cay 2
Vista Park 9
Vizcay 8

Wellington 9
West Stonebridge 8
Westbury 8
Westhaven 7
Weston Hills 9
Westridge 9
Whispering Oaks 5
Wilderness 6
Wildflower Ridge 7
Windsor Hills 10
Windsor Palms 10
Windward Cay 5
Windwood Bay 7
Winslow Estates 8
Woodbridge 3
Woodridge 9

Continued from page 23

On the other hand, some vacation-home companies, like rental-car agencies, don't assign you a specific home until the day you arrive. These companies provide photos of a typical home instead of making information available on each of the individual homes in their inventory. In this case, you have to take the company's word that the typical home pictured is representative and that the home you'll be assigned will be just as nice.

How the Vacation-Home Market Works

In the Orlando area, there are more than 26,000 rental homes, including stand-alone homes, single-owner condos (that is, not time-shares), and town homes. The same area has about 116,000 hotel rooms. Almost all the rental homes are occupied by their owners for at least a week or two each year; the rest of the year, the owners make the homes available for rent. Some owners deal directly with renters, while others enlist the assistance of a property-management company.

Incredibly, about 700 property-management companies operate in the Orlando–Kissimmee market. Most of these are mom-and-pop outfits that manage an inventory of 10 homes or less (probably fewer than 70 companies oversee more than 100 rental homes).

Homeowners pay these companies to maintain and promote their properties and handle all rental transactions. Some homes are made available to wholesalers, vacation packagers, and travel agents in deals negotiated either directly by the owners or by property-management companies on the owners' behalf. A wholesaler or vacation packager will occasionally drop its rates to sell slow-moving inventory, but more commonly the cost to renters is higher than when dealing directly with owners or management companies: Because most wholesalers and packagers sell their inventory through travel agents, both the wholesaler/packager's markup and the travel agent's commission are passed along to the renter. These costs are in addition to the owner's cut and/or the fee for the property manager.

Along similar lines, logic may suggest that the lowest rate of all can be obtained by dealing directly with owners, thus eliminating an intermediary. Though this is sometimes true, it's more often the case that property-management companies offer the best rates. With their marketing expertise and larger customer base, these companies can produce a higher occupancy rate than can the owners themselves. What's more, management companies, or at least the larger ones, can achieve economies of scale not available to owners regarding maintenance, cleaning, linens, even acquiring furniture and appliances (if a house is not already furnished). The combination of higher occupancy rates and economies of scale adds up to a win–win situation for owners, management companies, and renters alike.

Location, Location, Location

The best vacation home is one that is within easy commuting distance of the theme parks. If you plan to spend some time at SeaWorld and the Universal parks, you'll want something just to the northeast of Walt Disney World (between the World and Orlando). If you plan to spend most of your time in the World or Legoland Florida, the best selection of vacation homes is along US 192 to the south of the park.

Walt Disney World lies mostly in Orange County but has a small southern tip that dips into Osceola County, which, along with Polk County to the west of the World, is where most vacation homes and single-owner condos and town houses are. Zoning laws in Orange County (which also includes most of Orlando, Universal Studios, Sea-World, Lake Buena Vista, and the International Drive area) used to prohibit short-term rentals of homes and single-owner condos, but in recent years the county has loosened its zoning restrictions in a few predominantly tourist-oriented areas.

By our reckoning, about half the rental homes in Osceola County and all the rental homes in Polk County are too far away for commuting to be practical. You might be able to save a few bucks by staying farther out, but the most desirable homes to be found are in Vista Cay and in developments no more than 4 miles from Disney World's main entrance on US 192 (Irlo Bronson Memorial Highway), in Osceola County.

To get the most from a vacation home, you need to be close enough to commute in 20 minutes or less to your Orlando destination. This will allow for naps, quiet time, swimming, and dollar-saving meals you prepare yourself.

Shopping for a Vacation Home

The only practical way to shop for a rental home is on the web. This makes it relatively easy to compare different properties and rental companies; on the downside, there are so many owners, rental companies, and individual homes to choose from that you could research yourself into a stupor. Three main types of websites serve the home-rental game: those for property-management companies, which showcase a given company's homes and are set up for direct bookings; individual owner sites; and third-party listings sites, which advertise properties available through different owners and sometimes management companies as well. Sites in the last category will usually refer prospective renters to an owner's or management company's site for reservations.

We've found that most property-management sites are not very well designed and will test your patience to the max. You can practically click yourself into old age trying to see all the homes available or figure out where on earth they are. Nearly all claim to be "just minutes from Disney [or Universal]." (By that reasoning, we should list our homes; they're also just minutes from Disney . . . 570 minutes, to be exact!)

Many websites list homes according to towns (such as Auburndale, Clermont, Davenport, Haines City, and Winter Garden) or real estate developments (including Eagle Pointe, Formosa Gardens, Indian Ridge, and Windsor Palms) in the general Disney-Universal area, none of which you're likely to be familiar with. The information that counts is the distance of a vacation home or condo from your Orlando destination; for that you often must look for something like "4 miles from Universal" embedded in the home's description. If you visit a site that lists homes by towns or real estate developments, begin by looking at our map on pages 24–25, which shows where all these places are. If the map is unhelpful in determining distance, we suggest that you find another location for your stay.

The best websites provide the following:

- Numerous photos and in-depth descriptions of individual homes to make comparisons quick and easy
- Overview maps or text descriptions that reflect how far specific homes or developments are from your Orlando destination
- The ability to book the rental home of your choice on the site
- An easy-to-find phone number for bookings and questions

The best sites are also easy to navigate, let you see what you're interested in without your having to log in or divulge any personal information, and list memberships in such organizations as the Better Business Bureau and the Central Florida Vacation Rental Managers Association (visit **cfvrma.com** for the association's code of ethics).

Recommended Websites

After checking out dozens upon dozens of sites, here are the ones we recommend. All of them meet the criteria listed above. If you're stunned that there are so few of them, well, so were we. (For the record, we elected not to list some sites that met our criteria but whose homes are too far away from the Orlando-area attractions.)

All Star Vacation Homes (allstarvacationhomes.com) is easily the best of the management-company sites, with easily accessible photos and plenty of details about featured homes. All the company's rental properties are within either 4 miles of Walt Disney World or 3 miles of Universal Studios.

#1 Dream Homes (floridadreamhomes.com) has a good reputation for customer service and now has photos of and information about the homes in its online inventory.

Orlando's Finest Vacation Homes (orlandosfinest.com) represents both homeowners and property-management companies. Offering a broad inventory, the Orlando's Finest website features photos and information on individual homes. Though the info is not as detailed as that offered by the All Star Vacation Homes site, friendly sales agents can fill in the blanks.

Vacation Rentals by Owner (vrbo.com) is a nationwide vacation-homes listings service that puts prospective renters in direct contact with owners. The site is straightforward and always lists a large number of rental properties in Celebration, Disney's planned community situated about 8–10 minutes from the theme parks. Two similar listings services with good websites are **Vacation Rentals 411 (vacationrentals411.com)** and **Last Minute Villas (lastminutevillas.net)**.

The website for **Visit Orlando (visitorlando.com)** is the place to go if you're interested in renting a condominium at one of the many timeshare developments (click on "Places to Stay" at the site's home page). You can call the developments directly, but going through this website allows you to bypass sales departments and escape their high-pressure invitations to sit through sales presentations. The site also lists hotels and vacation homes.

Making Contact

Once you've found a vacation home you like, check around the website for a Frequently Asked Questions (FAQ) page. If there's not a FAQ page, here are some of the things you'll want to check out on the phone with the owner or rental company.

1. How close is the property to your vacation destination?
2. Is the home or condominium that I see on the Internet the one I'll get?
3. Is the property part of a time-share development?
4. Are there any specials or discounts available?
5. Is everything included in the rental price, or are there additional charges? What about taxes?
6. How old is the home or condo I'm interested in? Has it been refurbished recently?
7. What is the view from the property?
8. Is the property near any noisy roads?
9. What is your smoking policy?
10. Are pets allowed? (This consideration is as important to those who want to avoid pets as to those who want to bring them.)
11. Is the pool heated?
12. Is there a fenced backyard where children can play?
13. How many people can be seated at the main dining table?
14. Is there a separate dedicated telephone at the property?
15. Is high-speed Internet access available?
16. Are linens and towels provided?
17. How far are the nearest supermarket and drugstore?
18. Are child-care services available?
19. Are there restaurants nearby?
20. Is transportation to the parks provided?
21. Will we need a car?
22. What is required to make a reservation?
23. What is your change/cancellation policy?

24. When is checkout time?
25. What will we be responsible for when we check out?
26. How will we receive our confirmation and arrival instructions?
27. What are your office hours?
28. What are the directions to your office?
29. What if we arrive after your office has closed?
30. Whom do we contact if something goes wrong during our stay?
31. How long have you been in business?
32. Are you licensed by the state of Florida?
33. Do you belong to the Better Business Bureau and/or the Central Florida Vacation Rental Managers Association?

We frequently receive letters from readers extolling the virtues of renting a condo or vacation home. This endorsement by a family from Ellington, Connecticut, is typical:

> *Our choice to stay in a vacation home was based on cost and sanity. We've found over the last couple of years that our children can't share the same bed. We have also gotten tired of having to turn off the lights at 8 p.m. and lie quietly in the dark waiting for our children to fall asleep. With this in mind, we needed a condo/suite layout. We decided on the Sheraton Vistana Resort. We had a two-bedroom villa with full kitchen, living room, three TVs, and washer/dryer. I packed for half the trip and did laundry almost every night. The facilities offered a daily children's program and several pools, kiddie pools, and play-scapes. Located on FL 535, we had a 5- to 10-minute drive to most attractions, including SeaWorld, Disney, and Universal.*

A St. Joe, Indiana, family had a good experience renting a vacation home, writing:

> *We rented a home in Kissimmee this time, and we'll never stay in a hotel again. It was by far the nicest, most relaxing time we've ever had down there. Our rental home was within 10–15 minutes of all the Disney parks and 25 minutes from SeaWorld. We had three bedrooms, two baths, and an in-ground pool in a screened enclosure out back. We paid $90 per night for the whole shootin' match. We did spring for the pool heating, $25 per night extra in February. We used AAA Dream Homes Rental Company, and they did a great job by us. They provided us with detailed info before we went down, so we'd know what we needed to bring.*

A New Jersey family of five echoes the above:

> *I cannot stress enough how important it is if you have a large family (more than two kids) to rent a house for your stay! We had visited Orlando several times in the past by ourselves when we were newly-weds. Fast-forward 10 years later, when we took our three kids, ages 6 years, 4 years, and 20 months. We stayed at Windsor Hills Resort, which I booked through **globalresorthomes.com**. I was able to see all*

the homes and check availability when I was reserving the house. This development is 1.5 miles from the Disney Maingate. It took us about 10 minutes to drive there in the a.m., and we had no traffic issues at all.

ORLANDO'S BEST HOTELS *for* FAMILIES

WHAT MAKES A SUPER FAMILY HOTEL? Roomy accommodations, in-room fridge, great pool, complimentary breakfast, child-care options, and programs for kids are a few of the things The Unofficial Guide hotel team researched in selecting the top hotels for families from among hundreds of properties in the Orlando area. Some of our picks are expensive, others are more reasonable, and some are a bargain. Regardless of price, be assured that these hotels understand a family's needs.

Though all of the following hotels offer some type of shuttle to the theme parks, some offer very limited service. Call the hotel before you book and ask what the shuttle schedule will be when you visit. Because families, like individuals, have different wants and needs, we haven't ranked these properties; they're listed by zone and alphabetically.

Disney's Flamingo Crossings

In 2007, right before the global financial meltdown, Disney announced ambitious plans for a new 450-acre, Value-oriented hotel and restaurant complex, just beyond the western edge of the main Disney World property, at the intersection of Western Way and FL 429. Plans were quietly dropped when the Great Recession came. For years, nothing other than an abandoned website and some press releases remained.

Fast-forward to 2015, and construction has begun on the first two hotels, scheduled to open in early 2016. Both are Marriott brands: **TownePlace Suites,** an extended-stay hotel, and **SpringHill Suites** will have about 250 rooms each; we expect them to be near the $150- to $250-per-night price point. As budget suites, these rooms are targeting the sports groups that participate in events at Disney's Wide World of Sports complex. These two hotels will be adjacent and share parking, a pool, and a gym. Other planned amenities include batting cages, a basketball court, and a practice field capable of being configured for different sports. Assuming there's a market for these, the developer plans to build up to five more hotels in the same area.

INTERNATIONAL DRIVE & UNIVERSAL AREAS

Castle Hotel ★★★½

Rate per night $149–$219. **Pool** ★★★. **Fridge in room** Yes ($15/day). **Shuttle to parks** Yes (Universal, SeaWorld, and Wet 'n

8629 International Dr.
Orlando
☎ 407-345-1511 or
877-317-5753
castlehotelorlando.com

Wild). **Maximum number of occupants per room** 4. **Special comments** Full breakfast for up to 4 people for an additional fee ($12 for adults, children age 12 and under free with paying adult). Pets up to 50 pounds welcome ($150 nonrefundable fee).

YOU CAN'T MISS THIS ONE: It's the only castle on I-Drive. Previously a Holiday Inn and before that a DoubleTree, the Castle is now part of Marriott's Autograph Collection. A recent $6.5-million renovation left the hotel's over-the-top ambience refreshed but largely unchanged: Inside you'll find the same royal colors (purple predominates), opulent fixtures (antlers are a recurring motif), European art, and Renaissance music.

The 216 rooms and suites also retain the royal treatment, but the decor is a bit more tasteful and streamlined after the renovation. All rooms are fairly large and well equipped with flat-panel TV, minibar (fridge is available at an extra charge), free Wi-Fi, coffeemaker, iron and board, hair dryer, and safe. The Garden Bistro & Bar off the lobby serves full or Continental breakfast. For lunch or dinner, you might walk next door to Vito's Chop House (dinner only) or Café Tu Tu Tango (an Unofficial favorite). The heated circular pool is 5 feet deep and features a fountain in the center, a poolside bar, and a hot tub. There's no separate kiddie pool. Other amenities include the Poseidon Spa, a fitness center, gift shop, lounge, valet laundry service and facilities, and guest services desk with park passes for sale and babysitting recommendations. Security feature: Elevators require an electronic key card.

CoCo Key Hotel and Water Resort–Orlando ★★★½

7400 International Dr.
Orlando
☎ 407-351-2626 or
877-875-4681
cocokeyorlando.com

Rate per night $75–$108. **Pools** ★★★★. **Fridge in room** Yes. **Shuttle to parks** Yes (Universal, SeaWorld, Aquatica, and Wet 'n Wild). **Maximum number of occupants per room** 4. **Special comments** $24/night resort fee for use of the water park; day guests may use the water park for $24.95/person Monday–Friday ($26.95 on Saturday–Sunday; $21.95 for Florida residents).

NOT FAR FROM THE UNIVERSAL ORLANDO theme parks, CoCo Key combines a tropical-themed hotel with a canopied water park featuring three pools and 14 waterslides, as well as poolside food and arcade entertainment. A full-service restaurant serves breakfast and dinner; a food court offers family favorites such as burgers, chicken fingers, and pizza.

A unique feature of the resort is its cashless payment system, much like that on a cruise ship. At check-in, families receive bar-coded wristbands that allow purchased items to be easily charged to their room.

The unusually spacious guest rooms include 37-inch flat-panel TVs, free Wi-Fi, granite showers and countertops, and plenty of accessible outlets for electronics.

DoubleTree by Hilton Orlando at SeaWorld ★★★★½

10100 International Dr.
Orlando
☎ 407-352-1100 or
800-327-0363
**doubletreeorlando
idrive.com**

Rate per night $129–$179. **Pools** ★★★½. **Fridge in room** Standard in some rooms; available in others for $10/day. **Shuttle to parks** Yes (Disney, Universal, SeaWorld, and Aquatica). **Maximum number of occupants per room** 4. **Special comments** Good option if you're visiting SeaWorld or Aquatica. Pets welcome (1 per room, 25-pound limit, $75). $20/night resort fee.

ON 28 LUSH, TROPICAL ACRES with a Balinese feel, the DoubleTree is adjacent to SeaWorld and Aquatica water park. The 1,094 rooms and suites—classified as resort or tower—are suitable for business travelers or families. We recommend the tower rooms for good views and the resort rooms for maximum convenience. Laguna serves steak and seafood, along with breakfast; you can also get a quick bite at The Market or the pool bar. Relax and cool off at one of the three pools (there are two more just for kids), or indulge in a special spa treatment. A fitness center, mini-golf course and putting green, children's day camp, and game area afford even more diversions. The resort is about a 15-minute drive to Walt Disney World, a 12-minute drive to Universal, or a short walk to SeaWorld.

Hard Rock Hotel Universal Orlando ★★★★½

Rate per night $259–$464. **Pool ★★★★. Fridge in room** Yes. **Shuttle to parks** Yes (Universal, SeaWorld, Discovery Cove, Aquatica, and Wet 'n Wild). **Maximum number of occupants per room** 5 (double-queen) or 3 (king). **Special comments** Microwaves available for $15/day. Character dinner on Saturday. Pets welcome ($50/night).

5800 Universal Blvd. Orlando

☎ 407-503-2000 or 888-464-3617

hardrockhotel orlando.com

FOR YOUNGER ADULTS AND FAMILIES with older kids, the Hard Rock Hotel is the hippest place to lay your head. Opened in 2001, the Hard Rock Hotel is both Universal Orlando's least-expansive (but second most expensive) on-site resort and the closest resort to Universal's theme parks. The exterior has a California Mission theme, with white stucco walls, arched entryways, and rust-colored roof tiles. Inside, the lobby is a tribute to rock-and-roll style, all marble, chrome, and stage lighting.

The eight floors hold 650 rooms and 29 suites, with the rooms categorized into standard, deluxe, and club-level tiers. Standard rooms are 375 square feet. The Hard Rock Hotel completed a top-to-bottom "remastering" of its rooms in early 2015, giving the formerly masculine decor a major makeover, with light-gray walls and linens, pastel furniture, and colorful retro-inspired accents.

Standard rooms are furnished with two queen beds, with smooth, plush, comfortable linens and more pillows than you'll know what to do with. Rooms also include a flat-panel LCD TV, refrigerator, coffeemaker, and an alarm clock with a 30-pin iPhone docking port.

A six-drawer dresser and separate closet with sliding doors ensure plenty of storage space. In addition, most rooms have a reading chair and a small desk with two chairs. An optional rollaway bed, available at an extra charge, allows standard rooms to sleep up to five people.

Each room's dressing area features a sink and hair dryer. The bathroom is probably large enough for most adults to get ready in the morning while another person gets ready in the dressing area.

Guests staying in standard rooms can choose from one of three views: standard, which can include anything from walkways and parking lots to lawns and trees; garden view, which includes the lawn, trees, and (in some rooms) the waterway around the resort; and pool view, which includes the Hard Rock's expansive pool.

Deluxe rooms with king beds are around 500 square feet and can accommodate up to three people with an optional rollaway bed rental. These rooms feature a U-shaped sitting area in place of the second bed, and the rest of the amenities are the same as in standard rooms. Deluxe queen rooms are also 500 square feet and can hold up to five people using a pullout sofa.

The pool is an attraction unto itself; it is the place to see and be seen. Situated in the middle of the resort's C-shaped main building, the 12,000-square-foot pool includes a 250-foot waterslide, a sand beach, and underwater speakers so you can hear the music while you swim. Adjacent to the pool are a fountain play area for small children, a sand-volleyball court, hot tubs, and a poolside bar. The Hard Rock also has a small, functional fitness center. Like all Universal Orlando Resort hotels, the Hard Rock has a business center and video arcade.

On-site dining includes The Kitchen, a casual full-service restaurant open for breakfast, lunch, and dinner, featuring American food such as burgers, steaks, and salads. The Palm Restaurant is an upscale steak house available for dinner only. And, of course, the Hard Rock Cafe is just a short distance away at Universal CityWalk.

After its much-needed refurbishment, we rate the rooms at Hard Rock slightly ahead of the more-expensive Portofino Bay. While not exactly cheap, Hard Rock is a good value compared to, say, Disney's Yacht & Beach Clubs. What you're paying for at the Hard Rock is a short walk to the theme parks and Universal Express Unlimited first, and the room second.

Nickelodeon Suites Resort ★★★½

14500 Continental Gateway, Orlando
☎ 407-387-5437 or 877-NICK-111
nickhotel.com

Rate per night $149–$209. **Pools** ★★★★. **Fridge in room** Yes. **Shuttle to parks** Yes (Disney, Universal, SeaWorld, Aquatica, and Wet 'n Wild). **Maximum number of occupants per room** 8. **Special comments** Daily character breakfast; $35/night resort fee.

SPONGEBOB SQUAREPANTS, eat your heart out. This resort is as kid-friendly as they come. Decked out in all themes Nickelodeon, the hotel is sure to please any fan of TV shows such as *SpongeBob, Dora the Explorer,* and *Avatar: The Last Airbender,* to name a few. Nickelodeon characters from the channel's many shows hang out in the resort's lobby and mall area, greeting kids while parents check in.

Guests can choose from among 777 suites—one-bedroom Family Suites and two- and three-bedroom KidSuites—executed in a number of different themes—all very brightly and creatively decorated. All suites include kitchenettes or full kitchens; also standard are microwave, fridge, coffeemaker, TV, iron and board, hair dryer, and safe. KidSuites feature a semiprivate kids' bedroom with bunk or twin beds, pullout sleeper bed, 32-inch TV, CD player, and activity table. The master bedroom offers ample storage space that the kids' bedroom lacks.

Additional amenities include a video arcade, Studio Nick (which hosts several game shows a night for a live studio audience), a buffet (kids age 3 and younger eat free with a paying adult), a food court offering Subway and other choices, the full-service Nicktoons Cafe (offers character breakfasts), a convenience store, a lounge, a gift shop, a fitness center, a washer and dryer in each courtyard, and a guest-activities desk (buy attraction tickets and get babysitting recommendations). Not to be missed are the resort's two pools, Oasis and Lagoon. Oasis features a water park complete with water cannons, rope ladders, geysers, and dump buckets, as well as a hot tub for adults (with a view of the rest of the pool so you can keep an eye on little ones) and a smaller play area for younger kids. Kids will love the huge, zero-entry Lagoon Pool with 400-gallon dump bucket, plus a nearby basketball court and nine-hole mini-golf course. Pool activities for kids are scheduled several times a day, seasonally; some games feature the infamous green slime. Whatever you do, don't let your kids hear you say, "I don't know," while you're here—trust us.

Rosen Shingle Creek   ★★★★

Rate per night $179–$190. **Pools** ★★★★. **Fridge in room** Yes. **Shuttle to parks** Yes (Universal, SeaWorld, Discovery Cove, Aquatica, and Wet 'n Wild). **Maximum number of occupants per room** 4.

9939 Universal Blvd.
Orlando
☎ 407-996-9939 or
866-996-6338
rosenshinglecreek.com

BEAUTIFUL ROOMS (east-facing ones have great views) and excellent restaurants distinguish this mostly meeting- and convention-oriented resort. The pools are large and lovely and include a lap pool, a family pool, and a kiddie wading pool. There's an 18-hole golf course on-site, as well as a superior spa and an adequate fitness center. Child care is provided as well.

Though a state-of-the-art video arcade will gobble up your kids' pocket change, the real kicker, especially for the 8-years-and-up crowd, is a natural area encompassing lily ponds, grassy wetlands, Shingle Creek, and an adjacent cypress swamp. Running through the area is a nature trail complete with signs to help you identify wildlife. Great blue herons, wood storks, coots, egrets, mallard ducks, anhingas, and ospreys are common, as are sliders (turtles), chameleons, and skinks (lizards). Oh yeah, there are alligators and snakes too—real ones, but that's part of the fun.

If you stay at Shingle Creek and plan to visit the theme parks, you'll want a car. Shuttle service is limited, departing and picking up at rather inconvenient times and stopping at three other hotels before delivering you to your destination.

Universal's Cabana Bay Beach Resort   ★★★★

Rate per night $119–$210 standard rooms, $174–$294 suites. **Pools** ★★★★. **Fridge in room** Suites only. **Shuttle to parks** Yes (Universal, SeaWorld, Discovery Cove, Aquatica, and Wet 'n Wild). **Maximum number of occupants per room** 4 for standard rooms, 6 for suites. **Special comments** Character greeting in lobby on Friday. Pets not permitted.

6550 Adventure Way
Orlando
☎ 407-503-4000 or
888-464-3617
tinyurl.com/cabanabay

IF YOU'RE OBSESSED WITH VINTAGE 1950s and 1960s designs, and with finding a good value (we're guilty on both accounts), you may just fall in love with Cabana Bay Beach Resort, Universal's first on-site hotel aimed at the value and moderate markets. The mid-century modern aesthetic starts with the neon signage that welcomes you outside and continues inside with lots of windows, bright colors, and period-appropriate lighting and furniture. We think the resort would be right at home in the deserts of Palm Springs or Las Vegas, while our British friends say the decor reminds them of Butlins Bognor Regis resort circa 1985.

Whatever Cabana Bay reminds you of, we think you'll like it. Kids will love the two large and well-themed pools (one with a lazy river), the amount of space they have to run around in, the video arcade, and the vintage cars parked outside the hotel lobby. Adults will appreciate the sophisticated kitsch of the decor, the multiple lounges, the business center, and the on-site Starbucks. We think Cabana Bay is an excellent choice for price- and/or space-conscious families visiting Universal.

The hotel's closest competitor in the Orlando area is Disney's Art of Animation Resort, and the two share many similarities. Both have standard rooms and family suites. At 430 square feet per suite, Cabana Bay suites are about 135 square feet smaller than comparable suites at A of A and have only one bathroom. We found them well appointed for two to four people per room (though not for the six Loews claims as its capacity). Rack rates for the suites are about $140–$300 per night less than Art of Animation's.

Each family suite has a small bedroom with two queen beds, divided from the living area and kitchenette by a sliding screen; a foldout sofa in the living area offers additional sleeping space. The bath is divided into three sections: toilet, sink area, and shower room with additional sink. The kitchenette has a microwave, coffee-maker, and mini-fridge. A bar area allows extra seating for quick meals, and a large closet has enough space to store everyone's luggage. Built-in USB charging outlets for your devices are a thoughtful touch. Standard rooms have the same two queen beds but without the living area, kitchenette, or three-way bathroom. Instead, they get a mini-fridge with coffeemaker and an average-size single bathroom.

Recreational options include the 10-lane Galaxy Bowl (about $15 per person with shoe rental), poolside table tennis and billiards, and a large Jack LaLanne fitness center. Outdoor movies are shown nightly near the pool.

In addition to the Starbucks, a food court with seating area shows 1960s TV clips. Swizzle Lounge in the lobby, two pool bars, in-room pizza delivery, and table-service snacks and sandwiches at the Galaxy Bowl round out the on-site dining options. You'll find more restaurants and clubs nearby at the Royal Pacific Resort and Universal CityWalk.

Unlike the other Universal resorts, Cabana Bay offers no watercraft service to the parks—it's either take the bus or walk. In November 2014, a new pedestrian bridge opened connecting Cabana Bay to CityWalk and the rest of Universal Orlando, but we still recommend the bus service for most people. Cabana Bay guests are eligible for early entry at Universal but do not get a complimentary Universal Express pass.

Take care when driving into and out of the hotel's driveway on Adventure Way. If you miss the entrance, or make a right when exiting, you'll find yourself on a one-way road to I-4 West toward Disney, and you won't be able to make a U-turn until the FL 528 expressway.

Universal's Portofino Bay Hotel   ★★★★½

5601 Universal Blvd.
Orlando
☎ 407-503-1000 or
888-464-3617
**tinyurl.com
/portofinobay**

Rate per night $294–$479. **Pools** ★★★★. **Fridge in room** Minibar; fridge available for $15/day. **Shuttle to parks** Yes (Universal, SeaWorld, Discovery Cove, Aquatica, and Wet 'n Wild). **Maximum number of occupants per room** 5 (double-queen) or 3 (king). **Special comments** Character dinner on Friday. Pets welcome ($50/night).

IF YOU ARE IN SEARCH OF the ultimate European-style, spare-no-expense on-site experience, look no further than the Portofino Bay Hotel. Universal's top-of-the-line hotel evokes the Italian seaside city of Portofino, complete with a man-made Portofino Bay past the lobby. To Universal's credit, the layout, color, and theming of the guest room buildings are a good approximation of the architecture around the harbor in the real Portofino (Universal's version has fewer yachts, however).

Inside, the lobby is decorated with pink marble floors, white-wood columns, and arches. The space is both airy and comfortable, with side rooms featuring seats and couches done in bold reds and deep blues.

Portofino Bay was refurbished in 2013. Most guest rooms are 450 square feet and have either one king bed or two queen beds. King rooms sleep up to three people with an optional rollaway bed; the same option allows queen rooms to sleep up to five. Two room-view options are available: Garden rooms look out over the landscaping and trees (many of these are the east-facing rooms in the resort's east wing; others face one of the three pools); bay-view rooms face either west or south and overlook Portofino Bay, with a view of the piazza behind the lobby too.

Rooms come furnished with a 32-inch LCD flat-panel TV, a refrigerator, a coffeemaker, and an alarm clock with a 30-pin iPhone docking port. Other amenities include a small desk with two chairs, a comfortable reading chair with lamp, a chest of drawers, and a standing closet. Wi-Fi is $15 per day in guest rooms, free in the lobby. Beds are large, plush, and comfortable.

Guest bathrooms at Portofino Bay are the best on Universal property. We've seen smaller New York apartments! The best thing is the shower, which has enough water pressure to strip paint from old furniture, not to mention an adjustable spray nozzle that varies the water pulses to simulate everything from monsoon season in the tropics to the rhythmic thumps of wildebeest hooves during migrating season. We love it.

Portofino Bay has three pools, the largest of which is the Beach Pool, on the west side of the resort. Two smaller quiet pools sit at the far end of the east wing and to the west of the main lobby. The Beach Pool has a zero-entry design and a waterslide themed after a Roman aqueduct, plus a children's play area, hot tubs, and a poolside bar and grill. The Villa Pool has private cabana rentals for that Italian Riviera feeling. Rounding out the luxuries are the full-service Mandara Spa; a complete fitness center with weight machines, treadmills, and more; a business center; and a video arcade.

On-site dining includes three sit-down restaurants serving Italian cuisine; a deli; a pizzeria; and a café serving coffee and gelato. Some of the food prices go well beyond what we'd consider reasonable, even for a theme park hotel.

While we think Portofino Bay has some of Universal's best rooms, the prices put it on par with the Ritz-Carlton—something its good points can't quite justify. On the other hand, the Ritz isn't a short walk from The Wizarding World of Harry Potter.

Universal's Royal Pacific Resort ★★★★½

Rate per night $234–$404. **Pools** ★★★★. **Fridge in room** Yes. **Shuttle to parks** Yes (Universal, SeaWorld, Discovery Cove, Aquatica, and Wet 'n Wild). **Maximum number of occupants per room** 5 (double-queen) or 3 (king). **Special comments** Microwaves available for $15/day. Character breakfast on Sunday; character dinners on Monday, Wednesday, and Thursday. Pets welcome ($50/night).

6300 Hollywood Way
Orlando
☎ 407-503-1000 or
888-464-3617
**tinyurl.com
/royalpacific**

A FAVORITE OF YOUNG FAMILIES and solo travelers alike, the Royal Pacific is the least expensive and most relaxing of Universal's deluxe hotels. You may be tempted, as we were initially, to write off the Royal Pacific, which opened in 2002, as a knockoff of Disney's Polynesian Village Resort. There are indeed similarities, but the Royal Pacific is attractive enough, and has enough strengths of its own, for us to recommend that you try a stay there to compare for yourself.

The South Seas–inspired theming is both relaxing and structured. Guests enter the lobby from a walkway two stories above an artificial stream that surrounds the resort. Once you're inside, the lobby's dark teakwood accents contrast nicely with the enormous amount of light coming in from the windows and three-story A-frame roof. Palms line the walkway through the lobby, and through these you see that the whole lobby surrounds an enormous outdoor fountain.

The 1,000 guest rooms are spread among three Y-shaped wings attached to the main building. Standard rooms are 335 square feet and feature one king or two queen beds. King rooms sleep up to three people with an optional rollaway bed; queen rooms sleep five with that rollaway bed. The beds, fitted with 300-thread-count sheets, are very comfortable.

The rooms and hallways of Royal Pacific's first tower were refurbished in 2015, and the remainder will be done by early 2016, with modern monochrome wall treatments and carpets, accented with boldly colored floral graphics. Rooms include a 32-inch flat-panel LCD TV, a refrigerator, a coffeemaker, and an alarm clock with a 30-pin iPhone docking port. Other amenities include a small desk with two chairs, a comfortable reading chair, a chest of drawers, and a large closet.

A dressing area with sink is separated from the rest of the room by a wall. Next to the dressing area is the bathroom, with a tub, shower, and toilet. While they're acceptable, the bathroom and dressing areas at the Royal Pacific are our least favorite in the Universal resorts.

Jurassic Park Kids Suites have two rooms with a door connecting the kid's room to the main hotel room; only the main room has a door out to the hallway. The kid's room has two twin beds with light-up raptor slash marks on the headboards, while the rest of the room is fully themed to the *Jurassic Park* film, including on-set photos.

Guests in north- and west-facing rooms in Tower 1 are closest to the attractions at Islands of Adventure and can hear the roar from IOA's Incredible Hulk Coaster throughout the day and night. East-facing rooms in Towers 1 and 2 are exposed to traffic noise from Universal Boulevard and, more distantly, I-4. Quietest are south-facing pool-view rooms in Tower 1 and south-facing rooms in Tower 3.

As at the Hard Rock, the Royal Pacific's zero-entry pool includes a sand beach, volleyball court, play area for kids, hot tub, and cabanas for rent, plus a poolside bar and grill.

Amenities include a 5,000-square-foot fitness facility, a business center, a video arcade, two full-service restaurants, three bars, and a luau. Of the table-service restaurants, only Islands Dining Room is open for breakfast. Emeril Lagasse's Tchoup Chop, the other table-service option, is open for lunch and dinner (reservations recommended).

Universal's Sapphire Falls Resort   *(opens 2016)*

6601 Adventure Way Orlando

☎ 407-503-5000 or 888-464-3617

loewshotels.com /sapphire-falls-hotel

Rate per night $229–$264. **Pools** ★★★★. **Fridge in room** Yes. **Shuttle to parks** Yes (Universal, SeaWorld, Discovery Cove, Aquatica, and Wet 'n Wild). **Maximum number of occupants per room** 5 (double/queen) or 3 (king).

UNIVERSAL'S FIFTH ON-SITE LOEWS HOTEL, Sapphire Falls Resort, seeks to bring a sunny Caribbean island vibe to the moderate-price market when its 1,000 rooms open in summer 2016. Sandwiched between Royal Pacific and Cabana Bay—both physically and pricewise—Sapphire Falls sports all of the amenities of Universal's three Deluxe hotels, including water taxi transportation to the parks, with the crucial exception of complimentary Express Passes.

Water figures heavily at Sapphire Falls, whose namesake waterfalls form the scenic centerpiece of the resort. The zero-entry main pool features a white-sand beach, waterslide, children's play areas, fire pit, and cabanas for rent. A fitness room holds a sauna and hot tub. For dinner, Amatista Cookhouse offers table-service Caribbean dining, with an open kitchen and waterfront views. Club Katine serves tapas-style small plates near the pool bar's fire pit. New Dutch Trading Co. is an island-inspired grab-and-go marketplace, and Strong Water Tavern in the lobby has rum tastings and table-side ceviche.

Sapphire Falls also contains 131,000 square feet of meeting space and a business center. Covered walkways connect to a parking structure, which in turn connects to the meeting facilities at Royal Pacific, making the new sister properties ideal for conventions.

The rooms range from 364 square feet in a standard queen or king to 529 square feet in the 36 Kids' Suites, up to 1,358 square feet in the 15 Hospitality Suites. All rooms have a 49-inch flat-panel HDTV, mini-fridge, and coffeemaker.

LAKE BUENA VISTA & I-4 CORRIDOR

B Resort ★★★½

Rate per night $135–$172. **Pools** ★★★½. **Fridge in room** Yes. **Shuttle to parks** Yes (Disney only). **Maximum number of occupants per room** 4 plus child in crib. **Special comment** $22.50/night resort fee.

1905 Hotel Plaza Blvd.
☎ 407-828-2828 or
800-66-BHOTELS
bresortlvb.com

B RESORTS, a Florida hotel chain, relaunched the former Royal Plaza in the summer of 2014 after an extensive multiyear renovation. Located in the Downtown Disney Resort Area, within walking distance of shops and restaurants and situated 5 miles or less from the Disney parks, the 394-room hotel targets couples, families, groups, and business travelers.

Decorated in cool blues, whites, and grays, guest rooms and suites afford views of downtown Orlando, area lakes, and theme parks. Along with B Resorts-exclusive Blissful Beds, each room is outfitted with sleek modern furnishings and a large interactive flat-screen TV. Additional touches include a mini-fridge and gaming consoles (available on request). Some rooms are also equipped with bunk beds, kitchenettes, or wet bars.

Our most recent stay at the B Resort was in early 2015, and we enjoyed it quite a bit. Our standard room was spotlessly clean, and the room decor is fun without being faddy. The bathroom is spacious, with plenty of storage. The glass shower is well-designed and has good water pressure. There's absolutely nothing wrong with this hotel at this price point, except for the terrible traffic you have to endure every night because of Disney Springs. And that's a shame because it's not the hotel's doing. But if the B were on the other side of Disney Springs, we'd gladly stay here again.

A mom from Tennessee also likes the B Resort, especially when it's on sale:

The vibe of the B Resort was great—like a knockoff of the W, very bright and modern. The restaurant was great, and the zero-entry pool was good. The resort has a more adult feel, but I never felt out of place with my son. I found a deal on Orbitz for around $310 for three nights, with taxes and fees. If choosing between the B and Pop Century for a short stay, I'd take the B Resort hands down.

Amenities include free Wi-Fi, a spa, beauty salon, and fitness center. The main restaurant, American Q, serves a modern upscale take on classic barbecue in regional styles ranging from Carolina to Kansas City. Hungry guests can also choose from a poolside bar and grill; The Pickup, a grab-and-go shop just off the lobby that serves quick breakfasts, snacks, picnic lunches, and ice cream; and 24/7 in-room dining.

Other perks: a zero-entry pool with interactive water features; a kids' area; loaner iPads; Monscierge, a digital touch screen concierge and destination guide in the lobby; and more than 25,000 square feet of meeting and multiuse space. Though not served by Disney transportation, B Resort provides bus service to the Disney parks and Disney Springs.

Buena Vista Palace Hotel & Spa ★★★½

1900 E. Buena Vista Dr.
Lake Buena Vista
☎ 407-827-2727 or
866-397-6516
buenavistapalace.com

Rate per night $121–$226. **Pools** ★★★½. **Fridge in room** Yes. **Shuttle to parks** Yes (Disney only). **Maximum number of occupants per room** 4. **Special comments** Sunday character brunch available; $22/night resort fee.

THE BUENA VISTA PALACE IS upscale and conve-nient. Surrounded by an artificial lake and plenty of palms, the spacious pool area comprises three heated pools, the largest of which is partially covered; a whirlpool and sauna; a basketball court; and a sand-volleyball court. A pool concierge will fetch your favorite magazine or fruity drink. On Sunday, the Watercress Café hosts a character brunch ($25 for adults; $12 for children). The 897 guest rooms are posh and spacious; each comes with desk, coffeemaker, hair dryer, satellite TV with pay-per-view movies, iron and board, and mini-fridge. There are also 117 suites. In-room babysitting is available. One lighted tennis court, a European-style spa offering 60 services, a fitness center, an arcade, a playground, and a beauty salon round out amenities. Two restaurants and a mini-market are on-site. And if you aren't wiped out after time in the parks, consider dropping by the Lobby Lounge or the full-menu sports bar for a nightcap. *Note:* All these amenities and services come at a price—a $22-per-night resort fee will be added to your bill.

Four Seasons Resort Orlando at Walt Disney World Resort ★★★★★

10100 Dream Tree Blvd.
Golden Oak
☎ 407-313-7777
or 800-267-3046
**fourseasons.com
/orlando**

Rate per night $545–$845. **Pools** ★★★★★. **Fridge in room** Yes. **Shuttle to parks** Yes (Disney only). **Maximum number of occupants per room** 4 (3 adults or 2 adults and 2 children). **Special comment** The best pool complex in Walt Disney World.

AT 444 GUEST ROOMS, the Four Seasons Resort Orlando is simultaneously the largest hotel in the Four Seasons chain and the smallest on Disney property. It's also the best deluxe resort in the area, with comfort, amenities, and personal service that far surpass anything that Disney's Deluxes offer. If you're trying to fit a couple of days of relaxing, non-park time into your vacation, this is the hotel to choose.

Standard guest rooms average around 500 square feet and feature either one king bed with a sleeper sofa or two double beds (a crib is available in double rooms). Amenities include two flat-panel TVs, a coffeemaker, a small refrigerator, a work desk with two chairs, a personal digital video recorder (DVR) to record TV shows, and Bluetooth speakers for your personal audio. In keeping with the room's gadget-friendly spirit, each nightstand has four electrical outlets and two USB ports.

Bathrooms have glass-walled showers, a separate tub, marble vanities with two sinks, mosaic-tile floors, hair dryers, lighted mirrors, and a TV in the mirror above the sink.

Most rooms have an 80-square-foot balcony with table and chairs—perfect for your morning coffee or evening nightcap. Standard-view rooms look out onto the resort's lawns, gardens, and nearby homes in Golden Oak. Lake-view rooms—which overlook the lake, the Tom Fazio–designed Tranquilo Golf Club (formerly Osprey Ridge), or the pool—cost about $100 more per night than standard-view rooms. Park-view rooms, on floors 6–16, cost about $200 more per night than standard-view rooms and offer views of the Magic Kingdom's nightly fireworks. (Suites are available with views of Epcot too.)

The resort's 5-acre pool area is the best on Walt Disney World property, and the least crowded. It features an adult pool, a family pool, an 11,000-square-foot lazy river, and a splash zone with two 242-foot waterslides. To put this in perspective, the Four Seasons' pool area is about twice as large as Stormalong Bay at the Beach and Yacht Club Resorts but with only a third as many guests. Private pool cabanas are available for rent (around $200/day).

Capa, a Spanish-themed rooftop restaurant, serves seafood and steaks (open nightly, 6–10 p.m.; dress is resort casual, and reservations are recommended). Ravello, on the first floor, serves American breakfasts (6:30–11 a.m.) and Italian dinners (5:30–10 p.m.; reservations are recommended, and dress is smart casual). PB&G (Pool Bar and Grill) serves barbecued meats and salads by the main pool (11 a.m.–6 p.m.).

Service is excellent at the Four Seasons. About 25% of the staff transferred from other Four Seasons properties, bringing years of experience and knowledge to this resort. On one visit, the front desk receptionist walked us to our room after check-in, and we were often greeted by name as we walked through the resort.

At the hotel's Disney Planning Center, Disney cast members can help with reservations or any other Disney needs. Disney will also deliver your in-park purchases to the Four Seasons, but staying at the Four Seasons does not qualify guests for Extra Magic Hours, 60-day FastPass+ reservations, or use of Magical Express from the airport.

The hotel has a full-service spa and fitness center, as well as a beautiful late-checkout lounge that allows use of the showers and bathrooms in the spa.

Hilton Orlando Bonnet Creek ★★★★

Rate per night $119–$249. **Pool** ★★★★½. **Fridge in room** Yes. **Shuttle to parks** Yes (Disney only). **Maximum number of occupants per room** 4. **Special comment** $22/night resort fee.

14100 Bonnet Creek Resort Lane, Orlando
☎ 407-597-3600
hiltonbonnetcreek.com

THE HILTON BONNET CREEK is one of our favorite non-Disney hotels in Lake Buena Vista, and the value for the money beats anything in Disney's Deluxe category. Behind Disney's Caribbean Beach and Pop Century Resorts, this Hilton is much nicer than the one in the Downtown Disney Resort Area.

Standard rooms measure around 414 square feet and have either one king bed or two queen beds. The beds' mattresses and linens are very comfortable. Other features include a 37-inch flat-panel TV, a spacious work desk, an armoire, a small reading chair with floor lamp, a nightstand, and a digital clock. A coffeemaker, small refrigerator, ironing board, and iron are all standard, along with free wired and wireless Internet.

Bathrooms include tile floors with glass showers and a hair dryer. Unfortunately, the layout isn't as up-to-date as other hotels'—where many upscale hotel bathrooms have two sinks (so two people can primp at once), the Hilton's has only one. And where modern bathroom configurations often include a dressing area separate from the bath and a separate water closet for the commode, everything is in the bathroom here. That makes it harder for four-person families to get ready in the morning.

The Hilton's public areas are stylish and spacious. Families will enjoy the huge zero-entry pool, complete with waterslide, as well as the 3-acre lazy river. Even better, the Hilton staff run arts-and-crafts activities poolside during the day, allowing parents to grab a quick swim and a cocktail. Pool-facing cabanas are also available for rent at around $300 per day or $150 per half-day. If you're trying to stay in swimsuit shape, a nice fitness center sits on the ground floor.

The Hilton participates in the Waldorf Astoria's Kids Club next door, for children ages 5–12. A daytime program is available 10:30 a.m.–2:30 p.m., and an evening program is available 6–10 p.m. on Friday and Saturday. Price is $75 for the first child, $25 for each additional child.

There are more than a dozen restaurants and lounges between the Hilton and the Waldorf Astoria, with cuisine including an upscale steak house, Italian, sushi, tapas, a coffee bar, an American bistro, and breakfast buffet choices. Breakfast hours usually run 7–11:30 a.m., lunch 11:30 a.m.–5 p.m., and dinner 5–10 p.m. Reservations are recommended for the fancy places.

Hilton Orlando Lake Buena Vista ★★★★

1751 Hotel Plaza Blvd.
☎ 407-827-4000
hilton-wdwv.com

Rate per night $161–$241. **Pools** ★★★½. **Fridge in room** Minibar; mini-fridge available free on request. **Shuttle to parks** Yes (Disney theme and water parks only). **Maximum number of occupants per room** 4. **Special comments** Sunday character breakfast; $22/night resort fee.

LOCATED IN THE DOWNTOWN DISNEY RESORT AREA, the Hilton has rooms that are comfortable and nicer than some others in the DDRA, though the resort fees are outrageous and the decor is dated. It used to be the only hotel to offer Disney's Extra Magic Hours program to its guests (though that ended in December 2015). On-site dining includes Covington Mill Restaurant, offering sandwiches and pasta; Andiamo, an Italian bistro; and Benihana, a Japanese steak house and sushi bar. Covington Mill hosts a Disney-character breakfast on Sundays. The two pools are matched with a children's spray pool and a 24-hour fitness center. An exercise room and a game room are on-site, as is a 24-hour market. Babysitting is available, but there are no organized children's programs.

A Denver family of five found the Hilton's shuttle service lacking:

The transportation, provided by Mears, was unreliable. They did a better job of getting guests back to the hotel from the park than getting them to the park from the hotel. Shuttles from the hotel were randomly timed and went repeatedly to the same parks—skipping others and leaving guests to wait for up to an hour.

Holiday Inn Resort Lake Buena Vista ★★★½

13351 FL 535, Orlando
☎ 407-239-4500
or 866-808-8833
hiresortlbv.com

Rate per night $80–$164 **Pool** ★★★. **Fridge in room** Yes. **Shuttle to parks** Yes (Disney only). **Maximum number of occupants per room** 4–6. **Special comments** $15/night resort fee entitles guests to numerous perks, including use of fitness center and daily fountain drinks for kids. Pets welcome ($50–$75/night depending on weight).

THE BIG LURE HERE IS KIDSUITES—405-square-foot rooms, each with a separate children's area. The kids' area sleeps two to four children in one or two sets of bunk beds. The separate adult area has its own TV, safe, hair dryer, and mini-kitchenette with fridge, microwave, sink, and coffeemaker. Standard guest rooms offer these adult amenities. Other kid-friendly amenities include the tiny Castle Movie Theater, which shows movies all day, every day; a playground; an arcade with video games and air hockey, among its many games; and a basketball court. Other amenities include a fitness center for the grown-ups and a large free-form pool complete with kiddie pool and two whirlpools. Applebee's serves breakfast and dinner and offers an à la carte menu for dinner. There's also a mini-mart. More perks: Kids age 12 and younger eat free from a special menu when dining with one paying adult (maximum four kids per adult), and "Dive-Inn" poolside movies are shown on Saturday nights.

Hyatt Regency Grand Cypress ★★★★½

1 Grand Cypress Blvd.
Orlando
☎ 407-239-1234
grandcypress.hyatt.com

Rate per night $169–$334. **Pool** ★★★★★. **Fridge in room** Yes, plus minibar. **Shuttle to parks** Yes (Disney, Universal, and SeaWorld). **Maximum number of occupants per room** 4. **Special comment** $29/night resort fee.

THERE ARE MYRIAD REASONS to stay at the 1,500-acre Grand Cypress, but the pool ranks as reason number one. The 800,000-gallon tropical paradise has two 45-foot waterslides, waterfalls, and a suspension bridge, along with a waterslide tower, a splash zone, a pool bar, and kids' rock-climbing facilities.

   The 769 standard guest rooms are 360 square feet and have a Florida ambience, with green and reddish hues, touches of rattan, and private balconies. Amenities include a minibar, iron and board, safe, hair dryer, ceiling fan, and cable/satellite TV with pay-per-view movies and video games. Suite and villa accommodations offer even more amenities. Camp Hyatt provides supervised programs for kids ages 3–12; in-room babysitting is available. Six restaurants offer dining options, and four lounges provide nighttime entertainment.

Marriott Village at Lake Buena Vista ★★★

8623 Vineland Ave.
Orlando
☎ 407-938-9001
or 800-761-7829
marriottvillage.com

Rate per night $74–$189. **Pools** ★★★. **Fridge in room** Yes. **Shuttle to parks** Disney only, $7. **Maximum number of occupants**

per room 4 (Courtyard and Fairfield) or 5 (SpringHill). **Special comment** Free Continental breakfast at Fairfield and SpringHill.

THIS GATED HOTEL COMMUNITY INCLUDES a 388-room Fairfield Inn (★★★½), a 400-suite SpringHill Suites (★★★), and a 312-room Courtyard (★★★½). Whatever your budget, you'll find a room here to fit it. If you need a bit more space, book SpringHill Suites; if you're looking for value, try the Fairfield Inn; if you need limited business amenities, reserve at the Courtyard. Amenities at all three properties include fridge, cable TV, iron and board, hair dryer, and microwave. Cribs and rollaway beds are available at no extra charge at all locations. Swimming pools at all three hotels are attractive and medium-sized, featuring children's interactive splash zones and whirlpools; in addition, each property has its own fitness center. The incredibly convenient Village Marketplace food court includes Pizza Hut, Village Grill, Village Coffee House, and a 24-hour convenience store. Bahama Breeze and Golden Corral full-service restaurants are within walking distance. Other services and amenities include a Disney planning station and ticket sales, an arcade, and a Hertz car-rental desk. Shoppers will find the Orlando Premium Outlets adjacent. You'll get plenty of bang for your buck at Marriott Village.

Sheraton Lake Buena Vista Resort ★★★★

12205 S. Apopka Vineland Rd., Orlando
☎ 407-239-0444
sheratonlakebuena
vistaresort.com

Rate per night $163–$200. **Pool** ★★★★. **Fridge in room** Yes. **Shuttle to parks** Yes (Disney only). **Maximum number of occupants per room** 4–6. **Special comments** Dogs 80 pounds and under allowed; $19.95/night resort fee.

COMPRISING 400 GUEST ROOMS and 90 family junior suites, this resort has a sleek, modern feel. Amenities in each room include Sheraton Sweet Sleeper beds, free Wi-Fi, 42-inch HDTV, refrigerator, coffeemaker, hair dryer, safe, clock-radio, and iron and board. The family junior suites also provide bunk beds for children. Microwaves are available at an extra charge. The relaxing pool area features cabanas with food service (for a fee), and youngsters can enjoy the cascading waterfall and waterslide.

The Top of the Palms Spa offers massages, facials, manicures, and pedicures. Also on-site are two restaurants, a business center, a fitness center, an arcade, and a gift shop.

Sheraton Vistana Resort Villas ★★★★

8800 Vistana Centre Dr. Orlando
☎ 407-239-3100 or 866-208-0003
tinyurl.com/vistanaresort

Rate per night $127–$254. **Pools** ★★★½. **Fridge in room** Yes. **Shuttle to parks** Yes (Disney free; other parks for a fee). **Maximum number of occupants per room** 4–8. **Special comment** Though time-shares, the villas are rented nightly as well.

THE SHERATON VISTANA is deceptively large, stretching across both sides of Vistana Centre Drive. Because Sheraton's emphasis is on selling the time-shares, the rental angle is little known. But families should consider it; the Vistana is one of Orlando's best off-Disney properties. If you want a serene retreat from your days in the theme parks, this is an excellent base. The spacious villas come in one-bedroom, two-bedroom, and two-bedroom-with-lock-off models (which can be reconfigured as one studio room and a one-bedroom suite). All are decorated in beachy pastels, but the emphasis is on the profusion of amenities. Each villa has a full kitchen (including fridge/freezer, microwave, oven/range, dishwasher, toaster, and coffee-maker, with an option to pre-stock with groceries and laundry products), washer and dryer, TVs in the living room and each bedroom (one with DVD player), stereo with CD player in some villas, separate dining area, and private patio or balcony in most. Grounds offer seven swimming pools (three with bars), four playgrounds, two restaurants, game rooms, fitness centers, a mini-golf course, sports equipment rental (including bikes), and courts for basketball, volleyball, tennis, and shuffle-board. A mind-boggling array of activities for kids (and adults) ranges from crafts to games and sports tournaments. Of special note: Vistana is highly secure, with locked gates bordering all guest areas, so children can have the run of the place without parents worrying about them wandering off. The one downside: noise, both above (from being on the flight path of a helicopter tour company) and below (from International Drive). Bring a white noise machine or app for better sleep.

Waldorf Astoria Orlando   ★★★★½

14200 Bonnet Creek Resort Lane, Orlando
☎ 407-597-5500
waldorfastoria orlando.com

Rate per night $234–$424. **Pool** ★★★★. **Fridge in room** Yes. **Shuttle to parks** Yes (Disney only) **Maximum number of occupants per room** 4, plus child in crib. **Special comments** Good alternative to Disney Deluxe resorts; $30/night resort fee.

THE WALDORF ASTORIA is between I-4 and Disney's Pop Century Resort, near the Hilton Orlando at the back of the Bonnet Creek Resort property. Getting here requires a GPS or good directions, so be prepared with those before you travel. Once you arrive, however, you'll know the trip was worth it. Beautifully decorated and well manicured, the Waldorf is more elegant than any Disney resort. Service is excellent, and the staff-to-guest ratio is far lower than at Disney properties.

At just under 450 square feet, standard rooms feature either two queen beds or one king. A full-size desk allows you to get work done if it's absolutely neces-sary, and rooms also have flat-panel TVs, high-speed Internet, and Wi-Fi. The bathrooms are spacious and gorgeous, with cool marble floors, glass-walled show-ers, separate tubs, and enough counter space for a Broadway makeup artist. This space is so nice that we've debated whether we'd rather stay at Pop Century with three others or sleep in a Waldorf bathroom by ourselves.

Amenities include a fitness center, a spa, a golf course, six restaurants, and two pools (including one zero-entry pool for kids). Poolside cabanas are available for rent. The resort offers shuttle service to the Disney parks about every half hour, but check with the front desk for the exact schedule when you arrive. Runners will enjoy the relative solitude—it's about a 1-mile round-trip to the nearest busy road.

Wyndham Bonnet Creek Resort   ★★★★½

9560 Via Encinas Lake Buena Vista
☎ 407-238-3500 or 888-743-2687
wyndhambonnet creek.com

Rate per night $229–$359. **Pool** ★★★★. **Fridge in room** Yes. **Shuttle to parks** Yes (Disney only). **Maximum number of occupants per room** 4–12 depending on room/suite. **Special comment** A non-Disney suite hotel within Walt Disney World.

THIS CONDO HOTEL lies on the south side of Buena Vista Drive, about 0.25-mile east of Disney's Caribbean Beach Resort. The property has an interesting history: When Walt Disney began secretly buying up real estate in the 1960s under the names of numerous front companies, the land on which this resort stands was the last holdout and was never sold to Disney, though the company tried repeatedly to acquire it through the years. (The owners reportedly took issue with the way Disney went about acquiring land and preferred to see the site languish undeveloped.)

The 482-acre site was ultimately bought by Marriott, which put up a Fairfield Inn time-share development in 2004. The Wyndham is part of a luxury-hotel complex on the same site that includes a 500-room Waldorf Astoria (see previous profile), a 400-room Wyndham Grand, and a 1,000-room Hilton (see page 41). The development is surrounded on three sides by Disney property and on one side by I-4.

One- and two-bedroom condos have fully equipped kitchens, washers and dryers, jetted tubs, and balconies. Activities and amenities include two outdoor swimming pools, a lazy river float stream, a children's activities program, a game room, a playground, and miniature golf. Free scheduled transportation serves all the Disney parks. One-bedroom units are furnished with a king bed in the bedroom and a sleeper sofa in the living area; two-bedroom condos have two double beds in the second bedroom, a sleeper sofa in the living area, and an additional bath.

US 192 AREA

7888 W. US 192
Kissimmee
☎ 407-390-9888 or
888-390-9888
clarionsuites
kissimmee.com

Clarion Suites Maingate ★★★½

Rate per night $99–$169. **Pool** ★★★. **Fridge in room** Yes. **Shuttle to parks** Yes (Disney, Universal, and SeaWorld). **Maximum number of occupants per room** 6 for most suites. **Special comments** Free Continental breakfast served daily for up to two guests; additional breakfast $5.99 advance, $6.99 day of.

THIS PROPERTY HAS 150 SPACIOUS one-room suites, each with double sofa bed, microwave, fridge, coffeemaker, TV, hair dryer, and safe. The suites aren't lavish, but they're clean and contemporary, with muted deep-purple and beige tones. Extra bathroom counter space is especially convenient for larger families. The heated pool is large and has plenty of lounge chairs and moderate landscaping. A kiddie pool, whirlpool, and poolside bar complete the courtyard. Other amenities include an arcade and a gift shop. But Clarion's big plus is its location next door to a shopping center with about everything a family could need. There, you'll find 10 dining options, including Outback Steakhouse, Red Lobster, Subway, T.G.I. Friday's, and Chinese, Italian, and Japanese eateries; a Winn-Dixie Marketplace; a liquor store; a bank; a dry cleaner; and a tourist-information center with park passes for sale, among other services. All this is a short walk from your room.

Gaylord Palms Resort & Convention Center ★★★★½

6000 W. Osceola Pkwy.
Kissimmee
☎ 407-586-2000
gaylordpalms.com

Rate per night $257–$283. **Pool** ★★★★. **Fridge in room** Yes. **Shuttle to parks** Yes (Disney only). **Maximum number of occupants per room** 4. **Special comments** Probably the closest you'll get to Disney-level extravagance out of the World. $20/night resort fee.

THIS DECIDEDLY UPSCALE RESORT has a colossal convention facility and caters strongly to business clientele, but it's still a nice (if pricey) family resort.

Hotel wings are defined by the three themed, glass-roofed atriums they overlook. Key West's design is reminiscent of island life in the Florida Keys; Everglades is an overgrown spectacle of shabby swamp chic, complete with piped-in cricket noise and a robotic alligator; and the immense, central St. Augustine harks back to Spanish Colonial Florida. Lagoons, streams, and waterfalls cut through and connect all three, and walkways and bridges abound. A fourth wing, Emerald Bay Tower, overlooks the Emerald Plaza shopping and dining area of the St. Augustine atrium. These rooms are the nicest and the most expensive, and they're mostly used by convention-goers. Though rooms have fridges and alarm clocks with CD players (as well as other perks such as high-speed Internet access), the rooms themselves really work better as retreats for adults than for kids. However, children will enjoy wandering the themed areas and playing in the family pool (with water-squirting octopus). In-room child care is provided by Kid's Nite Out.

Orange Lake Resort   ★★★★½

Rate per night $107–$159. **Pools** ★★★★. **Fridge in room** Yes. **Shuttle to parks** Yes (fee varies depending on destination). **Maximum number of occupants per room** Varies. **Special comments** This is a time-share property, but if you rent directly through the resort as opposed to the sales office, you can avoid time-share sales pitches; $8/night resort fee.

8505 W. US 192
Kissimmee
☎ 407-239-0000 or
800-877-6522
orangelake.com

YOU COULD SPEND YOUR ENTIRE VACATION never leaving this property, about 6–10 minutes from the Disney theme parks. From its 10 pools and two mini-water parks to its golfing opportunities (36 holes of championship greens plus two 9-hole executive courses), Orange Lake offers an extensive menu of amenities and recreational opportunities. If you tire of lazing by the pool, try waterskiing, wakeboarding, tubing, fishing, or other activities on the 80-acre lake. There's also a live alligator show, exercise programs, organized competitive sports and games, arts-and-crafts sessions, and miniature golf. Activities don't end when the sun goes down. Karaoke, live music, a Hawaiian luau, and movies at the resort cinema are some of the evening options.

The 2,412 units are tastefully decorated and comfortably furnished, ranging from suites and studios to three-bedroom villas, all with fully equipped kitchens. If you'd rather not cook on vacation, try one of the seven restaurants scattered across the resort: two cafés, three grills, one pizzeria, and a fast-food eatery. If you need help with (or a break from) the kids, babysitters are available to come to your villa, accompany your family on excursions, or take your children to attractions for you.

Radisson Resort Orlando–Celebration   ★★★★

Rate per night $99–$155. **Pool** ★★★★½. **Fridge in room** Yes. **Shuttle to parks** Yes (Disney only). **Maximum number of occupants per room** 5. **Special comments** $20/night resort fee; kids age 10 and younger eat free with a paying adult at Mandolin's restaurant.

2900 Parkway Blvd.
Kissimmee
☎ 407-396-7000
or 800-634-4774
radissonorlando resort.com

THE POOL ALONE IS WORTH A STAY HERE, but the Radisson Resort gets high marks in all areas. The free-form pool is huge, with a waterfall and waterslide surrounded by palms and flowering plants, plus a smaller heated pool, two whirlpools, and a kiddie pool. Other outdoor amenities include two lighted tennis courts, sand volleyball, a playground, and jogging areas. Kids can also blow off steam at the arcade, while adults might visit the fitness center. Rooms are elegant, featuring Italian furnishings and marble baths. They're of ample size and include a minibar (some rooms), coffeemaker, TV, iron and board, hair dryer, and safe. Dining options include Mandolin's for breakfast (buffet) and dinner and a 1950s-style diner serving burgers, sandwiches, shakes, and Pizza Hut pizza, among other fare. A sports lounge with a 6-by-11–foot TV offers nighttime entertainment. Guest services can help with tours, park passes, car rental, and babysitting. While the hotel doesn't offer children's programs per se, there are plenty of activities, such as face painting by a clown, juggling classes, bingo, and arts and crafts at the pool.

LODGING *at* UNIVERSAL ORLANDO

UNIVERSAL HAS FIVE RESORT HOTELS. The 750-room Portofino Bay Hotel is a gorgeous property set on an artificial bay and themed like an Italian coastal town. The 650-room Hard Rock Hotel is an ultracool "Hotel California" replica, and the 1,000-room, Polynesian-themed Royal Pacific Resort is sumptuously decorated and richly appointed. All three are on the pricey side. The retro-style Cabana Bay Beach Resort, Universal's largest hotel, has 1,800 moderate- and value-priced rooms, plus amenities (bowling alley, lazy river) not seen at comparable Disney resorts. A fifth hotel, the Caribbean-styled Sapphire Falls Resort, opens in 2016 with 1,000 rooms priced between Royal Pacific and Cabana Bay. See the full profiles of Universal's hotels on pages 33–39.

BENEFITS OF STAYING ON-SITE AT UNIVERSAL ORLANDO

UNIVERSAL OFFERS PERKS to get theme park visitors into its hotels. All guests at any Universal Orlando Resort on-site hotel can take advantage of the following:

- Early Park Admission to The Wizarding World 1 hour before the public (see page 229)
- The ability to charge in-park purchases to the hotel-room key
- Free package delivery to the hotel room for any items purchased in the theme parks
- Free parking at the main CityWalk parking garage
- Free transportation to the theme parks and CityWalk
- Pool-hopping privileges to use any hotel's recreational facilities
- Free Wi-Fi Internet in all hotel rooms and public areas (faster speeds available for a fee)
- Free scheduled transportation to SeaWorld, Aquatica, and Wet 'n Wild via the Super Star Shuttle
- Free rental golf clubs, range balls, and transportation (for foursomes) to participating golf courses.

In addition, every guest staying at the three deluxe hotels (Portofino Bay, Hard Rock, and Royal Pacific) get the following benefits:

- Free Universal Express Unlimited Passes for both parks (see page 198)
- Priority seating at select restaurants in the parks and CityWalk

All these benefits are available from the moment you arrive until midnight on the day you check out. Even if your room won't be ready until the afternoon, you can register at your hotel as early in the morning as you like, leaving your bags and retrieving your Express Passes (if eligible) in time for the Early Park Admission hour. Then linger at the resort after your checkout time, taking advantage of your pool privileges until late in the evening.

The most valuable of these perks is the admission to The Wizarding World of Harry Potter 1 hour before the general public each morning, followed by the Universal Express Unlimited Passes for deluxe guests. It's hard to put a dollar value on the Early Park Admission, but two-park Universal Express Unlimited Passes are sold to the general public for $80–$160 per day, per person, excluding tax, depending on the time of year you visit. Universal says the pass is "a value of up to $89," which works out to $356 per day for a family of four. One night at Universal's Royal Pacific hotel costs anywhere from $234 to $404, excluding tax, depending on the season. If you were planning on staying at a comparable off-site deluxe hotel anyway, staying at the Royal Pacific gets your family two days of Universal Express Unlimited at little to no cost. During busy season, this can be a huge boon for parties of four or five. If you are traveling solo or as a couple, or are visiting at a slow time of year, calculate the cost of staying at Cabana Bay or Sapphire Falls and buying Express Passes upon arrival if they turn out to be necessary.

Some of the benefits are of questionable value. Free parking at the theme parks, for example, is of little use to anyone staying at the resort because it's probably just as much walking from the resort as it is from the garages. Having stayed at each of Universal's hotels, we think a sometimes-overlooked benefit is the ability to walk to the parks from your hotel. And it's not just the convenience—the walkways are pretty and almost serene at night, if you can ignore the whooshing noise from The Incredible Hulk Coaster. This Dallas-area family found foot accessibility to the parks to be Universal's biggest advantage over Walt Disney World's on-site hotels:

The simple convenience of being able to walk everywhere whenever you wanted was definitely worth the expense. Disney's shuttle or parking system is extensive. We tried the bus, but it gets bogged down by the stops. Parking your own vehicle meant parking and then using a tram to get to the gate. Magic Kingdom was the worst with its parking off-site; thereby, you cannot hop from park to park quickly. At Universal, with one parking area, everything was easily and quickly reachable. The girls discovered that they could enjoy the park early (with little wait time), walk back to the hotel to nap, and then go back to the park or CityWalk. They felt very grown-up being able to be on their own without us adults to slow them down. This was inconvenient at Disney due to the transport time.

UNIVERSAL ORLANDO VACATION PACKAGES

UNIVERSAL FREQUENTLY OFFERS vacation packages including hotel accommodations and theme park tickets via its in-house travel company, Universal Orlando Vacations. You can book a package yourself by calling ☎ 877-801-9720, or by visiting **universalorlando vacations.com** or your preferred travel agent. Universal Orlando Vacations booked more than 45 days in advance require only a $50 per-person deposit (airfare fully due at time of booking) that is fully refundable until 45 days out; after that, the penalty is $200 per package, though some event tickets may be nonrefundable.

Universal advertises its packages with enticing taglines like, "The Wizarding World from only $109 a night!" You've got to do the math, though, because sometimes it's difficult to see how buying the package can save money over buying each component separately.

Here's an example. A Wizarding World of Harry Potter Vacation Package in early 2015 offered a family of four (two adults and two kids under age 10) these components:

1. Four nights at a Universal on-site hotel (or off-site partner hotel)
2. Three days of park-to-park admission
3. Breakfast at The Three Broomsticks (one per person)
4. Breakfast at the Leaky Cauldron (one per person)
5. Special themed welcome parcel with owl plush, welcome letter, and home delivery of tickets
6. Early Park Admission to The Wizarding World of Harry Potter 1 hour before the general public

Staying at the Royal Pacific Resort, the package started at $1,726, including tax, during the value season, and cost $1,852 during regular season (April and May). There were significant restrictions, including blackout dates around spring break, Easter, and Memorial Day, and the stay had to occur on a Sunday–Thursday to qualify for that low rate; weekend nights were more expensive.

Here's the first thing to recognize: The last item—early admission to The Wizarding World—is automatically given to everyone who stays at a Universal resort. That is already included in the package, so it doesn't have any value by itself.

There are only three components to price: the hotel, tickets, and the breakfasts at The Three Broomsticks and Leaky Cauldron. Universal normally charges $14 for FedEx ticket delivery (discount ticket vendors deliver for free), and the stuffed toy would retail for around $15; the welcome letter has no monetary value. We checked Universal's website for the cost of the other components using various dates in early 2015 and ensured those dates would also qualify for the package above. Here's a typical cost per component:

- $968.40 for four nights (using "Stay More, Save More" discount) at Royal Pacific Resort, including tax (regular seasonal rate $1,210.52, including tax)
- $691.96 for the same three-day tickets from **undercovertourist.com**
- $120.90 for breakfast for four at The Three Broomsticks and Leaky Cauldron, including tax

The total cost if you bought each component separately is $1,781.26, a savings of almost $75 off the online package. You can still reserve breakfast in The Wizarding World through your hotel's ticket desk even without a package. Universal's price for the breakfast is $16 per adult and $12.39 per child, so it's easy enough to figure out what it costs. And you can always have lunch at The Three Broomsticks too, with the money you'll save by buying each item separately.

While it won't save you money, there are a few reasons why you might still want to book a Universal Orlando Vacations package. The first is if you can't afford to stay on-site but still want Early Park Admission to The Wizarding World. Booking a room at a Universal-area partner hotel as part of a package through Universal Orlando Vacations is the only way to get guaranteed early entry to the Harry Potter attractions, other than staying in an on-site hotel.

Another reason is if you are attending a special event at Universal Orlando that offers exclusive experiences for package buyers. For example, the Celebration of Harry Potter fan convention in January holds an after-hours party in The Wizarding World just for vacation-package purchasers. Occasionally, packages are offered with truly unique perks: Before the openings of Hogsmeade and Diagon Alley, a limited number of package holders were allowed into the new Wizarding Worlds weeks before the general public. These rare opportunities are only for the diehards because uncontrollable technical delays can always preempt previews without refunds.

HOTELS *and* MOTELS:
Rated and Ranked

IN THIS SECTION, WE COMPARE HOTELS in the four lodging areas defined earlier in this chapter. Additional hotels can be found at the intersection of US 27 and I-4, on US 441 (Orange Blossom Trail), and in downtown Orlando. Most of these require more than 30 minutes of commuting to Orlando attractions and thus are not rated. We also haven't rated lodging east of Siesta Lago Drive on US 192.

WHAT'S IN A ROOM?

EXCEPT FOR CLEANLINESS, state of repair, and decor, travelers pay little attention to hotel rooms. There is, of course, a clear standard of quality that differentiates Motel 6 from Holiday Inn, Holiday Inn from Marriott, and so on. Many guests, however, fail to appreciate that some rooms are better engineered than others. Making the room usable to its occupants is an art that combines both form and function.

Decor and taste are important. No one wants to stay in a room that's dated, garish, or ugly. But beyond decor, how "livable" is the room? In Orlando, for example, we've seen some beautifully appointed rooms that aren't well designed for human habitation. Even more than decor, your room's details and design elements are the things that will make you feel comfortable and at home.

ROOM RATINGS

TO EVALUATE PROPERTIES FOR THEIR QUALITY, tastefulness, state of repair, cleanliness, and size of their standard rooms, we have grouped the hotels and motels into classifications denoted by stars—the overall star rating. Star ratings in this guide apply only to Orlando-area properties and don't necessarily correspond to ratings awarded by Frommer's, Mobil, AAA, or other travel critics. Because stars have little relevance when awarded in the absence of recognized standards of comparison, we have tied our ratings to expected levels of quality established by specific American hotel corporations.

unofficial **TIP**
The key to avoiding disappointment is to snoop in advance. Ask how old the hotel is and when its guest rooms were last renovated.

Overall star ratings apply only to room quality and describe the property's standard accommodations. For most hotels, a standard accommodation is a room with one king bed or two queen beds. In an all-suite property, the standard accommodation is either a studio or a one-bedroom suite. In addition to standard accommodations, many hotels offer luxury rooms and special suites, which aren't rated in this guide. Star ratings for rooms are assigned without regard to whether a property has restaurant(s), recreational facilities, entertainment, or other extras.

In addition to stars (which delineate broad categories), we use a numerical rating system—the room-quality rating. Our scale is 0–100, with 100 being the best possible rating and zero (0) the worst. Numerical ratings show the difference we perceive between one property and another. For instance, rooms at both the Stay Sky Suites I-Drive Orlando and the Clarion Suites Maingate are rated three and a half stars (★★★½). In the supplemental numerical ratings, the former is an 82 and the latter a 76. This means that within the ★★★½ category, Stay Sky Suites has slightly nicer rooms than Clarion Suites.

The location column identifies the area in Orlando where you'll find a particular property. **WDW** indicates that the property is inside Walt Disney World. A **1** means it's on or near International Drive. Properties on or near US 192 (also known as Irlo Bronson Memorial Highway, Vine Street, and Space Coast Parkway) are indicated by a **3**, and those in the vicinity of Universal Orlando as **4**. All others are marked with

2 and for the most part are along FL 535 and the I-4 corridor, though some are in nearby locations that don't meet any other criteria.

Names of properties along US 192 also designate location (for example, Holiday Inn Maingate West). The consensus in Orlando seems to be that the main entrance to Disney World is the broad interstate-type road that runs off US 192. This is called the Maingate. Properties along US 192 call themselves Maingate East or West to differentiate their positions along the highway. So, driving southeast from Clermont or Florida's Turnpike, the properties before you reach the Maingate turnoff are called Maingate West, while the properties after you pass the Maingate turnoff are called Maingate East.

LODGING AREAS (see map on page 14)	
WDW Walt Disney World	
1 International Drive	**2** Lake Buena Vista and I-4 Corridor
3 US 192 (Irlo Bronson Memorial Highway)	**4** Universal Orlando Area

Cost estimates are based on the hotel's published rack rates for standard rooms. Each **$** represents $50. Thus a cost symbol of **$$$** means that a room (or suite) at that hotel will be about $150 a night; amounts over $200 are indicated by **$ x 5** and so on.

OVERALL STAR RATINGS		
★★★★★	Superior rooms	Tasteful and luxurious by any standard
★★★★	Extremely nice rooms	What you'd expect at a Hyatt Regency or Marriott
★★★	Nice rooms	Holiday Inn or comparable quality
★★	Adequate rooms	Clean, comfortable, and functional without frills—like a Motel 6
★	Super-budget	These exist but are not included in our coverage

We've focused on room quality and excluded consideration of location, services, recreation, or amenities. In some instances, a one- or two-room suite is available for the same price or less than that of a single standard hotel room.

If you've used an earlier edition of this guide, you'll notice that new properties have been added and many ratings and rankings have changed, some because of room renovation or improved maintenance or housekeeping. Lax housekeeping or failure to maintain rooms can bring down ratings.

Before you shop for a hotel, consider this letter from a man in Hot Springs, Arkansas:

We canceled our room reservations to follow the advice in your book and reserved a hotel highly ranked by The Unofficial Guide. *We wanted inexpensive but clean and cheerful. We got inexpensive but also dirty, grim, and depressing. The room spoiled the holiday for me aside from our touring.*

This letter was as unsettling to us as the bad room was to the reader—our integrity as travel journalists is based on the quality of the information we provide. When rechecking the hotel, we found that our rating was representative, but the reader had been assigned one of a small number of threadbare rooms scheduled for renovation.

Be aware that some chains use the same guest room photo in promotional literature for all their hotels and that the rooms at a specific property may bear no resemblance to the photo in question. When you or your travel agent calls, ask how old the property is and when the guest room you're being assigned was last renovated. If you're assigned a room that is inferior to your expectations, demand to be moved.

A WORD ABOUT TOLL-FREE TELEPHONE NUMBERS

AS WE'VE REPEATED SEVERAL TIMES in this chapter, it's essential to communicate with the hotel directly when shopping for deals and stating your room preferences. Most toll-free numbers are routed directly to a hotel chain's central reservations office, and the customer-service agents there typically have little or no knowledge of the individual hotels in the chain or of any specials those hotels may be offering. In our Hotel Information Chart (pages 62–72), therefore, we list the toll-free number only if it connects directly to the hotel in question; otherwise, we provide the hotel's local phone number. After you've reserved your room, you can check online to make sure the reservation is in order.

TOP 30 BEST HOTEL VALUES

IN THE CHART ON THE OPPOSITE PAGE, we look at the best combinations of quality and value in a room. Rankings are calculated without consideration for location or the availability of restaurant(s), recreational facilities, entertainment, and/or amenities.

A reader wrote to complain that he had booked one of our top-ranked rooms in terms of value and had been very disappointed in the room. We noticed that the room the reader occupied had a quality rating of ★★½. Remember that the list of top deals is intended to give you some sense of value received for dollars spent. A ★★½ room at $40 may have the same *value* as a ★★★★ room at $115, but that doesn't mean the rooms will be of comparable *quality*. Regardless of whether it's a good deal, a ★★½ room is still a ★★½ room.

TOP 30 BEST HOTEL VALUES

	HOTEL	LOCATION	QUALITY	ROOM RATING	COST ($ = $50)
1.	Rodeway Inn Maingate	3	★★½	59	$-
2.	Monumental Hotel	1	★★★★½	94	$$-
3.	Shades of Green	WDW	★★★★½	91	$$-
4.	Extended Stay America Orlando Lake Buena Vista	2	★★★★	83	$$-
5.	Extended Stay America Convention Center/Westwood	1	★★★★	84	$$-
6.	Holiday Inn Main Gate East	3	★★★★½	90	$$+
7.	Monumental MovieLand Hotel	1	★★★	68	$+
8.	Vacation Village at Parkway	3	★★★★½	91	$$+
9.	Motel 6 Orlando–I-Drive	1	★★★	66	$+
10.	Westgate Vacation Villas	2	★★★★½	90	$$+
11.	Super 8 Kissimmee/Maingate	3	★★★	70	$+
12.	Radisson Resort Orlando-Celebration	3	★★★★	86	$$
13.	Inn at Calypso	3	★★★½	82	$$-
14.	Westgate Town Center	2	★★★★½	93	$$+
15.	Hampton Inn & Suites Orlando–South Lake Buena Vista	3	★★★½	80	$$-
16.	Super 8 Kissimmee	3	★★½	60	$-
17.	Hilton Grand Vacations Club at SeaWorld	1	★★★★½	95	$$$-
18.	Extended Stay America Deluxe Orlando Theme Parks	4	★★★½	75	$$-
19.	Extended Stay America Orlando Theme Parks	4	★★★½	75	$$-
20.	Rosen Inn at Pointe Orlando	1	★★★½	75	$$-
21.	Hilton Orlando Bonnet Creek	1	★★★★	88	$$+
22.	Four Points by Sheraton Orlando Studio City	1	★★★★½	90	$$$-
23.	Quality Suites Turkey Lake	2	★★★	74	$+
24.	Legacy Vacation Club Orlando	3	★★★½	80	$$$-
25.	Knights Inn Maingate Kissimmee/Orlando	3	★★	58	$-
26.	Extended Stay America Orlando Convention Center	1	★★★	72	$+
27.	Orange Lake Resort	3	★★★★½	94	$$$-
28.	La Quinta Inn Orlando I-Drive	1	★★★	73	$$-
29.	Barefoot'n Resort	3	★★★★	85	$$+
30.	Ramada Convention Center I-Drive	1	★★★	65	$+

HOW THE HOTELS COMPARE

HOTEL	LOCATION	QUALITY	ROOM RATING	COST ($ = $50)
Four Seasons Resort Orlando at Walt Disney World Resort	WDW	★★★★★	98	$ x 9
Omni Orlando Resort at ChampionsGate	2	★★★★★	96	$+ x 5
Hilton Grand Vacations Club at SeaWorld	1	★★★★½	95	$$$-
Rosen Centre Hotel	1	★★★★½	95	$$$+
Disney's Animal Kingdom Villas (Kidani Village)	WDW	★★★★½	95	$- x 10
Bay Lake Tower at Disney's Contemporary Resort	WDW	★★★★½	95	$- x 12
Monumental Hotel	1	★★★★½	94	$$-
Orange Lake Resort	3	★★★★½	94	$$$-
Gaylord Palms Hotel & Convention Center	3	★★★★½	94	$$$+
Ritz-Carlton Orlando, Grande Lakes	1	★★★★½	94	$+ x 5
Westgate Town Center	2	★★★★½	93	$$+
Waldorf Astoria Orlando	2	★★★★½	93	$$$$+
JW Marriott Orlando Grande Lakes	1	★★★★½	93	$+ x 5
Hard Rock Hotel Orlando	4	★★★★½	93	$ x 8
Disney's Contemporary Resort	WDW	★★★★½	93	$+ x 9
Disney's Grand Floridian Resort & Spa	WDW	★★★★½	93	$- x 14
Villas at Disney's Grand Floridian Resort & Spa	WDW	★★★★½	93	$- x 13
DoubleTree by Hilton Orlando at SeaWorld	1	★★★★½	92	$$$+
Marriott's Grande Vista	1	★★★★½	92	$$$+
Westgate Lakes Resort & Spa	2	★★★★½	92	$$$+
Hilton Orlando	1	★★★★½	92	$$$$+
Villas of Grand Cypress	2	★★★★½	92	$- x 5
Hyatt Regency Grand Cypress	3	★★★★½	92	$- x 5
Marriott's Sabal Palms	2	★★★★½	92	$+ x 6
Universal's Portofino Bay Hotel	4	★★★★½	92	$+ x 8
Disney's Polynesian Village, Villas & Bungalows (studios)	WDW	★★★★½	92	$+ x 11
Disney's Polynesian Village Resort	WDW	★★★★½	92	$- x 12
Vacation Village at Parkway	3	★★★★½	91	$$+
Shades of Green	WDW	★★★★½	91	$$-
Disney's Animal Kingdom Villas (Jambo House)	WDW	★★★★½	91	$ x 8
Holiday Inn Main Gate East	3	★★★★½	90	$$+
Westgate Vacation Villas	2	★★★★½	90	$$+
Four Points by Sheraton Orlando Studio City	1	★★★★½	90	$$$-
Polynesian Isles Resort (Diamond Resorts)	3	★★★★½	90	$$$
Rosen Plaza Hotel	1	★★★★½	90	$$$+

HOW THE HOTELS COMPARE

HOTEL	LOCATION	QUALITY	ROOM RATING	COST ($ = $50)
Bohemian Celebration Hotel	2	★★★★½	90	$$$+
Renaissance Orlando at SeaWorld	1	★★★★½	90	$$$+
Marriott's Harbour Lake	2	★★★★½	90	$$$$-
Hyatt Regency Orlando	1	★★★★½	90	$$$$-
Lighthouse Key Resort & Spa	3	★★★★½	90	$$$$-
Liki Tiki Village	3	★★★★½	90	$$$$-
Grand Beach	1	★★★★½	90	$$$$-
Walt Disney World Dolphin	WDW	★★★★½	90	$$$$+
Walt Disney World Swan	WDW	★★★★½	90	$$$$+
Orlando World Center Marriott Resort	2	★★★★½	90	$$$$+
Wyndham Bonnet Creek Resort	2	★★★★½	90	$$$$+
Universal's Royal Pacific Resort	4	★★★★½	90	$+ x 6
Disney's Old Key West Resort	WDW	★★★★½	90	$+ x 8
Disney's Saratoga Springs Resort & Spa	WDW	★★★★½	90	$+ x 8
Disney's Beach Club Resort	WDW	★★★★½	90	$+ x 9
Villas at Disney's Wilderness Lodge	WDW	★★★★½	90	$- x 10
Disney's Beach Club Villas	WDW	★★★★½	90	$- x 10
Disney's BoardWalk Villas	WDW	★★★★½	90	$- x 10
Treehouse Villas at Disney's Saratoga Springs Resort & Spa	WDW	★★★★½	90	$- x 20
DoubleTree Universal	4	★★★★	89	$$$-
Courtyard Orlando Lake Buena Vista at Vista Centre	2	★★★★	89	$$$-
Sheraton Vistana Resort Villas	2	★★★★	89	$$$$-
Disney's Animal Kingdom Lodge	WDW	★★★★	89	$ x 8
Disney's Yacht Club Resort	WDW	★★★★	89	$- x 10
Disney's BoardWalk Inn	WDW	★★★★	89	$+ x 10
Hilton Orlando Bonnet Creek	1	★★★★	88	$$+
WorldQuest Orlando Resort	1	★★★★	88	$$$-
Caribe Royale All-Suite Hotel & Convention Center	1	★★★★	88	$$$+
Hilton Garden Inn Lake Buena Vista/ Orlando	2	★★★★	88	$$$+
Hilton Grand Vacations Club on I-Drive	1	★★★★	88	$$$+
Sheraton Lake Buena Vista Resort	2	★★★★	88	$$$+
Rosen Shingle Creek	1	★★★★	88	$$$+
Universal's Cabana Bay Beach Resort	4	★★★★	88	$$$$-
Hilton Orlando Lake Buena Vista	WDW	★★★★	87	$$$-
Mystic Dunes Resort & Golf Club	3	★★★★	87	$$$-
Wyndham Cypress Palms	3	★★★★	87	$$$
Westin Orlando Universal Boulevard	1	★★★★	87	$$$$+

HOW THE HOTELS COMPARE

HOTEL	LOCATION	QUALITY	ROOM RATING	COST ($ = $50)
Radisson Resort Orlando-Celebration	3	★★★★	86	$$
Embassy Suites Orlando–Lake Buena Vista Resort	2	★★★★	86	$$$+
Floridays Resort Orlando	1	★★★★	86	$$$$
Marriott's Cypress Harbour	1	★★★★	86	$ x 6
Disney's Fort Wilderness Resort (cabins)	WDW	★★★★	86	$- x 8
Disney's Wilderness Lodge	WDW	★★★★	86	$- x 9
Marriott's Imperial Palms	1	★★★★	86	$- x 9
Barefoot'n Resort	3	★★★★	85	$$+
Hawthorn Suites Lake Buena Vista	2	★★★★	85	$$+
Wyndham Orlando Resort I-Drive	1	★★★★	85	$$+
Residence Inn Orlando at SeaWorld	2	★★★★	85	$$$-
Legacy Vacation Club Lake Buena Vista	2	★★★★	85	$$$-
Homewood Suites by Hilton LBV-Orlando	2	★★★★	85	$$$$-
Marriott's Royal Palms	1	★★★★	85	$- x 6
Extended Stay America Convention Center/Westwood	1	★★★★	84	$$-
Star Island Resort & Club	3	★★★★	84	$$$+
Hyatt Place Orlando/Universal	4	★★★★	84	$$$+
Disney's Port Orleans Resort–French Quarter	WDW	★★★★	84	$- x 5
Extended Stay America Orlando Lake Buena Vista	2	★★★★	83	$$-
Buena Vista Suites	1	★★★★	83	$$$+
Disney's Coronado Springs Resort	WDW	★★★★	83	$- x 5
Disney's Port Orleans Resort–Riverside	WDW	★★★★	83	$- x 5
Inn at Calypso	3	★★★½	82	$$-
Courtyard Orlando LBV in Marriott Village	2	★★★½	82	$$+
Stay Sky Suites I-Drive Orlando	1	★★★½	82	$$+
CoCo Key Water Resort-Orlando	1	★★★½	82	$$+
Point Universal Orlando Resort, The	1	★★★½	82	$$+
Holiday Inn Resort Lake Buena Vista	2	★★★½	82	$$+
Radisson Hotel Orlando Lake Buena Vista	2	★★★½	82	$$$-
Castle Hotel	1	★★★½	82	$$$+
B Resort	WDW	★★★½	82	$$$+
Nickelodeon Suites Resort	1	★★★½	82	$$$$
Parkway International Resort	3	★★★½	82	$- x 5
Westgate Towers	2	★★★½	81	$$+
Homewood Suites by Hilton I-Drive	1	★★★½	81	$$$$-
Hampton Inn & Suites Orlando–South Lake Buena Vista	3	★★★½	80	$$-

HOW THE HOTELS COMPARE

HOTEL	LOCATION	QUALITY	ROOM RATING	COST ($ = $50)
Legacy Vacation Club Orlando	3	★★★½	80	$$$-
Comfort Inn Orlando–Lake Buena Vista	2	★★★½	80	$$
Hilton Garden Inn Orlando I-Drive North	1	★★★½	80	$$+
Hawthorn Suites Orlando Convention Center	1	★★★½	80	$$+
Fairfield Inn & Suites Near Universal Orlando Resort	4	★★★½	80	$$$-
Hilton Garden Inn Orlando at SeaWorld	1	★★★½	80	$$$-
Embassy Suites Orlando I-Drive/Jamaican Court	1	★★★½	80	$$$-
Residence Inn Orlando Convention Center	1	★★★½	80	$$$-
Buena Vista Palace Hotel & Spa	WDW	★★★½	80	$$$-
Disney's Art of Animation Resort	WDW	★★★½	80	$$$$-
SpringHill Suites Orlando Convention Center	1	★★★½	80	$$$$-
Orbit One Vacation Villas	3	★★★½	80	$$$$-
Disney's Caribbean Beach Resort	WDW	★★★½	80	$$$$+
Fairfield Inn & Suites Orlando Lake Buena Vista	2	★★★½	79	$$+
Holiday Inn in the Walt Disney World Resort	WDW	★★★½	79	$$$+
Courtyard Orlando I-Drive	1	★★★½	78	$$+
Park Inn by Radisson Resort and Conference Center	3	★★★½	78	$$$-
Clarion Suites Maingate	3	★★★½	76	$$
Palms Hotel & Villas	3	★★★½	76	$$+
Grand Lake Resort	1	★★★½	76	$$+
Hampton Inn Orlando/Lake Buena Vista	2	★★★½	76	$$$-
Quality Suites Lake Buena Vista	2	★★★½	76	$$$-
Quality Suites Royale Parc Suites	3	★★★½	76	$$$+
Extended Stay America Deluxe Orlando Theme Parks	4	★★★½	75	$$-
Extended Stay America Orlando Theme Parks	4	★★★½	75	$$-
Rosen Inn at Pointe Orlando	1	★★★½	75	$$-
Best Western Plus Universal Inn	4	★★★½	75	$$-
Hawthorn Suites Orlando I-Drive	1	★★★½	75	$$+
Fairfield Inn & Suites Orlando LBV in Marriott Village	2	★★★½	75	$$+
Embassy Suites Orlando I-Drive	1	★★★½	75	$$#-
Holiday Inn & Suites Orlando Universal	4	★★★½	75	$$$-
Wyndham Lake Buena Vista Resort	WDW	★★★½	75	$$+
DoubleTree Guest Suites	WDW	★★★½	75	$$$
Residence Inn Orlando Lake Buena Vista	2	★★★½	75	$$$+

HOW THE HOTELS COMPARE

HOTEL	LOCATION	QUALITY	ROOM RATING	COST ($ = $50)
Sonesta ES Suites Orlando	1	★★★½	75	$$$+
Best Western Premier Saratoga Resort Villas	3	★★★½	75	$$$$−
Quality Suites Turkey Lake	2	★★★	74	$+
Galleria Palms Kissimmee Hotel	3	★★★	74	$$−
Crown Club Inn	3	★★★	74	$$−
Fairfield Inn & Suites Orlando I-Drive/Convention Center	1	★★★	74	$$+
Best Western Lake Buena Vista Resort Hotel	WDW	★★★	74	$$$+
La Quinta Inn Orlando I-Drive	1	★★★	73	$$−
International Palms Resort & Conference Center	1	★★★	73	$$+
Disney's All-Star Movies Resort	WDW	★★★	73	$$$−
Disney's All-Star Music Resort	WDW	★★★	73	$$$−
Disney's All-Star Sports Resort	WDW	★★★	73	$$$−
Extended Stay America Orlando Convention Center	1	★★★	72	$+
Baymont Inn & Suites Celebration	3	★★★	72	$$
Ramada Plaza Resort and Suites Orlando I-Drive	1	★★★	72	$$+
Staybridge Suites Lake Buena Vista	2	★★★	72	$$$+
SpringHill Suites Orlando LBV in Marriott Village	2	★★★	71	$$$+
Disney's Pop Century Resort	WDW	★★★	71	$$$+
Super 8 Kissimmee/Maingate	3	★★★	70	$+
Hampton Inn I-Drive/Convention Center	1	★★★	70	$$+
Comfort Suites Universal	4	★★★	70	$$+
Monumental MovieLand Hotel	1	★★★	68	$+
Westgate Palace	1	★★★	68	$$$$−
Maingate Lakeside Resort	3	★★★	67	$$−
Enclave Hotel & Suites	1	★★★	67	$$$−
Hampton Inn Universal	4	★★★	67	$$$−
Motel 6 Orlando–I-Drive	1	★★★	66	$+
Comfort Inn I-Drive	1	★★★	66	$$−
Ramada Convention Center I-Drive	1	★★★	65	$+
Rosen Inn International Hotel	1	★★★	65	$$+
Best Western I-Drive	1	★★★	65	$$+
Magnuson Grand Hotel Maingate West	3	★★★	65	$$+
Clarion Inn & Suites at I-Drive	1	★★½	64	$+
Clarion Inn Lake Buena Vista	2	★★½	64	$$−
Hampton Inn South of Universal	1	★★½	64	$$$−

HOW THE HOTELS COMPARE

HOTEL	LOCATION	QUALITY	ROOM RATING	COST ($ = $50)
Silver Lake Resort	3	★★½	64	$$$
Floridian Hotel & Suites	1	★★½	63	$$-
La Quinta Inn Orlando-Universal Studios	4	★★½	63	$$-
Country Inn & Suites Orlando Universal	1	★★½	63	$$
Comfort Inn Maingate	3	★★½	62	$$+
Avanti Resort Orlando	1	★★½	62	$$+
Celebration Suites	3	★★½	61	$+
Super 8 Kissimmee	3	★★½	60	$-
Destiny Palms Maingate West	3	★★½	60	$+
Royal Celebration Inn	3	★★½	60	$+
Rodeway Inn Maingate	3	★★½	59	$-
Knights Inn Maingate Kissimmee/Orlando	3	★★	58	$-
Red Roof Inn Orlando Convention Center	1	★★	58	$+
Extended Stay Orlando Convention Center	1	★★	58	$$

HOTEL INFORMATION CHART

Avanti Resort Orlando ★★½ 8738 International Dr. Orlando, FL 32819 ☎ 407-313-0100 **avantiresort.com** LOCATION 1 ROOM RATING 62 COST ($=$50) $$+	**B Resort** ★★★½ 1905 Hotel Plaza Blvd. Lake Buena Vista, FL 32830 ☎ 407-828-2828 **bresortlbv.com** LOCATION WDW ROOM RATING 82 COST ($=$50) $$$+	**Barefoot'n Resort** ★★★★ 2754 Florida Plaza Blvd. Kissimmee, FL 34746 ☎ 407-589-2127 **barefootn.com** LOCATION 3 ROOM RATING 85 COST ($=$50) $$+
Bay Lake Tower at Disney's Contemporary Resort ★★★★½ 4600 N. World Dr. Lake Buena Vista, FL 32830 ☎ 407-824-1000 **tinyurl.com/baylaketower** LOCATION WDW ROOM RATING 95 COST ($=$50) $- X 12	**Baymont Inn & Suites Celebration** ★★★ 7601 Black Lake Rd. Celebration, FL 34747 ☎ 407-396-1100 **tinyurl.com/baymontcelebration** LOCATION 3 ROOM RATING 72 COST ($=$50) $$	**Best Western I-Drive** ★★★ 8222 Jamaican Ct. Orlando, FL 32819 ☎ 407-345-1172 **tinyurl.com/bwidrive** LOCATION 1 ROOM RATING 65 COST ($=$50) $$+
Best Western Lake Buena Vista Resort Hotel ★★★ 2000 Hotel Plaza Blvd. Lake Buena Vista, FL 32830 ☎ 407-828-2424 **lakebuenavistaresorthotel.com** LOCATION WDW ROOM RATING 74 COST ($=$50) $$$+	**Best Western Plus Universal Inn** ★★★½ 5618 Vineland Rd. Orlando, FL 32819 ☎ 407-226-9119 **tinyurl.com/bwuniversal** LOCATION 4 ROOM RATING 75 COST ($=$50) $$-	**Best Western Premier Saratoga Resort Villas** ★★★½ 4787 W. US 192* Kissimmee, FL 34746 ☎ 407-997-3300 **bestwesternpremier kissimmee.com** LOCATION 3 ROOM RATING 75 COST ($=$50) $$$$-
Bohemian Celebration Hotel ★★★★½ 700 Bloom St. Celebration, FL 34747 ☎ 407-566-6000 **celebrationhotel.com** LOCATION 2 ROOM RATING 90 COST ($=$50) $$$+	**Buena Vista Palace Hotel & Spa** ★★★½ 1900 E. Buena Vista Dr. Lake Buena Vista, FL 32830 ☎ 407-827-2727 **buenavistapalace.com** LOCATION WDW ROOM RATING 80 COST ($=$50) $$$-	**Buena Vista Suites** ★★★★ 8203 World Center Dr. Orlando, FL 32821 ☎ 407-239-8588 **bvsuites.com** LOCATION 1 ROOM RATING 83 COST ($=$50) $$$+
Caribe Royale All-Suite Hotel & Convention Center ★★★★ 8101 World Center Dr. Orlando, FL 32821 ☎ 407-238-8000 **cariberoyale.com** LOCATION 1 ROOM RATING 88 COST ($=$50) $$$+	**Castle Hotel** ★★★½ 8629 International Dr. Orlando, FL 32819 ☎ 407-345-1511 **castlehotelorlando.com** LOCATION 1 ROOM RATING 82 COST ($=$50) $$$+	**Celebration Suites** ★★½ 5820 W. US 192* Kissimmee, FL 34746 ☎ 407-396-7900 **suitesatoldtown.com** LOCATION 3 ROOM RATING 61 COST ($=$50) $+
Clarion Inn & Suites at I-Drive ★★½ 9956 Hawaiian Ct. Orlando, FL 32819 ☎ 407-351-5100 **tinyurl.com/clarionidrive** LOCATION 1 ROOM RATING 64 COST ($=$50) $+	**Clarion Inn Lake Buena Vista** ★★½ 8442 Palm Pkwy. Lake Buena Vista, FL 32836 ☎ 407-996-7300 **clarionlbv.com** LOCATION 2 ROOM RATING 64 COST ($=$50) $$-	**Clarion Suites Maingate** ★★★½ 7888 W. US 192* Kissimmee, FL 34747 ☎ 407-390-9888 **clarionsuiteskissimmee.com** LOCATION 3 ROOM RATING 76 COST ($=$50) $$

*US 192 is known locally as Irlo Bronson Memorial Highway.

HOTEL INFORMATION CHART

CoCo Key Water Resort–Orlando ★★★½
7400 International Dr.
Orlando, FL 32819
☎ 407-351-2626
cocokeyorlando.com
LOCATION 1
ROOM RATING 82
COST ($=$50) $$+

Comfort Inn I-Drive ★★★
8134 International Dr.
Orlando, FL 32819
☎ 407-313-4000
tinyurl.com/comfortidrive
LOCATION 1
ROOM RATING 66
COST ($=$50) $$-

Comfort Inn Maingate ★★½
7675 W. US 192*
Kissimmee, FL 34747
☎ 407-396-4000
comfortinnkissimmee.com
LOCATION 3
ROOM RATING 62
COST ($=$50) $$+

Comfort Inn Orlando–Lake Buena Vista ★★★½
8686 Palm Pkwy.
Orlando, FL 32836
☎ 407-239-8400
tinyurl.com/comfortinnlbv
LOCATION 2
ROOM RATING 80
COST ($=$50) $$

Comfort Suites Universal ★★★
5617 Major Blvd.
Orlando, FL 32819
☎ 407-363-1967
tinyurl.com/csuniversal
LOCATION 4
ROOM RATING 70
COST ($=$50) $$+

Country Inn & Suites Orlando Universal ★★½
7701 Universal Blvd.
Orlando, FL 32819
☎ 407-313-4200
countryinns.com/orlandofl_universal
LOCATION 1
ROOM RATING 63
COST ($=$50) $$

Courtyard Orlando I-Drive ★★★½
8600 Austrian Ct.
Orlando, FL 32819
☎ 407-351-2244
tinyurl.com/courtyardidrive
LOCATION 1
ROOM RATING 78
COST ($=$50) $$+

Courtyard Orlando LBV in Marriott Village ★★★½
8623 Vineland Ave.
Orlando, FL 32821
☎ 407-938-9001
tinyurl.com/courtyardlbvmarriottvillage
LOCATION 2
ROOM RATING 82
COST ($=$50) $$+

Courtyard Orlando LBV at Vista Centre ★★★★
8501 Palm Pkwy.
Lake Buena Vista, FL 32836
☎ 407-239-6900
tinyurl.com/courtyardlbv
LOCATION 2
ROOM RATING 89
COST ($=$50) $$$-

Crown Club Inn ★★★
105 Summer Bay Blvd.
Clermont, FL 34711
☎ 407-239-8315
crownclubinn.com
LOCATION 3
ROOM RATING 74
COST ($=$50) $$-

Destiny Palms Maingate West ★★½
8536 W. US 192*
Kissimmee, FL 34747
☎ 407-396-1600
destinypalmshotel.com
LOCATION 3
ROOM RATING 60
COST ($=$50) $+

Disney's All-Star Movies Resort ★★★
1901 W. Buena Vista Dr.
Lake Buena Vista, FL 32830
☎ 407-939-7000
tinyurl.com/allstarmovies
LOCATION WDW
ROOM RATING 73
COST ($=$50) $$$-

Disney's All-Star Music Resort ★★★
1801 W. Buena Vista Dr.
Lake Buena Vista, FL 32830
☎ 407-939-6000
tinyurl.com/allstarmusicresort
LOCATION WDW
ROOM RATING 73
COST ($=$50) $$$-

Disney's All-Star Sports Resort ★★★
1701 W. Buena Vista Dr.
Lake Buena Vista, FL 32830
☎ 407-939-5000
tinyurl.com/allstarsports
LOCATION WDW
ROOM RATING 73
COST ($=$50) $$$-

Disney's Animal Kingdom Lodge ★★★★
2901 Osceola Pkwy.
Lake Buena Vista, FL 32830
☎ 407-938-3000
tinyurl.com/aklodge
LOCATION WDW
ROOM RATING 89
COST ($=$50) $ X 8

Disney's Animal Kingdom Villas (Jambo House) ★★★★½
2901 Osceola Pkwy.
Lake Buena Vista, FL 32830
☎ 407-938-3000
tinyurl.com/akjambo
LOCATION WDW
ROOM RATING 91
COST ($=$50) $ X 8

Disney's Animal Kingdom Villas (Kidani Village) ★★★★½
3701 Osceola Pkwy.
Lake Buena Vista, FL 32830
☎ 407-938-7400
tinyurl.com/akkidani
LOCATION WDW
ROOM RATING 95
COST ($=$50) $- X 10

Disney's Art of Animation Resort ★★★½
1850 Animation Way
Lake Buena Vista, FL 32830
☎ 407-938-7000
tinyurl.com/artofanimationresort
LOCATION WDW
ROOM RATING 80
COST ($=$50) $$$$-

HOTEL INFORMATION CHART

Disney's Beach Club Resort ★★★★½ 1800 Epcot Resorts Blvd. Lake Buena Vista, FL 32830 ☎ 407-934-8000 **tinyurl.com/beachclubresort**	**Disney's Beach Club Villas** ★★★★½ 1800 Epcot Resorts Blvd. Lake Buena Vista, FL 32830 ☎ 407-934-8000 **tinyurl.com/beachclubvillas**	**Disney's BoardWalk Inn** ★★★★ 2101 N. Epcot Resorts Blvd. Lake Buena Vista, FL 32830 ☎ 407-939-6200 **tinyurl.com/boardwalkinn**
LOCATION WDW ROOM RATING 90 COST ($=$50) $+ X 9	LOCATION WDW ROOM RATING 90 COST ($=$50) $- X 10	LOCATION WDW ROOM RATING 89 COST ($=$50) $+ X 10
Disney's BoardWalk Villas ★★★★½ 2101 N. Epcot Resorts Blvd. Lake Buena Vista, FL 32830 ☎ 407-939-6200 **tinyurl.com/boardwalkvillas**	**Disney's Caribbean Beach Resort** ★★★½ 900 Cayman Way Lake Buena Vista, FL 32830 ☎ 407-934-3400 **tinyurl.com/caribbean beachresort**	**Disney's Contemporary Resort** ★★★★½ 4600 N. World Dr. Lake Buena Vista, FL 32830 ☎ 407-824-1000 **tinyurl.com/contemporarywdw**
LOCATION WDW ROOM RATING 90 COST ($=$50) $- X 10	LOCATION WDW ROOM RATING 80 COST ($=$50) $$$$+	LOCATION WDW ROOM RATING 93 COST ($=$50) $+ X 9
Disney's Coronado Springs Resort ★★★★ 1000 W. Buena Vista Dr. Lake Buena Vista, FL 32830 ☎ 407-939-1000 **tinyurl.com/coronadosprings**	**Disney's Fort Wilderness Resort** (cabins) ★★★★ 4510 N. Fort Wilderness Trl. Lake Buena Vista, FL 32830 ☎ 407-824-2837 **tinyurl.com/ftwilderness**	**Disney's Grand Floridian Resort & Spa** ★★★★½ 4401 Floridian Way Lake Buena Vista, FL 32830 ☎ 407-824-3000 **tinyurl.com/grandflresort**
LOCATION WDW ROOM RATING 83 COST ($=$50) $- X 5	LOCATION WDW ROOM RATING 86 COST ($=$50) $- X 8	LOCATION WDW ROOM RATING 93 COST ($=$50) $- X 14
Disney's Old Key West Resort ★★★★½ 1510 North Cove Rd. Lake Buena Vista, FL 32830 ☎ 407-827-7700 **tinyurl.com/oldkeywest**	**Disney's Polynesian Village Resort** ★★★★½ 1600 Seven Seas Dr. Lake Buena Vista, FL 32830 ☎ 407-824-2000 **tinyurl.com/polynesianresort**	**Disney's Polynesian Village, Villas & Bungalows** (studios) ★★★★½ 1600 Seven Seas Dr. Lake Buena Vista, FL 32830 ☎ 407-824-2000 **tinyurl.com/polynesianresort**
LOCATION WDW ROOM RATING 90 COST ($=$50) $+ X 8	LOCATION WDW ROOM RATING 92 COST ($=$50) $- X 12	LOCATION WDW ROOM RATING 92 COST ($=$50) $+ X 11
Disney's Pop Century Resort ★★★ 1050 Century Dr. Lake Buena Vista, FL 32830 ☎ 407-938-4000 **tinyurl.com/popcenturywdw**	**Disney's Port Orleans Resort– French Quarter** ★★★★ 2201 Orleans Dr. Lake Buena Vista, FL 32830 ☎ 407-934-5000 **tinyurl.com/portorleansfq**	**Disney's Port Orleans Resort– Riverside** ★★★★ 1251 Riverside Dr. Lake Buena Vista, FL 32830 ☎ 407-934-6000 **tinyurl.com/portorleans riverside**
LOCATION WDW ROOM RATING 71 COST ($=$50) $$$+	LOCATION WDW ROOM RATING 84 COST ($=$50) $- X 5	LOCATION WDW ROOM RATING 83 COST ($=$50) $- X 5
Disney's Saratoga Springs Resort & Spa ★★★★½ 1960 Broadway Lake Buena Vista, FL 32830 ☎ 407-827-1100 **tinyurl.com/saratogawdw**	**Disney's Wilderness Lodge** ★★★★ 901 Timberline Dr. Lake Buena Vista, FL 32830 ☎ 407-824-3200 **tinyurl.com/wildernesslodge**	**Disney's Yacht Club Resort** ★★★★ 1700 Epcot Resorts Blvd. Lake Buena Vista, FL 32830 ☎ 407-934-7000 **tinyurl.com/yachtclubwdw**
LOCATION WDW ROOM RATING 90 COST ($=$50) $+ X 8	LOCATION WDW ROOM RATING 86 COST ($=$50) $- X 9	LOCATION WDW ROOM RATING 89 COST ($=$50) $- X 10

*US 192 is known locally as Irlo Bronson Memorial Highway.

HOTEL INFORMATION CHART

DoubleTree by Hilton Orlando at SeaWorld ★★★★½
10100 International Dr.
Orlando, FL 32821
☎ 407-352-1100
doubletreeorlandoidrive.com

LOCATION 1
ROOM RATING 92
COST ($=$50) $$$+

Embassy Suites Orlando I-Drive ★★★½
8978 International Dr.
Orlando, FL 32819
☎ 407-352-1400
embassysuitesorlando.com

LOCATION 1
ROOM RATING 75
COST ($=$50) $$$−

Enclave Hotel & Suites ★★★
6165 Carrier Dr.
Orlando, FL 32819
☎ 407-351-1155
enclavesuites.com

LOCATION 1
ROOM RATING 67
COST ($=$50) $$$−

Extended Stay America Orlando Convention Center ★★★
6451 Westwood Blvd.
Orlando, FL 32821
☎ 407-352-3454
tinyurl.com/extendedstayocc

LOCATION 1
ROOM RATING 72
COST ($=$50) $+

Extended Stay Orlando Convention Center ★★
8750 Universal Blvd.
Orlando, FL 32819
☎ 407-903-1500
tinyurl.com/esccuniversal

LOCATION 1
ROOM RATING 58
COST ($=$50) $$−

Fairfield Inn & Suites Orlando Lake Buena Vista ★★★½
12191 S. Apopka-Vineland Rd.
Lake Buena Vista, FL 32836
☎ 407-239-1115
tinyurl.com/fairfieldlbv

LOCATION 2
ROOM RATING 79
COST ($=$50) $$+

DoubleTree Guest Suites ★★★½
2305 Hotel Plaza Blvd.
Lake Buena Vista, FL 32830
☎ 407-934-1000
doubletreeguestsuites.com

LOCATION WDW
ROOM RATING 75
COST ($=$50) $$$

Embassy Suites Orlando I-Drive/Jamaican Court ★★★½
8250 Jamaican Ct.
Orlando, FL 32819
☎ 407-345-8250
orlandoembassysuites.com

LOCATION 1
ROOM RATING 80
COST ($=$50) $$$−

Extended Stay America Convention Center/Westwood ★★★★
6443 Westwood Blvd.
Orlando, FL 32821
☎ 407-351-1982
tinyurl.com/extendedstay westwood

LOCATION 1
ROOM RATING 84
COST ($=$50) $$−

Extended Stay America Orlando Lake Buena Vista ★★★★
8100 Palm Pkwy.
Orlando 32836
☎ 407-239-4300
tinyurl.com/extendedlbv

LOCATION 2
ROOM RATING 83
COST ($=$50) $$−

Fairfield Inn & Suites Near Universal Orlando Resort ★★★½
5614 Vineland Rd.
Orlando, FL 32819
☎ 407-581-5600
tinyurl.com/fairfielduniversal

LOCATION 4
ROOM RATING 80
COST ($=$50) $$$−

Fairfield Inn & Suites Orlando LBV in Marriott Village ★★★½
8615 Vineland Ave.
Orlando, FL 32821
☎ 407-938-9001
tinyurl.com/fairfieldlbv marriottvillage

LOCATION 2
ROOM RATING 75
COST ($=$50) $$+

DoubleTree Universal ★★★★
5780 Major Blvd.
Orlando, FL 32819
☎ 407-351-1000
doubletreeorlando.com

LOCATION 4
ROOM RATING 89
COST ($=$50) $$$−

Embassy Suites Orlando–Lake Buena Vista Resort ★★★★
8100 Lake Ave.
Orlando, FL 32836
☎ 407-239-1144
embassysuiteslbv.com

LOCATION 2
ROOM RATING 86
COST ($=$50) $$$+

Extended Stay America Deluxe Orlando Theme Parks ★★★½
5610 Vineland Rd.
Orlando, FL 32819
☎ 407-370-4428
tinyurl.com/esvineland

LOCATION 4
ROOM RATING 75
COST ($=$50) $$−

Extended Stay America Orlando Theme Parks ★★★½
5620 Major Blvd.
Orlando, FL 32819
☎ 407-351-1788
tinyurl.com/extendeduniversal

LOCATION 4
ROOM RATING 75
COST ($=$50) $$−

Fairfield Inn & Suites Orlando I-Drive/Convention Center ★★★
8214 Universal Blvd.
Orlando, FL 32819
☎ 407-581-9001
tinyurl.com/fairfieldocc

LOCATION 1
ROOM RATING 74
COST ($=$50) $$+

Floridays Resort Orlando ★★★★
12562 International Dr.
Orlando, FL 32821
☎ 407-238-7700
floridaysresortorlando.com

LOCATION 1
ROOM RATING 86
COST ($=$50) $$$$

HOTEL INFORMATION CHART

Floridian Hotel & Suites ★★½ 7531 Canada Ave. Orlando, FL 32819 ☎ 407-212-3021 **thefloridianhotel.com** LOCATION 1 ROOM RATING 63 COST ($=$50) $$–	**Four Points by Sheraton Orlando Studio City** ★★★★½ 5905 International Dr. Orlando, FL 32819 ☎ 407-351-2100 **fourpointsorlandostudiocity .com** LOCATION 1 ROOM RATING 90 COST ($=$50) $$$–	**Four Seasons Resort Orlando at Walt Disney World Resort** ★★★★★ 10100 Dream Tree Blvd. Golden Oak, FL 32836 ☎ 407-313-7777 **fourseasons.com/orlando** LOCATION WDW ROOM RATING 98 COST ($=$50) $ X 9
Galleria Palms Kissimmee Hotel ★★★ 3000 Maingate Ln. Kissimmee, FL 34747 ☎ 407-396-6300 **galleriakissimmeehotel.com** LOCATION 3 ROOM RATING 74 COST ($=$50) $$–	**Gaylord Palms Hotel & Convention Center** ★★★★½ 6000 W. Osceola Pkwy. Kissimmee, FL 34746 ☎ 407-586-0000 **gaylordpalms.com** LOCATION 3 ROOM RATING 94 COST ($=$50) $$$+	**Grand Beach** ★★★★½ 8317 Lake Bryan Beach Blvd. Orlando, FL 32821 ☎ 407-238-2500 **diamondresorts.com /grand-beach** LOCATION 1 ROOM RATING 90 COST ($=$50) $$$$–
Grand Lake Resort ★★★½ 7770 W. US 192* Kissimmee, FL 34747 ☎ 407-396-3000 **dailymanagementresorts.com** LOCATION 1 ROOM RATING 76 COST ($=$50) $$+	**Hampton Inn & Suites Orlando–South Lake Buena Vista** ★★★½ 4971 Calypso Cay Way Kissimmee, FL 34746 ☎ 407-396-8700 **tinyurl.com/hamptonsouthlbv** LOCATION 3 ROOM RATING 80 COST ($=$50) $$–	**Hampton Inn I-Drive/ Convention Center** ★★★ 8900 Universal Blvd. Orlando, FL 32819 ☎ 407-354-4447 **tinyurl.com/hamptonocc** LOCATION 1 ROOM RATING 70 COST ($=$50) $$+
Hampton Inn Orlando/Lake Buena Vista ★★★½ 8150 Palm Pkwy. Orlando, FL 32836 ☎ 407-465-8150 **tinyurl.com/hamptonlbv** LOCATION 2 ROOM RATING 76 COST ($=$50) $$$–	**Hampton Inn South of Universal** ★★½ 7110 S. Kirkman Rd. Orlando, FL 32819 ☎ 407-345-1112 **tinyurl.com/hamptonkirkman** LOCATION 1 ROOM RATING 64 COST ($=$50) $$$–	**Hampton Inn Universal** ★★★ 5621 Windhover Dr. Orlando, FL 32819 ☎ 407-351-6716 **tinyurl.com/hamptonuniversal** LOCATION 4 ROOM RATING 67 COST ($=$50) $$$–
Hard Rock Hotel Orlando ★★★★½ 5800 Universal Blvd. Orlando, FL 32819 ☎ 407-503-2000 **hardrockhotelorlando.com** LOCATION 4 ROOM RATING 93 COST ($=$50) $ X 8	**Hawthorn Suites Lake Buena Vista** ★★★★ 8303 Palm Pkwy. Orlando, FL 32836 ☎ 407-597-5000 **hawthornlakebuenavista.com** LOCATION 2 ROOM RATING 85 COST ($=$50) $$+	**Hawthorn Suites Orlando Convention Center** ★★★½ 6435 Westwood Blvd. Orlando, FL 32821 ☎ 407-351-6600 **hawthornsuitesorlando.com** LOCATION 1 ROOM RATING 80 COST ($=$50) $$+
Hawthorn Suites Orlando I-Drive ★★★½ 7975 Canada Ave. Orlando, FL 32819 ☎ 407-345-0117 **tinyurl.com/hawthornidrive** LOCATION 1 ROOM RATING 75 COST ($=$50) $$+	**Hilton Garden Inn Lake Buena Vista/Orlando** ★★★★ 11400 Marbella Palm Ct. Orlando, FL 32836 ☎ 407-239-9550 **tinyurl.com/hgilakebuenavista** LOCATION 2 ROOM RATING 88 COST ($=$50) $$$+	**Hilton Garden Inn Orlando at SeaWorld** ★★★½ 6850 Westwood Blvd. Orlando, FL 32821 ☎ 407-354-1500 **tinyurl.com/hgiseaworld** LOCATION 1 ROOM RATING 80 COST ($=$50) $$$–

*US 192 is known locally as Irlo Bronson Memorial Highway.

HOTEL INFORMATION CHART

Hilton Garden Inn Orlando I-Drive North ★★★½
5877 American Way
Orlando, FL 32819
☎ 407-363-9332
tinyurl.com/hiltonidrive

LOCATION 1
ROOM RATING 80
COST ($=$50) $$+

Hilton Grand Vacations Club at SeaWorld ★★★★½
6924 Grand Vacations Way
Orlando, FL 32821
☎ 407-239-0100
tinyurl.com/hgvseaworld

LOCATION 1
ROOM RATING 95
COST ($=$50) $$$–

Hilton Grand Vacations Club on I-Drive ★★★★
8122 Arrezzo Way
Orlando, FL 32819
☎ 407-465-2600
tinyurl.com/hgvidrive

LOCATION 1
ROOM RATING 88
COST ($=$50) $$$+

Hilton Orlando ★★★★½
6001 Destination Pkwy.
Orlando, FL 32819
☎ 407-313-4300
thehiltonorlando.com

LOCATION 1
ROOM RATING 92
COST ($=$50) $$$$+

Hilton Orlando Bonnet Creek ★★★★
14100 Bonnet Creek Resort Ln.
Orlando, FL 32821
☎ 407-597-3600
hiltonbonnetcreek.com

LOCATION 1
ROOM RATING 88
COST ($=$50) $$+

Hilton Orlando Lake Buena Vista ★★★★
1751 Hotel Plaza Blvd.
Lake Buena Vista, FL 32830
☎ 407-827-4000
hilton-wdwv.com

LOCATION WDW
ROOM RATING 87
COST ($=$50) $$$–

Holiday Inn & Suites Orlando Universal ★★★½
5905 Kirkman Rd.
Orlando, FL 32819
☎ 407-351-3333
hiuniversal.com

LOCATION 4
ROOM RATING 75
COST ($=$50) $$$–

Holiday Inn in the Walt Disney World Resort ★★★½
1805 Hotel Plaza Blvd.
Lake Buena Vista, FL 32830
☎ 407-828-8888
hiorlando.com

LOCATION WDW
ROOM RATING 79
COST ($=$50) $$$+

Holiday Inn Main Gate East ★★★★½
5711 W. US 192*
Kissimmee, FL 34746
☎ 407-396-4222
holidayinnmge.com

LOCATION 3
ROOM RATING 90
COST ($=$50) $$+

Holiday Inn Resort Lake Buena Vista ★★★½
13351 FL 535
Orlando, FL 32821
☎ 407-239-4500
hiresortlbv.com

LOCATION 2
ROOM RATING 82
COST ($=$50) $$+

Homewood Suites by Hilton I-Drive ★★★½
8745 International Dr.
Orlando, FL 32819
☎ 407-248-2232
homewoodsuitesorlando.com

LOCATION 1
ROOM RATING 81
COST ($=$50) $$$$–

Homewood Suites by Hilton LBV-Orlando ★★★★
11428 Marbella Palm Ct.
Orlando, FL 32836
☎ 407-239-4540
tinyurl.com/homewood suiteslbv

LOCATION 2
ROOM RATING 85
COST ($=$50) $$$$–

Hyatt Place Orlando/ Universal ★★★★
5895 Caravan Ct.
Orlando, FL 32819
☎ 407-351-0627
orlandouniversal.place.hyatt .com

LOCATION 4
ROOM RATING 84
COST ($=$50) $$$+

Hyatt Regency Grand Cypress ★★★★½
1 Grand Cypress Blvd.
Orlando, FL 32836
☎ 407-239-1234
grandcypress.hyatt.com

LOCATION 2
ROOM RATING 92
COST ($=$50) $– X 5

Hyatt Regency Orlando ★★★★½
9801 International Dr.
Orlando, FL 32819
☎ 407-284-1234
orlando.regency.hyatt.com

LOCATION 1
ROOM RATING 90
COST ($=$50) $$$$–

Inn at Calypso ★★★½
5001 Calypso Cay Way
Kissimmee, FL 34746
☎ 407-997-1400
calypsocay.com/the-inn.php

LOCATION 3
ROOM RATING 82
COST ($=$50) $$–

International Palms Resort & Conference Center ★★★
6515 International Dr.
Orlando, FL 32819
☎ 407-351-3500
internationalpalms.com

LOCATION 1
ROOM RATING 73
COST ($=$50) $$+

JW Marriott Orlando Grande Lakes ★★★★½
4040 Central Florida Pkwy.
Orlando, FL 32837
☎ 407-206-2300
jw-marriott.grandelakes.com

LOCATION 1
ROOM RATING 93
COST ($=$50) $+ X 5

HOTEL INFORMATION CHART

Knights Inn Maingate Kissimmee/Orlando ★★ 7475 W. US 192* Kissimmee, FL 34747 ☎ 407-396-4200 **tinyurl.com/knightsinnmgk** LOCATION 3 ROOM RATING 58 COST ($=$50) $-	**La Quinta Inn Orlando I-Drive** ★★★ 8300 Jamaican Ct. Orlando, FL 32819 ☎ 407-351-1660 **tinyurl.com/lqidrive** LOCATION 1 ROOM RATING 73 COST ($=$50) $$-	**La Quinta Inn Orlando–Universal Studios** ★★½ 5621 Major Blvd. Orlando, FL 32819 ☎ 407-313-3100 **tinyurl.com/lquniversal** LOCATION 4 ROOM RATING 63 COST ($=$50) $$-
Legacy Vacation Club Lake Buena Vista ★★★★ 8451 Palm Pkwy. Lake Buena Vista, FL 32836 ☎ 407-238-1700 **legacyvacationresorts.com** LOCATION 2 ROOM RATING 85 COST ($=$50) $$$-	**Legacy Vacation Club Orlando** ★★★½ 2800 N. Poinciana Blvd. Kissimmee, FL 34746 ☎ 407-997-5000 **legacyvacationresorts.com** LOCATION 3 ROOM RATING 80 COST ($=$50) $$$-	**Lighthouse Key Resort & Spa** ★★★★½ 8545 W. US 192* Kissimmee, FL 34747 ☎ 321-329-7000 **lighthousekeyresort.com** LOCATION 3 ROOM RATING 90 COST ($=$50) $$$$-
Liki Tiki Village ★★★★½ 17777 Bali Blvd. Winter Garden, FL 34787 ☎ 407-239-5000 **likitiki.com** LOCATION 3 ROOM RATING 90 COST ($=$50) $$$$-	**Magnuson Grand Hotel Maingate West** ★★★ 7491 W. US 192* Kissimmee, FL 34747 ☎ 407-396-6000 **tinyurl.com/magnusongrand** LOCATION 3 ROOM RATING 65 COST ($=$50) $$+	**Maingate Lakeside Resort** ★★★ 7769 W. US 192* Kissimmee, FL 34747 ☎ 407-396-2222 **maingatelakesideresort.com** LOCATION 3 ROOM RATING 67 COST ($=$50) $$-
Marriott's Cypress Harbour ★★★★ 11251 Harbour Villa Rd. Orlando, FL 32821 ☎ 407-238-1300 **tinyurl.com/cypressharbour villas** LOCATION 1 ROOM RATING 86 COST ($=$50) $ X 6	**Marriott's Grande Vista** ★★★★½ 5925 Avenida Vista Orlando, FL 32821 ☎ 407-238-7676 **tinyurl.com/marriotts grandevista** LOCATION 1 ROOM RATING 92 COST ($=$50) $$$+	**Marriott's Harbour Lake** ★★★★½ 7102 Grand Horizons Blvd. Orlando, FL 32821 ☎ 407-465-6100 **tinyurl.com/harbourlake** LOCATION 2 ROOM RATING 90 COST ($=$50) $$$$-
Marriott's Imperial Palms ★★★★ 8404 Vacation Way Orlando, FL 32821 ☎ 407-238-6200 **tinyurl.com/imperialpalmvillas** LOCATION 1 ROOM RATING 86 COST ($=$50) $- X 9	**Marriott's Royal Palms** ★★★★ 8404 Vacation Way Orlando, FL 32821 ☎ 407-238-6200 **tinyurl.com/marriottsroyal palms** LOCATION 1 ROOM RATING 85 COST ($=$50) $- X 6	**Marriott's Sabal Palms** ★★★★½ 8805 World Center Dr. Orlando, FL 32821 ☎ 407-238-6200 **tinyurl.com/marriottssabal palms** LOCATION 2 ROOM RATING 92 COST ($=$50) $+ X 6
Monumental Hotel ★★★★½ 12120 International Dr. Orlando, FL 32821 ☎ 407-239-1222 **monumentalhotelorlandofl .com** LOCATION 1 ROOM RATING 94 COST ($=$50) $$-	**Monumental MovieLand Hotel** ★★★ 6233 International Dr. Orlando, FL 32819 ☎ 407-351-3900 **monumentalmovielandhotel .com** LOCATION 1 ROOM RATING 68 COST ($=$50) $+	**Motel 6 Orlando-I-Drive** ★★★ 5909 American Way Orlando, FL 32819 ☎ 407-351-6500 **tinyurl.com/motel6idrive** LOCATION 1 ROOM RATING 66 COST ($=$50) $+

*US 192 is known locally as Irlo Bronson Memorial Highway.

HOTEL INFORMATION CHART

Mystic Dunes Resort & Golf Club ★ ★ ★ ★
7600 Mystic Dunes Ln.
Kissimmee, FL 34747
☎ 407-396-1311
mystic-dunes-resort.com

LOCATION	3
ROOM RATING	87
COST ($=$50)	$$$–

Nickelodeon Suites Resort
★ ★ ★ ½
14500 Continental Gateway
Orlando, FL 32821
☎ 407-387-5437
nickhotel.com

LOCATION	1
ROOM RATING	82
COST ($=$50)	$$$$

Omni Orlando Resort at ChampionsGate ★ ★ ★ ★ ★
1500 Masters Blvd.
ChampionsGate, FL 33896
☎ 407-390-6664
tinyurl.com/omnichampions gate

LOCATION	2
ROOM RATING	96
COST ($=$50)	$+ X 5

Orange Lake Resort
★ ★ ★ ★ ½
8505 W. US 192*
Kissimmee, FL 34747
☎ 407-239-0000
tinyurl.com/orangelake resortorlando

LOCATION	3
ROOM RATING	94
COST ($=$50)	$$$–

Orbit One Vacation Villas
★ ★ ★ ½
2950 Entry Point Blvd.
Kissimmee, FL 34741
☎ 407-396-1300
tinyurl.com/orbit1villas

LOCATION	3
ROOM RATING	80
COST ($=$50)	$$$$–

Orlando World Center Marriott Resort ★ ★ ★ ★ ½
8701 World Center Dr.
Orlando, FL 32821
☎ 407-239-4200
marriottworldcenter.com

LOCATION	2
ROOM RATING	90
COST ($=$50)	$$$$+

Palms Hotel & Villas ★ ★ ★ ½
3100 Parkway Blvd.
Kissimmee, FL 34747
☎ 407-396-2229
thepalmshotelandvillas.com

LOCATION	3
ROOM RATING	76
COST ($=$50)	$$+

Park Inn by Radisson Resort and Conference Center
★ ★ ★ ½
3011 Maingate Ln.
Kissimmee, FL 34747
☎ 407-396-1400
parkinn.com/hotel-orlando

LOCATION	3
ROOM RATING	78
COST ($=$50)	$$$–

Parkway International Resort
★ ★ ★ ½
6200 Safari Trl.
Kissimmee, FL 34746
☎ 407-396-6600
parkwayresort.com

LOCATION	3
ROOM RATING	82
COST ($=$50)	$– X 5

The Point Universal Orlando Resort ★ ★ ★ ½
7389 Universal Blvd.
Orlando, FL 32819
☎ 407-956-2000
thepointorlando.com

LOCATION	1
ROOM RATING	82
COST ($=$50)	$$+

Polynesian Isles Resort
(Diamond Resorts) ★ ★ ★ ★ ½
3045 Polynesian Isles Blvd.
Kissimmee, FL 34746
☎ 407-396-1622
polynesianisle.com

LOCATION	3
ROOM RATING	90
COST ($=$50)	$$$

Quality Suites Lake Buena Vista ★ ★ ★ ½
8200 Palm Pkwy.
Orlando, FL 32836
☎ 407-465-8200
qualitysuiteslbv.com

LOCATION	2
ROOM RATING	76
COST ($=$50)	$$$–

Quality Suites Royale Parc Suites ★ ★ ★ ½
5876 W. US 192*
Kissimmee, FL 34746
☎ 407-396-8040
royaleparcsuitesorlando.com

LOCATION	3
ROOM RATING	76
COST ($=$50)	$$$+

Quality Suites Turkey Lake
★ ★ ★
9350 Turkey Lake Rd.
Orlando, FL 32819
☎ 407-351-5050
qualitysuitesorlandolbv.com

LOCATION	2
ROOM RATING	74
COST ($=$50)	$+

Radisson Hotel Orlando Lake Buena Vista ★ ★ ★ ½
12799 Apopka–Vineland Rd.
Orlando, FL 32836
☎ 407-597-3400
tinyurl.com/radissonlbv

LOCATION	2
ROOM RATING	82
COST ($=$50)	$$$–

Radisson Resort Orlando-Celebration ★ ★ ★ ★
2900 Parkway Blvd.
Kissimmee, FL 34747
☎ 407-396-7000
tinyurl.com/radissonoc

LOCATION	3
ROOM RATING	86
COST ($=$50)	$$

Ramada Convention Center I-Drive ★ ★ ★
8342 Jamaican Ct.
Orlando, FL 32819
☎ 407-363-1944
tinyurl.com/ramadaidrive

LOCATION	1
ROOM RATING	65
COST ($=$50)	$+

Ramada Plaza Resort and Suites Orlando I-Drive ★ ★ ★
6500 International Dr.
Orlando, FL 32819
☎ 407-345-5340
tinyurl.com/ramadaplazaidrive

LOCATION	1
ROOM RATING	72
COST ($=$50)	$$+

HOTEL INFORMATION CHART

Red Roof Inn Orlando Convention Center ★★ 9922 Hawaiian Ct. Orlando, FL 32819 ☎ 407-352-1507 **tinyurl.com/redroofkiss** LOCATION 1 ROOM RATING 58 COST ($=$50) $+	**Renaissance Orlando at SeaWorld** ★★★★½ 6677 Sea Harbor Dr. Orlando, FL 32821 ☎ 407-351-5555 **tinyurl.com/renorlando seaworld** LOCATION 1 ROOM RATING 90 COST ($=$50) $$$+	**Residence Inn Orlando at SeaWorld** ★★★★ 11000 Westwood Blvd. Orlando, FL 32821 ☎ 407-313-3600 **tinyurl.com/residenceinn seaworld** LOCATION 2 ROOM RATING 85 COST ($=$50) $$$-
Residence Inn Orlando Convention Center ★★★½ 8800 Universal Blvd. Orlando, FL 32819 ☎ 407-226-0288 **tinyurl.com/resinnconvention center** LOCATION 1 ROOM RATING 80 COST ($=$50) $$$-	**Residence Inn Orlando Lake Buena Vista** ★★★½ 11450 Marbella Palm Ct. Orlando, FL 32836 ☎ 407-465-0075 **tinyurl.com/residenceinnlbv** LOCATION 2 ROOM RATING 75 COST ($=$50) $$$+	**Ritz-Carlton Orlando, Grande Lakes** ★★★★½ 4012 Central Florida Pkwy. Orlando, FL 32837 ☎ 407-206-2400 **grandelakes.com** LOCATION 1 ROOM RATING 94 COST ($=$50) $+ X 5
Rodeway Inn Maingate ★★½ 5995 W. US 192* Kissimmee, FL 34747 ☎ 407-396-4300 **tinyurl.com/rodewaymaingate** LOCATION 3 ROOM RATING 59 COST ($=$50) $-	**Rosen Centre Hotel** ★★★★½ 9840 International Dr. Orlando, FL 32819 ☎ 407-996-9840 **rosencentre.com** LOCATION 1 ROOM RATING 95 COST ($=$50) $$$+	**Rosen Inn at Pointe Orlando** ★★★½ 9000 International Dr. Orlando, FL 32819 ☎ 407-996-8585 **roseninn9000.com** LOCATION 1 ROOM RATING 75 COST ($=$50) $$-
Rosen Inn International Hotel ★★★ 7600 International Dr. Orlando, FL 32819 ☎ 407-996-1600 **roseninn7600.com** LOCATION 1 ROOM RATING 65 COST ($=$50) $$+	**Rosen Plaza Hotel** ★★★★½ 9700 International Dr. Orlando, FL 32819 ☎ 407-996-9700 **rosenplaza.com** LOCATION 1 ROOM RATING 90 COST ($=$50) $$$+	**Rosen Shingle Creek** ★★★★ 9939 Universal Blvd. Orlando, FL 32819 ☎ 407-996-9939 **rosenshinglecreek.com** LOCATION 1 ROOM RATING 88 COST ($=$50) $$$+
Royal Celebration Inn ★★½ 4944 W. US 192* Kissimmee, FL 34746 ☎ 407-396-4455 **royalcelebrationorlando.com** LOCATION 3 ROOM RATING 60 COST ($=$50) $+	**Shades of Green** ★★★★½ 1950 W. Magnolia Palm Dr. Lake Buena Vista, FL 32830 ☎ 407-824-3400 **shadesofgreen.org** LOCATION WDW ROOM RATING 91 COST ($=$50) $$-	**Sheraton Lake Buena Vista Resort** ★★★★ 12205 S. Apopka–Vineland Rd. Orlando, FL 32836 ☎ 407-239-0444 **sheratonlakebuenavistaresort .com** LOCATION 2 ROOM RATING 88 COST ($=$50) $$$+
Sheraton Vistana Resort Villas ★★★★ 8800 Vistana Centre Dr. Orlando, FL 32821 ☎ 407-239-3100 **tinyurl.com/vistanavillas** LOCATION 2 ROOM RATING 89 COST ($=$50) $$$$-	**Silver Lake Resort** ★★½ 7751 Black Lake Rd. Kissimmee, FL 34747 ☎ 407-397-2828 **silverlakeresort.com** LOCATION 3 ROOM RATING 64 COST ($=$50) $$$	**Sonesta ES Suites Orlando** ★★★½ 8480 International Dr. Orlando, FL 32819 ☎ 407-352-2400 **sonesta.com/orlando** LOCATION 1 ROOM RATING 75 COST ($=$50) $$$+

*US 192 is known locally as Irlo Bronson Memorial Highway.

HOTEL INFORMATION CHART

SpringHill Suites Orlando Convention Center ★★★½
8840 Universal Blvd.
Orlando, FL 32819
☎ 407-345-9073
tinyurl.com/shsconvention center

LOCATION	1
ROOM RATING	80
COST ($=$50)	$$$–

SpringHill Suites Orlando LBV in Marriott Village ★★★
8601 Vineland Ave.
Orlando, FL 32821
☎ 407-938-9001
tinyurl.com/springhillmarriott village

LOCATION	2
ROOM RATING	71
COST ($=$50)	$$$+

Star Island Resort & Club
★★★★
5000 Avenue of the Stars
Kissimmee, FL 34746
☎ 407-997-8000
star-island.com

LOCATION	3
ROOM RATING	84
COST ($=$50)	$$$+

Staybridge Suites Lake Buena Vista ★★★
8751 Suiteside Dr.
Orlando, FL 32836
☎ 407-238-0777
tinyurl.com/staybridgelbv

LOCATION	2
ROOM RATING	72
COST ($=$50)	$$$+

Stay Sky Suites I-Drive Orlando ★★★½
7601 Canada Ave.
Orlando, FL 32819
☎ 407-581-2151
stayskysuitesidriveorlando.com

LOCATION	1
ROOM RATING	82
COST ($=$50)	$$+

Super 8 Kissimmee ★★½
1815 W. Vine St.
Kissimmee, FL 34741
☎ 407-847-6121
tinyurl.com/super8kiss

LOCATION	3
ROOM RATING	60
COST ($=$50)	$–

Super 8 Kissimmee/Maingate
★★★
5875 W. US 192*
Kissimmee, FL 34746
☎ 407-396-8883
tinyurl.com/super8maingate

LOCATION	3
ROOM RATING	70
COST ($=$50)	$+

Treehouse Villas at Disney's Saratoga Springs Resort & Spa ★★★★½
1960 Broadway
Lake Buena Vista, FL 32830
☎ 407-827-1100
tinyurl.com/saratogawdw

LOCATION	WDW
ROOM RATING	90
COST ($=$50)	$– X 20

Universal's Cabana Bay Beach Resort ★★★★
6550 Adventure Way
Orlando, FL 32819
☎ 407-503-2000
tinyurl.com/cabanabay

LOCATION	4
ROOM RATING	88
COST ($=$50)	$$$$–

Universal's Portofino Bay Hotel ★★★★½
5601 Universal Blvd.
Orlando, FL 32819
☎ 407-503-1000
tinyurl.com/portofinobay

LOCATION	4
ROOM RATING	92
COST ($=$50)	$+ X 8

Universal's Royal Pacific Resort ★★★★½
6300 Hollywood Way
Orlando, FL 32819
☎ 407-503-3000
tinyurl.com/royalpacific

LOCATION	4
ROOM RATING	90
COST ($=$50)	$+ X 6

Vacation Village at Parkway
★★★★½
2949 Arabian Nights Blvd.
Kissimmee, FL 34747
☎ 407-396-9086
dailymanagementresorts.com

LOCATION	3
ROOM RATING	91
COST ($=$50)	$$+

Villas at Disney's Grand Floridian Resort & Spa ★★★★½
4401 Floridian Way
Lake Buena Vista, FL 32830
☎ 407-824-3000
tinyurl.com/grandfloridian villas

LOCATION	WDW
ROOM RATING	93
COST ($=$50)	$– X 13

Villas at Disney's Wilderness Lodge ★★★★½
901 Timberline Dr.
Lake Buena Vista, FL 32830
☎ 407-824-3200
tinyurl.com/wlvillas

LOCATION	WDW
ROOM RATING	90
COST ($=$50)	$– X 10

Villas of Grand Cypress
★★★★½
1 N. Jacaranda
Orlando, FL 32836
☎ 407-239-4700
grandcypress.com

LOCATION	2
ROOM RATING	92
COST ($=$50)	$– X 5

Waldorf Astoria Orlando
★★★★½
14200 Bonnet Creek Resort Ln.
Lake Buena Vista, FL 32830
☎ 407-597-5500
waldorfastoriaorlando.com

LOCATION	2
ROOM RATING	93
COST ($=$50)	$$$$+

Walt Disney World Dolphin
★★★★½
1500 Epcot Resorts Blvd.
Lake Buena Vista, FL 32830
☎ 407-934-4000
swandolphin.com

LOCATION	WDW
ROOM RATING	90
COST ($=$50)	$$$$+

Walt Disney World Swan
★★★★½
1200 Epcot Resorts Blvd.
Lake Buena Vista, FL 32830
☎ 407-934-3000
swandolphin.com

LOCATION	WDW
ROOM RATING	90
COST ($=$50)	$$$$+

HOTEL INFORMATION CHART

Westgate Lakes Resort & Spa ★★★★½ 10000 Turkey Lake Rd. Orlando, FL 32819 ☎ 407-345-0000 **westgateresorts.com/lakes** LOCATION 2 ROOM RATING 92 COST ($=$50) $$$+	**Westgate Palace** ★★★ 6145 Carrier Dr. Orlando, FL 32819 ☎ 407-996-6000 **westgateresorts.com/palace** LOCATION 1 ROOM RATING 68 COST ($=$50) $$$$–	**Westgate Towers** ★★★½ 7600 West US 192* Kissimmee, FL 34747 ☎ 407-396-2500 **westgateresorts.com/towers** LOCATION 2 ROOM RATING 81 COST ($=$50) $$+
Westgate Town Center ★★★★½ 7700 Westgate Blvd. Kissimmee, FL 34747 ☎ 407-396-2500 **westgateresorts.com /town-center** LOCATION 2 ROOM RATING 93 COST ($=$50) $$+	**Westgate Vacation Villas** ★★★★½ 7700 Westgate Blvd. Kissimmee, FL 34747 ☎ 407-239-0510 **westgateresorts.com /vacation-villas** LOCATION 2 ROOM RATING 90 COST ($=$50) $$+	**Westin Orlando Universal Boulevard** ★★★★ 9501 Universal Blvd. Orlando, FL 32819 ☎ 407-233-2200 **westinorlandouniversal.com** LOCATION 1 ROOM RATING 87 COST ($=$50) $$$$+
WorldQuest Orlando Resort ★★★★ 8849 Worldquest Blvd. Orlando, FL 32821 ☎ 407-387-3800 **worldquestorlando.com** LOCATION 1 ROOM RATING 88 COST ($=$50) $$$–	**Wyndham Bonnet Creek Resort** ★★★★½ 9560 Via Encinas Lake Buena Vista, FL 32830 ☎ 407-238-3500 **wyndhambonnetcreek.com** LOCATION 2 ROOM RATING 90 COST ($=$50) $$$$+	**Wyndham Cypress Palms** ★★★★ 5324 Fairfield Lake Dr. Kissimmee, FL 34746 ☎ 407-397-1600 **cypresspalms.com** LOCATION 3 ROOM RATING 87 COST ($=$50) $$$
Wyndham Lake Buena Vista Resort ★★★½ 1850 Hotel Plaza Blvd. Lake Buena Vista, FL 32830 ☎ 407-828-4444 **wyndhamlakebuenavista.com** LOCATION WDW ROOM RATING 75 COST ($=$50) $$+	**Wyndham Orlando Resort I-Drive** ★★★★ 8001 International Dr. Orlando, FL 32819 ☎ 407-351-2420 **wyndham.com/hotels /MCOWD** LOCATION 1 ROOM RATING 85 COST ($=$50) $$+	

*US 192 is known locally as Irlo Bronson Memorial Highway.

PART TWO

BUSCH GARDENS
TAMPA BAY

SPANNING 335 ACRES, Busch Gardens combines elements of a zoo and a theme park. Formerly owned by Anheuser-Busch (free beer samples were once a hallmark of the franchise), the Busch Gardens parks in Florida and Williamsburg, Virginia, along with the SeaWorld parks, were sold in 2009 to financial conglomerate The Blackstone Group. Rather symbolic of the buyout, the parks' Clydesdale horses are gone, though the Busch name remains.

The park is divided into nine African-themed regions (as you encounter them moving counterclockwise through the park): Morocco, Egypt, Nairobi, Pantopia, Congo, Jungala, Stanleyville, Sesame Street Safari of Fun, and Bird Gardens. A haven for thrill-ride fanatics, the park has several roller coasters that are consistently rated among the top five in the country. Busch Gardens is more than thrill fare, however, with beautiful landscaping, excellent shows, and really wonderful children's play areas.

With the wildlife of Disney's Animal Kingdom and the thrills of Universal's Islands of Adventure, some may wonder, why leave Orlando for a day at Busch Gardens in Tampa? For those who love roller coasters, Busch Gardens boasts seven (eight when Cobra's Curse opens in 2016), three in the super-coaster category. No other area attraction can top that in terms of thrills. Nor can Busch Gardens be matched in its ability to offer a balanced day of fun for all ages. Those who shy away from roller coasters will find plenty to do at the park, with its abundance of animal exhibits, children's rides, gardens, shows, and shops.

unofficial **TIP**
Busch Gardens is close to Tampa, including the city's museums and other attractions.

In addition, the drive is easy and only about 90 minutes from Orlando. With Florida's fickle weather, it could be raining in Orlando but bright and sunny in Tampa, so it's a good idea to check the weather if you're rained out of O-town. Of course, this holds true in reverse, and, unlike at Disney, where most of the rides are indoors, any rain will cause the closing of most of the rides at Busch Gardens.

GETTING THERE

BUSCH GARDENS IS ABOUT 70 MILES from Walt Disney World. The trip should take about an hour and a half, depending on traffic and the construction that plagues I-4. The best way to get there is via I-275. Driving west on I-4, there are signs for Busch Gardens, but ignoring them will save you a long journey through Tampa city streets. Proceed instead to the junction of I-275 and go north. Take Exit 50 onto East Busch Boulevard/FL 580, turn left, and drive a little more than 2 miles; the entrance to Busch Gardens will be on your left. Parking is $17 in a lot across the street from the park (trams are provided) and $22 in a preferred lot closer to the main entrance, which fills up quickly.

ADMISSION PRICES

BEFORE PURCHASING TICKETS to Busch Gardens, consider some of the following choices, which are similar to the options offered by its sister park, SeaWorld. As with SeaWorld, the best option for most visitors to Busch Gardens is a one-day pass. Busch Gardens has discontinued most of its multiday tickets in favor of package deals and annual passes. However, several options will get you a lot more time in the park for slightly more money than the cost of a one-day ticket. If you're planning to spend time at other Orlando theme parks, consider the Three-Park Pass, which, in addition to Busch Gardens, includes admission to SeaWorld and Busch Gardens's Adventure Island water park. Discounts are available for Florida residents, AAA members, disabled visitors, senior citizens, and military personnel.

> **ONE-DAY TICKET** Adults **$97** + tax • Children ages 3-9 **$92**+ tax • Children under age 3 **Free**

Busch Gardens Annual Pass

This pass is the best deal for admission to Busch Gardens. For the price of less than two general admission tickets, you can return to the park an unlimited amount of times for an entire calendar year. It includes free general parking and 10% off merchandise and food purchases.

> **BUSCH GARDENS ONE-YEAR PASS** Adults and children age 3 and older **$156** + tax • Seniors age 65 and older **$148** + tax • Children under age 3 **Free**

> **BUSCH GARDENS TWO-YEAR PASS** Adults and children age 3 and older **$235** + tax • Seniors age 65 and older **$227** + tax • Children under age 3 **Free**

Multipark Annual Pass

These passes allow unlimited admission to Busch Gardens, SeaWorld, and/or Adventure Island for one or two years and include free general parking, as well as 10% off merchandise and food purchases in each of the parks.

BUSCH GARDENS AND ADVENTURE ISLAND ONE-YEAR PASS Adults and children age 3 and older **$192** + tax • Seniors age 65 and older **$184** + tax • Children under age 3 **Free**

BUSCH GARDENS AND ADVENTURE ISLAND TWO-YEAR PASS Adults and children age 3 and older **$292** + tax • Seniors age 65 and older **$286** + tax • Children under age 3 **Free**

BUSCH GARDENS AND SEAWORLD ONE-YEAR PASS Adults and children age 3 and older **$216** + tax • Seniors age 65 and older **$208** + tax • Children under age 3 **Free**

BUSCH GARDENS AND SEAWORLD TWO-YEAR PASS Adults and children age 3 and older **$317** + tax • Seniors age 65 and older **$309** + tax • Children under age 3 **Free**

BUSCH GARDENS, ADVENTURE ISLAND, AND SEAWORLD ONE-YEAR PASS Adults and children ages 3 and older **$252** + tax • Seniors age 65 and older **$244** + tax • Children under age 3 **Free**

BUSCH GARDENS, ADVENTURE ISLAND, AND SEAWORLD TWO-YEAR PASS Adults and children ages 3 and older **$352** + tax • Seniors age 65 and older **$344** + tax • Children under age 3 **Free**

Platinum Passes

The Platinum Passes include admission to 11 parks across the country (including Busch Gardens, SeaWorld, Adventure Island, and Aquatica), as well as free parking, ride-again privileges on some rides, reserved seating at some shows, and 10% off merchandise and food purchases in the park(s).

ONE-YEAR PLATINUM PASS Adults and children age 3 and older **$336** + tax • Seniors age 65 and older **$328** + tax • Children under age 3 **Free**

TWO-YEAR PLATINUM PASS Adults and children age 3 and older **$506** + tax • Seniors age 65 and older **$498** + tax • Children under age 3 **Free**

Orlando FlexTicket Plus

This pass is good for up to 14 consecutive days at six parks: Busch Gardens, Universal Studios Florida, Universal's Islands of Adventure, SeaWorld Orlando, Aquatica, and Wet 'n Wild. There's a version that excludes Busch Gardens, so be sure to get the one you want.

FLEXTICKET PLUS Adults **$415.43** • Children ages 3–9 **$399.45** • Children under age 3 **Free**

QUICKQUEUE

MUCH LIKE UNIVERSAL ORLANDO'S EXPRESS PASS, Busch Gardens sells a QuickQueue service that lets you skip the line at the most popular coasters and rides. Passes start at $19.99 per person per day for one-time use, or $34.99 for unlimited daily use; prices rise with the crowds. Unless you are visiting in peak season and have a lot more money than time, we suggest hitting the big attractions at opening and skipping the QuickQueue pass unless it's absolutely essential. On slower days, the pass is practically useless.

Continued on page 78

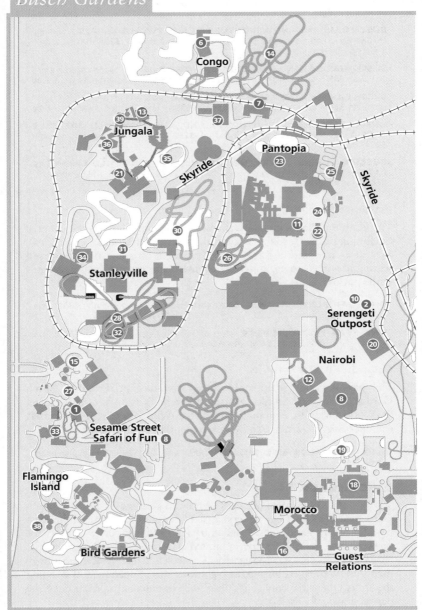

Busch Gardens

Congo

Jungala

Skyride

Pantopia

Skyride

Stanleyville

Serengeti
Outpost

Nairobi

Sesame Street
Safari of Fun

Flamingo
Island

Morocco

Bird Gardens

Guest
Relations

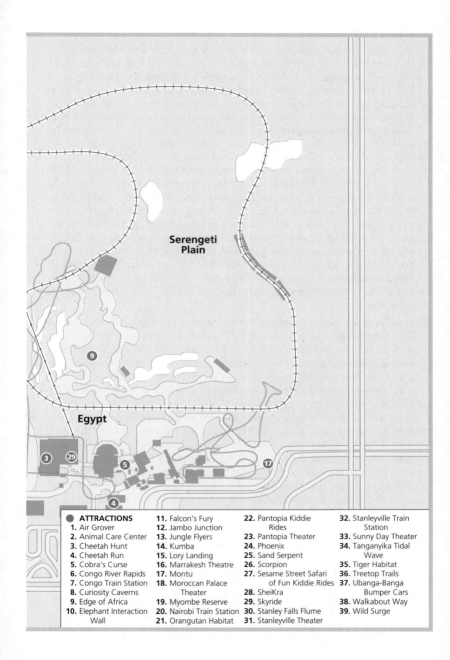

● ATTRACTIONS
1. Air Grover
2. Animal Care Center
3. Cheetah Hunt
4. Cheetah Run
5. Cobra's Curse
6. Congo River Rapids
7. Congo Train Station
8. Curiosity Caverns
9. Edge of Africa
10. Elephant Interaction
   Wall
11. Falcon's Fury
12. Jambo Junction
13. Jungle Flyers
14. Kumba
15. Lory Landing
16. Marrakesh Theatre
17. Montu
18. Moroccan Palace
   Theater
19. Myombe Reserve
20. Nairobi Train Station
21. Orangutan Habitat
22. Pantopia Kiddie
   Rides
23. Pantopia Theater
24. Phoenix
25. Sand Serpent
26. Scorpion
27. Sesame Street Safari
   of Fun Kiddie Rides
28. SheiKra
29. Skyride
30. Stanley Falls Flume
31. Stanleyville Theater
32. Stanleyville Train
   Station
33. Sunny Day Theater
34. Tanganyika Tidal
   Wave
35. Tiger Habitat
36. Treetop Trails
37. Ubanga-Banga
   Bumper Cars
38. Walkabout Way
39. Wild Surge

Continued from page 75

ARRIVING

NORMAL PARK HOURS VARY month to month and sometimes day to day but range from 10 a.m.–6 p.m. during the off-season to 9 a.m.–9 p.m. during holidays. The park stays open until midnight on Friday and Saturday nights mid-June–mid-August. Unlike other local attractions, Busch Gardens does not allow you through the turnstiles before the scheduled opening time. We recommend checking the website (**buschgardenstampa.com**) for exact hours of operation. Visiting during peak season equals waiting in long lines. Busch Gardens also draws crowds of locals, so avoid visiting on weekends or holidays.

Even when crowds are low, it requires a lot of planning and hustling to see Busch Gardens in one day. In particular, expect to spend a lot of time getting oriented and consulting park maps and signage. With no central hub and few connecting walkways, it's very easy to get lost. Go slow until you have a feel for where you are in the park, or you could spend some frustrating time retracing your steps. Of course, group ages and personal tastes will eliminate some rides and exhibits. Groups without children, for instance, don't need to budget time for kiddie rides. However, even selective touring may not afford enough time to enjoy the park fully. Below are a few tips that may help.

PLAN AHEAD Busch Gardens is crammed full of rides and exhibits; the first time many visitors see it, they develop a glazed look in their eyes and begin a crazed tour. Somehow, we doubt that these folks see even half of what the park offers. Instead, determine in advance what you really want to see. For many groups this involves compromise: Parents may not want to spend as much time as children on rides, whereas older kids may want to steer clear of many of the zoological exhibits. If children are old enough, we recommend splitting up after determining a few meeting times and locations for checking in throughout the day. Alternately, parents may want to plan kids' rides around the live-entertainment schedule, placing children safely in line and then attending a performance of a nearby show while the youngsters wait and ride. Note that bags, cameras, and other belongings are not permitted on most of the thrill rides; for 50¢, you can temporarily stow such items in lockers near the ride entrances. Thrill-ride enthusiasts should bring a roll of quarters to pay for the lockers.

ARRIVE EARLY As with other Central Florida attractions, arriving early is the single most effective strategy for efficient touring and avoiding long waits in line. Leave Orlando around 7 a.m. to arrive a little before 8:30 a.m. during peak season. Give yourself an extra half hour during other times, when the park doesn't open until 9:30 a.m. or 10 a.m. Have a quick breakfast before leaving, or eat in the car to save time. To save a few dollars and some time, purchase your tickets online and print them out before leaving for Busch Gardens. But if you did not buy them online, purchase tickets (either at the windows or through the self-service kiosks), and be at the turnstile ready to roll when the gate opens at either 9 or 9:30 a.m. First thing in the morning, there should be no lines and relatively few people. Rides that require up to an hour (or more) wait later in the day can be experienced in less than 15 minutes first thing in the morning. Following are three ways to hit the five major coasters at prime times with as little waiting in line as possible:

ROUTE 1: Ride Cheetah Hunt (the closest coaster to the front of the park) first thing, and then head to Cobra's Curse (opens 2016), then Montu, followed by Kumba; save SheiKra for mid- to late afternoon.

ROUTE 2: After riding Cheetah Hunt first, continue onto Stanleyville to ride SheiKra, followed by Kumba; hit Montu and finally Cobra's Curse (opens 2016) late in the day.

ROUTE 3: Head to Cheetah Hunt first, and then Cobra's Curse (opens 2016), followed by Montu. Then backtrack past the entrance to Stanleyville to SheiKra. Because Kumba is located in the rear of the park, it will not be as crowded in the morning, and you should be able to ride all the major coasters within 2 hours of the park's opening. This route is only practical with very small groups on off-peak days, when the park isn't packed. Even on slower days, you will find a slight line at SheiKra, Cheetah Hunt, and Cobra's Curse with this route, but you should still be able to check the coasters off your list first thing in the morning and free up the rest of your day for other attractions.

unofficial **TIP**
The live cheetahs that live near Cheetah Hunt are sent out on runs a couple of times during morning hours, but in the afternoon they lay about in the shade, though naturalists do discuss the animals. For a better chance of seeing the handsome cats doing their cheetah-race thing, follow the first of these suggested coaster-riding routes.

BE PREPARED TO WALK AND WALK AND WALK Busch Gardens is huge and requires lots of walking. Bring strollers for little ones, and consider wheelchairs for others who tire quickly. Both stroller and wheelchair rentals are available at the rentals desk, located in the fourth gift shop on the right as you enter the main gate. Reservations can be made ahead of time online or by calling ☎ 888-800-5447. Single strollers cost $15 plus tax, while double strollers cost $19 plus tax, and wheelchairs are available for $18 plus tax. Four-wheel electric scooters, also known as electronic convenience vehicles (ECVs), are available for $50 plus tax. Guests renting the scooters must be at least 18 years old. You can reserve wheelchairs and strollers 1–180 days ahead of time (24 hours in advance minimum) online at **seaworldparks.com/en/buschgardens-tampa/dine-and-shop/shopping/stroller-rental-shop.**

Once you've secured transportation, you'll need to find your way around the park. Make sure to have all the members in your group grab a park map; show schedules are printed on the reverse side. Due to the park's confusing layout, you'll appreciate having the navigational assistance of your entire group. With all of the calories burned walking around this large park, be aware of keeping everyone fed.

You might want to stop for group meals, as eateries are widely spaced, and roving snack vendors are sometimes scarce.

AVOID BOTTLENECKS An early arrival will help you avoid the bottlenecks at most of the major attractions. As for smaller rides, if there's a line, don't wait. Go see a show or visit the animal exhibits that usually have no wait. Then return to the rides later in the day, when lines should subside.

CONTACTING BUSCH GARDENS

FOR MORE INFORMATION, call ☎ 888-800-5447. In addition to park information, the Busch Gardens website (**buschgardenstampa .com**) features an animal information database.

ATTRACTIONS

MOROCCO

Marrakesh Theatre ★★★

| APPEAL BY AGE | PRESCHOOL ★★½ | GRADE SCHOOL ★★½ | TEENS ★★½ |
| YOUNG   ADULTS ★★ | | OVER 30   ★★ | SENIORS   ★½ |

What it is Song-and-dance show. **Scope and scale** Diversion. **When to go** Check daily entertainment schedule. **Authors' rating** Modestly entertaining; ★★★. **Duration of show** 20 minutes.

DESCRIPTION AND COMMENTS The theater holds a variety of performances, but most are of the song-and-dance nature. The show playing on our last visit was a cover-song montage of Motown hits. As with previous years, a live band backs a group of singers-cum-dancers, with the entire ensemble decked out in appropriate wardrobe and hair. The performers have fine voices, are good up-tempo dancers, and cheerfully prompt the audience to sing along.

TOURING TIPS Rows of wrought iron patio seats fill this outdoor theater. They are not on an incline, and it is difficult to see the stage from the back. Arrive 10 minutes early to get the best seats near the front of the house. Rows to the right or left of the stage also offer great views.

Moroccan Palace Theater/*Iceploration* ★★★

| APPEAL BY AGE | PRESCHOOL ★★★½ | GRADE SCHOOL ★★★½ | TEENS ★★½ |
| YOUNG   ADULTS ★★½ | | OVER 30   ★★ | SENIORS   ★★ |

What it is Musical show on ice, featuring some dandy costumes and skaters. **Scope and scale** Diversion. **When to go** Check daily entertainment schedule. **Authors' rating** Interesting, but the skaters aren't performing those big-point routines you're used to seeing at the Olympics; ★★★. **Duration of show** 30 minutes.

DESCRIPTION AND COMMENTS The stage *is* covered with ice, which is groomed every day, but the surface is not large enough to allow for truly exciting skating displays, which often require the skaters to be moving at a high rate of speed. Rather, this show involves some synchronized passes by three or four costumed troupers, a few lifts, and a few spins by the featured skaters. The story consists of a grandfather magically transporting his high-tech young grandson to a rain forest, the South Pole, and the

Great Barrier Reef to get the lad to see the wonder of nature. On the plus side, the production is enlivened by colorful costumes and animal puppets, some impressive set pieces that are brought to life with large-scale video projections, and an inoffensive original sound track.

TOURING TIPS It's best to see this show during a break in your day of activities; it's an opportunity to get out of the Florida heat and humidity. There are no bad seats in the theater because the stage is rather shallow, front to back. If you are around during Christmas time, the special seasonal ice show is much more athletic and emotionally involving.

Myombe Reserve ★★★

| APPEAL BY AGE | PRESCHOOL ★★★ | GRADE SCHOOL ★★★ | TEENS ★★½ |
| YOUNG   ADULTS ★★½ | OVER 30 ★★★ | | SENIORS   ★★★ |

What it is Gorilla habitat. Scope and scale Major attraction. When to go Anytime before 4 p.m. Authors' rating Great theming, informative; ★★★.

DESCRIPTION AND COMMENTS A mist-filled path through a lush landscape leads you to this beautiful habitat filled with waterfalls, thick vegetation, and marshland. The first section is home to several chimpanzees that romp through the trees and greenery. The second area features large gorillas. Only one or two of the animals are regularly visible, but at least one can usually be found napping in front of the glass. Two overhead monitors play a video full of interesting information about each animal in the habitat, including how they interact with each other. Chalkboards throughout the exhibit provide facts and figures about the animals.

TOURING TIPS The animals are usually most active before 11 a.m., but check your schedule or the sign in front of the exhibit for guided tour times. After riding Montu, you can snake through this exhibit, which exits into Nairobi, on your way to Kumba. Bronze sculptures of gorillas and chimpanzees, placed throughout the exhibit, provide some fun photo opportunities. Climb onto the giant gorilla at the entrance or join the train of chimpanzees combing through each other's hair for a unique snapshot.

Exclusive Park Experiences ★★★½

| APPEAL BY AGE | PRESCHOOL ★★★ | GRADE SCHOOL ★★★★ | TEENS ★★★ |
| YOUNG   ADULTS ★★★★ | OVER 30 ★★★½ | | SENIORS   ★★★½ |

What it is Guided tours on the plain and behind the scenes. Scope and scale Major attraction. When to go Call ☎ 888-800-5447 for a schedule. Special comment Must be at least 5 years old (see descriptions below for further restrictions). Authors' rating Worthwhile for animal enthusiasts or the affluent, but can be too expensive for the average visitor; ★★★½.

DESCRIPTION AND COMMENTS Busch Gardens offers a wide variety of exclusive park experiences, but many of them contain overlapping locations, so pick the one that is right for you. Though you can book all the tours listed below on the day of your visit at the Tours Information and Reservation Center near the main gate, the limited capacity of the tours causes them to sell out early most of the year. During peak seasons, you should call weeks in advance. The number for reservations is ☎ 888-800-5447 or visit **seaworldparks.com/en/buschgardens-tampa/attractions/exclusive-park-experiences** to book online. Check-in for all tours is at the Serengeti Outpost, near the Animal Care Center in Nairobi.

None of the tour prices include park admission, unless noted, and the prices vary due to the length and capacity of each tour. Prices are the same for all participants, regardless of age. Though the tours are worthwhile for animal enthusiasts, many—if not all—are too expensive for the average visitor. All prices below are listed without tax.

- **SERENGETI SAFARI** *$29–$39 per person depending on season, 30 minutes.* Guides drive you in an open-back truck into the Serengeti Plain for up close encounters with some of the tamer animals. A zoologist accompanies the trip and doles out information on all of the animals you encounter. The highlight of the trip is feeding the antelope and giraffes. It's a treat to watch the long tongue of a giraffe remove the leaves from a prickly branch while adeptly avoiding thorns. Bring your camera!

- **JUNGALA INSIDER** *$29 per person, 45 minutes.* The tour gives visitors an up close look at Jungala's inhabitants, including the Bengal tigers and orangutans. Zookeepers are on hand to answer any questions. Wheelchairs cannot be accommodated.

- **KEEPER FOR A DAY** *$250 per person, 6½ hours.* If you're a zoo enthusiast ready to shell out some big cash to fulfill a personal dream, then this may be worth considering. Shadow a zookeeper for a morning with some of the herbivores on the Serengeti Plain and spend an afternoon with the Busch Gardens's avian team. If you're going to spend this kind of money, be sure to call ahead and get a detailed itinerary for the day you're visiting. You must be at least 13 years of age and 52 inches tall, and children ages 13–17 must be accompanied by an adult. Park admission and lunch is included in the price. Wheelchairs cannot be accommodated. Reservations must be made at least seven days in advance.

- **HEART OF AFRICA TOUR** *$39 per person, 1½ hours.* Join the keepers for behind-the-scenes time with hippos, cheetahs, and even lions. Open to those age 10 and older; wheelchairs cannot be accommodated.

- **ANIMAL CARE CENTER BEHIND THE SCENES** *$29 per person, 1¼ hours.* For visitors who always wanted to be a veterinarian, this tour takes them behind the glass walls of the Animal Care Center, where they get hands-on time with X-rays, microscopes, and other life-saving medical equipment. Open to age 8 and older; be warned that you may witness an actual surgery or medical procedure.

TOURING TIPS Two different half- and full-day guided tours of the park are also available, and their prices are $100–$200 plus tax and park admission. The selling point is one-time, front-of-the-line access to most of the major rides and/or front seats at all of the shows and/or an Adventure Tour. If you're in the mood for the VIP treatment, call ☎ 888-800-5447 for more information.

EGYPT

Cheetah Hunt ★★★★½

APPEAL BY AGE	PRESCHOOL †	GRADE SCHOOL ★★★★½	TEENS ★★★★★
YOUNG ADULTS ★★★★★		OVER 30 ★★★★★	SENIORS ★★★★½

† *Preschoolers are generally too short to ride.*

What it is Roller coaster. **Scope and scale** Super-headliner. **When to go** Immediately after park opening. **Special comment** 48″ minimum height requirement.

Authors' rating Can't-disappoint run even for coaster fans; ★★★★½. **Duration of ride** 3½ minutes, including loading and unloading.

DESCRIPTION AND COMMENTS Located in the area that formerly included both the beloved Clydesdales' stables and the monorail station, this roller coaster is an attractive pairing of the latest in thrill rides and the eternal allure of beautiful big cats.

The park is famous for its high-speed rides. Busch officials label Cheetah Hunt a launch coaster, driven by a series of magnets—officially, a linear synchronous motor propulsion system. It is the park's first coaster whose onward surge is not powered simply by gravity after the climb to the starting hill. Instead, Cheetah Hunt boasts three bursts of acceleration—up to 30 miles per hour as it starts, as well as at unexpected moments; suddenly up to 60 miles per hour; and after a slower stretch, back up to 40.

The riders climb to a height of 102 feet—providing a magnificent if rapid view of the animal-filled Serengeti Plain—before plunging 130 feet as they rush through a trench. The 16-passenger trains race through several rolling turns and a full inversion—you're held in place by shoulder bars that are double-locked with a belt attached to the seat—over the 4,429-foot track. Thrill seekers experience four times the pull of gravity. The ride's designer told us that he was inspired by the Endor forest speeder bike chase from *Return of the Jedi;* after experiencing the tight twisting track of the coaster's climactic riverbed run, you'll understand exactly what he meant. Having said that, Cheetah Hunt is designed to be smooth and accessible to a wide range of riders who may be intimidated by SheiKra, Montu, and Kumba; though it will put a smile on your face, Cheetah Hunt won't make you scream your head off like those powerhouse coasters.

Five of the trains can operate simultaneously; park executives estimate that they can move 1,370 passengers per hour.

TOURING TIPS Because it has the lowest height requirement of any major coaster in Busch Gardens and it's close to the entrance, Cheetah Hunt is typically swamped when the park first opens each day. When you enter the park, circle to your right around the Guest Services building and check the wait time for the Cheetah Hunt.

kids **Cheetah Run** ★★★★

| APPEAL BY AGE | PRESCHOOL ★★★★★ | GRADE SCHOOL ★★★★★ | TEENS ★★★★★ |
| YOUNG ADULTS ★★★★★ | | OVER 30 ★★★★★ | SENIORS ★★★★★ |

What it is Live-animal attraction. **Scope and scale** Headliner. **When to go** Check park map for first scheduled interaction of the day. **Authors' rating** I'll be sure to stop here both entering and leaving the park; ★★★★.

DESCRIPTION AND COMMENTS Located next to the Cheetah Hunt coaster, the attraction highlights the cheetah, fastest of all land animals.

Visitors, standing inside an African-themed, covered area, view the park's dozen cheetahs through large windows. The cheetahs are trained to chase a feathery lure, and, one at a time, will pursue the lure past the windows, for just over 100 feet. This viewing arrangement is similar to the one at the Edge of Africa lion habitat.

To pass the time between the animals' runs, visitors can use touch screens to learn more about the cheetahs, as well as about the Busch

Gardens/SeaWorld efforts to help them. Among the facts: The cheetah is the only big cat that cannot retract its claws, but those give the animal more traction during its high-speed chases. Other adaptations include a small head for less wind resistance and a tail that moves much like a boat's rudder to help the running animal steer itself. Much of this knowledge also is presented live by the trainers during brief but scheduled afternoon presentations. Unless motivated by instinct, the animals race along their path after the lure only in the mornings, when the weather is cooler. In the afternoon, the exhibit is an educational viewing with the trainers standing or squatting next to the lovely animals at rest. Some cheetahs are almost always viewable in a shaded area, where they can stroll about or plop down beneath the trees.

TOURING TIPS The keepers offer their presentations and the runs three or four times a day total, but they do *not* have the runs every day; if it's raining, there is no running. On the other hand, visitors can see occasional public presentations of the youngest cheetahs, Tendai (meaning "thankful") and Thabo (meaning "joy"), born in late 2014.

Because it is among the newest animal attractions in Busch Gardens, Cheetah Run is usually swamped when the park first opens. When you enter, circle to your right around the Guest Services building and you'll quickly reach the live-cheetah viewing area; check the wait time for the Cheetah Hunt. You might make this a multiple-visit area: in the morning to see the cheetahs running and in the afternoon for the simple lesson and to admire them in repose. If you want to get out of the heat, the Crown Colony Café is just a few yards away.

Cobra's Curse *(opens 2016)*

What it is Family-friendly spinning roller coaster. Scope and scale Headliner. When to go First thing after Cheetah Hunt or at the end of the day. Special comment 42″ minimum height requirement. Duration of ride More than 3½ minutes.

DESCRIPTION AND COMMENTS Cobra's Curse joins Busch Gardens's impressive roller-coaster lineup in 2016 as a family-focused stepping-stone between the Air Grover kiddie coaster and Cheetah Hunt's high-speed launch. Located in the Egypt area behind the defunct King Tut's Tomb walk-through, the 2,100 feet of steel track for Cobra's Curse required partial rerouting of the Serengeti Express train tracks. It's topped by an 80-foot-tall snake sculpture that riders confront face-to-face. A first-of-its-kind design from Germany's MACK Rides, the new coaster takes eight riders at a time, seated back-to-back in tandem cars, up an elevator-like vertical 70-foot lift, before sending them spinning in circles at up to 40 miles per hour.

TOURING TIPS Parts of the old Tut's Tomb will be repurposed as an air-conditioned queue for Cobra's Curse. That's a good thing, because with a broad appeal but an hourly capacity of just more than 1,000 riders per hour, the line is sure to be lengthy. Take this one for a spin as soon after opening as possible (preferably right after Cheetah Hunt), or save it until last.

Edge of Africa ★★★½

APPEAL BY AGE	PRESCHOOL ★★★½	GRADE SCHOOL ★★★★	TEENS ★★★
YOUNG ADULTS ★★★	OVER 30 ★★★½		SENIORS ★★★½

What it is Walking tour of animal habitats. **Scope and scale** Headliner. **When to go** Crowds are minuscule in the afternoon, and the animals are fairly active. **Authors' rating** Good presentation; ★★★½.

DESCRIPTION AND COMMENTS This walking safari features hippopotamuses, giraffes, lions, meerkats, hyenas, and vultures in naturalistic habitats. The area was designed for up close viewing, many times with just a pane of glass between you and the animals. Exhibits of note are the hippopotamus habitat and the hyena area. The hippos wade in 5-foot-deep water filled with colorful fish, all visible through the glass wall. In the hyena habitat, open safari vehicles are built into the glass, offering a great photo opportunity if you climb in when the animals come near.

TOURING TIPS Animals are most active during feedings and during the chats by keepers; check the park map for times of the keeper talks. Feeding times are not regularly scheduled, so the animals don't fall into a pattern that would not exist in the wild. Employees are usually willing to tell you feeding times for the day. It might be a hike to return to this area, but seeing the lions chomp into raw meat is definitely worth it.

There is a hidden entrance to this area between Cobra's Curse and the restrooms near Montu. This is useful if you ride the roller coasters before seeing the animals. An entrance from Nairobi also makes this area more easily accessible.

Montu   ★★★★★

APPEAL BY AGE	PRESCHOOL †	GRADE SCHOOL ★★★★	TEENS ★★★★★
YOUNG ADULTS ★★★★½		OVER 30 ★★★½	SENIORS ★★½

† Preschoolers are generally too short to ride.

What it is Inverted steel super roller coaster. **Scope and scale** Super-headliner. **When to go** Before 10 a.m. or after 4 p.m. **Special comment** 54″ minimum height requirement. **Authors' rating** Incredible; ★★★★★. **Duration of ride** About 3 minutes.

DESCRIPTION AND COMMENTS Seats hang below the track and riders' feet dangle on this intense inverted roller coaster, which is among the top 20 in the country and among the best we've ever ridden. The fast-paced but extremely smooth ride begins with a 13-story drop. Riders are then hurled through a 104-foot inverted vertical loop. Speeds reach 60 miles per hour as riders are accelerated through more dizzying loops and twists, including an Immelman, an inverse loop named after German World War I fighter pilot Max Immelman.

TOURING TIPS Depending on which route you take, try to ride in the morning or later in the afternoon to avoid waits that can be as long as an hour (or even more). If lines are still long, however, don't be discouraged. As many as 32 riders can pile onto each train, so even the longest line will move quickly and steadily.

If you have time, ride twice, first near the back of the train and then in the front row. In the back, you'll glimpse a sea of dangling feet in front of you and be surprised by each twist and turn because you can't see where the track is headed, just legs swooping through the air. Riding in the front gives you a clear, unobstructed view of everything around you, including the huge trees dozens of feet below you on the first drop. If you have to choose one or the other, we definitely recommend the front row. Look for the special front-seat queue once you enter the load station. The wait for the front is usually an extra 20 minutes, but it's worth it for the thrill.

Skyride ★★★

APPEAL BY AGE	PRESCHOOL ★★	GRADE SCHOOL ★★½	TEENS ★★
YOUNG ADULTS ★★	OVER 30 ★★½		SENIORS ★★★

What it is Scenic transportation to Stanleyville train station. **Scope and scale** Minor attraction. **When to go** In the morning; lines can be long in the afternoon. **Authors' rating** Slow, in a park noted for its speed rides; ★★★. **Duration of ride** 4 minutes.

DESCRIPTION AND COMMENTS This aerial tram travels between Egypt, close to the Cheetah Hunt, and Stanleyville, close to Kumba. It offers great views of the Serengeti Plain and its wild inhabitants as well as the roller coasters. You can board at either terminus, but you must wait in line again to take a return trip.

TOURING TIPS If the lines are small, you may use the Skyride as a shortcut from Montu to Kumba and SheiKra. The shortcut may work only early in the morning because if the lines are not short, this ride takes longer than walking; however, it's still faster than the train.

NAIROBI

Animal Care Center ★★★½

APPEAL BY AGE	PRESCHOOL ★★	GRADE SCHOOL ★★★	TEENS ★★½
YOUNG ADULTS ★★★	OVER 30 ★★★		SENIORS ★★★½

What it is Walk-through veterinary clinic. **Scope and scale** Minor attraction. **When to go** Anytime, especially mornings, when medical procedures are scheduled. **Authors' rating** Informative and air-conditioned; ★★★½. **Duration of ride** About 8 minutes.

DESCRIPTION AND COMMENTS To give guests a deeper look into the veterinary services it provides to its nonhuman employees, Busch Gardens has supplemented Jambo Junction with a colorful (and blissfully cool) Animal Care Center, where you can witness animal check-ups and even surgeries through large glass windows. The Animal Care Center is featured on the ABC TV series *The Wildlife Docs,* so you may spot a reality TV star during your stay. Handsomely designed but a bit dry for the little ones when there isn't an active operation on display, this walk-through diversion is extremely similar to Rafiki's Planet Watch at Disney's Animal Kingdom, only without the cartoon characters or inconvenient train ride.

TOURING TIPS Stop in any time you need a break from the elements, but the most interesting examinations always occur before lunchtime; ask an employee in the morning what's on the doc's docket for the day.

Curiosity Caverns ★★½

APPEAL BY AGE	PRESCHOOL ★★½	GRADE SCHOOL ★★★½	TEENS ★★½
YOUNG ADULTS ★★★	OVER 30 ★★★		SENIORS ★★½

What it is Walk-through exhibit of "odd" animals. **Scope and scale** Minor attraction. **When to go** Anytime. **Authors' rating** A cool break; ★★½.

DESCRIPTION AND COMMENTS This seems to be a catchall for types of animals not exhibited elsewhere in the park. You'll see snakes and other reptiles behind glass, including a Burmese python and an anaconda, though the exhibit also has a three-toed sloth, bats, and a laughing kookaburra bird (which did not appear to be in the mood for laughter on our last visit).

TOURING TIPS The cooler climate inside Curiosity Caverns makes it an ideal place for reptiles, as well as humans, to hide from the heat and the glare outside.

Elephant Interaction Wall   ★★

APPEAL BY AGE	PRESCHOOL ★★★	GRADE SCHOOL ★★★	TEENS ★★
YOUNG ADULTS ★★		OVER 30 ★★	SENIORS ★★½

What it is Elephant habitat. **Scope and scale** Minor attraction. **When to go** During interaction times. **Authors' rating** ★★.

DESCRIPTION AND COMMENTS Endangered Asian elephants roam a dry dirt pen. A large pool is deep enough for these huge animals to submerge themselves and escape the Florida heat. The pen is surprisingly small; it's too bad the elephants can't roam the larger Serengeti Plain.

TOURING TIPS Visit during enrichment times, when trainers interact with the animals and speak with guests. The daily entertainment schedule doesn't list enrichment times for all the animals, so you should ask a keeper.

Jambo Junction   ★★★½

APPEAL BY AGE	PRESCHOOL ★★½	GRADE SCHOOL ★★★½	TEENS ★★
YOUNG ADULTS ★★★		OVER 30 ★★½	SENIORS ★★★

What it is Animals on display. **Scope and scale** Minor attraction. **When to go** Anytime. **Authors' rating** Super cute; ★★★½.

DESCRIPTION AND COMMENTS Busch Gardens is home to more than 2,700 animals, and many of the females often give birth to young. The park also rescues ill or orphaned animal infants, including a sizable number of endangered species. The animal nursery in Jambo Junction houses these infants, but other animals, such as flamingos, lemurs, cuscuses, sloths, and opossums, are also presented to the guests. No matter which animals are on display, you're sure to come down with a small case of the warm fuzzies.

TOURING TIPS The attraction contains more animals in pens outside the main facility. The best time to stop by is during the daily scheduled Animal Ambassador sessions (usually at 1 p.m.), when you may get the chance to feed a feathered friend.

Serengeti Express   ★★

APPEAL BY AGE	PRESCHOOL ★★½	GRADE SCHOOL ★★½	TEENS ★★
YOUNG ADULTS ★★		OVER 30 ★★★	SENIORS ★★★½

What it is Train tour through the Serengeti Plain and around the park. **Scope and scale** Minor attraction. **When to go** Afternoon. **Authors' rating** Relaxing; ★★. **Duration of ride** 12 minutes through animal area exiting at next station; 35 minutes round-trip.

DESCRIPTION AND COMMENTS Riding this train gives your feet a break and provides the best view of the animals along the Serengeti Plain. Because it's quite poky, we don't recommend it as an alternate means of transportation, but the 12-minute trip from the Nairobi station through the Serengeti Plain to the Congo station is worth the time if you're not racing to ride the coasters. Onboard guides identify the animals you see and tell a little about their history and habits. The train will take you close to the ostriches, wildebeests, and white rhinos.

TOURING TIPS Because the train runs counterclockwise, sit on the left-hand side for the best view of the entire plain. If you board at the Nairobi station, get off at the Congo station for Kumba or the Congo River Rapids; get off at Stanleyville for Tanganyika Tidal Wave or the Sesame Street Safari of Fun children's area.

PANTOPIA

Falcon's Fury   ★★★★

| APPEAL BY AGE | PRESCHOOL † | GRADE SCHOOL ★★★½ | TEENS ★★★★½ |
| YOUNG ADULTS ★★★★½ | | OVER 30 ★★★★ | SENIORS ★★½ |

† *Preschoolers are generally too short to ride.*

What it is A face-down plunge from a 300-plus-foot drop tower. **Scope and scale** Super-headliner. **When to go** Before lunch, immediately after the major coasters. **Special comment** 54″ minimum height requirement. **Authors' rating** A real scream! ★★★★. **Duration of ride** About 90 seconds.

DESCRIPTION AND COMMENTS Busch Gardens added another record-breaking scream producer in 2014: a 300-foot plummet, with the riders facing down toward their onrushing doom. Falcon's Fury is the centerpiece of Pantopia, the pan-cultural land with an eye-popping color palette that replaced the drab former Timbuktu theme.

At the base of a 335-foot freestanding column (the tallest such tower in North America when it opened), 32 passengers at a time climb into seats and pull down an over-the-shoulder safety bar with a comfortable padded chest restraint. You're then lifted approximately 300 feet above the pavement, affording an excellent view of downtown Tampa before the seats rotate forward 90 degrees so that you are facing down. After a random number of seconds (a particularly nerve-racking touch) the seats are released into true free fall for more than 5 seconds, reaching speeds of 60 miles per hour. Just before you reach the ground, your seat is returned to an upright position as 3.5 g's of braking force are applied, so that your feet (not face) touch terra firma first.

Falcon's Fury isn't for the fainthearted, and even a single glance at it from the parking lot is enough to make thrill-ride addicts apprehensive; this thing makes Disney's Tower of Terror look like a kiddie bounce house. But the truth is that the anticipation on the way up is the worst part; once the free fall begins, your prone position prevents your stomach from leaping into your mouth, and you're free to enjoy a brief moment of zero-g weightlessness before the brakes bring you to a surprisingly smooth stop. If you can get up the nerve, this is the closest you'll come to skydiving without strapping on a parachute.

TOURING TIPS The ride, which replaced the Sandstorm carnival spinner, is only able to hoist and drop fewer than 1,000 riders per hour. That should translate to long lines, but the ride's intimidation factor seems to limit its audience, usually resulting in modest waits even at peak times. Even so, you should ride Falcon's Fury in the morning immediately after riding the major roller coasters. If the line is short, you may want to take two plunges; you'll be able to relax and enjoy the view (and the fall) much easier the second time around.

kids Kiddie Rides ★★½

APPEAL BY AGE	PRESCHOOL ★★★	GRADE SCHOOL †	TEENS †
YOUNG ADULTS †		OVER 30 †	SENIORS †

† Not designed for older kids and adults.

What they are Pint-size carnival rides. Scope and scale Minor attraction. When to go Anytime. Authors' rating Good diversion for children; ★★½.

DESCRIPTION AND COMMENTS Nothing fancy, but these attractions help kids who aren't old enough to ride the thrillers feel that they aren't being left out. Another set of kiddie rides can be found in the Sesame Street Safari of Fun area.

TOURING TIPS These rides are strategically placed near the adult attractions in this area (Falcon's Fury, Scorpion, and Phoenix), so one parent can keep the kids occupied while another rides. The classic carousel is quite lovely and entertaining for all ages.

Pantopia Theater/*Opening Night Critters* ★★★

APPEAL BY AGE	PRESCHOOL ★★★½	GRADE SCHOOL ★★★½	TEENS ★★★
YOUNG ADULTS ★★½		OVER 30 ★★★	SENIORS ★★★

What it is Trained animal show. Scope and scale Minor attraction. When to go Anytime. Authors' rating ★★★. Duration of show 30 minutes.

DESCRIPTION AND COMMENTS This large air-conditioned theater used to show 3-D movies, but it was repurposed during the Pantopia makeover as the home for Busch Gardens's latest trained animal show. Critters both domestic and exotic, many rescued from shelters, are put through their paces in this slapstick backstage comedy. The animals are undeniably adorable, and the impressive behaviors they exhibit are on par with those in similar shows at SeaWorld (*Pets Ahoy!*) and Universal Studios Florida (*Animal Actors on Location*). But the trainers are not allowed to simply demonstrate their craft; they must sing and dance, with predictable results. Skip this one unless you have pet-crazy kids or need to escape the heat.

TOURING TIPS The showtimes are posted on your park map, and there may be as few as two performances per day. Sit under a pole-mounted hoop for an avian flyby in the finale, and head to the front of the theater immediately after the show to meet some of the stars.

Phoenix ★★

APPEAL BY AGE	PRESCHOOL †	GRADE SCHOOL ★★★	TEENS ★★★
YOUNG ADULTS ★★½		OVER 30 ★★½	SENIORS ★

† Preschoolers are generally too short to ride.

What it is Swinging pendulum ride. **Scope and scale** Minor attraction. **When to go** Anytime. **Special comments** 48″ minimum height requirement; not for those prone to motion sickness. **Authors' rating** Dizzying; ★★. **Duration of ride** 5 minutes.

Motion Sickness

DESCRIPTION AND COMMENTS A large wooden boat swings back and forth, starting slowly and then gaining speed before making a complete circle with passengers hanging upside down.

TOURING TIPS Remove glasses and anything in your shirt pockets to avoid losing them when the boat is suspended upside down for several seconds.

kids Sand Serpent ★★★

APPEAL BY AGE	PRESCHOOL ★★★	GRADE SCHOOL ★★★½	TEENS ★★
YOUNG ADULTS ★★		OVER 30 ★★	SENIORS ★

What it is Kiddie coaster. **Scope and scale** Minor attraction. **When to go** Line is usually relatively short compared with the big coasters, but an early stop would be wise because the line grows as the day goes on. **Special comments** 46″ minimum height requirement; must be at least 6 years old. **Authors' rating** Fun for the little coaster lovers; ★★★. **Duration of ride** Approximately 3 minutes.

DESCRIPTION AND COMMENTS Hairpin turns and mini-drops make this a good choice for thrill seekers who aren't yet tall enough to take on the big coasters.

TOURING TIPS This was originally named the Cheetah Chase and was renamed once the new Cheetah Hunt and Cheetah Run attractions opened. The line moves quickly here but builds in the afternoon due to its proximity to other kiddie rides. This is also a good place to wait for the super-coaster riders in your party.

Scorpion ★★★

APPEAL BY AGE	PRESCHOOL †	GRADE SCHOOL ★★★½	TEENS ★★½
YOUNG ADULTS ★★★		OVER 30 ★★★	SENIORS ★★

† *Preschoolers are generally too short to ride.*

What it is Roller coaster. **Scope and scale** Headliner. **When to go** After 2 p.m. **Special comment** 42″ minimum height requirement. **Authors' rating** Quick but exciting; ★★★. **Duration of ride** 1½ minutes.

DESCRIPTION AND COMMENTS This coaster pales in comparison with big sisters Kumba and Montu. In spite of its small stature, with speeds of 50 miles per hour, a 360-degree vertical loop, and three 360-degree spirals, it's nothing to sneeze at.

TOURING TIPS Lines are rarely long for this attraction, but because the coaster doesn't have the high capacity of Kumba or Montu, the line moves slowly. Ride after the major coasters and Falcon's Fury, or save the ride for the afternoon, when the wait is almost always shorter.

CONGO

Congo River Rapids ★★★½

APPEAL BY AGE	PRESCHOOL ★★★½	GRADE SCHOOL ★★★½	TEENS ★★★½
YOUNG ADULTS ★★★		OVER 30 ★★★	SENIORS ★★★½

What it is Whitewater raft ride. **Scope and scale** Headliner. **When to go** After 4 p.m. **Special comment** You will get soaked. **Authors' rating** A great time but not worth more than a 45-minute wait; ★★★½. **Duration of ride** 3 minutes.

DESCRIPTION AND COMMENTS Whitewater raft rides have become somewhat of a theme park standard, and this version is pretty much the status quo. Twelve riders sit on a circular rubber raft as they float down a jungle river, jostling and spinning in the waves and rapids. Scary signs warn of dangerous crocodiles in the "river," but no beasts (robotic or otherwise) ever show themselves. It is possible to avoid getting drenched through the sheer luck of where your boat goes, but in the end, getting very wet is almost guaranteed due to both water jets operated by mischievous onlookers on a bridge and a final gauntlet of giant water jets that soaks almost every raft that passes through. There's nothing like the helpless feeling of watching your boat drift into the path of one of these mega fire hoses.

TOURING TIPS Wear a poncho, either your own or one purchased at nearby concession huts. Stow as much clothing in the lockers at the dock as you can take off and remain decent (especially socks—nobody likes squishy feet). There is no watertight center console on these rafts. Also, know that long lines are inevitable for this slow-loading and slow-unloading attraction. We recommend that you ride the roller coasters first, saving this attraction for later in the morning or afternoon. The cute monkeys on display make waiting in the first third of the line fairly entertaining.

Kumba ★★★★½

APPEAL BY AGE	PRESCHOOL †	GRADE SCHOOL ★★★★	TEENS ★★★★
YOUNG ADULTS ★★★★		OVER 30 ★★★★	SENIORS ★★

† Preschoolers are generally too short to ride.

What it is Steel super roller coaster. **Scope and scale** Super-headliner. **When to go** Before 11 a.m. or after 2:30 p.m. **Special comment** 54" minimum height requirement. **Authors' rating** Excellent; ★★★★½. **Duration of ride** Approximately 3 minutes.

DESCRIPTION AND COMMENTS Kumba's dramatic loops rise above the treeline in the Congo area, with a trainload of screaming riders twisting skyward. Just like sister coaster Montu, Kumba is one of the best in the country. Unlike Montu's, Kumba's trains sit on top of the track as it roars through 3,900 feet of twists and loops. Reaching speeds of 60 miles per hour, Kumba is certainly fast, but it also offers an incredibly smooth ride. This is good because the coaster's intense corkscrews will churn your insides something fierce. Thrilling elements include a diving loop, a camelback with a 360-degree spiral, and a 108-foot vertical loop. Kumba resembles Islands of Adventure's Incredible Hulk Coaster (another Bolliger & Mabillard creation) without the initial launch or boring back half; Kumba maintains its ferocious pace from the first drop to the final brake run like few rides can.

TOURING TIPS Kumba will be the last coaster you ride in the morning taking either route 1, 2, or 3. Following route 1, it will be after Montu; with routes 2 and 3, it will follow SheiKra. Just like Montu and SheiKra, as many as 32 riders can brave Kumba at once, so even if there is a line, the wait shouldn't be unbearable. Kumba is one of the few coasters ever to make Seth gray out from excessive g-forces; whether that's a warning or an endorsement depends on your tolerance.

Ubanga-Banga Bumper Cars ★★½

APPEAL BY AGE	PRESCHOOL ★★★	GRADE SCHOOL ★★★	TEENS ★★★
YOUNG ADULTS ★★½		OVER 30 ★★	SENIORS ★

What it is Bumper car ride. **Scope and scale** Minor attraction. **When to go** Anytime. **Authors' rating** ★★½. **Duration of ride** Approximately 2 minutes, depending on park attendance.

DESCRIPTION AND COMMENTS Basic carnival bumper car ride.

TOURING TIPS Don't waste time waiting in the usually very long line for this attraction if you're on the roller-coaster circuit. However, because this ride is right next to Kumba, it is a perfect place for kids and others in your group to wait for those braving the coaster.

JUNGALA

kids Jungle Flyers ★½

APPEAL BY AGE	PRESCHOOL ★★½	GRADE SCHOOL ★★★½	TEENS ★
YOUNG ADULTS †		OVER 30 †	SENIORS †

† Not designed for older kids and adults.

What it is Zip line. **Scope and scale** Minor attraction. **When to go** Early in the morning. **Special comments** 48" minimum height requirement; restricted to children ages 6–13. Parents can ride along, but the total weight cannot exceed 210 pounds. **Authors' rating** Poor call; ★½. **Duration of ride** 2 minutes.

DESCRIPTION AND COMMENTS At the top of a long flight of stairs in Jungala lies Jungle Flyers. Here, six small chairs, which each seat two people, shoot back and forth across short zip lines. The chairs have hang gliding wings attached to their tops, the only theming. Parents can ride along, but anyone over the age of 13 cannot ride without a child.

TOURING TIPS You'd think that theme parks would learn from the mistakes of their competition, but this ride proves that it's not always the case. Pteranodon Flyers is one of the biggest time wasters at Universal's Islands of Adventure, yet Busch Gardens has gone ahead and come up with a rather similar ride without the high-quality theming. The only thing Busch Gardens has managed to duplicate is the wait time. Unless there's no one here and your child meets all of the height and weight requirements, skip it.

Orangutan Habitat ★★★

APPEAL BY AGE	PRESCHOOL ★★★½	GRADE SCHOOL ★★★½	TEENS ★★½
YOUNG ADULTS ★★★		OVER 30 ★★★	SENIORS ★★★½

What it is Zoological exhibit. **Scope and scale** Major attraction. **When to go** Anytime. **Authors' rating** Great to see the guys when they're active; ★★★.

DESCRIPTION AND COMMENTS Directly beside the Tiger Habitat is a place where guests can view these great apes playing in large environs, complete with high wires and a moat. The depth of the enclosure, coupled with its many egresses, can make it difficult to spot the somewhat reclusive primates. Fortunately, Busch Gardens has provided quarter-operated telescopes, located on the enclosure's bridge, to make spotting these guys easier.

TOURING TIPS This is a good place to go if a tour group is crowding the Tiger Habitat. On occasion, you'll see the orangutans skittering along the high wires, but more often, you'll only spot a tuft of orange fur or nothing at all. The same viewing opportunities (minus the rope tricks) hold true for two other small enclosures nearby, which house the flying foxes and the gibbons.

kids Tiger Habitat ★★★★

APPEAL BY AGE	PRESCHOOL ★★★★½	GRADE SCHOOL ★★★★½	TEENS ★★★½
YOUNG ADULTS ★★★★		OVER 30 ★★★★	SENIORS ★★★½

What it is Zoological exhibit. Scope and scale Headliner. When to go Anytime. Authors' rating Big cats; ★★★★.

DESCRIPTION AND COMMENTS Thick glass panes separate viewers from this highly endangered species. Viewing areas surround the habitat, which makes actually seeing the inhabitants not only much more likely but also more thrilling. A small ladder leads into a tiny glass bubble, where one visitor at a time can peer up into a secluded part of the reserve.

If you are lucky enough to experience it, the tigers occasionally swim in the small stream, and the glass partition lets you see their feline feet treading water (not a perspective you'd ever want to have in the wild).

TOURING TIPS This viewing area is one of the best for any species at the park. Check with trainers early in the day for the tiger tug-of-war schedule, which sets groups of visitors against the pulling power of a Bengal tiger; a partition is in between the two species, of course.

kids Treetop Trails ★★★

APPEAL BY AGE	PRESCHOOL ★★★½	GRADE SCHOOL ★★★½	TEENS ★★
YOUNG ADULTS ★½		OVER 30 ★★	SENIORS ★★

What it is Climbing playground. Scope and scale Minor attraction. When to go Anytime. Authors' rating Fun escape; ★★★.

DESCRIPTION AND COMMENTS A series of cargo nets and wooden bridges links together this multistoried playground. Though not as intricate as, say, Camp Jurassic at Islands of Adventure, this area lets kids run free and makes a nice counterpart to Sesame Street Safari of Fun.

Its proximity to dining and benches makes it a good place for weary parents to rest and for kids to expend some excess energy (though they will need some of it to make it through the rest of the park).

TOURING TIPS Some of the tunnels are too small for adults to fit in without hunching over, so it's best to sit below and watch the kids from a stationary vantage point. Up top, there is a good view down at the Wild Surge, where you can wave at all the folks standing in line.

Wild Surge ★★½

APPEAL BY AGE	PRESCHOOL ★★★½	GRADE SCHOOL ★★★½	TEENS ★★
YOUNG ADULTS ★½		OVER 30 ★★	SENIORS ★★

What it is Spire with two rows of seats that rise and drop. **Scope and scale** Minor attraction. **When to go** Early. **Authors' rating** Time waster; ★★½. **Duration of ride** 1 minute.

DESCRIPTIONS AND COMMENTS Hidden in the center of a circle of rocks, this basic carnival ride sends up to 14 people to the top of a spire, and then drops, lifts, and again drops them back down. It only free-falls part of the way, so it's fine for younger kids.

TOURING TIPS With only one low-capacity ride, wait times can exceed 45 minutes on busy days. Actual ride time is only about a minute, but load times make this a 3-minute ordeal. This is a clumsy and ill-conceived ride, and with the exception of the neighboring Jungle Flyers, it ranks up there with the worst wait-time-to-thrill ratio in the park.

kids SESAME STREET SAFARI OF FUN

Air Grover ★★★

APPEAL BY AGE	PRESCHOOL ★★★★	GRADE SCHOOL ★★★½	TEENS †
YOUNG ADULTS †	OVER 30 †		SENIORS †

† Not designed for older kids and adults.

What it is Lazy steel-track coaster. **Scope and scale** Headliner. **When to go** Before noon or after 4 p.m. **Special comments** 38" minimum height requirement; children 38"–41" must be accompanied by a rider at least 14 years old. **Authors' rating** Those on the ground need to pinch themselves to stay awake while watching; ★★★. **Duration of ride** About 45 seconds.

DESCRIPTION AND COMMENTS Once the kiddies' lap bars are locked, the cars slowly take off. They move slowly up an incline to a height of perhaps 20 feet, and then slowly move down and through two 360-degree helixes, before easing back to the platform.

TOURING TIPS Unlike most roller coasters, riders do *not* want to hurry to claim the front car: The view from there is blocked by a massive Grover figure.

Kiddie Rides ★★★½

APPEAL BY AGE	PRESCHOOL ★★★★	GRADE SCHOOL ★★★½	TEENS †
YOUNG ADULTS †	OVER 30 †		SENIORS †

† Not designed for older kids and adults.

What they are Playland for the stroller and tyke set. **Scope and scale** Headliner. **When to go** Before your littlest ones get too pooped. **Special comment** 56" *maximum* height requirement. **Authors' rating** Time to turn the teens loose while you watch the nippers; ★★★½.

DESCRIPTION AND COMMENTS This area looks like the mall on the day after Thanksgiving. Kiddie rides include a pint-size merry-go-round and tiny auto track with just two, two-seat cars on it, plus a hard-floored splash pool that requires at least watertight diapers for the youngest.

Adults and teens can accompany little ones on the three-story-high cargo-netted playground at Elmo's Treehouse. Roped-in bridges between the higher stations lead to a central jungle gym of cargo nets. For adults not wanting to accompany children across the netting, a central staircase leads to the upper-level play area.

TOURING TIPS Height restrictions vary between 36 and 56 inches, though adults are allowed to walk in the overhead cargo-net areas with the kids.

Adults need to study the park map to understand what is where because only the downsized Air Grover roller coaster and the theater stand out from the poorly signed entrances to some attractions.

Sunny Day Theater ★★★

APPEAL BY AGE	PRESCHOOL ★★★★	GRADE SCHOOL ★★★	TEENS †
YOUNG ADULTS †	OVER 30 †		SENIORS †

† Not designed for older kids and adults.

What it is Stage with shows featuring humans inside Sesame Street character costumes. **Scope and scale** Minor attraction. **When to go** Check daily entertainment schedule. **Special comment** Unless your kids are younger than age 8, they will likely be squirming before the end of the show. **Authors' rating** Those metal benches sure seem hard, even before the show is done; ★★★. **Duration of show** 15 minutes.

DESCRIPTION AND COMMENTS Moving about and waving their arms or paws to the sound track, the familiar characters offer their gentle version of education. For instance, the show *"A" Is for Africa* has the dancers holding up pictures of animals, while the prerecorded narration talks about the critters' habits and habitats and encourages the audience to imitate the animals' noises.

TOURING TIPS This small theater is the first element of the Sesame Street area if you have turned left at the park entrance and passed through Morocco. While the youngest kids may be content to sit through a show, if they glance just next door, they are liable to be drawn to Air Grover, the mini roller coaster. A better plan than stopping here first is to let the nippers enjoy the rides and active play areas, and then return to the theater.

STANLEYVILLE

SheiKra ★★★★★

APPEAL BY AGE	PRESCHOOL †	GRADE SCHOOL ★★★	TEENS ★★★★½
YOUNG ADULTS ★★★★½	OVER 30 ★★★★		SENIORS ★★

† Preschoolers are generally too short to ride.

What it is Quick steel-track dive coaster. **Scope and scale** Super-headliner. **When to go** Before 11 a.m. or after 4 p.m. **Special comment** 54" minimum height requirement. **Authors' rating** It rides like the commercial; ★★★★★. **Duration of ride** 3 minutes.

DESCRIPTION AND COMMENTS This attraction is 200 feet tall, making it the tallest coaster in the state of Florida (for now), and it's one of only nine dive coasters that exist anywhere. (A dive coaster is a ride with a completely vertical drop.) Also incorporated are twists, swooping turns, a second huge plunge, and a tunnel of mist. The drops aren't just steep— riders hurtle down at an average of 70 miles per hour. The car has three rows with eight seats across, so there are no bad seats. Any seat on Shei-Kra is second only to the front row of Montu, especially since the coaster's floor was removed.

TOURING TIPS You cannot take anything on this ride and must use a locker (50¢) found across from the entrance; there are also cubbies for last-minute things you might have in shirt or blouse pockets. If you are planning on hitting any of the nearby water rides soon after, keep your gear in the locker.

Stanley Falls Flume ★★½

APPEAL BY AGE	PRESCHOOL ★★★		GRADE SCHOOL ★★★		TEENS ★★
YOUNG	ADULTS ★★	OVER	30 ★★½	SENIORS	★★½

What it is Water-flume ride. **Scope and scale** Major attraction. **When to go** After 3 p.m. **Special comment** 46″ minimum height requirement to ride alone. **Authors' rating** Nothing too exciting; ★★½. **Duration of ride** 3 minutes.

DESCRIPTION AND COMMENTS Logs drift along a winding flume before plummeting down a 40-foot drop. There is almost no theming on this ride, but because the little ones can ride with an adult, it's a good way for small children (who are ready for it) to enjoy a moderate thrill. Riders are only slightly splashed on the final big drop.

TOURING TIPS This ride is exciting without being scary or jarring. During peak season, save it for the late afternoon, when lines will be shorter.

kids **Stanleyville Theater/*Madagascar Live: Operation Vacation*** ★★★

APPEAL BY AGE	PRESCHOOL ★★★★		GRADE SCHOOL ★★★★		TEENS ★★★
YOUNG	ADULTS ★★	OVER	30 ★★	SENIORS	★★

What it is High-energy musical review. **Scope and scale** Major attraction. **When to go** Consult website or park map insert for each day's showtimes. **Authors' rating** There's so much action onstage that it's entertaining despite the slimmest of story lines; ★★★. **Duration of show** 20 minutes.

DESCRIPTION AND COMMENTS This live-action musical is based on the highly popular Madagascar series of films from Dreamworks Animation. Humans inside characters' costumes, penguins, a lion, a meerkat, and more romp around the stage alongside six dancers, two singers, and a four-piece band. The dancing and singing is almost constant, with the dancers and costumed characters briefly stepping down from the stage and into the aisles of the revamped (now covered and air-conditioned) Stanleyville Theater.

TOURING TIPS The six dancers mix moves ranging from cheerleading routines to hip-shaking stuff you might see on a club floor, so if you want to watch their feet, sit several rows back from the front of the elevated stage. During the lower-attendance months of fall and spring, this show is staged only on weekends with scheduled meet and greets with the *Madagascar* characters on weekdays.

Tanganyika Tidal Wave ★★½

APPEAL BY AGE	PRESCHOOL †		GRADE SCHOOL ★★★		TEENS ★★★
YOUNG	ADULTS ★★★	OVER	30 ★★★	SENIORS	★★

† *Preschoolers are generally too short to ride.*

What it is Quick, super water-flume ride. **Scope and scale** Headliner. **When to go** Before 11 a.m. or after 3 p.m. **Special comments** 48″ minimum height requirement; you will get soaked. **Authors' rating** A long wait for a very short thrill; ★★½. **Duration of ride** 2 minutes.

DESCRIPTION AND COMMENTS The Tanganyika Tidal Wave was king before the Orlando parks realized that a super water-flume ride should entertain you as well as get you wet. Consequently, this ride pales in comparison with Splash Mountain at Walt Disney World or Jurassic Park River Adventure at Islands of Adventure. It does do a spectacular job of getting you soaked, however. Riders board a 25-passenger boat and slowly float past empty stilt houses and ominous skulls before making the climb to the top of a steep drop. The cars are specifically designed to throw the water onto the passengers, guaranteeing a soggy experience.

TOURING TIPS If you didn't get enough water on the ride, stand on the bridge crossing the splash pool. An enormous wall of water shoots from each dropping car, fully drenching onlookers. If you want the visuals without the bath, a glass wall in the area blocks the water and is one of the most fun diversions in the park.

As you exit the attraction, or if you choose not to ride, visit Orchid Canyon. This gorgeous area features many varieties of orchids growing around waterfalls in artificial rocks.

BIRD GARDENS
Lory Landing ★★★

| APPEAL BY AGE | PRESCHOOL ★★★ | GRADE SCHOOL ★★★ | TEENS ★★★ |
| YOUNG   ADULTS ★★★ | | OVER 30   ★★★ | SENIORS   ★★★½ |

What it is Interactive aviary. Scope and scale Major attraction. When to go Birds are hungrier in the morning but don't mind an afternoon snack. Authors' rating Cute; ★★★.

DESCRIPTION AND COMMENTS Many area attractions feature aviaries, but this is by far the biggest and the best. Tropical birds from around the world dot the lush landscape, fill the air in free flight, and are displayed in habitats. Purchase a nectar cup for $5, and some of these delightful creatures will be eating right out of your hand. Many will land on your hands, arms, shoulders, or even head, making this attraction a nightmare for those with bird-in-the-hair phobia. The illustrated journal of a fictitious explorer helps differentiate the many species, including lorikeets, hornbills, parrots, and avocets.

TOURING TIPS Try to visit before lunch because the birds usually get their fill of nectar by early afternoon.

kids Walkabout Way ★★★½

| APPEAL BY AGE | PRESCHOOL ★★★★ | GRADE SCHOOL ★★★★ | TEENS ★★★½ |
| YOUNG   ADULTS ★★★½ | | OVER 30   ★★★½ | SENIORS   ★★★ |

What it is A chance to feed kangaroos and wallabies, plus a small aviary. Scope and scale Minor attraction. When to go Anytime, but check park map for scheduled keepers' chats and feedings. Authors' rating ★★★½.

DESCRIPTION AND COMMENTS Walkabout Way is a path between the large cages holding wallabies and both red and gray kangaroos. Feed is for sale if you want to have the oddly sweet-looking creatures nuzzle your hand, or you can watch the pros do it several times a day. The Walkabout is adjacent to the smallish Aviary Walk-Thru. There are no informational handouts on the birds nor plaques to identify them, but the aviary does include kookaburras.

TOURING TIPS This far corner of the park is quiet, and you may find a bit of solace by the pond near the aviary.

DINING

BUSCH GARDENS OFFERS A SIMILAR SELECTION of food as sister park SeaWorld. Fast food costs about $8–$10 per person, not including drinks. The menu at **Bengal Bistro** in the Jungala area is typical: A breaded fish sandwich or Italian sub is $9, and a kid's hot dog with a souvenir plate or a spicy chicken sandwich is $8. All of these come with a side item such as fries. There is some variety among the dining spots. For instance, carved deli sandwiches on freshly baked bread and southwest veggie wraps are a favorite at **Zagora Café.**

For amazing views of the Serengeti Plain, try a meal at **Crown Colony Café.** The menu features salads, pizza, and chicken strips. Entrées are about $7–$11.

The 1,000-seat, air-conditioned **Dragon Fire Grill** is a nice break from the outside heat. Bare wooden tables surround a stage, where dancers and singers perform shows several times throughout the day. Busch Gardens has gotten good feedback on the new menu introduced here in 2015, which features open-kitchen-style culinary stations serving Italian (flatbread pizza, chicken with pasta), Asian (teriyaki, tempura, lo mein), Southwestern (tortilla salads, empanadas), and American (rotisserie chicken, barbecue ribs, burgers) cuisines. There's also a Starbucks kiosk for your caffeine fix. Keeping in mind that the Dragon Fire Grill serves food court style and feeds thousands daily, the food is not bad, and the prices are reasonable, with entrées for less than $12.

The **Zambia Smokehouse** is an indoor-outdoor restaurant, and it's positioned next to the SheiKra monster coaster, allowing great views of the screaming passengers and the ride's impressive swoops and drops. Entrées such as ribs, chicken, and brisket are smoked for several hours and are reasonably priced, ranging $8–$16.

The All-Day Dining Deal (all-you-can-eat) lets you eat in each of six restaurants (excluding baby back ribs) for $33 (plus tax) for adults and $17 for kids ages 3–9. You get one entrée, one side or dessert, and one soft drink each time through the line, but sharing is not allowed.

SHOPPING

THERE'S PLENTY OF BUSCH GARDENS–LOGO MERCHANDISE, but visitors looking for something more should be happy with the diverse selection. Find nature-themed gifts, such as wind chimes and jewelry, as well as gifts fashioned from recycled items, at **Xcursions** in Bird Gardens. African gifts and crafts, including clothing, brass urns, and leather goods, can be found throughout the park. Most have reasonable prices, though some larger, intricate items can be more expensive. For that hard-to-shop-for adult, try the **Emporium,** the largest gift shop in the park, which features handcrafted items from many countries. Happily for guests, it is located by the front gate, so you can buy those souvenirs on the way out. Like SeaWorld, Busch Gardens offers a vast array of kid-pleasing stuffed animals; kids and parents should be happy with the prices.

PART THREE

LEGOLAND FLORIDA

AS THE GUIDEBOOK YOU'RE HOLDING RECOUNTS, Central Florida is thick with theme parks, amusement parks, and water parks, which are wrapped around any number of specialty topics. Each place works hard to differentiate itself from the competition.

Unlike the massive parks that emphasize cartoon heroes, action movies, or living creatures, Legoland Florida has no similar competition: Nowhere else in the Sunshine State is there something such as a Tinkertoy Town or an Erector Set Village.

But there *are* six other Legolands: three in Europe; one north of San Diego, California; and one in Malaysia, with Legoland Dubai scheduled to open in 2016. The original park opened in 1968 in Billund, Denmark, and the word *Lego* is a contraction of the Danish words that translate as "play well."

What filled that first 9-acre site more than 40 years ago is still a major lure for Legoland Florida: giant models of real-life buildings, vehicles, and people, all made from the tiny plastic bricks. Legoland Florida is the largest of this breed and reportedly used an estimated 58 *million* bricks to create its models.

While it has one entire area, Miniland, filled by these intricate models, it also has four roller coasters among its more than 50 attractions. Though the coasters launch and plunge their riders at various speeds, none of these rides are the whipsaw attractions that draw adrenaline junkies to the larger theme parks.

Legoland is designed for the chief users of the plastic blocks, kids 2–12 years old, with only a nod to the adults who bring them here. While several of the park's pint-size rides are just for the kiddies, others, such as the Quest for Chi boat ride, accommodate all members of the family to make it more of a group experience. Many of the rides require a taller "responsible" person to accompany the shortest guests.

The park also opens a spacious water park for the warmer months, closing usually in September and reopening in the late spring. The water park includes various slides and a wave pool, and these six attractions have minimum heights ranging from 36 to 48 inches. The water park has an additional admission cost.

In addition to the brick models and kiddie-size rides, Legoland Florida boasts naturally shaded areas, benches on which to relax, and lots of tables holding the plastic bricks, all thoughtfully placed by the waiting lines for rides to occupy the younger guests.

But there are a few missteps in general too. For a park devoted to the youngest park goers, many of the walkways are simply too narrow to allow easy passage—especially with the number of strollers and double strollers that guests bring. Crowds admiring the numerous models of Miniland can create gridlock on those sidewalks.

Also, there is a tendency to exaggerate the titles of some rides. There is no rally (or race) for the Big Rig Rally, no jousting on the Royal Joust, no racing on the AquaZone Wave Racers, and no revenge at the Pharaoh's Revenge. Not a major flaw, but why promise something that will not be delivered?

Also, there are height minimums for almost every ride, including five of the six water park rides. If the parents dutifully march their kid to the large rulers at such rides and learn the child is too short, the parents had best be ready to explain why "all" the other kids are going on the ride but their little ones can't. To ward off the whining, stop by Guest Relations for a free color-coded height indicator wristband so that your kid will only have to be measured once.

GETTING THERE

LEGOLAND FLORIDA IS ROUGHLY 35 MILES and 45 minutes west of Walt Disney World. From the Orlando area, take I-4 West and exit onto US 27 South. Continue on this road about 19 miles. Turn right at FL 540/Cypress Gardens Boulevard. The park is 4 miles away on the left. Look for green mileage signs that point the way.

Strollers are available for rent for $10 for a one-seater, $15 for dual seats. Also, wheelchairs may be rented for $12, and electric convenience vehicles, the powered wheelchairs, are $37.

Locker rentals are $5, $7, or $12, depending on the size.

Parking is $17 per car, or $15 if purchased in advance online. Campers and RVs pay $18, but motorcycles are only $10. You can upgrade to preferred parking closest to the park gate for $22. Or you can take the shuttle from I-Drive 360 at 8401 Universal Boulevard for $5 per person; make reservations at least 24 hours in advance at **florida.legoland.com/buy-tickets/legoland-shuttle** or by calling ☎ 877-350-5346, and arrive at the location by 8:30 a.m. on the day of departure.

ADMISSION PRICES

TICKETS ARE AVAILABLE for single-day and two-day admissions—a cheap option if your kids are so young that they might tire before sampling many of the attractions. There are also annual passes and combo tickets for the regular park and the water park, plus parking passes. Buying tickets online is a good way to save a few dollars on most of the ticket options. Because Legoland uses a flexible staffing plan, it will discount your web-purchased admission if you specify the exact day(s) you'll visit. See the park's website, **florida.legoland.com,** for vacation packages that include hotel stays as well.

LEGOLAND ONLY ONE DAY PICK-A-DATE (purchased in advance for a specific date) Adults **$74** + tax • Children ages 3–12 and seniors age 60 and older **$67** + tax

LEGOLAND ONLY ONE DAY (flexible dates, valid for 1 year from purchase) Adults **$89** + tax • Children ages 3–12 and seniors age 60 and older **$82** + tax

COMBO LEGOLAND AND WATER PARK ONE DAY PICK-A-DATE (purchased in advance for a specific date) Adults **$89** + tax • Children ages 3–12 and seniors age 60 and older **$82** + tax • Children age 2 and younger **$3** + tax

COMBO LEGOLAND AND WATER PARK ONE DAY (purchased at gate) Adults **$104** + tax • Children ages 3–12 and seniors age 60 and older **$97** + tax • Children age 2 and younger **$3** + tax

Annual Passes

Annual passes provide unlimited admission to Legoland Florida for a year, plus occasional discounts and invitations to special events. Legoland annual passes are available in three levels: the Awesome Pass grants one-year unlimited admission to both the theme and water parks; 10% discounts on food, merchandise, and hotel stays; and Bonus Brick Time (also known as early entry) during the busy season. The Awesomer Pass adds free standard parking at Legoland, as well as unlimited entry to Madame Tussauds, SeaLife Aquarium, and the Orlando Eye at I-Drive 360. The Awesomest Pass piles on admission to every Merlin-owned attraction across America. Online discounts are available for Florida residents, and Florida K-12 teachers can show their pay stub and teaching certificate for a free annual pass.

Awesome Pass **$119** + tax	Florida Resident Awesome Pass **$99** + tax
Awesomer Pass **$149** + tax	Awesomest Pass **$269** + tax

CONTACTING LEGOLAND FLORIDA

FOR MORE INFORMATION, visit the website at **florida.legoland.com,** which has updates about the park. For general information, call ☎ 877-350-LEGO (5346).

unofficial **TIP**
As with all the theme parks, get to the parking lot entrance a few minutes before the park's opening time.

Even when crowds are low, it requires a lot of planning to take in all of Legoland Florida in anything approaching a smooth path. Several factors contribute to this:

- Different guests will want to do different things—true for most multi-person groups at most parks.
- The timing of the live shows and films, in places distant from one another, can throw detours in your linear path.

- Many of the paths are narrow, so congestion is frequent.
- But the real hindrance to a smooth tour is that Legoland is divided into 12 sections. And like Busch Gardens, there is no central focus to aim for, nor any sidewalk approaching a straight route to let you easily walk to every zone.

Following is a relatively relaxing, general touring plan for enjoying Legoland that doesn't require much backtracking. If, however, you really want to minimize your time in line and are up for a little extra walking, use the One-Day Touring Plan on page 123.

If you view the map for this chapter, you might plan your tour by dividing Legoland into two horizontal slices. After entering, straight ahead is The Grand Carousel of Fun Town; youngsters enjoy this tame merry-go-round, and more than a few adults climb aboard for the nostalgia. After the carousel, turn to the right and traverse Duplo Valley (for the littlest kids only). But just beyond this area is World of Chima, based on a fairly new animated show on the Cartoon Network and, of course, the tie-in line of special bricks. There is a super-headliner ride in Chima, but beware of going there too soon. Riders *will* get wet, and you might not want to start your day in squishy shoes and damp clothes. On this suggested park itinerary, by keeping to your right, you'll enter Lego Kingdoms; its Dragon coaster is primo and thus has the longest lines in this zone.

Next, work through the Land of Adventure. Its best ride is Coaster-saurus, a fine wooden coaster, while the Lost Kingdom Adventure ride lets you fire lasers at targets as your car whisks through a pharaoh's tomb. Next you come to Lego City and the amusing slapstick *Big Test Live Show* at the open-air theater.

Now the path gets tricky: If you have young ones, they'll enjoy the driving and boating "schools," while older kids and the adults will want to board the Flying School roller coaster.

Adjacent to this Lego City zone is the water park; let's save that for last, when the afternoon heat demands a break. Similarly, the lovely remnants of the Cypress Gardens landscaped area are a pleasant respite from the hustle-bustle, but few youngsters will prefer a look at flowering shrubs over a chance to steer a battery-driven car or to climb aboard one of the simple round-and-round rides.

Still in Lego City, there's an interactive family contest, in which adults or older kids and their younger siblings climb into pretend fire trucks and police cars and try to beat the other groups in staging a rescue. The competition is fun.

But now comes another choice: Are your youngsters really into building with the famous plastic bricks, or would they prefer more rides? If the former, head to your right and Imagination Zone, with its five venues for designing things with the blocks and/or engaging in competitions with their creations. Otherwise, leave Lego City and walk more or less straight to Lego Technic, with its Lego Technic Project X coaster and two way-less-exciting rides.

You can double back now to the adjacent Imagination Zone for being creative with the bricks, or stroll to your right and the Pirate's Cove amphitheater to view one of the water-ski shows that (sort of) recall the exhibitions that made Cypress Gardens famous more than 50 years ago.

Then it's on to Miniland, where strikingly clever models of major Florida landmarks, major cities, and Star Wars are located. Allow time for admiring the numerous models because some are animated and/or have sound tracks, and the detailing is remarkable. Moving on, steer to your right, entering Fun Town, and be sure to catch one of the 4-D films at the Fun Town Theater. Pay a visit to Heartlake City, and explore the World of Chima if you skipped it earlier.

unofficial **TIP**

Because most of the rides cater to young (read: small) children, the time to load and unload a ride may well exceed the time of the ride itself.

For those who still have stamina or enthusiasm, try not to tear your paper map of the park as you figure out how to double back to your favorite attractions. And now might be the time to walk back to the water park.

ATTRACTIONS

LEGOLAND RIDE MINIMUM HEIGHTS range from 30 to 48 inches; some rides have age minimums or maximums, and some require a "responsible" person of a minimum height to accompany the smallest riders. Most ride queues include convenient play areas where kids can build blocks while one parent waits in line.

THE BEGINNING
Island in the Sky   ★★½

APPEAL BY AGE	PRESCHOOL ★★★	GRADE SCHOOL ★★★½	TEENS ★★
YOUNG ADULTS ★★★	OVER 30 ★★½		SENIORS ★★★½

What it is Enclosed platform that rises about 100 feet and rotates. **Scope and scale** Minor attraction. **When to go** Good way to begin your day in Legoland, by getting an aerial view of the park as you enter. **Special comment** Children shorter than 48" must be accompanied by a responsible rider at least 48" tall. **Authors' rating** Worth a look; ★★½. **Duration of ride** 6½ minutes.

DESCRIPTION AND COMMENTS This iconic remnant of Cypress Gardens offered a better view when the panorama below was a couple of sleepy hamlets and orange groves to the horizon. Now it's urban sprawl, RV parks, and a lot less grove.

TOURING TIPS Show up whenever you want, but don't delay your park tour to do this first.

FUN TOWN
Factory Tour   ★½

APPEAL BY AGE	PRESCHOOL ★★★	GRADE SCHOOL ★★★★	TEENS ★★½
YOUNG ADULTS ★★	OVER 30 ★½		SENIORS ★

Legoland

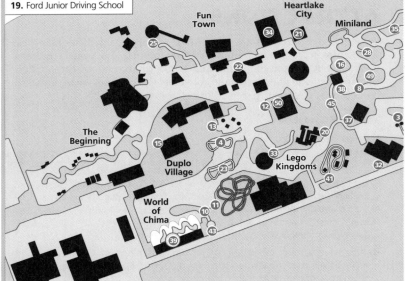

ATTRACTIONS
1. AquaZone Wave Racers
2. *Battle for Brickbeard's Bounty Water Ski Show*
3. Beetle Bounce
4. Big Rig Rally
5. Boating School
6. Build & Test
7. Build-A-Raft River
8. California
9. Coastersaurus
10. Cragger's Swamp
11. The Dragon
12. Duplo Farm
13. Duplo Playtown
14. Duplo Splash Safari
15. Factory Tour
16. Florida State
17. Flying School
18. Ford Driving School
19. Ford Junior Driving School
20. The Forestmen's Hideout
21. *Friends to the Rescue Live Show*
22. The Grand Carousel
23. Granny's Jalopies
24. Hero Factory
25. Island in the Sky
26. Joker Soaker
27. Kid Power Towers
28. Las Vegas
29. Lego Mindstorms
30. Lego Technic Project X
31. Lego Wave Pool
32. Lost Kingdom Adventure
33. Merlin's Challenge
34. Mia's Riding Adventure
35. New York City
36. *NFPA Big Test Live Show*
37. Pharoah's Revenge

Lake Eloise

Pira

Fun Town

Heartlake City

Miniland

The Beginning

Duplo Village

World of Chima

Lego Kingdoms

What it is Shop with an overview of how Legos are made. **Scope and scale** Diversion. **When to go** If you need to get out of the heat or rain. **Authors' rating** Barely worth the time; ★½. **Duration of tour** 10 minutes, for video and mock assembly line.

DESCRIPTION AND COMMENTS A video uses stop-action of a Lego worker touring a factory where the bricks are made, with minor accidents that might amuse the under-7 set. After the brief video, you enter a pretend

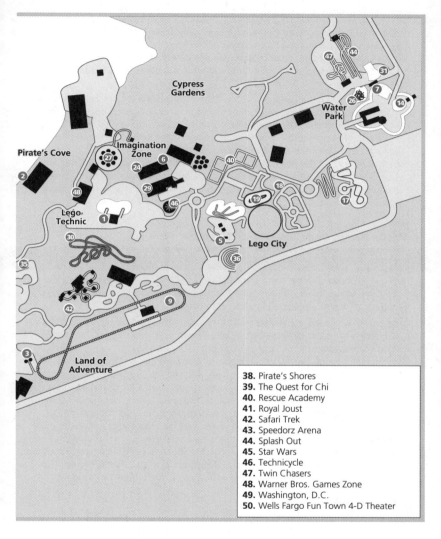

Cypress
Gardens

Water
Park

Pirate's Cove

Imagination
Zone

Lego
Technic

Lego City

Land of
Adventure

38. Pirate's Shores
39. The Quest for Chi
40. Rescue Academy
41. Royal Joust
42. Safari Trek
43. Speedorz Arena
44. Splash Out
45. Star Wars
46. Technicycle
47. Twin Chasers
48. Warner Bros. Games Zone
49. Washington, D.C.
50. Wells Fargo Fun Town 4-D Theater

factory line showing plastic pieces moving along and being molded. Then, surprise, you exit into a large gift shop, selling model kits, how-to books, and individual Lego pieces by weight.

TOURING TIPS This is just the first of nine merchandise stores in the park; skip this one so that you don't have to lug the purchases for hours (or leave your purchases at Package Pick-Up). You can always stop here on the way out.

The Grand Carousel ★★½

APPEAL BY AGE	PRESCHOOL ★★★★		GRADE SCHOOL ★★½		TEENS ★★
YOUNG	ADULTS ★½		OVER 30 ★½		SENIORS ★

What it is Two-deck merry-go-round. **Scope and scale** Minor attraction. **When to go** Either upon first entering or just before leaving the park. **Special comment** Children shorter than 48″ must be accompanied by a responsible rider at least 48″ tall. **Authors' rating** Slowgoing entertainment; ★★½. **Duration of ride** 1½ minutes, but loading time is 5 minutes.

DESCRIPTION AND COMMENTS The Grand Carousel is in your path shortly after entering the park. You can either sit in a sort of open coach or climb aboard one of the 32 horses, which, like most everything else in the park, is designed to resemble a Lego brick creation. The horses go up and down slowly, and there are seat belts for young riders.

TOURING TIPS If the line waiting to ride is short when you encounter the carousel, you might as well quickly put the little nippers on something simple. But after the youngest riders, there is a big gap in who might enjoy this—sort of leaping to the over-30 crowd wanting to recall their own childhood rides.

Wells Fargo Fun Town 4-D Theater ★★★½

APPEAL BY AGE	PRESCHOOL ★★★★	GRADE SCHOOL ★★★★½		TEENS ★★★
YOUNG	ADULTS ★★½	OVER 30 ★★½		SENIORS ★★

What it is Shows 3-D cartoon films with added effects. **Scope and scale** Major attraction. **When to go** Check daily entertainment schedule. **Authors' rating** Entertaining; ★★★½. **Duration of show** 12 minutes.

DESCRIPTION AND COMMENTS The spacious theater rotates three films, showing each two or three times daily. The films are all stop-action involving various characters made of Lego bricks in good-versus-evil-type melodramas. One of the flicks, *Legends of Chima,* is an exceptionally clever parody of *Lord of the Rings* writ small, and the hit *Lego Movie* characters Emmet and Wyldstyle are back in a brand-new short film, debuting in January 2016. Also, if you have a Legoland Discovery Center near your hometown, these same films may be showing there. In addition to the 3-D images, fans blow cold air, spray a water mist, or drop snowflakes from the ceiling. All of these effects are unexpected and add fun to the viewing.

TOURING TIPS No strollers are allowed in the theater. If you think your young ones won't tolerate wearing the 3-D glasses, don't bother entering. But this is a great place to escape the heat and/or rain typical of Florida.

HEARTLAKE CITY

LEGOLAND'S NEWEST AND SMALLEST LAND, Heartlake City is squarely aimed at the girl-centric Lego Friends product line's female fans, who can play with an interactive musical fountain or take selfies with life-size Lego sculptures of Andrea, Emma, Mia, Olivia, and Stephanie. Squeezed into this slender lakeside are a spinning ride and live show, along with an ice cream shop and a faux newsroom, where you can pay to have your image placed in front of a cartoon background using a green screen.

Friends to the Rescue Live Show   ★★★

APPEAL BY AGE	PRESCHOOL ★★★	GRADE SCHOOL ★★★½	TEENS ★
YOUNG ADULTS ★	OVER 30 ★½		SENIORS ★½

What it is Live musical show. Scope and scale Minor attraction. When to go Check daily entertainment schedule. Special comment 48″ minimum height requirement. Authors' rating For tween girls only; ★★★. Duration of show 20 minutes.

DESCRIPTION AND COMMENTS   Andrea is putting on a big concert at the Heartlake Hall, but she can't pull it off without the help of all her friends and the audience. The actresses are plucky enough as they dance and sing along karaoke-style to forgettable original songs, but anyone who isn't a 9-year-old girl will likely nod off before it's over. On the plus side, the theater is nicely air-conditioned.

TOURING TIPS   Seat the kids on the floor down front so they'll be pulled into the audience-participation dance segments.

Mia's Riding Adventure   ★★★

APPEAL BY AGE	PRESCHOOL ★★½	GRADE SCHOOL ★★★½	TEENS ★★★
YOUNG ADULTS ★★½	OVER 30 ★★½		SENIORS ★★

What it is Horse-themed spinning ride. Scope and scale Minor attraction. When to go Early in the morning or at the end of the day. Special comment 48″ minimum height requirement. Authors' rating Deceptively adorable; ★★★. Duration of ride About 90 seconds.

DESCRIPTION AND COMMENTS   You may have seen a Zamperla Disk'O ride—where riders sit in a spinning circle while sliding back and forth on a U-shaped half-pipe track—at your local fair or amusement park, but you've never seen one quite like Legoland's custom equestrian version. Twenty-four jockeys securely straddle horse-shaped seats, facing outward as their faux fillies smoothly gallop back and forth.

TOURING TIPS   This is a great starter ride for girls intimidated by coasters geared to their bigger brothers. Even adults who have never experienced this type of carnival spinner may be surprised by the thrills it can deliver. Unfortunately, it is only capable of serving about 600 riders per hour, so hit it first thing or save it for the end of your day.

DUPLO VALLEY

DUPLO BRICKS ARE THE LARGER VERSION designed for smaller hands, and this zone at Legoland is for the youngest visitors. It also holds an air-conditioned playroom when Florida's heat becomes too much.

Big Rig Rally   ★★★

APPEAL BY AGE	PRESCHOOL ★★★★	GRADE SCHOOL ★★★	TEENS —
YOUNG ADULTS —	OVER 30 —		SENIORS —

What it is Guided ride on an oval track. Scope and scale Minor attraction. When to go Only when in Duplo Valley. Special comments 36″ minimum height requirement; children 36″–48″ must be accompanied by a responsible rider at least 48″ tall. Authors' rating Entertaining only for young kids; ★★★. Duration of ride 2 minutes.

DESCRIPTION AND COMMENTS The youngest kids climb in to mock trucks—again, shaped as if they were formed by Lego bricks—have a seat belt fastened around them, and pretend to drive the trucks as they move around a track.

TOURING TIPS Because the wee ones might believe that they really are steering when they turn the wheel, they can enjoy this ride and might want to ride it more than once.

Duplo Farm ★★½

APPEAL BY AGE	PRESCHOOL ★★★★	GRADE SCHOOL ★★★	TEENS —
YOUNG ADULTS —	OVER 30 —		SENIORS —

What it is Unstructured play area. Scope and scale Minor attraction. When to go Whenever the youngsters need to burn off energy. Authors' rating Entertaining only for young kids; ★★½.

DESCRIPTION AND COMMENTS This indoor space includes several structures that are supposed to be a house, a farm, and more, with slides and lots of windows to peek through. There are also Lego-style statues of some farm animals. This is the place for kids to run around while their parents stand just inside the door, watching the action but not joining in.

TOURING TIPS Duplo Valley is located to the right just after entering the gates. It's the adults' call as to whether to let the littlest kids spend time in all of Duplo Valley's attractions or to find a better way to use up the price of admission.

Duplo Playtown ★★

APPEAL BY AGE	PRESCHOOL ★★★½	GRADE SCHOOL ★★★	TEENS —
YOUNG ADULTS —	OVER 30 —		SENIORS —

What it is Open play area. Scope and scale Minor attraction. When to go Before the youngest ones get hooked on the rides. Authors' rating ★★.

DESCRIPTION AND COMMENTS This is the outdoor version of the farm, covered only by shade trees. A few structures to climb around in, slide down from, and peek out of.

TOURING TIPS A chance to meet other tots and maybe get in a game of follow-the-leader. Go anytime while in Duplo Valley.

Granny's Jalopies ★★½

APPEAL BY AGE	PRESCHOOL ★★★★½	GRADE SCHOOL ★★★★	TEENS —
YOUNG ADULTS —	OVER 30 —		SENIORS —

What it is Mock cars ride on a track. Scope and scale Minor attraction. When to go Only when in Duplo Valley. Special comments 36" minimum height requirement; children 36"–48" must be accompanied by a responsible rider at least 48" tall. Authors' rating Entertaining for youngest kids; ★★½. Duration of ride 1 minute, 40 seconds.

DESCRIPTION AND COMMENTS As with the Big Rig Rally, children are belted in to old-timey convertibles, with a backseat for parents or older siblings, for a guided ride around a track. The cars are linked together, resembling a loosely connected train.

TOURING TIPS Riders are allowed to continue after completion of one cycle as long as no other kids are waiting to climb in the cars.

WORLD OF CHIMA

Cragger's Swamp ★½

APPEAL BY AGE	PRESCHOOL ★★★★	GRADE SCHOOL ★★½	TEENS —
YOUNG ADULTS —		OVER 30 —	SENIORS —

What it is Water squirts up at irregular intervals from the pavement around a cargo-netted area. **Scope and scale** Diversion. **When to go** For the youngest kids, unless the heat has gotten to you. **Special comment** Toddlers in diapers are not allowed in this play area. **Authors' rating** This is an effort to keep the kids entertained; ★½.

DESCRIPTION AND COMMENTS Water jets are water jets, and all but the youngest park visitors will have seen them someplace else. The theming with plastic-block critters and the cargo-net fencing lend interest.

TOURING TIPS Remember that if you let your children play in this, they will be wetter than a carp within a few minutes—and that may not be comfortable for them for the rest of the day. So you may want to schedule this for cooling off, rather than to begin your park tour.

The Quest for Chi ★★★½

APPEAL BY AGE	PRESCHOOL ★★★★	GRADE SCHOOL ★★★★★	TEENS ★★★★★
YOUNG ADULTS ★★★★		OVER 30 ★★★	SENIORS ★★

What it is Boat ride in which passengers can aim a water cannon at both the stationary plastic-block models along the course and at the folks who chose not to ride but to watch—*they have water cannons too*. **Scope and scale** Super-headliner. **When to go** You *could* make this your first stop—the water ride is that much fun—but see our Touring Tips below. **Special comments** Children shorter than 48" must be accompanied by a responsible rider at least 48" tall; infants are not allowed. **Authors' rating** Surprising amount of fun on the water ride, and a chance to escape the oppressive heat of Florida's five-month summers; ★★★½. **Duration of ride** 5–6 minutes; passengers can only board or leave one at a time, which slows the beginning and end of the ride.

DESCRIPTION AND COMMENTS The backstory: All the boat passengers have been recruited to help good guy Laval the Lion retrieve the mystical Chi, an orb that supplies energy to all living things but which has been swiped by Laval's former BFF, Cragger the Crocodile. Fortunately for us, all the animals in Chima speak pretty good English, so we've learned the need for this pursuit from the monitors that are playing while we've waited in the fan-cooled, and covered, back-and-forth queue to board the ride. Eight passengers can sit in each boat; they sit four to a row, facing in opposite directions. Mounted in front of each rider is a water cannon whose force of spray is controlled by the passenger turning a handle. By aiming and firing the water cannon, the passengers can squirt the dozens of plastic-block statues of the baddies (or Laval's plastic helpers) as the boats float gently by. Water-sensing targets are supposed to activate animations along the way, but on our last visit, most of the effects were broken, and the few that operate are unimpressive. Passengers can also try to squirt riders in other boats, as well as spectators on the surrounding walkway.

TOURING TIPS Signs outside the entrance—a giant, fanciful, open lion's mouth—caution that riders will get wet. That's the cue to either don the rain ponchos you cleverly brought with you or to buy new ones from the nearby gift shop—$5 for kids, $6 for adults. Most of the dousing comes from the 1,000 gallons of water falling off Mount Cavora (in the cartoon series, it floats in the air; here, it is 23 feet tall but is atop a 32-foot-high pole—on the park map it looks like a rotten avocado dripping on the attractions below). Guests seated on the left side of the boat (the far side from the loading dock) get the most direct drenching from Mount Cavora but can't aim their guns to return fire at the spectators squirting them.

Speedorz Arena ★½

APPEAL BY AGE	PRESCHOOL ★★★½	GRADE SCHOOL ★★★★½	TEENS ★
YOUNG ADULTS —		OVER 30 —	SENIORS —

What it is Kids aim tiny motorized vehicles through an obstacle course. **Scope and scale** Diversion. **When to go** Anytime, especially if the line to ride Quest for Chi is long. **Authors' rating** The kids we watched got bored after a few minutes; ★½.

DESCRIPTION AND COMMENTS In the animated TV series, the creatures speak English, walk on their hind legs, and even ride wheeled vehicles. This diversion focuses on those vehicles: A covered circular platform is divided into 14 wedge-shaped slices, with an attendant standing in the center of the platform. The attendant gives the kids fistfuls of tiny versions of the cartoon vehicles. The players poke a thin plastic rod through a hole in the vehicle to charge a friction motor, and then each player sets the vehicle down in his or her area and tries to aim the vehicle so that it goes through obstacles such as a ring, a ramp, or tower—all made of Lego bricks. No points are scored nor prizes given. The children can play by themselves or challenge neighbors to races.

TOURING TIPS No height limit, as long as the child can see over the top of the playing surface—though we noted the youngest children didn't understand that to charge the motor, the plastic rod had to go into a certain hole, not just any open space on the vehicle.

LEGO KINGDOMS

The Dragon ★★★½

APPEAL BY AGE	PRESCHOOL ★★★½	GRADE SCHOOL ★★★★	TEENS ★★★★
YOUNG ADULTS ★★★½		OVER 30 ★★★	SENIORS ★★★

What it is Roller coaster. **Scope and scale** Headliner. **When to go** Anytime. **Special comments** 40" minimum height requirement; children 40"–48" must be accompanied by a responsible adult. **Authors' rating** Odd intro to the coaster, which is brief but fun; ★★★½. **Duration of ride** 3 minutes.

DESCRIPTION AND COMMENTS Created around Cypress Gardens's Okeechobee Rampage family coaster, The Dragon spends 2 minutes slowly moving through a castle occupied by Lego statues of everyone from the scullery lad to the friar, from the king to a steam-hissing, head-bobbing dragon. But once outside, the coaster climbs a metal track and spends just over a minute speeding through banked curves. Guests who have visited The Wizarding World of Harry Potter will notice a strong similarity between this coaster and Flight of the Hippogriff.

TOURING TIPS It's worth the wait in line, which is under cover but outdoors; the ceiling fans here help some against the heat and humidity.

The Forestmen's Hideout ★★★½

APPEAL BY AGE	PRESCHOOL ★★★½	GRADE SCHOOL ★★★★	TEENS —
YOUNG ADULTS —	OVER 30 —		SENIORS —

What it is Open play area. **Scope and scale** Minor attraction. **When to go** Before the day gets too hot. **Special comments** Restricted to children ages 5–12; children younger than age 7 must be accompanied by a responsible adult. **Authors' rating** ★★★½.

DESCRIPTION AND COMMENTS Cargo-net ramps flow like giant cobwebs around free-form wooden structures, with both open and tube slides letting the kids come back down from two elevated areas. The surface is a cushioned rubber matting, protection against falls.

TOURING TIPS Fine place to let parents rest on benches while the kids burn off energy. You might suggest that your young ones start a game of tag or follow-the-leader—sure to keep them happily busy.

Merlin's Challenge ★★½

APPEAL BY AGE	PRESCHOOL ★★★½	GRADE SCHOOL ★★★	TEENS ★½
YOUNG ADULTS —	OVER 30 —		SENIORS —

What it is Cars circling a hub. **Scope and scale** Minor attraction. **When to go** Anytime. **Special comments** 36″ minimum height requirement; children 36″–48″ must be accompanied by a responsible rider at least 48″ tall. **Authors' rating** Recalls tame midway rides; ★★½. **Duration of ride** 1 minute, 40 seconds.

DESCRIPTION AND COMMENTS Two-passenger cars rotate around a central hub and rise over three small hills. The round-and-round action lasts less than 2 minutes, though loading and unloading the 23 cars can take more than a minute.

TOURING TIPS No reason to hurry your party toward this ride, but rather let the kiddies watch a rotation of the cars and then decide if they want to wait in line. Children, or the smallest person in the car, must sit on the inside nearest the hub.

Royal Joust ★★

APPEAL BY AGE	PRESCHOOL ★★★½	GRADE SCHOOL ★★★	TEENS —
YOUNG ADULTS —	OVER 30 —		SENIORS —

What it is Ride around a track. **Scope and scale** Minor attraction. **When to go** Unless the kids insist on riding The Dragon coaster, let them try the plastic horses here first. **Special comments** Restricted to children ages 4–12 and less than 170 pounds; 36″ minimum height requirement. **Authors' rating** A yawner except for the youngest; ★★. **Duration of ride** A little more than 2 minutes.

DESCRIPTION AND COMMENTS OK, we didn't *really* think that they would give children lances and set them off on horseback to ride against each other. But this is 180 degrees in the opposite direction: Lego-brick horses bob slightly as they move along their track, going toward a few Lego-brick people and structures. However, nothing actually touches anything because the kids have only the mock reins to hold on to, and many don't bother with that.

TOURING TIPS Because each horse saddle is a one-seater, no one can accompany the littlest riders. However, they are belted onto their steed, and parents can line a railing to photograph their little ones.

LAND OF ADVENTURE

Beetle Bounce ★★

APPEAL BY AGE	PRESCHOOL ★★★	GRADE SCHOOL ★★★	TEENS ★
YOUNG ADULTS ★		OVER 30 —	SENIORS —

What it is A small drop tower. **Scope and scale** Diversion. **When to go** Anytime. **Special comment** 36″ minimum height requirement. **Authors' rating** For anyone over the age of 9, forget this; ★★. **Duration of ride** 1 minute.

DESCRIPTION AND COMMENTS Two side-by-side benches can each seat seven riders. Once the lap bar is lowered, the benches rise about 15 feet, then drop, rise, drop, rise. . . . Everything is done slowly over the course of the 1-minute ride.

TOURING TIPS Have the kids wait for this one only if the line for the adjacent Lost Kingdom Adventure ride is too long.

Coastersaurus ★★★★½

APPEAL BY AGE	PRESCHOOL ★★★★	GRADE SCHOOL ★★★★½	TEENS ★★★★★
YOUNG ADULTS ★★★★★		OVER 30 ★★★★½	SENIORS ★★★★½

What it is Roller coaster. **Scope and scale** Super-headliner. **When to go** Get there early, so you can stand in line for a second ride. **Special comments** 36″ minimum height requirement; children 36″–48″ must ride with a responsible rider at least 48″ tall. **Authors' rating** One of the top two rides in this park; ★★★★½. **Duration of ride** 1 minute, 20 seconds.

DESCRIPTION AND COMMENTS This wooden roller coaster was named the Triple Hurricane when it was purpose-built and installed for Cypress Gardens. Now the train of 10 two-person cars begins with a rise of 40 feet and then dips, rises, and curves through a jungle dotted with dinosaurs made of you-know-what. With speeds up to 21 miles per hour, the ride lasts just under 1½ minutes. Mindful of their young target demographic, Legoland officials scaled down the thrills on all the coasters to what they call pink-knuckle rides. But the clickety-clack of a wooden coaster is something special.

TOURING TIPS If your group likes coasters, then plan your path to reach Coastersaurus as soon as you enter the park.

Lost Kingdom Adventure ★★★

APPEAL BY AGE	PRESCHOOL ★★	GRADE SCHOOL ★★★½	TEENS ★★★
YOUNG ADULTS ★★		OVER 30 ★★	SENIORS ★★

What it is Aim at sensor targets with a laser as you ride past them. **Scope and scale** Major attraction. **When to go** Anytime, but it's an especially good way to briefly get out of the heat. **Special comments** 34″ minimum height requirement; children 34″–42″ must ride with a responsible rider at least 42″ tall. **Authors' rating** You are moving through a shooting gallery; ★★★. **Duration of ride** 3 minutes, 20 seconds.

DESCRIPTION AND COMMENTS The two-person cars move slowly through a pharaoh's tomb, with each passenger firing a pistol emitting lasers. You aim at glowing discs on the various objects and statues that you pass by; your score is tallied in a digital readout in front of you. Though not a bad ride, Lost Kingdom Adventure feels simplistic after experiencing Toy Story Midway Mania! or Men In Black Alien Attack, and we've found that the guns frequently malfunction, leading to frustrations.

TOURING TIPS The backstory—why *are* you in a tomb, firing at these discs?—is not clear, but once you start aiming your laser pistol, it's unimportant because you're competing with your fellow rider. No prize, though, just the satisfaction of being the sharper shooter.

Pharaoh's Revenge ★★½

APPEAL BY AGE	PRESCHOOL ★★★½	GRADE SCHOOL ★★★½	TEENS ★★
YOUNG ADULTS —		OVER 30 —	SENIORS —

What it is Shooting game. **Scope and scale** Diversion. **When to go** Anytime. **Authors' rating** A chance to shoot the gun Mom won't let you have at home; ★★½.

DESCRIPTION AND COMMENTS In a cargo-netted enclosure, kids on two levels can fire foam balls at each other with various types of stationary shooters.

TOURING TIPS Many kids (read: boys) can't resist playing with the guns. Parents or teenagers are best stationed in the lower pit, where they can send foam balls up vacuum tubes to the upper floor for the kids to launch.

Safari Trek ★★½

APPEAL BY AGE	PRESCHOOL ★★★	GRADE SCHOOL ★★★	TEENS —
YOUNG ADULTS —		OVER 30 —	SENIORS —

What it is Tame ride along a rail. **Scope and scale** Minor attraction. **When to go** Anytime. **Special comments** 34" minimum height requirement; children 34"–48" must ride with a responsible rider at least 48" tall; maximum age is 12; maximum weight is 170 pounds. **Authors' rating** Another pretend-you-steer ride for youngsters; ★★½. **Duration of ride** 2 minutes.

DESCRIPTION AND COMMENTS In Lego-brick jeeps painted with zebra stripes, kids pretend to steer past a jungle of brick animal statues. One elephant squirts water at the passing vehicle, a hippo lets out a roar as the jeep passes by, meerkats chirp, and the macaws are beautifully colored.

TOURING TIPS Third-best entrée on the slim menu of Land of Adventure, so navigate to Safari Trek right after experiencing Coastersaurus and Lost Kingdom Adventure.

LEGO CITY

Boating School ★★★

APPEAL BY AGE	PRESCHOOL ★★½	GRADE SCHOOL ★★★	TEENS —
YOUNG ADULTS —		OVER 30 —	SENIORS —

What it is Boats move slowly around several curves in a water tank. **Scope and scale** Minor attraction. **When to go** Anytime. **Special comments** 34" minimum height requirement; children 34"–48" must ride with a responsible rider at least 48" tall. **Authors' rating** Chance for youngsters to play captain; ★★★. **Duration of ride** About 5 minutes.

DESCRIPTION AND COMMENTS The two-seater miniature boats, again resembling Lego-brick constructions, use electric motors operated by a foot pedal. The passengers do indeed steer their boat, and perhaps because the water offers less traction than the driving school's wheeled vehicles on the roads, the boats seem to head from side to side in the canal, seldom staying on a straight line. Sometimes the ride-along adult or older (taller) kids help with the steering.

The ride attendants will use poles or even step into the canal, which is about 30 inches deep, to physically move the boats away from the walls or other boats if there is a floating traffic jam.

TOURING TIPS Before you let them board, make sure that your youngsters aren't afraid of being away from you while on the water—the boats travel several yards from, and occasionally face away from, onlookers' viewpoints.

Flying School ★★★★

APPEAL BY AGE	PRESCHOOL †	GRADE SCHOOL ★★★★½	TEENS ★★★★★
YOUNG ADULTS ★★★★★	OVER 30 ★★★★½		SENIORS ★★★★

† Preschoolers are generally too short to ride.

What it is Metal roller coaster on which your feet dangle free. **Scope and scale** Super-headliner. **When to go** If you like coasters, head here as soon as you get to the park. **Special comments** 44″ minimum height requirement; children 44″–52″ must be accompanied by a responsible rider at least 52″ tall; maximum height is 6′5″. **Authors' rating** The real deal for thrills; ★★★★. **Duration of ride** Just over a minute.

DESCRIPTION AND COMMENTS This is one of the coasters that Legoland kept when it took over the defunct Cypress Gardens. It was originally called the Swamp Thing—if you look closely just before you board, you can still see the name faintly painted on the structure. It is an inverted roller coaster: Two riders sit side by side in a suspended carrier that has no floor, so the extra thrill is looking down past your dangling legs.

Up to 20 can ride at a time over the 1,122 feet of track. It takes 30 seconds for the two-person seats to ascend the first hill of about 49 feet, and then it's 45 seconds of whipping around curves, with modest plunges. You'll be thankful for the shoulder bars and may wish for some sort of head brace.

TOURING TIPS This coaster can be far more painful than its statistics should suggest, and it is particularly hard on middle-aged necks, so unless you're a credit-counting coaster junkie (or your kids drag you bodily into the seat), consider skipping this despite the high rating.

Ford Driving School ★★★½

APPEAL BY AGE	PRESCHOOL —	GRADE SCHOOL ★★★½	TEENS —
YOUNG ADULTS —	OVER 30 —		SENIORS —

What it is Drivers propel and steer around a track. **Scope and scale** Major attraction. **When to go** First thing in the morning, or immediately after experiencing the roller coasters. **Special comment** Restricted to children ages 6–13. **Authors' rating** Parents love to watch—and shout at—their young drivers; ★★★½. **Duration of ride** A little over 3 minutes.

DESCRIPTION AND COMMENTS The next step up for would-be motorists after the Junior Driving School. One driver per vehicle, which they propel by stepping on a pedal and which they fully steer. This course includes intersections, curves, and working traffic lights. The 20 or more cars on the course move slowly, and bumpers all around prevent any damage. Unlike the Magic Kingdom's speedway, these cars aren't on rails, and drivers are expected to observe the rules of the road if they want to earn a souvenir driver's license.

TOURING TIPS Parents enjoy this view of their youngsters—but then, they aren't handing over keys to the family automobile for years to come. You'll want to hurry over to the fenced viewing area to claim space for watching and/or filming.

Ford Junior Driving School ★★½

APPEAL BY AGE	PRESCHOOL ★★½	GRADE SCHOOL ★★½	TEENS —
YOUNG ADULTS —	OVER 30 —		SENIORS —

What it is Cars move slowly around a track. **Scope and scale** Minor attraction. **When to go** First thing in the morning, or immediately after experiencing the roller coasters. **Special comment** Restricted to children ages 3–5. **Authors' rating** ★★½. **Duration of ride** 3 minutes.

DESCRIPTION AND COMMENTS The littlest park goers climb into tiny cars, and when they depress a pedal, electric batteries slowly propel the car around an oval track. The kids really do steer, and the attendants are kept busy lifting the front end of the cars away from the curbs and back to the "street."

Big photo op for the parents. It takes about 75 seconds to complete one lap, if the driver stays away from the side curbs. A remote switch turns on the car batteries for about 2 minutes, before the ride halts and the cars are loaded and unloaded.

TOURING TIPS Good place to let the youngest kids pretend to be a grown-up, so head here after the Boating School.

NFPA Big Test Live Show ★★★★

APPEAL BY AGE	PRESCHOOL ★★★★½	GRADE SCHOOL ★★★★½	TEENS ★★★½
YOUNG ADULTS ★★★½	OVER 30 ★★★		SENIORS ★★★

What it is Live action slapstick routine. **Scope and scale** Headliner. **When to go** Check daily schedule for showtimes. **Authors' rating** Surprisingly amusing for all ages; ★★★★. **Duration of show** 20 minutes.

DESCRIPTION AND COMMENTS Held in an amphitheater near both the Coastersaurus and Flying School rides, this comedy show features four acrobatic types pretending to qualify for the volunteer fire department. The gags center on a clever, mock hook and ladder, with a telescoping ladder, and include blunders and wetting down a few rows of the audience. The motto the volunteers—and viewers—learn: "Put the wet stuff on the hot stuff." The performers also do the stop, drop, and roll and thus probably get across that basic emergency reaction.

TOURING TIPS There are no bad seats in the covered, open-air theater, and ushers and recorded announcements inform the audience that the first three rows are in the splash zone. During the show, the splashing is pretty low-key, but youngsters love it.

Rescue Academy ★★★½

APPEAL BY AGE	PRESCHOOL ★★½	GRADE SCHOOL ★★★½	TEENS ★★½
YOUNG ADULTS ★★	OVER 30 ★★		SENIORS ★★

What it is Competition using self-propelled vehicles. **Scope and scale** Major attraction. **When to go** Anytime. **Special comments** 34" minimum height requirement; children 34"–48" must be accompanied by a responsible rider at least 48" tall. **Authors' rating** Rare chance for parents to get involved with kids; ★★★½. **Duration of ride** 2 minutes.

DESCRIPTION AND COMMENTS Adults or older kids are encouraged to join the little children in one of four rescue vehicles—two fire trucks and two police cars. The older passengers vigorously pump handles up and down to propel the vehicle several yards toward a building; its windows are painted either with flames or jail inmates trying to break out. Everyone piles off the vehicles and, again, the older folks pump a handle, this time to provide water to a nozzle that their younger teammates aim at holes in the window. When enough water goes into a hole, the flames are put out or the jailbreak is foiled, and that team hops back onto its vehicle and reverses course. No prize other than satisfaction to the winner.

TOURING TIPS The riders seem to enjoy this one, including the working-together aspect, and with up to 16 guests going on each ride, the queue moves quickly. But it's worth the wait for even a few rounds in front of you.

LEGO TECHNIC
AquaZone Wave Racers ★★½

APPEAL BY AGE	PRESCHOOL ★★★½	GRADE SCHOOL ★★★	TEENS —
YOUNG ADULTS —	OVER 30 —		SENIORS —

What it is Make-believe flying boats skim the water as they move in a circle. **Scope and scale** Minor attraction. **When to go** Anytime. **Special comments** 40" minimum height requirement; children 40"–52" must be accompanied by a responsible rider at least 52" tall. **Authors' rating** Limited appeal to older children; ★★½. **Duration of ride** 2½ minutes.

DESCRIPTION AND COMMENTS Two can ride, front and back, in this vehicle, but only the person in the front seat can steer. And "steering" is pretty limited: The driver can cause the vehicle to turn inward, toward the hub around which the ride rotates, but nothing more, nor can the driver make the vehicle rise or lower in its path. Two hubs operate simultaneously, but the vehicles are never close to each other. This is a prime example of Legoland's philosophy that expects youngsters to buy into the idea that they are controlling the ride somehow. Most of the time, the "control" is minimal.

TOURING TIPS Again, younger kids enjoy the motion of the ride, but you'll need to judge their patience at waiting for their turn—the ride is only a minor attraction.

Lego Technic Project X ★★★★

APPEAL BY AGE	PRESCHOOL ★★★★	GRADE SCHOOL ★★★★½	TEENS ★★★★
YOUNG ADULTS ★★★★	OVER 30 ★★★		SENIORS ★★★

What it is Tame version of the old Wild Mouse. **Scope and scale** Headliner. **When to go** As with all four coasters, head here early; otherwise, be ready to wait in line. **Special comments** 42" minimum height requirement; children 42"–48" must ride with someone at least 14 years old. **Authors' rating** Fun ride, and one of the longer ones too; ★★★★. **Duration of ride** 2 minutes.

DESCRIPTION AND COMMENTS Imported and revamped from the Legoland park in England, this coaster launches one four-passenger car about every 30–40 seconds. After slowly ascending a hill, the car navigates a series of U-turns, some sharp ones taken more rapidly than some wider ones, so that riders don't know what to expect. The track dips slightly a few times before you're back in the station. The drops and curves are far wilder than those found in any of Orlando's Wild Mouse-style steel coasters.

TOURING TIPS The back-and-forth queue has an adjacent area with Legos for kids to play with during the wait, which can climb to 45 minutes during the weekend. The line is covered but open on the sides, as are most of the queuing areas in this park, so there is protection from the sun but not the heat.

Technicycle ★★★

APPEAL BY AGE	PRESCHOOL ★★★★	GRADE SCHOOL ★★★★½	TEENS ★★★
YOUNG ADULTS —		OVER 30 ★★	SENIORS ★★

What it is Rotating ride on which pedaling faster causes the vehicle to rise. Scope and scale Minor attraction. When to go Anytime. Special comments 36" minimum height requirement; children 36"–42" must be accompanied by a responsible rider at least 42" tall. Authors' rating Fun ride for younger kids; ★★★. Duration of ride 1½ minutes.

DESCRIPTION AND COMMENTS At last, a ride on which the passengers actually have a significant effect. Of course, everything is relative: In this case, two people ride on a whacky-looking vehicle with a wing above and propeller behind. It hangs from an overhead support. As the riders pedal faster, the vehicle rises while rotating around a central hub. But the ride lasts just 1 minute.

TOURING TIPS This is one of the few rides, such as Lego City's Rescue Academy, on which participants are expected to use some energy—all the more reason to get that adult riding with the little ones.

PIRATE'S COVE

Battle for Brickbeard's Bounty Water Ski Show ★★★½

APPEAL BY AGE	PRESCHOOL ★★★★½	GRADE SCHOOL ★★★★½	TEENS ★★★★
YOUNG ADULTS ★★★½		OVER 30 ★★★	SENIORS ★★★½

What it is Demonstration of water-skiing tricks, with a theme to the action. Scope and scale Super-headliner. When to go Check the daily performance schedule; typically at least four shows per day. Authors' rating You don't see this sort of skiing exhibition much now; ★★★½. Duration of show 20 minutes.

DESCRIPTION AND COMMENTS Undoubtedly, there are grandparents attending each performance who can remember seeing this sort of spectacle either live—probably here at the former Cypress Gardens—or on TV, maybe even on ESPN a few years back. As a strong gesture to its Cypress Gardens heritage, Legoland stages a pirate-themed show weak on plot—pirates clash with the princess and her soldiers to regain their pirate ship—but pretty good on the skiing techniques. None of the old-style skiing pyramids are demonstrated, but quite a few ramps are taken, and as many as four skiers are towed at a time.

TOURING TIPS There are no bad seats in the covered amphitheater, but the first four rows are in the splash zone. It's actually more like a sprinkle zone—until the pirates surprise the youngsters chosen to man the water cannon. The pirates simply put a hand up in front of the cannon's modest stream, forcing the water backward against the kids.

MINILAND

ONE OF THE WONDERS of all the Legolands is Miniland, site of the incredible models made from the little plastic blocks. Here, reportedly more than 30 million bricks have been used to create themed areas including **Washington, D.C., New York City, Las Vegas, a pirate display, Florida, California,** and an homage to the **Star Wars** franchise.

Artisans termed master model builders create these spectacles, generally on a 1:20 scale. Some of the specific models include animated aspects or sound tracks. For instance, yellow cabs roll through New York's Times Square, and boats glide past Florida beaches and on Washington's Potomac River. At the Daytona International Speedway area, visitors will be able to race tiny cars around a slotted track in front of the grandstand. Row upon row of model trucks and cars fill the infield at the track.

Also in the Florida section are Miami Beach and its gaudy South Beach Deco hotels, as well as the iconic Kennedy Space Center, complete with the massive Vehicle Assembly Building, a space shuttle on the launchpad, and the Rocket Garden. Here, too, are St. Augustine and its centuries-old Spanish fort, Mallory Square in Key West, the Everglades, and buildings and streetcars from downtown Tampa, about an hour's drive to the west of Legoland. (Nothing representing Orlando, which is closer, but why publicize the competition?)

The Las Vegas model includes iconic hotels such as Luxor Las Vegas, Excalibur, and Treasure Island, plus the Stratosphere tower and Paris Las Vegas's Eiffel Tower. There's even a sound track of noise recorded on the famed Strip.

The Washington area has miniature re-creations of the White House (it measures about 5-by-4-feet), the Capitol, the Washington Monument, the Lincoln and Jefferson Memorials, and the Smithsonian's Castle. An animated marching band parades in front of the Capitol.

Using about 2 million blocks, New York City includes Rockefeller Plaza with tiny water fountains, the Statue of Liberty, the Empire State Building (more than 10 feet tall), the Guggenheim Museum, and the Bronx Zoo.

The California models include San Francisco's landmark Golden Gate Bridge, serpentine Lombard Street, and its familiar painted row houses. Los Angeles displays include Grauman's Chinese Theatre, the Hollywood Bowl, and, of course, the Hollywood sign.

The pirate section features a battle between two ships floating on a sizable body of water that fronts a village where another ship is under construction. These detailed ship models are impressive.

Legoland Florida opened its impressive Star Wars section about a year after the rest of the park debuted. The Star Wars site holds about 2,000 models, composed of more than 1.5 million of the little plastic bricks, that reflect machines or creatures from all six of the films plus the TV series *Clone Wars*. Park visitors can push buttons to cause motion and sound with some of the figures. And if you have a favorite character, take the time to bend down and look for him, her, or it here.

IMAGINATION ZONE

WITH ONE ENTRANCE MARKED by a 7-foot-tall head of Albert Einstein, this area essentially is the place where kids and grown-ups finally get to use both their minds and hands—and to play full-time with the blocks. A bonus: The play areas are enclosed and air-conditioned, providing a great escape from heat and humidity. Except for one actual ride, the standard ratings used elsewhere in the book are not relevant for Imagination Zone.

Build & Test

Kids (and adults) can create miniature cars from bricks and wheels that are supplied, and then race their creations against others on a digitally timed track.

Hero Factory

This special area offers fans the chance to build their favorite space-exploration creatures, based on that line of Lego characters. The room is cleared every 15 minutes if it reaches capacity; otherwise, kids can (and will) build for an unlimited length of time.

Kid Power Towers ★★½

APPEAL BY AGE	PRESCHOOL ★★★	GRADE SCHOOL ★★★★	TEENS ★★★
YOUNG ADULTS ★★	OVER 30 ★★		SENIORS ★★

What it is Riders propel themselves up and down. **Scope and scale** Minor attraction. **When to go** Anytime. **Special comments** 40″ minimum height requirement; children 40″–48″ must be accompanied by a responsible rider at least 48″ tall. **Authors' rating** Requires a little upper-arm strength; ★★½. **Duration of ride** 1½ minutes.

DESCRIPTION AND COMMENTS Three towers resembling giant stacks of—what else?—Lego bricks accommodate up to eight people at a time. Sitting in two-person carriers, kids and adults pull down on ropes to hoist themselves to the top of a tower for a slightly elevated view of the park and nearby Lake Eloise. They come back down by easing on the hoisting ropes, after a 1½-minute ride.

TOURING TIPS A play area of Lego bricks occupies youngsters during the wait to board.

Lego Mindstorms

The sharper kids can build computerized robots out of Legos to roll across a tabletop and follow commands to perform simple actions, such as moving or dislodging items. This is a sample of what older Lego devotees, including plenty of adults, create from the more-expensive kits and parts.

Though there is no posted age requirement at Mindstorms, the area is designed for children in third through sixth grades, so be honest in evaluating your kids' capabilities before strolling over to this attraction.

Warner Bros. Games Zone

You didn't think you could escape video games completely, did you? Here are stations for numerous G-rated games, most with a Lego tie-in but featuring such pop-culture icons as Star Wars, Indiana Jones, and Batman. You can utilize iPads, Xbox consoles, and video kiosks to play.

CYPRESS GARDENS

IN A NICE TRIBUTE to one of the original and nonmechanized, non-automated, and/or noncomputerized Florida parks, Legoland has retained 39 acres of the original Cypress Gardens. It's lovingly landscaped—azaleas and camellias are resplendent in the spring—and its paths include bridges over streams from adjacent Lake Eloise. Of course it's not entirely natural: More of the Lego-brick animals are scattered here. The vintage Oriental Gardens and iconic Florida Pool (built for Esther William's 1953 film *Easy to Love*) were both restored in 2014, and the ginormous banyan tree that's been growing there since 1939 is showing no signs of stopping.

WATER PARK

A SEASONAL ATTRACTION that costs $15 for adults, $3 for those younger than age 3, in addition to the Legoland entrance ticket, this park rents both lockers and towels. It has a snack stand and gift shop. The water park is located at the far end of Legoland from its entrance.

Because you can't enjoy the water park without splashing around and getting wet, it is impractical to plan on going in and out of the water park to visit the various non–water park rides without drying off first. The water park is a remedy against the heat, but you'll want to save it for the latter part of your Legoland visit.

Build-A-Raft River   ★★★½

APPEAL BY AGE	PRESCHOOL ★★★★½	GRADE SCHOOL ★★★★½	TEENS ★★★★
YOUNG ADULTS ★★★½	OVER 30 ★★★		SENIORS ★★★

What it is Clever upgrade on the lazy river. Scope and scale Major attraction. When to go When you want a leisurely float. Authors' rating Great, interactive idea; ★★★½.

DESCRIPTION AND COMMENTS The water park includes a 1,000-foot-long canal with a gentle current; guests grab a large, clear inner tube that has been modified: The upper rim can accept snap-on, oversize, floating Lego bricks. Each tube becomes a personalized creation, with as many bricks as the rider wants to add. This revolutionizes the traditional lazy tube float: Each rider has his or her own work of art, which can be changed constantly. The concept is clever, but the path itself is short and under-themed (aside from a few spritzing statues) in comparison to lazy rivers in Orlando.

TOURING TIPS Float down the river when you just want to cool off and relax for a while.

Duplo Splash Safari   ★★★

APPEAL BY AGE	PRESCHOOL ★★★★	GRADE SCHOOL ★★★	TEENS —
YOUNG ADULTS —	OVER 30 —		SENIORS —

What it is Shallow play pool for the youngest kids. Scope and scale Diversion. When to go The place to take your youngest kids while at the water park. Special comment Children younger than age 12 must be accompanied by an adult age 18 or older. Authors' rating Kids make of this what they will; ★★★.

DESCRIPTION AND COMMENTS The pool has a few gentle slides. Kids can turn the wheels on some happy-looking animal statues to squirt water, and a lifeguard stands in the water.

TOURING TIPS Set the littlest ones here; height restrictions can prevent them from using other parts of the water park.

Joker Soaker   ★★★★

APPEAL BY AGE	PRESCHOOL ★★★★★	GRADE SCHOOL ★★★★★	TEENS ★★★★
YOUNG ADULTS ★★½		OVER 30 ★★½	SENIORS ★★½

What it is Zany place to get doused. **Scope and scale** Major attraction. **When to go** Anytime during your water park visit. **Special comments** 36″ minimum height requirement; 42″ minimum height requirement to ride the slides. **Authors' rating** Fun times, boosted by the surprise factor; ★★★★.

DESCRIPTION AND COMMENTS A bizarre, brilliantly colored, multistory structure holds fountains plus buckets of various sizes that fill and tip, unexpectedly, on the thrill seekers waiting below. There are slides of varying lengths and a wading pool too.

TOURING TIPS If your kids might be uncomfortable in the wave pool, this is the best bet for letting them enjoy some free-form playtime.

Lego Wave Pool   ★★★½

APPEAL BY AGE	PRESCHOOL ★★★★	GRADE SCHOOL ★★★★½	TEENS ★★★★½
YOUNG ADULTS ★★★★		OVER 30 ★★★	SENIORS ★★★

What it is Especially wide, gentle wave pool. **Scope and scale** Major attraction. **When to go** Good alternative to the big slides and Build-A-Raft. **Special comment** 42″ minimum height requirement. **Authors' rating** ★★★½.

DESCRIPTION AND COMMENTS Mankind has been drawn to the oceans' shoreline thousands of years before someone thought we should wear swimsuits. This pool is both quite wide and has a gentle wave action—it can accommodate oodles of people, even those not quite ready to swim on their own. The water gets just about deep enough to swim in toward the walled end of the pool. Otherwise, you're going to bob about.

TOURING TIPS Most everyone will enjoy this pool, but the smallest (and presumably youngest) kids are not allowed in, so you might need to plan how to divide and still chaperone your brood.

Splash Out   ★★★★

APPEAL BY AGE	PRESCHOOL —	GRADE SCHOOL ★★★★★	TEENS ★★★★★
YOUNG ADULTS ★★★★		OVER 30 ★★★	SENIORS ★★

What it is Giant waterslides. **Scope and scale** Super-headliner. **When to go** As with all the coasters, the waterslides have their devotees, so come early. **Special comment** 48″ minimum height requirement. **Authors' rating** Rapid plunges; ★★★★. **Duration of ride** About 3 minutes.

DESCRIPTION AND COMMENTS Riders climb to a 60-foot height, and then choose between one enclosed or two open waterslides to zip down. The legs may give out from the climbing before the sliding ceases to be fun.

TOURING TIPS Another attraction that prohibits the smallest kids from taking part, so you ought to determine what to substitute for them.

Twin Chasers ★★★★

APPEAL BY AGE	PRESCHOOL —	GRADE SCHOOL ★★★★★	TEENS ★★★★★
YOUNG ADULTS ★★★★★		OVER 30 ★★★½	SENIORS ★★

What it is Spiraling waterslides. **Scope and scale** Super-headliner. **When to go** Early, while your legs can still repeatedly carry you to the top. **Special comment** 48″ minimum height requirement. **Authors' rating** Fun ride; ★★★★. **Duration of ride** About 4 minutes.

DESCRIPTION AND COMMENTS Two people can fit in one of the rafts used to navigate the 375-foot-long, twisting, turning slides. The slides are enclosed part of the way and open part of the way. Because you're zipping down within a closed tube part of the time, as well as navigating several turns, this set of slides offers a different sort of thrill.

TOURING TIPS Unless you just want to float or swim against the wave-pool current, this is the water park's top feature, so head here first.

DINING

THE PARK OFFERS A FEW MORE CHOICES than the standard burger and fries. For instance, the spacious **Market Restaurant** is located before any ride or attraction. It offers salads ($5.99) and soups ($4.50). For bigger appetites, dinner plates include a half roast chicken or Norwegian roast salmon, plus two sides, for $9.99. Or you can order sides, including rice and a vegetable medley, separately for $4.50 each. Also on the menu: kung pao sirloin and vegetable pad Thai, $9.49 each. There are also bakery items, milk shakes, and a specialty coffee stand, as well as a good number of vegetarian options.

But you can also get midway-style food: Just a few yards from the Market Restaurant is the much-smaller **Granny's Apple Fries.** These are Granny Smith apple slices coated in a flour mixture and then deep-fried, dusted with a cinnamon-sugar mix, and served with a cup of vanilla-cream dipping sauce. There are nearly a dozen more fast-food places throughout Legoland. Legoland's food tends to be slightly lower in cost and quality than comparable comestibles at Orlando's parks; the all-you-can-eat pizza buffet is particular dire, but the burgers aren't awful.

SHOPPING

THIS IS WHERE THE UBIQUITOUS GIFT SHOPS of other large theme parks have an edge: They don't all sell the same thing. But at Legoland, it's all about the bricks. They do come in an incredible range of colors, sizes, and shapes beyond the square or rectangular block. The individual bricks are sold by the weight. Six retail locations essentially sell only bricks—one of them is reserved just for girls—and detailed how-to-build books, while other shops specialize in Lego logo apparel, character costumes, and tchotchkes. Don't be too disappointed to discover that the prices here are usually higher than at your local toy store or Amazon.com, and they don't carry coveted out-of-production lines like Harry Potter.

LEGOLAND HOTEL

IF SPENDING YOUR DAY SURROUNDED BY LEGOS isn't enough, you can lay your head at the hotel that bricks built—but don't worry, your pillow won't be made of plastic. Opened in 2015, the Legoland Hotel is steps from the park entrance and boasts 152 rooms, all of which boast king-size beds in the adult sleeping area, and a separate kids' bedroom with bunk beds and its own entertainment center. Standard rooms sleep five, while VIP suites can accommodate up to nine; both include mini-fridges, coffeemakers, multiple TVs, and free Wi-Fi. Each hotel floor is themed to a different Lego genre—Pirate, Adventure, Kingdom, or Friends—and you can upgrade to a premium themed room for additional in-room decor; even the elevators get in on the act with a disco light and sound show.

Legoland Hotel guests can take advantage of a daily character buffet breakfast at Bricks Restaurant (included in the room charge) and Bonus Brick Time early entry to select attractions in the park, along with character meet and greets, games, and model-building parties in the evening. Bricks also offers a character buffet dinner ($20 for adults; $13 for children ages 7–12; $8 for children ages 3–6), and parents can unwind with a cocktail at the Skyline Café while their kids play in the lobby. Master Model Builder Workshops are also popular, so be sure to sign up for one of the limited spots at registration as soon as you check in. The pool and splash-play areas are attractive, if not especially elaborate, with fun floating foam bricks to build with and full waterside bar service.

Rack rates can be steep, starting around $120 for a parking lot view in the slow season and going up to $500 or more a night, plus a $20-per-day resort fee and an optional $20-per-stay valet parking fee.

ONE-DAY TOURING PLAN

THIS ONE-DAY TOURING PLAN INCLUDES all of the park's attractions for both younger children (ages 3–5, or less than 36 inches in height) and older children (ages 6–13 and more than 40 inches tall). Skip any attraction that does not interest you or for which your child is not yet tall enough.

The touring plan suggests visiting Legoland's shows and films immediately after lunch. Work the shows into the schedule in the order that is most convenient for you; it's rare for many of the shows to play to a capacity audience, and you shouldn't have trouble getting in to the next performance.

1. Arrive at the park entrance 30 minutes before official opening (45 minutes if you need to buy admission). Obtain a guide map and daily entertainment schedule.

2. If you have children ages 3–5, head to the Ford Junior Driving School

in Lego City as soon as the park opens, and ride. If your children are older, ride the Ford Driving School instead. Finally, if you have children from both age groups, visit the Junior Driving School before the Driving School.

3. Experience the Rescue Academy, also in Lego City. (34" min. height requirement)

4. Try Boating School in Lego City. (34" min. height requirement)

5. Ride Flying School in Lego City if your children are at least 44" tall and willing enough to ride.

6. If you have children ages 3–5, head to Duplo Valley and ride Big Rig Rally and Granny's Jalopies. (36" min. height requirement)

7. Take the Safari Trek in Land of Adventure. (34" min. height requirement)

8. Try Beetle Bounce in Land of Adventure. (36" min. height requirement)

9. Ride Coastersaurus. (36" min. height requirement)

10. Take the Lost Kingdom Adventure. (34" min. height requirement)

11. If time permits before lunch, let the kids play in the Pharaoh's Revenge play set in Land of Adventure.

12. Eat lunch and work in any shows you want to see.

13. Tour the Miniland buildings.

14. Tour the Duplo Farm in Duplo Valley.

15. Ride Merlin's Challenge in Lego Kingdoms. (36" min. height requirement)

16. Ride The Dragon. (40" min. height requirement)

17. Try Royal Joust, also in Lego Kingdoms. (36" min. height requirement)

18. If time permits, set the kids loose to run around in the Forestmen's Hideout.

19. Take the Quest for Chi boat ride in the World of Chima. You will get wet. (48" min. height requirement) Children under 48" can get soaked in the nearby Cragger's Swamp water play area.

20. Ride Project X in Lego Technic. (40" min. height requirement)

21. Take a spin on the AquaZone Wave Racers in Lego Technic. (40" min. height requirement)

22. Experience Technicycle. (36" min. height requirement)

23. Try the Grand Carousel in Fun Town.

24. Ride Mia's Riding Adventure in Heartland City

25. Ride Island in the Sky in The Beginning, if both you and your kids are up for it.

26. Tour Cypress Gardens if time permits.

27. Try the Kid Power Towers if time permits. (40" min. height requirement)

PART FOUR

GATORLAND

IN THESE DAYS OF GENIAL ZOOKEEPERS, it's hard to imagine a man like Florida showman Owen Godwin, who established Gatorland in 1949. More of a reptile-fixated P. T. Barnum than an environmental enthusiast, Godwin traveled the world collecting toothy critters for his zoo collection of gators and "jungle crocs." But the days of aggressive collecting are gone. Most of the alligators are born right in the Gatorland swamp, and Gatorland naturalists will tell you of their efforts to rehabilitate injured or displaced animals brought to them from all over Florida.

For more than 65 years, Gatorland has existed as a roadside wonder. Before the days of magic castles and studio back lots, tourists flocked to the Sunshine State for its beaches and wildlife. Sprinkled along the highways that linked the state's natural attractions were tiny outposts of tourism—must-see roadside stops meant to break up the monotony of travel. Gatorland fell into this category. The park was ripe with tourist appeal—who can resist a park that hawks Florida's most infamous resident, the alligator?

unofficial **TIP**
For those who want variety in their sightseeing itinerary, this is the place for a real change of pace.

Today, Gatorland seems to disappear in the clutter of touristy Orlando. But rather than fall victim to its own kitsch or wither in the Disney glare, Gatorland has adapted enough to proudly call itself "Orlando's best half-day attraction." It doesn't try to be one of the highfalutin theme parks in its backyard. Though the attraction has grown to 110 acres, the whole place is barely big enough for a good-size Walt Disney World parking lot. But nowhere else will you see this many gators and crocs, and nowhere else are they celebrated with such abandon. In short, Gatorland is a hallmark of Old Florida made good.

The park recently added a zip line, at heights up to 65 feet above the ground. The zip line carries the brave over ponds holding Cuban crocodiles, known to jump out of the water to snatch the occasional low-flying bird. It comes with a big ol' price tag too—more than the cost of admission (though it does include park admission).

GETTING THERE

FROM DISNEY Take US 192 (or the Central Florida GreeneWay, if you don't mind paying a few bucks in tolls) to US 441/Orange Blossom Trail. Turn left. Gatorland is on your right.

FROM ORLANDO Take I-4 to Exit 72 (FL 528/Beachline Expressway). In 2.5 miles, take Exit 3A to John Young Parkway, and head south. In 2.7 miles, turn left onto Deerfield Boulevard. In 1.4 miles, make a right onto US 441/Orange Blossom Trail. Gatorland is about 1.6 miles south, between the Osceola Parkway and FL 417/Central Florida GreeneWay. Parking is free.

ADMISSION PRICES

FOLLOWING ARE THE FULL ADMISSION PRICES at press time. Coupons are available in Gatorland brochures (found at kiosks throughout Orlando), and discounted prices are available at **gatorland.com.** The park offers AAA, AARP, and Florida-resident discounts. A special Photographers Pass allows bird-watchers to enter the park early and/or stay until dusk on select days January–June; prices range from $10 to upgrade a single-day pass for early or late access to $80 for an annual Photo Pass.

One-Day Pass   Adults **$26.99** + tax • Children ages 3-12 **$18.99** + tax • Children under age 3 **Free**
Annual Pass (unlimited admission for one year from the first day of use) Adults **$45.99** + tax • Children ages 3-12 **$31.99** + tax • Children under age 3 **Free**

ARRIVING

GATORLAND IS OPEN DAILY 10 a.m.–6 p.m. Gators don't mind rain (and most observation walkways have canopies), so the attraction is open rain or shine.

Gatorland bills itself as a half-day attraction, which makes it the perfect alternative when you don't have a full day to spend at Walt Disney World, SeaWorld, or the Kennedy Space Center Visitor Complex.

unofficial **TIP**
Plan your visit to this park around the shows.

Plan to spend about 3–4 hours to see it well. However, the park lends itself to any type of schedule. With nearby parking and the park's manageable size, it is easy to come and go. A small-gauge railroad ride traverses part of the park and passes local flora and fauna in their natural swampy habitat.

Shows and feeding times are scheduled throughout the day, with performances repeated about every 3 hours, beginning shortly after park opening, then after lunch, and again midafternoon. Performances are scheduled for easy back-to-back viewing.

Check the show schedule when you arrive. Because the shows are can't-miss attractions, plan your schedule around them. Plenty of diversions are near each show area.

Stroller and wheelchair rentals are available near the entrance. A single stroller is $10, while a double stroller is $15. Wheelchairs are

Gatorland

● **ATTRACTIONS**
1. Adventure Hour
2. Allie's Barnyard Petting Zoo
3. Alligator Breeding Marsh
4. Bobcat Bayou
5. Cuban crocs
6. Dog Gone Gator, Chester
7. Emu enclosure
8. Flamingo Island
9. Gator Gully Splash Park
10. *Gator Jumparoo Show*
11. Gators, and More Gators
12. Gator Wrestlin' Stadium/*Gator Wrestlin' Show*
13. Gatorland Express Train Station
14. Giant tortoise
15. Jungle Crocs of the World
16. Nile crocs
17. Ol' Owl House
18. Panther Springs
19. Parrot Playground
20. Pops, the Giant Alligator
21. Python House
22. Raccoon Hut
23. Saltwater crocs
24. Screamin' Gator Zip Line
25. Snakes of Florida
26. Swamp Walk
27. *Up Close Encounters*
28. Very Merry Aviary
29. White Gator Swamp

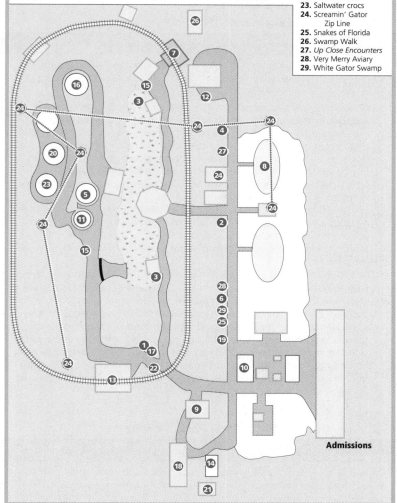

Admissions

available for $10, and electronic convenience vehicles (ECVs) rent for $25.

CONTACTING GATORLAND

FOR MORE INFORMATION, contact Gatorland at ☎ 800-393-JAWS (5297) or **gatorland.com.**

■❙ ATTRACTIONS

Alligator Breeding Marsh ★★★½

APPEAL BY AGE	PRESCHOOL ★★		GRADE SCHOOL ★★		TEENS ★★
YOUNG	ADULTS ★★★		OVER 30 ★★★		SENIORS ★★★

What it is A breeding ground for gators in a picturesque setting. **Scope and scale** Diversion. **When to go** At the warmer part of the day. **Authors' rating** The quiet heart of Gatorland; ★★★½.

DESCRIPTION AND COMMENTS The alligator breeding marsh is one of Gatorland's most unexpected attractions. Set in the middle of a park of zoo-like cages and enclosures, this large body of water is home to nearly 200 alligators in their natural setting. You're looking at the real ranch behind all the wrestlin' and jumpin'. A flotilla of a couple dozen gators hovering placidly by your feet is enough to make you reconsider leaning over the railing for a better photo. Try out each floor of the three-story observation tower for different (and safely distant) perspectives.

　　The marsh is also a haven for bird-watchers. Every year, more than 4,000 birds make their home at Gatorland, including green, blue, and tri-colored herons; cattle egrets; and cormorants. At feeding time, the trees along the boardwalk marsh fill with waterbirds, including several rare and protected species.

TOURING TIPS For the best view, bring binoculars. It is truly spectacular to feed the gators here (a bag of fish is $5). There is a smaller feeding area elsewhere, but you'll get more of a show if you take the goodies here. On one visit, a family brought several loaves of bread to feed the gators. It was a fascinating sight, and it attracted what seemed like hundreds of creatures. Check the trees on your right as you walk toward the petting farm, with the marsh behind you. During summer visits, they host hundreds of nesting egrets and herons, with the accompanying chirps of their young. Because the second level of the observation tower is above the trees, it provides a rare look at these birds.

kids Gator Gully Splash Park ★★★

APPEAL BY AGE	PRESCHOOL ★★★		GRADE SCHOOL ★★★★		TEENS ★★½
YOUNG	ADULTS ★★★		OVER 30 ★★		SENIORS ★

What it is A wet and dry playground for kids. **Scope and scale** Major attraction. **When to go** When the temperature kicks up a notch. **Authors' rating** A welcome way to cool down; ★★★.

DESCRIPTION AND COMMENTS Small children will go berserk when they see this Old Florida–themed water playground. Gatorland really shines here, with an attraction that rivals the children's areas located at other Orlando-area parks. You'll find several interactive fountains and other water-soaking games. Nearby, a dry playground is available for those who don't want to get wet.

TOURING TIPS   There are changing rooms nearby if you want to bring a spare set of dry clothes.

Gator Jumparoo Show   ★★★★

APPEAL BY AGE	PRESCHOOL ★★★	GRADE SCHOOL ★★★★	TEENS ★★★½
YOUNG ADULTS ★★★		OVER 30 ★★★	SENIORS ★★★

What it is It's gators: They jump, and you watch—from a distance. Scope and scale Super-headliner. When to go Check entertainment schedule. Authors' rating Yikes! ★★★★. Duration of show 15 minutes.

DESCRIPTION AND COMMENTS   This is, as they say, the marrow that has kept visitors circulating through Gatorland for almost 70 years. Visitors gather around a square pond framed by wooden boardwalks (thankfully with high railings). A trainer ventures out to a fragile-looking cupola on the water, and then the fun begins. Everyone is encouraged to stamp their feet on the boards, which lets the alligators know that supper's ready. The reptiles come gliding in from adjacent ponds, and the trainer yells and waves to attract them. Plucked chickens are strung up on wires over the water, and them gators commence to jumpin'. Trainers also dangle treats over the water, and gators snatch the food right from their hands. After you see a 10-foot-long 300-pounder leap head-high out of the water to crunch some poultry, you'll spend the rest of your time at Gatorland nervously skirting the railings. Visit the nonthreatening lorikeet aviary to calm down if necessary.

TOURING TIPS   There's no seating here, so be sure to arrive at least 10 minutes before showtime to stake your claim along the railing.

Gator Wrestling Stadium/*Gator Wrestlin' Show*   ★★★★

APPEAL BY AGE	PRESCHOOL ★★½	GRADE SCHOOL ★★★★½	TEENS ★★★★½
YOUNG ADULTS ★★★★		OVER 30 ★★★½	SENIORS ★★★½

What it is Where man (especially his head) was not meant to go. Scope and scale Super-headliner. When to go Check entertainment schedule; usually three shows daily. Authors' rating Not to be missed; ★★★★. Duration of show 15 minutes.

DESCRIPTION AND COMMENTS   There are no bad views in the 800-seat stadium. There is one seat, however, that most audience members would rather not have. That's the perch on the back of an alligator in a sandy pit in the middle of the theater. Here, a wisecracking fool keeps the audience spellbound with his courage—or reckless disregard for bodily integrity—for 15 minutes. The show features two "crackers," the nickname for Florida ranchers who often cracked their whips to get their animals to move. Enlisting their best Foghorn Leghorn impressions, the two play off of each other while one unfortunate soul wrestles the gator, opens its mouth, and even (gulp!) places his chin under its snout.

TOURING TIPS   Arrive a bit early to see the "wrestlers" warming up. Though every side offers a good view, the red bleachers typically have the best vantage point.

Gatorland Express Railroad ★★½

APPEAL BY AGE	PRESCHOOL ★★★		GRADE SCHOOL ★★★		TEENS ★
YOUNG ADULTS ★½		OVER 30 ★★		SENIORS ★★½	

What it is A circling train. **Scope and scale** Diversion. **When to go** Anytime for a quick rest of your feet. **Authors' rating** Can a gator hijack a train? ★★½. **Duration of ride** 6 minutes.

DESCRIPTION AND COMMENTS Given the park's small size, the train isn't really necessary as transportation. But it's good for a break and for getting a different view of the natural areas. Chances are that the nutty guy who narrates your ride will turn up again later in the gator-wrestling or *Jumparoo* show.

TOURING TIPS It costs an extra $2 to ride the train, but you can tack the fee onto your ticket when you arrive. The train is a good way to see the park and rest your feet, but skip it if you don't need the break.

Gatorland Zoo ★★½

APPEAL BY AGE	PRESCHOOL ★★★		GRADE SCHOOL ★★★		TEENS ★★
YOUNG ADULTS ★★½		OVER 30 ★★		SENIORS ★★	

What it is A collection of animal displays. **Scope and scale** Diversion. **When to go** Between shows. **Authors' rating** Fun, but not as cool as gators; ★★½.

DESCRIPTION AND COMMENTS Dozens of animal exhibits line the 150-foot main walkway, including Florida white-tailed deer, emus, llamas, snakes, turtles, tortoises, and birds. Allie's Barnyard petting zoo—always a favorite among young children—contains the usual collection of goats, sheep, and the occasional exotic calf. The walk-through Very Merry Aviary is stocked with lorikeets, multicolored birds that are trained to land on visitors' shoulders to drink nectar from a cup (available for $2). Baby alligators are sometimes on display here, and a special Snakes of Florida exhibit highlights local serpents.

TOURING TIPS Zoo exhibits are near both main show areas and are perfect fillers between other shows. Bring a handful of quarters to buy animal food. It's a minimal cost for a big thrill.

Jungle Crocs of the World ★★★½

APPEAL BY AGE	PRESCHOOL ★★		GRADE SCHOOL ★★★½		TEENS ★★★
YOUNG ADULTS ★★★		OVER 30 ★★★½		SENIORS ★★★½	

What it is A rare collection of international crocodiles. **Scope and scale** Headliner. **When to go** Around feeding time. **Authors' rating** Insidiously catchy theme song; ★★★½. **Duration of show** 10 minutes (feeding show).

DESCRIPTION AND COMMENTS As you step onto the boardwalk leading you to this animal exhibit, you'll soon notice how the park revels in its own cheese factor. Speakers lining the walkway play a song devoted entirely to founder Owen Godwin and his many adventures to claim this collection of "jungle crocs." This song, a close relative to *The Beverly Hillbillies* theme, will not leave your brain for at least an hour after departing Gatorland. But eventually, you come to the crocodile habitats. There are four total, featuring crocodiles from North and South America, Cuba, Asia, and Africa's Nile

River. This exhibit features a rare collection of crocodiles, such as the Cuban crocodile. The smallest and most dangerous of breeds, Cuban crocs can leap from the water like dolphins to catch birds in flight. This area includes plenty of sight gags, including a downed plane and pup tents that mysteriously lack any human beings.

TOURING TIPS Be sure to stick around for a feeding session, listed on the show schedule. On our latest visit, however, the feeding times were not listed, so you may need to ask.

Screamin' Gator Zip Line ★★★★½

APPEAL BY AGE	PRESCHOOL —	GRADE SCHOOL ★★★★	TEENS ★★★★★
YOUNG ADULTS ★★★★★		OVER 30 ★★★★½	SENIORS ★★★★½

What it is A zip line that includes passing over some crocodiles and alligators. Scope and scale Super-headliner. Special comments 37″ minimum height requirement; must be 60–275 pounds to ride. Authors' rating A great thrill on a well-operated zip line; ★★★★½. Duration of experience 1 hour, 15 minutes.

DESCRIPTION AND COMMENTS The zip line whooshes the daring above ponds holding Cuban crocodiles and above the Alligator Breeding Marsh. While the crocs are noted for jumping out of the water for handouts, it's more likely that they'll be dozing in the sun or lolling in their water when you zip by overhead. Plus, zippers are harnessed to metal cables with backup buckles for safety.

The route covers about 1,200 feet, with five intermediate platforms to zip to. Distances between the tree house–like platforms range from 200 to 520 feet, and on the last and longest glide, zippers are paired for a race to the finish. Riders can expect to zip along as fast as 30 miles per hour. The cables are up to 65 feet above the ground and its scaly attractions. On our trip, the two guides conducted a rapid safety check of each participant before allowing them to leave any platform—the most concern we've ever experienced at a zip line.

A suspension bridge leads to the last platform. Participants are again hooked to an overhead cable by one of their safety lines, and then have to take measured strides to reach the next plank in the gently swaying bridge; it's not as easy as it looks, but there are cables on each side to hold.

Including a brief video, the safety orientation, stepping into your safety harness and donning your helmet, and the walk through the park to reach the first tower, experiencing the Screamin' Gator will take about 1 hour, 15 minutes. But the overall time depends on how many are in your group, and only one group is allowed on the lines at a time. Reservations are a must.

TOURING TIPS Call ahead to reserve a time for this attraction; the price includes admission to the park. While there is a minimum weight requirement of 60 pounds, we saw a smaller child dressed in the harness and helmet who was held by her father for each of the five glides—all four of their pulley and safety lines were hooked to the cable. There is even a specially adapted zip experience for those with lower-body mobility challenges. Riders take an elevator to a platform over the breeding marsh and, in a special safety harness, zip down a single purpose-built line at a lower height than the standard course. The cost is also lower, only $15.

Swamp Walk ★★★

APPEAL BY AGE	PRESCHOOL ★	GRADE SCHOOL ★	TEENS ★
YOUNG ADULTS ★★½	OVER 30 ★★★		SENIORS ★★★

What it is Boardwalk through undisturbed nature. **Scope and scale** Diversion. **When to go** When you need some quiet time. **Authors' rating** Natural Florida; ★★★.

DESCRIPTION AND COMMENTS Cross the swinging bridge that leads to a boardwalk trail through a beautiful natural swamp. So far removed from the rest of the attractions that many visitors fail to discover it, the walk is easily one of the most exotic and unusual promenades to be found in all of Florida. The swamp is actually part of the headwaters for the Florida Everglades, the critically important south Florida swampland hundreds of miles away. Winding gracefully with no apparent impact on the environment, the walk, flanked by towering cypress trees and draped with Spanish moss, disappears deep into the lush, green swamp. Simultaneously tranquil and serene yet bursting with life, the swamp radiates primeval loveliness.

TOURING TIPS Visit the Swamp Walk before sunset, when the mosquitoes come out to feast on unsuspecting Gatorland tourists. There is no fence underneath the railing, so keep an eye on the little ones, though the mere idea that a gator is in this swamp should be enough to keep them in line.

Up Close Encounters ★★★

APPEAL BY AGE	PRESCHOOL ★★	GRADE SCHOOL ★★★	TEENS ★★
YOUNG ADULTS ★★★	OVER 30 ★★½		SENIORS ★★

What it is Educational hands-on animal show. **Scope and scale** Minor attraction. **When to go** When not at the other shows; usually held three times a day. **Authors' rating** Creepy and fun; ★★★. **Duration of show** 15 minutes.

DESCRIPTION AND COMMENTS This small stadium hosts a show-and-tell of whatever creatures—mostly snakes—the keepers might have in Gatorland's bag of tricks that day. The keepers hold the venomous critters aloft, but visitors can actually handle some of the more passive creatures, such as birds or animals borrowed from the petting zoo. Gatorland provides a home for lots of captured or injured wildlife, including animals confiscated from illegal pet traders. One keeper offered to let us hold some friendly snakes and a giant emperor scorpion, creepy-crawly as can be. We respectfully declined.

TOURING TIPS Our bad example aside, the best way to enjoy the show is to get close to the creatures and interact. Though the knowledgeable Gatorland naturalists can tell you a lot about the snakes and other animals, the real thrill comes from holding them yourself. If you are not selected to hold the animals during the show, you may hold most of them afterward, including the Burmese python, for a $5 fee.

◼ ADVENTURE TOURS

GATORLAND OFFERS FOUR DIFFERENT up close encounters with the alligators. The **Rookie Wrestling** tour allows guests to sit atop a gator (with the gator's mouth taped, of course, and the trained pro in charge); it's $10 for the experience, and photos cost extra. The **Adventure Hour** takes guests behind the scenes of the breeding marsh for $10. During the **Gator Night Shine** tour, guests look for, and toss hot dogs to, gators at night for $19.99. The **Trainer for a Day** program allows you to handle baby gators and some reptiles, get close to some of the big critters, and best (?) of all, get into the sandy gator-wrestling pit with the trainer and his foe, all for $125 (participants must be at least 12 years of age; program begins at 8 a.m. and lasts 2 hours). For tour reservations, call ☎ 800-393-JAWS (5297) or visit **gatorland.com**.

DINING

unofficial TIP
Ever try gator meat? This could be your chance, and you may be pleasantly surprised.

DINING AT GATORLAND can be either an adventure or a nonevent. Its regular menu items are nothing spectacular, but, then again, they are also fairly inexpensive by Orlando theme park standards. A burger is about $4.39, and a kids' meal is about $6.59. The menu is varied, however, and includes chicken breast and a fish-and-chips basket.

But who comes to Gatorland to eat a hot dog? No true adventurer can visit without trying at least a bite of gator meat. **Pearl's Patio Smokehouse** features gator nuggets. In humanity's never-ending quest to reduce all animals to nugget form, this is one of the less impressive examples. Yes, the gator nuggets *do* taste like chicken, though spicier and much tougher. They come with barbecue dipping sauces to mask any unfamiliar tastes. If you see a nearby gator eyeing you accusingly, console yourself with the thought that he'd do the same to you—only with less barbecue sauce and a lot more screaming.

SHOPPING

IF YOU ARE LOOKING FOR A TACKY FLORIDA SOUVENIR for that prized spot on your mantel, Gatorland is the place. Similar to shops that line US 192, the park hawks everything gator-related you could ever imagine—and even a few things you would, in a sane world, never even consider. There are also several merchandise carts throughout the park, as well as two unique photo locations.

PART FIVE

HOLY LAND EXPERIENCE

AN ENTIRELY NEW KIND OF THEME PARK opened in Orlando in early 2001. The Holy Land Experience is a re-creation of biblical-era Israel by way of evangelical Christianity. Don't expect a Jehovah Coaster or Red Sea Flume, though—this park is only for thrills of the spiritual kind. The Holy Land Experience has more in common with passive attractions like Gatorland than with places like Walt Disney World or Universal Studios. The park is currently owned by Trinity Broadcasting Network, which beams evangelical TV programs it films here to the entire world.

At 15 acres, this park is tiny by local standards. It's packed with a half dozen exhibits and re-creations of structures dating from 1450 BC to the first century AD, elaborately crafted by the same company that built parts of Walt Disney World and Universal's Islands of Adventure. The theming and detail are meticulous and impressive. Costumed performers roam the park and interact with guests, sometimes assembling for performances or impromptu congregations.

unofficial **TIP**
Not built in a day: You'll notice a similar attention to detail here as in some Disney parks.

Which brings up a big caveat: Though the historical re-creations might interest period enthusiasts, straight history is not really the focus here. Some Jewish groups have expressed concern about the appropriation of Jewish history and ritual for a Christian-themed park. Because it's ministry-operated, the park is very open about its evangelical mission. Every exhibit, show, performance, and shop is geared toward the Christian faith—essentially the born-again version. No one will treat you rudely or force you to participate in anything that makes you uncomfortable, but you can no more escape Christianity at the Holy Land Experience than you could escape Mickey Mouse at Walt Disney World. If that's not your cup of tea, then this place is not for you.

unofficial **TIP**
Come to Holy Land Experience only if you're interested in all things Christian.

If Christian-oriented touring suits you and your family, the Holy Land Experience is a singular attraction. Tremendous press coverage and high initial attendance proved that its creators have hit on something unique. However, a general tourism slump and declining crowds led to a huge increase in ticket prices, making the Holy Land Experience less of a deal than it once was. The park's small size makes it a manageable outing, though, and the needs of the elderly, disabled, or foreign tourist get special attention here. In fact, most guests tend to be adults or seniors. Despite the often cutting-edge theming and production values, children are likely to get bored after more than a few hours here.

GETTING THERE

THE HOLY LAND EXPERIENCE is very easy to find because it's located right off I-4 near Universal Orlando. From Disney World or points south, take I-4 East to Exit 78 (just past Universal Orlando and the Florida Turnpike). The Holy Land Experience is just off the exit ramp, on the west side of I-4. From Orlando, take I-4 West for 5 miles to Exit 78. Parking is free.

ADMISSION PRICES

ONE-DAY PASS Adults **$50** • Children ages 6–18 **$35** • Children ages 3–5 **$20** • Children under age 3 **Free**

ARRIVING

THE HOLY LAND EXPERIENCE is open Tuesday–Saturday, with special programs during holidays (call ahead for details). Hours are 10 a.m.–6 p.m.; closed January 1, Thanksgiving, and December 25–26. Visitors may purchase tickets at the booth near the front entrance or online at **holylandexperience.com.** If you or a family member require transportation within the park, you can borrow a wheelchair by leaving a driver's license; strollers are not rented.

Most of this small park is meant to be enjoyed on a walk-through basis at your own pace, but there are several shows and presentations to see. Many of the shows are 25–45 minutes long, and several key live dramas are performed only once per day. The tour of the Scriptorium is about 55 minutes; the presentation on Christ's death and Resurrection, titled *Passion of the Christ,* is now 75 minutes long. Thanks to the show schedule, a thorough tour of the Holy Land Experience takes at least a full operating day (and guests are helpfully provided with a suggested two-day itinerary), assuming you want to experience every element. Our advice is to check the daily schedule, either online or once you arrive at the park, and make a point of seeing the featured exhibits, using the various live performances and presentations as filler. Because some of the live performances are held only once daily, be sure to arrive a few minutes before 10 a.m. if you want to catch all of the shows.

The Holy Land Experience

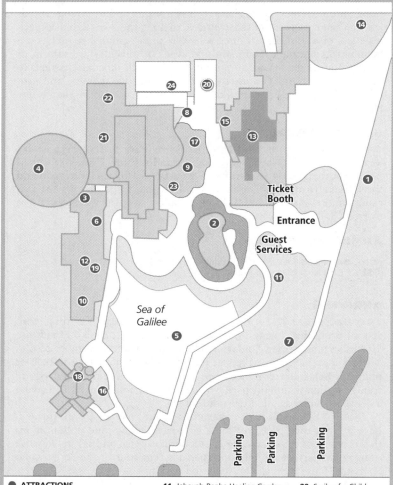

Sea of Galilee

Ticket Booth

Entrance

Guest Services

Parking   Parking   Parking

● **ATTRACTIONS**
1. Bethlehem Village Loop
2. Calvary's Garden Tomb
3. Christus Gardens
4. Church of All Nations
5. Crystal Living Waters
6. Dr. Paul F. Crouch Antiquities Collection
7. Garden of Eden
8. Garden of Gethsemane
9. *Holy Communion with Jesus*
10. House of Judea
11. Jehovah-Rapha Healing Garden
12. Jerusalem Model AD 66
13. Jerusalem Street Market
14. Jesus Boat
15. JUCE Explode Youth Center
16. Living Word Prayer Gardens
17. Qumran Caves
18. The Scriptorium for Biblical Antiquities
19. Shofar Auditorium
20. Smile of a Child Adventure Land
21. Temple Plaza (Herod's Temple)
22. Theater of Life
23. Tiny Town of Bethlehem
24. Wilderness Tabernacle

CONTACTING THE HOLY LAND EXPERIENCE

FOR INFORMATION ABOUT TICKETS, hours, or special presentations, contact the Holy Land Experience at ☎ 800-447-7235 or 407-872-2272, or **holylandexperience.com.**

ATTRACTIONS

IN ADDITION TO THE FOLLOWING ATTRACTIONS, the Holy Land Experience also contains many large models of items from Jesus's time, including Herod's temple, Qumran Caves (where the Dead Sea Scrolls were discovered), and the bell tower at the Church of Nativity in Israel. Gardens are scattered throughout the park, allowing guests a place to pray or rest. The gardens, though not large, do include re-creations of the Gardens of Eden and Gethsemane. Holy Land Experience also does a spectacular job decorating the park exterior and parking lot with Christmas lights, which can be admired on winter nights without paying admission.

Calvary's Garden Tomb ★½

APPEAL BY AGE	PRESCHOOL ★	GRADE SCHOOL ★	TEENS ★
YOUNG ADULTS ★★	OVER 30 ★★		SENIORS ★★½

What it is Re-creation of Christ's empty tomb and setting for dramatic and historical presentations. **Scope and scale** Diversion. **When to go** Anytime. **Authors' rating** Not much to see; ★½. **Duration of show** 15–20 minutes; check presentation schedule.

DESCRIPTION AND COMMENTS Visitors wind their way along a highly attenuated version of the Via Dolorosa ("way of suffering"), which Jesus walked on his way to Calvary to be crucified. Within a few paces, you end up in a garden with Jesus's tomb as its centerpiece, the door stone rolled away to reveal its emptiness.

TOURING TIPS This is an especially similar re-creation of the Garden Tomb in Israel—serene and poignant. Plan to pause here while passing through to another attraction.

Christus Gardens ★★★

APPEAL BY AGE	PRESCHOOLERS ★★	GRADE SCHOOL ★★½	TEENS ★★½
YOUNG ADULTS ★★½	OVER 30 ★★★		SENIORS ★★★

What it is Wax statues in dioramas. **Scope and scale** Minor attraction. **When to go** Anytime. **Authors' rating** ★★★.

DESCRIPTION AND COMMENTS These statues, reportedly almost a century old, were brought to the park in 2012 from a display in Tennessee. In seven dioramas, the handsomely created figures portray the life, death, and Resurrection of Jesus.

TOURING TIPS Christus Gardens is actually a small indoor venue. It is not well marked, so look for the entrance on your left after you've passed the Temple Plaza in front of the Temple of Herod, and before you reach the Church of All Nations.

Crystal Living Waters ★★★

APPEAL BY AGE	PRESCHOOL ★★	GRADE SCHOOL ★★★	TEENS ★★
YOUNG ADULTS ★★½		OVER 30 ★★★	SENIORS ★★★

What it is Computer-controlled dancing waters. **Scope and scale** Diversion. **When to go** Anytime. **Authors' rating** ★★★. **Duration of show** About 15 minutes.

DESCRIPTION AND COMMENTS Located in the pond between The Scriptorium Center and Esther's Banquet Hall, this brings to mind the dancing waters in front of the Bellagio hotel in that modern-day Gomorrah, Las Vegas. But this is on a much smaller scale. Recorded religious music, including hymns, plays, but the fountains are not synchronized to that.

TOURING TIPS Though the daily schedule lists the fountains at just twice a day, they were spurting often during a recent summer-day visit. There are no seats arranged facing the fountains, but outdoor seating at Esther's Banquet Hall has a fair view.

Forgiven ★★★

APPEAL BY AGE	PRESCHOOL —	GRADE SCHOOL ★½	TEENS ★★
YOUNG ADULTS ★★★		OVER 30 ★★★	SENIORS ★★★

What it is Three vignettes about Christ forgiving the sins of believers. **Scope and scale** Headliner. **When to go** May be offered just once a day, so check daily schedule. **Authors' rating** Variations on a theme; ★★★. **Duration of show** 45 minutes.

DESCRIPTION AND COMMENTS A well-crafted, if repetitive, amalgamation of Jesus speaking to biblical figures and explaining that he wipes away the penalties of their sins if they will accept him. The show moves quickly enough, but the lesson could be learned with one less vignette—after all, the audience consists of people who have paid to give witness to their faith. The performers, as many as a dozen on stage at once, are quite good, though some sound more earnest than others. The musical background is a recording, as is the applause sound track that follows the last vignette.

TOURING TIPS Church of All Nations is the largest venue in the park, seating about 2,000. However, the majority of these seats are on rather steep risers, so if you have mobility issues and would prefer to sit on the ground floor, be sure to arrive at least 15 minutes before the scheduled showtime.

The Four Women Who Loved Jesus ★★½

APPEAL BY AGE	PRESCHOOL —	GRADE SCHOOL —	TEENS ★★
YOUNG ADULTS ★★½		OVER 30 ★★½	SENIORS ★★★

What it is Vignettes on the Amazing Grace. **Scope and scale** Major attraction. **When to go** Check daily schedule for performance times. **Authors' rating** ★★½. **Duration of show** 25 minutes.

DESCRIPTION AND COMMENTS This production is typical of the live performances in the park and is shown at the Church of All Nations. The women, three of whom know each other, gather after Jesus's arrest and help explain to a "harlot," who has also been touched by Jesus, why each of the others knows him. Typical of the teaching nature of the dialogue, each of the four women recites the line, "I love you for the rest of my life." Mood music plays almost continuously during this 25-minute show; the lighting is just right; and as Jesus, other followers, and centurions gather, as many as 11 actors occupy the stage.

TOURING TIPS Only one performance is held per day, at the Church of All Nations. This is typically the first major show of the morning, so you should be able to find a last-minute seat more easily here than at the afternoon productions.

The Fullness of Time Has Come ★★★

APPEAL BY AGE	PRESCHOOL ★★★	GRADE SCHOOL ★★★½	TEENS ★★★½
YOUNG ADULTS ★★★½		OVER 30 ★★★	SENIORS ★★★

What it is Nativity play. Scope and scale Major attraction. When to go See schedule for showtime. Authors' rating ★★★. Duration of show 35 minutes.

DESCRIPTION AND COMMENTS Introduced in the winter of 2014 as a seasonal show, this reimagined Christmas pageant proved so popular that it's now performed daily year-round. All the expected elements of a Nativity play are present—Mary, manger, and so on—but this time the birth of Christ is shown from the angels' point of view, as they prepare to announce Jesus's arrival to the world.

TOURING TIPS One of the more elaborate shows at Holy Land Experience, this production employs large-scale sets and shiny costumes to make the familiar tale more theatrical. Only one performance is held per day, at the Church of All Nations, so show up at least 15 minutes early for the best seats.

Holy Communion with Jesus ★★★½

APPEAL BY AGE	PRESCHOOL —	GRADE SCHOOL ★★	TEENS ★★★
YOUNG ADULTS ★★★		OVER 30 ★★★★	SENIORS ★★★★

What it is Reenactment of Jesus coming to the Last Supper. Scope and scale Major attraction. When to go Repeated about a half dozen times a day. Authors' rating ★★★½. Duration of show 10 minutes.

DESCRIPTION AND COMMENTS Just beyond the entrance, guests can walk into a high-ceilinged room that is supposed to be the Upper Room, where Jesus and the disciples had the Last Supper. Each guest is presented with a tiny wooden goblet holding a thimbleful of grape juice and a tiny square of unleavened bread. The only furnishing in the room is a long wooden table, and guests can sit at it or stand on one side of it.

An actor portraying John enters from the other side of the table, offers a soliloquy, and leads the assembled in a prayer. Then the actor portraying Jesus—and be aware that more than one actor portrays Jesus each day in the park—enters from the far side of the table and speaks to the assembled. At times his face is serene; at times, his voice breaks, as he forecasts what will happen to him. He leads a Communion, and as John then leads the guests in a hymn, Jesus passes among them, touching each person as he looks him or her in the eye.

As with all of the live performances in the Holy Land Experience, the young actors seem to embrace the dignity of their roles so that this Communion is almost poignant.

TOURING TIPS Signage is not a strong point in the Holy Land Experience, so guests may only *happen* upon the Qumran Caves—where the Upper Room is located—after passing through the main entrance and then through a small courtyard that includes restrooms. The Upper Room itself is spacious, and the only table is quite large, so that many more than 12 visitors can be seated. Fear not: The actor portraying Jesus moves through the room and touches or speaks briefly to every person, so don't worry if you don't get one of the chairs.

The Jerusalem Model AD 66   ★★★½

APPEAL BY AGE	PRESCHOOL ★	GRADE SCHOOL ★★	TEENS ★★★
YOUNG ADULTS ★★★	OVER 30 ★★★½		SENIORS ★★★½

What it is Elaborate replica of ancient Jerusalem. **Scope and scale** Headliner. **When to go** After experiencing the Scriptorium; check daily schedule for presentation times. **Authors' rating** Very cool; ★★★½. **Duration of show** 25 minutes.

DESCRIPTION AND COMMENTS This is touted as "the world's largest indoor model of first-century Jerusalem." The 25-foot-wide model is meant to represent Jerusalem circa AD 66, including the Temple of Jerusalem as rebuilt by Herod while the Romans ruled the city. You can examine the model on your own, but a guided lecture is much more informative because there are no plaques to reveal what is represented. The lecture covers what everything in the model is, the history of the era, where Jesus went during the last week of his life, and more.

TOURING TIPS This headliner has only a few scheduled presentations, so be sure to consult the daily schedule to fit a visit into your plans. Try to make it to the first presentation of the morning to ensure touring flexibility later in the day.

Legna   ★★½

APPEAL BY AGE	PRESCHOOL —	GRADE SCHOOL ★★★	TEENS ★★½
YOUNG ADULTS ★★½	OVER 30 ★★		SENIORS ★★

What it is A surprisingly lighthearted live production explaining that Jesus forgives all who believe in Him. **Scope and scale** Major attraction. **When to go** Check daily schedule for performance times. **Authors' rating** ★★½. **Duration of show** 45 minutes.

DESCRIPTION AND COMMENTS In *Legna* (*angel* spelled backwards), the apostle Peter explains to his young friend Rhoda how Christ sent an angel to free him from a Roman jail. But Rhoda guesses that it might have been in answer to her prayers to Jesus to help Peter. The surprising comic relief in this skit is supplied by the angel, who pretends to slip, get fouled up in his wings, and even offers a joke or two. When the jailed Peter says he can't go with the angel because he's in chains, the angel answers, "Clap off"—mocking the commercials for sound-detecting off/on switches for table lamps. As he utters those words, Peter's chains fall to the floor. Another comical skit recounts the story of Daniel and the lion's den.

TOURING TIPS If you've brought children, be sure to check the daily show schedule for *Legna*—it is aimed at youngsters but may be offered only once a day at the Church of All Nations.

Passion of the Christ Live Drama   ★★★★

APPEAL BY AGE	PRESCHOOL ★★½	GRADE SCHOOL ★★★½	TEENS ★★★★
YOUNG ADULTS ★★★★½	OVER 30 ★★★★½		SENIORS ★★★★½

What it is Musical interpretation of Christ's Crucifixion. **Scope and scale** Superheadliner. **When to go** See entertainment schedule for showtimes, typically just once a day. **Authors' rating** ★★★★. **Duration of show** 75 minutes.

DESCRIPTION AND COMMENTS Located in the Church of All Nations, this show lets you become witness to Christ's Crucifixion and Resurrection. Though at the outset of the performance you may believe that you'll need to use your imagination to see Christ—Holy Land has a tendency to employ rousing speeches over visual props—an actor does portray the King of kings. Songs accompany the Crucifixion, but all are tempered and reverent. You will not leave singing any of the tunes, but may find yourself uplifted at his sacrifice.

TOURING TIPS There is just one presentation, usually in the afternoon. This is an extravaganza, utilizing most of the 30-plus stage performers and even some of the guides from Guest Services to fill out the crowd scenes. The Church of All Nations auditorium holds 2,000 people, but it's smart to arrive at least 15 minutes before the scheduled start to have a better choice of seats. Note that while this show isn't as gory as the Mel Gibson movie that shares its name, the violence can be quite graphic; parental discretion is advised.

The Scriptorium Center for Biblical Antiquities ★★★★

APPEAL BY AGE	PRESCHOOL ★	GRADE SCHOOL ★★½	TEENS ★★½
YOUNG ADULTS ★★★	OVER 30 ★★★		SENIORS ★★★½

What it is Walk-through exhibit detailing the history of the Bible itself. **Scope and scale** Super-headliner. **When to go** Immediately on entering the park. **Authors' rating** World-class collection, not to be missed; ★★★★. **Duration of show** 55 minutes; presentations every hour.

DESCRIPTION AND COMMENTS This museum showcases a fascinating collection of biblical antiquities, some dating from thousands of years ago. Exhibits include ancient cuneiform, scrolls, Gutenberg and Tyndale Bibles, manuscripts, and more. Spotlights shine on particular objects while narration explains their historical and religious significance. Theming and attention to detail are the best of anywhere in the park, and the Holy Land Experience's overriding evangelism is also front and center. The walk-through ends in a modern home setting that is conspicuously Bible-free, which is meant to inspire reflection on how we can bring the Good Book back into our collective lives. (We first thought that we'd mistakenly wandered into someone's living quarters, until a man in monk's robes appeared and assured us that it was all part of the program.)

TOURING TIPS Most guests initially visit the attractions near the park entrance. Proceeding immediately to the Scriptorium will get you through it with the first batch of guests (only three people were in our group) and free you up for other attractions and shows.

Shofar Auditorium/Shows and Lectures ★★★

APPEAL BY AGE	PRESCHOOL ★★½	GRADE SCHOOL ★★★½	TEENS ★★★
YOUNG ADULTS ★★★½	OVER 30 ★★★★		SENIORS ★★★★

What it is Myriad of musicals and lectures. **Scope and scale** Minor attractions. **When to go** See entertainment schedule for showtimes; not all shows are performed each day. **Authors' rating** ★★★.

DESCRIPTION AND COMMENTS Many different shows and a series of lectures all take place in Shofar Auditorium. The auditorium is located inside the same building as Jerusalem AD 66; the entrance is through the gift shop. The auditorium looks like the inside of many modern churches, with rows of chairs facing the stage, and is decorated in red velvet with Grecian columns. Two large screens can be found at either end of the main stage and are incorporated into the shows and presentations.

The shows that take place in the Shofar Auditorium change seasonally and recently have been aimed squarely at young guests. Current titles include *David & Goliath,* a "fun drama about defeating the giants in your life," and *Ignite Your Light!,* an interactive show that offers kids the chance to dress up as angels while playing Scripture-centric games.

None of the shows dazzled us or contained significant differences in production elements. In addition to the shows, Shofar Auditorium also hosts a series of lectures that are usually insightful. Most of the lecturers have doctoral degrees in theology or a corresponding field, and though the lectures change daily, the amount of in-depth history and thorough research is more than most local clergy have time to include in their sermons.

TOURING TIPS Check the park schedule for showtimes. You shouldn't need to arrive more than 5 minutes before a performance to get a decent seat.

Smile of a Child Adventure Land ★★★

APPEAL BY AGE	PRESCHOOL ★★★½	GRADE SCHOOL ★★★★	TEENS ★★½
YOUNG ADULTS ★½		OVER 30 —	SENIORS ½

What it is Children's play area. Scope and scale Major attraction. When to go Anytime. Authors' rating Small but useful; ★★★.

DESCRIPTION AND COMMENTS This addition to the Holy Land Experience gives the little ones a place to get away from the more info-heavy lectures and presentations. The play area consists of a cave meant to resemble the belly of a whale (complete with Jonah), a screening room with beanbag chairs, a small climbing wall, and a theater shaped like Noah's Ark, which occasionally hosts short plays. It's good that the area's here, but don't expect it to be on par with a Disney attraction.

TOURING TIPS The area comes off as a concession for parents whose kids grow bored in the first hour or so of touring. Unfortunately, the tiny size of the kids' area won't hold most children's attention for more than a few minutes, though the air-conditioned screening room makes a good place for exhausted youths to rest.

Theater of Life ★½

APPEAL BY AGE	PRESCHOOL ★	GRADE SCHOOL ★	TEENS ½
YOUNG ADULTS ★		OVER 30 ★½	SENIORS ★½

What it is A smaller theater used for both a variety of live presentations and films. Scope and scale Minor attraction. When to go See entertainment schedule for showtimes; not all shows are performed each day. Authors' rating ★½.

DESCRIPTION AND COMMENTS This venue is sort of a catchall. Events may include half hour karaoke sessions (religious tunes only) once or twice a day, and films range from repeated showings of a 25-minute presentation on the Resurrection to a 20-minute Christmas-themed animated film.

TOURING TIPS Check the daily presentation schedule on the back of the park map or on the website to see what appeals to you.

The Wilderness Tabernacle/*The Ark of the Covenant*
★★

APPEAL BY AGE	PRESCHOOL —	GRADE SCHOOL —	TEENS ★★
YOUNG ADULTS ★★½	OVER 30 ★★½		SENIORS ★★½

What it is Depiction of how Jews were told to observe the Day of Atonement.
Scope and scale Barely a diversion. **When to go** Only to get out of the rain.
Authors' rating ★★. **Duration of show** 20 minutes.

DESCRIPTION AND COMMENTS After watching this one-man performance,
with its recorded narration carrying the minimal action, you may wonder
why it is being staged. Precepts of Judaism are mentioned many times
throughout the Holy Land Experience; the celebratory song "Hava Nagila"
even plays over the sound system when you pass the ticket office. Still,
Christians may be confused as to why the Holy Land Experience bills this
presentation—about how ancient Jews observed their holiest day, Yom
Kippur—as a major attraction. The sole actor portrays Moses's brother,
Aaron, the high priest, and speaks only a few sentences during the 20 long
minutes that this performance occupies. The light-and-smoke display
when the Ark is opened at the end won't impress anyone who remembers
the first Indiana Jones film, but it is about the closest thing to special
effects that you'll find in the park.

TOURING TIPS Showtimes are posted at the theater entrance and on the
park map. Arrive at least 5 minutes early to claim a viewing spot. Better
yet, don't, especially if you have any qualms about the park's sometimes
clumsy co-opting of other cultures to promote its agenda.

DINING

THE ONLY RESTAURANT OF NOTE is an American/Middle Eastern-
themed eatery called **Esther's Banquet Hall,** named after the heroine of
the Jewish holiday Purim. The menu features fresh daily chef's specials,
hot entrées, and gourmet desserts, along with kids' meals. Other refresh-
ment options include **Martha's Kitchen** (ice cream and cold drinks), **Last
Snack** (foot-long hot dogs), and the deliciously dubbed **Holy Grounds
Coffee Shop.** Food service starts shutting down around 3:15 p.m., so
plan on eating dinner outside the park.

SHOPPING

AT THE PARK'S ENTRANCE, the **Jerusalem Street Market** is the main
shopping venue. Various costumed craftspeople hawk their wares, and
a cluster of stores sells a variety of souvenirs. Typical gifts such as Bibles
and crosses are available, but there are also more exotic choices such as
mosaics, horn shofars, olive-wood crèches, antievolution place mats,
and plush toy camels and lambs. Another small gift shop geared toward
books and the history of Bible-making can be found in the Scriptorium,
and another can be found outside the Shofar Auditorium.

PART SIX

KENNEDY SPACE CENTER

YOU MAY BE OLD ENOUGH TO REMEMBER the excitement and anticipation of the early days of space exploration. If not, you've probably seen the movies. Regardless, the pioneer spirit of the space program—sparked when President John F. Kennedy promised to land a man on the moon and return him safely—is contagious.

Since the summer of 1963, Kennedy Space Center has been the training area and launch site for most major U.S. space programs, including Project Mercury's manned orbital missions, Project Apollo's voyages to the moon, and the space shuttle program. In addition, weather and communications satellites are regularly put into orbit from here. Kennedy Space Center Visitor Complex is thoroughly modern and offers some of the attractions and amenities of a contemporary theme park. The complex does a wonderful job of capturing the spirit of adventure—and the uncertainty—of the early days of America's space program. It also offers a unique glimpse into the latest NASA advancements and some interesting visions of where the future of space exploration may lead.

Aware of the sometimes wide gulf of interests between the average tourist and the hard-core space junkie, the Visitor Complex is much more engaging and kid-friendly than in the past. Serious space cadets can still visit some of the authentic installations and buildings, such as the massive Vehicle Assembly Building, Launch Control Center, and the two launchpads. Other visitors can marvel at gee-whiz exhibits, IMAX 3-D movies, and giant rockets. Even so, be sensitive to your group's likes and dislikes, especially when it comes to the specialty tours—some of which are hours long and involve lengthy bus rides.

In June 2013, the Visitor Complex opened its most jaw-dropping—and inspiring—exhibit: Space Shuttle *Atlantis*. That's exactly what visitors almost come nose to heat-streaked nose with. For devotees, this alone might be worth the price of admission. The tours at Kennedy Space Center are most enjoyable for those with a serious interest in the space program and, other than the *Atlantis* exhibit, a high tolerance for touring at a distance. Even then, you may not be happy. But with the end of the space shuttle program, the Visitor Complex instituted several new bus tours with an "I almost touched it" aspect to the focus of each. However, the operation of some of these new tours is contingent on the use of the launch facilities by commercial interests, which might require the facilities to again be closed to the public.

GETTING THERE

KENNEDY SPACE CENTER VISITOR COMPLEX is an easy day trip from most Central Florida attractions. From Orlando, take FL 528 (also called both the Bee Line Highway Toll Road and the Beachline Expressway) east. (A round-trip on the Beachline will cost about $5 in tolls, so have some cash handy.) Turn onto FL 407 north, then FL 405 east, and follow it to the Kennedy Space Center Visitor Complex. You can also take Colonial Drive/FL 50 and travel east to FL 405. Parking is $10 per automobile, $5 per motorcycle, and $15 per motor home/RV. Annual pass holders receive complimentary parking with proof of a valid annual pass.

ADMISSION PRICES

THE STANDARD ADMISSION BADGE includes the Kennedy Space Center Tour, both IMAX 3-D films, and all attractions and exhibits at the Visitor Complex. KSC Up-Close Tours are priced separately. The annual pass includes free parking and merchandise discounts.

STANDARD ADMISSION Adults **$50** + tax • Children ages 3–11 **$40** + tax • Children under age 3 **Free**

UP-CLOSE TOURS (plus standard admission required) Adults **$25** + tax • Children ages 3–11 **$19** + tax | Children under age 3 **Free**

ATLANTIS ANNUAL PASS Adults **$89** + tax • Children ages 3–11 **$71** + tax • Children under age 3 **Free**

EXPLORER VIP ANNUAL PASS Adults **$139.36** + tax • Children ages 3–11 **$109.36** + tax • Children under age 3 **Free**

Astronaut Training Experience

If you're really into the astronaut thing, the Astronaut Training Experience (or ATX, as it's called) takes visitors age 14 and older and their parent or guardian through a half day of the training that astronauts use to get ready for a launch, including training simulators, mock mission-control access, and a final simulated launch and orbit. ATX Family allows the whole family to participate, but

unofficial **TIP**
To infinity and beyond: Take kids with a real interest in becoming an astronaut on the ATX.

children must be age 7 or older. Call ☎ 866-737-5235 for more information or to make reservations. Or reserve a spot via the website, **kennedyspacecenter.com.**

> **ATX CORE PROGRAM** (must be age 14 or older to participate) **$175** + tax per person; fee includes admission to the Visitor Complex
>
> **ATX FAMILY** (must be age 7 or older to participate) Adults and children age 12 and older **$175** + tax • Children ages 7-11 **$165**

Zero-G Weightless Flight

The Zero-G flight near Kennedy Space Center is for the more adventurous and affluent but is only offered a few days a year. An independent group, not the Space Center, takes off from the Space Coast Regional Airport in nearby Titusville. Once airborne, the pilot takes the modified 727 plane through a series of parabolic maneuvers. After a 45-degree ascent to 34,000 feet altitude, the plane heads downward, creating a zero-gravity atmosphere for about 30 seconds, and then repeats the maneuver over and over again. The price tag for the flight is out of our budget at $4,950 plus tax. Group rates are available, and tickets can be purchased online at **gozerog.com** or by phone at ☎ 800-937-6480.

ARRIVING

KENNEDY SPACE CENTER VISITOR COMPLEX is usually open 9 a.m.–5:30 p.m., though closing times vary by season. Call ahead before making the drive. Also note that even though there are no more space shuttle launches, other rockets do lift off from the Space Center, usually to service the International Space Station, and from the adjacent Cape Canaveral Air Force Station; the Visitor Complex may provide special viewing opportunities for these launches. Visit **kennedyspacecenter.com/events.aspx?type=rocket-launches** to learn if any space shots are scheduled during your vacation.

*un*official **TIP**
This facility's tour can take an entire day, so be sure that everyone in your group is truly interested in seeing everything there is to see before you board the bus.

The two IMAX movies are 40–45 minutes each, and the bus tours can take from 2½ to more than 3 hours. If this leaves you feeling overwhelmed, you're right—though the footprint of the Visitor Complex itself is quite small compared to commercial theme parks, there's a lot of ground to cover here. The wrong approach is to race from attraction to attraction in one day. Instead, take it slow and soak in some of the better attractions, leaving the others behind. The annual pass, which costs just $25 more than a one-day admission, is the perfect solution, letting you absorb all there is to see and do. Also, the special bus tours are timed so that you cannot take more than two of them in one day.

Most visitors should start their day with some of the exhibits at the hub, which provide an informative background on space history. Then, if you've found one that really meets your interests, head for the generic bus tour. Buses leave every 15 minutes, but if your timing is off, you can stand a full 15 minutes before boarding, and then sit on the bus for a few minutes before taking off. Buses visit Launch Complex 39 and drop everyone off at the fascinating Apollo/Saturn V Center; on weekends the buses typically stop at a multistory observation platform that has a nice panoramic look at the working end of the Space Center: the Vehicle Assembly Building, Launch Control Center, and the two launchpads. The gem is the Apollo/Saturn V Center, with a moon rock you can touch, re-creations (using video and animatronics) of a launch sequence and the first landing on the moon, and its breathtaking Saturn V rocket.

After the bus tour, see at least one of the IMAX movies. The five-and-a-half-story screens provide amazing views, and the sound systems are excellent. There are always two movies playing at alternate times. The movies are included in your general admission ticket, and there's a full concession stand in the lobby. Scarfing down popcorn while venturing through space in 3-D—what could be better?

CONTACTING KENNEDY SPACE CENTER

FOR MORE INFORMATION about Kennedy Space Center, call ☎ 866-737-5235. The Space Center will mail you a brochure about tours, as well as launch schedule information. You can also visit **kennedy spacecenter.com,** which has a page about educational tours offered, as well as a section on NASA history.

■ ATTRACTIONS

VISITOR COMPLEX
Astronaut Encounter ★★★

APPEAL BY AGE	PRESCHOOL ½	GRADE SCHOOL ★★★	TEENS ★½
YOUNG ADULTS ★★★	OVER 30 ★★★		SENIORS ★★★½

What it is Talk with a real live astronaut. **Scope and scale** Minor attraction. **When to go** See daily schedule. **Authors' rating** A bit forced; ★★★.

DESCRIPTION AND COMMENTS Usually twice a day, a NASA astronaut appears in the Astronaut Encounter Theater for a meet and greet. The astronaut's opening act is a Visitor Complex emcee who warms up the crowd with some fun space facts and nutty science tomfoolery, assisted by a kid volunteer from the audience. The emcee then introduces the astronaut, who talks about his or her particular mission(s) in space. A different astronaut will give the lecture on different days. The quality of the lecture varies on each astronaut's mission; a biologist may not excite the children as much as a shuttle pilot.

After the talk, the astronaut will take questions. The Q&A can be dull, so if you want to make it interesting, come with your own questions or have the children come up with questions during the presentation (questions about the dangers of space are good leads to more exciting stories).

Children do seem intrigued, but they don't appear to have the astronaut hero worship more popular with preceding generations.

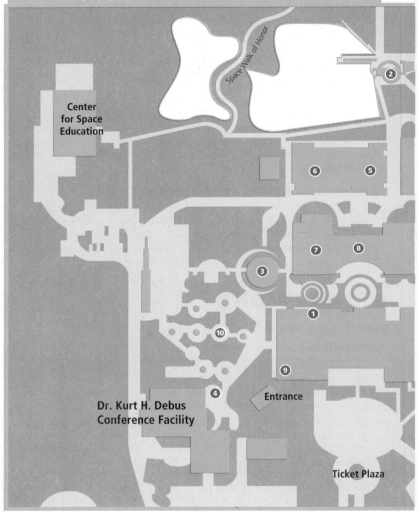

Kennedy Space Center Visitor Complex

Center for Space Education

Space Walk of Honor

②

⑥   ⑤

⑦   ⑧

③

①

⑩

⑨

④   Entrance

Dr. Kurt H. Debus
Conference Facility

Ticket Plaza

For an even more intimate astronaut encounter, sign up for Lunch with an Astronaut. As the name implies, this involves sharing a meal with an astronaut, who first shows a video about life on the space shuttle, and then gives a personalized presentation about his or her own space experiences. A Q&A follows, as well as a chance to take photos with the astronaut. The lunch experience begins at 12:15 and includes a buffet meal; the menu varies but usually includes salad, chicken, fish, and mac and cheese for the kids. Cost including admission to the Visitor Complex is $80 plus tax for adults, $60

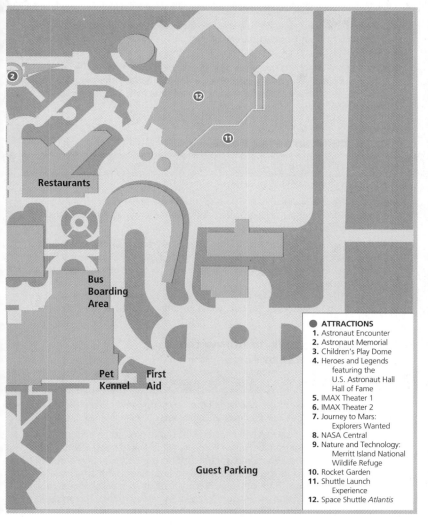

Restaurants

Bus
Boarding
Area

Pet   First
Kennel   Aid

Guest Parking

● **ATTRACTIONS**
1. Astronaut Encounter
2. Astronaut Memorial
3. Children's Play Dome
4. Heroes and Legends
       featuring the
       U.S. Astronaut Hall
       Hall of Fame
5. IMAX Theater 1
6. IMAX Theater 2
7. Journey to Mars:
       Explorers Wanted
8. NASA Central
9. Nature and Technology:
       Merritt Island National
       Wildlife Refuge
10. Rocket Garden
11. Shuttle Launch
        Experience
12. Space Shuttle *Atlantis*

plus tax for kids ages 3–11, or $30 for adults ($16 kids) as an upgrade if you already purchased entry. Call ☎ 866-737-5235 for advance reservations or purchase online at **kennedyspacecenter.com.** Tickets for Lunch with an Astronaut can also be purchased at the Visitor Complex, but same-day tickets may already be sold out.

TOURING TIPS Check the daily entertainment schedule for times. If kids get bored, the spread-out seats make it easy to tactfully get up and wander off to another attraction.

Astronaut Memorial ★★★

APPEAL BY AGE	PRESCHOOL ½	GRADE SCHOOL ½	TEENS ★★
YOUNG ADULTS ★★	OVER 30 ★★★		SENIORS ★★★

What it is A memorial to those who died for space exploration. **Scope and scale** Minor attraction. **When to go** At the end of the tour. **Authors' rating** Touching tribute; ★★★.

DESCRIPTION AND COMMENTS The entire memorial tilts, while mirrors direct the sun's rays onto glass names etched in a black marble slab. You probably won't want to spend a great deal of time here, but it's a poignant thing to see.

kids Children's Play Dome ★★½

APPEAL BY AGE	PRESCHOOL ★★★	GRADE SCHOOL ★★	TEENS †
YOUNG ADULTS †	OVER 30 †		SENIORS †

† Not designed for teenagers or adults.

What it is A kiddie playground. **Scope and scale** Diversion. **When to go** If your older kids are looking at the Rocket Garden, supervise the young ones here. **Authors' rating** Small but cute; ★★½.

DESCRIPTION AND COMMENTS This little playground, under cover from the hot sun, is a nice diversion for kids. With two stories, a cushioned floor, slides, and netting, it is similar to kids' areas at other attractions, but a space theme prevails.

TOURING TIPS One adult can take the older kids to an IMAX movie or on a stroll through the Rocket Garden, while another supervises the little ones here.

Heroes and Legends, featuring the U.S. Astronaut Hall of Fame ★★★

APPEAL BY AGE	PRESCHOOL ★★	GRADE SCHOOL ★★★	TEENS ★★½
YOUNG ADULTS ★★½	OVER 30 ★★½		SENIORS ★★★

What it is Complex of exhibits and astronaut honor roll. **Scope and scale** Major attraction. **When to go** Anytime. **Authors' rating** Current version, ★★★; new version, TBD.

DESCRIPTION AND COMMENTS In 2015, KSC broke ground on a brand-new home for the U.S. Astronaut Hall of Fame, which is set to open in late 2016. The new Heroes and Legends attraction will house the collection of astronaut memorabilia and mementos (including equipment and small spacecraft, flight patches, and personal items) that is currently found in a separate facility outside the Visitor Complex. When complete, the updated Hall of Fame will feature 360-degree multimedia presentations that leverage 3-D projections, holograms, and virtual reality technology to let visitors vicariously experience what astronauts like John Glenn and Neil Armstrong went through.

The current Hall of Fame itself takes up one room, listing those honored and inducted so far. Another room sports an array of simulators that will be of the most interest to kids, allowing them to land a shuttle, dock with the space station, and engage in other space pursuits. It was unconfirmed at press time if the simulators would be included in the new attraction.

TOURING TIPS The new Heroes and Legends venue will be located between the entry plaza and the rocket garden, making it the first thing visitors encounter. See it briefly at the beginning of the day if you arrive early, or save it for late when the rest of the crowds have moved on.

Until the new attraction opens, the original Hall of Fame is situated down the road from the Visitor Complex. It requires a 10-minute drive to get there. You will need to use your own vehicle because buses do not run to the Hall of Fame.

The new attraction is expected to be included in regular admission. For now, you may purchase either a regular Kennedy Space Center Visitor Complex admission, which includes admission to the Astronaut Hall of Fame and is good for two days, or just purchase a ticket at the Hall of Fame for $27 plus tax for adults and $23 plus tax for children ages 3–11. This is a good last stop before heading to the hotel, as long as you do not want to ride any of the simulators. The lines at the end of the day are as tedious as any major theme park's, and the rewards are not up to the wait. The Hall of Fame stays open until 6 p.m.; closing times for the Visitor Complex vary by season, but due to the long lines, a midday excursion (barring IMAX presentation or bus tour) is a better plan.

IMAX Films ★★★★

APPEAL BY AGE	PRESCHOOL ★★	GRADE SCHOOL ★★★½	TEENS ★★★½
YOUNG ADULTS ★★★★		OVER 30 ★★★★	SENIORS ★★★★

What they are Large-format 3-D films projected onto huge screens with incredible sound systems. **Scope and scale** Super-headliner. **When to go** Check daily entertainment schedule; perfect during rain or midafternoon heat. **Authors' rating** Excellent; ★★★★. **Duration of shows** 40–45 minutes.

DESCRIPTION AND COMMENTS Kennedy Space Center (KSC) offers two excellent IMAX films each day:

• *JOURNEY INTO SPACE 3-D* KSC's newest IMAX 3-D film takes a look back at the history of NASA's past accomplishments and gives a peek into its future plans for extraterrestrial exploration. Narrated by Sir Patrick Stewart (who *Star Trek* fans will agree is a much more appropriate narrator than Tom Cruise, host of the Space Station documentary that this film replaced), *Journey Into Space* splices in-depth interviews with Commander Chris Ferguson, an astronaut who flew on the final space shuttle mission, with ultra-sharp imagery shot in space on IMAX cameras. The film's finale looks beyond today's technology (like the International Space Station and Hubble Telescope) to imagine the first mission to Mars, visualizing a multiyear voyage to the red planet in the in-development Orion crew capsule.

• *HUBBLE 3-D* Narrated by Leonardo diCaprio and filmed by the crews of three space shuttle missions, this film documents the demanding efforts to repair—and repair again—the Hubble Space Telescope. The scenes of astronauts delicately, or sometimes forcefully, working to replace parts of the telescope are at first interesting but become repetitive. The best images are of the stunning views captured by Hubble that seem to propel us inside galaxies and nebulae—the colors and shapes are breathtaking. A charming touch: The film begins and ends to the version of "Somewhere Over the Rainbow" sung by the late Hawaiian Iz Kamakawiwo'ole.

TOURING TIPS Regardless of which movie you choose, we recommend sitting toward the back of the theater for the best view and to fully experience the awesome sound system. You will need to arrive early because these theaters are fairly small. Standard theater fare is sold in the lobby.

Journey to Mars: Explorers Wanted ★★½

APPEAL BY AGE	PRESCHOOL ½	GRADE SCHOOL ★★½	TEENS ★★★
YOUNG ADULTS ★★★		OVER 30 ★★	SENIORS ★★

What it is Exhibits and brief presentation about the future of space travel. **Scope and scale** Minor attraction. **When to go** While waiting for the bus or IMAX films. **Authors' rating** Plea to continue the journey; ★★½.

DESCRIPTION AND COMMENTS A collection of hands-on exhibits that speculate on where our space travelers will go and how they will get there. Some exhibits are educational and straightforward, such as many dealing with the various Mars landers and the Pathfinder mission (you can even sign up to send your signature to the Red Planet on the next mission). Other exhibits go on flights of fancy about how futuristic spacecraft will work and about potential colonization of other planets. For 10 minutes on the half hour, a presenter speaks in rosy terms about what space exploration has gained us on Earth, and then yields to video sound bites from aerospace workers on how much more there is to learn.

TOURING TIPS An easy walk-through, with nothing too surprising. Kids will like the touching-encouraged exhibits. Hit this one as filler when needed.

NASA Central ★★½

APPEAL BY AGE	PRESCHOOL ½	GRADE SCHOOL ★½	TEENS ★★
YOUNG ADULTS ★★½		OVER 30 ★★★	SENIORS ★★★

What it is Live launch briefings and artifacts on display. **Scope and scale** Diversion. **When to go** After visiting *Atlantis*. **Authors' rating** Happens only twice a day, but a good way to get in the know; ★★½.

DESCRIPTION AND COMMENTS The artifacts are neat, but most enjoyable are the live briefings that occasionally take place, depending on upcoming or recent launches. Space Center communicators and live footage from throughout the complex give a glimpse into what is happening at the Space Center, or at the International Space Station, the day of your visit.

TOURING TIPS Visit just days before a launch and you'll catch the real action, which could include live video from the International Space Station. If you visit when LC 39 is closed for a launch, this will probably be as close as you get.

Nature and Technology: Merritt Island National Wildlife Refuge ★★

APPEAL BY AGE	PRESCHOOL ½	GRADE SCHOOL ★½	TEENS ★½
YOUNG ADULTS ★★		OVER 30 ★★	SENIORS ★★

What it is Small exhibit on the coexistence of local wildlife and high technology. **Scope and scale** Diversion. **When to go** Anytime. **Authors' rating** Unremarkable; ★★.

DESCRIPTION AND COMMENTS Even though it's harmless enough, this walk-through exhibit is largely uninspired, though the pine interior and two dozen or so taxidermic animals make a drastic juxtaposition to the metal shells of the adjacent Rocket Garden. Small displays catalog the lives and habits of the thousands of wild animals in the Merritt Island National Wildlife Refuge as well as the Canaveral National Seashore, including bald eagles, alligators, snakes, wild pigs, sea turtles, manatees, and so on.

TOURING TIPS Skip this one unless you're killing time while someone else is on the bus or in the movie theater. Or duck in during the rain or hot summer sun, but it's only good for about a 30-minute detour.

Rocket Garden ★★★

APPEAL BY AGE	PRESCHOOL ½	GRADE SCHOOL ★★	TEENS ½
YOUNG ADULTS ½		OVER 30 ★★	SENIORS ★★

What it is Outdoor rocket display. Scope and scale Diversion. When to go Before you head home. Authors' rating Unique; ★★★.

DESCRIPTION AND COMMENTS Rockets, spacecraft, and antennae dot a vast lawn. The big rockets take center stage and are the perfect backdrop for group photos. Space enthusiasts and grade-schoolers may enjoy the climb-in replicas of Mercury, Gemini, and Apollo capsules.

TOURING TIPS Morning and afternoon guided tours are offered. Check the sign near the garden entrance for times.

Shuttle Launch Experience ★★★½

APPEAL BY AGE PRESCHOOL ★★	GRADE SCHOOL ★★★½	TEENS ★★★½
YOUNG ADULTS ★★★	OVER 30 ★★★½	SENIORS ★★★

What it is Simulation of a space launch. Scope and scale Super-headliner. When to go Make this your first stop. Authors' rating So close, yet so far; ★★★½. Duration of ride 25 minutes.

DESCRIPTION AND COMMENTS This attraction is housed in a six-story facility in the far right corner of the park. A long gantry switches back and forth to an anteroom where guests stand en masse to watch a 10-minute introduction video. It's a bit reminiscent of the scene where Dorothy first meets the Wizard of Oz. Narration by space shuttle commander Charlie Bolden (now the head of NASA) fills the room with anticipation as it warns riders of the perils of space travel; it closes with smoke machines and lights simulating the ignition of the rockets.

Riders then form a queue and get another 5- to 10-minute talk about how this is their last chance to opt out of the ride and watch the video in a motion-free zone.

Finally, riders board, strap in, and get bounced around a little bit while looking at a blue screen. They then disembark from the 2-minute experience through a large, spiraling hall filled with celestial factoids.

TOURING TIPS Bolden's continued narration during the shuttle experience does a fine job of stealing the realism and any tension that had been built up (not his fault, of course). The subpar graphics is the other major factor that contributes to this ride's underwhelming experience. With all the money KSC spent on both the facility and the theming, it should have invested a few more bucks for a good film instead of something that looks like an aging flight simulator. It's much closer to the jerky Wild Arctic helicopter simulator at SeaWorld than the more captivating Star Tours at Disney's Hollywood Studios.

Space Shuttle *Atlantis* ★★★★★

What it is The Space Shuttle *Atlantis* and about 60 touch screens and simulators. *Atlantis* flew 33 missions in space between October 1985 and July 2011, which was the final flight of the space shuttle program. **Scope and scale** Super-headliner. **When to go** You might want to take one of the basic bus tours of the Space Center's buildings and structures first to build appreciation for this attraction. **Authors' rating** It will be a favorite memory; ★★★★★.

DESCRIPTION AND COMMENTS The NASA bosses were smart enough to know that once the space shuttle program ended in 2011, the vehicles themselves would be in huge demand. Most of the shuttles were doled out to various museums, but the *Atlantis,* which touched down July 21, 2011, after flying the last of its 33 shuttle missions, was put on display here beginning in June 2013.

The entrance to this six-story structure is flanked by same-size copies of the liftoff systems for all shuttles: an enormous orange external fuel tank and a pair of white, solid rocket boosters. The fuel tank stands 184 feet tall, and visitors can walk underneath it as they enter the building. The structure is clad in orange-yellow tiling, to represent the flames of liftoff, and gray-silver, representing the underside shielding of the orbiters.

Visitors enter a movie theater that can hold 250 people: In addition to the large screen in front, other screens cover part of the sides and reach overhead. A 12-minute film depicts a 1969 meeting at the Manned Spacecraft Center in Houston, where NASA executives were told to design and construct something new—a reusable spaceship to use in building the International Space Station. The film includes actual footage of failures NASA experienced while trying to create the shuttle. Finally, 12 years later, the first space shuttle does lift off.

The screen is filled with the familiar image of the ignition sequence, the billowing clouds of smoke, and a NASA announcer proclaiming that *Atlantis* has achieved liftoff. With that, the front screen lifts up, and the audience is just a few yards from the *Atlantis.*

The orbiter hangs from the ceiling, tilted so that visitors can see inside the open cargo bay and walk under the extended cargo boom, named the Canadarm. You will also see evidence of the wear on the heat tiles, sustained during the *Atlantis*'s 33 liftoffs and reentries and more than 125 million miles of travel about 220 miles above Earth.

A series of touch screen panels—there are about 40 of them on three levels—allows the visitor to look at a cross section of the orbiter, and then touch a chosen area to read more about what took place there. Other screens have details on each of the program's 135 shuttle missions. Small domed kiosks allow visitors to perform a virtual space walk.

Climbing a nearby set of stairs, visitors come to a full-size model of the Hubble Space Telescope, larger than a school bus. Information pylons review shuttle missions that were deployed to repair the telescope.

A scale replica of the International Space Station offers smaller, or at least more-agile, guests the opportunity to climb through a clear tube (just like the astronauts do) through a copy of part of the station's interior.

On the next level, the discussion centers on the orbiter's reentry and its decline in speed from more than 17,000 mph while orbiting to "just" 247 mph as it glided to a landing at the Space Center.

To imagine the reentry, during which the pilot had to guide the shuttle through slow S curves to decrease speed, youngsters can trot through a series of curved barriers and plop down on a large slide that descends to the ground level at the same angle of descent the orbiter used.

Various simulators allow guests to operate the Canadarm to remove a payload from the cargo bay, dock the orbiter with the Space Station, land the orbiter at the Cape, and even operate the 400-foot-tall crane that raised and moved the orbiters within the Vehicle Assembly Building. Most of these simulators have time limits. In 2015 KSC installed a new exhibit, located on the ground floor directly beneath *Atlantis,* that pays tribute to the loss of space shuttles *Challenger* and *Columbia*. In addition to personal mementos from the fallen astronauts, the Forever Remembered memorial is the first time that NASA has ever publicly displayed fragments recovered from the destroyed spaceships; a 12-foot section of the *Challenger*'s body, emblazoned with an American flag, and a window from *Columbia*'s cockpit, are presented respectfully in a dimly lit hall.

TOURING TIPS You might be fascinated by simply staring at the *Atlantis* as you circle it. But there are about 20 simulators and another 40 or so touch screens, plus brilliantly illustrated static information displays. (Some have tiny panels that attract the attention of grade-schoolers or middle-school viewers for easy science lessons.) You could spend 90 minutes at this attraction, but a number of features at the Visitor Complex are timed, so be careful how you plan your day here.

As the park's newest—and, we think, most impressive—static attraction, the Space Shuttle *Atlantis* exhibit is sure to be busy all day long. If you follow our general advice of reaching the park as soon as it opens, head first for Space Shuttle *Atlantis*. Then take a bus tour(s) or view an IMAX film, and perhaps you'll want to return to *Atlantis* in the late afternoon, when attendance at the Space Center has thinned. Remember, there are dozens of hands-on exhibits surrounding the orbiter.

KENNEDY SPACE CENTER BUS TOUR

BUSES RUN EVERY 15 MINUTES and make either one or two stops, depending on the season, around Kennedy Space Center. Depending on the day of the week, the tour stops at the LC 39 Observation Gantry or travels through the Space Center and then stops at the Apollo/Saturn V Center, where you tour at your own pace. The bus ride itself is a little less than 2 hours, but with your time in the center, figure on 3 hours. The bus that drops you off will not be the same one that picks you up, so if you buy presents at the gift shops, you will have to carry them with you for the remainder of the tour.

In transit, there's no staring into "space." TV monitors show informative segments on space exploration to prepare you for the next destination. Think of this time as cramming for an exam. If possible, sit near the front of the bus, on the right side, for a better view of buildings in the area. Also, if you're lucky, an alert bus driver will point out signs of wildlife—which include an impressive bald eagle's nest, sunning or floating alligators, perhaps a manatee or wild pig—along the way to the following stops:

Apollo/Saturn V Center ★★★★

APPEAL BY AGE	PRESCHOOL ★★★	GRADE SCHOOL ★★★★	TEENS ★★★
YOUNG ADULTS ★★★½	OVER 30 ★★★★		SENIORS ★★★★

What it is Exhibit celebrating the race to the moon. **Scope and scale** Super-headliner. **When to go** Anytime. **Authors' rating** Where else can you touch a moon rock?; ★★★★.

DESCRIPTION AND COMMENTS The Apollo/Saturn V Center is a gigantic building (actually constructed around the enormous Saturn V!) with several displays. All guests enter a holding area, where you'll see a 9-minute film on the race to the moon. The film is good, but things only get better.

The next stop is the Firing Room Theater, which catapults you back in time to December 1, 1968, for the launch of the first successful manned mission to the moon. Actual remnants of the original 1960s firing room, including countdown clocks and launch consoles, set the mood. Once the show is under way, three large screens take you back to that day with original footage from the Space Center. During this 10-minute presentation, you'll sense the stress of the launch commanders and feel as though you're experiencing the actual launch through some fun special effects.

This is a pride-inducing presentation that prepares you for the real meat and potatoes of the Apollo/Saturn V Center—the actual 363-foot Saturn V moon rocket. When the doors of the Firing Room Theater open, guests are instantly overwhelmed by the size of the rocket. The amount of power the rocket produced on blastoff (7½ million pounds of thrust) could light up New York City for an hour and 15 minutes. In addition, this room is filled with space artifacts, including the van used to transport astronauts to the launchpad, a lunar module, and Jim Lovell's Apollo 13 space suit. But there are more than just dusty relics here. Kennedy Space Center does a great job of telling the history of the era, with storyboards along the walls to document the highlights of each Apollo mission.

Another excellent exhibit at the Apollo/Saturn V Center is the Lunar Theater, where Neil Armstrong narrates a suspenseful documentary about his trip to the moon with Apollo 11. Younger generations may be a little shocked at how close the "eagle" came to missing its landing. The set of Lunar Theater enhances the 12-minute film with a few eccentric tricks; the whole production is short, touching, and inspired.

TOURING TIPS If you're traveling with kids, they may well be restless by now. Check out the interactive exhibits or maybe step outside. A patio near the dining area is a good spot for your family to get some fresh air.

LC 39 Observation Gantry ★★½

APPEAL BY AGE	PRESCHOOL ★★	GRADE SCHOOL ★★★	TEENS ★★
YOUNG ADULTS ★★½	OVER 30 ★★★		SENIORS ★★★½

What it is Observation area that focuses on the launchpad. **Scope and scale** Major attraction. **When to go** Anytime. **Authors' rating** Unless you buy a ticket for one of the specialty bus tours, this is as close as you'll get to the historic launchpads; ★★½.

DESCRIPTION AND COMMENTS The LC 39 exhibits celebrate the space shuttle—the first spacecraft designed to be reusable. A 7-minute film at the LC 39 Theater, narrated by shuttle astronaut Marsha Ivins, explains how NASA engineers and technicians serviced the shuttle before launch. After the film, the doors open to dump you into a room with model displays. From here, head to the observation gantry, which puts you roughly a mile away from Launch Pads 39A and 39B, the only sites used for launching the shuttle. These are also the pads from which the Saturn V rockets blasted off to the moon during the Apollo program.

TOURING TIPS You'll be tempted to race to the observation gantry, but watching the film first provides for a better appreciation of the views offered there. The intricate launchpad model should be your first stop once the movie doors have opened. The model runs through a launch every few minutes, so to see the pieces move, wait for the countdown.

Once at the observation gantry, look for the Crawlerway path, a road nearly as wide as an eight-lane highway and more than 3 miles long. It was constructed to bear the weight of the Crawler-Transporter (6 million pounds) that moved the huge rockets from the Vehicle Assembly Building to the launchpads.

OTHER TOURS

KSC Up-Close Explore Tour and Launch Control Center Tour ★★★★

APPEAL BY AGE	PRESCHOOL ★★	GRADE SCHOOL ★★★	TEENS ★★★½
YOUNG ADULTS ★★★★	OVER 30 ★★★★½		SENIORS ★★★★½

What it is Bus tours to areas that have been closed to the public for decades. **Scope and scale** Super-headliner. **When to go** Check the daily schedule; the tours are planned so that visitors cannot ride more than one in a day. **Special comments** Tours may be canceled or altered due to launch activity. Also, KSC Up-Close tours may not be offered in the future, due to possible demands for use of the facilities by commercial firms launching rockets. **Authors' rating** If these tours are offered, do pay for the once-in-a-lifetime experience; ★★★★. **Duration of tour** 2–2½ hours.

DESCRIPTION AND COMMENTS Depending on the tour, you will stand outside the 525-foot-tall Vehicle Assembly Building, where a guide and color photo murals explain how the space shuttles and even the 363-foot-tall Saturn V rockets were maneuvered upright by overhead cranes. Or you will spend about 50 minutes in the firing room of the Launch Control Center, where 200 real rocket scientists and other experts sat before computer consoles monitoring dozens of space shuttle launches. The tour guides were all longtime employees in other support jobs at the Space Center and offer personal as well as historical trivia during their narrations.

TOURING TIPS The tours each cost $25 for adults, $19 for children ages 3–11, plus tax. You should order your tickets online (**kennedyspacecenter .com/ksc-tours.aspx**) because of the limited touring schedules. The two tours are offered only once a day, at competing times. But before reserving your tour, do check the times of the IMAX films, so that you can experience as much of the Visitor Complex as possible each day you are there.

Cape Canaveral: Then and Now   ★★★½

| APPEAL BY AGE | PRESCHOOL ★★ | GRADE SCHOOL ★★½ | TEENS ★★½ |
| YOUNG ADULTS ★★★½ | OVER 30 ★★★★ | | SENIORS ★★★★ |

What it is Bus tour to Cape Canaveral. **Scope and scale** Headliner. **When to go** Check the daily schedule. **Special comments** Tour was suspended at press time but may return; photo ID required. **Authors' rating** A piece of NASA history; ★★★½. **Duration of tour** 3–3½ hours.

DESCRIPTION AND COMMENTS Situated about 15 miles from Kennedy Space Center, Cape Canaveral Air Station is an active launch facility where unmanned rockets are sent into space on NASA, military, and commercial missions. Even more interesting, though, is Cape Canaveral's place in history as the original home of the U.S. space program. It is here that the early Mercury missions, as well as the first Americans, were launched into space. And unlike the main bus excursion, with its faraway viewing, this tour allows you to actually explore these historical locations firsthand. Elements of the main KSC Bus Tour are included in this tour as well.

A highlight of the tour is the Air Force Space and Mission Museum, home of the world's largest outdoor collection of missiles on display.

TOURING TIPS You are not allowed to tour at your own pace and must depart with the same group on the same bus. This tour costs an extra $25 plus tax for adults and $19 plus tax for children ages 3–11 in addition to the regular admission, and is for true space aficionados only.

Does your child dream of becoming an astronaut? Maybe you remember the exact day Neil Armstrong set foot on the moon. If so, seeing a live launch is truly awe-inspiring and will leave you with a memory that you'll never forget.

While NASA's famed space shuttles no longer operate, the government has contracted with commercial companies to stage several more missions to service the International Space Station, into 2016. At the present time, Visitor Complex officials believe that while launch viewing will be included in regular admission for most launches, it may also offer off-site viewing opportunities for an additional fee. KSC officials suggest checking the website for details: **kennedyspacecenter.com.**

Launches can also be seen outside of Kennedy Space Center along US 1 in Titusville and along US A1A in Cape Canaveral and Cocoa Beach. All of these locations can be reached from FL 528 (Beeline Highway toll road) east. You should arrive early (about 3 hours in advance), however, because many locals line the streets for launches.

Be aware that some of the attractions at the Kennedy Space Center Visitor Complex may be closed the day of a launch for safety reasons. If you do want to be at the center for a launch, arrive at least 2 hours before the scheduled lift-off. Also, though this problem has lessened now that NASA's space shuttles are no longer launched, there can be sizable traffic jams leaving the area within minutes after a rocket lifts off. If you are viewing from one of the nearby highways, plan to visit one of the many nearby beaches until roads are clear.

DINING

THE NEAREST RESTAURANTS to the Visitor Complex are almost a dozen miles away on the mainland. However, you'll find pizza, pasta, burgers, turkey wraps, and chicken Caesar salads (all less than $8); barbecue pork (slightly more than $8); hot dogs (different sizes for adults and kids); and occasional specialty items at the **Orbit Café,** where you can sit inside or outside. However, there is no shade over the outdoor tables, and the grackles and seagulls can be annoying. The **Rocket Garden Café** has outside tables only, overlooking the iconic Rocket Garden, but it offers a more imaginative cuisine, such as conch fritters ($7.50); steak salad, vegetable frittata, or chicken empanada ($9.50 each); and flatbread pizza ($12.50). There is only one other snack stand in the Visitor Complex for a quick bite, though the IMAX theater has a nice concession stand if you long for Raisinets or other traditional candies. A picnic area beside the Constellation Sphere makes a nice alfresco dining spot.

SHOPPING

LET YOUR KIDS TRY astronaut ice cream in the gift shop. There are three shops here: the smallish **Voyagers,** to your left just after you pass the ticket gate; the much-larger, two-story **Space Shop;** and one at the Apollo/Saturn V Center. Don't be shy—try the freeze-dried ice cream sandwich or freeze-dried strawberries. You also can find snow globes, space shuttle gummy candy, books for various age levels, T-shirts, flight jackets, kid-size flight suits, and more. Prices vary, and while you might find the T-shirt/ball-cap combo for just $20, you'll also note the hoodies priced at $60. Remember that the less you buy when you first arrive, the less you'll have to carry—and the less you'll have to remember to take with you off the tour buses. There are no rental lockers at the Visitor Complex.

PART SEVEN

SEAWORLD

A WORLD-CLASS MARINE-LIFE THEME PARK, SeaWorld is the odd middle child of Central Florida's mega-parks—without the allure of Mickey Mouse or the glitz of the movie-studio attractions. For years, this park succeeded by appealing to those who appreciated the wonder of sea creatures such as killer whales and dolphins. Walt Disney World may have cornered the market on make-believe, but SeaWorld offered the unique opportunity of watching people interact with live animals.

As competition for tourists' time increased and Disney ventured into the wild-animal business with its Animal Kingdom, SeaWorld created new interactive encounters that can't be found at any other area park. SeaWorld also added thrill rides, including a flight simulator, multiple roller coasters, and a hybrid flume-coaster. Combined with the charm of the animals, these attractions and several entertaining shows have created a whole new SeaWorld that isn't just for the fish-and-whale crowd. Many *Unofficial Guide* readers consider the park to be a favorite part of an Orlando vacation.

unofficial **TIP**
If you and, yes, even your kids, tire of imitation animals like Minnie and Mickey, try a day at SeaWorld.

A family from England writes:

The best-organized park [is] SeaWorld. The printout we got on arrival had a very useful show schedule, told us which areas were temporarily closed due to construction, and had a readily understandable map. Best of all, there was almost no queuing. We rated this day so highly that it is the park we would most like to visit again.

A woman from Alberta, Canada, gives her opinion:

We chose SeaWorld as our fifth day in Orlando. What a pleasant surprise! It was every bit as good (and in some ways better) than WDW itself. Well worth the admission, an excellent entertainment value, educational, well run, and better value for the dollar in food services.

A reader from Sylvania, Georgia, believes Disney could learn a thing or two from SeaWorld:

Disney ought to take a look at how well this place is run. I know they don't have the same crowds or the exciting rides, but there is still a lot of entertainment here and never a wait. This allows you to set your pace without worrying about what you'll have to miss. You'll see it all no matter how you do it, you'll come away feeling that you got better value for your dollars, you won't feel as tired as a Disney day, and you will probably learn more too. The only downside is that you'll probably be hungry. Food is not one of the park's assets.

On top of its accumulated charms, SeaWorld also boasts its aquatic sub-park, Discovery Cove. Here, you can swim with live dolphins. All of this makes SeaWorld a great way to shift gears from the Mouse race, while still enjoying the big production values of a major theme park desti-

unofficial **TIP**
There's more than just marine life at this well-organized park to keep everyone entertained.

nation. Unfortunately, we'd be remiss not to mention the elephant—or orca, rather—in the room. The 2010 death of trainer Dawn Brancheau and the 2013 film *Blackfish* have brought questions about SeaWorld's care for its large marine mammals into the mainstream media. We've personally seen both how much SeaWorld's frontline employees care about their animal charges, and the challenging circumstances that they sometimes operate under. Both extremes of the argument—that SeaWorld should immediately release its killer whales to the wild and that SeaWorld should completely dismiss any criticism—seem equally untenable. But even if you have no interest whatsoever in the issue, it's impossible to ignore how the controversy has affected the park. As SeaWorld's stock and profits have precipitously fallen, so have mainte-nance and operations standards. On our latest visit, we were distressed to see peeling paint, damaged displays, and malfunctioning equipment in far too many attractions, while staffing cutbacks have made queues crawl far slower than their maximum capacity, making a modestly busy weekday feel like a holiday crowd. Newly installed SeaWorld Parks CEO Joel Manby, who was lauded for his work with Herschend Family Entertainment, is attempting to turn things around with new thrill rides and animal enclosures as the chain celebrates its 50th anniversary. But for the moment, returning guests better brace themselves; though the animals are still as enthralling as ever, the theme park side of SeaWorld may not live up to your warm memories.

GETTING THERE

SEAWORLD IS ABOUT 10 MILES EAST of Walt Disney World. Take I-4 to FL 528/Beachline Highway East. Exit at the first ramp, which is International Drive. Turn left off the exit ramp. Turn right at Central Florida Parkway. The entrance to SeaWorld is on the right just prior to a large SeaWorld sculpture. Car and motorcycle parking is $17, and preferred parking is available for $20 in a lot closer to the main entrance that fills up quickly. RV and camper parking is $22. Discovery Cove is directly across the Central Florida Parkway from SeaWorld. Parking at the Discovery Cove lot is free.

Strollers are available for rent for $15 (single) or $25 (double). Wheelchairs are $12, and electronic convenience vehicles (ECVs) are $50. All-day lockers—located outside the park exit, behind Shamu's Emporium, and inside Antarctica—cost $10 for a small locker, $13 for a large locker, or $15 for a jumbo locker; a $10 refundable key deposit is required. If you just want to stow items before a ride, you can rent one-time use lockers at Journey to Atlantis, Kraken, Manta, and Shamu's Happy Harbor for $1 for the first hour, $2 for each additional hour.

ADMISSION PRICES

EXCEPT UNDER THE MOST CROWDED CONDITIONS, a typical visitor can see most (if not all) of SeaWorld in one solid day of touring, so a One-Day Pass makes sense. However, several options will get you a lot more time in the park for slightly more money than a one-day ticket. If you're planning to spend time at other local theme parks, consider the money-saving Orlando FlexTicket, good for admission to five or six parks (depending on the version you purchase). Several deals combine SeaWorld admission with tickets for sister parks Busch Gardens and the water park Adventure Island, both in Tampa. Discounts are available for Florida residents, AAA members, disabled visitors, senior citizens, and military personnel. All tickets, even the FlexTicket, can be purchased on the park's website (**seaworld.com**). Purchasing tickets online, from an authorized vendor, or from an authorized ticket agent in Orlando will save you from the logjam at the park ticket kiosks, and purchasing online also will save you a few dollars. SeaWorld is also the first major area park to experiment with airline-style variable pricing; if you order online, you can get a weekday-only ticket for up to $27 below the any-day gate price. If you fail to obtain tickets in advance, try the electronic ticket machines located outside SeaWorld's main gate and to the right of the ticket kiosks. To use the machines, bring your credit card and your patience. The touch screen interface is temperamental at best, and the purchase process more complicated than necessary. Follow the instructions as you would with an ATM. When you are finished—it will take about 3–5 minutes per purchase—the machine will print out your tickets.

unofficial **TIP**
It's a major time- and money-saver to pay admission before heading to the park.

ONE-DAY PASS Adults **$97** + tax • Children ages 3–9 **$92** + tax • Children under age 3 **Free**

14-DAY PASS TO SEAWORLD ORLANDO AND AQUATICA Age 3 and older **$135** + tax • Children under age 3 **Free**

14-DAY PASS TO SEAWORLD ORLANDO AND BUSCH GARDENS Age 3 and older **$145** + tax • Children under age 3 **Free**

14-DAY PASS TO SEAWORLD ORLANDO, AQUATICA, AND BUSCH GARDENS Age 3 and older **$165** + tax • Children under age 3 **Free**

Fun Card

This pass is good only for residents of Florida and is by far the best deal for admission to SeaWorld, but there are a few catches. For the same price as the One-Day Pass, you get unlimited admission to SeaWorld through December 31. There's also a combination ticket that allows admission to both Busch Gardens and SeaWorld. Fun Cards don't get free parking or other Annual Pass–holder benefits.

SEAWORLD ORLANDO FUN CARD Adults **$97** + tax • Children ages 3-9 **$92** + tax • Children under age 3 **Free**

SEAWORLD ORLANDO AND BUSCH GARDENS FUN CARD Age 3 and older **$169** + tax • Children under age 3 **Free**

Annual Passes

These allow unlimited admission to either SeaWorld alone or a combination of SeaWorld, Aquatica, or Busch Gardens for one or two years and include free general parking and 10% off merchandise and food purchases in the park(s). The Platinum includes admission to 10 parks across the country and also includes free parking, ride-again privileges on some rides, and 10% off food and merchandise purchases in the park(s).

ONE-YEAR ANNUAL PASS Age 3 and older **$156** + tax • Children under age 3 **Free**

TWO-YEAR ANNUAL PASS Age 3 and older **$235** + tax • Children under age 3 **Free**

SEAWORLD AND AQUATICA ONE-YEAR PASS Age 3 and older **$192** + tax • Children under age 3 **Free**

SEAWORLD AND AQUATICA TWO-YEAR PASS Age 3 and older **$292** + tax • Children under age 3 **Free**

SEAWORLD AND BUSCH GARDENS ONE-YEAR PASS Age 3 and older **$216** + tax • Children under age 3 **Free**

SEAWORLD AND BUSCH GARDENS TWO-YEAR PASS Age 3 and older **$317** + tax • Children under age 3 **Free**

SEAWORLD, AQUATICA, AND BUSCH GARDENS ONE-YEAR PASS Age 3 and older **$252** + tax • Children under age 3 **Free**

SEAWORLD, AQUATICA, AND BUSCH GARDENS TWO-YEAR PASS Age 3 and older **$352** + tax • Children under age 3 **Free**

PLATINUM PASSPORT (one year) Age 3 and older **$336** + tax • Children under age 3 **Free**

PLATINUM PASSPORT (two years) Age 3 and older **$506** + tax • Children under age 3 **Free**

Orlando FlexTicket

This pass is good for up to 14 consecutive days at six parks: Busch Gardens, Universal Studios Florida, Universal's Islands of Adventure, SeaWorld, Aquatica, and Wet 'n Wild. There's also a version that excludes Busch Gardens, so be sure to get the one you want. Prices include tax.

FLEXTICKET Adults **$394.03** • Children ages 3-9 **$378.05**

FLEXTICKET PLUS Adults **$415.43** • Children ages 3-9 **$399.45**

Continued on page 166

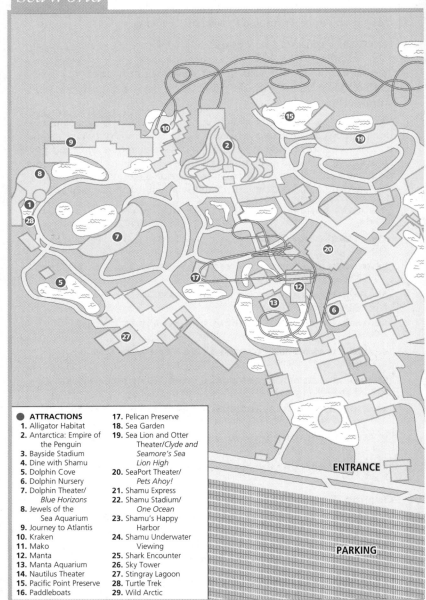

SeaWorld

ATTRACTIONS
1. Alligator Habitat
2. Antarctica: Empire of the Penguin
3. Bayside Stadium
4. Dine with Shamu
5. Dolphin Cove
6. Dolphin Nursery
7. Dolphin Theater/ *Blue Horizons*
8. Jewels of the Sea Aquarium
9. Journey to Atlantis
10. Kraken
11. Mako
12. Manta
13. Manta Aquarium
14. Nautilus Theater
15. Pacific Point Preserve
16. Paddleboats
17. Pelican Preserve
18. Sea Garden
19. Sea Lion and Otter Theater/*Clyde and Seamore's Sea Lion High*
20. SeaPort Theater/ *Pets Ahoy!*
21. Shamu Express
22. Shamu Stadium/ *One Ocean*
23. Shamu's Happy Harbor
24. Shamu Underwater Viewing
25. Shark Encounter
26. Sky Tower
27. Stingray Lagoon
28. Turtle Trek
29. Wild Arctic

ENTRANCE

PARKING

Continued from page 163

QuickQueue

Like Busch Gardens, SeaWorld offers a paid line-skipping service called QuickQueue. Participating attractions include all the roller coasters, Antarctica: Empire of the Penguin, Turtle Trek, Wild Arctic, and the Sky Tower. QuickQueue costs between $19 and $34 (depending on season) per person per day for unlimited usage; single-use QuickQueue passes can be purchased for some rides using SeaWorld's mobile app. If you arrive before opening and follow our touring advice, QuickQueue shouldn't be necessary, but it's a welcome luxury if you arrive midmorning on a busy day.

ARRIVING

SEAWORLD OFFICIALLY OPENS AT 9 A.M. Ropes to the north side of the park drop at 10 a.m., except during the busiest times of year, when the entire park opens all at once. Closing time fluctuates from 6 or 7 p.m. in the late fall and winter to 9 or 10 p.m. in the summer and on holidays.

Exploring SeaWorld takes a full day. Because the majority of attractions are shows, it won't be a mad rush to avoid lines like at other theme parks. However, avoiding the rare long wait and large crowds requires getting there early during busy times of the year. Like other area parks, SeaWorld opens its turnstiles at either 8:30 a.m. or 8:45 a.m. depending on the season, which means that you can enter the park before the scheduled opening. You can only wander around a limited area with a bakery and a few shops, however. Nonetheless, during peak season, we suggest that you arrive no later than 8:20 a.m., allowing time to park and purchase tickets. At other times, arriving at 8:40 a.m. should give you a jump on the crowds.

While a member of your party purchases tickets, have another track down a SeaWorld map. Map-toting employees are usually positioned in front of the ticket booth. While waiting for the park to open, plan your attack.

During peak season, if you're a fan of water thrill rides, locate the quickest route to Journey to Atlantis, which combines elements of a water ride and dry roller coaster. When the ropes drop, head straight there. You'll be tempted to stop at animal exhibits along the route, but save those for later. The line for Journey to Atlantis will be most manageable early in the day.

Otherwise, head straight to Empire of the Penguin. If the wait there is more than 30 minutes, try again in the early evening. If roller coasters are your thing, head for the Manta coaster first, and then ride Empire of the Penguin. The coaster is clearly visible from the main entrance. After Manta (or Empire of the Penguin, depending on which you rode first), hustle over to Kraken, located at the back of the park between Journey to Atlantis and Antarctica: Empire of the Penguin.

When attendance isn't at its highest, lines for Journey to Atlantis and Kraken can be quite short. Because Manta is located close to the park entrance, its lines are only short immediately after park opening, regardless of season. At those slower times of the year, or if you don't like water rides or coasters, plan to hurry to Dolphin Cove in the Key West area when the park opens. In addition to beating the bulk of the crowd, you'll get to see the animals at their most active time in the morning. But if the dolphins are one of your main reasons for visiting SeaWorld, use your morning visit to book an appointment for an up close interaction at the mint-green house on the left side of the pool.

Arrange the remainder of your day around the show schedule. Attractions encircle a large lagoon, and the best strategy to see it all is to travel clockwise. This tactic depends on the entertainment schedule, of course, but at the very least, allow time to see the attractions in the area surrounding each show. You will save time and energy by not roaming aimlessly, and there's not much point in rushing—the entertainment schedule is not designed for immediate back-to-back viewing of shows.

Walt Disney World might be known for its friendly, informative cast members, but it certainly hasn't cornered the market. At each animal exhibit in SeaWorld, you can find pleasant and extremely knowledgeable employees who will share interesting information and answer any questions.

SeaWorld also allows visitors to view training sessions that occur at many of the show stadiums. A schedule for these sessions isn't published, but if you're near any of the stadiums between shows, pop in. You can also hang out a bit after a show to possibly catch some unscripted action.

CONTACTING SEAWORLD

FOR MORE INFORMATION, call ☎ 877-557-7404 or visit the SeaWorld website at **seaworldorlando.com.** If you or your children are interested in learning more about the park's animals before visiting, SeaWorld also maintains a website designed for students and teachers at **seaworld.org.** If you have an iPhone or Android, download the official SeaWorld app for maps, showtimes, games, and the ability to skip lines.

▌ ▌ ATTRACTIONS

Alligator Habitat ★★

APPEAL BY AGE	PRESCHOOL ★★½	GRADE SCHOOL ★★½	TEENS ★★★
YOUNG ADULTS ★	OVER 30 ★½		SENIORS ★★

What it is Outdoor alligator viewing. **Scope and scale** Diversion. **When to go** Anytime. **Authors' rating** Easy to miss; ★★.

DESCRIPTION AND COMMENTS The exhibit is located on the walkway directly beside the entrance to Turtle Trek. The docile gators don't move much except at feeding times, which occur randomly throughout the day, but asking a nearby attendant may get you the schedule for your visit.

TOURING TIPS This is not Gatorland, and the guys in the habitat are small, but for those who've never seen Florida's most famous residents, it's worth a peek.

Antarctica: Empire of the Penguin ★★★½

APPEAL BY AGE	PRESCHOOL ★★★½	GRADE SCHOOL ★★★★	TEENS ★★★★
YOUNG ADULTS ★★★★		OVER 30 ★★★★	SENIORS ★★★★

What it is Combination dark ride and penguin exhibit. Scope and scale Super-headliner. When to go First 30 minutes the park is open. Special comments Attraction temperature is set for the comfort of the penguins. There are two versions of this ride, and the wild version has a 42″ minimum height requirement (there's no height requirement for the mild version). Authors' rating Wildlife component is exceptional; ★★★½. Duration of ride 4 minutes. Loading speed Moderate.

DESCRIPTION AND COMMENTS Antarctica: Empire of the Penguin is the largest expansion project in the park's history at 4 acres. It encompasses shops, a restaurant, and a beverage station, as well as a dark ride and an extensive penguin viewing area, all carved into a canyon of faux ice and rocks. At the Empire's center is, what else, the South Pole, here represented by a sort of barber pole with a reflective globe on top. Pleasant enough during the day, the area is particularly compelling after dark with the white and periwinkle-blue hues of the ice peaks illuminated both from within and without.

The centerpiece of the theme area is the combination Empire of the Penguin dark ride and live penguin exhibit. For the ride, you can choose a mild or wild version. Concerning the latter, it spins and bumps, but to call it wild is a bit over the top. Both mild and wild renditions glide through the same scenes. We preferred the mild ride because it's easier to see the various scenes if you're not spinning around, plus the "thrills" you're missing hardly surpass Dumbo.

The experience begins with a preshow introducing Puck, a newly hatched gentoo penguin. After the preshow, you come to a junction where you have to make your mild versus wild decision. Next you board an eight-person "Antarctic saucer" and get under way. The saucer's movements are controlled by a one-of-a-kind, motion-based, trackless ride system developed by Oceaneering International, the same company that created, among others, the ride system for The Amazing Adventures of Spider-Man at Islands of Adventure. Each battery-powered saucer consists of an upper and lower platform. You sit atop the upper platform, which provides up-and-down and swaying movement. The base (lower) platform allows omnidirectional lateral movement. The overall effect is that of randomly floating.

You drift through a convoluted ice cavern bathed in more colors than Ben & Jerry has flavors. Projections of Puck chronicle his growth and development leading up to his first leap into the sea. His timing is bad, however, and he's hardly splashed down before being beset by a leopard seal. Naturally he survives, but the fish sandwich he was craving will have to wait.

An interesting aspect is that, as you progress through the ride, the temperature continues to drop until it bottoms out at about 30°F, the ambient temperature of the live penguin habitat at the end. Presumably SeaWorld could have separated the penguins from the people with a plexiglass wall, allowing the viewing area to be heated, but then guests might linger overlong observing the colony. Trust us—if you board the ride wearing a T-shirt, shorts, and flip-flops, you will not spend half the day admiring the penguins.

Disembarking from the ride, you enter the penguin habitat, housing almost 250 birds, including gentoo, king, rockhopper, and Adélie penguins. You can view the tuxedoed residents either above or below water. The habitat is by far the highlight of the overall experience. Lighting is consistent with light at Antarctica for any given time of year. Thus, if you visit during the summer, which is winter in Antarctica, you may find the exhibit a little dark for your tastes. You can stay and watch as long as you want or, more to the point, as long as you can stand the cold. The exhibit is fun for the penguins too— they love it when you do jumping jacks. The length of the experience varies according to how long you stand shivering in the habitat, but the preshow, the ride, and 10 minutes viewing the penguins would put the total time at about 20 minutes plus. Despite the impressive technology in play, the ride's placid pacing and poor computer graphics can't live up to the expectations raised by the awe-inspiring exterior, and the attraction's best element will be blown past by many warmth-seeking riders. If you wait more than 20 minutes for this attraction, you'll likely end up disappointed.

TOURING TIPS If you're inordinately fond of penguins, it's probably worth it to bring a sweater and a jacket (you can store them in a locker when not in use). For the rest, you'll most likely surrender to the cold before you're really ready to leave, but that's the way SeaWorld planned it. Because it's new, the ride draws huge crowds as soon as the park opens, and there's lots more competition early in the day for the Empire of the Penguin ride because, unlike the Kraken and Manta coasters, the ride is available to all ages and sizes. To avoid a long wait, arrive 30 minutes before the park opens, admission in hand, and ride first thing. From the park entrance, bear left around the Manta lagoon past the Manta Aquarium and the Pelican Preserve. At the T-intersection, go left, and then take your first right along the back side of the Dolphin Theater. You'll see Antarctica ahead and on your right. If Manta is more important than Antarctica, ride it first, and then head for the penguins. After the penguins, ride Kraken.

The Empire of the Penguin ride saw waits of more than an hour during the summer of 2015, which is not surprising, because it can accommodate only about 1,000 guests per hour. If you encounter a wait longer than 30 minutes when you arrive at Antarctica, your best bet is to try again after sunset. Waits during the evening hours average 25 minutes or less.

kids *Blue Horizons*/**Dolphin Theater** ★★½

APPEAL BY AGE PRESCHOOL ★★★½	GRADE SCHOOL ★★★★	TEENS ★★★
YOUNG ADULTS ★★★	OVER 30 ★★½	SENIORS ★★½

What it is A dolphin, bird, and acrobatics show. Scope and scale Headliner. When to go Check daily entertainment schedule. Authors' rating A hodgepodge of animals and humans doing tricks that we've seen before; ★★½. Duration of show Less than 25 minutes.

DESCRIPTION AND COMMENTS The *Blue Horizons* show—which includes dolphins, macaws, acrobats, high divers, spraying water, a huge set with an enormous truss, and a loud ballad score—is one of the premier attractions at SeaWorld. With all of these elements, the show should succeed.

Unfortunately, it contains critical flaws. The plot is minimal: Creatures of the sea and sky show us the way to become guardians of Earth. Despite the many disparate elements, the show contains lulls in action.

The show opens with a young woman named Marina opening a door into a fantasy world, and after that, the plot goes hither and yon. Without some foreknowledge—and even with it—the later appearance of a lady in bird costume with her minions of birdman-acrobats is somewhat disconcerting and confusing. This lady is *supposed* to represent the Spirit of the Sky, while her male counterpart in the water is *supposed* to represent the Spirit of the Sea. Instead, he comes across as the young woman's interspecies love interest, partly because of his dolphin-gray costume that counters the young woman's pink costume, but more because of a bit too much frolicking.

The title, *Blue Horizons,* is derived from the horizon line where sky and sea meet. The young woman wants to be part of the sky and the sea, and so does the set. The set's scale is impressive but the look is less so; the large orbs attached to the backdrop are meant to simultaneously represent clouds and bubbles but look like poorly painted globs of glue.

Later in the show, four male high divers perform simple maneuvers on the way into the pool, and then two other fellows, wearing odd toe-to-head costumes with feathered headpieces, do some bungee maneuvers toward the pool as they hang from elastic cords.

Even with the flaws, the show's animal stunts are interesting—and for those who have never seen trained dolphins leap into the air or propel human trainers across the pool, both above and below the water, even impressive. The cetaceans perform a few synchronized maneuvers, use their tails to splash water on the front rows, and spin underwater while two flights of three macaws fly about accompanied by a symphonic score.

Still, most of these watery tricks are not new, and the choreography seems as if too many ideas were thrown out on the table back at SeaWorld HQ, but no one said, "Let's not do that." This show appeals mainly to the youngsters or to those who never saw *Flipper* on TV decades ago.

TOURING TIPS The audience can enter the Dolphin Theater from either the left, near the Dolphin Cove pool, or the right, beneath the coils of the Manta ride. Wheelchair users may enter in the center of the stadium, using a less-steep ramp. Try to arrive at least 20 minutes before the show starts to get the best seats: middle-height rows, middle of the theater. Remember that there is a splash zone for the first few rows, but the spraying is not as intense as it is at the killer whale show. Seats in the very back have their view of the high dives obscured by the stadium's roof.

Clyde and Seamore's Sea Lion High/ Sea Lion and Otter Stadium   ★★★½

APPEAL BY AGE PRESCHOOL ★★★★	GRADE SCHOOL ★★★★	TEENS ★★★
YOUNG ADULTS ★★★½	OVER 30 ★★★	SENIORS ★★★

What it is Show featuring sea lions, otters, and a walrus. Scope and scale Headliner. When to go Check daily entertainment schedule. Authors' rating Unabashed cornball comedy; ★★★½. Duration of show 30 minutes.

DESCRIPTION AND COMMENTS One of three headlining shows at Sea-World, the signature sea lion production was completely overhauled for

2015 with a new set, script, and high school theme. Before the show starts, a comical crossing guard warms up the seated audience with physical shtick while "helping" seat arriving guests. He doesn't mock incoming individuals as mercilessly as the previous show's pirate mime did, nor is he quite as funny.

The show proper puts us inside Sea Lion High just before graduation, with our sea lion stars Clyde and Seamore set to flunk out and lose their scholarships unless they can pass four finals before day's end. One at a time, the pair tackle drama class (re-creating scenes from *Jaws*), chemistry (learning that all drains do lead to the ocean), dance (doing the tango with a rose in their mouths), and gym (featuring a climactic high dive). The goofy story line features a hysterical lunch-lady cameo and copious kid-friendly bathroom humor, while taking some clever pokes at teen movie tropes that parents raised on movies directed by John Hughes will chuckle at. It also takes a self-aware and self-deprecating stance by winking to the audience when (not if) the sea lions make mistakes. Due to the strong ensemble work between trainers and animals—including the supporting otter and walrus cast members—as well as the better-than-average script that showcases the animals' talents, this refreshed show is once again the funniest and fastest paced performance at SeaWorld.

TOURING TIPS   This attraction draws a crowd, so attempt to arrive up to 45 minutes ahead of showtime. Take the first dozen rows' splash-zone signs seriously; the water cannons installed around the set mean business.

Dolphin Cove   ★★★★

| APPEAL BY AGE PRESCHOOL ★★★ | GRADE SCHOOL ★★★★ | TEENS ★★★★ |
| YOUNG ADULTS ★★★★ | OVER 30 ★★★★ | SENIORS ★★★★ |

What it is Outdoor dolphin habitat. **Scope and scale** Major attraction. **When to go** In the morning to register for scheduled interactions. **Authors' rating** Impressive; ★★★★.

DESCRIPTION AND COMMENTS   This sprawling, 2-acre habitat is filled with a community of swimming and leaping dolphins. Any guest can stand in a small section along one side of the pool and observe the dolphins. A path along the opposite side of the pool leads to an overlook area with excellent views and a great photo location. Next to the overlook is a walkway to an underwater viewing area that provides the best glimpse of these mammals in action. The interior walkway is air-conditioned and one of the most memorable sights at SeaWorld.

TOURING TIPS   SeaWorld has ceased selling fish for guests to feed to the dolphins (so as to better manage their diets) and restricted access to portions of the habitat where guests can touch the creatures. Instead, you must register for an extra-cost Dolphin Encounter, where, for $15 per person, you'll get 5 minutes of up close interaction with a bottlenose. You can shake fins, have a splash battle, play fetch with floating balls, and pose for photos (for an additional fee, natch). Book your encounter at the Reservations Counter near the front entrance or at the greenhouse near the dolphin pool; sign up early because slots can fill up before lunch. Also be aware that Dolphin Cove closes as early as 6 p.m., even on nights when the park is open late.

Dolphin Nursery   ★★

APPEAL BY AGE	PRESCHOOL ★		GRADE SCHOOL ★★		TEENS ★
YOUNG ADULTS ★★			OVER 30 ★★		SENIORS ★★

What it is Outdoor pool for expectant dolphins or mothers and calves. **Scope and scale** Diversion. **When to go** Anytime. **Authors' rating** Only worth a quick glimpse unless a baby is present; ★★.

DESCRIPTION AND COMMENTS Seeing this tiny pool that used to be the sole dolphin experience at SeaWorld should make you appreciate Dolphin Cove and Discovery Cove all the more. But the small size is perfect for its current purpose—providing a separate area for pregnant dolphins and new moms and calves. Stop by for a quick glance if it's an expectant dolphin. Stay longer if there's a baby in the pool.

TOURING TIPS This area will be roped off and guests understandably kept away when a dolphin goes into labor. Because it's near the park entrance, swing by on your way out to see if the area has reopened, and you might be able to view mom and baby.

Just behind the Dolphin Nursery is a pleasant and secluded area. Follow the path next to the pool and seat yourself on a smallish wall topped by decorative paving stones. You'll be partially shaded by tall bamboo trees and can still enjoy a view of the nursery pool.

kids Journey to Atlantis   ★★

APPEAL BY AGE	PRESCHOOL †		GRADE SCHOOL ★★★		TEENS ★★★
YOUNG ADULTS ★★½			OVER 30 ★★		SENIORS ★★

† Preschoolers are generally too short to ride.

What it is Water ride and roller coaster combo. **Scope and scale** Headliner. **When to go** Before 10 a.m. or after 4 p.m. during peak season; avoid visiting immediately after a Dolphin Theater show. **Special comments** 42" minimum height requirement; pregnant women or people with heart, back, or neck problems should not ride. **Authors' rating** Once cheesy but fun, now just cheesy; ★★. **Duration of ride** 6 minutes. **Loading speed** Moderate.

DESCRIPTION AND COMMENTS Riders board eight-passenger boats and plunge down a nearly vertical 60-foot waterfall before careening through a mini–roller coaster. Though this ride is housed in a truly impressive edifice that spouts fire and water, the payoff inside is pretty meager. The attraction supposedly takes guests on a voyage through Atlantis as they try to avoid an evil spirit, but even after several trips, we still didn't have a good grasp on this story line (what's up with that goldfish, or sea horse, or whatever it was?). And though the effects weren't extraordinary when working, so many of them are now malfunctioning or muted that whatever point the ride once had is made completely moot. For that reason, and because of an "it's over before you know it" feeling, we have to give the ride lower marks than those of Disney's Splash Mountain and Universal's Dudley Do-Right's Ripsaw Falls.

TOURING TIPS Closer to sunset, the special effects in this attraction are more intense because the darker evening sky helps keep light from leaking into the ride when the boats travel outdoors. However, during peak seasons, the wait in line can be an hour or longer, and we don't think

Journey to Atlantis is worth that much of your time. For best results, arrive early and dash to this attraction when the park opens at 9 a.m. (or immediately after riding Manta and/or Antarctica) to minimize the wait. Then stop by in the evening and ride again if the line isn't too long.

Journey to Atlantis will get you wet, especially in the front seats. If you want to minimize the drenching, bring a poncho or purchase one at the gift shop at the attraction. Place any items that you don't want to get soaked, such as cameras, in the pay lockers near the entrance to the queue. Free bins are available at the loading dock, but they are not secured. Jewels of the Seas Aquarium is a single round room tucked inside the ride's gift shop, whose walls and floor are covered in aquatic habitats containing luminescent jellyfish, clown fish, and other colorful creatures. You'll pass by it while exiting the attraction, or you can enter it without waiting in the queue.

Kraken ★★★★

APPEAL BY AGE	PRESCHOOL †	GRADE SCHOOL ★★★★	TEENS ★★★★
YOUNG ADULTS ★★★½		OVER 30 ★★★	SENIORS ★

† Preschoolers are generally too short to ride.

What it is Roller coaster. **Scope and scale** Super-headliner. **When to go** Immediately following a ride on Manta or Empire of the Penguin. **Special comments** 42″ minimum height requirement; pregnant women or people with heart, back, or neck problems should not ride. **Authors' rating** A real brain rattler; ★★★★. **Duration of ride** 3 minutes. **Loading speed** Moderate.

DESCRIPTION AND COMMENTS The impressive coaster, named after the mythological underwater beast, features a top speed of 65 miles per hour, a length of more than 4,000 feet, and a first drop of 144 feet. This floorless coaster puts riders in 32 open-sided seats, in eight rows, riding on a pedestal above the track. It's a sort of combination of the newer inverted coasters (where riders dangle in seats, rather than sit in cars) with the open ceiling of a traditional coaster. The net effect is that nothing up, down, or sideways blocks your view, an especially amazing effect on that first big drop—when it seems as though you're about to plunge right into a lake.

Despite its overall great fun, be warned that this coaster does not offer the smoothest ride. You will be jerked around a bit, and repeated rides may lead to woozy crab-walking.

TOURING TIPS This extremely popular coaster draws crowds, and with recent slow operations, it struggles to come anywhere close to moving 1,600 riders per hour (its theoretical maximum capacity). Even in peak season, the ride may not open until 10 a.m., and large lines will build once it does. We suggest that you arrive when the park opens; ride Manta, Antarctica, and Journey to Atlantis; and then immediately line up for Kraken's opening. You must put your large items in a pay locker while riding, or leave them with a non-rider.

Mako *(opens summer 2016)*

What it is Shark-inspired steel hyper-coaster. **Scope and scale** Super-headliner. **When to go** Before 10 a.m. or after 4 p.m. **Special comments** 54″ minimum height requirement. **Duration of ride** 3¼ minutes. **Loading speed** Moderate.

DESCRIPTION AND COMMENTS Gliding into the park like a shark silently stalking its prey, Mako will make its debut at SeaWorld in summer 2016, barely a year after construction began, as Orlando's tallest and fastest roller coaster—or at least until I-Drive's Skyscraper Polercoaster gets built. This latest Bolliger & Mabillard–manufactured scream machine will be the first in town to reach a height of 200 feet, and the 28-passenger trains will hit speeds of up to 73 miles per hour along the 4,760 feet of track, which will stretch along International Drive behind the existing Shark Encounter. Mako's design will emphasize out-of-seat air time over upside-down inversions, with nine distinct moments of weightlessness in the course. In addition to the physical thrills, guests get to explore ancient shipwrecks as they approach the ride and experience 48,000 watts of surround sound effects as the coaster cars dive over pedestrians' heads near the ride's finale.

For those unwilling to take the plunge, an adjacent Sharks Realm aquarium will supplement the existing Shark Encounter exhibits, creating an entire shark-themed mini-land.

TOURING TIPS With no dangling legs or loop-the-loops, Mako is intended to be less intense than Manta and Kraken, though it should still pack quite a bite. If open during your visit, ride first thing in the morning, or immediately after experiencing Manta and Antarctica.

Manta ★★★★★

APPEAL BY AGE PRESCHOOL †	GRADE SCHOOL ★★★★	TEENS ★★★★★
YOUNG ADULTS ★★★★★	OVER 30 ★★★★★	SENIORS ★★★★

† *Preschoolers are generally too short to ride.*

What it is Inverted steel super roller coaster. **Scope and scale** Super-headliner. **When to go** Before 10 a.m. or after 4 p.m. **Special comment** 54″ minimum height requirement. **Authors' rating** So much action that it's hard to take it in on just one ride; ★★★★★. **Duration of ride** 2½ minutes. **Loading speed** Moderate.

DESCRIPTION AND COMMENTS The king of SeaWorld rides, Manta is a steel coaster on which riders are arranged four across lying facedown beneath the expanse of a giant manta ray–shaped carriage. The coaster soars and swoops through a pretzel loop, a 360-degree in-line roll, and two corkscrews—not to mention a first drop of 113 feet. There are four inversions while Manta reaches a height of 140 feet and speeds of more than 55 miles per hour. But don't worry—lying facedown puts you in the perfect position to throw up. Actually, the ride is relatively smooth, though the action seems nonstop. If you get sick, it will be from the bugs you pick out of your teeth (keep your mouth closed at all times—you're supposed to be a ray, not a bat). The queuing area passes aquarium windows displaying rays and vividly colored fish.

TOURING TIPS Riders are not allowed to carry backpacks or shoulder bags on Manta; they must be left with non-riders or in nearby lockers that rent for $1. Before climbing into the Manta seats, riders with non-lacing shoes must leave them in wire baskets hanging at the exit fence. On busy days, up to three coaster trains can operate, serving about 1,000 guests per hour; on slower days, only one, so riders who have finished the course may hang, facing down, for another minute and a half while the carrier in front of theirs is loaded.

Which row you sit in makes more of a difference on Manta than most coasters. In the front row, the ride is relatively gentle and scenic; sitting in the back, you'll pull enough g's at the bottom of the inverted loop to make a jet pilot pass out.

Children too short for Manta or those park goers who don't want to accompany others on the ride can pass the time viewing a bevy of rays, a large Pacific octopus, darling sea horses, and more in the adjacent Manta Aquarium. Don't miss the two unique features: a ceiling aquarium where you can walk beneath swimming fish, and a crawl-into aquarium where smaller guests can pop their heads up into an underwater bubble.

kids *One Ocean/Shamu Stadium* ★★★★

| APPEAL BY AGE PRESCHOOL ★★★★½   GRADE SCHOOL ★★★★★   TEENS ★★★★★ |
| YOUNG ADULTS ★★★★★   OVER 30 ★★★★½   SENIORS ★★★★½ |

What it is Killer whale show. **Scope and scale** Super-headliner. **When to go** Check daily entertainment schedule. **Authors' rating** Designed to be the premier live-animal event at SeaWorld; ★★★★. **Duration of show** 25 minutes.

DESCRIPTION AND COMMENTS Following the shocking death of a trainer working with one of the killer whales just after a performance in February 2010, SeaWorld withdrew its orca trainers from the tanks at all of its parks. Now, no trainers will be in the water during any killer whale performances—at any SeaWorld park. Yet the theme of this show, *One Ocean,* which debuted in April 2011, is that humans and animals are connected, that ours is "one world united by one ocean," the narration says.

One Ocean has as many as six orcas at one time in the tank, fronting the 6,000-seat Shamu Stadium. Usually performing in pairs and the occasional foursomes, the mighty mammals swim and leap and even soar from the water for a full somersault. Typically, at least two orcas are simultaneously swimming past fountains, through curtains of water, and under shooting jets of water.

As with most celebrities, these killer whales are known by stage names—most notably, Shamu and Baby Shamu. Actually, at least 20 orcas have been born in the various SeaWorlds, so the animals on display here are of varying sizes and ages. While the orcas are all undeniably awe-inspiring, watching them go back and forth in similar patterns for nearly half an hour frankly gets a bit boring, and the nature footage screened on the blotchy Jumbotron (which is completely illegible from the stadium's sides) aren't any more compelling. It's also embarrassing watching the trainers try to dance and clap to the insipid soft rock sound track; apparently anyone with stage presence is sent to the sea lion show.

One thing has not changed from the previous choreographed show: The famous splash zone—the half-dozen or more rows of seats closest to the tank—is still a gonna-get-wet area for the guests there. Depending on which whales are doing the splashing with their tails, gallons and gallons of 55°F salt water are flung into those first rows. When the largest of the orcas performs that trick, it is a real crowd-pleaser, with the audience howling and cheering as folks get splashed. And some in the crowd, especially the under-12 set, make it a point to be in the water's path. During the summer and holidays, SeaWorld stages special versions of its Shamu shows just before the park closes. The orca's act remains pretty much the same, but the music is swapped out for rock and roll (or gospel, depending on the season), and the animal antics are supplemented with a brief pyrotechnic finale, launched over the lake behind the stadium. As far as fireworks go, SeaWorld's current displays are closer in quality to Universal's than Disney's and don't equal the old *IllumiNations*-esque laser show, which was watched from the now-unused Bayside Stadium. If you didn't see the daytime Shamu show, you should stick around for the evening one, but it's probably not worth waiting around for if you've already seen everything in the park long before showtime.

TOURING TIPS We're not kidding when we say gallons of chilly salt water. You will get soaked in the first few rows. If you or the kids think you're up for it, you might want to bring some extra clothes to change into after the cold shower. You should leave your cameras with someone out of the range of the corrosive salt water. Though this is a large stadium, you must arrive at least 20 minutes before the scheduled start to get a seat. Warming up the crowd before the shows is a video on training the orcas. There may be as few as two shows a day or as many as four; check the daily schedule for the times.

kids Pacific Point Preserve ★★★

APPEAL BY AGE	PRESCHOOL ★★★½	GRADE SCHOOL ★★★½	TEENS ★★★
YOUNG ADULTS ★★★		OVER 30 ★★★	SENIORS ★★★

What it is Outdoor sea lion habitat. **Scope and scale** Major attraction. **When to go** Feeding times (scattered throughout the day). **Authors' rating** Fun and startling; ★★★.

DESCRIPTION AND COMMENTS Let the sound of more than 50 barking sea lions and harbor seals lead you to this nifty area tucked behind Sea Lion and Otter Stadium. An elevated walkway behind a glass partition surrounds the sunken habitat. The animals can be found sunning themselves on the rocky terrain or lounging in the shallow waves. More often, though, they'll be barking impatiently—perhaps very impatiently—for a snack. Though these animals aren't trained, a few of the sea lions will improvise cute antics for food, such as mimicking you sticking out your tongue. Sometimes, they get so excited about a possible meal that their barking reaches amazing, earsplitting levels.

TOURING TIPS If you participate in a feeding, which costs $5 for one tray of fish (or $20 for five), watch out for the large, aggressive birds that lurk in this area. They are poised to steal the fish right out of your hand, snatch one in midair as you toss it to the sea lions, or even land on your head or shoulders to make a grab for the goods (we saw this happen twice).

Look closely at the animals and you might spot some adorable sea lion or harbor seal pups—especially if you visit during spring or summer.

Pets Ahoy!/SeaPort Theater ★★★½

APPEAL BY AGE	PRESCHOOL ★★★	GRADE SCHOOL ★★★	TEENS ★★½
YOUNG ADULTS ★★★		OVER 30 ★★★	SENIORS ★★★

What it is Show featuring trained pets. **Scope and scale** Major attraction. **When to go** Check daily entertainment schedule. **Authors' rating** The truth about cats and dogs? ★★★½. **Duration of show** 25 minutes.

DESCRIPTION AND COMMENTS Despite its cornball name—SeaWorld's need to uphold its nautical theme seems to exceed its need to reel in a crowd—the show remains a draw due to the elaborate integration of the beach-town set with the animals who inhabit it. The show is a series of skits that each imitate a Rube Goldberg machine: A dog pulls a lever that signals a cat to run across the stage that, in turn, signals a different cat to climb a rope onto a roof, and so on. The skits are accented with sound effects and music, as well as a basic plot that always ends with a humorous, if predictable, twist. The humans mostly remain mute and offstage (assuming that the animals remember their cues), aside from a brief mid-show interlude to introduce a special performer—such as a 140-pound Great Dane—and to plead on behalf of the local animal shelter, from where many of the cast members were rescued. At the end of the show, you can talk to the trainers and get close to the animals. Keep your eyes open, kids; you might spot a few creatures that Mom has *never even considered* for pets. We think that this is the funniest of the trained animal shows in the Orlando parks, and it's the only one that's air-conditioned (an important bonus).

TOURING TIPS SeaPort Theater is located on The Waterfront between the Sky Tower and the southern bridge that leads to Shamu Stadium. The theater is small, but because the show is not a headliner, seats are often available.

kids Shamu Express ★★½

APPEAL BY AGE	PRESCHOOL ★★★	GRADE SCHOOL ★★★½	TEENS ★★
YOUNG ADULTS ★½		OVER 30 ★★	SENIORS ★★

What it is Children's roller coaster. **Scope and scale** Minor attraction. **When to go** Avoid visiting after a Shamu show. **Special comment** Open 10 a.m.–1 hour before park closing. **Authors' rating** Thrill ride for kids; ★★½.

DESCRIPTION AND COMMENTS With Kraken towering over the park, riders under 42 inches tall may feel left out of the roller coaster market. Sea-World consoles its younger riders with the Shamu Express, located in Shamu's Happy Harbor. The coaster is very small, with only 800 feet of track, but the ride is smooth and makes a great starter coaster. Besides, who can resist cars shaped like the park's biggest star?

TOURING TIPS The roller coaster holds only 28 guests at a time, but the short track keeps the lines from piling up. Still, avoid the Shamu Express, and all of Happy Harbor, directly before and after performances at Shamu Stadium.

kids Shamu's Happy Harbor ★★★½

APPEAL BY AGE	PRESCHOOL ★★★	GRADE SCHOOL ★★★	TEENS ★
YOUNG ADULTS ★		OVER 30 ★	SENIORS ★★

What it is Children's play area. **Scope and scale** Minor attraction. **When to go** Avoid visiting after a Shamu show. **Special comments** Open 10 a.m.–1 hour before park closing; some attractions here have a maximum height requirement. **Authors' rating** A nice oversize playground; ★★★½.

DESCRIPTION AND COMMENTS Four stories of net span this 3-acre children's play area. Children and brave adults can climb, crawl, and weave through this net jungle. Other activities include an air bubble where kids under 54 inches tall can bounce and play, as well as an interactive submarine with several water cannons and fountains. An area for smaller kids (they must be under 42 inches tall) includes a standard ball-filled room and several playground contraptions. Standard carnival rides with aquatic theming are also located here.

TOURING TIPS Parents can grab a cool drink and relax at Coconut Cove while watching their children play. Most adults should stay clear of the patience-testing, headache-causing, steel drum area, where kids are allowed to bang to their hearts' content.

Shamu Underwater Viewing ★★★

APPEAL BY AGE	PRESCHOOL ★★	GRADE SCHOOL ★★★	TEENS ★★½
YOUNG ADULTS ★★★		OVER 30 ★★★	SENIORS ★★★

What it is Whale viewing area. **Scope and scale** Minor attraction. **When to go** Avoid visiting immediately before or after a Shamu show. **Authors' rating** Good look at these incredible animals; ★★★.

DESCRIPTION AND COMMENTS Go behind the scenes at Shamu Stadium for a peek at the stars of the show in their 1.5 million–gallon pool. Check the above-water viewing area for a training session or a veterinary visit. When standing "next to" these animals in the underwater viewing area, be prepared to be awestruck by their enormous size.

TOURING TIPS When the animals are not active, or not even present, this area is not worth visiting. Check with the SeaWorld employee usually stationed nearby for the best times to visit on a particular day.

Have your camera ready at the underwater viewing area. The whales usually slowly circle the pool, offering an amazing backdrop for a group photo.

Shark Encounter ★★★½

APPEAL BY AGE	PRESCHOOL ★★★	GRADE SCHOOL ★★★½	TEENS ★★★★
YOUNG ADULTS ★★★½		OVER 30 ★★★½	SENIORS ★★★½

What it is Exhibit of sharks, eels, and other dangerous sea creatures. **Scope and scale** Major attraction. **When to go** Anytime. **Authors' rating** Pleasantly creepy; ★★★½.

DESCRIPTION AND COMMENTS This walk-through exhibit immerses you (almost literally) in the frightening world of dangerous marine life. First, you are surrounded by moray eels as you walk through an acrylic tube at the bottom of a large aquarium. These eels peer out from lairs in an artificial tropical reef or undulate through the water. Next are several large aquariums housing poisonous fish, including the beautiful but lethal scorpion fish and the puffer fish, one of the world's deadliest. Then get ready for the grand finale—a 600,000-gallon tank filled with six species of sharks, including bull sharks, nurse sharks, and lemon sharks, as well as dozens of enormous grouper and other smaller fish. An entire wall of a large room gives a comprehensive view of this beautifully lit tank. Its amazing creatures will glide next to you and directly overhead as you pass through an acrylic tunnel. As you exit the tunnel, you'll learn that it supports 500 tons of salt water, but if necessary, it could handle nearly five times that weight—the equivalent of more than 370 elephants. A reassuring thought.

TOURING TIPS The crowd usually bottlenecks at the eel habitat. If possible, worm your way through the initial backup. The tube is fairly long, and you'll find the same great view with a smaller crowd near the other end.

You can get in on the feeding yourself, daily, at a small pool at the entrance to the exhibit. Purchase a tray of fish for $5 (five trays for $20) and toss them cheerfully to small hammerhead and nurse sharks.

Sky Tower ★★½

APPEAL BY AGE	PRESCHOOL ★★	GRADE SCHOOL ★★	TEENS ★★
YOUNG ADULTS ★★½		OVER 30 ★★½	SENIORS ★★★

What it is Scenic aerial ride. Scope and scale Minor attraction. When to go Anytime, though it's quite beautiful at night. Special comment While it previously cost additional, the Sky Tower is now free. Authors' rating ★★½. Duration of ride Nearly 7 minutes. Loading speed Slow.

DESCRIPTION AND COMMENTS Who doesn't enjoy getting a bird's-eye view of things? Plus, a ride to the top of the tower is somewhat calming. The tower has two levels of enclosed seats that rotate as they rise for great views of the park. It's amazing how serene the park looks—and how tiny the killer whales appear—from the top. On a clear day, you can see many other interesting sites, including downtown Orlando, the top of Spaceship Earth at Epcot, and the unmistakable toaster shape of Disney's Contemporary Resort.

TOURING TIPS This attraction closes if lightning or high winds pop up, and both are frequent in Central Florida. It also doesn't run during the peak season's nighttime fireworks display. The Sandbar Lounge at the bottom of the tower serves a variety of refreshments. Lines have been much longer for this glacially slow loader ever since it became included in park admission. If you must ride it, do so near opening or at the very end of the day.

Stingray Lagoon ★★★

APPEAL BY AGE	PRESCHOOL ★★	GRADE SCHOOL ★★★½	TEENS ★★★
YOUNG ADULTS ★★★		OVER 30 ★★★	SENIORS ★★½

What it is Stingray pool. Scope and scale Minor attraction. When to go Feeding times. Authors' rating Ray-riffic; ★★★.

DESCRIPTION AND COMMENTS The shallow water in this waist-high pool is filled with dozens of undulating stingrays. After the death of world-renowned zoologist Steve Irwin (the "Croc Hunter") in 2006 due to a stingray attack, these creatures seem even more menacing than before. However, all of the stingrays at SeaWorld continue to have their barbs removed, so they are not a threat to visitors. They may seem ominous, but they are actually quite mellow, and you shouldn't be afraid to stick your fingers into the tank and feel their silky skin.

TOURING TIPS Though a small tray of fish costs $5 (five trays for $20), don't miss feeding these graceful creatures. (Feedings are scheduled throughout the day.) The fish are slimy, and the tail end must be carefully placed between two fingers, but even the most squeamish in our group enjoyed the stingrays swimming over their hands and lightly sucking the food into their mouths.

kids Turtle Trek ★★★

APPEAL BY AGE	PRESCHOOL ★★★		GRADE SCHOOL ★★★½	TEENS ★★★
YOUNG	ADULTS ★★½	OVER 30 ★★½		SENIORS ★★

What it is Indoor/outdoor manatee and sea turtle habitats, with a 3-D animated film. **Scope and scale** Headliner. **When to go** Anytime. **Authors' rating** Remarkable animals in an easily viewed habitat, plus a 3-D film; ★★★. **Duration of show** 6 minutes for film.

DESCRIPTION AND COMMENTS This area is the repurposed Manatee Rescue attraction. Now you can look down on a tank of freshwater fish plus four manatees and, next to it, a tank of saltwater fish and several sea turtles. When you go to the belowground viewing area, a guide discusses the turtles and the dangers from man and predator to the hatchlings. Then you're given 3-D glasses and ushered into a domed, 360-degree projection area. On this unusual screen, 34 projectors show an animated film that lasts 6 minutes. The 3-D film gives the effect of viewing the ocean through the viewpoint of a sea turtle. While the virtual first-person odyssey—from hatching on a beach and surviving a crab attack to evading sharks and fishnets so you can return home to breed—should be immersive, obtrusive projector lights, murky images, and inconsistent animation intrude on the illusion. Small kids could find the film overwhelming, and adults are likely to find it anticlimactic. Not discussed in either the live presentation or the movie is that the manatees are also on the endangered species list. You only need to observe the horrendous scars from a boat propeller on the back of one of these manatees to see what is happening. All of the docile creatures in this exhibit were injured in the wild and have been rescued by SeaWorld. For most of the rescued animals, this is the last part of their rehabilitation, though none of the 11 sea turtles here can be returned to the wild, government conservationists have decreed.

TOURING TIPS To accommodate the maximum number of viewers in the domed theater, attendants count noses before allowing everyone to flow in to the two viewing rooms belowground. But once inside those rooms, there is no crowd control, so you may not get an unobstructed view of the two tanks. The solution: Immediately edge to the front toward the big windows of the first viewing room. On occasion, SeaWorld rescues orphaned baby manatees. Check with an educator in the area to find out if any are in the exhibit, if they might be bottle-fed, and at what time. It's pure, distilled cuteness.

Wild Arctic ★★★½

APPEAL BY AGE	PRESCHOOL ★★★	GRADE SCHOOL ★★★★	TEENS ★★★
YOUNG	ADULTS ★★★	OVER 30 ★★½	SENIORS ★★

What it is Simulator ride and animal exhibit. **Scope and scale** Major attraction. **When to go** Avoid going immediately following a Shamu show; waits will be shorter before 11 a.m. and after 4 p.m. **Authors' rating** Animal exhibit is better than the simulator; ★★★½. **Duration of ride** 5 minutes for simulator. **Loading speed** Moderate.

DESCRIPTION AND COMMENTS Wild Arctic combines a mediocre simulator ride with a spectacular animal habitat, featuring blubbery walruses and sweet-faced beluga whales. The usually long line gives you the option of not riding the simulator—a great idea if you're prone to motion sickness, or have experienced the superior simulators at Disney and Universal. Unfortunately, skipping the simulator will not allow you to enter Wild Arctic much sooner; you will still have to watch the simulator's movie before entering.

The simulator provides a bumpy ride aboard a specially designed 59-passenger "helicopter." Once passengers are safely strapped in, the ride ostensibly takes visitors to a remote Arctic research station (the wildlife habitat). On the way, riders fly over polar bears and walruses, but, of course, things go horribly wrong. A storm blows through, the engine inconveniently fails during an avalanche, and there is much wailing and gnashing of teeth. The loud hullabaloo and dated effects amount to nothing in particular, and in the end you make it to the station unscathed.

As you step off the simulator, or if you bypass it, you'll enter a cavernous, fog-filled room. A walkway on the far side overlooks a large pool that is home to a few beluga whales and, if you're lucky, some cute harbor seals. This room establishes the Arctic theme, but unless it's feeding time, the animals rarely surface here. Gigantic walruses often lounge near the glass or swim lazily by.

As you descend farther into the exhibit, you'll discover a deep, underwater viewing area, which gives you a real sense of the walruses' immense size. If it's quiet, you also can hear the deep, reverberating vocalizations of these large beasts. This is also the best location to catch a glimpse of the beluga whales. Looking like puffy, bulbous dolphins, these gentle creatures glide through the water. On occasion, a few playful harbor seals will join them. These crazy critters will come right up to the glass for a staring match with you.

TOURING TIPS Wild Arctic has two queues: By Air, which is for the simulator, and By Land, which still makes you watch the simulator movie but without all the jarring effects of the ride. Given the below-par quality of the simulator ride, we recommend skipping it if there's any line to speak of. If you are sneaky, you can enter the walk-through's exit through the gift shop and explore with no wait whatsoever. The animals are definitely worth seeing, though. As in all animal exhibits, several SeaWorld educators are scattered around to answer any questions.

The simulator holds nearly 60 riders, who flood the animal area after each trip. Hang back behind the crowd for a few minutes when the simulator off-loads and wait for the masses to clear. Then you can have the area next to the beluga whales mostly to yourself until the ride dumps off the next group.

If this isn't close enough to the whales for you, try the Beluga Interaction Program, where you can swim with, feed, and even attempt to signal to these sub-Arctic mammoths. The price for this program is not cheap (starting at $119 for adults or kids), and you need to make reservations online or by calling ☎ 888-800-5447. Participants must be at least 10 years of age; children under the age of 14 must be accompanied by a paying adult. For $59 and up, the Wild Arctic Up-Close tour takes guests age 8 and older behind the scenes for a 75-minute hands-on (though out-of-water) animal interaction.

TOURS

Behind-the-Scenes Tours ★★★★

APPEAL BY AGE	PRESCHOOL ★★★		GRADE SCHOOL ★★★½		TEENS ★★★★
YOUNG ADULTS ★★★★		OVER 30 ★★★★		SENIORS ★★★★	

What it is Get up close and personal with, and even touch and feed, the critters. **Scope and scale** Major attraction. **When to go** Advance reservations are a must. The tour times vary by the day, and on the day of your program you'll be instructed to check in (usually at the reservations desk) at least 30 minutes before your tour starts. **Special comment** Prices for the tours are $29–$119 for age 10 and up and $9–$59 for children ages 3-9. **Authors' rating** A wonderful experience; ★★★★.

DESCRIPTION AND COMMENTS Park staff lead groups, usually with a maximum of 16, behind the scenes to speak with the animals' caretakers, hear about the differences and peculiarities between animals of the same species, and, if these are performers, learn how they are trained.

The educational side may be too much for youngsters, but everyone loves the big event of each of the several tours: getting to touch and be photographed with a penguin, shark, or dolphin, or to feed stingrays, seals, and sea lions.

The basic 75-minute Behind-The-Scenes Tour includes interactions with penguins and a small shark and is priced starting at only $29 for adults, $9 for kids ages 3–9. Two shorter tours, the Sea Lion & Otter Up-Close Tour (1 hour: $44 for adults; $24 for kids 3–9) and Penguin Up-Close Tour (45 minutes: $59 for adults; $39 for kids 3–9), are built around specific species, while the Beluga Interaction Program and Wild Arctic Up-Close Tours (see page 181) are focused on residents of that attraction. Finally, the 6-hour Expedition Guided Tour combines front-of-the-line access to all the rides and reserved seating for three shows with animal feeding experiences, as well as unlimited all-day dining for yourself. Guided tours start at $79 for adults and $59 for children ages 3–9; much pricier private VIP tours are available on request if you don't want to be grouped with other families. Some VIP tours are offered only during the winter holiday season.

TOURING TIPS You must stop by the guided-tour counter at the front of the park on the day of your visit or reserve a spot on the park's website (**seaworldorlando.com**). If you want to take one of the tours, make a reservation online because spots fill quickly and it's first come, first served.

Taking an hour out of your SeaWorld visit for these tours will require careful planning, but for sea-life enthusiasts, it's a neat experience. Longer tours are also available, and the price increases with each of these tours, but places such as the Dolphin Nursery may be worth a few extra dollars.

Marine Mammal Keeper Experience ★★★

APPEAL BY AGE	PRESCHOOL †		GRADE SCHOOL †		TEENS ★★★★
YOUNG ADULTS ★★★★		OVER 30 ★★★		SENIORS ★★½	

† Preschoolers and grade-schoolers are not old enough to participate.

What it is Chance to shadow a SeaWorld trainer for a day. **Scope and scale** Major attraction. **When to go** Program begins at 6:30 a.m. **Special comments** Costs $399 plus tax (admission is included); participants must be at least 13 years old; 52" minimum height requirement. **Authors' rating** Extremely expensive but worth it for enthusiasts; ★★★.

DESCRIPTION AND COMMENTS Shadow a SeaWorld trainer during this 7-hour program. Learn through hands-on experience how SeaWorld staff members care for and train their animals, from stuffing vitamins into a slimy fish to positive-reinforcement training techniques. The fee includes lunch and a T-shirt.

TOURING TIPS Attendance for this program is limited to four people per day. Calling up to six months ahead is best, but cancellations do occur. For information and reservations, call ☎ 888-800-5447. Participants must be in good physical condition and at least 13 years old.

DINING

SEAWORLD OFFERS MUCH MORE than the usual theme park fare of burgers and fries. The food for the most part is very good, and prices are a bit lower than at Disney World.

Your feasting can begin at **Cypress Bakery,** which opens at 8:30 a.m. during the busy season and 8:45 a.m. otherwise. Choose from an array of wonderful pastries, cakes, and muffins to enjoy while you plan your day.

For a more toothsome experience, try **Sharks Underwater Grill** at the Shark Encounter attraction, which offers "Floribbean" cuisine served next to floor-to-ceiling windows on the shark tank. Appetizers cost $7–$15, and entrées run $29–$36 at this full-service eatery. The menu here offers sustainable seafood, steaks, chicken, and fresh salads.

SeaWorld's answer to the character meals with costumed mascots that other theme parks offer is **Dine with Shamu,** which lets you munch on a buffet meal while trainers put a multiton orca through its paces. Don't worry—plexiglass shields prevent you from getting soaked by playful splashing while you eat. The menu includes salads, jambalaya, pork loin, pepper steak, and pasta, along with chicken nuggets and hot dogs for the kids. The cost starts at $29 plus tax for adults, $19 plus tax for children ages 3–9.

For quick service, try **Mango Joe's Café** for grilled burgers and sandwiches, or **Seafire Inn** for fajitas and rice bowls. Along the Waterfront, there are several options, including the **Spice Mill,** a walk-up café with selections such as grilled-chicken Caesar salads, beef or garden burgers, and low-fat vegetable chili. **Voyager's Smokehouse** offers baby back ribs and smoked chicken, as well as kids' meals of chicken nuggets, hot dogs, or mac and cheese—with the option of substituting carrots for the standard side of fries.

Across from the SeaPort Theater is **Seaport Pizza,** with four kinds of pizza by the slice. Beyond Shamu Stadium and the Nautilus Theater, and worth the walk, the pleasant **Terrace Garden Buffet** has seating indoors and out. The menu is limited to barbecue ribs, chicken, and salad.

Park goers can also buy an All-Day Dining Option—$33 for adults, $18 for children—and get one entrée, one side or dessert, and one drink per visit to any of six restaurants, as well as buy-one/get-one-free snacks and beverages at selected carts. Unlike at Busch Gardens, SeaWorld's unlimited dining plan is valid on ribs and sampler platters.

SHOPPING

UNLIKE AT DISNEY, shopping at SeaWorld isn't an attraction in and of itself. There is, of course, a huge selection of SeaWorld merchandise. Some of it is unique, and prices are relatively reasonable. Fans of ocean wildlife can find a vast array of marine merchandise, ranging from high-quality, expensive sculptures to T-shirts, beach towels, and knickknacks. Children will be overwhelmed by the huge selection of stuffed animals, and parents will be pleased by their low prices—many small- to medium-size toys are priced under $10.

Along the Waterfront area, there are more shopping selections, such as the **Tropical Trading Company** with goods from Africa, Bali, and Indonesia, among other origins, and do-it-yourself shops such as a bead store and a doll factory. For a unique souvenir, ask a pearl diver at **The Oyster's Secret** near the Sky Tower to retrieve a shellfish while you watch through underwater windows; they'll extricate the organic gem inside and send it home with you for $16.95.

DISCOVERY COVE

INSPIRED BY A LARGE NUMBER OF REQUESTS for dolphin swims, as well as the success of the original Dolphin Interaction Program, SeaWorld created Discovery Cove in 2000. This intimate sub-park is a welcome departure from the hustle and bustle of other Orlando parks; the relaxed pace here could be the overstimulated family's ticket back to mental health. With a focus on personal service and one-on-one animal encounters, Discovery Cove admits only 1,200 guests per day. The park is also an all-inclusive experience, so once you enter, you don't need to open your wallet; provided are all meals, snacks, and beverages plus all animal interactions and swim gear, even parking and a pass to SeaWorld and Aquatica. The tranquil setting and unobtrusive theming make this park unique for Central Florida. Why, there are only two gift shops! And you don't even have to walk through them to get out!

The main draw at Discovery Cove is the chance to swim with an Atlantic bottlenose dolphin, from among the 45 here. The 30-minute dolphin swim experience is open to visitors age 6 and older who are comfortable in the water. The experience begins with an orientation led by trainers and an opportunity for participants to ask questions before entering the Dolphin Lagoon. Next, groups of six to eight guests wade into shallow water for an introduction to one of the dolphins in its habitat. Though this is not an inexpensive endeavor, the singular nature of the experience cannot be overstated. The dolphins are playful,

Discovery Cove

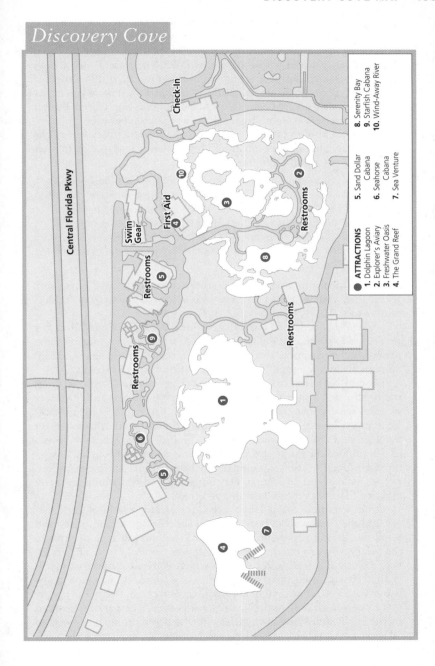

Check-In

Central Florida Pkwy

First Aid

Swim Gear

Restrooms

Restrooms

Restrooms

Restrooms

ATTRACTIONS
1. Dolphin Lagoon
2. Explorer's Aviary
3. Freshwater Oasis
4. The Grand Reef

5. Sand Dollar Cabana
6. Seahorse Cabana
7. Sea Venture

8. Serenity Bay
9. Starfish Cabana
10. Wind-Away River

friendly, and frankly amazing to be around. This is as hands-on as it gets. Be aware that you're dealing with a powerful, mischievous animal in its element, so don't be surprised if you get splashed, squirted, or even affectionately bonked with a flipper or fluke. The trainers are always in control, though, so there is nothing to fear. Overall, if this is to your taste at all, it's not to be missed. Authors' rating? Five stars, if you forget the outrageously inflated prices for souvenir photos and videos; budget to be extorted if you want visual evidence of your experience.

Be careful about planning who does what at Discovery Cove. The perils of being left out are illustrated by this letter sent in by a mother of three from Croydon, England:

> Only two of the five [in our group] swam with the dolphins because that is the only booking we could get. We would recommend that all people in the party swim with the dolphins to avoid the awful, sad feeling of being left out that three of us had. The two children refused to look at their brother, and Dad just wanted to go home. Dad felt guilty, and what was supposed to be the highlight of the trip turned into a downer.

Not an ideal situation. If you're visiting Discovery Cove as a group, try to time your visit so everyone who wants to swim with the dolphins can.

SeaWorld added The Grand Reef in June 2011. The Grand Reef is a pool—holding almost a million gallons of salt water—and surrounding sandy beaches covering nearly 2½ acres. In the water are about 10,000 animals, including roughly 125 species of fish, rays, and sharks.

Grand Reef guests can wander over bridges to tiny islands, relax on the beach, and simply wade around to observe the fish and 90 pieces of coral from above the surface. Or visitors can pay $59 for the Sea-Venture experience: Don a diving helmet to walk below the water, get up close views of sharks and venomous lionfish—through a window—and hand-feed the tamer species. Fresh air is pumped through a hose—no SCUBA certification is required. The helmeted guests, in groups limited to six, descend a ladder to play aquanaut and walk among the fish and rays. The SeaVenture lasts about 1 hour.

Other exhibit areas at Discovery Cove include the Explorer's Aviary and the Freshwater Oasis. You can snorkel or swim in the Grand Reef, the habitat for thousands of exotic fish and dozens of rays. In the aviary, you can touch and feed gorgeous tropical birds. The Freshwater Oasis is a freshwater pool in which you can swim or wade. It is stocked with marmosets (small monkeys) and, though not in the water with you, charming Asian small-clawed otters—they only grow to 11 pounds, so they look like miniature otters. The park is threaded by the freshwater Wind-Away River, in which you can float or swim to all these areas. Pleasant beaches, with hammocks, lounges, and chairs, serve as pathways connecting the attractions.

Guests at Discovery Cove need not be exceptional swimmers—the water is shallow and so heavily salted that it's very difficult not to float. Watchful lifeguards are omnipresent. You'll need to wear your swimsuit and pool shoes as well as a cover-up. On rare days when it's too cold to swim in Orlando, guests are provided with wet suits. The park also supplies masks and snorkels, and you get to keep the snorkel (after all, nobody wants to reuse those). Discovery Cove provides fish-friendly sunscreen: Guests may not use their own sunscreen. You must also remove all watches and jewelry (except wedding bands), as they might end up getting swallowed by the animals if you lose them. Free lockers enable you to stow everything you need to put away, all day. Comfortable, clean, well-appointed bathrooms and showers are also provided.

GETTING THERE

DISCOVERY COVE IS LOCATED directly across the Central Florida Parkway from SeaWorld. Parking is free.

PRICES AND RESERVATIONS

DISCOVERY COVE IS OPEN 7:30 A.M. or 9 a.m. to 5:30 p.m. daily year-round. Because admission is limited to 1,200 guests per day, you should purchase tickets in advance by calling ☎ 877-4-DISCOVERY (877-434-7268) or by visiting **discoverycove.com.** There are two admission options. The all-inclusive Dolphin Swim Day Resort package, depending on month and day of the week, is $229–$429, plus tax, per person and includes the dolphin swim; breakfast, lunch, snacks, and beverages throughout the day; unlimited access to the Grand Reef, Explorer's Aviary, Freshwater Oasis, Serenity Bay, and Wind-Away River; and the use of beach umbrellas, lounge chairs, towels, lockers, and swim and snorkel gear.

If you're not interested in the dolphin swim, the Day Resort Package is $169–$249 (depending on season), plus tax, per person for the day and includes everything but the dolphin encounter. Discovery Cove admission includes parking at Discovery Cove as well as a 14-day, unlimited-use pass to SeaWorld Orlando and Aquatica, making the high price tag a bit easier to swallow. For only $25 more, you can add unlimited admission to Busch Gardens in Tampa Bay for 14 consecutive days. The passes are valid before or after your Discovery Cove visit.

The Trainer for a Day package includes everything the all-inclusive dolphin package does, along with a second enhanced dolphin experience and backstage tours of the dolphin and shark areas. Admission to participate is $428–$658, plus tax (depending on season).

ARRIVING

THE PARK ESSENTIALLY has two opening times: During the busy summer and end-of-the-year seasons, it will open at 7:30 a.m. for check-in; the rest of the year, it opens at 9 a.m. It is essential to arrive before the park opens, especially during the summer season, so that you can be among the first guests to register for your dolphin interaction. Guests are assigned time slots for the dolphin swims throughout the day, but you're not assigned your time slot until you show up on the day of your reservation. The later you register, the later in the day your dolphin swim will be, and summer thunderstorms can force afternoon interactions to be canceled altogether. Dolphins are generally more active in the morning, and once you do the interaction, you can spend the rest of your day lazily snorkeling or snoozing on the beach (without worrying about missing your appointment with Flipper).

On registering, you'll be asked to provide a credit card number. You'll then be issued a lanyard card with your picture on it. This card corresponds to the credit card you just gave, so it can be used for purchases anywhere in Discovery Cove. This means you can stow your wallet or purse in a locker for your whole stay. The locker key is also on a lanyard, so it's very easy to keep up with everything.

You'll be assigned one of three cabanas as your meeting place for the dolphin interaction. These are easy to find because Discovery Cove is really not that large. Show up about 5 minutes before your assigned time. A trainer will give a short orientation, and then it's off to the dolphin swim. Enjoy. Following your dolphin encounter, linger until the park closes to enjoy the facilities, not to mention the free food and drink. By the way, the adult beverages are free-flowing but light on the booze, so you may get a pleasant buzz but are unlikely to encounter bumbling drunks.

PART EIGHT

UNIVERSAL ORLANDO

THE UNIVERSAL ORLANDO RESORT is located on 840 acres inside the city of Orlando, about 8 miles northeast of Walt Disney World (which is actually in Lake Buena Vista). The resort consists of two theme parks—**Universal Studios Florida** and **Universal's Islands of Adventure**—along with Loews-operated Universal hotels and the **CityWalk** dining, nightlife, and shopping complex. Wet 'n Wild, a nearby water park, is also marketed under the Universal Orlando banner.

Universal Studios Florida (USF) opened in June 1990. At the time, it was almost four times the size of Disney's Hollywood Studios (originally known as Disney-MGM Studios), and much more of its facility was accessible to visitors. Like Disney's parks, USF is spacious, beautifully landscaped, meticulously clean, and delightfully varied in its entertainment. Its rides are exciting and innovative and, like many Disney attractions, focused on familiar and/or beloved movie characters or situations.

With only one theme park, Universal played second fiddle to Disney's juggernaut for almost a decade. Things began to change when Universal opened Islands of Adventure (IOA) in 1999. Adding a second park, along with the CityWalk nightlife complex and on-site resort hotels, made Universal a legitimate two-day destination and provided Universal with enough critical mass to begin serious competition with Disney for tourists' time and money.

In 2007 Universal's management made one bold bet: securing the rights to build a Harry Potter–themed area within IOA. Harry, it was thought, was possibly the only fictional character extant capable of trumping Mickey Mouse, and Universal went all out, under author J. K. Rowling's watchful and exacting eye, to create a setting and attractions designed to be the envy of the industry. The Wizarding World of Harry Potter–Hogsmeade, as the new land was called, opened at IOA in 2010 and was an immediate hit; it was followed in

Continued on page 192

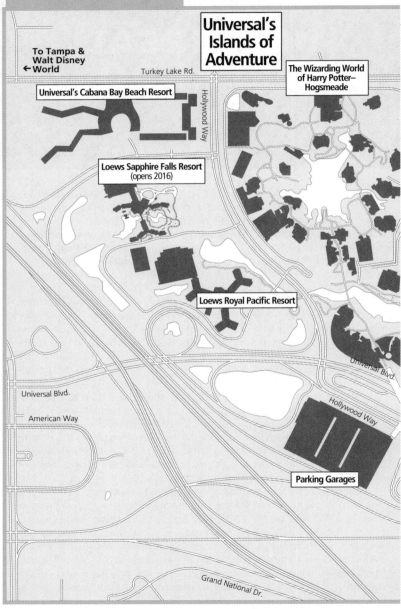

Universal Orlando

To Tampa &
Walt Disney
← World

Turkey Lake Rd.

Hollywood Way

Universal's
Islands of
Adventure

The Wizarding World
of Harry Potter–
Hogsmeade

Universal's Cabana Bay Beach Resort

Loews Sapphire Falls Resort
(opens 2016)

Loews Royal Pacific Resort

Universal Blvd.

Universal Blvd.

American Way

Hollywood Way

Parking Garages

Grand National Dr.

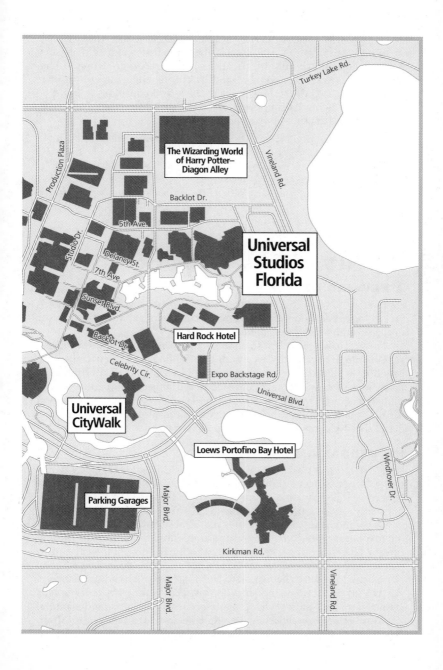

Continued from page 189

2014 by The Wizarding World of Harry Potter–Diagon Alley at USF.

Now, USF and IOA are state-of-the-art parks vying with Disney parks, whose attractions are decades older on average. None of Disney's latest attractions are the kind of cutting-edge, super-headliner attractions that Universal has built recently and continues to build.

Even hard-core Disney fans, such as this Moncton, Nebraska, reader, are beginning to pay attention:

> *I'm a huge fan of all things Disney, so it pains me a little to say that the highlight of our most recent trip was actually Universal Orlando. Not because Disney World isn't spectacular—it always is—but because Universal's themed Harry Potter experience is by far the most immersive I've ever had. Disney has to be a little nervous. Responding to Pottermania with an Avatar land just doesn't seem like a good move— Disney on the defensive! But hey, a little competition is healthy.*

A **UNIVERSAL PRIMER**

A NEW KID ON THE BLOCK

UNIVERSAL HAS DEVELOPED into a major, world-class, multi-faceted resort destination—one that we can no longer adequately cover in the several dozen pages allocated here.

Therefore, we're excited to announce *The Unofficial Guide to Universal Orlando,* by Seth Kubersky with Bob Sehlinger and Len Testa. This brand-new guide is the most comprehensive on Universal Orlando in print, with almost 400 pages devoted to the subject. Though we'll continue to cover Universal Orlando in this book, we strongly recommend the new guide for all of the tips, insights, elaborations, and attention to detail that we can't accommodate in these pages.

UNIVERSAL ON THE WEB

IF, JUDGING FROM THE PLENITUDE of independent Disney World websites, you expect a similar number of such sites for Universal, you'd be wrong. Though some Disney sites cover Universal in some (usually minimal) way, independent Universal sites are practically nonexistent.

Of the independent Disney sites that deal with Universal, we recommend **mousesavers.com** for hotel and admission discounts, plus touring tips for The Wizarding World of Harry Potter. For comprehensive information and discussion, try **parkscope.net** and **orlandoparksnews.com.** For discussion boards dedicated to Universal, go to **orlandounited.com.** For crowd projections and touring tips, check our own **touringplans .com.** News and park developments are available at **orlandosentinel .com** and **orlandoweekly.com; jimhillmedia.com** offers insider information on attractions, new technologies, and updates in the parks. Finally, there's the official Universal Orlando website, **universalorlando.com.**

UNIVERSAL ADMISSIONS (prices include tax)		ADULTS	AGES 3–9
BASE TICKETS	One-Day Base Ticket	$109	$103
	Two-Day Base Ticket	$160	$149
	Three-Day Base Ticket	$170	$160
	Four-Day Base Ticket	$181	$170
PARK HOPPING	One-Day Park-to-Park Ticket	$157	$151
	Two-Day Park-to-Park Ticket	$208	$197
	Three-Day Park-to-Park Ticket	$218	$208
	Four-Day Park-to-Park Ticket	$229	$218
ANNUAL PASSES	Power Annual Pass	$256	$256
	Preferred Annual Pass	$357	$357
	Premier Annual Pass	$511	$511

Universal also offers a free app for iOS and Android that displays wait times and interactive maps while you're inside the parks, using the resort's free Wi-Fi (connect to **xfinitywifi** and accept the legal terms).

COST

UNIVERSAL'S ADMISSION POLICY largely emulates Disney's Magic Your Way program. A one-day, one-park Base Ticket is on par with those at the Disney parks; multiday single-park Base Tickets, however, are significantly less expensive at Universal. Park-hopping (or Park-to-Park, in Universal parlance) passes can be much more expensive at Disney, where, for example, a four-day Park Hopper ticket costs a little over 70% more than what you'd pay at Universal.

Be aware that you *must* have Park-to-Park admission to ride the Hogwarts Express train between IOA and USF; single-park tickets may be upgraded at Guest Services or the train stations.

As at Disney, passes expire 14 days after the first use. Prices listed above are what you'd pay online and include tax; unlike Disney, however, Universal offers discounts when you purchase passes online at **universalorlando.com,** including $20-per-pass discounts on multiday tickets plus other time-limited specials. Passes purchased online are printable, can be used at the turnstiles, and are good for 14 days beginning with the day of first use. Though Universal discounts multiday tickets online, one-day admissions are slightly more expensive than at the gate; nevertheless, they're probably worth it for the convenience.

The **Three-Park Unlimited** ticket is good for 14 consecutive days of Park-to-Park admission at both USF and IOA, plus Wet 'n Wild. Three-Park Unlimited tickets are sold by a number of third-party vendors, but not directly by Universal at this time. Only a few dollars more than the four-day Park-to-Park ticket, this ticket is poorly publicized but a great value if you like waterslides and aren't buying an Annual Pass for your extended stay.

The five-park, 14-day **Orlando FlexTicket** allows unlimited entry to Universal Studios Florida (USF), Universal's Islands of Adventure (IOA), SeaWorld, Aquatica, and Wet 'n Wild and costs $394.03 for adults and $378.05 for children ages 3–9, tax included. The six-park, 14-day **Orlando Flex Ticket Plus,** providing unlimited entry to USF, IOA, SeaWorld, Aquatica, Wet 'n Wild, and Busch Gardens, costs $415.43 for adults and $399.45 for children. Buy the tickets online at the websites of the participating parks, or get them at a discount at **officialticketcenter.com.** Flex Tickets are a good deal only if you visit all of the parks covered.

The main Universal Orlando information number is ☎ 407-363-8000. Reach Guest Relations at ☎ 407-224-4233; order tickets by mail at ☎ 407-224-7840. The numbers for Lost and Found are ☎ 407-224-4244 (USF) and 407-224-4245 (IOA); press 2 to be connected.

Ticket Savings from Third-Party Vendors

The lowest possible prices on electronically delivered Universal tickets that we're aware of are through **Orlando Ticket Connection** (**orlandoticketconnection.com**), which undercuts Universal's online prices on park-to-park tickets by $5–$10. We'd love to hear from readers who have had experiences (good or bad) with Orlando Ticket Connection. **Parksavers** (**parksavers.com**) sells Universal tickets for a few dollars more than Orlando Ticket Connection, but be aware that their buyers receive a printable voucher that must be redeemed at the park with a photo ID, instead of going straight to the turnstiles.

Dreams Unlimited Travel (**dreamsunlimitedtravel.com**) charges the same for Universal tickets as the official website, but it does offer exclusive one- and two-day park-to-park passes bundled with discounted round-trip transportation from Disney-area hotels via Mears (see page 197). Its tickets are purchased directly through Universal's secure website and can be printed at home or retrieved from will-call kiosks.

Universal charges $14 for domestic FedEx shipping of tickets ($19 for international delivery). If you want physical tickets mailed to you for the cheapest price and can order at least two weeks before your trip, consider using an online ticket wholesaler, such as **The Official Ticket Center** (**officialticketcenter.com**) or **Undercover Tourist** (**undercovertourist.com**). Official Ticket Center advertises all its prices inclusive of tax and USPS Certified shipping, and it has the lowest bottom-line cost on physical Universal Orlando tickets that we've found, usually within pennies of Orlando Ticket Connection's e-delivery price.

unofficial **TIP**
In order, Mondays, Sundays, and Saturdays are the best days to visit Universal Orlando.

A WORD ABOUT CROWDS

YOU'VE PROBABLY READ ABOUT the huge crowds that inundate The Wizarding World outposts at both Universal parks. The reports are true, but they present an unbalanced view of the crowds at the Universal parks overall. To get a quantitative grip on crowding, let's look at attendance figures compared with the size of the parks. On a day of average attendance, USF and Disney's Hollywood Studios see about the same number of guests per acre. However, USF has 22 attractions, while DHS has only 16. Therefore, the crowds are distributed among more attractions at USF, making it seem less crowded. Contrasting the Magic Kingdom with IOA, the latter averages 203 guests per day, per acre, while the Magic Kingdom—the attendance leader of all the world's theme parks—registers a whopping 495 guests per day, per acre. Depending on how you define attractions, however, the Magic Kingdom has about 42, versus 26 at Islands of Adventure. Even so, there are still one-and-a-half as many guests for each Magic Kingdom attraction as there are for each IOA attraction.

unofficial **TIP**
Get to the park with your admission already purchased about 45 minutes before official opening time. Arrive 60 minutes before official opening time if you need to buy admission. **Be aware that you can't do a comprehensive tour of both Universal parks in a single day.**

HOW MUCH TIME TO ALLOCATE

TOURING UNIVERSAL STUDIOS FLORIDA, including one meal and a visit to Diagon Alley, takes about 10–12 hours. One reader laments:

> *There's a lot of standing at USF, and it isn't as organized as DHS. Many of the attractions don't open until 10 a.m. We weren't able to see nearly as many attractions at Universal as we were at DHS during the same amount of time.*

As the reader observes, some USF attractions don't open until 10 a.m. or later. Most theater attractions don't schedule performances until 11 a.m. or after. This means that early in the day, all park guests are concentrated among the limited number of attractions in operation.

You won't have to worry about any of this if you use our Universal Studios touring plans. We'll keep you one jump ahead of the crowd and make sure that any given attraction is running by the time you get there.

LODGING AT UNIVERSAL ORLANDO

UNIVERSAL HAS FIVE RESORT HOTELS. The 750-room **Portofino Bay Hotel** is a gorgeous property set on an artificial bay and themed like an Italian coastal town. The 650-room **Hard Rock Hotel** is an ultracool Hotel California replica, and the 1,000-room, Polynesian-themed **Royal Pacific Resort** is sumptuously decorated and richly appointed. All three are on the pricey side. The retro-style **Cabana Bay Beach Resort,** Universal's largest hotel, has 1,800 moderate- and value-priced rooms, plus amenities (such as a bowling alley and lazy river) not seen at comparable Disney resorts. A fifth hotel, the Caribbean-style **Sapphire Falls Resort,** opens in 2016 with 1,000 rooms priced between those at Royal Pacific and Cabana Bay.

Like Disney, Universal offers a number of incentives for visitors to stay at its hotels. Perks available include delivery to your on-site hotel room of purchases made in the parks, tickets and reservation information from hotel concierges, priority dining reservations at select

Universal restaurants, and the ability to charge purchases to your room account.

Universal charges a $20-per-night self-parking fee ($27 for valet) at its luxury resorts ($12 per night at Cabana Bay, self-parking only); day guests pay $22 for self-parking and $32 for valet. Free buses and water taxis serve Universal Studios Florida, Islands of Adventure, CityWalk, SeaWorld, Aquatica (SeaWorld's water park), and Wet 'n Wild. Hotel guests (except for those at Cabana Bay and Sapphire Falls) may use the Universal Express program without limitation all day long and are also eligible for "next available" table privileges at CityWalk restaurants and similar priority admission to Universal Orlando theme park shows. The most valuable perk to most Universal resort guests, however, is admission to The Wizarding Worlds of Harry Potter at Islands of Adventure and at Universal Studios Florida 1 hour before the general public.

ARRIVING AT UNIVERSAL ORLANDO

UNIVERSAL ORLANDO CAN BE ACCESSED from eastbound I-4 by taking Exit 75A and turning left at the top of the ramp onto Universal Boulevard. If you're traveling westbound on I-4, use Exit 74B and then turn right on Hollywood Way. There are also entrances off Kirkman Road to the east, Turkey Lake Road to the north, and Vineland Road to the west. Universal Boulevard connects the International Drive area to Universal via an overpass bridging I-4. Turkey Lake and Vineland Roads are particularly good alternatives when I-4 is gridlocked.

Two multistory parking garages hold 20,000 cars; signs from all four entrances route you to the parking structures. Parking is $20 for cars and $22 for RVs, trailers, and other large rigs. Regular parking drops to $5 between 6 and 10 p.m. and is free after 10 p.m. Preferred parking is offered during the day for $25, but we've scored spaces just as good or better using the regular parking, especially when we've arrived before 10:30 a.m. An advantage of preferred parking, however, is that you'll park faster because the ratio of cars choosing preferred to regular is about 1 to 13. In addition to the garages, valet parking is available at CityWalk for $15 for a visit of up to 2 hours or $35 for longer than that. If you're a Universal hotel guest, park in the hotel lot and walk, take a free water taxi to CityWalk, or catch a shuttle bus to the parking garages' central hub.

The two rectangular garages lie along a north–south axis, with the pedestrian walkways leading to the theme parks running along the west, or long, side of each building. Because the garages are two-thirds as wide as they are long, the farther your parking place is from the west side, the worse it will be. This is why preferred parking is often not as close as regular parking—with the former, you'll be closer to the covered walkways to the parks, but if your particular space is toward the east side of the garage, you'll end up farther away than a guest who chose regular parking and was assigned a space closer to the west side of the structure.

We strongly recommend that you take a photo of the name and number of your section, level, and row. Sections are named for movies—*Jurassic Park, King Kong,* and the like. The first numeral of the number following the section name tells you what deck level you're on, and the remaining numbers specify the row. So if a sign tells you that you're on King Kong 410, you're in the King Kong section on the fourth floor in Row 10.

From the garages, moving sidewalks deliver you to CityWalk. From here, you can access the main entrances of both Universal Studios Florida and Islands of Adventure. Unlike at Disney parks, there are no trams, so depending on where in the garage your car is parked, you'll have an 8- to 20-minute hike to the theme park entrances even if you use the (sometimes) moving walkways.

If you're staying at Walt Disney World and you don't have a car, **Mears Transportation** will shuttle you from your hotel to Universal and back for $20. Pickup and return times are at your convenience. To schedule a shuttle, call ☎ 855-463-2776.

From three Denver college-aged women who tried Mears:

We took a Mears shuttle from Disney to Universal, and I would not recommend it. It's $20 a person and takes a very long time to get you there. It stops at SeaWorld and a couple of other places before Universal Studios. We didn't look into cab fares, but if we had a car, it would have been cheaper and easier to drive it over to Universal. We waited 45 minutes for the shuttle to pick us up from Universal.

For guests staying at Universal's on-site hotels, the **SuperStar Shuttle** will deliver you from Orlando International Airport to Universal and back again. Unlike Disney's similar Magical Express program, the SuperStar Shuttle isn't free; round-trip transfers are $35 per person (kids under age 3 are free) and can be added to your Universal Vacations package. Call ☎ 866-604-7557 for details.

Taxis and ride-share services (such as **Uber** and **Lyft**) are also readily available to and from the resorts. A one-way taxi ride is $35–$45 (plus tip) depending on which Disney hotel you are leaving from, and it may be cheaper than a shuttle if you have three to five people. In other cities, the advantage to Uber and Lyft is that they charge about 30–40% less than a traditional taxi. Orlando, however, has mandated that ride-sharing services charge the same per-mile as taxis, negating their price advantage. (At press time, Uber was still charging its lower rates while it negotiates with the city.) In addition, the ride-share companies are not currently authorized to operate on Orlando International Airport property (as scary signage warns arriving visitors on their way to baggage claim) and are in litigation with the airport authority over their status. All transportation services drop off and pick up from the lower level of Universal's main parking hub, from which you can walk to CityWalk and the parks.

UNIVERSAL EXPRESS

LIKE WALT DISNEY WORLD'S FastPass+, Universal Express is a system whereby guests can skip the line and experience an attraction via a special queue with little or no waiting. Unlike FastPass+, Universal Express is not free. Two versions are available, both of which require you to cough up more money beyond your park admission:

Universal Express is free to guests at all Universal hotels except Cabana Bay Beach and Sapphire Falls Resorts; they may use the Express lines all day long simply by flashing the pass they get at check-in. This is especially valuable during peak season.

Guests staying at Cabana Bay, Sapphire Falls (opens 2016), or a non-Universal hotel can purchase Universal Express for an extra $35–$150 (depending on the season), which provides line-jumping privileges at each Universal Express attraction at a given park.

A Kansas City family of four liked the hotel Express Pass:

The Express Pass that you get "free" by staying at one of the resorts is a lifesaver. We never waited in line more than 15 minutes, and it was usually closer to 5. For my roller coaster–loving family, this was great. We didn't have a scheduled time to ride anything like Disney, so we could stray from our plan and re-ride Hulk or Rockit over and over again, which we did. The two Universal parks are close together, so park-hopping doesn't require a shuttle ride.

You can purchase Universal Express for one or both parks and for either single (one ride only on each participating attraction) or unlimited use. The number of Express Passes is limited each day, and they can sell out. Increase your chances of securing passes by buying and printing them at home off Universal's website. Speaking of participating attractions, more than 90% of rides and shows are covered by Universal Express, a much higher percentage than those covered by FastPass+ at Walt Disney World.

You can also buy Universal Express at the theme parks' ticket windows, just outside the front gates, but it's faster to do so inside the parks.

unofficial **TIP**
Universal Express is not valid at the headliner Harry Potter attractions: Forbidden Journey, Escape from Gringotts, and Hogwarts Express.

At Universal Studios Florida, it's available at **Super Silly Stuff;** at Islands of Adventure, you can buy Universal Express at **Jurassic Outfitters, Toon Extra,** and the **Marvel Alterniverse Store.** It's also available up to eight months in advance at **universalorlando.com.** You'll need to know when you plan on using it, though, because prices vary depending on the date.

No matter which version of Universal Express you use, it works the same: Present your pass to a greeter at each attraction entrance, get it scanned for verification, and enjoy your expedited entertainment. At shows, you can present your pass for priority seating 15 minutes before showtime, but that's less of a perk because Universal's large theaters rarely fill up.

A New York mom had a trouble-free experience but questions the value of the investment:

> We bought Universal Express, but it was neither necessary nor consistently effective. By arriving at park opening, we were able to see many attractions right away without needing the passes at all. They helped on about three attractions between the two parks—a poor return for an investment of $156. On Dudley Do-Right, we still had to wait 30 minutes even with Express, whereas with Disney's free FastPass+ we never waited more than 5 minutes for an attraction. The only aspect of UE that was better than FP+ is that touring order was unaffected: UE could be used whenever you first approached an attraction instead of your having to come back later.

UNIVERSAL EXPRESS FOR RESORT GUESTS This program allows guests at all Universal resorts except Cabana Bay and Sapphire Falls to bypass the regular line anytime and as often as desired simply by flashing a pass they get at check-in. Be aware that neither Harry Potter and the Forbidden Journey nor Pteranodon Flyers at IOA is a Universal Express attraction, nor is Harry Potter and the Escape from Gringotts at USF or the inter-park Hogwarts Express train. Again, however, all Universal hotel guests, including those staying at Cabana Bay and Sapphire Falls, may enter one or both parks' (depending on the season) Wizarding World outposts an hour before they open to the public. Which park you may enter on any particular day, and which attractions will be operating, are at Universal's discretion and may rotate among the hotels to manage demand.

A father from Snellville, Georgia, discovered that it was cheaper for his family to stay at a Universal resort than buy Universal Express:

> We got a room at the Royal Pacific Resort for $349 on a Saturday night, which allowed us to use Universal Express Saturday and Sunday. The room cost $43.63 per person per day, while an [à la carte] Express Pass this same weekend would have cost $56 per person per day, and we still would have had to pay for a hotel.

IS UNIVERSAL EXPRESS WORTH IT? The answer depends on the season you visit, hours of park operation, and crowd levels. Attendance has jumped at both parks since the opening of each Harry Potter land, especially at Universal Studios Florida since Diagon Alley opened. However, the big-ticket rides in Hogsmeade and Diagon Alley don't participate in Universal Express, so you don't get to cut in line at Universal's most in-demand attractions. Still, if you want to sleep in and arrive at a park after opening, Express is an effective, albeit expensive, way to avoid long lines at the non-Potter headliner attractions, especially during holidays and busy times.

If, however, you arrive 30 minutes before park opening and use our touring plans (see pages 232 and 260), you should experience the lowest possible waits at both parks. We encourage you to try the plans first, but if waits for rides become intolerable, you can always buy Express in the parks, provided it hasn't sold out (an infrequent occurrence).

Finally, you'll want to devise a convenient way to keep track of your pass, as this Bluffton, Indiana, dad found out a little too late:

> I wish I'd known ahead of time to bring a lanyard to hang our Universal Express Pass on.

How Universal Express Affects Crowd Conditions at Attractions

This system dramatically affects crowd movement (and touring plans) in the Universal parks. A woman from Yorktown, Virginia, writes:

> People in the Express line were let in at a rate of about 10 to 1 over the regular-line folks. This created bottlenecks and long waits for people who didn't have the Express privilege at the very times when it's supposed to be easier to get around!

SINGLES LINES

ANOTHER TIME-SAVING OPTION is the singles line. Several attractions have this special line for guests riding alone. As Universal employees will tell you, this line is often just as fast as the Express line. We strongly recommend using the singles line whenever possible—it will decrease your overall wait and leave more time for repeat rides or just bumming around the parks. Note, though, that some queues (particularly Forbidden Journey's and Escape from Gringotts's) are attractions in themselves and deserve to be experienced during your first ride.

U-BOT

THIS RIDE-RESERVATION SYSTEM works much like Universal Express but incorporates the small U-Bot device. Guests can purchase access to the device at any Express kiosk (buying access online is currently not an option). Once you have your U-Bot, you can use it to reserve ride times for any Universal Express attraction, but note that you can make only one reservation at a time. The U-Bot will vibrate and display a message telling you when it's time to ride. Next, you take your U-Bot to the ride's Express entrance, where the attraction greeter will scan your device and admit you to the Express queue. U-Bot costs considerably less than an Express Pass (usually by about $10–$20).

LOCKERS

UNIVERSAL ENFORCES A MANDATORY locker system at its big thrill rides. On most rides, all bags, purses, and other objects too large to be secured in a pocket must be placed in a locker. A strict "no loose items" policy is enforced at The Incredible Hulk Coaster, Hollywood Rip Ride Rockit, and Dragon Challenge. At these rides, guests are required to pass through an airport-style security screening to ensure that no phones, keys, or even spare change enter the queue.

Lockers outside these attractions are free for an amount of time that depends on the length of the standby line. So if the line is 30 minutes, for example, and the ride itself is 10 minutes, you get 40 minutes plus a small cushion of about 15 minutes. The lockers then cost $3 for each half hour after that, with a $20 maximum.

The locker banks are easy to find; each bank has a small computer in the center. When the sun is bright, the screen is almost impossible to read, so have someone block the sun or use a different computer. After selecting your language, you press your thumb onto the keypad and have your fingerprint scanned. We've seen people walk away cursing at this step, having repeated it over and over with no success. Don't press down too hard—the computer can't read your thumbprint that way. Instead, take a deep breath and lightly place your thumb on the scanner.

After you do your thumb scan, you'll receive a locker number. Write it down! When you return from your ride, go to the same kiosk machine, enter your locker number, and scan your thumb again. At Guest Relations, family-size lockers are available for $10 for the entire day, but remember that only the person who used his or her thumb to get the locker can retrieve anything from it.

UNIVERSAL, KIDS, AND SCARY STUFF

THOUGH THERE'S PLENTY FOR YOUNGER CHILDREN to enjoy at the Universal parks, most major attractions can potentially make kids under age 8 wig out. At Universal Studios Florida, forget **Hollywood Rip Ride Rockit, Men in Black Alien Attack, Revenge of the Mummy, The Simpsons Ride,** *Terminator 2: 3-D,* and **Transformers: The Ride 3-D.** The first part of **E. T. Adventure** is a little dicey for a few preschoolers, but the end is all happiness and harmony. There are some scary visual effects on both the **Hogwarts Express** train that runs between the two parks and **Escape from Gringotts,** even though both are billed as family rides. Interestingly, very few families report problems with *Universal Orlando's Horror Make-Up Show.* Anything we haven't listed is pretty tame.

At Universal's Islands of Adventure, watch out for **The Amazing Adventures of Spider-Man, Doctor Doom's Fearfall, Dragon Challenge, Harry Potter and the Forbidden Journey, The Incredible Hulk Coaster, Jurassic Park River Adventure,** and *Poseidon's Fury.* **Skull Island** is visually and psychologically intense; it may be too much for little ones. **Popeye & Bluto's Bilge-Rat Barges** is wet and wild, but most younger children handle it well. **Dudley Do-Right's Ripsaw Falls** is a toss-up, to be considered only if your kids like water-flume rides. *The Eighth Voyage of Sindbad Stunt Show* includes some explosions and startling special effects, but again, kids tolerate it well. Nothing else should pose a problem.

CHILD SWAP "Switching off" at Universal is similar to Disney's version. The entire family goes through the whole line together before being split into riding and non-riding groups near the loading platform. The non-riding parent and child(ren) wait in a designated room, usually with some sort of entertainment (for example, Forbidden Journey at IOA shows the first 20 minutes of *Harry Potter and the Sorcerer's Stone* on a loop), a place to sit down, and sometimes restrooms with changing tables. At any theme park, the best tip we can give is to ask the greeter in front of the attraction what you're supposed to do.

BLUE MAN GROUP

NO PIECE OF ENTERTAINMENT better encapsulates the "Universal Difference" than Blue Man Group's nightly performances at CityWalk. Cirque du Soleil's *La Nouba*—the closest equivalent at Walt Disney World—is epic, opulent, and elegant, appealing to infants and grandparents alike. Blue Man Group, in comparison, is intimate, offbeat, occasionally ornery, with elements of avant-garde performance art that are as likely to provoke a loud "What the hell?" as applause. Both are phenomenal pieces of theater in their own right, and well worth every penny. But Disney doesn't provide ponchos to patrons seated in the first four rows for protection against flying paint.

The three blue men of the Blue Man Group are just that—blue— and bald and mute. Wearing black clothing and skullcaps slathered with bright-blue grease paint, they deliver a fast-paced show that uses music (mostly percussion) and multimedia effects to make light of contemporary art and life in the information age. The Universal act is just one expression of a franchise that started with three friends in New York's East Village. Now you can catch their zany, wacky, smart stuff in New York, Las Vegas, Boston, Chicago, and Berlin, among other places. The 1-hour, 45-minute Orlando production was updated and reimagined in 2012 to reflect cultural changes in the use of technology in daily life; it includes some segments similar to those seen in other cities but isn't identical.

Funny, sometimes poignant, and always compelling, Blue Man Group pounds out vital, visceral tribal rhythms on complex instruments (made of PVC pipes) that could pass for industrial intestines, and makes seemingly spontaneous eruptions of visual art rendered with marshmallows and a mysterious goo. The weekly supplies include 25.5 pounds of Cap'n Crunch, 60 Twinkies, 996 marshmallows, and 9.5 gallons of paint. If all this sounds silly, it is, but it's also strangely thought-provoking and deals with topics such as the value of modern art, the ubiquity and addictive nature of tablet devices, the way rock music moves you, and how we're all connected. (*Hint:* It's not the Internet.)

A live percussion band backs Blue Man Group with a relentless and totally engrossing industrial dance riff. The band resides in long, dark alcoves above the stage. At just the right moments, the lofts are lit to reveal a group of pulsating neon-colored skeletons.

Audience participation completes the Blue Man experience. The blue men often move into the audience to bring guests on stage. At the end of the show, giant glowing balloons drop from the rafters for the audience to bat around like beach balls. And a lot of folks can't help standing up to dance and laugh. Magicians for the creative spirit that resides in us all, Blue Man Group makes everyone a coconspirator in a joyous explosion of showmanship.

This show is decidedly different and requires an open mind to be appreciated. It also helps to be a little loose, because, like it or not, everybody gets sucked into the production and leaves the theater a little bit lighter in spirit. If you don't want to be pulled onstage to become a part of the improvisation, don't sit in the first half-dozen or so rows.

The Universal Box Office (☎ 888-340-5476 or 407-258-3626) is open 7 a.m.–7 p.m. EST, or you can buy tickets online at **universal orlando.com.** Advance tickets at the Universal Orlando website run $60–$110 for adults, $30–$57 for children; tickets purchased at the box office cost $10 more. The show isn't recommended for kids under age 3, but they may attend without a ticket if they sit on a lap. AAA members and Preferred and Premiere Annual Pass holders save 20% on up to six tickets, and students with school ID can buy two tickets for $34 on the day of the show, if any are left. You can also save a few dollars by bundling a Blue Man Group ticket with theme park admission or a meal at CityWalk. All Blue Man Group tickets include free CityWalk club admission after the show.

A $20 VIP upgrade option includes access to the Bluephoria private lounge 45 minutes before and after the show, two free drinks (alcoholic or soft), and a photo op with a Blue Man. The lounge is undersized, but the drinks alone are almost worth the upgrade, and the brief meet and greet is a great bonus.

The show is staged in the Sharp Aquos Theatre, which was originally the Nickelodeon soundstage. It can be accessed from CityWalk by following the path between Hard Rock Cafe and Hollywood Rip Ride Rockit, or by exiting Universal Studios Florida through the side gate near Despicable Me Minion Mayhem. Center seats in rows B, C, and D go for a premium price; we recommend center seats in rows E–L, at least nine rows back from the stage.

UNIVERSAL ORLANDO DINING PLAN

UNIVERSAL HAS REPLACED its former all-you-care-to-eat fast-food Meal Deals with a **Quick Service Universal Dining Plan** that provides one quick-service meal (including an entrée and soft drink), another soft drink, and one snack. The cost is $19.99 for adults and $12.99 for kids age 9 and younger, plus tax. It's valid at most quick-service eateries in both parks (including **Three Broomsticks** at The Wizarding World of Harry Potter–Hogsmeade, the **Leaky Cauldron** in Diagon Alley, and **Fast Food Boulevard** in Springfield U.S.A.) and a smattering at Universal CityWalk, but not at any hotel eateries.

Virtually every entrée at participating venues can be purchased with a quick-service meal credit, even combo platters that include a side salad or milk shake. A few of the most expensive items, such as whole pizzas, aren't covered. For your nonalcoholic beverages, you can choose from a regular-size fountain soda; bottled water, juice, or sports drink; or coffee, cocoa, or tea (including tall Starbucks brews). Eligible snacks include churros, pretzels, popcorn, ice cream (regular-size cup or cone, or novelty bar), funnel cakes, cookies, and pastries. Some larger items from snack vendors, such as turkey legs and hot dogs, count as a quick-service meal.

You can buy the Quick Service Dining Plan in advance, but instead, take advantage of your ability to buy into the plan on a day-by-day basis at any participating restaurant after you've already made your menu selection. If your entrée and drink add up to at least $15 before tax and you aren't eligible for any discounts, it's probably in your best interest to ask the cashier to sell you a Quick Service plan. The few extra dollars will net you another drink (worth about $3) and snack (worth $3–$6) for the afternoon, saving you $1–$4. Order a rib platter and soda with a dining plan, and your second drink and snack are essentially free. On the other hand, if you order an $8 cheese pizza and a $3 bag of chips, you'll lose about $3 on the deal. The dining-plan cards aren't tied to a particular person, so they can be traded among family members, and unused credits hold their value as long as you hold onto the card.

A **Table Service Universal Dining Plan** is also offered to on-site hotel guests buying vacation packages, but it's an even worse bargain. It costs $51.99 per adult per day ($17.99 for kids) and includes everything the Quick Service Dining Plan does, plus one table-service meal (entrée, soft drink, and select dessert, minus tip) per day. Unfortunately, fewer than a dozen restaurants on property participate, none of which are in the hotels—which is strange, because the only way to buy the Table Service Dining Plan is as part of a Universal Orlando Vacations hotel package. The Table Service Dining Plan probably wouldn't be a great deal even if Universal gave it away "free," as Disney does with its dining plan; at full price, you're basically throwing money away.

UNIVERSAL STUDIOS FLORIDA

WHEN UNIVERSAL STUDIOS began developing its first Orlando property, the park was originally envisioned along the lines of the long-established Hollywood Studio Tour, with the majority of the guest experiences occurring during an extensive tram tour of the limited-access back lot, along with a handful of rides and shows in the front of the park. When Disney aped that exact game plan for WDW's Hollywood Studios park, Universal did a dramatic 180 with its designs, breaking out the tram tour's iconic encounters—King Kong, Earthquake, and Jaws—into their own headliner attractions, each of which easily exceeded its Disney contemporaries in technology and thrill (if not reliability) upon Universal Studios Florida's (USF's) 1990 debut.

Since the turn of the millennium, the two parks have gone in different directions. Whereas Disney's Hollywood Studios (DHS) essentially abandoned its production facilities long ago, USF test-markets TV pilots to guests and has limited actual filming, some of which visitors can attend. More important, Universal has updated, upgraded, or entirely replaced nearly every attraction that opened in the 1990s, replacing King Kong with Revenge of the Mummy, Back to the Future with The Simpsons Ride, and Jaws with The Wizarding World of Harry Potter–Diagon Alley. With each renovation came groundbreaking advancements in ride hardware and special effects. In contrast, only one truly innovative attraction has opened at DHS in the past decade: 2008's Toy Story Midway Mania! While work is now underway to revitalize DHS, at the moment it offers only 5 real rides, versus USF's 10 major moving attractions. If the last time you visited Universal was in the early 2000s, you literally won't recognize the majority of the park.

USF is laid out in a P-configuration, with the rounded part of the *P* sticking out disproportionately from the stem. Beyond the main entrance, a wide boulevard stretches past several shows and rides to the park's New York area. Branching off this pedestrian thoroughfare to the right are four streets that access other areas of the park and intersect a promenade circling a large lake. The area of USF open to visitors is a bit smaller than Epcot.

The park is divided into seven areas: **Hollywood, New York, Production Central, San Francisco, Woody Woodpecker's KidZone, World Expo,** and **The Wizarding World of Harry Potter–Diagon Alley.** In most of USF, where one area begins and another ends is blurry, but no matter. Guests orient themselves by the major rides, sets, and landmarks and refer, for instance, to "New York," "the waterfront," "over by E. T.," or "by Mel's Diner."

In diametric contrast, The Wizarding World of Harry Potter–Diagon Alley is an immersive themed area whose scope and scale exceed those of its older sibling at Islands of Adventure. We discuss Diagon Alley and its attractions in their own section, starting on page 220.

Springfield U.S.A., part of World Expo and the setting of the long-running animated comedy *The Simpsons,* is a themed area—more like window dressing for a once-sterile part of the park—with **The Simpsons Ride** as its centerpiece. Rounding out that attraction are a spinning ride and several *Simpsons*-themed restaurants, including a real-life Moe's Tavern.

Because the majority of USF attractions really aren't thematically integrated into the areas of the park in which they reside, we present them alphabetically rather than by area.

Services and amenities include stroller and wheelchair rental, lockers, diaper-changing and infant-nursing facilities, car assistance, and foreign-language assistance. Most of the park is accessible to disabled

Continued on page 208

Universal Studios Florida

1. *Animal Actors on Location*
2. *The Blues Brothers Show*
3. Curious George Goes to Town
4. *A Day in the Park with Barney*
5. Despicable Me Minion Mayhem
6. E.T. Adventure
7. *Fear Factor Live*
8. Fievel's Playland
9. Harry Potter and the Escape from Gringotts
10. Hogwarts Express
11. Hollywood Rip Ride Rockit
12. Kang & Kodos' Twirl 'n' Hurl
13. Men in Black Alien Attack
14. Ollivanders
15. Revenge of the Mummy
16. *Shrek 4-D*
17. The Simpsons Ride
18. *Terminator 2: 3-D*
19. Transformers: The Ride 3-D
20. *Universal's Cinematic Spectacular* (seasonal)
21. *Universal Orlando's Horror Make-Up Show*
22. Woody Woodpecker's Nuthouse Coaster

Parade Route: ● ● ● ● ● ● ● ● ● ● ● ●

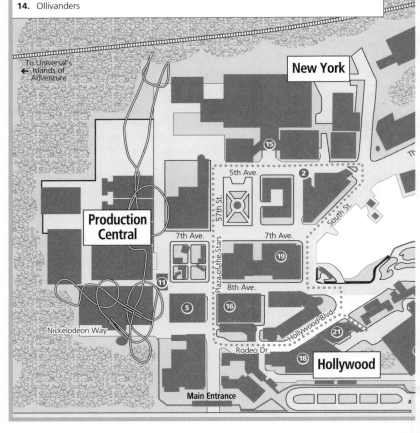

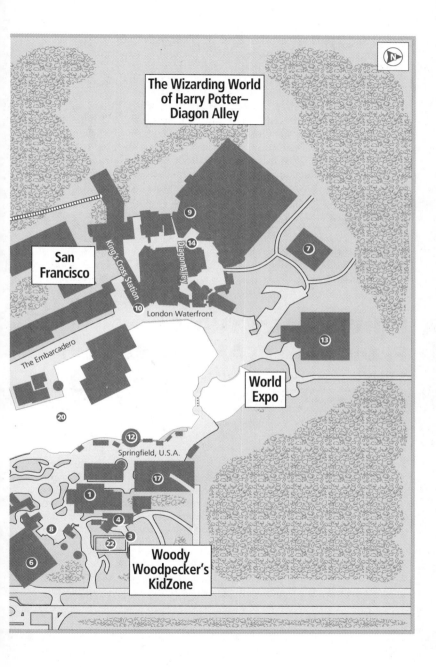

Continued from page 205

guests, and TDDs are available for the hearing-impaired. Almost all services are in the **Front Lot,** just inside the main entrance.

At press time, several major USF attractions were closed for redevelopment. The entire San Francisco area, including *Beetlejuice Graveyard Revue* and *Disaster!*, is being transformed into a new Fast & Furious ride (scheduled to open in 2017) in which guests will join Vin Diesel and his crew of hot-rodding outlaws on a 3-D high-speed chase inspired by the hit film franchise. The *Twister . . . Ride It Out* special effects demonstration will become a new motion simulator featuring *Tonight Show* host Jimmy Fallon. And the Lucile Ball tribute museum is being transformed into an interactive Hello Kitty store. Finally, most of Woody Woodpecker's KidZone (excluding the E. T. ride) is slated to be replaced by a new Nintendo-themed land.

NOT TO BE MISSED AT UNIVERSAL STUDIOS FLORIDA		
• Harry Potter and the Escape from Gringotts	• Men in Black Alien Attack	• Terminator 2: 3-D
	• Ollivanders	• Transformers: The Ride 3-D
• Hogwarts Express	• Revenge of the Mummy	
• Hollywood Rip Ride Rockit	• The Simpsons Ride	• *Universal Orlando's Horror Make-Up Show*

UNIVERSAL STUDIOS FLORIDA ATTRACTIONS

Animal Actors on Location (Universal Express) ★★★½

APPEAL BY AGE	PRESCHOOL ★★★★	GRADE SCHOOL ★★★★	TEENS ★★★
YOUNG ADULTS ★★★	OVER 30 ★★★★		SENIORS ★★★★

What it is Animal-tricks and comedy show. **Scope and scale** Major attraction. **When to go** After you've experienced all rides. **Authors' rating** Cute li'l critters; ★★★½. **Duration of show** 20 minutes. **Probable waiting time** 25 minutes.

DESCRIPTION AND COMMENTS This show integrates video segments with live sketches, jokes, and animal tricks performed onstage. The idea is to create eco-friendly family entertainment. Several of the animal thespians are veterans of TV and movies; many were rescued from shelters. What sets *Animal Actors* apart is the use of varied and unusual kinds of animals, and the opportunity to see the animals being trained on stage. The show usually makes use of audience volunteers (mostly children) in a couple of segments. Sit in the center of the stadium about halfway up for the best chance to be selected.

TOURING TIPS Check the daily entertainment schedule for showtimes. You shouldn't have any trouble getting in.

The Blues Brothers Show ★★★½

APPEAL BY AGE	PRESCHOOL ★★★	GRADE SCHOOL ★★★½	TEENS ★★★½
YOUNG ADULTS ★★★½	OVER 30 ★★★★		SENIORS ★★★★

What it is Blues concert. **Scope and scale** Diversion. **When to go** Scheduled showtimes. **Special comments** A party in the street. **Authors' rating** Energetic; ★★★½. **Duration of show** 12 minutes. **Probable waiting time** None.

DESCRIPTION AND COMMENTS Held on the corner of the New York area, across from the lagoon, *The Blues Brothers Show* features Jake and Elwood performing a few of the hit songs from the classic 1980 movie musical, including "Soul Man" and "Sweet Home Chicago." The brothers are joined on stage by Jazz the saxophone player and his girlfriend, Mabel the waitress, who belts an Aretha Franklin cover to start the show.

TOURING TIPS Check the daily entertainment schedule for showtimes. The audience stands on the street during the 12-minute show, without cover or shade.

A Day in the Park with Barney (Universal Express)   ★★★

APPEAL BY AGE	PRESCHOOL ★★★★★	GRADE SCHOOL ★★★	TEENS ★★
YOUNG ADULTS ★★★		OVER 30 ★★★	SENIORS ★★★

What it is Live-character stage show. **Scope and scale** Major children's attraction. **When to go** Anytime. **Authors' rating** A great hit with preschoolers; ★★★. **Duration of show** 20 minutes, plus 5-minute preshow and character greeting after the show. **Probable waiting time** 15 minutes.

DESCRIPTION AND COMMENTS The cuddly purple dinosaur of public-TV fame leads a sing-along with the help of the audience and sidekicks Baby Bop and BJ. A short preshow gets the kids lathered up before they enter Barney's Park (the theater). Interesting theatrical effects include wind, falling leaves, clouds and stars in the simulated sky, and snow. After the show, Barney poses for photos with parents and children inside the theater or in the indoor playground at the theater exit.

TOURING TIPS If your child likes Barney, this show is a must. Unfortunately, we heard rumors at press time that Barney may be calling it quits at USF in the near future.

Despicable Me Minion Mayhem *(Universal Express)* ★★★★

APPEAL BY AGE	PRESCHOOL ★★★★	GRADE SCHOOL ★★★★	TEENS ★★★★
YOUNG ADULTS ★★★★		OVER 30 ★★★★	SENIORS ★★★★

What it is Motion-simulator 3-D ride. **Scope and scale** Major attraction. **When to go** The first hour after park opening or after 5 p.m. **Special comments** Expect *long* waits in line. **Authors' rating** Great fun; ★★★★. **Duration of ride** 5 minutes. **Average wait in line per 100 people ahead of you** 7 minutes; assumes all simulators in use. **Loading speed** Moderate–slow.

Motion Sickness

DESCRIPTION AND COMMENTS This motion-simulator system premiered as the Funtastic World of Hanna-Barbera when the park opened in 1990; was used again in Jimmy Neutron's Nicktoon Blast, which replaced the former in 2003; and was retained for the attraction's third and current incarnation as Despicable Me Minion Mayhem, which opened in summer 2012.

As with the former attractions, Despicable Me Minion Mayhem involves the motion simulators moving and reacting in sync with a cartoon projected on an IMAX-like screen. Though the simulators have been updated, the most significant upgrade is incorporated in the projection system, which employs high-definition 3-D digital technology.

The story combines elements from the animated movie *Despicable Me,* starring Gru, the archvillain, along with his adopted daughters and his diminutive yellow Minions. During the queue and preshow, you visit Gru's house and are then ushered into his lab, where you're turned into a Minion. The ride ends with a disco dance party that you join as you exit.

TOURING TIPS The ride is just inside the USF main entrance, making crowding a problem. If you're on hand at park opening and you ride Despicable Me first, you'll have a short wait. However, you'll set yourself up for a long wait at nearby Hollywood Rip Ride Rockit. If the coaster is a priority for you, ride it first and then return to Despicable Me immediately afterward. If by that time the wait is intolerable, try again in the late afternoon. Stationary seating is available for those prone to motion sickness and for children less than 40 inches tall.

E. T. Adventure *(Universal Express)* ★★★½

APPEAL BY AGE	PRESCHOOL ★★★★	GRADE SCHOOL ★★★★	TEENS ★★★
YOUNG ADULTS ★★★		OVER 30 ★★★★	SENIORS ★★★★

What it is Indoor adventure ride based on the beloved movie. **Scope and scale** Major attraction. **When to go** During the first 90 minutes the park is open. **Special comments** 34″ minimum height requirement. **Authors' rating** A happy reunion; ★★★½. **Duration of ride** 4½ minutes. **Average wait in line per 100 people ahead of you** 5 minutes. **Loading speed** Moderate.

DESCRIPTION AND COMMENTS Guests board a bicycle-like conveyance to escape with E. T., The Extra-Terrestrial, from earthly law enforcement officials and journey to his home planet. Concerning the latter, where E. T. is reunited with family and friends, Len Testa likens it to *The Wizard of Oz*'s Technicolor scene, only reenacted with a cave full of naked mole rats. (C'mon, Len, where's the love?) The attraction is similar to Peter Pan's Flight at the Magic Kingdom, only longer and weirder.

A Baton, North Carolina, reader with perhaps too much time on his hands got to wondering:

Why do the inhabitants of E. T.'s home planet, who presumably have never visited Earth, speak better English than he does?

TOURING TIPS Most preschoolers and grade-school children love E. T. We think it's worth a 20- to 30-minute wait, but no longer than that. Lines build quickly after 10:30 a.m., and waits can reach 2 hours on busy days. Ride in the morning or late afternoon. On peak days, a time-saving single-rider line is occasionally opened.

Fear Factor Live (Universal Express) ★★½

APPEAL BY AGE	PRESCHOOL ★	GRADE SCHOOL ★★	TEENS ★★★★
YOUNG ADULTS ★★★		OVER 30 ★★★	SENIORS ★★

What it is Live version of the gross-out-stunt TV show. **Scope and scale** Headliner. **When to go** 6–8 shows daily; crowds are smallest at the first and second-to-last shows. **Authors' rating** *Ewwww;* ★★½. **Duration of show** 30 minutes. **Probable waiting time** 25 minutes.

DESCRIPTION AND COMMENTS *Fear Factor Live* is a stage version of the uniquely stomach-turning reality show that ran on NBC from 2001 to 2006 and again from 2011 to 2012. In the theme park iteration, six volunteers compete for one prize; this varies but is always a package that contains Universal goodies ranging from park tickets to T-shirts. Contestants must be 18 years or older (with a photo ID to prove it) and weigh at least 110 pounds. Those demented enough to volunteer should arrive at least 75 minutes before showtime to sign papers and complete some obligatory training for the specific competitive events. Anyone who doesn't wish to compete in the stage show itself can sign up for the Critter Challenge or the Food Challenge. With an adult's permission, volunteers as young as age 16 can compete in the latter.

The stage show is performed in a covered theater and consists of three different challenges. In the first, all six contestants are suspended two-and-a-half stories in the air and try to hang on to a bar as long as possible. The difficulty is compounded by heavy-duty fans blasting the contestants' faces (as you can imagine, this stunt requires exceptional upper-body strength).

Once the first two contestants are eliminated, it's time for a brief intermission called the Desert Hat Ordeal. This involves a brave audience member–lunatic who has signed up for the Critter Challenge. Prepared with eye goggles and a mouthpiece, the volunteer is put in a chair with a glass case over his or her head. A wheel is spun to determine what will be crawling over the volunteer's head; the creepy-crawly choices include spiders, snakes, roaches, and scorpions. The only incentive to participate is a free photo of the ordeal for contestants to take to their therapists.

Back at the main competition, the four remaining contestants are split into two teams to compete in the Eel Tank Relay. This consists of one team member grabbing beanbags out of a tank full of eels and throwing them to his or her partner to catch in a bucket. Audience members drench the contestants with high-powered water guns, further spicing up the event. The duo who buckets the most beanbags wins, going on to compete against each other in the final round for the $400 prize package.

As the stage is prepared for the finale, the folks who volunteered for the Food Challenge are split into two teams and invited to drink a mixture of curdled milk, mystery meat, and various live bugs that are all blended together on stage. The team that drinks the most of the mixture within the time limit wins a glamorous plastic mug that says, "I Ate a Bug," a convenient euphemism for "I have the brain of a nematode."

The last event has the two remaining contestants scramble up a wall to retrieve flags, jump into a car that is lifted in the air, and then jump out of the car to retrieve more flags. The first player to remove a rocket launcher from the backseat of the car and hit a target on the stage wall wins.

It's our duty to confess that this is one of our least favorite shows in any theme park, anywhere, ever. You have been warned.

TOURING TIPS If you've ever wanted a chance to test your mettle (sanity?), *Fear Factor Live* may be your big chance. Participants for the physical stunts are chosen early in the morning and between performances outside the theater, so head there first thing if you want to be a contestant. The contestants for the skeevier stunts, like the bug-smoothie drinking, are chosen directly from the audience. Sit close to the front and wave your hands like crazy when it comes time for selection. Finally (and seriously), this show is too intense and gross for kids age 8 and under.

Fievel's Playland ★★★

APPEAL BY AGE	PRESCHOOL ★★★★	GRADE SCHOOL ★★★★	TEENS —
YOUNG ADULTS —		OVER 30 —	SENIORS —

What it is Children's play area with waterslide. **Scope and scale** Minor attraction. **When to go** Anytime. **Authors' rating** A much-needed attraction for preschoolers; ★★★. **Probable waiting time** 20–30 minutes for the waterslide; otherwise, no waiting. **Loading speed** Slow for the waterslide.

DESCRIPTION AND COMMENTS This whimsical playground in Woody Woodpecker's KidZone features ordinary household items reproduced on a giant scale, as a mouse would experience them. Preschoolers and grade-schoolers can climb nets, walk through a huge boot, splash in a sardine-can fountain, seesaw on huge spoons, and climb onto a cow skull. Most of the playground is reserved for preschoolers, but a combo waterslide and raft ride is open to all ages.

TOURING TIPS Most of Fievel's Playland requires no waiting, so you can stay as long as you want. Younger children love the oversize items, and there's enough to keep teens and adults busy while little ones let off steam. The waterslide–raft ride is open to everyone but is extremely slow-loading and carries only 300 riders per hour. With an average wait of 20–30 minutes, the 16-second ride isn't worth the trouble. Also, you're highly likely to get soaked. Lack of shade is a major shortcoming of the entire attraction—the playground is scorching during the heat of the day.

Hollywood Rip Ride Rockit *(Universal Express)* ★★★★

APPEAL BY AGE	PRESCHOOL —	GRADE SCHOOL ★★★★	TEENS ★★★★½
YOUNG ADULTS ★★★★½		OVER 30 ★★★★½	SENIORS ★★★½

What it is High-tech roller coaster. **Scope and scale** Headliner. **When to go** Immediately after park opening. **Special comments** 51" minimum height requirement; expect long waits in line. **Authors' rating** Woo-hoo! (and ouch!); ★★★★. **Duration of ride** 2½ minutes. **Average wait in line per 100 people ahead of you** 3–5 minutes. **Loading speed** Moderate.

Motion Sickness

DESCRIPTION AND COMMENTS Hollywood Rip Ride Rockit is USF's candidate for the most technologically advanced coaster in the world. Well, we know how long that distinction lasted, but for sure this ride has some features that we've never seen before. Let's start with the basics: Rip Ride Rockit is a sit-down X-Car coaster that runs on a 3,800-foot steel track, with a maximum height of 167 feet and a top speed of 65 miles an hour. Manufactured by German coaster maker Maurer Söhne, X-Car vehicles are more maneuverable than most other kinds and use less restrictive restraints, making for an exhilarating ride.

You ascend—vertically—at 11 feet per second to crest the 17-story-tall first hill, the highest point reached by any roller coaster in Orlando, until Mako in SeaWorld opens in 2016. The drop is almost vertical, too, launching you into Double Take, a loop inversion in which you begin on the inside of the loop, twist to the outside at the top (so you're upright), and then twist back inside the loop for the descent. Double Take stands 136 feet tall, and its loop is 103 feet in diameter at its widest point. You next hurl (no, not that kind of hurl!) into a stretch of track shaped like a musical treble clef. As on Double Take, the track configuration on Treble Clef is a first. Another innovation is Jump Cut, a spiraling negative-gravity maneuver. Usually on coasters, you experience negative gravity on long, steep, vertical drops; with Jump Cut you feel like you're in a corkscrew inversion, but you never actually go upside down. Other high points include a 95-degree turn, a downhill into an "underground chasm" (gotta love those Universal PR wordsmiths!), and a final incline loop banked at 150 degrees.

The ride starts in the Production Central area; weaves into the New York area near the former *Twister . . . Ride It Out,* popping out over the heads of guests in the square below; and then storms out and over the lagoon separating Universal Studios Florida from Islands of Adventure.

Each train consists of two cars, with riders arranged two across in three rows per car. Each row is outfitted with color-changing LEDs and high-end audio and video technology for each seat. Like Rock 'n' Roller Coaster at Disney's Hollywood Studios, the "Triple R" features a musical sound track, but in this case you can choose the genre of music you want to hear as you ride: classic rock, country, disco, pop, or rap. When it's over, Universal flogs a digital-video rip of your ride, complete with the sound track you chose, that you can upload to YouTube, Facebook, and the like.

From a Whalton, England, mom:

A fabulous, gut-wrenching coaster that thrilled the socks off my 8- and 9-year-olds. (Mum found it a bit too brutal to repeat.)

A perhaps-jaded Easton, Connecticut, coaster aficionado offers this:

The loud music blasting in our ears canceled out the sound of the coaster. If only they had a "None of the Above: Silence" selection. The singles-line hint was a real time-saver.

When Hollywood Rip Ride Rockit premiered in 2009, it was pretty smooth. Alas, the wheels on the cars haven't held up well in the hot Florida sun. While perfectly safe, Rip Ride Rockit now subjects you to a lot of side-to-side jarring. To crib a phrase from Tina Turner, some folks like it easy . . . and some folks like it *rough.*

TOURING TIPS Hollywood Rip Ride Rockit can put more trains on the tracks simultaneously than any other coaster in Florida, which results in an hourly capacity of about 1,500 riders. Because the ride is so close to the USF entrance, it's a crowd magnet, creating bottlenecks from park opening on. Your only chance to ride without a long wait is to be one of the first to enter the park when it opens.

Kang & Kodos' Twirl 'n' Hurl   ★★★

APPEAL BY AGE	PRESCHOOL ★★★★	GRADE SCHOOL ★★★	TEENS ★★★
YOUNG ADULTS ★★★		OVER 30 ★★★	SENIORS ★★

What it is Spinning ride. **Scope and scale** Minor attraction. **When to go** After The Simpsons Ride. **Special comments** Rarely has a long wait. **Authors' rating** The world's wittiest spinner; ★★★. **Duration of ride** 1½ minutes. **Average wait in line per 100 people ahead of you** 21 minutes. **Loading speed** Slow.

DESCRIPTION AND COMMENTS The Twirl 'n' Hurl is primarily eye candy for Springfield U.S.A. Think of it as Dumbo with Bart's sense of humor: Guests ride around in little flying saucers while the alien narrators, Kang and Kodos, hold pictures of Simpson characters. You can make the characters speak and spin by steering your craft to the proper altitude. All the while, Kang exhorts you (loudly) to destroy Springfield and makes insulting comments about humans. Preschoolers enjoy the ride, while older kids crack up over the gags.

TOURING TIPS You can dig the narration from the sidelines rather than queue up for this slow-loading midway ride. If you have folks who are hot to ride, get them on whenever there are 50 or fewer guests in line.

Men in Black Alien Attack *(Universal Express)*   ★★★★½

APPEAL BY AGE   PRESCHOOL ★★   GRADE SCHOOL ★★★★★   TEENS ★★★★★
YOUNG ADULTS ★★★★★   OVER 30 ★★★★★   SENIORS ★★★★

What it is Interactive dark thrill ride. **Scope and scale** Super-headliner. **When to go** During the first 90 minutes the park is open. **Special comments** May induce motion sickness; 42″ minimum height requirement. Switching-off option provided (see page 201). **Authors' rating** Buzz Lightyear on steroids; not to be missed; ★★★★½. **Duration of ride** 4½ minutes. **Average wait in line per 100 people ahead of you** 5 minutes. **Loading speed** Moderate–fast.

DESCRIPTION AND COMMENTS Men in Black Alien Attack brings together Will Smith and Rip Torn (as Agent J and MIB director Zed) for an interactive sequel to the hit film. The story line has you volunteering as a Men in Black (MIB) trainee. After an introductory warning that aliens "live among us" and articulating MIB's mission to round them up, Zed expounds on the finer points of alien spotting and familiarizes you with your training vehicle and your weapon, an alien "zapper." You then load up and are dispatched on an innocuous training mission that immediately deteriorates into a situation where only you can prevent aliens from taking over the universe. If you saw the movie, you understand that the aliens are mostly giant bugs and that zapping them involves blasting them into myriad gooey body parts. Thus, the meat of the ride (pardon the pun) consists of careening around Manhattan in your MIB vehicle and shooting aliens. Targets above you score the most points; look for aliens behind second-story windows. If you're good enough, you can max out with 999,999 points.

Men in Black is interactive in that your marksmanship and ability to blast yourself out of some tricky situations will determine how the story ends. Also, you're awarded a personal score (as at the Magic Kingdom's Buzz Lightyear's Space Ranger Spin) and a score for your car. There are about three dozen possible outcomes and literally thousands of different ride experiences determined by your pluck, performance, and, in the final challenge, your intestinal fortitude.

TOURING TIPS Each alien figure has sensors that activate special effects and respond to your zapper. Aim for the eyes and keep shooting until the aliens' eyes turn red. Also, many of the aliens shoot back, causing your vehicle to veer or spin; in the mayhem, you might fail to notice that another vehicle runs beside you on a dual track. At a certain point, you can shoot the flashing "vent" on top of this other car and make its occupants spin around. Of course, they can do the same to you.

Avoid a long wait and ride during the first 90 minutes the park is open, or try the single-rider line if you don't mind splitting your group. You can re-ride by following the signs for the child swap at the top of the exit stairs.

Revenge of the Mummy *(Universal Express)*   ★★★★½

APPEAL BY AGE	PRESCHOOL ★★	GRADE SCHOOL ★★★★	TEENS ★★★★★
YOUNG ADULTS ★★★★½		OVER 30 ★★★★	SENIORS ★★★½

What it is Combination dark ride and roller coaster. **Scope and scale** Super-headliner. **When to go** The first hour the park is open or after 6 p.m. **Special comments** 48″ minimum height requirement. Switching-off option provided (see page 201). **Authors' rating** Killer! Not to be missed; ★★★★½. **Duration of ride** 3 minutes. **Average wait in line per 100 people ahead of you** 7 minutes. **Loading speed** Moderate.

DESCRIPTION AND COMMENTS It's hard to wrap your mind around this attraction, but trust us when we say that you're in for a very strange experience. Here, quoting Universal, are some of the things you can look forward to: "authentic Egyptian catacombs"; "high-velocity show-immersion system" (Huh? Quickie baptism?); "magnet-propulsion launch wave system"; "a 'Brain Fire' [!] that hovers [over guests] with temperatures soaring to 2,000°F"; and "canopic jars containing grisly remains."

When you read between the lines, Revenge of the Mummy is an indoor dark ride based on the Mummy flicks, where guests fight off "deadly curses and vengeful creatures" while flying through Egyptian tombs and other spooky places on a high-tech roller coaster. As far as special effects go, they're pretty good: video effects, animatronics, lighting, and enough fire-spewing gas vents to rotisserie a chicken. The endings (yes, plural) are pretty clever.

The queuing area serves to establish the story line: You're in a group touring a set from the Mummy films when you enter a tomb where the fantasy world of film gives way to the real thing. Along the way, you're warned about a possible curse. The visuals are rich and compelling as the queue makes its way to the loading area, where you board a clunky, jeeplike vehicle. The ride begins as a slow, very elaborate dark ride, passing through various chambers, including one where flesh-eating scarab beetles descend on you. Suddenly your vehicle stops, then drops backward and rotates. Here's where you're shot at high speed up the first hill of the roller coaster part of the ride. We won't divulge too much, but the coaster part of the ride offers its own panoply of surprises (there are no barrel rolls or upside-down stuff, however). And though it's a wild ride by anyone's definition, the emphasis remains as much on the visuals, robotics, and special effects as on the ride itself.

TOURING TIPS Diagon Alley, Hollywood Rip Ride Rockit, and Despicable Me Minion Mayhem have diminished the early-morning crowds. Nevertheless, try to ride during the first hour the park is open. If lines are long, try the singles line, which is often more expedient than Universal Express. Concerning motion sickness, if you can ride Space Mountain without ill effect, you should be fine on Revenge of the Mummy. Finally, note that the Mummy's queue contains enough scary business to frighten little kids all on its own.

Shrek 4-D *(Universal Express)*   ★★★½

APPEAL BY AGE	PRESCHOOL ★★★	GRADE SCHOOL ★★★★★	TEENS ★★★★★
YOUNG ADULTS ★★★★★		OVER 30 ★★★★★	SENIORS ★★★★★

What it is 3-D movie with air, water, and smell effects. **Scope and scale** Headliner. **When to go** The first hour the park is open or after 4 p.m. **Authors' rating** The snarkiest 3-D show in town; ★★★½. **Duration of show** 20 minutes. **Probable waiting time** 16 minutes.

DESCRIPTION AND COMMENTS Based on characters from the hit movie, the preshow presents the villain from the movie, Lord Farquaad, as he appears on various screens to describe his posthumous plan to reclaim his lost bride, Princess Fiona, who married Shrek. The plan is posthumous because Lord Farquaad ostensibly died in the movie, and it's his ghost making the plans, but never mind. Guests then move into the main theater, don their 3-D glasses, and recline in seats equipped with "tactile transducers" and "pneumatic air propulsion and water spray nodules capable of both vertical and horizontal motion." As the 3-D film plays, guests are also subjected to smells relevant to the on-screen action (oh, boy).

Technicalities aside, *Shrek 4-D* is a mixed bag. It's frantic, laugh-out-loud funny, and iconoclastic. Concerning the last, the film takes a good poke at Disney, with Pinocchio, the Three Little Pigs, and Tinker Bell (among others) all sucked into the mayhem. But the video quality and 3-D effects are dated by today's ultra-HD standards, the story line is incoherently disconnected from the clever preshow, and the franchise's relevance has faded since the lackluster fourth film. On the upside, in contrast to Disney's *It's Tough to Be a Bug!*, *Shrek 4-D* doesn't generally freak out kids under age 7.

TOURING TIPS Universal claims that it can move about 2,400 guests per hour through *Shrek 4-D,* but the show's location at the front of the park and directly across from Despicable Me Minion Mayhem translates to heavy traffic in the morning. If you see lines longer than 20 minutes, try visiting during mealtimes or in the last 2 hours the park is open. There's not much in the film or preshow to scare small children.

The Simpsons Ride *(Universal Express)*   ★★★★

APPEAL BY AGE	PRESCHOOL ★★	GRADE SCHOOL ★★★★	TEENS ★★★★
YOUNG ADULTS ★★★★		OVER 30 ★★★★	SENIORS ★★★½

What it is Mega–simulator ride. **Scope and scale** Super-headliner. **When to go** During the first hour the park is open. **Special comments** 40″ minimum height requirement; not recommended for pregnant women or people prone to motion sickness. Switching-off option provided (see page 201). **Authors' rating** Despicable Me with attitude; not to be missed; ★★★★. **Duration of ride** 4⅓ minutes, plus preshow. **Average wait in line per 100 people ahead of you** 5 minutes. **Loading speed** Moderate.

Motion Sickness

DESCRIPTION AND COMMENTS The Simpsons Ride is based on the Fox animated series that is now TV's longest-running sitcom. Featuring the voices of Dan Castellaneta (Homer), Julie Kavner (Marge), Nancy Cartwright (Bart), Yeardley Smith (Lisa), and other cast members, the attraction takes a wild, humorous poke at thrill rides, dark rides, and live shows "that make up a fantasy amusement park dreamed up by the show's cantankerous Krusty the Clown."

Two preshows involve *Simpsons* characters speaking sequentially on different video screens around the line area. Their comments help define the characters for guests who are unfamiliar with the TV show. The attraction is a simulator ride similar to Star Tours at Disney's Hollywood Studios and Despicable Me Minion Mayhem (see page 209), but with a larger screen more like that of Soarin' at Epcot. The ride vehicles hold eight guests in two rows of four.

The story line has the conniving Sideshow Bob secretly arriving at Krustyland, the aforementioned amusement park, and plotting his revenge on Krusty and Bart, who, in a past *Simpsons* episode, revealed that Sideshow Bob had committed a crime for which he'd framed Krusty. Sideshow Bob gets even by making things go wrong with the attractions that the Simpsons (and you) are riding.

Like the show on which it's based, The Simpsons Ride definitely has an edge, and more than a few wild hairs. Like *Shrek 4-D,* it operates on several levels. There will be jokes and visuals that you'll get but will fly over your children's heads—and most assuredly vice versa.

TOURING TIPS Though not as rough and jerky as its predecessor, Back to the Future—The Ride, it's a long way from being tame. Skip it if you're an expectant mom or prone to motion sickness. Some parents may find the humor too coarse for younger kids.

Terminator 2: 3-D (*Universal Express*) ★★★★

APPEAL BY AGE	PRESCHOOL ★★★	GRADE SCHOOL ★★★★	TEENS ★★★★
YOUNG ADULTS ★★★★★		OVER 30 ★★★★★	SENIORS ★★★★

What it is 3-D thriller mixed-media presentation. **Scope and scale** Super-headliner. **When to go** After 3:30 p.m. **Special comments** One of the nation's best theme park theater attractions; very intense for some preschoolers and grade-schoolers. **Authors' rating** Furiously paced; not to be missed; ★★★★. **Duration of show** 20 minutes, including 8-minute preshow. **Probable waiting time** 20–40 minutes.

DESCRIPTION AND COMMENTS The evil "cop" from *Terminator 2* battles Arnold Schwarzenegger's T-100 cyborg character. In case you missed the Terminator flicks, here's a refresher: A bad robot arrives from the future to kill a nice boy. Another bad robot—who has been reprogrammed to be good—pops up to save the boy. The bad robot chases the boy and the good robot, menacing the audience in the process.

The attraction, like the films, is all action, and you really don't need to understand much. What's interesting is that it uses 3-D film and a theater full of sophisticated technology to integrate the real with the imaginary. Images seem to move in and out of the film, not only in the manner of traditional 3-D but also in reality: Remove your 3-D glasses a moment, and you'll see that the guy on the motorcycle is actually onstage.

TOURING TIPS The 700-seat theater changes audiences about every 19 minutes. Even so, because the show is popular, expect to wait about 30 minutes. We suggest that you save *Terminator* and other theater presentations until you've experienced all the rides. Families with young children will be relieved to know that the violence characteristic of the movie series is largely absent from the attraction—there's suspense and action, but not much blood and guts.

Transformers: The Ride 3-D   ★★★★★

APPEAL BY AGE   PRESCHOOL ★★★   GRADE SCHOOL ★★★★★   TEENS ★★★★★
YOUNG ADULTS ★★★★★   OVER 30 ★★★★★   SENIORS ★★★★

What it is Multisensory 3-D dark ride. **Scope and scale** Super-headliner. **When to go** First 30 minutes the park is open or after 4 p.m. **Special comments** Must be 40″ tall to ride; single-rider line available. **Authors' rating** Not to be missed; ★★★★★. **Duration of ride** 4½ minutes. **Average wait in line per 100 people ahead of you** 3 minutes. **Loading speed** Moderate-fast.

DESCRIPTION AND COMMENTS Hasbro's Transformers—those toy robots from the 1980s that you twisted into trucks and planes—have been, well, transformed into director Michael Bay's recent movie franchise. In 2013, Transformers fans at Universal Studios Florida finally received a theme park attraction befitting their pop-culture idols. Recruits to this cyber-tronic war enlist by entering the N.E.S.T. Base (headquarters of the heroic Autobots and their human allies). Inside, in the queue, video monitors catch you up on the backstory. Basically, the Decepticon baddies are after the Allspark, source of cybernetic sentience. Your job is to safeguard the shard. The highly vexing evil Megatron and his pals Starscream and Devastator threaten the mission, but don't worry—we have Sideswipe and Bumblebee on the bench to back us up.

Transformers harnesses the same traveling simulator system behind Islands of Adventure's Amazing Adventures of Spider-Man, and it ups the ante with photo-realistic high-definition imagery, boosted by dichroic 3-D glasses that produce remarkably sharp, vivid visuals. The plot amounts to little more than a giant game of keep-away, and the uninitiated will likely be unable to tell one meteoric mass of metal from another, but you'll be too dazzled by the debris whizzing by to notice. The ride's mix of detailed (though largely static) set pieces and video projections bring these colossi to life in one of the most intense, immersive thrill rides found in any theme park.

Two millennials had, shall we say, a visceral take on Transformers:

The illusion of being smashed through an office building is pretty convincing. If you've ever wondered what it would like to be eaten, digested, and pooped out of a giant robot, this is the ride for you.

Hopefully, it's also a ride for those who don't exactly see Transformers as a ride down the alimentary canal. Robots poop? Who knew?

TOURING TIPS This ride draws crowds—your only solace is that The Wizarding World of Harry Potter–Diagon Alley draws even larger throngs. Follow our touring plan to minimize waits. The single-rider line will get you on board faster, but as singles lines go, this is one of the slower ones and will be closed off if it becomes backed up. Finally, it's hard to focus on the fast-moving imagery from the front row; center seats in the second and third rows provide the best perspective.

Universal Orlando's Horror Make-Up Show
(Universal Express)   ★★★★½

APPEAL BY AGE   PRESCHOOL ★★★   GRADE SCHOOL ★★★★   TEENS ★★★★
YOUNG ADULTS ★★★★★   OVER 30 ★★★★   SENIORS ★★★★

What it is Theater presentation on the art of makeup. **Scope and scale** Major attraction. **When to go** After you've experienced all rides. **Special comments** May frighten young children. **Authors' rating** A gory knee-slapper; not to be missed; ★★★★½. **Duration of show** 25 minutes. **Probable waiting time** 20 minutes.

DESCRIPTION AND COMMENTS The *Horror Make-Up Show* is a brief but humorous look at how basic monster-movie special effects are done. The show includes onstage demonstrations of effects such as blood-spurting fake knives and rubber limbs, plus how mechanical effects are combined with rubber masks to transform human heads into wolf-shaped skulls. Film clips are interspersed throughout the presentation, showing how computer-generated special effects are blended into live-action films. This may be Universal's most entertaining live show. While there's plenty of fake blood thrown around, the script is mostly funny. The hosts' running commentary about horror-film making is interspersed with plenty of pop-culture jokes for the kids.

TOURING TIPS The *Horror Make-Up Show* is the sleeper attraction at Universal. Its humor and tongue-in-cheek style transcend the gruesome effects, and most folks (including preschoolers) take the blood and guts in stride. But it's the exception that proves the rule, as this reader relates:

> *My 7- and 9-year-olds had no problem with* Terminator *but were scared by the* Horror Make-Up Show *(despite my telling them the guy was not really cutting anyone's arm off!). We ended up leaving before the show was over.*

Universal's Cinematic Spectacular: 100 Years of Movie Memories ★★★½ *(seasonal when park is open late)*

APPEAL BY AGE	PRESCHOOL ★★★	GRADE SCHOOL ★★★★	TEENS ★★★½
YOUNG ADULTS ★★★★		OVER 30 ★★★★	SENIORS ★★★★

What it is Fireworks, dancing fountains, and movies. **Scope and scale** Major attraction. **When to go** 1 show a day, usually at park closing. **Special comments** Movie trailers galore. **Authors' rating** Good effort; ★★★½. **Duration of show** 15–20 minutes. **Probable waiting time** None.

DESCRIPTION AND COMMENTS This is USF's big nighttime event, designed to cap your day at the park. Shown on the lagoon in the middle of the park, the presentation runs through film clips and music from the first 100 years of Universal's biggest movies. The scenes are projected onto three enormous "screens" made by spraying water from the lagoon into the air (similar to *Fantasmic!* at Disney's Hollywood Studios). Fireworks and colored lights are also used to good effect throughout the presentation, which is narrated by God himself—well, actually, Morgan Freeman. It's an enjoyable way to end your day at the park.

Reviews are generally either mixed or positive. This mom of two liked it:

> *My family really enjoyed the show. It didn't have the same emotional impact as [Disney's]* Wishes, *but it was entertaining. There were so many great movies we hadn't thought about in ages!*

If you've been experiencing USF attractions throughout the day, you've already been exposed to most of the characters and memorable scenes referenced in the nighttime show. Reliving them again so soon may seem redundant, though dozens of films are referenced that aren't otherwise honored in the parks.

TOURING TIPS The ends of the lagoon are not recommended for viewing. The best spot is directly across the lagoon from Richter's Burger Company, where the sidewalk makes a small protrusion overlooking the water. Because acquiring a spot here can be very difficult during peak season, we recommend arriving at least 45 minutes ahead of time.

Before the show begins, realize that not all of the movie clips may be suitable for young viewers. The horror montage, for example, mixes excerpts from hoary black-and-white monster movies with potentially fright-inducing clips from films such as *The Birds, Halloween, Psycho, The Silence of the Lambs,* and *Tales from the Crypt.*

Finally, just as Disney does with *Fantasmic!,* Universal offers a dinner package for the *Cinematic Spectacular.* As of now, the only restaurant option is Lombard's Seafood Grille; the cost is $45 for adults and $13 for kids, including tax and tip. After the meal, you'll go to a special seating area to watch the show and enjoy a dessert buffet. It's a decent option if you're in the mood for seafood and you planned to see the show anyway. Reservations are required and can be made online (**tinyurl.com/cinematicspectacular dining**) or by phone (☎ 407-224-7554, Monday–Saturday, 7:30 a.m.–10 p.m.; Sunday, 7:30 a.m.–9 p.m. Eastern time).

Woody Woodpecker's Nuthouse Coaster and Curious George Goes to Town ★★½

APPEAL BY AGE   PRESCHOOL ★★★★   GRADE SCHOOL ★★★½   TEENS —
YOUNG   ADULTS   —   OVER   30   —   SENIORS   —

What it is Interactive playground and kids' roller coaster. **Scope and scale** Minor attraction. **When to go** Anytime. **Special comments** 36″ minimum height requirement for coaster. **Authors' rating** *The* place for rambunctious kids; ★★½. **Average wait in line per 100 people ahead of you** 5 minutes for the coaster. **Loading speed** For the coaster, *slooow.*

DESCRIPTION AND COMMENTS These two kid-friendly attractions reside, along with Fievel's Playland (see page 212), in Woody Woodpecker's KidZone. The Nuthouse Coaster is small enough for kids to enjoy but sturdy enough for adults, though its moderate speed might unnerve some smaller children. Adjacent is Curious George Goes to Town, an interactive playground that exemplifies the Universal obsession with wet stuff; in addition to innumerable spigots, pipes, and spray guns, two giant roof-mounted buckets periodically dump a thousand gallons of water on unsuspecting visitors below. Kids who want to stay dry can mess around in the foam-ball playground, also equipped with chutes, tubes, and ball-blasters.

TOURING TIPS Visit after you've experienced all the major attractions. Rumor has it that the KidZone may be closing in the near future.

THE WIZARDING WORLD OF HARRY POTTER–DIAGON ALLEY

WHEN UNIVERSAL opened The Wizarding World of Harry Potter at Islands of Adventure, it created a paradigm shift in the Disney–Universal theme park rivalry. Not only did Universal trot out some groundbreaking ride technology, but it also demonstrated that it could trump Disney's most distinctive competence: the creation of infinitely detailed and totally immersive themed areas. To say that The Wizarding World was a game changer is an understatement of the first order.

It was immediately obvious that Universal would build on its Potter franchise success—but how and where? Universal's not sitting on 27,000-plus acres like Disney, so real estate was at a premium. If Potterville was going to grow, something else had to go. Conventional wisdom suggested The Wizarding World expansion would gobble up The Lost Continent section of Islands of Adventure, and that may happen yet. But looking at the ledger, it was clear that the older Universal Studios Florida theme park could use a boost.

It just so happened that a substantial chunk of turf at USF was occupied by the aging Jaws ride and its contiguous themed area. The space would allow for substantial development; plus, its isolated location—in the most remote corner of the park—was conducive to creating a totally self-contained area where Potter themes could be executed absent any distraction from neighboring attractions. In short, it was perfect.

So how would the new Potter area tie in to the original at IOA? And what Harry Potter literary icons could be exploited? It was pretty clear that a new suburb of Hogsmeade wasn't going to cut it. Turns out that the answer was virtually shouting from the pages of the Harry Potter novels, which observe a clear dichotomy of place—plots originate in London and then unfold at distant Hogwarts.

Two London sites that figure prominently in the Potter saga brim with attraction possibilities: Diagon Alley, a secret part of London that is a sort of sorcerers' shopping mall; and the King's Cross railroad station, where wizarding students embark for the train trip to Hogwarts.

Following much deliberation and consultation with Warner Bros. and author J. K. Rowling, the final design called for a London-waterfront street scene flanking Universal Studios Lagoon. The detailed facades, anchored by the **King's Cross** railroad station on the left and including **Grimmauld Place** and **Wyndham's Theatre,** recall West London scenes from the books and movies. **Diagon Alley,** secreted behind the London street scene, is accessed through a secluded entrance in the middle of the facade. Like Hogsmeade at IOA, Diagon Alley features shops and restaurants in addition to three attractions and live entertainment.

Diagon Alley covers 20 acres—about the same area as the Hogsmeade original—but offers about two-and-a-half times the pedestrian space, since it doesn't have space- (and people-) eating outdoor roller coasters. With only one high-capacity ride (**Harry Potter and the Escape from Gringotts**), along with an enlarged version of the **Ollivanders** wand-shop experience in Hogsmeade and the **Hogwarts Express** train connecting the two Wizarding Worlds, the new area's increased elbow room is somewhat offset by a relatively reduced hourly capacity of the attractions, making Diagon Alley's maximum capacity approximately 8,000, about double Hogsmeade's occupancy limit.

In the attraction department, Universal once again came out swinging for the fences. As before with Harry Potter and the Forbidden

Journey, the headliner attraction for the expansion is high-tech and cutting-edge—and once again a dark ride, but this time of the roller coaster genre. The labyrinthine passages and caverns of Gringotts Wizarding Bank, the financial institution of choice for the wizarding set, are the setting of this plot-driven 3-D dark ride–coaster.

Though Gringotts is Diagon Alley's headliner, we think that the most creative element in the two-park Potter domain is the Hogwarts Express, which re-creates the train trip from London to Hogwarts and vice versa. Serving as both an attraction and transportation between USF and IOA, the Express unifies the two disparately located Wizarding Worlds.

Diagon Alley in Detail

Diagon Alley and its London waterfront are sandwiched between the San Francisco and World Expo areas of the park, about as far from Universal Studios Florida's main entrance as you can get. From the park entrance, turn right on Rodeo Drive to Mel's Diner; from here, circumnavigate the lagoon counterclockwise, keeping it to your left until you reach the entrance to the London waterfront, where wrought iron fencing surrounds a parklike promenade. You can also access the London waterfront from the San Francisco area by walking clockwise around the lagoon and then taking a shoreline bypass along the embankment to the World Expo side of the Potter-themed area. Here you can access London through the gateway closest to the *Fear Factor Live* stadium. A third option is to take Hogwarts Express from Islands of Adventure, which exits at the London waterfront area.

Having arrived at the London area, take a moment to spot Kreacher (the house elf regularly peers from a second-story window above 12 Grimmauld Place) and chat with the Knight Bus conductor and his Caribbean-accented shrunken head. Also notable are snack and souvenir stands and a towering statue-topped fountain.

Now enter Diagon Alley next to the Leicester Square marquee in the approximate center of the building facades. As in the books and films, the unmarked portal is concealed within a magical brick wall that is ordinarily reserved for wizards and the like. (Unfortunately, the wall doesn't actually move, due to safety concerns.) However, the endless queue of Muggles (plain old humans) in shorts and flip-flops will leave little doubt where that entryway is.

Once admitted, look down the alley to the rounded facade of **Gringotts Wizarding Bank,** where a 40-foot fire-breathing Ukrainian Ironbelly dragon (as seen in *Harry Potter and the Deathly Hallows: Part 2*) perches atop the dome. To your left is the **Leaky Cauldron,** the area's flagship restaurant, serving authentically hearty British pub fare such as bangers and mash, cottage pie, and Guinness stew. You order and get your drinks at a counter; then you're seated with a candle that helps servers deliver food direct to your table. You can top off your meal with potted chocolate and sticky toffee pudding for dessert, or step around the corner to **Florean Fortescue's Ice-Cream Parlour** for unusual hard-pack flavors such as clotted cream, Earl Grey and lavender, and chocolate chili. Butterbeer soft-serve tastes almost exactly like the drinks, and you can get it at Florean Fortescue's in a cup ($4.99), waffle cone ($5.99), or plastic souvenir sundae glass ($10.99). If you only want a cup of Butterbeer without toppings, the soft-serve is also served off menu at **The Hopping Pot** and **The Fountain of Fair Fortune,** where you'll find a much shorter wait. If all that eating makes you thirsty, a variety of alcoholic and virgin novelty drinks are poured at The Hopping Pot and Fountain of Fair Fortune. Try the Wizard's Brew (a heavy porter) or Dragon Scale (a hoppy amber), or the Fishy Green Ale (mint boba tea with balls of blueberry juice) or Gillywater, which can be spiked with four different flavored elixirs. Of course, you can also get your Butterbeer or Pumpkin Juice fix.

Shopping is a major component of Diagon Alley in Potter lore; while Hogsmeade visitors went wild for the few wizardy shops there, Diagon Alley is the planet's wackiest mall, with a vastly expanded array of enchanted tchotchkes to declare bankruptcy over. Shops include **Weasleys' Wizard Wheezes,** a joke shop with many of the toys previously found in Hogsmeade's Zonko's, plus new gags such as Skiving Snackboxes and Decoy Detonators. Look up through the three-story store's glass ceiling for fireworks. **Wiseacre's Wizarding Equipment,** at the exit of Escape from Gringotts, sells crystal balls, compasses, and hourglasses. **Madam Malkin's Robes for All Occasions** stocks school uniforms, Scottish wool sweaters, and dress robes for wizards and witches. Adopt a plush cat, rat, owl, or hippogriff from the **Magical Menagerie. Shutterbutton's** will film your family in front of a green screen and insert you into a DVD of Potter scenes (about $70); **Quality Quidditch Supplies** sells golden snitches and jerseys for your favorite teams; and **Scribbulus** carries quills, notebooks, and similar school supplies. You can pay for all this loot in Gringotts bank notes, which you can purchase inside a money exchange overseen by an imperious interactive animatronic goblin, and then spend it anywhere within Universal Orlando (think Disney Dollars). In general, Diagon Alley's stores are larger and more plentiful than the tiny shops over in Hogsmeade, with carefully planned external and internal queues to corral waiting customers.

To the right of Escape from Gringotts is **Carkitt Market,** a canopy-covered plaza where short live shows are staged every half hour or so. *Celestina Warbeck and the Banshees* (★★★★) showcases the singing sorceress swinging to jazzy tunes titled and inspired by J. K. Rowling herself, and *Tales of Beedle the Bard* (★★★½) recounts the "Three Brothers" fable from *Deathly Hallows* with puppets crafted by Michael Curry (who also created the puppets for *Festival of the Lion King* and *Finding Nemo—The Musical*).

Intersecting Diagon Alley near the Leaky Cauldron is **Knockturn Alley,** a labyrinth of twisting passageways where the Harry Potter bad guys hang out. A covered walk-through area with a projected sky creating perpetual night, it features spooky special effects in the faux shop windows (don't miss the creeping tattoos and crawling spiders) and **Borgin and Burkes,** which sells objects from the dark side of magic (watch out for the mummified hand!).

With the opening of Diagon Alley, Universal also introduced interactive wands ($45) to the parks, supplementing the nonfunctional replica wands ($35) that continue to be sold at **Ollivanders** (see page 228) and in the smaller selection at **Wands by Gregorovitch.** Medallions embedded in the ground designate a couple dozen locations split between the two Wizarding Worlds, where hidden cameras in storefront windows can detect the waving of these special wands and respond to the correct motions with special effects both projected and practical. You might use the swish and flick of Wingardium Leviosa to levitate one object or the figure four Locomotor spell to animate another. It's a much more thematically satisfying form of interactivity than the gimmicky games found at the Magic Kingdom, but it can take some practice to get the hang of spell casting; wizards wander around the area to assist novices and demonstrate spells (though they may not loan their wands), but queues to trigger some effects can grow six deep at peak times. A map provided with each wand purchase details the location and movement for most effects, but there are some secret ones to discover on your own.

Discover is an important word in Diagon Alley—this incredibly intricate area feels like an actual place you can explore and get lost in, much like, say, Epcot's Morocco Pavilion or Disneyland's New Orleans Square. We can't overstate how seamlessly Diagon's designers have rendered the illusion of a living world, topping even Disney California Adventure's Cars Land. *Immersion* is an often-overworked buzzword in themed entertainment, but Diagon Alley exemplifies it, enveloping fans in Potter's world to a degree that far exceeds Hogsmeade's high standards. And even if you aren't a follower of the franchise, you may find yourself falling for it after experiencing Universal's incarnation.

Diagon Alley Attractions

Harry Potter and the Escape from Gringotts ★★★★★

APPEAL BY AGE	PRESCHOOL ★★	GRADE SCHOOL ★★★★	TEENS ★★★★★
YOUNG ADULTS ★★★★★		OVER 30 ★★★★★	SENIORS ★★★★

What it is Super-high-tech 3-D dark ride with roller coaster elements. **Scope and scale** Super-headliner. **When to go** Immediately after park opening or just before closing. **Special comments** Expect *looong* waits in line; 42″ minimum height requirement. **Authors' rating** The ultimate realization of "Ride the Movies"; not to be missed; ★★★★★. **Duration of ride** 4½ minutes. **Average waiting time per 100 people ahead of you** 4 minutes. **Loading speed** Moderate–fast.

DESCRIPTION AND COMMENTS Owned and operated by goblins, Gringotts is the Federal Reserve of the wizarding economy and the scene of memorable sequences from the first and final Potter installments. It's known for its toppling column facade, chandelier-adorned lobby, and bottomless caverns (and the heart-stopping rail carts running through them). The theme park adaptation is the centerpiece of Diagon Alley and the ultimate expression of the virtual reality rides that Universal has been refining since IOA opened.

Like Forbidden Journey at IOA, Harry Potter and the Escape from Gringotts incorporates a substantial part of the overall experience into its elaborate queue, which (like Hogwarts Castle) even non-riders should experience. You enter through the bank's lobby, where you're critically appraised by glowering animatronic goblins. Your path takes you to a "security checkpoint," where your photo will be taken (to be purchased afterward as an identity lanyard in the gift shop, natch), and past animated newspapers and office windows where the scenario is set up.

Unlike Forbidden Journey, however, Gringotts doesn't rush you through its queue but rather allows you to experience two full preshows before approaching the ride vehicles. In the first, goblin banker Blordak and Bill Weasley (Ron's curse-breaking big brother) prepare you for an introductory tour of the underground vaults. Then you're off for a convincing simulated 9-mile plunge into the earth aboard an "elevator" with a bouncing floor and ceiling projections. All this is before you pick up your 3-D glasses (identical to those at Transformers: The Ride 3-D) and ascend a spiral staircase into the stalactite-festooned boarding cave where your vault cart awaits.

Also unlike Forbidden Journey, and indeed all the rest of The Wizarding World, Gringotts is not set in a nebulous "moment frozen in time" where incidents from various stories simultaneously coexist. Instead, you enter the bank at the exact moment that Harry, Ron, Hermione, and Griphook arrive to liberate the Hufflepuff Cup Horcrux from Bellatrix Lestrange's vault. But in this retelling of *Deathly Hallows: Part 2*'s iconic action scene, you (as Muggles opening new bank accounts) are ingeniously integrated into the action. Familiar film moments featuring the vaults' guardian dragon play out in the background as Bellatrix and Voldemort menace you with snakes and sinister spells, whereupon the heroic trio pauses its quest to save your hapless posteriors. The storytelling—much more coherent than Forbidden Journey's—may disorient Potter purists, but it's an intelligent way to allow fans to relive a favorite adventure without merely rehashing the plot.

Gringotts's ornately industrial ride vehicles consist of two-car trains, each holding 24 people in rows of four. The ride merges Revenge of the Mummy's indoor-coaster aspects with The Amazing Adventures of Spider-Man's seamless integration of high-resolution 3-D film (the finale dome completely surrounds your car) and massive sculptural sets (some of the rockwork inside is six stories tall), while adding a few new tricks, such as independently rotating cars and motion-simulator bases built into the track.

The result is a ride that, though it doesn't break completely new ground as Forbidden Journey and Spider-Man did, combines favorite innovations from its predecessors in an exhilarating new way. It isn't quite the perfect attraction that some might be anticipating. The visuals are sometimes murky and the dialogue difficult to discern. And it's slightly disappointing that no animatronic figures, moving set pieces, or actual pyrotechnics appear in the ride, though you will get spritzed with water, blasted with warm air, and sprayed with fog—this is Universal, after all. Finally, though Helena Bonham Carter and Ralph Fiennes reprised their screen roles, Daniel Radcliffe and Emma Watson did not. Harry and pals' CGI stand-ins look OK, as they're never seen up close, but Hermione's voice double is dreadful.

Nitpicks aside, whether Escape from Gringotts is *the* greatest themed thrill ride of all time or merely *one* of the greatest can be happily debated by park fans until the next great leap forward comes along.

To these New England honeymooners, there's not much to debate:

Gringotts is a terrific ride! Less intense than the Forbidden Journey but still full of surprises.

TOURING TIPS Gringotts is the pot of gold at the end of Universal's rainbow that a kazillion crazed guests are racing toward. Though the interior line is gorgeous and air-conditioned, the mostly unshaded outdoor extended queue holds 4,000 guests—you don't want to be at the end of it. If you're a Universal resort guest and you qualify for early entry, use it. During off-season when USF doesn't offer Early Park Admission, day guests who arrive before official opening may be allowed to queue for Gringotts before it begins running. Otherwise, try the attraction around lunchtime or in the late afternoon; wait times usually peak after opening but become reasonable later in the day. Just be aware that the queue may shutter to new arrivals before the park closes if the posted wait time exceeds the remaining operating hours by more than 60 minutes, or even earlier if the ride breaks down. Be warned that, as with any ride this advanced, Gringotts can be expected to experience some downtime almost daily. Most operational interruptions are brief and resolved within 10 or 15 minutes.

As far as physical thrills go, Gringotts falls somewhere between Seven Dwarfs Mine Train and Space Mountain, with only one short (albeit unique) drop and no upside-down flips. It was designed to be less intense (read: less nauseating) than Forbidden Journey and therefore more appealing to families, with fewer height, weight, and size restrictions. The restraints are similar to Revenge of the Mummy's, with bars across your lap and shins, but slightly more restrictive. Use the test seat to the left of the front entrance if you're unsure, and request the third or sixth row for additional legroom.

The ride feels noticeably different depending on which row you're seated in. The front is closest to the action and has the scariest view of the drop; 3-D effects look better farther back. The sixth row gets the most coaster action, especially from the initial fall, but the screens are slightly distorted. The far right seat in row 4 is the sweet spot.

As is the case with most of Universal's thrill rides, you must leave your bags in a free locker. Luckily, unlike at Hogwarts Express, the lockers are separated from the attraction entrance, greatly improving guest flow. Universal Express is *not* currently accepted at this attraction. If you don't have bags and don't mind breaking up your group, the singles line will cut your wait to about a third of the posted time, but you'll skip all the preshows past the lobby; we don't advise this option until after your first ride.

Hogwarts Express   ★★★★½

What it is Transportation attraction. **Scope and scale** Super-headliner. **When to go** Immediately after park opening. **Special comments** Expect lengthy waits in line. A Park-to-Park pass is required to ride. **Authors' rating** A moving experience; not to be missed; ★★★★½. **Duration of ride** 4 minutes. **Average waiting time per 100 people ahead of you** 7 minutes. **Loading speed** Moderate.

DESCRIPTION AND COMMENTS Part of the genius of creating Diagon Alley at USF is that it's connected to Hogsmeade at Islands of Adventure (see page 244) by the Hogwarts Express, just as in the novels and films. The counterpart to Hogsmeade Station in IOA is Universal Studios' King's Cross station, a landmark London train depot that has been re-created a few doors down from Diagon Alley's hidden entrance. (It's important to note that King's Cross has a separate entrance and exit from Diagon Alley: You can't go directly between them without crossing through the London waterfront.)

The passage to Platform 9¾, from which Hogwarts students depart on their way to school, is concealed from Muggles by a seemingly solid brick wall, which you'll witness guests ahead of you dematerializing through. (Spoiler: The Pepper's Ghost effect creates a clever but congestion-prone photo op, but you experience only a dark corridor with whooshing sound effects when crossing over yourself.)

Once on the platform, you'll pass a pile of luggage (including an owl cage with an animatronic Hedwig) before being assigned to one of the three train cars' seven compartments. The train itself looks exactingly authentic to the nth degree, from the billowing steam to the brass fixtures and upholstery in your eight-passenger private cabin. Along your one-way Hogwarts Express journey, you'll see moving images projected beyond the windows of the car rather than the park's backstage areas, with the streets of London and the Scottish countryside rolling past outside your window. The screen isn't 3-D, but it's slightly curved to conceal the edges and create a convincing illusion of depth. Even more impressive are the frosted-glass doors you enter through, which turn out to be amazing screens that make it seem as if someone is standing on the other side. You experience a different presentation coming and going, and in addition to pastoral scenery, there are surprise appearances by secondary characters (Fred and George Weasley, Hagrid) and threats en route (bone-chilling Dementors, licorice spiders), augmented by sound effects in the cars.

Hogwarts Express isn't an adrenaline rush in the same way that Escape from Gringotts is, but for those invested in Potter lore, it may be even more emotionally thrilling. And unlike most Potter attractions, it can be experienced by the whole family, regardless of size.

TOURING TIPS There's a capacity-versus-authenticity issue front and center with Hogwarts Express—and if you know J. K. Rowling's reputation for perfectionism where adaptations of her books are concerned, you know the sticky wicket this presented for Universal. The train cars from the films and novels are divided into private compartments that seat eight, but replicating those compartments means fewer seats and longer load-ing times (and longer queues too). As a result, its carrying capacity is rel-atively small because the track can accommodate only two trains, each moving in a different direction and passing one another in the middle of the journey. This leaves Universal with a few crowd-mitigating options:

First, because using the train for a one-way trip involves park-hopping, one-way passengers will need a valid park-to-park ticket. Disembarking passengers must enter the second park and, if desired, queue again for their return trip. You'll be allowed (nay, encouraged) to upgrade your 1-Park Base Ticket at the station entrance.

Second, Universal Express is, ironically, unavailable for Hogwarts Express, at least for the time being.

Third, if the line becomes too long, Universal may limit you to only one one-way ride per day. If you wish to take a same-day return trip, you could be relegated to a secondary queue that promises to be exponentially slower than the already glacial standby queue. (Thankfully, this has only been enforced a couple of times.)

Despite all these challenges, Hogwarts Express managed to move 1 mil-lion riders in its first month of operation, surprising everyone with its opera-tional efficiency. As a result, lines rarely exceed 15 minutes in the morning and evening, though the queue may swell to an hour in midafternoon. The walk from one train station to the other is just under a mile and takes 20 min-utes at a moderate pace. If the posted wait is 15 minutes or less, it is typically quicker to take the train than to walk to the other Wizarding World.

Guests exiting in Hogsmeade have a chance to take a photo with the locomotive before it backs out for its next run. Guests departing from Hog-smeade should pose with the static train outside the station before they queue up.

Ollivanders ★★★★

APPEAL BY AGE	PRESCHOOL ★★★★	GRADE SCHOOL ★★★★★		TEENS ★★★★
YOUNG ADULTS ★★★★		OVER 30 ★★★½		SENIORS ★★★½

What it is Combination wizarding demonstration and shopping op. **Scope and scale** Major attraction. **When to go** After riding Harry Potter and the Escape from Gringotts. **Special comment** Audience stands. **Authors' rating** Enchanting; ★★★★. **Duration of show** 6 minutes. **Probable waiting time per 100 people ahead of you** 7 minutes.

DESCRIPTION AND COMMENTS Ollivanders, located in Diagon Alley in the books and films, somehow sprouted a branch location in Hogsmeade at IOA (see page 249). Potter scholars pointed out this misplacement, but the wand shop stayed put and became one of the more popular features of The Wizarding World. It also became a horrendous bottleneck, with long lines where guests roasted in an unshaded queue. In the Diagon Alley version, Ollivanders assumes its rightful place, and with much larger digs. At IOA, only 24 guests at a time can experience the little drama where wands choose a wizard (rather than the other way around). At USF, the shop has three separate choosing chambers, turning it from a popular curiosity into an actual attraction. As for the IOA location, it continues to operate.

TOURING TIPS If your young 'un is selected to test-drive a wand, be forewarned that you'll have to buy it if you want to take it home.

Touring Strategy

The Wizarding World of Harry Potter–Diagon Alley is the queen of the hop in the theme park world in 2015 and beyond. Because of the crowds, experiencing Diagon Alley without interminable waits is a challenge—if you visited The Wizarding World of Harry Potter–Hogsmeade during its first three years at IOA, you know of what we speak. Hogsmeade opened with three rides and Ollivanders; now it has four rides plus the wand shop. As discussed earlier, Diagon Alley has another Ollivanders and only two rides, one of which, Hogwarts Express, it shares with Hogsmeade in IOA. Because only half of each day's total train passengers can board at the USF station, Diagon Alley in essence has only one-and-a-half rides, plus Ollivanders and the various shops, to entertain the expected masses. In other words, it's crazy, folks.

When Early Park Admission is offered, USF admits eligible on-site resort guests 1 hour before the general public, with the turnstiles opening up to 90 minutes before the official opening time. Early entry is a tremendous perk if you're staying on-property, but you'll still be competing with thousands of other resort guests, so arrive at least 30 minutes before early entry starts; during peak season, showing up on the very first boat or bus from your hotel is recommended. If you're a day guest visiting on an Early Park Admission day, Diagon Alley will already be packed when you arrive. Even when USF doesn't offer Early Park Admission, all guests may enter Diagon Alley from the front gates up to 30 minutes before park opening, and hotel guests in IOA will arrive via Hogwarts Express a little after that, though Harry Potter and the Escape from Gringotts doesn't begin operating until close to official opening time.

Universal has multiple operational options for allowing guests into USF's Wizarding World. On low- to moderate-attendance days, you'll be able to stroll in and out of Diagon Alley without restriction. On days of heavy attendance, barricades may limit access to the London waterfront, forcing guests to queue near *Fear Factor Live* and enter Diagon Alley at a controlled pace, exiting only toward San Francisco. If the park is so busy that Diagon Alley reaches maximum capacity, free timed-entry return tickets specifying when you can visit will be distributed from touch screen kiosks located between Men in Black Alien Attack and *Fear Factor Live*. Guests are given a selection of 1-hour return windows, assuming any are still available. Once your time comes, report to the gates at the end of London near *Fear Factor Live*. On the busiest days, standby queues may snake from *Fear Factor Live* behind Men in Black Alien Attack toward The Simpsons Ride, but waiting in these is strongly discouraged. By late afternoon you should almost always be able to waltz right into Diagon Alley without a wait. (Gringotts itself is, of course, another story.)

When the park opens for early entry, eligible guests will be walked around the lake clockwise to Diagon Alley. At rope drop for regular operations, day guests are led counterclockwise to the London waterfront through World Expo. When crowd-control measures are in place during busy days, hustling to the waterfront counterclockwise through the Simpsons area is the most direct path to the ticket kiosks and standby entrance.

On the upside, the rush to Diagon Alley diminishes crowds and waits at other attractions. The downside to that upside: Those who can't enter Diagon Alley right away spread to nearby attractions, particularly Men in Black Alien Attack and to a lesser extent The Simpsons Ride and Revenge of the Mummy. Diagon Alley spillover affects wait times at these attractions all day, so experience them as early as possible.

LIVE ENTERTAINMENT *at* UNIVERSAL STUDIOS FLORIDA

IN ADDITION TO THE SHOWS PROFILED PREVIOUSLY, USF offers a wide range of street entertainment. Costumed comic book and cartoon characters (Shrek, SpongeBob SquarePants, Woody Woodpecker) roam the park for photo ops supplemented by look-alikes of movie stars, both living and deceased, plus the towering, talking Transformers cyberstars, which can be said to be neither. Musical acts also pop up.

In 2012 USF introduced the Disney-like **Universal's Superstar Parade** (★★★½), featuring dancers and performers, four large and elaborate floats inspired by cartoons, and a very mixed bag of street-prowling Universal characters. The parade stops twice for a highly choreographed ensemble number. Though impressive in its scope and coordination, the performance is well-nigh impossible to take in from any given viewing spot. The same floats are trotted out individually at various times of day for mini-shows and character meet and greets.

The parade, which is marked on the park map, begins at the Esoteric Pictures gate in Hollywood between *Universal Orlando's Horror Make-Up Show* and Cafe La Bamba. It turns right, then immediately makes a hard left around Mel's Drive-In, and follows the waterfront past Transformers toward San Francisco. From there it turns left at Louie's Pizza and proceeds along 5th Avenue, past Revenge of the Mummy. At the end of 5th Avenue, the parade takes a left onto 57th Avenue/Plaza of the Stars and heads toward the front of the park, where it makes another left onto Hollywood Boulevard, from whence it disappears backstage through the gate where it entered. The best viewing spots are along 5th Avenue, on the front steps of faux buildings in New York.

If you miss part of the parade in the New York area, you can scoot along the waterfront to Mel's Diner and catch it as it comes down Hollywood Boulevard. If you plan to leave the park after watching the parade on the New York streets, you can use the same route to access Hollywood Boulevard and the park exit before the parade arrives.

DINING *at* UNIVERSAL STUDIOS FLORIDA

MUCH OF THE QUICK SERVICE at Universal Studios Florida is utterly unremarkable: burgers, pizza, pasta, chicken fingers, sandwiches, and salads. The mediocre food is matched by the predictable theming in the park's original fast-food joints: American diner? Check. New York Italian? Got it. We're a little surprised that there's not a Chinese-takeout place next to a laundry in the San Francisco section.

unofficial **TIP**
We advise heading to Universal CityWalk (see page 391) if you're looking for good-quality food.

The expansion in 2013 of the Springfield U.S.A. themed area revitalized USF's quick-service scene by bringing a number of wacky *Simpsons*-inspired eateries to life along **Fast Food Boulevard,** including **Krusty Burger, The Frying Dutchman** for seafood, **Cletus' Chicken Shack, Luigi's Pizza, Lard Lad Donuts, Lisa's Teahouse of Horror, Bumblebee Man's Taco Truck, Duff Brewery,** and **Moe's Tavern.** Serving sizes are large, and the food quality is an improvement over your run-of-the-mill theme park fare, with dozens of menu items (including tater tots and curly fries) that aren't available in any other quick-service location.

An Ambler, Pennsylvania, couple sampled the offerings:

> The doughnuts at Lard Lad were fresh, flavorful, and surprisingly delicious. (Mmm . . . doughnuts . . .) The Flaming Moe is an overpriced glass of orange soda with dry ice on the bottom—for $8, it should have some alcohol in it or be larger. The queuing for Krusty Burger was frustrating during the lunch rush—they let only a few guests up to the food court area at a time—but once you go through the line and pay, an employee shows you to a table. Lunch for the four of us cost $88 with two beers and that one overpriced Flaming Moe. Duff beer was essentially a less-delicious Heineken. My husband's Krusty Burger was pretty good; my chicken-and-waffle sandwich was excellent but had too much sauce on it.

The best quick-service food in USF can currently be found at the **Leaky Cauldron.** Diagon Alley's flagship restaurant serves authentically hearty British pub fare such as bangers and mash, cottage pie, toad-in-the-hole, Guinness stew, and a ploughman's platter for two of Scotch eggs and imported cheeses. When you're done, head over to **Florean Fortescue's Ice-Cream Parlour** for some delicious Butterbeer ice cream.

USF's two sit-down restaurants are **Finnegan's Bar and Grill,** in New York, and **Lombard's Seafood Grille,** in San Francisco. Finnegan's serves typical bar food—burgers and wings—as well as fish-and-chips and other takes on Irish cuisine. Lombard's is the better restaurant, but it's not in the same stratosphere as Disney's Hollywood Brown Derby (in quality or price). Each week, on select evenings, Universal characters show up for dinner at the three deluxe resort hotels.

At the **Superstar Character Breakfast**, guests dine with characters from *Despicable Me, SpongeBob SquarePants, Hop,* and *Dora the Explorer.* Cost, including tax, is $27.50 for adults and $14 for kids. Call ☎ 407-224-3663 for reservations, or book at **universalorlando.com.**

There's also a weekly character breakfast at **Jake's** located in the Royal Pacific Resort ($29 adults; $16 kids); make a reservation by calling ☎ 407-503-3463.

UNIVERSAL STUDIOS FLORIDA TOURING PLANS

BUYING ADMISSION TO UNIVERSAL STUDIOS FLORIDA

ONE OF OUR BIG GRIPES ABOUT USF is that there are never enough ticket windows open in the morning to accommodate the crowds. Therefore, we strongly recommend that you buy your admission in advance. Passes are available online or by mail from USF at ☎ 800-711-0080 and at the concierge desks or attractions box offices of many Orlando-area hotels.

Many hotels that sell Universal admissions don't issue actual passes. Instead, the purchaser gets a voucher that can be redeemed for a pass at the theme park. Fortunately, the voucher-redemption window is separate from the park's ticket-sales operation. In addition, tickets bought online can be printed at home and contain a bar code that can be read at the turnstiles.

UNIVERSAL STUDIOS FLORIDA ONE-DAY TOURING PLAN

THIS PLAN IS FOR GUESTS without Park-to-Park tickets and includes every recommended attraction at USF. If a ride or show is listed that you don't want to experience, skip that step and proceed to the next. Move quickly from attraction to attraction, and if possible, hold off on lunch until after experiencing at least six rides.

1. Buy your admission in advance and call ☎ 407-363-8000 the day before your visit for the official opening time.

2. Arrive at USF 90–120 minutes before the official opening time if Early Park Admission is offered and you're eligible, or 30–45 minutes before opening for day guests. Get a park map as soon as you enter.

3. Early-entry guests should ride Harry Potter and the Escape from Gringotts if it's operating. If it's not, enjoy the rest of Diagon Alley but don't get in line.

4. Before early entry ends, hotel guests should exit Diagon Alley and ride Despicable Me Minion Mayhem. Day guests should wait in the front lot until permitted to ride Despicable Me.

5. Ride Hollywood Rip Ride Rockit.

6. Experience Transformers: The Ride 3-D.

7. Ride Revenge of the Mummy in New York.

8. Ride Men in Black Alien Attack in World Expo.

9. Ride The Simpsons Ride.

10. Ride Kang & Kodos' Twirl 'n' Hurl if 50 or fewer people are in line.

11. Ride E. T. Adventure in Woody the Woodpecker's KidZone.

12. Work in *Animal Actors on Location* around lunch (we recommend Fast Food Boulevard), according to the daily entertainment schedule.

13. See *Universal Orlando's Horror Make-Up Show* and *Terminator 2: 3-D* according to the daily entertainment schedule.

14. See *Shrek 4-D* in Production Central.

15. By this time, you should be able to enter Diagon Alley without waiting, even on busy days. Ride Harry Potter and the Escape from Gringotts. If this is your first ride, take the standby queue. For re-rides, use the single-rider line. The Gringotts queue may close before the rest of the park if the posted wait time exceeds remaining operating hours by more than 60 minutes.

17. See the wand ceremony at Ollivanders and buy a wand if you wish.

18. Tour Diagon Alley. Browse the shops, explore the dark recesses of Knockturn Alley, and discover the interactive effects. If you're hungry, try the Leaky Cauldron or Florean Fortescue's Ice-Cream Parlour.

19. See the *Celestina Warbeck* and *Tales of Beedle the Bard* shows.

20. Chat with the Knight Bus conductor and his shrunken head. Also look for Kreacher in the window of 12 Grimmauld Place, and listen to the receiver in the red phone booth.

21. If scheduled, see *Universal's Cinematic Spectacular* from Central Park (directly across the lagoon from Richter's Burger Company), Duff Brewery, or the embankment in front of London.

THE BEST OF UNIVERSAL STUDIOS FLORIDA AND ISLANDS OF ADVENTURE IN ONE DAY

THIS TOURING PLAN is for guests with one-day Park-to-Park tickets who wish to see the highlights of Universal Studios Florida and Islands of Adventure in a single day. The plan uses Hogwarts Express to get from one park to the other and then back again; you can walk back to the first park for the return leg if the line is too long. The plan includes a table-service lunch at Mythos (make reservations online a few days before your visit) and dinner at the Leaky Cauldron; during holiday periods, you may need to substitute a quick-service snack for one or both meals to fit in all of the plan's attractions. See page 262.

UNIVERSAL'S
ISLANDS *of* ADVENTURE

IN THE SUMMER OF 1999, Universal launched its second major theme park, **Islands of Adventure (IOA)**. From its very inception, IOA was designed to directly compete with Disney's Magic Kingdom. The park has more kid-friendly rides and cartoon characters (like Fantasyland), thrill rides in a sci-fi city (like Tomorrowland), and a jungle river with robot creatures (like Adventureland). Its layout—a central entry corridor leading to a ring of connected lands—even mimics the classic Disneyland model, with one major exception: Instead of a hub and castle in the center, Universal built a large lagoon, whose estuaries separate the park's thematically diverse "islands" (actually peninsulas).

*un*official **TIP**
Roller coasters at Islands of Adventure are the real deal—not for the faint of heart or for little ones.

Disney and Universal officially downplay their fierce competition, pointing out that any new theme park or attraction makes Central Florida a more marketable destination. Behind closed doors, however, the two companies share a Pepsi-versus-Coke rivalry that keeps both working hard to gain a competitive edge. The good news is that all this translates into bigger and better attractions for you to enjoy.

BEWARE OF THE WET AND THE WILD

THOUGH WE'VE DESCRIBED Universal's Islands of Adventure as a direct competitor to the Magic Kingdom, know this: Whereas most Magic Kingdom attractions are designed to be enjoyed by guests of any age, attractions at Islands of Adventure are created largely for an under-40 population. The roller coasters at Universal are serious with a capital *S*, making Space Mountain and Big Thunder Mountain Railroad look about as frightening as Dumbo. In fact, 9 of the top 14 attractions at IOA are thrill rides; of these, 3 will not only scare the crap out of you but will also drench you with water.

For families, there are three interactive playgrounds as well as six minor attractions that young children will enjoy. Of the top rides, only the two in Toon Lagoon (described later) are marginally appropriate for little kids, and even on these rides your child needs to be fairly hardy.

NOT TO BE MISSED AT UNIVERSAL'S ISLANDS OF ADVENTURE	
• The Amazing Adventures of Spider-Man	• Dragon Challenge
• Harry Potter and the Forbidden Journey	• Hogwarts Express
• The Incredible Hulk Coaster	• Jurassic Park River Adventure
• Popeye & Bluto's Bilge-Rat Barges	• Skull Island: Reign of Kong (*opens 2016*)

GETTING ORIENTED AT UNIVERSAL'S ISLANDS OF ADVENTURE

BOTH UNIVERSAL THEME PARKS are accessed via the Universal CityWalk entertainment complex. After crossing CityWalk from the parking garages, bear right to Universal Studios Florida or left to Universal's Islands of Adventure.

Islands of Adventure is laid out much like Epcot's World Showcase—arranged in a large circle surrounding a lagoon—but it evinces the same thematic continuity present in the Magic Kingdom. Each "land," or "island" in this case, is self-contained and visually consistent in its theme.

You first encounter the Moroccan-style **Port of Entry,** where you'll find Guest Services, lockers, stroller and wheelchair rentals, ATM banking, lost and found, and shopping. From Port of Entry, moving clockwise around the lagoon, you access **Marvel Super Hero Island, Toon Lagoon, Jurassic Park, The Wizarding World of Harry Potter–Hogsmeade, The Lost Continent,** and **Seuss Landing.** There is no in-park transportation to move you between lands.

UNIVERSAL'S ISLANDS *of* ADVENTURE ATTRACTIONS

MARVEL SUPER HERO ISLAND

THIS ISLAND, WITH ITS FUTURISTIC AND RETRO-FUTURE design and comic book signage, offers shopping, dining, and attractions based on Marvel Comics characters.

The Amazing Adventures of Spider-Man
(Universal Express) ★★★★★

APPEAL BY AGE	PRESCHOOL ★	GRADE SCHOOL ★★★★★	TEENS ★★★★★
YOUNG ADULTS ★★★★½	OVER 30 ★★★★½		SENIORS ★★★★★

What it is Indoor adventure simulator ride based on Spider-Man. **Scope and scale** Super-headliner. **When to go** During the first 40 minutes the park is open. **Special comment** 40″ minimum height requirement. **Authors' rating** One of the best attractions anywhere; not to be missed; ★★★★★. **Duration of ride** 4½ minutes. **Average waiting time per 100 people ahead of you** 5 minutes. **Loading speed** Fast.

DESCRIPTION AND COMMENTS The Amazing Adventures of Spider-Man—covering 1½ acres and combining moving ride vehicles, 3-D film, and live action—was enhanced in 2012 with a complete high-definition digital upgrade. Thirteen reanimated 3-D scenes fuse almost seamlessly with the actual sets and props, so that in many instances guests cannot tell until the action begins whether they're looking at a movie screen or an actual brick wall. The total package is astonishing—frenetic yet fluid, and visually rich. The ride is wild yet very smooth. Though the attractions are not directly comparable, Spider-Man is technologically ahead of The

Continued on page 238

Universal's Islands of Adventure

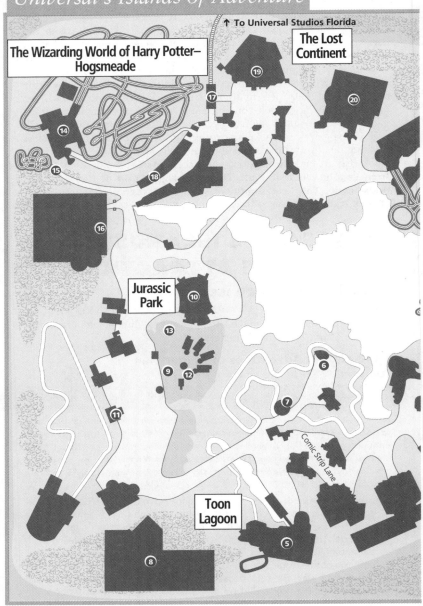

↑ To Universal Studios Florida

The Lost Continent

The Wizarding World of Harry Potter–Hogsmeade

Jurassic Park

Toon Lagoon

Comic Strip Lane

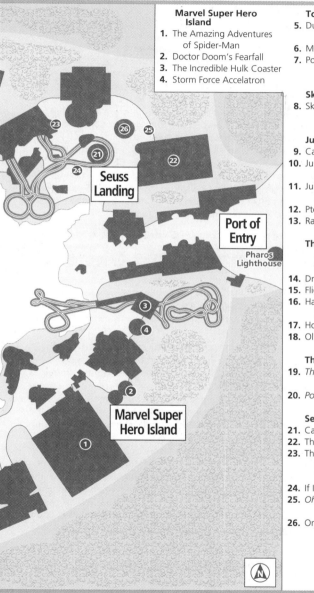

Marvel Super Hero Island
1. The Amazing Adventures of Spider-Man
2. Doctor Doom's Fearfall
3. The Incredible Hulk Coaster
4. Storm Force Accelatron

Toon Lagoon
5. Dudley Do-Right's Ripsaw Falls
6. Me Ship, *The Olive*
7. Popeye & Bluto's Bilge-Rat Barges

Skull Island
8. Skull Island: Reign of Kong (opens 2016)

Jurassic Park
9. Camp Jurassic
10. Jurassic Park Discovery Center
11. Jurassic Park River Adventure
12. Pteranodon Flyers
13. Raptor Encounter

The Wizarding World of Harry Potter– Hogsmeade
14. Dragon Challenge
15. Flight of the Hippogriff
16. Harry Potter and the Forbidden Journey
17. Hogwarts Express
18. Ollivanders

The Lost Continent
19. *The Eighth Voyage of Sindbad Stunt Show*
20. *Poseidon's Fury*

Seuss Landing
21. Caro-Seuss-el
22. The Cat in the Hat
23. The High in the Sky Seuss Trolley Train Ride!
24. If I Ran the Zoo
25. *Oh! The Stories You'll Hear!*
26. One Fish, Two Fish, Red Fish, Blue Fish

Seuss Landing

Port of Entry

Pharos Lighthouse

Marvel Super Hero Island

Continued from page 235

Twilight Zone Tower of Terror at Disney's Hollywood Studios—which is to say that it will leave you in awe.

The story line is that you're a reporter for the *Daily Bugle* newspaper (where Peter Parker, also known as Spider-Man, works as a mild-mannered photographer), when it's discovered that evildoers have stolen—we promise we're not making this up—the Statue of Liberty. You're drafted on the spot by your cantankerous editor to go get the story. After speeding around and being thrust into a battle between good and evil, you experience a 400-foot "sensory drop" from a skyscraper roof all the way to the pavement. Spidey is less frantic and frenetic than the similar Transformers ride at USF and features more dialogue and humor. Some folks who get motion sickness on Transformers find that they can tolerate this ride better.

TOURING TIPS If you were on hand at park opening, ride after experiencing Harry Potter and the Forbidden Journey, Dragon Challenge, and The Incredible Hulk Coaster. If you elect to bypass all the congestion at Forbidden Journey, ride after Dragon Challenge and the Hulk. If you arrived more than 15 minutes after park opening, skip Wizarding World attractions and ride Spider-Man after the Hulk.

Doctor Doom's Fearfall *(Universal Express)*   ★★★

APPEAL BY AGE	PRESCHOOL ★	GRADE SCHOOL ★★★★½	TEENS ★★★★½
YOUNG ADULTS ★★★★		OVER 30 ★★★½	SENIORS ★★

What it is Vertical ascent and free fall. **Scope and scale** Headliner. **When to go** First 40 minutes the park is open. **Special comment** 52″ minimum height requirement. **Authors' rating** More bark than bite; ★★★. **Duration of ride** 40 seconds. **Average waiting time per 100 people ahead of you** 18 minutes. **Loading speed** Slow.

DESCRIPTION AND COMMENTS Here you are (again), strapped into a seat with your feet dangling. You're blasted 200 feet up in the air and then allowed to partially free-fall back down. Imagine the midway game wherein a macho guy swings a sledgehammer, propelling a metal sphere up a vertical shaft to ring a bell—on this ride, you're the metal sphere.

That prospect sounds worse than it actually is—the scariest part of the ride by far is the apprehension that builds as you sit, strapped in, waiting for the ride to launch. Blasting up and falling down are actually pleasant.

TOURING TIPS We've seen glaciers that move faster than the line for Doctor Doom's Fearfall. If you want to ride without investing half a day, be one of the first to ride. If you're on hand at opening time, being among the first isn't too difficult (mainly because the nearby Wizarding World, Hulk, and Spider-Man attractions are bigger draws). Fortunately, as this reader discovered, Doctor Doom also has a singles line that's nearly always open:

If you ask a staff member for the single-rider line, they'll send you through the exit in the arcade. Then just follow the signs.

The Incredible Hulk Coaster *(Universal Express)*
★★★★½

APPEAL BY AGE	PRESCHOOL ★	GRADE SCHOOL ★★★★½	TEENS ★★★★★
YOUNG ADULTS ★★★★★		OVER 30 ★★★★½	SENIORS ★★

What it is Roller coaster. **Scope and scale** Super-headliner. **When to go** During the first 40 minutes the park is open. **Special comment** 54" minimum height requirement. **Authors' rating** A coaster-lover's coaster; not to be missed; ★★★★½. **Duration of ride** 2¼ minutes. **Average waiting time per 100 people ahead of you** 9 minutes. **Loading speed** Moderate.

Motion Sickness

DESCRIPTION AND COMMENTS There is, as always, a story line, but for this attraction it's of no importance whatsoever. What you need to know about this attraction is simple: You'll be shot like a cannon-ball from 0 to 40 mph in 2 seconds, and then you'll be flung upside down 100 feet off the ground, which will, of course, induce weight-lessness. From there it's a mere six rollovers punctuated by two plunges into holes in the ground before you're allowed to get out and throw up.

Seriously, the Hulk is a great roller coaster, one of the best in Florida, providing a ride comparable to that of Montu (Busch Gardens) with the added thrill of an accelerated launch (instead of the more typical uphill crank). At press time, a major refurbishment of the Hulk coaster—from track to launch mechanism to theming—was in progress, which should restore the ride's original smoothness and update the 1990s-era queue.

TOURING TIPS Our advice is to skip The Wizarding World attractions in the early morning and ride The Incredible Hulk Coaster first thing. Alternatively, if you insist on going to Hogsmeade at rope drop (or if you are eligible for Early Park Admission), you should ride Hulk immediately after you've enjoyed the Potter attractions. Universal provides electronic lockers near the entrance of the Hulk to deposit any items that might depart your person during the Hulk's seven inversions. Be prepared to pat down your pockets for loose change, or you'll be pulled aside for a TSA-style wanding after triggering the metal detectors.

When you reach the boarding area, note that the Hulk has a separate line for those who want to ride in the first row. A singles line is available during peak times, but you may not notice it at first, as this reader attests:

The single-rider line is kind of hard to find—ask where it is. I stood in the standby line for 20 minutes before I realized my mistake.

Storm Force Accelatron *(Universal Express)*   ★★½

APPEAL BY AGE	PRESCHOOL ★★★★★	GRADE SCHOOL ★★★½	TEENS ★★★
YOUNG ADULTS ★★★½	OVER 30 ★★½		SENIORS —

What it is Covered spinning ride. **Scope and scale** Minor attraction. **Special comment** May induce motion sickness. **When to go** During the first hour the park is open. **Authors' rating** Spiffed-up teacups; ★★½. **Duration of ride** 1½ minutes. **Average waiting time per 100 people ahead of you** 21 minutes. **Loading speed** Slow.

Motion Sickness

DESCRIPTION AND COMMENTS Storm Force is a spiffed-up version of Disney's nausea-inducing Mad Tea Party. Here, you spin to the accompaniment of a simulated thunderstorm and swirling sound and light. A story line loosely ties this midway-type ride to the Marvel Super Hero Island area, but it's largely irrelevant and offers no advice on keeping your lunch down.

TOURING TIPS Ride early or late to avoid long lines. If you're prone to motion sickness, keep your distance.

TOON LAGOON

THIS LAND TRANSLATES cartoon art into real buildings and settings. Whimsical and gaily colored, with rounded and exaggerated lines, Toon Lagoon is Universal's answer to the old Mickey's Toontown Fair in the Magic Kingdom—only you have about a 60% chance of drowning at Universal's version. Comic Strip Lane, Toon Lagoon's main street, features shops and eateries that tie in to the comic strip theme, featuring vintage Sunday-funnies favorites such as *Beetle Bailey, The Family Circus,* and *Blondie*—in other words, intellectual property that Universal could get for cheap. (The characters, though classic, are probably unrecognizable to anybody younger than Generation X.) Comic Strip Lane is a great place for photo ops with cartoon characters in their own environment.

Dudley Do-Right's Ripsaw Falls *(Universal Express)* ★★★½

APPEAL BY AGE	PRESCHOOL ★½	GRADE SCHOOL ★★★★½	TEENS ★★★★
YOUNG ADULTS ★★★★		OVER 30 ★★★★½	SENIORS ★★★★

What it is Flume ride. **Scope and scale** Major attraction. **When to go** Before 11 a.m. **Special comment** 44″ minimum height requirement. **Authors' rating** A minimalist Splash Mountain; ★★★½. **Duration of ride** 5 minutes. **Average waiting time per 100 people ahead of you** 9 minutes. **Loading speed** Moderate.

DESCRIPTION AND COMMENTS Inspired by the *Rocky and Bullwinkle* cartoons, this ride features Canadian Mountie Dudley Do-Right as he tries to save Nell from the evil Snidely Whiplash. Story line aside, it's a flume ride, with the inevitable big drop at the end. Universal claims that this is the first flume ride to "send riders plummeting 15 feet below the surface of the water." Actually, though, you're just plummeting into a tunnel.

The only problem with this attraction is that everyone inevitably compares it to Splash Mountain at the Magic Kingdom. The flume is as good as Splash Mountain's, and the final drop is a whopper, but the theming and the visuals aren't even in the same league. Taken on its own terms, however, Dudley Do-Right is a darn good flume ride.

TOURING TIPS This ride will get you wet, but on average not as wet as you might expect. If you want to stay dry, however, arrive prepared with a poncho or at least a big garbage bag with holes cut out for your head and arms. After riding, take a moment to gauge the timing of the water cannons that go off along the exit walk—this is where you can really get drenched. Ride after experiencing the Marvel Super Hero rides.

Me Ship, *The Olive* ★★★

APPEAL BY AGE	PRESCHOOL ★★★★★	GRADE SCHOOL ★★★★½	TEENS ★★
YOUNG ADULTS ★★		OVER 30 ★★½	SENIORS ★★

What it is Interactive playground. **Scope and scale** Minor attraction. **When to go** Anytime. **Authors' rating** Colorful and appealing for kids; ★★★.

DESCRIPTION AND COMMENTS *The Olive* is Popeye's three-story boat come to life as an interactive playground. Younger children can scramble around in Swee'Pea's Playpen, while older sibs shoot water cannons at riders trying to survive the adjacent Bilge-Rat Barges.

TOURING TIPS If you're into the big rides, save this for later in the day.

Popeye & Bluto's Bilge-Rat Barges *(Universal Express)*
★★★★

APPEAL BY AGE   PRESCHOOL ★½   GRADE SCHOOL ★ ★ ★ ★ ★   TEENS ★ ★ ★ ★½
YOUNG ADULTS ★ ★ ★ ★   OVER 30 ★ ★ ★ ★   SENIORS ★ ★ ★ ★

What it is Whitewater raft ride. **Scope and scale** Major attraction. **When to go** Before 11 a.m. **Special comment** 42" minimum height requirement. **Authors' rating** Bring your own soap; not to be missed; ★★★★. **Duration of ride** 4½ minutes. **Average waiting time per 100 people ahead of you** 5 minutes. **Loading speed** Moderate.

DESCRIPTION AND COMMENTS This whitewater raft ride includes an encounter with an 18-foot-tall octopus. Engineered to ensure that everyone gets drenched, the attraction even provides water cannons so that non-participants ashore can fire at those aboard. The rapids are rougher and more interesting, and the ride longer, than Animal Kingdom's Kali River Rapids. But Bilge-Rat Barges doesn't surpass Disney's raft ride for visuals and theming.

TOURING TIPS If you didn't drown on Dudley Do-Right, here's a second chance. You'll get a lot wetter from the knees down on this ride, so use your poncho or garbage bag and ride barefoot with your britches rolled up. This ride often opens an hour after the rest of the park. Experience the barges in the morning after the Marvel Super Hero attractions and Dudley Do-Right. If you've forgotten your wet wear, you might want to put off riding until last thing before leaving the park. Most preschoolers enjoy the barges—those who don't react more to the way the rapids look than to the roughness of the ride.

SKULL ISLAND

SKULL ISLAND: REIGN OF KONG is both an attraction and an entire "island" unto itself, located between Toon Lagoon's Dudley Do-Right's Ripsaw Falls and Thunder Falls Terrace restaurant in Jurassic Park.

Skull Island: Reign of Kong *(opens summer 2016)*

What it is Indoor-outdoor truck safari with 3-D effects. **Scope and scale** Super-headliner. **When to go** Immediately after park opening or just before closing. **Special comment** 34" minimum height requirement. **Authors' rating** Not yet rated; not to be missed. **Duration of ride** More than 4½ minutes. **Average waiting time per 100 people ahead of you** TBD. **Loading speed** TBD.

DESCRIPTION AND COMMENTS This attraction isn't exactly based on the 2005 *King Kong* remake (though director Peter Jackson did consult on the design), nor is it directly tied to the *Kong: Skull Island* film scheduled for release in 2017. Rather, the ride is an original adventure set in the 1930s, which begins as you pass beneath a stone archway, shaped like a massive monkey skull, and start exploring the elaborate, immersive queue. Pathways wind through dense foliage and an ancient temple inhabited by a hostile indigenous tribe before leading you to your transportation, which is an oversize open-sided "expedition vehicle" that superficially resembles the trucks at Animal Kingdom's Kilimanjaro Safari.

Your ride starts with a short loop outside through the jungle (which may be bypassed in inclement weather), ending at the massive torch-framed doors in the center of Skull Island's imposing 72-foot-tall facade. The doors open, allowing you to enter a subterranean maze of corridors and caverns in which you'll be assaulted by all manner of prehistoric beasts and bugs. After barely surviving a series of multisensory near misses with various nasties, you come to an encounter with King Kong himself, brought to life through enormous 3-D screens, similar to the *King Kong 360 3-D* attraction on Universal Studios Hollywood's tram tour. Finally, just when you think it's all over, you'll have one last face-to-face with the "eighth wonder of the world," only this time in the fur-covered flesh.

TOURING TIPS Skull Island promises to be epic in every sense, from the monumental exterior to the length of the experience, said to be one of the longest in the resort. It also promises to attract queues of equally epic proportions. On the plus side, Kong should draw some guests away from The Wizarding World of Harry Potter, helping rebalance the park. You'll want to visit Skull Island first thing in the morning, or immediately following the Hogsmeade attractions if you're using Early Park Admission.

The minimum height requirement is just 34 inches—one of the lowest in the resort—and is designed to be physically accessible to most members of the family. However, on a sensory and psychological level, it's extremely intense; if you or your little one has a fear of darkness, insects, or man-eating monsters, you may want to forgo the monkey.

JURASSIC PARK

JURASSIC PARK is a Steven Spielberg film franchise about a theme park with real dinosaurs. Jurassic Park at Islands of Adventure is a real theme park (or at least a section of one) with fictitious dinosaurs.

Camp Jurassic ★★★½

APPEAL BY AGE	PRESCHOOL ★★★★★	GRADE SCHOOL ★★★★½	TEENS ★
YOUNG ADULTS ★★		OVER 30 ★★★	SENIORS ★★

What it is Interactive play area. **Scope and scale** Minor attraction. **When to go** Anytime. **Authors' rating** Creative playground, confusing layout; ★★★½.

DESCRIPTION AND COMMENTS Camp Jurassic is a great place for children to cut loose. A sort of antediluvian Tom Sawyer Island, it allows kids to explore lava pits, caves, mines, and a rain forest.

TOURING TIPS Camp Jurassic will fire the imaginations of the under-13 set—if you don't impose a time limit on the exploration, you could be here awhile. The confusing layout intersects the queuing area for Pteranodon Flyers.

Jurassic Park Discovery Center ★★½

APPEAL BY AGE	PRESCHOOL ★★★	GRADE SCHOOL ★★★★	TEENS ★★★
YOUNG ADULTS ★★★		OVER 30 ★★★	SENIORS ★★★

What it is Interactive natural-history exhibit. **Scope and scale** Minor attraction. **When to go** Anytime. **Authors' rating** Definitely worth checking out; ★★½.

DESCRIPTION AND COMMENTS This interactive educational exhibit mixes fiction from the movie *Jurassic Park,* such as using fossil DNA to bring dinosaurs to life, with skeletal remains and other paleontological displays. One exhibit lets guests watch an animatronic raptor being hatched. Another allows you to digitally "fuse" your DNA with a dinosaur's to see what the resultant creature would look like.

TOURING TIPS Cycle back after experiencing all the rides or on a second day. Most folks can digest this exhibit in 10–15 minutes.

Jurassic Park River Adventure *(Universal Express)*
★★★★

APPEAL BY AGE	PRESCHOOL ★	GRADE SCHOOL ★★★★		TEENS ★★★★
YOUNG ADULTS ★★★★		OVER 30 ★★★★½	SENIORS ★★★★★	

What it is Indoor-outdoor river-raft adventure ride based on the *Jurassic Park* movies. **Scope and scale** Super-headliner. **When to go** Before 11 a.m. **Special comment** 42″ minimum height requirement. **Authors' rating** Better than its Hollywood cousin; not to be missed; ★★★★. **Duration of ride** 6½ minutes. **Average waiting time per 100 people ahead of you** 5 minutes. **Loading speed** Fast.

DESCRIPTION AND COMMENTS Guests board boats for a water tour of Jurassic Park. Everything is tranquil as the tour begins, and the boat floats among large herbivorous dinosaurs such as brontosauruses and stegosauruses. Then, as word comes in that some of the carnivores have escaped their enclosure, the tour boat is accidentally diverted into Jurassic Park's maintenance facilities. Here, the boat and its riders are menaced by an assortment of hungry meat-eaters led by the ubiquitous *T. rex.* At the climactic moment, the boat and its passengers escape by plummeting over an 85-foot drop.

TOURING TIPS Once you're under way, there's a little splashing but nothing major until the big drop at the end of the ride. Fortunately, not all that much water lands in the boat, so you don't get all that wet.

A Honolulu reader thinks Jurassic Park doesn't pass the smell test:

The Jurassic Park ride is a lot of fun—so fun, in fact, that you won't realize how truly HEINOUS the water that drenches you during the climactic splashdown is until much later. We sat in the front row for the ride and got soaked. Three hours later, my girlfriend and I realized that we reeked.

Young children must endure a double whammy on this ride. First, they're stalked by giant, salivating (sometimes spitting) reptiles; then they're sent catapulting over the falls. Unless your children are fairly hardy, wait a year or two before you spring the River Adventure on them.

Because the Jurassic Park section of IOA is situated next to The Wizarding World of Harry Potter–Hogsmeade, the boat will experience heavy crowds earlier in the day. Try to ride before 11 a.m.

Pteranodon Flyers ★★

APPEAL BY AGE	PRESCHOOL ★★★½	GRADE SCHOOL ★★★★	TEENS ★★★★
YOUNG ADULTS ★★★½		OVER 30 ★★★	SENIORS ★★★★

What it is Kiddie suspended coaster. **Scope and scale** Minor attraction. **When to go** When there's no line. **Special comment** Adults and older children must be accompanied by a child between 36″ and 52″ tall. **Authors' rating** All sizzle, no steak; ★★. **Duration of ride** 1¼ minutes. **Average waiting time per 100 people ahead of you** 28 minutes. **Loading speed** More sluggish than a hog in quicksand.

DESCRIPTION AND COMMENTS This is Islands of Adventure's biggest blunder. Engineered to accommodate only 170 persons per hour, the ride dangles you on a swing below a track that passes over a small part of Jurassic Park. We recommend skipping this one. Why? Because the next ice age will probably end before you reach the front of the line! And your reward for all that waiting? A 1-minute-and-15-second ride.

TOURING TIPS Photograph the pteranodon as it flies overhead. You're probably looking at something that will someday be extinct.

Raptor Encounter ★★★½

APPEAL BY AGE	PRESCHOOL ★★	GRADE SCHOOL ★★★★	TEENS ★★★★
YOUNG ADULTS ★★★½		OVER 30 ★★★½	SENIORS ★★★

What it is Photo op with lifelike dinosaur. **Scope and scale** Minor attraction. **When to go** Check park map or attraction for appearance times. **Authors' rating** Clever girl! Sure to scare the spit out of small kids; ★★★½. **Duration of encounter** About a minute. **Probable waiting time** 30 minutes.

DESCRIPTION AND COMMENTS Just when everyone thinks that Disney has a lock on the meet and greet market, between its talking Mickeys and *Frozen* sisters, Universal does the impossible—breeds a live velociraptor and makes it pose for pictures! OK, it isn't actually a real dinosaur on display just outside the Jurassic Park Discovery Center, inside a portion of the long-closed Triceratops Encounter walk-through attraction. In fact, it's an amazingly realistic puppet, created by Michael Curry (who created designs for Disney's *Lion King* and *Finding Nemo* musicals, as well as Diagon Alley's *Tales of Beedle the Bard* show) and brought to life by talented performers.

Several times each hour, the blue siren lights around the sunken predator paddock signal the arrival of Lucy or Ethel, the park's new semi-tame stars. A game warden briefs one family at a time regarding proper safety procedures (convey calm assurance, move in slowly, and try not to smell like meat) before they step up for a photo. Don't peer too closely over the edge of the raptor enclosure; you'll spot the cleverly camouflaged legs of the puppeteer inside and spoil the illusion. A Photo Connect photographer will take your picture with his or her camera (included with Star Card packages) or your own, and selfies are also encouraged—just don't be surprised if the dino snaps when you say, "Smile!"

TOURING TIPS The Raptor Encounter has quickly become quite popular, and with limited capacity and little shade, this can become an unpleasant wait. If appearance times aren't printed on the park map, check with a team member outside the paddock entrance and arrive at least 15 minutes before a scheduled session; 20-minute appearances begin around 11 a.m. and occur about every half hour until 6 p.m. Don't try to touch the raptor, or you may come home minus a hand—surreptitiously feeding your offspring to the dinosaurs is also discouraged by management.

THE WIZARDING WORLD OF HARRY POTTER-HOGSMEADE

IN WHAT MAY PROVE TO BE the competitive coup of all time between theme park archrivals Disney and Universal, the latter inked a deal with Warner Brothers Entertainment to create a "fully immersive"

Harry Potter–themed environment based on the best-selling children's books by J. K. Rowling and the companion blockbuster movies from Warner Brothers. The books have been translated into 74 languages, with more than 450 million copies sold in more than 200 territories around the world. The movies have made more than $7.7 billion worldwide, making Harry Potter the second highest-grossing film franchise in history. The project was blessed by Rowling, who is known for tenaciously protecting the integrity of her work. In the case of the films, she demanded that Warner Brothers be true, to an almost unprecedented degree, to the books on which the films were based.

The 20-acre Wizarding World is an amalgamation of landmarks, creatures, and themes that are faithful to the films and books. You access the area through an imposing gate that opens onto **Hogsmeade,** depicted in winter and covered in snow. This is The Wizarding World's primary shopping and dining venue. Exiting Hogsmeade, you first glimpse the towering castle housing **Hogwarts School of Witchcraft and Wizardry,** flanked by the **Forbidden Forest** and **Hagrid's Hut.** The grounds and interior of the castle contain part of the queue for the super-headliner **Harry Potter and the Forbidden Journey.** Universal has gone all out on the castle, with the intention of creating an icon even more beloved and powerful than Cinderella Castle at Disney's Magic Kingdom.

"What a Long Strange Trip It's Been"

That Grateful Dead lyric is awfully appropriate when recounting the evolution of The Wizarding World–Hogsmeade. A Harry Potter theme park (or themed area) has been the chop-licking dream of the amusement industry for a decade. First, of course, there were the books, which against all odds trumped texting and TV to lure a broad age range of youth back to the printed page. Next came the movies. In securing the film rights, Warner Brothers, along with several unsuccessful suitors, learned the most important thing about exploiting the Harry Potter phenomenon: J. K. Rowling is boss.

As the Potter juggernaut took the world by storm, entertainment conglomerates began approaching Rowling about theme park rights. When she spurned a Universal Studios Florida concept for a show based on the Potter characters, industry observers were certain that she had struck a deal with Disney. In fact, Disney was in talks with Rowling about a stand-alone Harry Potter theme park. For her part, Rowling had no problem visualizing what she wanted in a theme park, but from Disney's point of view, what Rowling wanted was operationally problematic, if not altogether impossible. Never an entity to concede control, Disney walked.

Universal caught Rowling on the rebound and brought her to Orlando to tour Islands of Adventure. Among other things, Universal officials squired her around The Lost Continent section of the park, impressing her with its detailed theme execution and showing her how, with a little imagination, it could be rethemed. Rowling saw the potential but wasn't much more flexible with Universal than she was with Disney. From her perspective, getting a themed area right couldn't be any harder than getting a movie right, so she insisted that Stuart Craig, her trusted production designer for the films, be responsible for faithfully re-creating sets from the movies. Universal, on fire to land Harry Potter, became convinced that the collaboration could work.

But theme parks and movies are two very different things. With a film, a set has to look good only for a few moments and then it's on to something else. With a theme park, a set has to look good 12–16 hours a day, in all manner of weather, and with tens of thousands of tourists rambling through it in need of food, drink, restrooms, protection from rain, and places to rest. With The Wizarding World–Hogsmeade, Rowling's insistence on authenticity occasioned conundrums not anticipated by the theme park designers, who, for example, logically assumed that guests would like to see the interior of Hagrid's Hut. No problem—a walk-through attraction will serve nicely. Of course, there's the Americans with Disabilities Act, so we'll need ramps both in and out of the hut. No way, say the movie people: Hagrid's Hut in the films had steps, so the theme park version must have them too.

Bone Up

We don't have room to explain all the Potter allusions and icons that are incorporated into The Wizarding World. Because they so accurately replicate scenes from the books and films, it helps immeasurably to be well versed in all things Harry. If it's been awhile since you've seen one of the movies or read one of the novels, you can brush up by watching the first four flicks in the series, in particular *Harry Potter and the Goblet of Fire* and *Harry Potter and the Sorcerer's Stone* (*Harry Potter and the Philosopher's Stone* outside India and the United States). For an easy memory jog, check out the films' trailers at YouTube. If you know nothing at all about Harry Potter, you'll still have fun, but to truly appreciate the nuance and detail, we suggest that you hit the books.

Getting In

Crowds are certainly larger during summer and holidays, but because of The Wizarding World's overwhelming popularity, you'll encounter lines even at slower times of year. During peak periods, hotel guests may be allowed into IOA 1 hour before the general public, while all guests are usually admitted through the turnstiles into Port of Entry 30 minutes before the official opening time.

Wizarding World crowd management has been a work in progress for Universal. Now, with six years of operation under its belt, Universal has settled on a flexible system predicated on the expected level of attendance for any given day. (Similar procedures are in place at Diagon Alley; see page 220.) No matter the crowd level, if you're staying in one of Universal's on-site hotels and you have early-entry privileges for The Wizarding World, use them, arriving as early during the early-entry period as possible.

On most days of the year, from the slowest off-season through the busiest summer weeks, you can enter and depart The Wizarding World of Harry Potter–Hogsmeade as you please. The waits for the rides will still be more than an hour at times, but gaining entry to the themed area itself is not an issue.

On days when the park is busiest, such as during spring break or between December 25 and January 1, access to Hogsmeade may be limited for part of the day. Barricades are placed at both entrances to The Wizarding World–Hogsmeade once the area reaches maximum occupancy. You can then go to touch screen ticket kiosks outside the Jurassic Park Discovery Center and obtain a free return ticket (not unlike the old paper Fastpasses at Walt Disney World) to come back during your choice of designated time windows. You do not need your admission ticket to receive a timed-return ticket, and one person can retrieve a time for your entire party (up to nine people). At the specified time, return to the Lost Continent entrance and present your pass to the barricade crew to gain entry.

*un*official **TIP**
If you leave The Wizarding World while the entrance barriers are in place and you wish to return, you'll either have to wait in line to get another pass (provided they haven't all been distributed) or wait until late in the day, when the barricades come down as crowds disperse.

The return time on your pass depends on crowd conditions and how many Universal resort guests are in The Wizarding World–Hogsmeade before the park opens to the general public. Depending on demand, your possible return times may be many hours in the future, and it's possible (though extremely rare) for return tickets to run out entirely. Another factor that will affect your wait is how well Harry Potter and the Forbidden Journey is operating because this is what those in line are waiting for. If the ride comes up on schedule and runs trouble-free, everything runs smoothly. If Forbidden Journey experiences problems, though, especially first thing in the morning, it gums up the works for everyone.

On these peak days, a standby queue may also be erected in the waterfront landing behind the Jurassic Park Discovery Center; because more guests can enter only as others leave, this line can be painfully slow, so a return ticket is strongly suggested. It is common for the entrance barricades to be removed during the last hour or two the park is open, thus presenting the opportunity to come and go as you please.

Once admitted to Hogsmeade, you'll still have to wait for each ride, store, and concession, as well as for the area's one restaurant. Because Hogsmeade has less elbow room than Diagon Alley, it will reach maximum occupancy and require return tickets on days when

Diagon does not, and feel more crowded once you finally get inside.

Note that guests arriving on Hogwarts Express disembark outside of Hogsmeade and must still retrieve a ticket before entering. The timed-return tickets are neither needed nor accepted for Hogwarts Express itself.

However complicated, it's all doable, as a multigenerational Grosse Pointe, Michigan, family attests:

> *Convinced of your rectitude, we went without fear to Universal. We made it to Harry Potter by 8:05, were out of the Forbidden Journey and on the Hippogriff by 8:30, and had our Butterbeer by 9.*

Ladies and Gentlemen, Start Your Broomsticks

The Wizarding World–Hogsmeade is in the northwest corner of Islands of Adventure, between The Lost Continent and Jurassic Park. From the IOA entrance, the most direct route there is through Port of Entry then right, through Seuss Landing (staying to the left of Green Eggs and Ham) and The Lost Continent, to the Hogsmeade main gate. The alternative route is to cross the bridge connecting The Lost Continent with Jurassic Park, and then turn right after entering the latter area. Note that the bridge is closed on slower days.

For the moment, though, let's begin our exploration at The Wizarding World's main entrance, on The Lost Continent side. Passing beneath a stone arch, you enter the village of Hogsmeade. The **Hogwarts Express** locomotive sits belching steam on your right. The village setting is rendered in exquisite detail: Stone cottages and shops have steeply pitched slate roofs; bowed multipaned windows; gables; and tall, crooked chimneys. Add cobblestone streets and gas streetlamps, and Hogsmeade is as reminiscent of Sherlock Holmes as it is of Harry Potter.

Your first taste—literally—of the Harry Potter universe comes courtesy of **Honeydukes.** Specializing in Potter-themed candy such as Acid Pops (no flashbacks, guaranteed), Tooth Splintering Strong Mints, and Fizzing Whizzbees, the sweet shop offers no shortage of snacks that administer an immediate sugar high. There's also a small bakery inside; while we highly recommend the Cauldron Cakes, the big draw is the elaborately boxed Chocolate Frogs. The chocolate inside isn't anything special, but the packaging looks as if it came straight from a Harry Potter film, complete with lenticular wizard trading card.

Next door to Honeydukes and set back from the main street is **Three Broomsticks,** a rustic tavern serving English staples such as fish-and-chips, shepherd's pie, Cornish pasties, and turkey legs; kids' fare includes the obligatory mac and cheese and chicken fingers. To the rear of the tavern is the **Hog's Head** pub, which serves a nice selection of beer as well as The Wizarding World's signature nonalcoholic brew, Butterbeer (see page 250). Three Broomsticks and the Hog's

Head were carved out of The Lost Continent's popular Enchanted Oak Tavern, which was Potterfied pretty effectively in its reincarnation, though a good deal of seating capacity was sacrificed. To dine at Three Broomsticks anytime from its opening until roughly 8 p.m., you'll have to wait in a long queue during busier times of year.

unofficial **TIP**
The only restrooms in The Wizarding World at IOA, labeled PUBLIC CONVENIENCES, are in the middle of Hogsmeade. Remember where they are—especially if you're planning to ride Forbidden Journey or Dragon Challenge and you're prone to motion sickness.

Roughly across the street from the pub, you'll find benches in the shade at the **Owlery,** where animatronic owls (complete with lifelike poop) ruffle and hoot from the rafters. Next to the Owlery is the **Owl Post,** where you can have mail stamped with a Hogsmeade postmark before dropping it off for delivery (an Orlando postmark will also be applied by the real USPS). The Owl Post also sells stationery, toy owls, and the like. Here, once again, a nice selection of owls preens on the timbers overhead. You access the Owl Post in either of two ways: through an interior door following the wand-choosing demonstration at Ollivanders (see below), or through **Dervish and Banges,** a magic-supplies shop that's interconnected with the Owl Post. You can't enter through the Owl Post's front door on busy days, when it serves exclusively as an exit. Because it's so difficult to get into the Owl Post, IOA sometimes stations a team member outside to stamp your postcards with The Wizarding World postmark.

Next to the Owl Post is the previously mentioned **Ollivanders** (★★★★), a musty little shop stacked to the ceiling with boxes of magic wands. Here, following a script from the Potter books, you can pick out a wand or, in an interactive experience, let it pick you. This is one of the most truly imaginative elements of The Wizarding World: A wand-keeper sizes you up and presents a wand, inviting you to try it out; your attempted spells produce unintended, unwanted, and highly amusing consequences. Ultimately, a wand chooses you, with all the attendant special effects. It's great fun, but the tiny shop can accommodate only about 24 guests at a time. Usually just one person in each group gets to be chosen by a wand, and then the whole group is dispatched to the Owl Post and Dervish and Banges to make purchases. Wand prices range from $25 for a no-frills model to $45 for an interactive gizmo that triggers special effects hidden inside shop windows throughout Hogsmeade. The wand experience is second in popularity only to Harry Potter and the Forbidden Journey—lines build quickly after opening, and there's little to no shade. If Ollivanders is a priority, go there first thing in the morning or after 7:30 p.m. The average wait time during summer and other busy periods is 45–85 minutes between 9:30 a.m. and 7:30 p.m. If you're just looking to buy a wand without the interactive experience, a cart is usually set up between Filch's Emporium of Confiscated Goods and the Flight of the Hippogriff exit, with little to no wait.

At the far end of the village, the massive **Hogwarts Castle** comes into view, set atop a rock face and towering over Hogsmeade and the entire Wizarding World. Follow the path through the castle's massive gates to the entrance of Harry Potter and the Forbidden Journey. Below the castle and to the right, at the base of the cliff, are the Forbidden Forest, Hagrid's Hut, and the **Flight of the Hippogriff** children's roller coaster. In the village, near the gate to Hogwarts Castle, is **Filch's Emporium of Confiscated Goods,** which offers all manner of Potter-themed gear, including Quidditch clothing, magical-creature toys, film-inspired chess sets, and, of course, Death Eater masks (breath mints extra).

In keeping with the stores depicted in the Potter films, the shopping venues in The Wizarding World–Hogsmeade are small and intimate—so intimate, in fact, that they feel congested when they're serving only 12–20 shoppers. With so many avid Potter fans, lines for the shops develop most days by 9:30 or 10 a.m., creating a phenomenon we've never seen in our 33 years of covering theme parks: The lines for the shops are longer than the lines for Dragon Challenge and Flight of the Hippogriff—at 11 a.m., there was frequently a 30- to 40-minute wait to get into the shops, but a less-than-20-minute wait to ride the coasters. Filch's Emporium is the only shop in The Wizarding World that you can enter during high season without waiting in line; the problem is that it doubles as the exit for Forbidden Journey. As throngs of riders flow out continuously, trying to enter Filch's is not unlike swimming upstream to spawn; still, it's a whole lot better than standing in lines for the other shops. Because the stores are so jammed, IOA sells some Potter merchandise, including wands, through street vendors and in Port of Entry shops.

At the end of the village and to the left is the walkway to **Jurassic Park,** the themed area contiguous to The Wizarding World.

The Butterbeer Craze

Butterbeer is a nonalcoholic, cream soda–like beverage served from a tap, with a butterscotch-y head that's added after the drink is poured. There's also a frozen version that's sort of like a slushie. Both were invented for The Wizarding World and had to meet J. K. Rowling's stringent specifications, which, among other things, required natural sugar (don't ask for Butterbeer Lite). We didn't expect to like it but were pleasantly surprised: It's tasty and refreshing, albeit *really* sweet. A 16-ounce soda in a plastic cup goes for $4.99, while the frozen version is $5.99. The same soda in a Harry Potter souvenir cup sells for an additional $8 with no discount on refills. The hot version is sold in a 12-ounce paper cup for $4.99.

*un*official **TIP**
At J. K. Rowling's request, no brand-name soft drinks are available in The Wizarding World—if you want a Coke, you'll have to go to The Lost Continent or Jurassic Park.

It seems that everyone in the park is dead set on trying Butterbeer, as confirmed by Universal's sale of its 5 millionth cup in December 2012. Unfortunately, at IOA the ambrosial liquid is sold only at Three Broomsticks, at the Hog's Head pub, and by two street vendors—and that means, once again, long waits. Many guests buy from the outside vendors, waiting 30 minutes or more in line to be served. We recommend that you try your luck at the Hog's Head—the wait here is generally 10 minutes or less, and often there's nobody in line, even when the outdoor carts have lines 30 people deep only 20 feet away. Once served, you can relax with your drink at a table in the pub or out on the rear patio. Be aware that the outdoor vendors charge a few cents more and don't honor Annual Pass discounts.

Wizarding World Entertainment

Nearly every retail space sports some sort of animatronic or special effects surprise. At Dervish and Banges, the fearsome Monster Book of Monsters rattles and snarls at you as Nimbus 2001 brooms strain at their tethers overhead. At the Hog's Head pub, the titular porcine part, mounted behind the bar, similarly thrashes and growls. Street entertainment at the Forbidden Journey end of Hogsmeade includes *The Frog Choir* (★★★), composed of four singers, two of whom are holding large amphibian puppets sitting on pillows. The 10-minute show is followed by a photo op. Though cute, *The Frog Choir* probably isn't worth going out of your way for. The 6-minute *Triwizard Spirit Rally* (★★★½) showcases dancing, martial arts, and acrobatics.

Dragon Challenge *(Universal Express)*   ★★★★

APPEAL BY AGE	PRESCHOOL ★	GRADE SCHOOL ★★★★★	TEENS ★★★★½
YOUNG ADULTS ★★★★★		OVER 30 ★★★★½	SENIORS ★★★

What it is Roller coaster. **Scope and scale** Headliner. **When to go** Immediately after Harry Potter and the Forbidden Journey. **Special comment** 54″ minimum height requirement. **Authors' rating** Almost as good as the Hulk coaster; not to be missed; ★★★★. **Duration of ride** 2½ minutes. **Average waiting time per 100 people ahead of you** 9 minutes. **Loading speed** Moderate.

DESCRIPTION AND COMMENTS Dragon Challenge, formerly Dueling Dragons and part of The Lost Continent, was renamed and incorporated into The Wizarding World in 2010. The story line is that you're preparing to compete in the Triwizard Tournament from *Harry Potter and the Goblet of Fire.* As you wind through the long, long queue, you pass through tournament tents and dark passages that are supposed to be under the stadium. You'll see the Goblet of Fire on display and hear the distant roar of the crowd in the supposed stadium above you.

Riders board one of two coasters—Chinese Fireball or Hungarian Horntail—that are launched moments apart on tracks that are closely intertwined. The tracks are configured so that you get a different experience on each. The trains are dispatched sequentially instead of simultaneously, so it looks as if one train is chasing another.

Because this is an inverted coaster, your view of the action is limited unless you're sitting in the front row. Regardless of where you sit, there's plenty to keep you busy. Dragon Challenge is the highest coaster in the park and also claims the longest drop at 115 feet, plus five inversions. It's a smooth ride all the way.

Coaster fans argue about which seat on which train provides the wildest ride. We prefer the front row of Horntail for the visuals during the close call with the castle and the last row of Fireball for added g-forces during the more intense inversions.

TOURING TIPS Use the restrooms before getting in line. The queuing area for Dragon Challenge is the longest, most convoluted affair we've ever seen, winding endlessly through a maze of faux subterranean passages. After what feels like a comprehensive tour of Mammoth Cave, you finally emerge at the loading area, where you must choose between Chinese Fireball or Hungarian Horntail. Of course, at this critical juncture, you're as blind as a mole rat from being in the dark for so long. Our advice is to follow the person in front of you until your eyes adjust to the light.

Waits for Dragon Challenge, one of the best coasters in the country, rarely exceed 30 minutes before 11 a.m. Ride after experiencing Harry Potter and the Forbidden Journey. Even if there's no line to speak of, it takes 10–12 minutes just to navigate the passages and not much less time to exit after riding. There used to be a shortcut from the exit back into the queue for re-rides, but since Universal began enforcing the mandatory locker policy with metal detectors outside the castle, everyone must be inconveniently inspected before each trip. Finally, if you don't have time to ride both coasters, the *Unofficial* crew unanimously prefers Chinese Fireball.

Flight of the Hippogriff *(Universal Express)* ★★★

APPEAL BY AGE   PRESCHOOL ★★★½   GRADE SCHOOL ★★★★   TEENS ★★★
YOUNG ADULTS ★★½   OVER 30 ★★★½   SENIORS ★★★

What it is Kiddie roller coaster. **Scope and scale** Minor attraction. **When to go** First 90 minutes the park is open. **Special comment** 36" minimum height requirement. **Authors' rating** A good beginner coaster; ★★★. **Duration of ride** 1 minute. **Average waiting time per 100 people ahead of you** 14 minutes. **Loading speed** Slow.

DESCRIPTION AND COMMENTS Below and to the right of Hogwarts Castle, next to Hagrid's Hut, the Hippogriff is short and sweet but not worth much of a wait. Potter fans will want to ride to see Hagrid's Hut and an adorable animatronic of Buckbeak.

TOURING TIPS Have your kids ride soon after the park opens while older sibs enjoy Dragon Challenge. Check out Hogwarts Castle from the cliff bottom and Hagrid's Hut above the path for the regular line.

Hogwarts Express ★★★★½

APPEAL BY AGE   PRESCHOOL ★★★★   GRADE SCHOOL ★★★★★   TEENS ★★★★
YOUNG ADULTS ★★★★½   OVER 30 ★★★★½   SENIORS ★★★★½

What it is Transportation attraction. **Scope and scale** Super-headliner. **When to go** Immediately after park opening. **Special comments** Expect lengthy waits in line; requires Park-to-Park admission. **Authors' rating** Not to be missed; ★★★★½. **Duration of ride** 4 minutes. **Average waiting time per 100 people ahead of you** 7 minutes. **Loading speed** Moderate.

DESCRIPTION AND COMMENTS See page 226 for a full review.

TOURING TIPS Because the Hogsmeade Station doesn't include the cool Platform 9¾ effect found at the King's Cross end, expect waits for the one-way trip to be shorter here. A Park-to-Park ticket is required to board, and all guests exit at Universal Studios Florida outside of the London waterfront, so the train isn't a shortcut into Diagon Alley.

The Hogsmeade Station lies within the footprint of the Dragon Challenge roller coaster and provides pedestrian access to Hogsmeade and IOA's Lost Continent themed area. On days of low to average attendance, disembarking guests will be allowed directly into Hogsmeade, less than a minute's walk away. On days of heavy attendance, they'll be directed to the bridge between The Lost Continent and Jurassic Park, where they'll have to either queue to enter Hogsmeade or obtain a free timed-entry ticket to visit The Wizarding World at a specified time.

If you wish to experience the train, do so before the queue builds in midafternoon. If the line grows very long, guests wishing to ride a second time in one day may be relegated to a slower re-ride queue.

Harry Potter and the Forbidden Journey ★★★★★

| APPEAL BY AGE | PRESCHOOL ★ | GRADE SCHOOL ★★★★½ | TEENS ★★★★★ |
| YOUNG ADULTS ★★★★★ | OVER 30 ★★★★★ | | SENIORS ★★★★★ |

Motion Sickness

What it is Motion-simulator dark ride. **Scope and scale** Super-headliner. **When to go** Immediately after park opening. **Special comments** Expect *long* waits in line; 48" minimum height requirement. **Authors' rating** Marvelous for Muggles and not to be missed; ★★★★★. **Duration of ride** 4¼ minutes. **Average waiting time per 100 people ahead of you** 4 minutes. **Loading speed** Fast.

DESCRIPTION AND COMMENTS This ride provides the only opportunity at Universal Orlando to come in contact with Harry, Ron, Hermione, and Dumbledore as portrayed by the original actors. Half the attraction is a series of preshows, setting the stage for the main event, a dark ride. You can get on the ride in only 10–25 minutes using the singles line, but everyone should go through the main queue at least once.

From Hogsmeade you reach the attraction through the imposing Winged Boar gates and progress along a winding path. Entering the castle on a lower level, you walk through a sort of dungeon festooned with various icons and prop replicas from the Potter flicks, including the Mirror of Erised from *Harry Potter and the Sorcerer's Stone.* You later emerge back outside and into the Hogwarts greenhouses. Cleverly conceived and executed, with some strategically placed mandrakes to amuse you, the greenhouses compose the larger part of the Forbidden Journey's queuing area. If you're among the first in the park and in the queue, you'll move through this area pretty quickly. Otherwise . . . well, we hope you like plants. The greenhouses are not air-conditioned, but fans move the (hot) air around. Blessedly, there are water fountains but, alas, no restrooms.

Having finally escaped horticulture purgatory, you reenter the castle, moving along its halls and passageways. One chamber you'll probably remember from the films is a multistory gallery of portraits, many of whose subjects come alive when they take a notion. You'll see for the first time the four founders of Hogwarts: Helga Hufflepuff holding her famous cup,

Godric Gryffindor and Rowena Ravenclaw nearby, and the tall, moving portrait of Salazar Slytherin straight ahead. The founders argue about Quidditch and Dumbledore's controversial decision to host an open house at Hogwarts for Muggles (garden-variety mortals). Don't rush through the gallery—the effects are very cool, and the conversation is essential to understanding the rest of the attraction.

Next up, after you've navigated some more passages, is Dumbledore's office, where the chief wizard appears on a balcony and welcomes you to Hogwarts. The headmaster's appearance is your introduction to Musion Eyeliner technology—a high-definition video-projection system that produces breathtakingly realistic, three-dimensional, life-size moving holograms. The technology uses a special foil that reflects images from HD projectors, producing holographic images of variable sizes and incredible clarity. After his welcoming remarks, Dumbledore dispatches you to the Defence Against the Dark Arts classroom to hear a presentation on the history of Hogwarts.

As you gather to await the lecture, Harry, Ron, and Hermione pop out from beneath an invisibility cloak. They suggest that you ditch the lecture in favor of joining them for a proper tour of Hogwarts, including a Quidditch match. After some repartee among the characters and a couple of special effects surprises, it's off to the Hogwarts Official Attraction Safety Briefing and Boarding Instructions Chamber—OK, we made up the name, but you get the picture. The briefing and instructions are presented by animated portraits, including an etiquette teacher. Later on, even the famed Sorting Hat gets into the act. All this leads to the Room of Requirement, where hundreds of candles float overhead and you board the ride.

After all the high-tech stuff in your queuing odyssey, you'll naturally expect to be wowed by your ride vehicle. Surely it's a Nimbus 3000 turbo-broom, a phoenix, a hippogriff, or at least the Weasleys' flying car. But no, what you'll ride on the most technologically advanced theme park attraction in America is . . . a *bench*? Yep, a bench.

A bit anticlimactic, perhaps, but as benches go, this one's a doozy, mounted on a Kuka robotic arm. When not engaged in Quidditch matches, a Kuka arm is a computer-controlled robotic arm similar to the kind used in heavy manufacturing. If you think about pictures you've seen of automotive assembly plants, Kuka arms are like those long metal appendages that come in to complete welds, move heavy stuff around, or fasten things. With the right programming, the arms can handle just about any repetitive industrial tasks thrown at them (see **kuka-robotics.com** for more info).

Bear with us for a moment; you know how we *Unofficial*s like techno-geekery. When you put a Kuka arm on a ride platform, it provides six axes—six degrees of freedom—with synchronized motion that can be programmed to replicate all the sensations of flying, including broad swoops, steep dives, sharp turns, sudden stops, and fast acceleration. Here's where it gets really good: Up to now, when Kuka arms and similar robotic systems have been employed in theme park rides, the arm has been anchored to a stationary platform. In Forbidden Journey, the arm is mounted on a ride vehicle that moves you through a series of action scenes projected all around you. The movement of the arm is synchronized to create the motion that corresponds to what's happening in the film. When everything works right, it's mind-blowing.

High-tech troubles aside, is the attraction itself ultimately worthy of the hype? In a word, *yes*! Your 4¼-minute adventure is a headlong sprint through the most thrilling moments from the first few Potter books: You'll soar over Hogwarts Castle, narrowly evade an attacking dragon, spar with the Whomping Willow, get tossed into a Quidditch match, and fight off Dementors inside the Chamber of Secrets. Scenes alternate between enormous physical sets, complete with animatronic creatures, elaborate lighting effects, and high-definition video-projection domes that surround your field of view, similar to Soarin' or The Simpsons Ride. Those Kuka-powered benches really do "levitate" in a manner that feels remarkably like free flight, and while you don't go upside down, the sensation of floating on your back or being slung from side to side is certainly unique.

The seamless transitions between screens and sets, and the way the domes appear to remain stationary in front of you while actually moving (much like Dreamfinder's dirigible in the original Journey into Imagination at Epcot), serve to blur the boundary between actual and virtual better than any attraction before it. The greatest-hits montage plotline may be a bit muddled, but the ride is enormously effective at leaving you feeling like you just survived the scariest scrapes from the early educational career of The Boy Who Lived.

Having experienced Forbidden Journey for ourselves, we have two primary bones to pick. First, Islands of Adventure team members rush you through the queue. To understand the story line and get the most out of the attraction, you really need to see and hear the entire presentation in each of the preshow rooms. This won't happen unless, contrary to the admonishments of the team members, you just park yourself and watch a full run-through of each preshow. Try to find a place to stop where you can let those behind you pass and where you're as far away from any staff as possible. As long as you're not creating a logjam, the team members will leave you alone as often as not.

Another alternative is to tell the greeter at the castle entrance that you want to take the **castle-only tour.** This self-guided experience lets guests who don't want to ride view the many features of the castle via a different queue. You can pause as long as you desire in each of the various chambers and savor the preshows without being herded along. At the end, if you decide to ride, ask to be guided to the singles line—using this strategy, you'll maximize your enjoyment of the castle while minimizing your wait for the ride. Note that the castle-only tour is often unavailable on peak-attendance days.

Another gripe: The dialogue in the preshows is delivered in English accents of varying degrees of intelligibility, and at a very brisk pace. Add an echo effect owing to the cavernous nature of the preshow rooms, and it can be quite difficult for Yanks to decipher what's being said. This is especially evident in the staccato repartee between Harry, Ron, and Hermione in the Defence Against the Dark Arts classroom.

TOURING TIPS Harry Potter and the Forbidden Journey has quickly become the most popular attraction at Islands of Adventure, and one of the most in-demand theme park attractions in America. The only way to ride without a prohibitive wait is to be one of the first through the turnstiles in the morning or to visit after 7:30 or 8 p.m.

Upon entering Forbidden Journey's outside queue, you have two choices: left line or right line. They are unmarked, but the left line is for those who have bags or loose items and therefore require a locker (no charge). Our wait-time research has shown that in some cases, not needing a locker can save you as much as 30 minutes of standing in line. If you do need to stow your stuff, be aware that the Forbidden Journey locker area is small, crowded, and confusing. It may make more sense to pay the $3 to stash your things in the lockers beside Dragon Challenge.

Universal warns you to secure or leave behind loose objects, which most people interpret to mean eyeglasses, purses, ball caps, and the like. However, the ride makes a couple of moves that will empty your trousers faster than a master pickpocket—ditto and worse for shirt pockets. When these moves occur, your stuff will clatter around like quarters in a slot machine tray. Much better to use the small compartment built into the seat back for keys, coins, phone, wallet, and pocket Bible. Be prepared, however: Team members don't give you much time to stow or retrieve your belongings.

The single-rider line is likewise unmarked, as relatively few guests use it. Whereas on most attractions the wait in the singles line is one-third the wait in the standby line, at Forbidden Journey it can be as much as one-tenth. Because the individual seating separates you from the other riders whether your party stays together or not, the singles line is a great option. To get there, enter the right (no-bags) line and keep left all the way into the castle. Past the locker area, take the first left into the singles line.

If you see a complete iteration of each preshow in the queue and then experience the ride, you'll invest 25–35 minutes even if you don't have to wait. If you elect to skip the preshows—the Gryffindor Common Room, where you receive safety and loading directions, is mandatory—and use the singles line, you can get on in about 10–25 minutes at any time of day. At a time when the posted wait in the regular line was 2 hours, we rode and were out the door in 15 minutes using the singles line.

Universal has toned down the Kuka programming to help reduce motion sickness, but we nonetheless recommend that you ride on a full stomach. If you start getting queasy, fix your gaze on your feet and try to exclude as much from your peripheral vision as possible.

If you have a child who doesn't meet the minimum height requirement of 48 inches, a child-swapping option is provided at the loading area.

The seats accommodate a wide variety of body shapes and sizes. Each bench has specially modified seats at either end. Though these allow many more people to ride, it's possible that guests of size can't fit in them. The best

unofficial **TIP**
Even if your child meets the height requirement, consider carefully whether Forbidden Journey is an experience he or she can handle—because the seats on the benches are compartmentalized, kids can't see or touch Mom or Dad if they get frightened.

way to figure out whether you can fit in a regular seat or one of the modified ones is to sit in one of the test seats outside the queue or just inside the castle. After you sit down, pull down on the safety harness as far as you can. One of three safety lights will illuminate: A green light indicates that you can fit into any seat, a yellow light means that you should ask for one of the modified seats on the outside of the bench, and a red light means that the harness can't engage enough for you to ride safely.

In addition, IOA team members select guests of all sizes "at random" to plop in the test seats, but they're really looking for large people or those who have a certain body shape. Team members handle the situation as diplomatically as possible, but if they suspect you're not the right size, you'll be asked to sit down for a test. For you to be cleared to ride, the overhead restraint has to click three times; once again, it's body shape rather than weight (unless you're over 300 pounds) that's key. Most team members will let you try a second time if you don't achieve three clicks on the first go. Passing the test by inhaling sharply is not recommended unless you can also hold your breath for the entire 4-plus minutes of the ride.

With The Wizarding World and especially Forbidden Journey soaking up so many guests in IOA, waits for attractions in the other themed areas are minimal up to around 11 a.m.

THE LOST CONTINENT

The Eighth Voyage of Sindbad Stunt Show
(Universal Express) ★★½

APPEAL BY AGE	PRESCHOOL ★★	GRADE SCHOOL ★★★½	TEENS ★★★
YOUNG ADULTS ★★★		OVER 30 ★★½	SENIORS ★★½

What it is Theater stunt show. **Scope and scale** Major attraction. **When to go** Any time on the daily entertainment schedule. **Authors' rating** Explosively awful; ★★½. **Duration of show** 17 minutes. **Probable waiting time** 15 minutes.

DESCRIPTION AND COMMENTS A story about Sindbad the Sailor is the glue that (loosely) binds this stunt show featuring water explosions, 10-foot-tall circles of flame, and various other eruptions and perturbations. Not unlike an action movie that substitutes a mind-numbing succession of explosions, crashes, and special effects for plot and character development, the production is so vacuous and redundant (not to mention silly) that it's hard to get into the spirit of the thing. A 2015 refurbishment freshened up the fisticuffs and updated some pop-culture references, while adding an inane audience-participation preshow. The "improvements" weren't enough to upgrade our opinion of the production. When our researchers went to review *Sindbad,* one team member passed, explaining that the show is like a colonoscopy—once every 10 years is enough.

TOURING TIPS See *The Eighth Voyage* after you've experienced the rides and the better-rated shows.

Poseidon's Fury *(Universal Express)* ★★★½

APPEAL BY AGE	PRESCHOOL ★★	GRADE SCHOOL ★★★½	TEENS ★★½
YOUNG ADULTS ★★★		OVER 30 ★★★	SENIORS ★★★

What it is High-tech theater attraction. **Scope and scale** Headliner. **When to go** After experiencing all the rides. **Special comment** Audience stands throughout. **Authors' rating** ★★★½. **Duration of show** 17 minutes, including preshow. **Probable waiting time** 25 minutes.

DESCRIPTION AND COMMENTS In the first incarnation of this story, the Greek gods Poseidon and Zeus duked it out, with Poseidon as the heavy. Poseidon fought with water, and Zeus fought with fire, though both sometimes resorted to laser beams and smoke machines. In the current incarnation, the rehabilitated Poseidon now tussles with an evil wizardish guy—named Lord Darkenon, of all things—and they fight with fire, water, lasers, and smoke machines. As you might have inferred, the story is somewhat incoherent, but the special effects are still amazing, as is the theming of the preshow area. The plot unfolds in installments as you pass through a couple of antechambers and finally into the main theater. Though the production plods a bit at first, it wraps up with quite an impressive flourish. *Poseidon* is far and away the best of the Islands of Adventure theater attractions (its only competition is *Sindbad*).

TOURING TIPS If you're still wet from Dudley Do-Right, the Bilge-Rat Barges, or the Jurassic Park River Adventure, you might be tempted to cheer the evil wizard's flame jets in hopes of finally drying out. Our money, however, is on Poseidon—it's legal in Florida for theme parks to get guests wet, but setting them on fire is frowned upon.

Frequent explosions, dark, and noise may frighten younger children. Catch *Poseidon* after getting your fill of the rides.

SEUSS LANDING

THIS 10-ACRE THEMED AREA is based on Dr. Seuss's famous children's books. Buildings and attractions replicate his whimsical style, with exaggerated features, bright colors, and rounded lines. Seuss Landing has four rides; **If I Ran the Zoo,** an interactive play area populated by Seuss creatures; and *Oh, the Stories You'll Hear!,* a live musical show.

Caro-Seuss-el *(Universal Express)* ★★★

APPEAL BY AGE   PRESCHOOL ★★★★★   GRADE SCHOOL ★★★★   TEENS ★★★
YOUNG ADULTS ★★★   OVER 30 ★★★½   SENIORS ★★★★

What it is Merry-go-round. **Scope and scale** Minor attraction. **When to go** Before 11 a.m. **Authors' rating** Wonderfully whimsical; ★★★. **Duration of ride** 2 minutes. **Average waiting time per 100 people ahead of you** 9 minutes. **Loading speed** Slow.

DESCRIPTION AND COMMENTS Totally outrageous, this full-scale, 56-mount merry-go-round is made up entirely of Dr. Seuss characters.

TOURING TIPS Even if you're too old or you don't want to ride, Caro-Seuss-el is worth an inspection.

The Cat in the Hat *(Universal Express)* ★★★½

APPEAL BY AGE   PRESCHOOL ★★★★½   GRADE SCHOOL ★★★★   TEENS ★★½
YOUNG ADULTS ★★½   OVER 30 ★★½   SENIORS ★★★

What it is Indoor adventure ride. **Scope and scale** Major attraction. **When to go** Before 11:30 a.m. **Special comment** 36″ minimum height requirement. **Authors' rating** Dr. S. would be proud; ★★★½. **Duration of ride** 3½ minutes. **Average waiting time per 100 people ahead of you** 5 minutes. **Loading speed** Moderate.

DESCRIPTION AND COMMENTS Guests ride on "couches" through 18 different sets inhabited by animatronic Seuss characters, including The Cat in the Hat, Thing 1 and Thing 2, and the beleaguered goldfish who tries to maintain order in the midst of bedlam.

TOURING TIPS This is fun for all ages. Try to ride early. The ride's energetic spinning has been greatly dampened, and a new height minimum was imposed, reducing its appeal for both tykes and teens.

The High in the Sky Seuss Trolley Train Ride!
(Universal Express) ★★★½

APPEAL BY AGE   PRESCHOOL ★★★★★   GRADE SCHOOL ★★★½   TEENS ★★★
YOUNG   ADULTS ★★★   OVER 30 ★★★   SENIORS ★★★★

What it is Elevated train. **Scope and scale** Major attraction. **When to go** Before 11:30 a.m. **Special comments** A relaxed look at the park; 40" minimum height requirement. **Authors' rating** ★★★½. **Duration of ride** 3½ minutes. **Average waiting time per 100 people ahead of you** 9 minutes. **Loading speed** Molasses.

DESCRIPTION AND COMMENTS Trains putter along elevated tracks while a voice reads a Dr. Seuss story over the train's speakers. As each train makes its way through Seuss Landing, it passes a series of animatronic characters in scenes that are part of the story being told. Little tunnels and a few mild turns make this a charming ride.

There are two tracks at the station. As you face the platform, to your left is the Beech track, which is aquamarine; to your right is the Star track, which is purple. Each track offers a different story.

TOURING TIPS The trains are small, fitting about 20 people, and the loading speed is glacial. Ride at the end of the day or first thing in the morning.

One Fish, Two Fish, Red Fish, Blue Fish
(Universal Express) ★★★

APPEAL BY AGE   PRESCHOOL ★★★★★   GRADE SCHOOL ★★★½   TEENS ★★½
YOUNG   ADULTS ★★★½   OVER 30 ★★★   SENIORS ★★★

What it is Wet version of Dumbo the Flying Elephant. **Scope and scale** Minor attraction. **When to go** Before 10 a.m. **Authors' rating** Who says you can't teach an old ride new tricks?; ★★★. **Duration of ride** 2 minutes. **Average waiting time per 100 people ahead of you** 9 minutes. **Loading speed** Slow.

DESCRIPTION AND COMMENTS Imagine Dumbo with Seuss-style fish instead of elephants and you have half the story—the other half involves yet another opportunity to drown. Guests steer their fish up or down 15 feet in the air while traveling in circles. At the same time, they try to avoid streams of water projected from "squirt posts."

TOURING TIPS We don't know what it is about this theme park and water, but you'll get wetter than at a full-immersion baptism.

DINING *at* UNIVERSAL'S ISLANDS *of* ADVENTURE

OF IOA'S GUSTATORY OFFERINGS, we like **Three Broomsticks,** The Wizarding World of Harry Potter's counter-service restaurant, which serves Boston Market–style rotisserie chicken, plus fish-and-chips, shepherd's pie, and barbecue ribs. A similar menu (minus the Potter theming or crowds) is available at **Thunder Falls Terrace** in Jurassic Park. The **Hog's Head** pub, a short walk from Three Broomsticks, serves beer, wine, mixed drinks, and the obligatory Butterbeer. We're also fond of the gyros at **Fire**

Eater's Grill and the sandwiches at **Blondie's.** Finally, we'd be remiss if we didn't tell you to skip the green eggs at the **Green Eggs and Ham Cafe.**

IOA has two sit-down restaurants: **Confisco Grille,** in Port of Entry, and **Mythos Restaurant,** in The Lost Continent. Confisco is fine for pizza and drinks. Despite its Hellenic-sounding name, Mythos isn't a Greek restaurant; rather, like a typical Applebee's or Chili's, it serves something-for-everyone fare, including Italian risotto, Asian noodles, and Mexican fish tacos, plus steaks and burgers. Nothing on the menu stands out as either very good or very bad, so stick with appetizers and drinks.

UNIVERSAL'S ISLANDS *of* ADVENTURE TOURING PLANS

DECISIONS, DECISIONS

WHEN IT COMES TO TOURING IOA efficiently in a single day, you have two basic choices, and as you might expect, there are trade-offs. The Wizarding World of Harry Potter–Hogsmeade sucks up guests like a Hoover, and the 20-acre section of the park will be quickly overrun by crowds on days of moderately heavy attendance. Because of Harry Potter and the Forbidden Journey's several preshows, it takes about 25 minutes to experience, even if you don't have to wait, which compounds the challenge of creating an optimal touring plan.

If you're intent on experiencing Harry Potter and the Forbidden Journey first thing, be at the turnstiles waiting to be admitted at least 30 minutes before the park opens. Once you're admitted, move as swiftly as possible to The Wizarding World, then ride Forbidden Journey, followed by Flight of the Hippogriff and Dragon Challenge, in that order.

If the rides operate as designed, you're golden. You can get Hogsmeade out of the way in about an hour, and be off to other must-see attractions before the park gets crowded. Then come back to The Wizarding World late in the day to explore Hogsmeade and the shops. If, on the other hand, the ride suffers technical difficulties, you may be stuck in line a long while, during which time the crowds will have spread to other areas of IOA. By the time you exit Forbidden Journey, there will be long lines for all of the park's other popular attractions.

Unless you have Early Park Admission privileges at IOA, a much better choice (and the path we follow in our recommended touring plans) is to skip Potterville first thing. Instead, enjoy other attractions in IOA, starting at Marvel Super Hero Island. The good news is that The Wizarding World usually clears out in the afternoon and is often empty in the last hour, even on busy days. You can ride Forbidden Journey with a minimal wait if you step in the queue shortly before closing time.

UNIVERSAL'S ISLANDS OF ADVENTURE ONE-DAY TOURING PLAN

THIS TOURING PLAN is for guests without Park-to-Park tickets and is appropriate for groups of all sizes and ages. It includes thrill rides that may induce motion sickness or get you wet. If the plan calls for you to experience an attraction that doesn't interest you, simply skip it and go to the next step. Be aware that the plan calls for some backtracking. If you have young children in your party, customize the plan to fit their needs and take advantage of child swap at thrill rides.

1. Buy your admission in advance and call ☎ 407-363-8000 the day before your visit for the official opening time.

2. Arrive at IOA 75–90 minutes before the official opening time if Early Park Admission is offered and you're eligible, or 30–45 minutes before opening for day guests. Get a park map as soon as you enter.

3. Early-entry guests should ride Harry Potter and the Forbidden Journey. Ride Flight of the Hippogriff and Dragon Challenge as well if you have time.

4. Exit Hogsmeade before early entry ends, and head to Marvel Super Hero Island to ride The Incredible Hulk Coaster. Guests without early entry should start at this step.

5. Ride The Amazing Adventures of Spider-Man.

6. Backtrack to ride Doctor Doom's Fearfall.

7. Continue clockwise and ride Dudley Do-Right's Ripsaw Falls in Toon Lagoon.

8. Ride Popeye & Bluto's Bilge-Rat Barges.

9. Take the Jurassic Park River Adventure.

10. Explore Camp Jurassic.

11. Check out the exhibits in the Jurassic Park Discovery Center.

12. Cross the bridge bypassing Hogsmeade to Lost Continent, and ride the High in the Sky Seuss Trolley Train Ride! in Seuss Landing.

13. Ride the Caro-Seuss-el.

14. Ride One Fish, Two Fish, Red Fish, Blue Fish.

15. Ride The Cat in the Hat.

16. Return to Lost Continent and eat lunch at Mythos.

17. Experience *Poseidon's Fury.*

18. See the next scheduled performance of *The Eighth Voyage of Sindbad Stunt Show.*

19. Chat with the Mystic Fountain before or after the *Sindbad* show.

20. Enter The Wizarding World of Harry Potter–Hogsmeade, and ride Dragon Challenge, or walk through the queue to see the Triwizard Tournament artifacts.

21. See the *Frog Choir* or *Triwizard Spirit Rally* perform on the small stage outside Hogwarts.

22. Ride Flight of the Hippogriff.

23. Ride Harry Potter and the Forbidden Journey. If the wait is more than 30 minutes, request a castle tour to experience the queue, and then use the single-rider line.

24. See the wand ceremony at Ollivanders and buy a wand if you wish.

25. Have dinner at Three Broomsticks.

26. See the stage show you didn't see earlier. Pose for a picture with the Hogwarts Express conductor, and explore the shops and interactive windows around Hogsmeade. Sample (or at least smell) some sweets at Honeydukes.

27. Revisit any favorite attractions, or remain in Hogsmeade until closing, enjoying the atmosphere.

THE BEST OF UNIVERSAL STUDIOS FLORIDA AND ISLANDS OF ADVENTURE IN ONE DAY

THIS TOURING PLAN is for guests with one-day Park-to-Park tickets who wish to see the highlights of Universal Studios Florida and Islands of Adventure in a single day. The plan uses Hogwarts Express to get from one park to the other and then back again; you can walk back to the first park for the return leg if the line is too long. The plan includes a table-service lunch at Mythos (make reservations online a few days before your visit) and dinner at the Leaky Cauldron; during holiday periods, you may need to substitute a quick-service snack for one or both meals to fit in all of the plan's attractions.

1. Buy your admission in advance; call ☎ 407-363-8000 the day before your visit for the official opening time.

2. Arrive at USF 90–120 minutes before the official opening time if Early Park Admission is offered and you're eligible, or 30–45 minutes before opening for day guests. Line up at the shortest open turnstile, and get a park map as soon as you enter. **Alternative:** If only IOA is open for Early Park Admission and you're eligible, arrive at IOA's turnstiles 75–90 minutes before the official opening time. Ride Harry Potter and the Forbidden Journey. Ride Flight of the Hippogriff and Dragon Challenge as well if you have time. Take the Hogwarts Express to King's Cross Station before USF officially opens for the day, and continue at the next step.

3. Early-entry guests should ride Harry Potter and the Escape from Gringotts if it is operating. If Gringotts is not operating, enjoy the rest of Diagon Alley but don't get in line.

4. Before early entry ends, hotel guests should exit Diagon Alley and ride Despicable Me Minion Mayhem. Day guests should wait in the front lot until permitted to ride Despicable Me.

5. Ride Hollywood Rip Ride Rockit.

6. Experience Transformers: The Ride 3-D in Production Central.

7. Ride Revenge of the Mummy in New York.

8. Ride Men in Black Alien Attack in World Expo.

9. Ride The Simpsons Ride.

10. Ride E. T. Adventure in Woody Woodpecker's KidZone.

11. Ride Hogwarts Express from King's Cross Station to IOA. Have your Park-to-Park ticket ready.

12. Ride Dragon Challenge in The Wizarding World of Harry Potter–Hogsmeade.

13. Eat lunch at Mythos in Lost Continent or Three Broomsticks in Hogsmeade.

14. Ride The Cat in the Hat in Seuss Landing.

15. Ride The Incredible Hulk Coaster on Marvel Super Hero Island.

16. Ride The Amazing Adventures of Spider-Man.

17. Continue clockwise through Toon Lagoon, and take the Jurassic Park River Adventure.

18. Enter Hogsmeade, and ride Flight of the Hippogriff if the wait isn't too long.

19. Ride Harry Potter and the Forbidden Journey. If the wait is more than 30 minutes, request a castle tour to experience the queue, and then use the single-rider line.

20. Return to Universal Studios Florida using the Hogwarts Express from Hogsmeade Station, or walk back to the other park if the posted wait exceeds 20 minutes.

21. See the next showing of *Universal Orlando's Horror Make-Up Show* upon returning to USF. If the remaining *Horror Make-Up* showtimes aren't convenient, substitute with *Terminator 2: 3-D*.

22. By this time, you should be able to enter Diagon Alley without waiting, even on busy days. Ride Harry Potter and the Escape from Gringotts. If this is your first ride, take the standby queue. For re-rides, use the single-rider line. The Gringotts queue may close before the rest of the park if the posted wait time exceeds remaining operating hours by more than 60 minutes.

23. See the wand ceremony at Ollivanders and buy a wand if you wish.

24. Tour Diagon Alley. Browse the shops, explore the dark recesses of Knockturn Alley, and discover the interactive effects. If you're hungry, try the Leaky Cauldron or Florean Fortescue's Ice-Cream Parlour.

25. See the *Celestina Warbeck* and *Tales of Beedle the Bard* shows.

26. Chat with the Knight Bus conductor and his shrunken head. Also look for Kreacher in the window of 12 Grimmauld Place, and listen to the receiver in the red phone booth.

27. If scheduled, watch *Universal's Cinematic Spectacular* from Central Park (directly across the lagoon from Richter's Burger Company), Duff Brewery, or the embankment in front of London.

PART NINE

The WATER PARKS and WATER SPORTS

WET 'N WILD, AQUATICA, *and* ADVENTURE ISLAND *versus* DISNEY WATER PARKS

DISNEY'S WATER PARKS, and to a somewhat lesser extent Aquatica by SeaWorld, are distinguished more by their genius for creating an integrated adventure environment than by their slides and individual attractions. At the Disney and SeaWorld water parks, both eye and body are deluged with the strange, exotic, humorous, and beautiful. Both Disney water parks are stunningly landscaped. Parking lots, street traffic, and so on are far removed from the swimming areas and out of sight. Also, each park has its own story to tell, a whimsical tale that forms the background for your swimming experience. Once you've passed through the turnstile, you're enveloped in a fantasy setting that excludes the outside world. This holds true for Aquatica by SeaWorld as well, albeit on a more modest scale, and with an aquatic theme rather than a background story.

unofficial TIP
Water parks are one area where the heightened thrills of the non-Disney water rides may outweigh the decor of the Disney water parks.

For many, however, the novelty of the theme is quickly forgotten once they hit the water, and the appreciation of being in an exotic setting gives way to enjoying specific attractions and activities. In other words, your focus narrows from the general atmosphere of the park to the next slide you want to ride. Once this occurs, the most important consideration becomes the quality and number of attractions and activities available and their accessibility relative to crowd conditions. Viewed from this perspective, the non-Disney water parks, especially Universal's Wet 'n Wild, give Disney more than a run for its money. Wet 'n Wild and Aquatica are located in the bustling International Drive tourist area; Adventure Island is located in Tampa. On its own merits, Adventure Island isn't worth a special trip from the Orlando area. But it's a fine way to pass the morning if you've spent the night in Tampa after a visit to Busch Gardens. Plus, the tamer rides and lighter crowds as compared to the Orlando parks are a nice break for the younger members of your family.

Universal is currently constructing the new Volcano Bay water park just south of Cabana Bay Beach Resort, which (according to permit filings) will feature 13 attractions reaching up to 200 feet tall. The new water park will have a tiki vibe, including a volcano, and is being pitched by Universal's publicists as the world's first "water theme park," implying that immersive theming on par with Disney will accompany the next-generation thrill slides. The new park is scheduled to open in 2017, and Wet 'n Wild will close December 31, 2016. What happens to it after that is anyone's guess; the land will most likely be used for more hotels. Until that happens, Wet 'n Wild continues to operate as Orlando's fourth-most popular water park.

A FLUME-TO-FLUME COMPARISON

THE TABLE ON THE NEXT PAGE provides a sense of what each water park offers, inside and outside Walt Disney World. In standard theme park jargon, the water parks refer to their various features, including slides, as attractions. Some individual attractions consist of several slides. If each slide at a specific attraction is different, we count them separately. Runoff Rapids at Blizzard Beach, for example, offers three corkscrew slides, each somewhat different. Because most guests want to experience all three, we count each individually. At the Toboggan Racers attraction (also at Blizzard Beach), there are eight identical slides, side by side. There's no reason to ride all eight, so we count the whole attraction as one slide.

Do the numbers tell the story? In the case of Wet 'n Wild, they certainly do. If you can live without the Disney and SeaWorld parks' theme setting or story line, Wet 'n Wild offers more attractions and more variety than any of the other parks. Plus, mid-June–mid-August, Wet 'n Wild is open until 9 p.m., offering live bands and dancing nightly. Even if you don't care about the bands or dancing, summer nights are more comfortable, lines for the slides often are shorter, and you don't have to worry about sunburn.

Generally speaking, during the day, you'll find Adventure Island in Tampa the least crowded of the parks, followed by Wet 'n Wild. The Disney and SeaWorld parks quite often sell out by about 11 a.m. This is followed by long waits for all the slides.

unofficial **TIP** Wet 'n Wild's later summer hours may mean shorter lines for the slides in the evenings.

Though not approaching Disney's or SeaWorld's standard for aesthetic appeal and landscaping, both Wet 'n Wild and Adventure Island are clean and attractive. In the surf- and wave-pool department, Aquatica's side-by-side wave and surf pools edge out Disney's Typhoon Lagoon. Whereas its surf pools produce 6-foot waves that you can actually bodysurf, the wave pools at the other parks offer

A FLUME-TO-FLUME COMPARISON					
	Blizzard Beach	Typhoon Lagoon	Wet 'n Wild	Adventure Island	Aquatica
SLIDES					
Vertical Speed Body Slide	1	1	2	1	—
Vertical Speed Tube Slide	1	—	—	—	4
Twisting Body Slide	—	—	4	4	—
Camel Hump Body Slide	1	—	1	—	—
Camel Hump Mat Slide	1	—	—	—	—
Camel Hump Tube Slide	—	—	1	2	—
Corkscrew Mat Slide	—	—	1	5	1
Corkscrew Body Slide	—	3	—	—	1
Open Corkscrew Tube Slide	3	4	2	3	—
Dark Corkscrew Tube Slide	1	—	2	1	2
FLUMES					
1- to 3-person Raft Flume	3	2	3	1	2
4- to 5-person Raft Flume	1	1	2	1	—
Total Slides	**12**	**11**	**18**	**18**	**10**
OTHER ATTRACTIONS					
Interactive Water Ride	1	1	—	1	—
Wave Pool	1	1	1	1	1
Surf Pool	—	1	1	1	1
Snorkeling Pool	—	1	—	—	—
Floating River	1	1	1	1	2
Isolated Children's Area	2	2	3	2	2
Other Attractions Total	**5**	**7**	**6**	**6**	**6**
Total Slides and Attractions	**17**	**18**	**24**	**24**	**16**

only bobbing action. All of the parks have outstanding water-activity areas for younger children, and each park features at least one unique attraction: Blizzard Beach has a 1,200-foot water bobsled; Adventure Island has a multistage slide broken up with pools of water; and Sea-World Aquatica's Loggerhead Lane float stream passes through a fish grotto with hundreds of exotic fish to view. Typhoon Lagoon takes fish-watching a step further with its Shark Reef, where you can snorkel among live fish.

Did we mention the giant toilet bowl? Wet 'n Wild has an attraction dubbed The Storm. The ride actually looks like a lot of fun, but in all honesty it strongly resembles a huge commode. Riders wash down a chute to gain speed, and then circle around a huge bowl before dropping into a pool below. This must be how that goldfish you flushed in third grade felt.

Prices for one-day admission are about the same at Blizzard Beach, Typhoon Lagoon, SeaWorld Aquatica, Wet 'n Wild, and Adventure

Island. Discount coupons are often available in free local visitor magazines for Wet 'n Wild.

WET 'N WILD

WET 'N WILD (on International Drive in Orlando, one block east of I-4 at Exit 75A; ☎ 800-992-WILD (9453) or 407-351-1800; **wetnwildorlando.com**) is a non-Disney water park option. Unlike Typhoon Lagoon and Blizzard Beach, in which scenic man-made mountains and integrated themes create a colorful atmosphere, Wet 'n Wild's only themes appear to be concrete, plastic, and water. Fortunately, the thrill, scope, and diversity of its rides make Wet 'n Wild an excellent alternative to the Disney swimming parks. Besides, contrary to what some Disney execs might believe, their water isn't any wetter.

Mears Transportation operates a shuttle to Wet 'n Wild that stops three times a day at Disney hotels. It's the same shuttle that commutes between Walt Disney World and Universal Orlando. Cost is $20 round-trip for guests age 3 and older. There is no free transportation to Wet 'n Wild from Disney property. If you are staying outside of Walt Disney World or Lake Buena Vista, or along US 192, you'll need a rental car or ride share. If you're staying on International Drive, you can take the **International Drive trolley** (visit **iridetrolley.com** for schedules and fees). If you drive, there is a large Wet 'n Wild parking lot that charges $13 per day for cars and $17 for RVs. Parking is ample; just be sure to hold the kids' hands when crossing the street.

You can buy your Wet 'n Wild tickets at the main gate or at **wetnwildorlando.com**. Prices are $57 + tax for adults and $52 + tax for children ages 3–9. Call beforehand for annual passes, special deals, and discounts for those in the military, AAA members, Florida residents, and groups. For the same price as (or for $10 less than, during certain promotions) a single-day ticket, Wet 'n Wild offers a Length of Stay pass on its website that is good for 14 consecutive days. Ticket prices are similar to those of the Disney parks, but if you attend during the summer, the park is open late (hours vary, from 9:30 a.m. until 9 p.m. at the latest; call or visit the website for details), allowing visitors to hit the slides in the morning, go back to their hotels for lunch and a nap, and then return for a dip at night. Disney water parks typically close by 6 or 7 p.m.

When you get hungry, the main food pavilions are **Wild Tiki Lounge, Bubba's Fried Chicken, Riverside BBQ, Manny's Pizza,** and **Surf Grill,** together offering such staples as burgers, pizza, and barbecued-pork sandwiches as well as more-nutritious (and nontraditional) items such as veggie burgers and tabbouleh. Wait times are long—Wild Tiki has flat-panel TVs to keep you occupied—and prices are high but not outrageous. During the busier months, Riverside BBQ offers an all-day all-you-can-eat plan with unlimited entrées, desserts, and soft drinks. For guests whose budgets and impatience thresholds are less flexible, feel free to bring in a cooler of lunch fixings (remember, glass containers and alcoholic beverages are prohibited, but you can purchase beer inside).

All the slides outside the **Kids' Park** have a 48-inch height requirement except for multipassenger slides, for which the minimum height is 36 inches if an adult accompanies the short rider; the only exception to this is the Aqua Drag Racer, which has a 42-inch minimum height.

BODY AND MAT SLIDES

SLIDES AT WET 'N WILD INCLUDE Aqua Drag Racer, Mach 5, Bomb Bay, Der Stuka, and The Storm. **Aqua Drag Racer,** which opened in 2014, features four side-by-side slides, down which a quartet of "racers" are simultaneously dispatched face-first on foam mats. The slides start 65 feet off the ground as enclosed tubes that twist around each other, before opening up into parallel lanes for the final dash to the checkerboard finish line. The entire run is 350 feet long and takes a little more than 10 seconds to complete. The **Mach 5** tower, located to the left of the park entrance, consists of three mat slides. The mats increase your speed and eliminate the chafing often experienced on body slides. To go even faster, try to get a newer mat with a smoother bottom. They are easily distinguishable: The new mats have white handles, while the old mats have blue ones.

unofficial **TIP**
Though ride attendants say that all three of the Mach 5 slides are equal, the center slide appears to be the zippiest route to the bottom.

Among the body slides (those without mats or rafts) are **Bomb Bay** and **Der Stuka,** twin speed flumes with pitches up to 79 degrees that descend from the top of a six-story tower. On Bomb Bay you stand on a pair of doors that open, dropping you into the chute. You have to work up the nerve to launch yourself on Der Stuka. The lack of a fully enclosed tube (such as the one on the Humunga Kowabunga speed slide at Typhoon Lagoon) adds the (perhaps justifiable) fear of falling off the 250-foot slides, but their ability to float your stomach somewhere near your teeth is a pretty unforgettable thrill.

The Storm body slide, located near Bomb Bay and Der Stuka, is a hybrid ride: half slide, half toilet bowl. The steep slide creates enough momentum to launch riders into a few laps around the bowl below before they begin slipping toward the hole in the center, eventually falling into a 6-foot-deep pool. The ride is exhilarating and disorienting; when the lifeguard at the ending pool begins hollering, just stumble toward his voice and give him a thumbs-up.

RAFT AND TUBE RIDES

THE HEADLINERS AT WET 'N WILD are the raft and tube rides, including Brain Wash, Disco H2O, The Surge, Black Hole, The Flyer, and The Blast. **Brain Wash** is an extreme six-story tube ride with a 53-foot vertical drop into a 65-foot funnel; tubes hold two or four riders. **Disco H2O** holds up to four people in one raft, ushering them down a long tube into a 1970s-era nightclub complete with lights, music, and a disco ball. The basic design of the ride is similar to that of The Storm (a long tube into a bowl), only not as frantic and disorienting; the disco theme, coupled with the fluidity of the ride, makes it a main draw.

The Surge launches from the same tower as Disco H2O and uses the same four-person rafts. Riders spin down the open-air course, drifting high onto the walls on each banked corner. To reach the top of the walls, try to go with a full raft—as with all raft rides, the more riders squeezed in, the faster you'll all go. Directly across from The Surge's splashdown pool is the entrance for **Black Hole.** Bring a partner for this one; Black Hole requires two riders on each raft, and honestly, who wants to embark into endless murk without some company? As impressive as the ride seems from afar, the anxiety created by the gaping entrance is the most exciting part of the ride. Yes, it's dark—there is track lighting down the entire course—but besides the darkness, the ride lacks the dips and turns found on the other slides. If you're claustrophobic and scared of the dark, this isn't the ride for you; if tight spaces and inky blackness don't give you a rush, then this isn't the ride for you either.

The gentler raft rides are **The Flyer** and **The Blast.** Both launch from the same tower as the Mach 5, but their entrance is accessible through the Kids' Park. At the base of the entrance are one- and two-person rafts; these are only for The Blast, so don't carry them up to the tower to The Flyer entrance. The Flyer is a calmer, toboggan-style ride in which riders sit one behind the other; it's suitable for families with smaller children.

The Blast is a themed ride, like Disco H2O, and is the wettest you can get without swimming. The theme of The Blast appears to be a broken waterworks, complete with spinning dials and broken pipes, all painted in comic book red and yellow. From mist to falling water to spraying pipes, this is the best way to cool off at Wet 'n Wild.

OTHER ATTRACTIONS

THE CENTRAL FIXTURE at Wet 'n Wild, the **Wave Pool Surf Lagoon,** is on par with Blizzard Beach's. Unlike at Typhoon Lagoon, there's no surfing in this wave pool, but you can rent tubes at the main rental stand or go bobbing with your body. The wave-making machine takes long breaks every day, so when you walk by and see waves, be sure to wade in.

Another any-time-of-day option is the **Lazy River.** Unlike the Lazy River at Typhoon Lagoon, the Lazy River at Wet 'n Wild is misnamed: The circuit is short, the current fast. Don't even bother trying to walk upstream to catch a tube—it's better to swim down the river or wait patiently until one passes within reach.

Wet 'n Wild's 1-acre **Blastaway Beach,** located to your immediate left after you enter the main gate, has about a zillion things for the younger kids to do. Look for the oversize sand castle and the zany play area decorated in every color from the Crayola box. Also included are an upper and lower pool, totaling about 15,000 square feet, and more than 160 water jets, a cannon, waterfalls, and 15 slides.

AQUATICA *by* SEAWORLD

AQUATICA IS ACROSS INTERNATIONAL DRIVE from the back side of SeaWorld. From Kissimmee, Walt Disney World, and Lake Buena Vista, take I-4 East, exiting onto the Central Florida Parkway and then bearing left on International Drive. From Universal Studios, take I-4 West to FL 528; from there, exit onto International Drive. Admission costs about the same (or a few bucks less with online discounts) as the Disney water parks and Wet 'n Wild. If you don't want to wait in a queue to purchase tickets, buy them in advance at **aquaticabyseaworld .com** or use the credit card ticket machines to the left of Aquatica's main entrance. Parking costs $13 for cars and motorcycles, $17 for RVs.

As at the other water parks, there are lockers (using new self-service electronic locks instead of old-fashioned keys), towels, wheelchairs, and strollers to rent; gift shops to browse; and places to eat. The three restaurants are **WaterStone Grill,** offering specialty sandwiches, cheeseburgers, wraps, and salads; **Banana Beach Buffet,** an all-you-can eat venue dishing up pizza, hot dogs, and chicken; and **Mango Market,** a diminutive eatery serving sandwiches, wraps, and salads. WaterStone Grill and Mango Market serve beer.

Aquatica is comparable in size to the other water theme parks in the area. Attractively landscaped with palms, ferns, and tropical flowers, it's far less themed than Disney's Typhoon Lagoon and Blizzard Beach but much greener and more aesthetically appealing than Wet 'n Wild. Promotional material suggests that Aquatica is unique in its combination of SeaWorld's signature marine-animal exhibits with the expected water park assortment of wave pools, slides, and creek floats. Marine exhibits, however, stop and end with a float-through tank of tropical fish and a pool of black-and-white Commerson's dolphins. Ads for the park show guests viewing the dolphins as they descend through a clear tube at the end of the **Dolphin Plunge** body slide. The reality is that you are flushed through the clear tube so fast, with so much water splashing around your face, that it's pretty much impossible to see anything. At Aquatica, the best option by far is to view the dolphins from the walkway surrounding the exhibit or from the subsurface viewing windows.

A Yorkshire, England, woman reacted to the Dolphin Plunge:

> *The slide had the longest queue in the park. We queued for the best part of an hour and all agreed that it was a waste of time! You can barely see through the transparent part of the tube where the dolphins are (if you're lucky!), the slide is short, and the see-through bit lasts about 2 seconds!*

RAFT AND TUBE RIDES

REGARDING THE DOLPHIN PLUNGE SLIDE, it's a corkscrewing romp through a totally dark tube until you blast through the clear tube at the end. Partly because of its location just inside the park entrance, and partly because of a relatively modest carrying capacity (approximately 280 people per hour), the slide stays mobbed all day. To experience the slide without a long wait, be on hand at park opening and ride first thing.

The first new slide at Aquatica in years, opened in 2014, **Ihu's Breakaway Falls** artfully blends hanging (without a noose) and being flushed down a really big toilet. But first you have to climb the equivalent of 10 stories of stairs. Once you haul yourself to the top of the tower and are revived, you step into one of three tubes with plexiglass doors. At some undetermined time (Aquatica staff dither around to build your anxiety), a trapdoor opens under you, gallowslike, and down you go. Each tube offers a different ride, but all three include big vertical drops, pitched drops, and corkscrews (the toilet part). A fourth tube at the top of the tower provides a wild but less intimidating ride, with the usual sit-down-and-off-you-go launch.

Other slides include **Tassie's Twisters,** in which an enclosed tube slide spits you into an open bowl where you careen around the edge much in the manner of the ball in a roulette wheel. Close to the Dolphin Plunge, Tassie's Twisters should be your second early-morning stop before heading to Ihu's.

After Breakaway Falls, head over to **Walhalla Wave** and **HooRoo Run,** both on the park's far right side. Both slides use circular rafts that can accommodate up to three people. Walhalla Wave splashes down an enclosed twisting tube, while HooRoo Run is an open-air run down a steep, straight, undulating slide. The same entrance serves both slides. Line up for Walhalla Wave (vastly more popular) on the right, for HooRoo Run on the left. Make Walhalla Wave your third slide of the day, followed by HooRoo Run.

Then pass along the right side of the children's adventure area, Walkabout Waters, to **Taumata Racer,** the park's highest-capacity slide with eight enclosed corkscrewing tubes.

The remaining slides are **Whanau Way** and **Omaka Rocka,** all the way across the park to the left of the entrance. Omaka Rocka is a wide-diameter, one-person, enclosed tube ride. The name derives from the wave action inside the tube, which washes you alternately up one side of the tube and then the other. Riders haul the single-person rafts up the stairs and select either the purple or aqua tube, and then whoosh down through three 40-foot open or half-pipe funnels, water curtains, and a final 360-degree spiral during a 50-second ride. Including the hike to the top, figure on spending 3 minutes for each climb and descent here. Sporting one corkscrew and a few twists, Whanau Way employs tubes that can carry one or two people. Because it's hard to see from the park entrance, Whanau Way doesn't attract long lines until midmorning.

Taken as a whole, the slides at Aquatica are not nearly as interesting, thrilling, or imaginative as those of its competitors, and aside from whisking you through a dolphin tank, they don't break any new ground. There are some variations among these slides: Tassie is in a two-person tube, sliders in Taumata use a mat, and the Dolphin is a body slide.

Dark slides are an essential part of almost every water-park lineup, but the technique seems overdone here. All slides other than HooRoo Run, Omaka Rocka, and Whanau launch you down these black holes, which makes for a very homogenized experience.

OTHER ATTRACTIONS

IN ADDITION TO THE SLIDES, Aquatica offers side-by-side wave pools, **Cutback Cove** and **Big Surf Shores.** This arrangement allows one cove to serve up bodysurfing waves while the other puts out gently bobbing floating waves. A spacious beach arrayed around the coves is the park's primary sunning venue. Shady spots, courtesy of beach umbrellas, ring the perimeter of the area for the sun-sensitive.

Loggerhead Lane and **Roa's Rapids** are the two floating streams. The former is a slow and gentle tube journey that circumnavigates the Tassie's Twisters slide. Its claim to fame is a section of the float where a plexiglass tunnel passes through the Fish Grotto, a tank populated by hundreds of exotic tropical fish and the relatively small Commerson's dolphins. Unique to Aquatica, Roa's Rapids is a much longer course with a very swift current. (The other water parks have floating creeks, but they're leisurely affairs where you can fall asleep in your tube.) Buoyancy vests are available, but most adults float or swim the stream. There are no rapids, but the flow is constricted from time to time, considerably increasing the already fast speed of the current. There's only one place to get in and out, so if you miss the takeout, you're in for another lap.

When it comes to children's water attractions, Aquatica more than equals the other area parks. In the back of the park, to the left of the wave pools, is **Kata's Kookaburra Cove,** featuring a wading pool and slides for the preschool crowd. But the real pièce de résistance is **Walkabout Waters.** If you have children under age 10, this alone may be worth the price of admission. Located in a calf-deep 15,000-square-foot pool, it's an immense three-story interactive playground set with slides, stairs, rope bridges, landings, and more. Water sprays, spritzes, pulsates, and plops at you from every conceivable angle. Randomly placed plastic squirting devices allow kids to take aim at unsuspecting adults, but the kids disperse quickly when either of two huge buckets dumps hundreds of gallons of water on the entire structure. It's impossible not to get wet. It's also impossible not to have fun.

ADVENTURE ISLAND

A SINGLE-DAY ADMISSION to Adventure Island is $49 plus tax for adults and children age 3 and older, and free for children under age 3 (save $5 when you purchase online). A one-year passport to Adventure Island is $120 for adults; a two-year passport is $170 for adults. Adventure Island also offers combination passports with up to three other parks—neighboring Busch Gardens, SeaWorld, and Aquatica—for one and two years, ranging $192–$336 for one year and $292–$506 for two years.

Adventure Island has different opening and closing times depending on the day of your visit. It may open as early as 9 a.m. and close as late as 9 p.m., with its longest days being on summer weekends. On slower days, the park is open 10 a.m.–5 p.m. The park is closed November–February, and open only on select days and weekends during March and October. Call ahead or check the website for park hours the day of your visit. You should arrive at the park at least 30 minutes before it opens, as the parking lot fills quickly, and during peak season it reaches capacity before noon. By arriving early, you'll be able to park directly in front of the main entrance and should be able to both purchase tickets and visit all of the attractions before any crowds begin to form.

Besides affording quick access to the ticket booth, parking close to the entrance is also helpful if you bring a picnic. Large coolers are permitted in the park, but glass containers, alcoholic beverages, and knives are prohibited. Though the theming at Adventure Island is light, there are some wonderful shaded picnic areas, which are to the left of the park entrance. We recommend the picnic tables under the live oaks between the Everglides and the Riptide. Quieter picnic spots, also in the shade, can be found behind the Riptide, and a gazebo—first come, first served—is located near the run-out pool for the Caribbean Corkscrew.

To purchase food within the park, stop by **Surfside Cafe** at the park's entrance or **Mango Joe's** in the rear of the park near the Volleyball Spike Zone. Surfside Cafe offers traditional grill food, but healthy choices such as salads are available. Unfortunately, seating here is all outside without any shade. Mango Joe's has a more diverse menu, including pizza, steak sandwiches, and veggie wraps. On busier summer days, a taco truck serves Tex-Mex street food with house-made chips and salsa.

When you want to buy food, you may find that your money is soaked. Adventure Island's solution to wet money is a scannable armband. Using a credit card or cash, you may preload an armband with the amount of money you would like to spend. When purchasing food or merchandise, swipe your armband and the money is deducted from your account. The program, available at Guest Services, is free, and any leftover money on the armband is fully refunded. The armband, cash, or credit card can be used at any of the snack bars and at the gift shop, where you can purchase sunscreen, swim equipment, or any other forgotten items (for a severe markup).

If you want to store any gear that you have purchased or brought, small lockers are available for $12 each, $3 of which is refunded to you on the return of your key, but only as a gift certificate to the gift shop. The locker keys come with a safety pin to clip to your clothing, and there is no fee for lost keys. Be aware, if you receive a key numbered between 1 and 650, your locker will be on an elevated wooden platform above a small lake. The slats in the platform are far apart, so be very careful about dropping anything as you open and close your locker; there's no way to get it back without persuading an employee to let you go swimming.

There is no finagling your way onto the rides if you don't meet the height requirements. For all of the major body slides or raft rides, you must be at least 42 inches tall, though a few require that you be at least 48 inches tall to ride. On some raft rides, children under 42 inches may ride with an adult if they can sit upright and wear a life vest. Some slides and other attractions have no height requirement. If we do not mention a height requirement for an attraction, you may assume that the height requirement is 42 inches.

To get to Adventure Island, follow the directions to Busch Gardens in Tampa in Part Two. Once you have arrived on East Busch Boulevard, continue to Busch Gardens. Turn left onto McKinley Drive, the first road past Busch Gardens, and you will find Adventure Island on your right. The park is set back from the road, and there is ample parking, which costs $12 for both cars and campers and is free for tour buses and motorcycles.

For more information, contact Adventure Island at ☎ 888-800-5447, or visit **adventureisland.com.**

RAFT RIDES

ADVENTURE ISLAND HOSTS SIX RAFT RIDES, and in clockwise order from the entrance, they are The Everglides, Calypso Coaster, Aruba Tuba, Colossal Curl, Key West Rapids, and the Wahoo Run. All of the raft rides are tame, but the Wahoo Run is as good a ride as any found at Wet 'n Wild.

The Everglides is the first ride you come to when you take a left at the entrance. At the bottom of the run-out pool, pick up a yellow sled. The sleds are rather heavy, but even children should have no problem carrying them up to the top of the 72-foot tower. To get down from the top, you can choose either of the two identical slides. Once you're settled in your sled, signal to the lifeguard that you are ready and then hold onto the side handles. A hydraulic ram lifts the back of your sled and pitches you forward down the slide. Though the drop is exhilarating, skipping across a 60-foot run-out pool is the high point of the ride. You can steer your sled by lightly pulling on the handles and leaning in the direction you want to go.

Across from the Everglides is the tower for **Aruba Tuba** and **Calypso Coaster.** Each ride requires different rafts and tubes, so check to make sure you have the transportation you want before you schlep it to the top of the tower (if you get confused as to which tube goes on which slide, pick up your tube from the run-out pool at the base of the slide that you want to ride). Aruba Tuba is green and requires either a single-person tube or a two-person raft. The slide has both open and enclosed portions, and as you spin around backward, the pitch-dark patches will take you by surprise. Aruba Tuba's curves are both plentiful and evenly spaced, creating a more docile and rhythmic run than Calypso Coaster's. The Calypso Coaster tube is white, and you may use either single-person blue tubes or double-person rafts. The slide is faster than Aruba Tuba and sends you high onto the walls. There are no steep pitches common on other raft rides, just a steady side-to-side motion. **Colossal Curl,** which replaced the park's 1980-vintage Gulf Scream slide, is a thrilling four-passenger family raft ride that gives riders a brief taste of watery weightlessness, thanks to a steep wave-shaped wall that rafts "surf" up and down at the finale of their 560-foot slide. Waterfalls and corkscrews enliven the mostly enclosed blue-green track up until that climax, which starts with a descent from 70 feet. Best of all, a conveyor belt lifts the clover-shaped tubes to the top of the tower for you.

The Adventure Island ride with the greatest lack of pitch is **Key West Rapids,** located in the back left corner of the park. You may ride in single-person tubes or in two-person rafts, but your total weight cannot exceed 300 pounds. Children under 54 inches tall may ride if they wear a life vest, available at stations around the park. From the top of the tower, you can see into Busch Gardens and down toward the greater Tampa area. Though the height exceeds that of almost all of the other attractions (except for Wahoo Run), the trip down Key West Rapids, interrupted with three small pools, is equivalent to a green trail on a ski mountain. The pools in the middle of the slide are unique, but there appears to have been a mild miscalculation in the strength of the pools' water jets that are supposed to push you across each pool to the next portion of the slide. Instead of being pushed via jets, you get tugged from one portion to the next by a lifeguard waiting in each pool. Though the ride down is meandering and slow, the final drop is steep, waking you up just in time to make your way to the next attraction.

In the opposite corner of the park from Key West Rapids is **Wahoo Run,** tucked away behind Runaway Rapids. Our favorite ride in the park, Wahoo Run seats up to five people with a combined weight of 800 pounds. Children under 42 inches tall may ride as long as they wear a life vest. There is no lap riding, so little guys must be able to sit up on their own. After everyone is on board, the raft is sent spinning as it descends through both open and enclosed sections of the slide. Unlike other enclosed slides, Wahoo Run has a wide enough diameter on its enclosed sections to keep claustrophobia at bay. Small waterfalls splash down on you as you enter and exit each of the enclosed sections. Even though these portions are pitch-black, there are no steep drops, so breathe easy. The ride is fast enough to keep thrill junkies entertained, but smooth enough for the entire family to enjoy.

BODY AND MAT SLIDES

THE BODY AND MAT SLIDES at Adventure Island are, for the most part, tamer than those at Wet 'n Wild. The calmer rides are on par with Disney's Typhoon Lagoon, though the slides are generally shorter than Disney's. These calmer, shorter slides allow younger guests moderate thrills without forcing them to ride through a whitewash of water that may frighten them. There are four attractions at Adventure Island that contain body or mat slides, and only one of them is moderately frantic. The four attractions are, in clockwise order beginning at the park's entrance, Riptide, Caribbean Corkscrew, Water Moccasin, and Runaway Rapids.

The only mat slide in the park, **Riptide** is not as fast or entertaining as Wet 'n Wild's Mach 5 mat slide, in part because all the mats at Riptide have corrugated bottoms, making them slower. The Riptide slide is also shorter than Mach 5, and though we would usually just write this off as a ride for younger kids, there is a 42-inch height requirement to ride. The attraction consists of two pink and two blue enclosed tubes that descend from the 55-foot tower. Four riders begin at the same time and race one another to the bottom. To get the most out of these mats, keep your feet off the slide, and move your body weight as far forward as comfortable while keeping your center of gravity pressed low. Take the turns high, and stay in the center of the slide for the straightaways. Other than that, the slides nearest the lifeguard stand toward the inside are a bit shorter than the outer slides.

Another enclosed slide is the **Caribbean Corkscrew** body slide. These two intertwined cylinders are twisted together like Twizzler candy and are just as likely to cause tooth loss. You will be unceremoniously ground and mashed about in the dark until you are finally spat out into the run-out pool.

A more amenable attraction is the **Water Moccasin,** located near Key West Rapids. Water Moccasin consists of three slides. The slides are set up like a mouth harp, with two slides curving around to each side of the pool and one flume dropping into the center. All of the slides are short, a benefit since the seams between each section of tubing have mild ridges that may sting your back as you pass over them. The truncated flume has the fewest seams and is also the fastest. There are no height requirements for Water Moccasin.

If you enjoy mellow, shorter slides, five such slides are available in **Runaway Rapids,** located in the rock formation to the right of the park's entrance. None of these slides has a height requirement. The rocks, which each slide weaves through, make up the best theming in the park. As you climb up the path through the rocks, it diverges in two directions. The path to the left takes you to the kiddie slide, numbered and named #1–Corkscrew Canal and #2–Little Squirt. The Corkscrew Canal wraps around a central post, while the Little Squirt takes you straight down. Children may wear life vests if they sit in the laps of adults. The path to the right winds through a crag in the rocks that contains a stream and a bench, and then rises up to the slides, numbered and named #3–Corkscrew Falls, #4–River of No Returns, and #5–Barracuda Run. Though all three slides are very similar, the ride is anything but. Corkscrew Falls is the fastest, River of No Returns is the rowdiest with plenty of sharp turns, and Barracuda Run is the most scenic, with bamboo and palm leaves overhead.

Though there is no height requirement, there is no lap riding or life vests allowed on these three slides.

OTHER ATTRACTIONS

ADVENTURE ISLAND HAS A FEW OTHER attractions that merit note. They are, again in clockwise order, the Rambling Bayou, Splash Attack, Fabian's Funport, the Endless Surf Wavepool, and the Paradise Lagoon. **Rambling Bayou** is a stream that encircles the left side of the park. Much larger than Wet 'n Wild's Lazy River, Rambling Bayou is more akin to the stream at Typhoon Lagoon. Though the theming isn't Disney-grade, palm trees and flower beds line the Rambling Bayou, giving you something to look at as you float around on your inner tube. The stream splits at one point; the left channel takes you back around immediately toward Riptide, while going right extends your ride, taking you through a greenhouse coated in Spanish moss. Be advised that there are sprinklers in the greenhouse, and the water is noticeably cooler than that of the stream. There are no height requirements for Rambling Bayou, but it's recommended that children under 42 inches wear a life vest; hand-held infants are prohibited. There are no lines here, and when the other attractions are crowded, wade into the stream, grab a tube, and wait until the crowds thin out for lunch.

Rambling Bayou will take you next to **Splash Attack,** a wet jungle gym. Splash Attack has no water underneath but plenty above. Perched atop the four slides, cargo nets, water cannons, tree house, and other contraptions is a 1,000-gallon bucket that dumps water onto its victims underneath every 7 minutes. Parents who want to watch their kids will be able to see them from a dry vantage point, but very little shade is available, so it's best to bring an umbrella or a bottle of sunscreen.

Fabian's Funport is another wet jungle gym located between the Spike Zone and the Endless Surf Wavepool. Fabian's Funport caters to a 50-inch-tall-and-under crowd, and though its play area is not as large as Wet 'n Wild's kids' zone, Fabian's miniature wave pool, water mushrooms, wet tunnels, and mini-aqueducts serve their purpose of keeping the little ones cool. The maximum water depth is 12 inches, and swim diapers are required.

Behind Fabian's Funport and Mango Joe's café is the **Spike Zone Volleyball Court.** The area does not see much activity unless a tournament is under way, but volleyballs are available at Mango Joe's for a refundable deposit. Sunbathers who want to savor the illusion of being at the beach should head here to lie out on the secluded sands.

For those interested in regular bathing, the **Endless Surf Wavepool** is the place to head. Located in the center of the park, it's impossible to miss. The wave pool is about the same size as Wet 'n Wild's wave pool, but at the head of the pool, replacing the big Wet 'n Wild sign, is a countdown clock that clicks off the time until the waves begin again. Unlike other wave pools, the Endless Surf Wavepool makes choppy waves only up to 5 feet high.

Paradise Lagoon is another large pool, sans the waves. Though swimming about is fun, the draw here is the three "cliff"-jumping platforms and two small slides, located at the back of the lagoon. Jumpers wait until a lifeguard sets the streetlight signal to green, and then jump the 10 feet—feet first only—into the pool. There are two staging areas, and facing the water from above, the left area contains both slides and one jumping platform. (Be sure to hold your nose when you go through the slides, or you'll come up spitting water.) The right area contains no slides but two cliff-jumping platforms. Though the 10-foot jump into the water is the same from both left and right, many jumpers will wait in line on the left for the platform next to the slides, while the other two platforms go unused. Skip the line and go to the right area, wait for the green light, and jump in.

 # WATER SPORTS

BUENA VISTA WATERSPORTS

Getting There

FROM DISNEY Take World Center Parkway to FL 535 (also called Kissimmee Vineland Road) and turn left. Just before you cross under I-4, you will see a small sign on your right for Buena Vista WaterSports. If you miss the sign, do not pass under I-4. Instead, take a right onto Vineland Avenue and pull into the parking lot. The parking lot is connected to Lake Bryan Drive. Buena Vista WaterSports is at 13245 Lake Bryan Drive, Orlando.

FROM ORLANDO Take I-4 to Exit 68 and go south on FL 535. You should be able to see the sign for Buena Vista WaterSports on your left almost immediately after you start south.

Admission Prices

Buena Vista WaterSports rents out Sea-Doo GTI personal watercraft that fit two to three people. The fee for a Sea-Doo is $105 per hour or $60 for 30 minutes. To drive, you need to be at least 17 years of age. Buena Vista will also tow you behind its competition ski boats on a **tube,** a **kneeboard, water skis,** or a **wakeboard.** The cost, including equipment rental, is $55 for 15 minutes, $95 for 30 minutes, or $165 for a full hour. Pontoon boat rentals are $125 for the first hour, $75 for each additional hour, or $300 for 4 hours. Canoe, kayak, and stand-up paddleboard rentals are $25 per hour. Though it's not stated, a "tips for tips" gratuity policy for personal instruction is the standard for most vacation activities.

Arriving

Located in an old lakeside mansion, Buena Vista WaterSports is only a 10-minute drive from Walt Disney World. Buena Vista is open daily year-round, weather permitting, but hours vary, so call before you go.

Once you've gotten off of the stress-filled freeways and byways of greater Orlando, you'll welcome the laid-back surfer atmosphere lakeside. The wicker chairs on the antebellum mansion's large wooden deck face the lake, and though we could tide ourselves over with a game of volleyball and a cooler filled with snacks, the action's on the water, so don't forget to bring a swimsuit, sunscreen, and a towel.

Be sure to call ahead before you come to Buena Vista WaterSports. The lakefront site holds many competitions throughout the summer. When these are under way, you will not be able to rent certain vessels or obtain lessons. The entire facility is also rented out for occasional parties, which will preclude you from using the site.

Contacting Buena Vista WaterSports

For information, call ☎ 407-239-6939 or visit **www.bvwatersports.com.**

ORLANDO WATERSPORTS COMPLEX

Admission Prices

All prices are listed without tax or equipment rental.

2 Hours $34 • **4 Hours $44** • **All-Day Pass $54** • **Monthly Pass $299**
Basic Equipment Rental $14–$34; basic gear includes a helmet and life vest; upgraded gear required for ramps and rails

Lessons

CABLE LESSONS Children age 10 and younger must take a lesson before being allowed to use the cable; 1-hour cable lessons are $90. Children age 10 and younger receive an additional 2-hour pass with the lesson. Kids over 10 and adults may optionally take a 20-minute cable lesson for $25. First-time riders can purchase a Get Up Guarantee, which includes 15 minutes of one-on-one instruction, a 4-hour cable pass, and equipment rental for $59. Call in advance to make a class reservation, especially if bringing kids under 10.

BOAT LESSONS 30 minutes, $120

STAND-UP PADDLEBOARDING LESSONS 1 hour, $25

Monthly, seasonal, and annual passes are available for $299–$1,199. There is a hefty $75 upgrade fee if you want to increase the length of your pass, so carefully consider which package you want before purchasing.

Getting There

Getting to the Orlando Watersports Complex can be rather difficult, though it is visible off of the Beachline Expressway (also called the Beachline Toll Road or FL 528). From I-4, take Exit 72 east. Take the Beachline east from Orlando toward Kennedy Space Center to Exit 4. Exit onto Orange Blossom Trail/US 441/Consulate Drive. Follow the signs to Orange Blossom Trail/US 441; then take a left on South Orange Blossom Trail. After 0.5 mile, turn right onto Landstreet Road and follow it 2 miles to the large yellow sign for the Orlando Watersports Complex at 8615 Florida Rock Road. Follow the road, cross the railroad tracks, and stick to the right. Within a few hundred yards you will be at the blue gates of the complex.

Arriving

Orlando Watersports is open daily, 10 a.m.–8 p.m., March–October. November–February, it is open daily, 11 a.m.–sunset.

The 50-acre complex features two **tow-cable courses for wakeboarding, water-skiing, kneeboarding,** and **wake-skating** (similar to wakeboarding except that your feet are not attached to the board). The novice park is larger and contains one small jump that you can ride over if you choose, but only if you wear a helmet. The advanced park is smaller and features large ramps, tabletops, and rails to slide on. The advanced park requires a helmet. To ride in the advanced park, you must first show your competence by completing at least one lap in the novice park.

The tow-cable system is moderately complex, so here is how it works. A single, thick, elevated cable, like those found on ski-resort chairlifts, moves around the perimeter of the pond at a constant speed. Permanently attached to the thick cable is a series of evenly spaced cable carriers (for explanation purposes, envision the cable carriers as large hooks). The last components of the system are the thin cables that dangle from the cable carriers. At the dangling end of the thin cables is the handle that the riders hold.

The departure area is a long dock that slopes down to the water. Riders wait their turn in a queue. When their turn is approaching, riders put on their boards and stand in ankle-deep water. Riders then take hold of the handle to a thin cable and stand by for the next cable carrier. As the cable carrier passes overhead, it unhooks the thin cable used by the previous rider and then hooks into the thin cable held by the waiting rider. Riders, if they hold on while being jerked forward, are now off the dock and skimming around the pond.

The novice pond has nine cable carriers, and the advanced pond has four; this means that only nine people can be on the novice pond at one time and only four on the advanced pond at one time. When the park is crowded, each rider is allowed one lap around the pond before he or she has to let go of the handle. To avoid crowds, arrive when the park opens. Within 2 hours after opening, the lines can become excessive. During the off-season or on slow days, riders are allowed as many as five laps around the pond before they have to let go. When your turn is up, or if you fall, let go of the handle and swim out of the way of other riders. Detach your board and finish swimming to the shoreline; then walk back around to the queue for another go.

Riders under the age of 18 need a release form signed by their parent or guardian for any activity at the Orlando Watersports Complex. Forms can be signed on-site or can be faxed to ☎ 407-816-9070.

Before you get in the water, you can store your gear in lockers on land. Lockers cost $3 but require an additional $5 deposit that is repaid when you return the key. There are also adequate changing facilities on-site (bring your towel, sunscreen, and swimsuit), and food is available at the concession stand.

Contacting Orlando Watersports Complex

For more information about site availability, contact Orlando Watersports Complex at ☎ 407-251-3100 or **aktionparks.com/orlando.**

PART TEN

GOLF *and*
MINIATURE GOLF

 GOLF

WALT DISNEY WORLD GOLF

RECENT YEARS HAVE BROUGHT A STREAM of big changes to Walt Disney World golf, but the final steps are complete with the November 2014 opening of the "new" Tranquilo Golf Club, and the upheaval seems to be over. In late 2011, after four decades, Disney stepped back from golf operations, turning maintenance and supervision of all its courses (except Tranquilo) over to Arnold Palmer Golf Management. Visitors will notice little change, but Disney is hoping to increase visibility for its golf offerings with Palmer at the reins—an Orlando resident, he's among the most famous and well-liked athletes in the history of the sport.

As for Disney's golf venues themselves, the **Magnolia** and **Oak Trail Golf Courses,** across Floridian Way from the Polynesian Village Resort, envelop the recreational complex of the Shades of Green military resort, and the pro shops and support facilities adjoin the hotel proper.

The **Palm Golf Course,** in the same complex, underwent a major renovation by Arnold Palmer in 2013. Updates include modernized bunkers (94 of them!) and tees, and completely rebuilt greens. It's business as usual for the **Lake Buena Vista Golf Course** at Saratoga Springs Resort & Spa, near Disney Springs.

The really big news is the reimagining of Disney's Osprey Ridge Golf Course as **Tranquilo Golf Club** at the new Four Seasons Orlando. Opened in November 2014, the course—which is also a certified Audubon wildlife sanctuary—is shared by the Four Seasons Resort Orlando (see hotel profile on page 40) and Golden Oak, a Disney-owned luxury residential development. Tom Fazio, who designed the original 1992 course, and is the most awarded living architect in terms of various golf-magazine course rankings, also did the redesign, which involved recontouring all the greens and renovating/adding bunkers. A new par-3 hole (#16) features deep bunkering and sand and a small target green. Overall, it is more challenging than the other Disney courses, which typically feature wide fairways and are forgiving, and is aimed more at the avid destination golfer. But equally important is the management by Four Seasons, which takes the same white-glove approach to its golf course portfolio as it does to its five-star hotels. The course is impeccably maintained, with perhaps the best conditioning of any in the Orlando area, and it has a stunning practice facility, clubhouse, and staff to match. Four Seasons also added a full-blown golf academy with both hourly and multiday instruction. It immediately jumped to number one in the entire region in ratings on the Golf Channel's consumer voting site **golfadvisor.com.** New carts feature GPS technology; the updated clubhouse has a well-equipped pro shop and a restaurant called Plancha, serving casual Cuban American fare in a lakeside setting. The course is open to the public, not just Four Seasons guests and Golden Oak residents. Though Tranquilo is no longer an official Disney golf course, we've included it here due to its proximity to the World.

Back at Walt Disney World, the Magnolia has undergone substantial renovations and upgrades over the past few years. Oak Trail is a nine-hole, par-36 course for beginners, and it's well suited to families. The other Disney courses are designed for the mid-handicap player and, while interesting, are quite forgiving. All courses are popular, with morning tee times at a premium, especially January–April. In addition to the golf courses, there are driving ranges and putting greens at each location.

*un*official **TIP**
To avoid the crowds, play on a Monday, Tuesday, or Wednesday, and sign up for a late-afternoon tee time.

Peak season for all courses is January–May, and off-season is May–October. Off-season and afternoon twilight rates are available. Carts, required at all courses except Oak Trail, are included in the greens fee. Tee times may be reserved 90 days in advance by Disney resort guests and 60 days in advance by day guests with a credit card. Proper golf attire, including spike-less shoes, is required. A collared shirt and Bermuda-length shorts or slacks meet the requirements.

Besides the ability to book tee times farther in advance, guests of Walt Disney World–owned resorts get other benefits that may sway a golfer's lodging decision. These include discounted greens fees, club rental, and charge privileges. The single most important, and least known, benefit is the provision of free round-trip taxi transportation between the golf courses and your hotel, which lets you avoid moving your car or dragging your clubs on Disney buses. (Cabs are paid with vouchers supplied to hotel guests.) Perhaps as a sign of tough economic times, Walt Disney World introduced discounted two-day, two-round passes at its four championship courses, taking about 30% off rates that are already good values.

The table on the next page summarizes prices for daily play at all Disney golf courses except Oak Trail; the cost of replaying the same course on the same day (if space is available) is half the full rate.

TYPE OF ADMISSION	OPENING–3 P.M.	3–4 P.M.	4 P.M.–CLOSING
Resort guest	$95	$59	$45
Resort guest, 2-round pass	$120	$120	$120
Day guest	$90	$55	$55
Day guest, 2-round pass	$125	$125	$125

For more information, call ☎ 407-939-GOLF (4653); to book a tee time online, go to **golfwdw.com**.

Lake Buena Vista Golf Course ★★★

ESTABLISHED 1971 DESIGNER Joe Lee STATUS Resort

2200 Club Lake Dr., Lake Buena Vista, FL 32830; ☎ 407-939-GOLF (4653)

TEES
- **Blue:** 6,745 yards, par 72, USGA 72.3, slope 133
- **White:** 6,281 yards, par 72, USGA 70.1, slope 130
- **Gold:** 5,910 yards, par 72, USGA 68.5, slope 125
- **Red:** 5,177 yards, par 72, USGA 69.7, slope 119

FACILITIES Pro shop, GPS, driving range, practice green, locker rooms, snack bar, food-and-beverage cart, and club and shoe rentals.

COMMENTS There are several memorable holes here, but this layout is the only one at Disney with housing on it—a lot of housing—which detracts from the golf experience. Nonetheless, the course itself is relatively pristine and was certified by Audubon International as a Cooperative Wildlife Sanctuary. The setting is geographically unique among the other layouts, tucked behind Saratoga Springs, and has a swampy feel reminiscent of the area's pre-Disney wetlands, with trees dripping Spanish moss. Narrow fairways and small greens emphasize accuracy over length.

Magnolia Golf Course ★★★½

ESTABLISHED 1970 DESIGNER Joe Lee STATUS Resort

1950 W. Magnolia/Palm Dr., Lake Buena Vista, FL 32830;
☎ 407-939-GOLF (4653)

TEES
- **Black:** 7,516 yards, par 72, USGA 76.0, slope 141
- **Blue:** 7,073 yards, par 72, USGA 74.0, slope 137
- **White:** 6,558 yards, par 72, USGA 71.6, slope 130
- **Gold:** 6,027 yards, par 72, USGA 69.0, slope 121
- **Red:** 5,127 yards, par 72, USGA 69.6, slope 126

FACILITIES Pro shop, GPS-equipped golf carts, driving range, practice green, locker rooms, food-and-beverage cart, and club and shoe rentals.

COMMENTS Another fine Joe Lee creation, Magnolia is Disney's longest course and features a whopping 97 bunkers, including the famous one in the shape of Mickey Mouse's head. But the layout is slightly less challenging than the Palm's. At more than 7,500 yards, this course may be the longest most guests ever have the opportunity to play.

Oak Trail Golf Course ★★½

ESTABLISHED 1980 DESIGNER Ron Garl STATUS Resort

1950 W. Magnolia/Palm Dr., Lake Buena Vista, FL 32830; ☎ 407-939-GOLF (4653)

TEES
- **White:** 2,913 yards, par 36, USGA 33.7, slope 119
- **Red:** 2,552 yards, par 36, USGA 32.3, slope 110

FEES Adults, $40; children age 17 and under, $21. Pull carts, $6 (course is walking only). A second round costs an additional $20.

FACILITIES Pro shop, driving range, practice green, locker rooms, food-and-beverage cart, and club and shoe rentals.

COMMENTS This Ron Garl nine-holer is a "real" course, not an executive par-3 like many nine-hole designs. Geared toward introducing children to the game, it also makes a good quick fix or warm-up before a round, and the walking-only layout is the only such routing at Walt Disney World.

Palm Golf Course ★★★★

ESTABLISHED 1970   DESIGNER Joe Lee   STATUS Resort

1950 W. Magnolia/Palm Dr., Lake Buena Vista, FL 32830;
☎ 407-939-GOLF (4653)

TEES
- **Blue:** 7,011 yards, par 72, USGA 73.7, slope 131
- **White:** 6,479 yards, par 72, USGA 71.4, slope 125
- **Gold:** 6,006 yards, par 69.2, USGA 71.4, slope 118
- **Red:** 5,262 yards, par 70.4, USGA 70.5, slope 126

FACILITIES Pro shop, driving range, practice green, locker rooms, food-and-beverage cart, and club and shoe rentals.

COMMENTS Completely renovated in 2013, with more-difficult bunkers and undulating greens. The greens play medium-fast to fast, so either go with a lot of spin and loft or try to bounce your shot on. Carts have GPS screens. Staff service is excellent. Beware the alligator in the water at hole #9 (not kidding).

Tranquilo Golf Club at Four Seasons Orlando

ESTABLISHED 2014   DESIGNER Tom Fazio   STATUS Resort

10100 Dream Tree Blvd., Golden Oak, FL 32830; ☎ 800-267-3046

TEES
- **Gold:** 6,901 yards, par 71, USGA 73.3, slope 127
- **Blue:** 6,450 yards, par 71, USGA 70.0, slope 124
- **White:** 6,015 yards, par 71, USGA 67.2, slope 118
- **Red:** 5,110 yards, par 71, USGA 63.9, slope 112

FEES $81–$205.

FACILITIES Pro shop, driving range, practice green, locker rooms, restaurant, and club and shoe rentals.

COMMENTS See summary on page 282.

GOLF BEYOND WALT DISNEY WORLD

Grand Cypress Golf Club

The greater Orlando area has enough high-quality courses (more than 150 of them!) to rival better-known golfing Meccas such as Scottsdale, Arizona, and Palm Springs, California. But unlike these destinations, with their endless private country clubs, Orlando is unique because almost all its courses are open for some sort of public play. It also has gotten less expensive with the entrance of several online companies discounting unsold last-minute tee times, up to several days in advance, a trend imported from other top golf locales, such as Las Vegas and Hawaii. Top choices include **www.lastminutegolfer.com, teetimes.com,** and **golfnow.com.** Unique to Orlando is the Golf Channel's (based here) take on Groupon, DealCaddy, which offers one steeply discounted Orlando special each day—for example, unlimited golf for one day at ChampionsGate Country Club, in season, for $55.

Of the many courses and resorts in the area, one stands head and shoulders above the rest, especially because it actually abuts Walt Disney World. Not only is the location of this course excellent, but the sprawling 1,500-acre **Grand Cypress Resort** is also superb in every other respect, with top-notch lodging, dining, and grounds, and an enormous fantasy-pool complex. Hotel choices are the full-service **Hyatt Regency,** which just finished renovating its guest rooms, or the **Villas at Grand Cypress,** an enclave of upscale rental homes. But the standout feature is the golf, which would be worth a trip regardless of where the resort was. The facilities are first-rate, from the luxurious clubhouse to the GPS-equipped carts. The golf club is also home to an excellent instructional facility, the **Grand Cypress Academy of Golf.**

Grand Cypress Golf Club, New Course ★★★★

ESTABLISHED 1988   DESIGNER Jack Nicklaus   STATUS Resort (Guests Only)

1 N. Jacaranda, Orlando, FL 32836; ☎ 407-239-4700 or ☎ 877-330-7377; **grandcypress.com**

TEES
- **Blue:** 6,720 yards, par 72, USGA 71.9, slope 121
- **White:** 6,106 yards, par 72, USGA 69.0, slope 115
- **Red:** 5,242 yards, par 72, USGA 69.2, slope 112

FEES $150–$175 ($120 in summer).

FACILITIES Pro shop, driving range, practice greens, locker rooms, restaurant, food-and-beverage cart, GPS-equipped golf carts, and club and shoe rentals.

COMMENTS The New Course is Jack Nicklaus's homage to the famous Old Course at St. Andrews, Scotland, the birthplace of golf. The first and last two holes are near-replicas of those at the Old Course; other features, such as the famous Swilcan Bridge and some of the huge bunkers, are re-created here. In between are Nicklaus's original holes, done in a links style, with double greens; pot bunkers; tall rough; and wide, hard fairways. As on most Scottish links courses, there are no trees, and the wind will play havoc with your shots when it's blowing. If you've never had a chance to play Scottish courses, the New is a reasonable facsimile that captures the spirit and history of the sport's earliest form.

Grand Cypress Golf Club ★★★★½
North, South, and East Courses

ESTABLISHED 1986   DESIGNER Jack Nicklaus   STATUS Resort (Guests Only)

1 N. Jacaranda, Orlando, FL 32836; ☎ 407-239-4700 or ☎ 877-330-7377;
grandcypress.com

NORTH/SOUTH TEES
- **Gold:** 7,208 yards, par 72, USGA 75.9, slope 142
- **Blue:** 6,643 yards, par 72, USGA 73.0, slope 138
- **White:** 6,066 yards, par 72, USGA 70.1, slope 131
- **Red:** 5,513 yards, par 72, USGA 72.8, slope 130

SOUTH/EAST TEES
- **Gold:** 6,953 yards, par 72, USGA 74.5, slope 138
- **Blue:** 6,392 yards, par 72, USGA 71.7, slope 135
- **White:** 5,840 yards, par 72, USGA 68.9, slope 129
- **Red:** 5,038 yards, par 72, USGA 69.7, slope 125

EAST/NORTH TEES
- **Gold:** 6,985 yards, par 72, USGA 74.6, slope 138
- **Blue:** 6,389 yards, par 72, USGA 71.5, slope 133
- **White:** 5,882 yards, par 72, USGA 69.0, slope 129
- **Red:** 5,047 yards, par 72, USGA 69.9, slope 125

FEES $150–$175 ($120 in summer).

FACILITIES Pro shop, driving range, practice greens, locker rooms, restaurant, food-and-beverage cart, GPS-equipped golf carts, and club rentals ($65) and shoe rentals ($20).

COMMENTS This course can be played in three different 18-hole combinations, but the South is the very best 9 at the resort, so try to book either North/South or South/East. The course is one of the most beautiful in Orlando, and water is found on 13 of the holes, creating additional peril. Many unique and interesting holes offer true risk–reward choices, such as shortcuts over lakes. The undulating greens are guarded by pot bunkers and grass depressions and are kept in superb shape. Unlike the New Course, this group of courses provides very few opportunities to bump and run the ball onto the green.

Other Standout Courses in Orlando

In addition to the Grand Cypress courses, the ones we've profiled in the following section also stand out. With the golf industry in a slump, no built-from-scratch new courses of note had opened since Rees Jones's **Waldorf Astoria Golf Club,** just outside of Walt Disney World, in 2009. That changed in early 2015 with the addition of the Country Club at ChampionsGate, the third 18-hole course in that facility. However, it won't last long—while the existing two courses are daily-fee, this is a private club anchored by real estate, with 800 homes planned, and as soon as enough are sold, it will close to the public. But it should be open for the foreseeable future, with very good conditions for a new course and reasonable greens fees, $110 or less in peak season. It is set apart from the other two in a gated community and does not yet have a permanent clubhouse. **Bella Collina Country Club,** another top area private club, succumbed to economic realities and has opened itself to limited public play, in the same price range, a move that the venerable **Windermere Country Club,** now open to nonmembers, made two years ago.

Arnold Palmer's Bay Hill Club & Lodge ★★★★

ESTABLISHED 1961   DESIGNER Dick Wilson   STATUS Resort

9000 Bay Hill Blvd., Orlando, FL 32819; ☎ 407-876-2429 or 888-422-9445; **bayhill.com**

TEES
- **Yellow:** 6,437 yards, par 72, USGA 71.3, slope 129
- **Blue:** 6,895 yards, par 72, USGA 72.3, slope 127
- **Green:** 7,381 yards, par 72, USGA 73.9, slope 136

FEES Lodging (for two) from $125 per night in summer to $240 per night in peak season, plus greens fees of $100–$180.

FACILITIES Lodging, pro shop, driving range, practice greens, locker rooms, restaurant, beverage cart, and shoe rentals.

COMMENTS Bay Hill is famous in the golf world as the home club of The King, Arnold Palmer, and is the site of his invitational tournament each year. You have to stay to play, and the luxury resort features a spa, fine dining, and a comprehensive golf academy. When he is in town, which is most of the time, Palmer makes a point of stopping by the clubhouse daily, and half the attraction of staying and playing here is to see him. The other half is the course. It consists of three nines, but it's the Challenger–Champion combination that is the most popular, and the one on which the PGA Tour event is played. This combo starts off with a roar, featuring the toughest opening hole on the PGA Tour, an uphill, 441-yard, dogleg left that is heavily bunkered, both in the fairway and around the green. Recent renovations by Palmer have made the course better than ever and include entirely new and better greens and tees throughout, plus substantial changes to eight holes.

ChampionsGate Golf Club

Three miles from Walt Disney World and close to Celebration lies one of the city's premier golf destinations. The complex includes an Omni hotel and the Florida headquarters of the world-renowned David Leadbetter Golf Academy. But the centerpieces of the $800 million, 1,500-acre facility are the two Greg Norman–designed courses. For more information, visit **championsgategolf.com.** A third course, the George Clifton–designed Country Club at ChampionsGate, opened in early 2015, set apart from the other two. This is a private club, but until enough homes are sold, it is open to public play. Golfers need to contact the club directly; it is separately managed.

ChampionsGate International Course ★★★★

ESTABLISHED 2000   DESIGNER Greg Norman   STATUS Public

1400 Masters Blvd., ChampionsGate, FL 33896; ☎ 407-787-4653 or 888-558-9301

TEES
- **Black:** 7,363 yards, par 72, USGA 76.8, slope 143
- **Blue:** 6,792 yards, par 72, USGA 74.1, slope 137
- **White:** 6,239 yards, par 72, USGA 71.5, slope 132
- **Gold:** 5,618 yards, par 72, USGA 68.0, slope 117

FEES $50–$140. Discounts available for Omni hotel guests.

FACILITIES Pro shop, driving range, practice greens, locker rooms, restaurant, GPS-equipped carts, beverage cart, and club and shoe rentals.

COMMENTS The tougher and more highly ranked of ChampionsGate's two layouts, with a USGA rating of 76.8, the International lives up to its name by re-creating the feel of the championship courses of the British Isles. Laid out in a links style, the course has carpetlike fairways framed by the stark, unfinished look of brown dunes, mounds, and severe pot bunkers.

ChampionsGate National Course ★★★½

ESTABLISHED 2000   DESIGNER Greg Norman   STATUS Public

1400 Masters Blvd., ChampionsGate, FL 33896; ☎ 407-787-4653 or 888-558-9301

TEES
- **Black:** 7,128 yards, par 72, USGA 75.2, slope 138
- **Blue:** 6,427 yards, par 72, USGA 71.9, slope 133
- **White:** 5,937 yards, par 72, USGA 69.1, slope 124
- **Gold:** 5,150 yards, par 72, USGA 65.3, slope 111

FEES $50–$120 Florida residents, $60–$140 nonresidents. Discounts available for Omni hotel guests.

FACILITIES Pro shop, driving range, practice greens, locker rooms, restaurant, GPS-equipped carts, beverage cart, and club and shoe rentals.

COMMENTS The kinder, gentler course at ChampionsGate, the National is a resort-style layout that ambles through 200 acres of citrus groves in a traditional parkland routing with far less water than the International. Deep greens welcome bump-and-run shots, and the length is manageable from every set of tees.

Falcon's Fire Golf Club ★★★★

ESTABLISHED 1993   DESIGNER Rees Jones   STATUS Public

3200 Seralago Blvd., Kissimmee, FL 34746; ☎ 407-239-5445; **falconsfire.com**

TEES
- **Gold:** 7,006 yards, par 72, USGA 73.2, slope 135
- **Blue:** 6,435 yards, par 72, USGA 71.0, slope 130
- **White:** 5,962 yards, par 72, USGA 68.5, slope 126
- **Red:** 5,388 yards, par 72, USGA 71.0, slope 123

FEES $39–$139 ($35 for guests age 15 and under). Fees include carts.

FACILITIES Pro shop, driving range, practice greens, restaurant, GPS-equipped carts, beverage cart, and club rentals.

COMMENTS The Rees Jones design of this bargain-priced daily-fee course features plenty of water hazards, especially on the harder back nine, and fast greens. The course is suitable for all abilities and, conveniently, is just 3 miles from Walt Disney World.

Orange County National Golf Center

Five miles north of Disney, in Winter Garden, lies Orlando's premier daily-fee public facility, winner of numerous industry awards and consistently named among the nation's top public clubs by most golf publications. Forty-five holes (including a nine-hole short course) and one of the country's best practice facilities (42 acres) occupy 922 verdant acres, without homes or other distractions—just pure golf. It's also easily the region's best value, with inexpensive on-site lodging and two-night, two-round packages ($223–$359 depending on season). For more information, visit **ocngolf.com.**

Crooked Cat ★★★★

ESTABLISHED 1997	DESIGNERS Isao Aoki, Davis Harman, and Phil Ritson	STATUS Public

16301 Phil Ritson Way, Winter Garden, FL 34787; ☎ 407-656-2626 or 888-727-3672

TEES
- **Q-School:** 7,493 yards, par 72, USGA 76.0, slope 139
- **Championship:** 6,927 yards, par 72, USGA 73.7, slope 132
- **Back:** 6,432 yards, par 72, USGA 71.4, slope 126
- **Middle:** 6,020 yards, par 72, USGA 66.8, slope 122
- **Forward:** 5,112 yards, par 72, USGA 69.6 slope 120

FEES $29–$89, varying by time of day, day of week, and time of year. Discounts for Florida residents and guests age 17 and under.
FACILITIES Lodging, GPS, pro shop, driving range, practice greens, locker rooms, restaurant, beverage cart, and club and shoe rentals.
COMMENTS Variety is the spice of life, and this partner to the very modern Panther Lake is a throwback to Scottish-style links courses, with few trees, wide fairways, and heather mixed in the rough. Large, sloped greens welcome bump-and-run shots but are protected by deep bunkers of both grass and sand. Crooked Cat is as well maintained as its sibling.

Panther Lake ★★★★½

ESTABLISHED 1997	DESIGNERS Isao Aoki, Davis Harman, and Phil Ritson	STATUS Public

16301 Phil Ritson Way, Winter Garden, FL 34787; ☎ 407-656-2626 or 888-727-3672

TEES
- **Q-School:** 7,350 yards, par 72, USGA 76, slope 139
- **Championship:** 6,849 yards, par 72, USGA 73.2, slope 132
- **Back:** 6,394 yards, par 72, USGA 71.2, slope 127
- **Middle:** 6,011 yards, par 72, USGA 69.2, slope 120
- **Forward:** 5,319 yards, par 72, USGA 70.8, slope 123

FEES $29–$89, varying by time of day, day of week, and time of year. Discounts for Florida residents and guests age 17 and under.
FACILITIES Lodging, GPS, pro shop, driving range, practice greens, locker rooms, restaurant, beverage cart, and club and shoe rentals.

COMMENTS Panther Lake was the nation's first course designed to showcase 18 signature holes, and no expense was spared to make the course beautiful, just as none is spared to keep it in excellent condition. The front nine is carved from Florida wetlands with water at every turn, while the much-different back has a Carolinas-like style with surprising elevation changes, stands of pines and oaks, and hard-to-hold greens emphasizing accuracy.

Reunion Resort

Reunion is a 2,300-acre resort and residential golf community with three courses, designed by Arnold Palmer, Tom Watson, and Jack Nicklaus. The resort also includes Annika Sorenstam's **Annika Academy.** (Sorenstam, now retired after the greatest career in the history of women's golf, lives here part-time, personally teaches several clinics, and focuses on this single location.) Reunion is the region's largest golf destination outside of Walt Disney World itself. For more information, visit **reunionresort.com.**

Nicklaus Course ★★★★

ESTABLISHED 2006   DESIGNER Jack Nicklaus   STATUS Resort (Guests Only)

7593 Gathering Dr., Reunion, FL 34747; ☎ 407-396-3199

TEES
- **Gold:** 7,244 yards, par 72, USGA 76.7, slope 147
- **Blue:** 6,537 yards, par 72, USGA 72.6, slope 142
- **White:** 6,260 yards, par 72, USGA 71.3, slope 140
- **Red:** 5,055 yards, par 72, USGA 65.4, slope 116

FEES Golf available only as part of inclusive lodging packages starting at $125 per night, with one round per night (two-night minimum stay).

FACILITIES Lodging, pro shop, driving range, practice greens, locker rooms, restaurant, beverage cart, and club and shoe rentals.

COMMENTS Nicklaus went for a flat parkland design here. This doesn't mean the course is easy, however, as he used a target-style layout, with forced carries of the tees to small landing areas in the fairways; small greens; and the constant temptation to go for it with risk–reward gambles over a variety of hazards, including water and sand. Water is in play on fully half the holes, and because the course is built through a bird sanctuary, it's quiet and pristine and a world apart from the city's hustle and bustle.

Palmer Course ★★★★

ESTABLISHED 2004   DESIGNER Arnold Palmer   STATUS Resort (Guests Only)

7593 Gathering Dr., Reunion, FL 34747; ☎ 407-396-3199

TEES
- **Black:** 6,916 yards, par 72, USGA 73.4, slope 137
- **Gold:** 6,419 yards, par 72, USGA 70.9, slope 132
- **Blue:** 6,058 yards, par 72, USGA 69.2, slope 128
- **White:** 5,529 yards, par 72, USGA 67.0, slope 116
- **Red:** 4,802 yards, par 72, USGA 63.3, slope 106

FEES Golf available only as part of inclusive lodging packages starting at $125 per night, with one round per night (two-night minimum stay).

FACILITIES Lodging, pro shop, driving range, practice greens, locker rooms, restaurant, beverage cart, and club and shoe rentals.

COMMENTS Palmer frames vast green fairways with numerous shapely white bunkers, and there's plenty of water, so much so that the course needs elaborate boardwalk-style cart bridges to whisk guests around. Still, the possibility for lost balls is offset by very generous fairways, with lots of room for errant drives, and this is the easiest of the three layouts here.

Watson Course ★★★★

ESTABLISHED 2004   DESIGNER Tom Watson   STATUS Resort (Guests Only)

7593 Gathering Dr., Reunion, FL 34747; ☎ 407-396-3199

TEES
- **Black:** 7,154 yards, par 72, USGA 74.7, slope 140
- **Gold:** 6,697 yards, par 72, USGA 72.2, slope 131
- **Blue:** 6,319 yards, par 72, USGA 70.6, slope 124
- **White:** 5,990 yards, par 72, USGA 69.4, slope 120
- **Red:** 5,395 yards, par 72, USGA 66.3, slope 114

FEES Golf available only as part of inclusive lodging packages starting at $125 per night, with one round per night (two-night minimum stay).

FACILITIES Lodging, pro shop, driving range, practice greens, locker rooms, restaurant, beverage cart, and club and shoe rentals.

COMMENTS Tom Watson is said to have made more than 40 site visits during construction to ensure that his British Isles–inspired masterpiece here was built correctly. Greens are huge but undulating, so getting on is no insurance against three- (or four-) putting. Bunkers are everywhere, from fairway hazards to greenside pot bunkers; from the back, where all the hazards come into play, this is one of Orlando's stiffest tests, yet the course gets appreciably easier as you move to shorter tees.

THE BEST OF THE REST
Shingle Creek Golf Club ★★★★

ESTABLISHED 2003   DESIGNER David Harman   STATUS Public

9939 Universal Blvd., Orlando, FL 32819; ☎ 407-996-9933 or 866-996-9933; **shinglecreekgolf.com**

TEES
- **Black:** 7,149 yards, par 72, USGA 74.7, slope 133
- **Gold:** 6,659 yards, par 72, USGA 72.1, slope 130
- **Blue:** 6,359 yards, par 72, USGA 70.4, slope 128
- **Silver:** 5,813 yards, par 72, USGA 68.2, slope 119
- **Ivory:** 5,099 yards, par 72, USGA 69.5 slope 122

FEES $99–$135; twilight, $55–$75. Further discounts for resort guests; golf and lodging packages also available.

FACILITIES Lodging, pro shop, driving range, practice greens, locker rooms, restaurant, GPS-equipped carts, beverage cart, and club and shoe rentals.

COMMENTS Hotelier Harris Rosen runs the state's largest privately owned hotel company. The flagship Shingle Creek Resort, a 1,500-room property, includes a golf course by David Harman of nearby Orange County National fame. The main feature is the namesake creek, originating some 10 miles north as part of the headwaters of the Everglades and meandering through the design, surrounded by native oaks and pines. Even in peak season, Shingle Creek is one of the very best golf values in the Orlando region, even more so for resort guests.

Waldorf Astoria Golf Club ★★★★

ESTABLISHED 2009   DESIGNER Rees Jones   STATUS Resort

14224 Bonnet Creek Resort Lane, Orlando, FL 32821; ☎ 407-597-3782; **waldorfastoriagolfclub.com**

TEES
- **Black:** 7,108 yards, par 72, USGA 74.9, slope 134
- **Blue:** 6,661 yards, par 72, USGA 72.9, slope 131
- **White:** 6,309 yards, par 72, USGA 71.4, slope 127
- **Green:** 5,990 yards, par 72, USGA 69.7, slope 125
- **Silver:** 5,089 yards, par 72, USGA 70.8, slope 127

FEES $95–$200 peak season; $90–$160 mid-season.

FACILITIES Lodging, pro shop, driving range, practice greens, locker rooms, restaurant, GPS-equipped carts, beverage cart, and club and shoe rentals.

COMMENTS The 482-acre Bonnet Creek Resort encompasses two hotels: a 497-room Waldorf Astoria and a 1,000-room Hilton. The Rees Jones–designed Waldorf Astoria course combines a classic parkland routing, where holes are separated by stands of towering pines, with the omnipresent lakes for which Florida golf is known. Several holes wrap dramatically along the shore or feature greens set against the water—in fact, only one hole from the 12th to 18th holes (#17) is dry. Private lessons are available.

Windermere Country Club ★★★

ESTABLISHED 1986   DESIGNER Ward Northrup   STATUS Semiprivate

2710 Butler Bay Dr. N., Windermere, FL 34786; ☎ 407-876-1112; **windermeregolf.com**

TEES
- **Blue:** 6,641 yards, par 72, USGA 71.6, slope 136
- **White:** 6,259 yards, par 72, USGA 69.9, slope 131
- **Gold:** 5,933 yards, par 72, USGA 68.3, slope 128
- **Red:** 5,375 yards, par 72, USGA 71.7, slope 127

FEES $49–$99; twilight, $24–$54.

FACILITIES Pro shop, driving range, practice greens, locker rooms, restaurant, carts, beverage cart, and club rentals.

COMMENTS Windermere is a private club that has begun allowing unrestricted outside play and also offers special deals to guests of the resort hotels within Universal Studios. Secluded, quiet, and parklike, the course is well maintained and offers a genteel member-for-a-day experience. Short by modern standards, it's challenging nonetheless: 13 holes have lakes in play, and the layout is heavily bunkered.

GOLF BEYOND ORLANDO

A SEISMIC SHIFT IN FLORIDA'S golf landscape occurred in late 2012, when two courses—Red and Blue—opened at the massive new 16,000-acre **Streamsong Resort,** midway between Orlando and Tampa. It's about an hour-and-15-minute drive from South Orlando, but a drive worth considering: The two layouts were immediately ranked first and second among all new courses in 2012 by *Golf Magazine,* and in the magazine's latest Top 100 You Can Play, they were both ranked in the top 16 in the entire country, while *Golf Digest* puts both in the top 24 U.S. publics. These are world-class destination courses.

The rugged site was a phosphate-mining operation in the 1960s and, unlike the rest of flat Florida, is graced with towering sand dunes up to 200 feet high—far more evocative of Scotland and Ireland than the United States. Streamsong is a pure golf resort, with no residential construction at all, and both courses encourage walking and employ caddies. Built on a base of sandy soil like the links courses of the British Isles, both play firm and fast and encourage running shots. They are the work of the world's two hottest golf-design firms: Tom Doak's Renaissance Golf (Blue) and the duo of Bill Coore and Ben Crenshaw (Red).

Streamsong has 12 guest rooms in its golf clubhouse, which also contains a full-service restaurant and a more casual bar and grill. There is also a luxurious full-service 216-room resort hotel with spa, pool, and more restaurants. Both courses stretch to about 7,250 yards, with five sets of tees, and cost $135 to walk or $160 to ride, with a caddy fee of $80 (for one or two golfers) and significant discounts for Florida residents ($75 to walk or $100 to ride).

For more information, call ☎ 863-428-1000 or visit **streamsong resort.com.**

▌█ MINIATURE GOLF

ORLANDO WOULDN'T BE A VACATION TOWN without miniature golf. Almost as abundant as fast-food chains, miniature golf courses dot the landscape on US 192, International Drive, FL 535, and inside Walt Disney World and Universal Orlando. Because courses have different themes, quality of play, costs, and such, the golf course profiles that follow offer comparisons as well as short reviews focusing on what makes each course unique, plus course location and contact information.

Most of the miniature golf in the greater Orlando area features long greens with few obstacles. You won't find ball-eating clowns or obnoxious windmills on any of the courses in town—the only places offering this ilk of in-course obstacles are the Universal and Disney courses. What you will find are 18–36 holes on clean grounds, trick shots, lots of cascading water, and a myriad of different themes.

The rules for miniature golf do differ from course to course, but the basics are fairly standard. The maximum amount of strokes per hole is six. When you hit the ball out-of-bounds or into a water trap, retrieve the ball and place it back on the course as close to the trap as possible; you will incur a one-stroke penalty. When you lose your ball in the water and you can't recover it, you can get another ball from the main booth, but you will incur a two-stroke penalty. There is no running at any of the courses, and all of the establishments are very wary about injury. By purchasing a ticket, you waive your right to sue if you fall or stumble, or get hit with a club or a ball. If you swing the putter back too far—as if making a slap shot in hockey—you will be asked to leave. The odds of injury are much greater crossing International Drive, so don't let that rule dissuade you from one of the best family games around.

Bonanza Golf ★★½

7761 W. US 192 (Irlo Bronson Memorial Highway), Kissimmee; ☎ 407-396-7536; **bonanzagolf.com**

Hours Daily, 9 a.m.–11 p.m. (last entry at 10:30 p.m.) **Cost** $9.95 + tax per person for one 18-hole course, $12.95 for 36 holes; second course may be played another day; free for children age 3 and under.

DESCRIPTION AND COMMENTS At the far end of US 192 are Bonanza Golf's two courses; the play on both is the same. Bonanza Golf has the longest greens of any of the courses (excluding Disney's Fantasia Fairway), but most are flat with a dogleg left or right. The long greens make the holes fairly easy, if not a bit bland.

The theming is supposedly a mining town but is light at best. We don't expect animatronics, but one prospector or a few pieces of mining equipment would animate this rather dull and uninspired course. Even the waterfall, which should add some charisma to the holes, faces out toward the parking lot. Still, the grounds are very clean, and most of the greens are in acceptable condition.

Congo River Kissimmee ★★★★½

4777 W. US 192, Kissimmee; ☎ 407 396-6900; **congoriver.com**

Hours Sunday–Thursday, 10 a.m.–11 p.m.; Friday–Saturday, 10 a.m.–midnight. **Cost** $11.99 + tax for adults; $9.99 + tax for children ages 5–9; free for one child younger than age 5.

DESCRIPTION AND COMMENTS A member of the Congo River family, the Kissimmee location is very similar to the other courses in theming and play, but it is by far the largest. There are two courses at the Kissimmee location, dubbed Stanley and Livingston. Stanley is less difficult than Livingston by six shots. Though we prefer the play on the Livingston course, the Stanley course is more scenic, with one hole on a boat and a path that takes you next to the crashed zebra-striped plane. The Kissimmee location is mountainous, filled with thin paths that make backtracking to the entrance difficult and can also make finding the next hole slightly confusing. The entire complex, including the air-conditioned bathrooms, is clean, and the greens are all in great condition. The staff is accommodating and very friendly. There is also a small arcade, an I-spy Exploration Game to play along the golf course, and an exhibit where you can pay to feed or take a photo with a live gator. Visit its website for admission discounts and a free scorecard app for your smartphone.

Congo River Orlando I-Drive ★★★★

5901 International Dr., Orlando; ☎ 407-248-9181; **congoriver.com**

Hours Sunday–Thursday, 10 a.m.–11 p.m.; Friday–Saturday, 10 a.m.–midnight. **Cost** $12.99 + tax for adults; $10.99 + tax for children ages 5–9; free for one child younger than age 5.

DESCRIPTION AND COMMENTS This Congo River course is the survivor after another member of the clan, about 0.5 mile away and near Wet 'n Wild, was closed. The grounds here are superbly clean, and the lies of the greens put the ball where you aim it. There is only one course, and the first nine holes are relatively level, making them handicapped accessible but not as challenging as holes at the other Congo River locations.

What sets this apart from its kin is the quality of theming. All the Congo River golf courses have African themes, but the execution here surpasses the others. To start, the course is built both around and within a large red-rock mountain. On the mountain, you will find a Land Rover stuck in a waterfall, a zebra-striped airplane sticking out of a slope, and caverns with skeletons. A great baobab tree caps off this I-Drive landmark. Even some of the holes are themed: Hole #7 is played on a dilapidated ship.

Congo River Orlando I-Drive also contains a few non-golf attractions. Like the two other Congo River courses, this course has a baby alligator pit with pieces of hot dog meat you can buy to feed the gators, but it also contains a pond filled with koi you can feed, a gift shop, a small arcade, and a game called Ubanki Hoops that consists of 18 basketball hoops slung in unorthodox ways. A scavenger hunt-style Exploration Game involves artifacts hidden in the theming; ask for a game card when picking up your golf equipment.

Congo River East Orlando ★★★★

12193 E. Colonial Dr., Orlando; ☎ 407-823-9700; **congoriver.com**

Hours Sunday–Thursday, 10 a.m.–11 p.m.; Friday–Saturday, 10 a.m.–midnight. **Cost** $12.49 + tax for adults; $10.49 + tax for children ages 5–9; free for one child younger than age 5.

DESCRIPTION AND COMMENTS This is the newest of the Congo River attractions. It is also the smallest, having only one 18-hole course, but it does offer the features of its siblings—gators and turtles to feed, the mock crashed airplane, waterfalls, and so on. It also has a fun addition to the round of golf—a scavenger hunt. On your card, you mark where you have located various items—you don't physically retrieve them—and if you are correct, you get a scratch-off card with prizes such as a free round of golf.

Fantasia Gardens ★★★★½

1205 Epcot Resorts Blvd., Lake Buena Vista; ☎ 407-560-4870; **disneyworld .disney.go.com/recreation/fantasia-gardens-fairways-miniature-golf**

Hours Daily, 10 a.m.–11 p.m. **Cost** $14 + tax for adults; $12 + tax for children ages 3–9; repeat rounds within 24 hours of playing are half-price with receipt.

DESCRIPTION AND COMMENTS Disney creativity is uncanny. A short walk from the Dolphin Hotel, Fantasia Gardens has two courses, one called Fantasia Gardens and the other called Fantasia Fairway. Though the greens have been bleached out by the sun and trodden down by tourists, Fantasia Gardens is one of the best courses in Orlando. What Disney excels at is not making difficult holes (they aren't) or making big rocky mountains to play on (none of those either), but instead making each hole unique. Each hole is themed after a different character from *Fantasia*, including Cupid, the flamingos, and the ballerina hippos. From holes that sound trumpets when you sink a putt to fountains on motion sensors that squirt water at you as you walk along, Disney has set the bar for creative design.

The Fantasia Fairway is, literally, a miniature golf course. There are grass greens and sand traps. The holes are long, some in excess of 100 feet. You can't use any irons, but you will have to putt farther than you ever have before. Both of these courses are open to non-Disney guests.

Gator Golf   ★½

6586 International Dr., Orlando; ☎ 407-363-2001; **idrivegatorgolf.com**

Hours Daily, 10 a.m.–10 p.m., but may close to new arrivals as early as 9 p.m. **Cost** $9.99 + tax for adults; $7.99 + tax for children ages 3–11; free for children age 2 and under; $4.99 to walk around the course to observe alligators.

DESCRIPTION AND COMMENTS You need only to walk around the place to realize that Gator Golf has seen better times. Major decorative pieces include a truck chassis more than a half-century old, an old tractor, a windmill (how are any of these related to the subtropical gator ponds they adorn?), and a waterfront boardwalk presentation for the first holes leading to the encircled pond at the back. Some of the fairway carpeting is torn, missing, or badly worn, and most of the holes lack the small rubber mats that serve as tee pads for the first putt. The paper (not cardboard) scorecard lacks pars for any of the 18 holes. Between the rampant graffiti, stagnant water features, and terrifying restrooms, there's really no worse place in Orlando for families to play a round of mini golf.

The big draw here would seem to be the several dozen alligators kept in various ponds depending on their size. Sadly for the gators, all of their ponds are overstocked compared to their habitat in Florida's remaining wilderness. A handler puts on daily wrestling shows with the gators, and you can take your photo with one for a $10 fee. The reptiles are mostly rescues and appear a bit too active and interested in the guests for comfort. You can buy hot dog meat for $5 to feed the alligators. The course also has turtles in display cases along the covered boardwalk by the first couple of holes, and tortoises outdoors.

Several of the holes are a few steps above the previous green, and the closing hole requires players to negotiate 16 steps—a factor for anyone with mobility issues or pushing a stroller. To find Gator Golf in the relentless clutter of I-Drive, look for the giant golf ball on a pole about 20 feet above the sidewalk and next to an alley. The signs also say MURPHY'S ARMS PUB. Parking is in the rear.

Hawaiian Rumble Adventure Golf, Buena Vista   ★★½

13529 S. Apopka-Vineland Rd., Orlando; ☎ 407-239-8300; **hawaiianrumbleorlando.com**

Hours Sunday–Thursday, 9 a.m.–10 p.m.; Friday–Saturday, 10 a.m.–11 p.m. **Cost** $9.95 + tax for age 3 and older; free for children age 2 and under; $12.95 + tax for 36-hole special.

DESCRIPTION AND COMMENTS Like the Hawaiian Rumble course on I-Drive, the course on FL 535 in Buena Vista has two courses named the Lani and the Kahuna. Though the Lani is supposed to be the more difficult, we didn't notice a significant difference between them. What is obvious is that Hawaiian Rumble Buena Vista pales next to the I-Drive locale. The greens at Buena Vista need some maintenance, and the play is relatively flat. There is a large volcano in the middle and a few flowers, but the theming ends there.

Other attractions include an air hockey table and an original *Ms. Pac-Man* machine. Visit its website for buy-one/get-one 50% off coupons.

Hawaiian Rumble Adventure Golf, I-Drive   ★★★

8969 International Dr., Orlando; ☎ 407-351-7733; **hawaiianrumbleorlando.com**

Hours Sunday–Thursday, 10 a.m.–11 p.m.; Friday–Saturday, 9 a.m.–midnight. **Cost** $9.95 + tax for age 3 and older; $12.95 + tax for 36-hole special; free for children age 2 and under.

DESCRIPTION AND COMMENTS Located next to WonderWorks on I-Drive. Parking is available just behind the course, but you will have to walk around the front to enter. One of the busiest courses in Orlando, Hawaiian Rumble features a 40-foot volcano, plenty of flora, fountains, and a series of streams. Unlike the heavily rock-themed Pirate's Cove locales or Congo Rivers, Hawaiian Rumble is a very flat course; you can play through the volcano but not on it.

There are two courses, the Kahuna and the Lani. Kahuna is easier and takes players through the volcano. Lani is very challenging. Hole #5 has a long uphill green ending in a jump over the stream. The 17th hole, where players hit the ball through a series of logs, is one of the more creative, and difficult, holes around.

There is a concession stand at the entrance, as well as a Ben & Jerry's ice cream parlor. This course has seen better days and isn't as attractive as some competitors in the area; there's a reason why it's one of the cheapest 36-hole courses on I-Drive.

Hollywood Drive-In Golf   ★★★★½

In Universal Orlando's CityWalk, 6000 Universal Blvd., Orlando; ☎ 407 802-4848; **hollywooddriveingolf.com**

Hours Daily, 9 a.m.–2 a.m. **Cost** 18 holes: $14.99 + tax for adults; $12.99 + tax for children ages 3–9. 36 holes: $26.98 + tax for adults; $22.98 + tax for children ages 3–9. Free for children age 2 and under. **Special comments** Guests playing 36 holes receive a free T-shirt. Buy tickets online for a discount.

DESCRIPTION AND COMMENTS So this is what money and imagination can do. On one edge of the Universal CityWalk entertainment complex, these 18-hole courses are awash in elaborate settings, props, and even audio. The theme is a drive-in movie showing two features: *Invaders from Planet Putt* and *The Haunting of Ghostly Greens*. Players can choose a single (18 holes) or double (36 holes) feature. The Invaders from Planet Putt course entertains with non-frightening statues and props such as rocket ships and little green men; a pretend newspaper box shows the Roswell, New Mexico, *Register* of July 8, 1947, with the blaring headline, "UFO SIGHTINGS CONTINUE." The Haunting of Ghostly Greens course features a giant spider, a graveyard, and a basement lab scene. This course is particularly nice at night but may creep out younger golfers. At various holes, the sound effects are a mooing cow, a chain saw, and a ray gun (we guess, as we've never actually *heard* a ray gun). The courses are quite easy, and the greens are in superb condition. Note that one of the courses is fully wheelchair accessible, while the other requires navigating some stairs.

If you aren't already on property, you must pay the usual parking fee ($20 for cars, $22 for RVs) to enter any part of Universal Orlando, which drastically boosts the price of playing these courses. As you exit the parking garages and moving sidewalks, Hollywood Drive-In Golf is on your immediate right, down one level. Universal Annual Pass holders, Florida residents, military, adults age 62 and older, and AAA members all get 10%–15% discounts on 18 holes. You can purchase online in advance, saving up to 13%, but online tickets can't be used on the same day they're purchased and aren't refundable if unused. There's also a free scorecard app for Apple and Android that you can download from the website in preparation for your putting.

Lost Caverns Adventure Golf ★★★★

6132 International Dr., Orlando; ☎ 407-264-0560; **lostcavernsgolf.com**

Hours Monday–Thursday, 10 a.m.–11 p.m.; Friday–Sunday, 10 a.m.–midnight. **Cost** First 18-hole course: $12 + tax per adult, $10 + tax per child. Second course is half price.

DESCRIPTION AND COMMENTS Lost Caverns golf, located in the shadow of Wet 'n Wild's waterslides, started life as a Congo River Golf, with similar (though less elaborate) African theming to the Congo course just up the road. After Congo River sold the location, the new owners rechristened it as Lost Caverns and refurbished the course, adding images of an Indiana Jones–esque cartoon mascot named Cliff Cavern, whose tween nieces help him guide golfers through two 18-hole courses. The well-maintained courses roam through caves, behind waterfalls, across rustic bridges, and up wooden stairs, so be prepared for a little hiking; if you require ADA accessibility, look elsewhere. Like Congo River, Lost Caverns also has gators to feed ($3 per bag) and be photographed with, as well as its own scavenger hunt game; spot all the hidden objects, and you could win free gator chow or another round of golf.

Mighty Jungle Golf ★★★½

7792 W. US 192, Kissimmee; ☎ 407-390-6453; **mightyjunglegolf.com**

Hours Sunday–Thursday, 10 a.m.–9 p.m.; Friday–Saturday, 10 a.m.–10 p.m. **Cost** $9.95 + tax for adults; $8.95 + tax for children ages 3–9; $2 for a second 18-hole course.

DESCRIPTION AND COMMENTS Tucked inside a retail/restaurant/lodging center off the busy highway, this nicely landscaped attraction sits next to a pleasant pond and has two fairly simple courses. The courses have an Africa theme with statues of animals sculpted to look real but not frightening. The putting surfaces are in fine shape, and the courses are fairly flat, meaning that there are no tough challenges to erode the fun of the game.

Pirate's Cove International Drive ★★★½

8501 International Dr., Orlando; ☎ 407-352-7378; **piratescove.net**

Hours Daily, 9 a.m.–11:30 p.m. **Cost** 18 holes: $12.50 + tax for adults; $11.50 + tax for children ages 4–12; free for children age 3 and under. 36 holes: $20.50 + tax for adults; $18.95 + tax for children ages 4–12; free for children age 3 and under.

DESCRIPTION AND COMMENTS Pirate's Cove on I-Drive is almost impossible to miss: It's located beside the Castle Hotel. Just keep an eye out for the pirate marooned in the middle of a lake. Pirate's Cove has two courses. The Captain's Course is easier, taking players along the front edge of the pond before they climb the hill. Plaques along the way aid the theme as they tell the story of pirate William Kidd. Blackbeard's Challenge is more difficult and offers plenty of opportunities to lose a ball in the water, including a large water gap shot on hole #9. The holes get harder as you proceed, and the fairways contain lots of rolling hills and sloping greens.

Though the course is very clean and the maintenance crew does its best, the course has some worn spots due to the high volume of visitors who spot it from I-Drive. Crowds here can be an issue, especially at night. If you like pirates and don't mind driving, you may want to play one of the other two pirate-themed courses in Orlando, even if their theming is not quite as involved. If you do visit, don't forget to take a photo op in the stockade.

Pirate's Cove Lake Buena Vista ★★★★

12545 FL 535, Lake Buena Vista; ☎ 407-827-1242; **piratescove.net**

Hours Daily, 9 a.m.–11 p.m. **Cost** 18 holes, $10.95 + tax for adults; $9.95 + tax for children ages 4–12; free for children age 3 and under. 36 holes: $15.95 + tax for adults; $14.95 + tax for children ages 4–12; free for children age 3 and under.

DESCRIPTION AND COMMENTS You will see this course every time you take I-4 through Orlando. Located in the rear of the Crossroads Shopping Center, this Pirate's Cove location is less crowded than its I-Drive sibling, and the Buena Vista locale offers the same high-caliber theming and challenging courses.

The courses' names are, yet again, Captain's Course and Blackbeard's Challenge. Captain Kidd's is the easier course, taking players to the top of the mountain as well as through the caverns under the waterfalls on holes #13 and #14, two of the more scenic holes in Orlando. Blackbeard's Challenge has fine lies, which means the ball goes where you aim it. A few long downhill shots, however, make hitting par difficult. The greens are tidy, and excluding the I-4 traffic, the setting, with the palms and flora adorning the top of the rocky hill, is excellent.

Pirate's Cove ★★★½

2845 Florida Plaza Blvd., Kissimmee; ☎ 407-396-7484; **piratesislandgolf.com**

Hours Daily, 10 a.m.–10 p.m. Call for seasonal hours. **Cost** 18 holes: $12 + tax for adults; $9 + tax for children ages 4–12; free for children age 3 and under. 36 holes: $17 + tax for adults; $14 + tax for children ages 4–12; free for children age 3 and under. $2 more for unlimited all-day play.

DESCRIPTION AND COMMENTS This mini golf course is tucked behind a shopping center next to Old Town and Fun Spot USA. Like the other Pirate's Cove course nearby, this one has a Captain's Course and a Blackbeard's Challenge course; however, the courses are operated by interrelated but independent companies, and the theming is not quite as strong, though plaques with pirate factoids at each hole add an educational touch.

But interesting holes—such as the 16th hole on the Captain's Course inside a cave on top of a hill—give it the requisite piratical ambience. The course is generally well shaded, and the grounds are absolutely spotless.

Because Pirate's Cove is hidden behind a Red Lobster, it gets little play. It's a nice secret course to go to when all the others are overcrowded.

Pirate's Island ★★★½

4330 W. Vine St., Kissimmee; ☎ 407-396-4660; **piratesislandgolf.com**

Hours Sunday–Thursday, 10 a.m.–10 p.m.; Friday–Saturday, 10 a.m.–11 p.m. **Cost** 18 holes, $11.50 + tax for adults; $9 + tax for children ages 4–12; free for children age 3 and under. 36 holes: $16.50 + tax for adults; $14 + tax for children ages 4–12; free for children age 3 and under. $2 more for unlimited all-day play.

DESCRIPTION AND COMMENTS Sibling of the Pirate's Cove course (see previous profile) also in Kissimmee and one of a half-dozen courses in the Southeast United States, Pirates Island naturally has a pirate theme too. Located in an urban setting, these two courses have a few shade trees and real grass to ease the view. No windmills here, but you'll find plenty of well-detailed nautical accessories. What makes this course enjoyable is the elbow room. Pirate's Island has more land than the other pirate courses, making its layout open and uncluttered. The entire place is immaculate, without even a leaf from those welcome shade trees cluttering the greens.

The Putting Edge ★★★½

5250 International Dr. (inside the Artegon Marketplace), Orlando; ☎ 407-248-0700; **puttingedge.com**

Hours Monday–Thursday, 11 a.m.–9:30 p.m.; Friday–Saturday, 11 a.m.–11 p.m.; Sunday, 11 a.m.–8 p.m. **Cost** $10.50 + tax for adults; $8.50 + tax for children age 12 and under. $2 more for unlimited all-day play.

DESCRIPTION AND COMMENTS Inside the Artegon Marketplace at the top of I-Drive, next to the Cinemark Theatres, is an underrated course. Though there is only one flat course, it is entirely under black lights. The theme here is aquatic. The music is also more tempered, with a mix of current Top 40 tunes. The edges of each hole are well marked, and each shot is moderately interesting. Younger players will enjoy both the easy shots and the charming theme, and the indoor location makes it a perfect rainy-day getaway.

Winter Summerland ★★★★

1548 W. Buena Vista Dr., Lake Buena Vista; ☎ 407-560-3000; **disneyworld .disney.go.com/recreation/winter-summerland-miniature-golf**

Hours Daily, 10 a.m.–11 p.m. **Cost** $14 + tax for adults; $12 + tax for children ages 3–9; repeat rounds within 24 hours of playing are half-price with receipt.

DESCRIPTION AND COMMENTS Inside Disney property, near the entrance to Blizzard Beach, you will find out what happens when the Imagineers set their minds to making an "ordinary" miniature golf course. There are two 18-hole courses, the Winter course and the Summer course. The play on each course is the same, but Winter features a snowy Christmas theme, while Summer features a sandy Christmas theme. Though Winter Summerland is small, the Imagineers have made each of the 36 holes unique. The in-course obstacles, such as sand and snow castles, all have interactive components. Some holes make noise, some blow air, and a few even attempt to block your shot! None of the holes are too difficult for children, making this an ideal family stop. One caveat: Winter Summerland's compactness may have you bumping elbows with other guests. The courses can be a mob scene both day and night.

PART ELEVEN

OLD TOWN *and* FUN SPOT USA

LOCATED SIDE BY SIDE ON US 192, Old Town and Fun Spot are in competition for tourists who are in search of entertainment without the flat-rate ticket prices found at the major theme parks. Even though Old Town has been a staple on this section of highway for more than 30 years, the newer Fun Spot USA is gaining in popularity, helped in part by its sister location (Fun Spot America) on International Drive.

Old Town and Fun Spot each have a unique feel, though the lack of a fence between the two may lead some guests to believe that the attractions share a common owner (they do not). Still, there's a bit of a synergy at work here. When you combine the rides at Fun Spot with the dining, shopping, and other activities at Old Town, they pose an interesting alternative for half-day touring, or an escape for those who don't want to spend their evenings within the confines of a major park.

OLD TOWN

THE LONGEVITY OF THIS FOUR-BLOCK MAIN STREET relies on its exclusive mixture of shopping, restaurants, carnival attractions, and thrill rides. Old Town is fashioned to be like a modern Mayberry with the fair in town. The atmosphere is akin to East Coast beach towns such as Ocean City, Maryland, or Myrtle Beach, South Carolina. Though the storefronts are attractive, Old Town has not undergone the Disney-style whitewash of magic and charm. At press time, Old Town was in the midst of a $10 million renovation. When complete in late 2016 or early 2017, the complex will sport an eye-catching new 1950s-themed entryway, an outdoor concert venue, repainted facades in the original color scheme, and 1,000 much-needed additional parking spaces. Old Town will also be installing new carnival rides, including a classically styled (but recently constructed) Ferris wheel. For the time being, nearly all of Old Town's attractions (aside from a few independently operated thrill rides) have been ripped out, including the iconic wheel that long stood at the entrance, so you'll need to step next door to Fun Spot to fulfill your fun fair needs.

As you walk down the street, you will pass storefronts ranging from trinket shops to spas, tattoo parlors to sunglass huts, and tobacco merchants to marionette dealers. Bars and restaurants are interspersed among the shops, as are a number of entertainment attractions.

Old Town also offers events throughout the year, including its famous weekly automotive shows. Classic cars roll in on Friday and Saturday nights to parade down Main Street. A live band, creating a spirited party atmosphere, accompanies most of these events.

One of the fine features about Old Town is that these shows, and admittance and parking in general, are all free. These perks allow potential patrons to peruse the storefronts, restaurants, rides, and other attractions before committing any cash. Because all you have to invest to visit Old Town is your time, it becomes a hard deal to pass up.

GETTING THERE

OLD TOWN IS LOCATED ON WEST US 192 (Irlo Bronson Memorial Highway), about 5 minutes from Disney World. From I-4, take Exit 64 east onto US 192. Old Town will be just over a mile ahead on your right.

ADMISSION PRICES

THE BUSINESS MODEL FOR OLD TOWN separates it from any amusement park in the area. Competing companies either lease or own each store and attraction, so one set of tickets or coupons is not valid for every experience (for example, laser tag tickets will not allow you to ride the Human Slingshot). The lack of a common currency frees you to spend as you see fit but also bumps up the prices on all of the rides; it appears that there is little profit sharing among companies. Currently, there are no wristbands or value packs available for Old Town attractions; you will need to purchase separate admission to each operating venue.

ARRIVING

OLD TOWN IS OPEN EVERY DAY of the year 10 a.m.–11 p.m. Most rides are open Monday–Friday, 4–11 p.m., and Saturday–Sunday, from noon on. Every Friday, starting at 4 p.m., Old Town hosts a show and parade of classic cars, manufactured between 1964 and 1988. On Saturday, beginning at 1 p.m., cars of pre-1980 vintage are on hand. Weather permitting, a live band plays during the car shows. There is also a doo-wop street party with line dancing every Wednesday, 6–9 p.m., and a Show 'n Shine cruise-in of classic Jeeps, trucks, and SUVs on Sundays starting at 4 p.m. As with admission to Old Town, these shows are free and are extremely popular, so arrive early or be prepared to hunt hard for a parking spot.

CONTACTING OLD TOWN

FOR MORE INFORMATION, call ☎ 407-396-4888 or visit **myold townusa.com**.

RIDES AND ATTRACTIONS

OLD TOWN PROPER CONSISTS OF FOUR BLOCKS on Main Street. Highlighting the diversity of ownership, and located between US 192 and the first retail/restaurant block of Old Town, are the Human Slingshot and the Vomatron (can you guess what that's supposed to make potential riders think?). While these attractions are adjacent to some of the Old Town rides, they are not part of Old Town. Attractions farther along the promenade include the Old Town Bull (think *Urban Cowboy* barroom ride) and Legends: A Haunting at Old Town, which are both located between blocks two and three; and The Great Magic Hall, located on block four.

The Great Magic Hall ★★★½

APPEAL BY AGE	PRESCHOOL ★★½	GRADE SCHOOL ★★★★	TEENS ★★★
YOUNG ADULTS ★★★½	OVER 30 ★★★½		SENIORS ★★★½

What it is Magic theater and shop. **Scope and scale** Major attraction. **Authors' rating** Small; ★★★½. **Duration of show** 30 minutes for one show, 2+ hours for Grand Magic Tour. **Cost** One show: $14. Grand Magic Tour: $22.

DESCRIPTION AND COMMENTS Obviously inspired by the famous Magic Castle in Los Angeles, The Great Magic Hall is a two-story temple to the ancient art of sleight of hand. Unlike the death-defying illusions featured in Vegas and on TV, The Great Magic Hall's prestidigitators focus on close-up tricks involving seemingly mundane props like playing cards, sewing needles, and pieces of string. You won't see an elephant disappear, but the intimate Victorian-themed performance spaces allow every audience member to be no farther than 15 feet from the magician, proving that there really is nothing up their sleeve.

   The Great Magic Hall is operated by Theatre Magic, the same folks who formerly ran the magic-trick demonstrations in several theme parks (including Universal Orlando). The hourly afternoon *Parlor Presents* shows are most similar to those free theme park presentations, with a member of the magic shop staff showing off tricks that are for sale afterward; the show we attended was a cut above the average, with some excellent card manipulations and a much softer sales pitch than in the parks. The early evening *Magician Tonight* sets feature a touring guest artist presenting his own personal repertoire, which might be a better bet.

   For the serious magic buff, the nightly Grand Magic Tour (which debuted in fall 2015) is an intense evening of illusion overload, in which you'll progress from room to room—each with an evocative name, such as The Passage of Impossibility or The Drawing Room of Deception—witnessing a different display of wizardry in each.

TOURING TIPS At press time, The Great Magic Hall was offering discounted tickets as low as $10 for adults and $8 for children. If you see the *Parlor Presents* show, you can see that evening's *Magician Tonight* for $4 more. Performances currently begin at 3 p.m. daily but are supposed to eventually start as early as 11 a.m. Visit **thegreatmagichall.com** or **facebook .com/thegreatmagichall,** or call ☎ 407-507-3987 for a current performance schedule.

Happy Days Bumper Cars ★★★

APPEAL BY AGE	PRESCHOOL ★★★	GRADE SCHOOL ★★★★	TEENS ★★½
YOUNG ADULTS ★★★		OVER 30 ★★★	SENIORS ★★½

What it is Disco-themed bumper cars. **Scope and scale** Minor attraction. **Special comment** 48" minimum height requirement. **Authors' rating** No deductibles; ★★★. **Duration of ride** 8–10 minutes. **Cost** $5 per person; $10 for unlimited rides and laser tag.

DESCRIPTION AND COMMENTS The cars are in better shape than some of the competition's but are nothing particularly special. Though the interior has a 1970s disco theme, the music is 1980s hair metal—we suppose it's a subtle message about the timelessness of bumper cars.

TOURING TIPS Not crowded; come anytime. Bumper cars do not have a reverse, so if you get stuck, just cock the wheel hard over and press the gas.

Happy Days Family Fun Track ★★★

APPEAL BY AGE	PRESCHOOL —	GRADE SCHOOL ★★★★	TEENS ★★★½
YOUNG ADULTS ★★½		OVER 30 ★★½	SENIORS ★★½

What it is Small go-cart track. **Scope and scale** Major attraction. **Special comments** 58" minimum height requirement to drive; no height requirement for passengers. **Authors' rating** Small; ★★★. **Duration of ride** 5 minutes. **Cost** $7 per person; $12 for two in double carts.

DESCRIPTION AND COMMENTS The go-cart track is one of the smallest in Orlando, but they did the best they could with the single oval track, having one of the longer sides bend inward to create two more turns and elevating the straightaway opposite. The simple shape allows you to pass other carts, but after 5 minutes, it becomes repetitive.

TOURING TIPS The carts are in rather poor shape compared with other local tracks, but their condition does not affect their speed. Still, Fun Spot is the place to go for go-carts. Being the only track at Old Town, Family Fun Track becomes very crowded in the evenings, but a full track is more exciting than an empty one. Once you've begun the race, you are forced to continue until it is completely over because opening the gate to pit row would halt all the other carts.

Happy Days Laser Tag ★★★

APPEAL BY AGE	PRESCHOOL ★★½	GRADE SCHOOL ★★★★	TEENS ★★★
YOUNG ADULTS ★★½		OVER 30 ★★★	SENIORS ★★½

What it is Real-life shoot-'em-up. **Scope and scale** Major attraction. **Special comments** 36" minimum height requirement; 9 players maximum. **Authors' rating** Good padding; ★★★. **Duration of attraction** 8–10 minutes. **Cost** $7 per person; $10 for unlimited bumper car rides and laser tag.

DESCRIPTION AND COMMENTS Forgoing the many partitions in Lazerworks at WonderWorks, Laser Tag at Old Town is fully padded with large air sacks. The room is smaller than at WonderWorks, but the padding allows shooters to dive and roll around to avoid getting hit, and with less cover to hide behind, you'll find yourself fully prone more often than not.

TOURING TIPS Because the course is inflatable, shoes are not permitted inside. All participants must come with clean socks or wear a provided pair.

The vests that register the tally are a bit cumbersome, and the lasers are hard to aim. Your best bet is to sneak up on people and to keep moving.

Human Slingshot ★★★½

APPEAL BY AGE	PRESCHOOL †	GRADE SCHOOL †	TEENS ★★★★½
YOUNG ADULTS ★★★★		OVER 30 ★★★★	SENIORS ★★

† *Preschoolers are generally too short to ride.*

What it is 180-foot slingshot. **Scope and scale** Major attraction. **Special comment** 44″ minimum height requirement. **Authors' rating** Scarier to watch than to ride; ★★★½. **Duration of ride** 4 minutes. **Cost** $25 per person.

DESCRIPTION AND COMMENTS The Slingshot is a massive steel V shape with flashing rainbow lights located near the front of Old Town. Riders latch into a two-person cart at the base of the V, where a bungee cord system runs down the legs of the V to the cart, like a slingshot. Once you're latched in, the tethered cart is pulled below the boarding area, then released, flinging riders 365 feet into the air, spinning head over feet the entire time. After the initial launch, the elastic cable makes for a smooth rise and fall. Surprisingly, the ride is almost peaceful, and less frightening than many of the major roller coasters in the area. Being more than 300 feet above the ground silences much surrounding noise, and the nighttime view is even better—for a few seconds at a time as you bob—than the Sky-Coaster's. As with most rides, the thrill is in the anticipation, not in the event. For $25, however, you're better off taking a helicopter for sightseeing or, for thrill junkies, paying out a few more bucks for the SkyCoaster.

TOURING TIPS The cart must have two people in it to keep balanced; a ride operator will go with you if you can't convince any of your friends or family. Riding at night is more thrilling, but long lines begin after 7 p.m. During high season, the wait can be more than an hour long. Watching everyone else is almost better than riding it yourself, though. A USB thumb drive with photographic proof of your ordeal is available for an additional $20.

Legends: A Haunting at Old Town ★★★★½

APPEAL BY AGE PRESCHOOL —	GRADE SCHOOL ★★★★	TEENS ★★★★½
YOUNG ADULTS ★★★★½	OVER 30 ★★★★½	SENIORS ★★★★

What it is An interactive walk-through haunted house. **Scope and scale** Headliner. **Special comments** Not recommended for youngsters. Open Thursday, 7–8:30 p.m., and Friday–Sunday, 7–11 p.m. Ghost tours: Tuesday–Thursday, 9 p.m. **Authors' rating** A taste of Halloween any time of year! ★★★★½. **Duration of attraction** Depends on how scared you are. **Cost** *Legends:* $15; *Ghosts of Old Town:* $20; *Legends* and *Ghosts of Old Town:* $30.

DESCRIPTION AND COMMENTS For years, one of Old Town's specialty attractions was the two-story Grimm's Haunted House. But in recent years it was open only a few nights a week as business fell off, perhaps because Grimm's hadn't kept up with fairly high-tech improvements in the industry. Grimm's let its lease go, and a consortium of just-dying-to-scare-you folks in Orlando and Dallas came together to revamp the place.

A twist on the usual haunted house, this is a tour of the grisly Ashdown and Son's Undertaking Establishment, established in 1889. Using veteran "scare" actors and new animatronics, lighting, and sound effects, the Legends attraction sends guests through the embalming room, undertaker's office, and dark hallways to reveal, in gruesome fashion, that not all of the funeral home's clients were dead when they arrived. The performances here are a cut above the usual bored booing, and the tone leans more toward creepy atmosphere with a touch of tongue-in-cheek humor rather than guts and gore. While there are a few graphic images and plenty of startles, the gross-out quotient is closer to Disney's Haunted Mansion (albeit with a bite) than Universal's Halloween Horror Nights. If you savor a good scare, this is one of the finest year-round haunted houses operating anywhere in America.

On select evenings, guests can pay an additional fee to join the Ghosts of Old Town, a narrated tour down the darkened streets of the amusement park, returning to the two-story funeral parlor for presentations on Victorian funeral practices, the paranormal, and local ghost tales. This is an Orlando attraction, not the Overlook Hotel, so any evidence of actual spirits is somewhat sketchy, but the tour guides do a terrific job of bringing their skeletal stories to life.

TOURING TIPS Leading up to Halloween, lines are as gruesome as the house, so try to stop in early if you're visiting in October. Buy your tickets in advance at **legendsoldtown.com** to save $3–$5 per person.

Old Town Bull ★★★

APPEAL BY AGE	PRESCHOOL —	GRADE SCHOOL ★★★	TEENS ★★½
YOUNG ADULTS ★★★½		OVER 30 ★★★½	SENIORS ★★

What it is Mechanical bull. **Scope and scale** Minor attraction. **Authors' rating** ★★★. **Duration of ride** 2 minutes. **Cost** $10 for adults; $7 for children.

DESCRIPTION AND COMMENTS As any fan of the 1970s classic movie *Urban Cowboy* already knows, a mechanical bull is a machine with a saddle that bucks riders up, down, and around, attempting to knock the rider off. It's the gear-and-motor approximation of bull riding found in rodeos. Old Town's bull is one and the same and has enough padding on the ground to minimize injuries, though you must sign a waiver before riding.

TOURING TIPS The ride doesn't open until later in the day when crowds are heavier.

Vomatron ★★★½

APPEAL BY AGE	PRESCHOOL †	GRADE SCHOOL †	TEENS ★★★★½
YOUNG ADULTS ★★★★		OVER 30 ★★★★	SENIORS ★★

† Young children are generally too short to ride.

What it is Ride elevating passengers 200 feet in the air in a circular motion. **Scope and scale** Major attraction. **Special comment** 44" minimum height requirement. **Authors' rating** Scarier to ride than to watch; ★★★½. **Duration of ride** 3 minutes. **Cost** $20 per person.

DESCRIPTION AND COMMENTS At either end of a single metal arm are two-seat buckets, which can turn over completely once the ride is in motion. The arm rotates around a center post, taking the buckets 200 feet up. Because they're at the end of the arm, the buckets reach a speed of 70 miles per hour, and the weight of the riders can cause the buckets to turn over. Hence the name Vomatron.

TOURING TIPS This ride opened in February 2012 and is among the newer attractions here. Because it can hold only four people at a time, the wait time can build as Old Town crowds grow during the evening. The Voma-tron and Human Slingshot open at 11 a.m. even on weekdays and do not shut down before midnight. But at the slowest times, this ride will operate with just one rider. To memorialize your near-death experience, Vomatron vends photos of your ride on a USB memory stick for an extra $15.

DINING

OLD TOWN HAS A WIDE VARIETY of dining options. There is Chinese food at **Bamboo Court,** Mexican at **Tex Mex,** and fast food at **Jimmy John's, Mr. Sushi,** and **A&W All American Food.** Our pick for the best deal in the park is **Flipper's Pizzeria,** located near the front entrance. Diners can get a single-topping personal pizza pie and a soda for $6.99 plus tax. For pizza in an amusement park setting, this is an exceptional deal. Checker's, Burger King, and a slew of local restaurants are located just outside of Old Town.

SHOPPING

NO MAIN STREET WOULD BE COMPLETE without shops, and shops line all four blocks of Old Town. Though Old Town contains more than 30 specialty shops—more than we can mention here—there aren't very many bargains, and don't expect flea market prices. They've hooked you with the attractions and atmosphere, and now it's time to unload a barrage of souvenirs, but that's no different from any other Florida park.

On the first block, you'll find **Groovy Store** packed with 1960s hip-pie memorabilia, **Old Town Leather** (a shop for bikers), **Annie's Gifts,** and the **Ocean Wave Surf Shop,** all on the right side of the street. **Puppets** sells marionettes; prices range from $8.50 for a small puppet to $50 for large puppets. Across the street is **Shoe Town,** a Magnetron magnet store, and **The British Isles Connection,** where you can stock up on English crisps, candy bars, and other staples for homesick visitors from the United Kingdom.

As Seen on TV is on the second block. Here you can buy all the questionable products that you've seen pitched on late-night info-mercials, only without the pain of paying shipping and handling fees. Next door is the **Old Town Portrait Gallery,** where your family can dress up in old-timey garb and pose for a sepia-tinted photo. **Electronic Town, Glitz** costume jewelry, and a caricature artist are also on the second block. **Kandlestix,** a candle outlet, is also on the second block.

On the third block, you will find **Vivian's Day Spa.** For $75 you can get a 1-hour therapeutic massage, and for $60 a French manicure. For $110, the Spa Serenity Package offers a 1-hour full-body massage, a 20-minute foot treatment, and a paraffin hand dip. This is a perfect stop for Mom while Dad takes the kids around. The third block also hosts a vacation-planning center with discount tickets and time-share come-ons, and an **Ink Spot** tattoo parlor that is open late, just in case you thought drinking was a good idea.

The fourth block hosts a **Made in the Shade Sunglasses** store, **Knives and Things,** and a couple shops selling Asian toys and novelties. **Filthy Rich** celebrity-inspired jewelry and **The General Store** are across the street. The General Store is themed to feel like a vintage hometown market, but instead of coffee cans and potatoes, you'll find Coca-Cola memorabilia and fake road signs. On the same side of the street is **Black Market Minerals,** an African-themed store with a collection of rocks, sculptures, and wind chimes.

FUN SPOT USA

LOCATED DIRECTLY BESIDE OLD TOWN, Fun Spot USA offers more thrill rides than its competition but less theming. Still, it seems to have a better grip on what will keep teenagers pleased, as well as a unified pricing scheme.

The park contains both go-cart tracks and carnival rides. But with the addition of big-time thrills, such as the SkyCoaster and a Wild Mouse–style ride, it's clearly the superior choice for adventure seekers.

Also, as at neighboring Old Town, admission and parking are both free. Fun Spot USA has a sister attraction on International Drive in nearby Orlando called Fun Spot America, which features a similar selection of go-cart tracks and carnival rides, plus an excellent wooden coaster (the only one in the area) and a mild suspended steel coaster. See page 320 in Part Twelve for details.

GETTING THERE

FUN SPOT USA IS LOCATED on West US 192 (West Irlo Bronson Memorial Highway), about 5 minutes from Walt Disney World. From I-4, take Exit 64 east onto US 192. Fun Spot will be just over a mile ahead on your right.

ADMISSION PRICES

EACH RIDE IS PRICED SEPARATELY and must be paid for with rechargeable debit cards that may be purchased from a ticket booth (located at four points around the park perimeter) or an automated vending machine. The roller coaster and two multilevel go-cart tracks cost $9 each; the two flat go-cart tracks are $6 each, as are the Hot Seat and Flying Bobs; and all remaining carnival and kiddie rides are $3 each. You get a bonus $4 credit for every $20 you put on a card. Cards retain their value indefinitely and may be used at either Fun Spot location.

Fun Spot offers three armbands. Each is good for the entire day. When selecting armbands, take the height and age of your group into consideration. There is no need to purchase armbands that are out of the height or age range of the rider. Unlimited armbands do not include the SkyCoaster or arcade games and are valid at both Fun Spot locations on the day purchased. If you arrive late enough in the evening, Fun Spot's two-day special can get you a second unlimited armband for free; ask at the ticket booth for details.

- **Single-Day Pass Over 54″ Tall** $44.95 + tax per person, unlimited go-cart tracks and rides (SkyCoaster not included)

- **Single-Day Pass Under 54″ Tall** $34.95 + tax per person, unlimited go-cart tracks and rides (SkyCoaster not included)

A seasonal pass, which offers unlimited rides at both Fun Spot parks until the end of the year, costs $75–$150, depending on the time of year purchased.

ARRIVING

FUN SPOT IS OPEN DAILY 10 a.m.–midnight during the summer months and end-of-the-year holiday season. The rest of the year, hours are Monday–Friday, 2 p.m.–midnight; Saturday–Sunday, 10 a.m.–midnight. Most of the rides are open noon–11 p.m. The attraction is closed on occasion for private parties. Parking and admission are free.

CONTACTING FUN SPOT

FOR MORE INFORMATION, call ☎ 407-397-2509 or visit **fun-spot .com.**

RIDES AND ATTRACTIONS

GO-CARTS The main draw at Fun Spot USA, as with Fun Spot America, are the go-carts. Concrete tracks allow Fun Spot patrons to operate go-carts rain or shine and create a smoother ride than the wooden planks at places such as Magical Midway. There are four tracks here that are on par with Fun Spot's other tracks, but due to this park's location next to Old Town, these tracks tend to be more crowded.

The four tracks are the Vortex, the Chaos, the Slick Track, and the Road Course. All of the tracks are color-coded to make them easy to distinguish.

The **Vortex** is the yellow, three-level, 800-foot track comprised of tight corkscrews at the back of the park. The biggest thrill occurs at its 36-foot apex, where the track makes a sharp, 20-degree descent for 100 feet. The collection of skid marks at the bottom is proof of its wild design. If you can ride only one go-cart at Fun Spot, make it this one. Riders are usually allowed five laps, totaling about 9 minutes, and must be at least 10 years old and 54 inches tall. It costs $9.

The longest track at Fun Spot is the 820-foot, blue **Chaos** track. The course is steeper than the Vortex but more timid due to the sharp twists and turns that make it difficult to pass other carts. There are plenty of hills and valleys, but after five laps and 8 minutes, you'll be ready to move along. As with the Vortex, riders must be at least 10 years old and at least 54 inches tall. The cost is $9.

The **Slick Track** is red. It's a simple oval course and the dullest, briefest race available. Skip this unless you're a die-hard NASCAR fan. Riders must be at least 8 years old and 56 inches tall. It costs $6.

The **Road Course** is green, and if you really want to test your driving skills, this is the track on which to do it. It's completely flat and packed with hairpin turns and short straightaways. The variety of angles in the course, from slow bends to hairpins, will both test your skill as a driver and allow you the opportunity to pass other carts. The unassuming flat track will have shorter lines because most guests will be drawn to the multistoried Vortex and Chaos tracks. Riders must be at least 12 years old and 56 inches tall. It costs $6.

ARCADE Fun Spot USA also has a 3,000-square-foot building next to its parking lot and entrance that contains more than five dozen typical arcade and video game consoles. You'll also find some air hockey tables here.

OTHER RIDES AND ATTRACTIONS

Flying Bobs ★★½

APPEAL BY AGE	PRESCHOOL ★★	GRADE SCHOOL ★★★	TEENS ★★★
YOUNG ADULTS ★★½		OVER 30 ★★	SENIORS ★½

What it is Circular coaster. **Scope and scale** Minor attraction. **Special comment** 42″ minimum height requirement to ride alone. **Authors' rating** ★★½. **Duration of ride** 3 minutes. **Cost** $6.

DESCRIPTION AND COMMENTS Located across from the Vortex track, Flying Bobs is another carnival standard. Cars, attached bumper-to-bumper, spin around a track, which is at an angle and shaped much like the tip of a lipstick. Disco beats blare, and when the ride starts spinning backward, you'll remember why you haven't ridden one of these since you were a kid.

TOURING TIPS The spinning can be a little nauseating but falls just short of needing our motion sickness warning.

Hot Seat ★★½

APPEAL BY AGE	PRESCHOOL ★★	GRADE SCHOOL ★★★	TEENS ★★★
YOUNG ADULTS ★★★		OVER 30 ★★	SENIORS ★½

What it is Big pendulum. **Scope and scale** Major attraction. **Special comment** 48″ minimum height requirement. **Authors' rating** ★★½. **Duration of ride** 3 minutes. **Cost** $6.

DESCRIPTION AND COMMENTS If you've ever wondered what's it like to be strapped to a giant's foot as he goes from a gentle walk to an all-out sprint, here's your chance. Side-by-side pendulums each have four seats attached to the bottoms. When they get swinging, riders get screaming.

It's a fun, rather short, way to spook parents and the easily mortified.

TOURING TIPS The ride is very similar to the Phoenix swinging boat at Busch Gardens, except that here you can see the ground beneath you. We're not sure why, but that makes this ride both more thrilling and less likely to turn your stomach.

kids Kid Spot ★★★

APPEAL BY AGE	PRESCHOOL ★★★★	GRADE SCHOOL ★★★	TEENS ★
YOUNG ADULTS ★★		OVER 30 ★★	SENIORS ★★½

What it is Kiddie rides. **Scope and scale** Minor attraction. **Special comment** 24"–42" minimum height requirements to ride alone. **Authors' rating** ★★★. **Duration of rides** 1–3 minutes. **Cost** $3.

DESCRIPTION AND COMMENTS A collection of classic kiddie rides sits near the parking lot in the front of the park. There are two sets of slides where you descend on burlap sacks, as well as miniature carnival rides where you can sit in one of eight biplanes (**Baron Planes**) or a truck (**Convoy**), all while circling a central hub. Other rides include a kiddie coaster (adults may accompany the smaller kids) and bumper cars (one set for kids, one for grown-ups). There's also a smallish carousel with 20 beautifully painted horses; it's a nostalgia trip for the grown-ups. A **Fun Slide, Happy Swing,** and castle-themed climbing structure round out the kiddie offerings.

TOURING TIPS This is on par with the kiddie rides at Fun Spot's I-Drive location. The only things missing are the bumper boats.

Paratrooper ★★

APPEAL BY AGE	PRESCHOOL ★★★	GRADE SCHOOL ★★★	TEENS ★★★
YOUNG ADULTS ★½		OVER 30 ★★	SENIORS ★★½

What it is Small, sideways Ferris wheel. **Scope and scale** Minor attraction. **Special comment** 46" minimum height requirement. **Authors' rating** ★★. **Duration of ride** 2 minutes. **Cost** $3.

DESCRIPTION AND COMMENTS A simplistic ride that spins around a central hub. Riders sit in carts that fit two people and that dangle from an object that looks like a giant umbrella. The attraction is located directly across from the Chaos go-cart track. This ride is far tamer than the attraction of the same name at Fun Spot's I-Drive location, which runs much faster and backwards. Don't confuse them!

TOURING TIPS A calm ride fine for older adults and younger children.

Rockstar Coaster ★★

APPEAL BY AGE	PRESCHOOL ★★½	GRADE SCHOOL ★★★½	TEENS ★★★
YOUNG ADULTS ★★		OVER 30 ★½	SENIORS ★

What it is Spinning Wild Mouse coaster. **Scope and scale** Major attraction. **Special comment** 48" minimum height requirement. **Authors' rating** ★★. **Duration of ride** 5 minutes. **Cost** $9.

DESCRIPTION AND COMMENTS Individual cars, which can spin around 360 degrees, ascend to the top of the track and then wind down through a series of hairpin curves. At each curve, riders are thrust against each other as the car spins around. Not that the quick spin isn't fun once, but the repetition of slamming against each other wears thin by the third turn, and with about 15 turns in all, you'll be happy to get off. Riders can somewhat control how much their ride vehicle spins as it proceeds down the length of track.

TOURING TIPS Why amusement parks, including parks as big as Disney (this ride is identical to Animal Kingdom's Primeval Whirl), continue to punish riders with these mouse coasters is beyond us. Skip this one if you have neck problems or if you don't like quick stops and starts.

Screamer ★★½

APPEAL BY AGE	PRESCHOOL ★★★	GRADE SCHOOL ★★★	TEENS ★★
YOUNG ADULTS ★★★		OVER 30 ★★	SENIORS ★★

What it is Spire drop. **Scope and scale** Minor attraction. **Special comment** 42″ minimum height requirement to ride alone. **Authors' rating** ★★½. **Duration of ride** 2 minutes. **Cost** $3.

DESCRIPTION AND COMMENTS This is yet one more rendition of a central spire where a group of riders goes to the top and then free-falls down. This ride holds eight guests at a time, and its height is in between that of Old Town's former Frog Hopper and The Super Shot.

TOURING TIPS Perhaps the least thrilling ride in the park.

Screaming Eagle ★★★

APPEAL BY AGE	PRESCHOOL ★★★★	GRADE SCHOOL ★★★★	TEENS ★★★
YOUNG ADULTS ★★		OVER 30 ★½	SENIORS ★

What it is Buckets revolving around a central axis. **Scope and scale** Minor attraction. **Special comment** 46″ minimum height requirement. **Authors' rating** A real thrill if you learn the trick; ★★★. **Duration of ride** 2 minutes. **Cost** $3.

DESCRIPTION AND COMMENTS A typical carnival ride with a nice view. Rudders allow the riders to control their up-and-down movement as the buckets fly in circles around the central axis.

TOURING TIPS This attraction is slow-loading, so be prepared to wait if you want to ride. The key to livening up this ride is learning how to make the cables "snap" by swiftly shifting the rudder from one side to another while coming around the arc of the curve. If done skillfully, you can make your vehicle fly sideways or even backwards! Watch **youtu.be/cdx78_rgNH4** to see Seth demonstrating the proper technique.

SkyCoaster ★★★★½

APPEAL BY AGE	PRESCHOOL ★★	GRADE SCHOOL ★★★★	TEENS ★★★★½
YOUNG ADULTS ★★★★½		OVER 30 ★★★★	SENIORS ★★

What it is A 300-foot-tall pendulum. **Scope and scale** Headliner. **Special comment** 42″ minimum height requirement. **Authors' rating** Adrenaline; ★★★★½. **Duration of ride** 6 minutes. **Cost** $40 for single-person flight; $35 per person for double-person flight; $30 per person for triple-person flight; or $20 if you already have an armband.

DESCRIPTION AND COMMENTS SkyCoaster is one of the most thrilling and expensive rides in Orlando. Situated over a pond, SkyCoaster looks like the buttress of a large suspension bridge. At 300 feet, the giant pendulum ride is the tallest such attraction in the world; from the top, you can see Epcot.

After suiting up in a harness resembling a knee-length apron, you proceed to a wooden platform in the center of the pond. Ride operators then raise you up and attach your harness to two cables, one to pull you aloft and one from which to swing. You are attached so that your head is toward the ground—you fly on your stomach like Superman—and then you're pulled backward to the top of the far tower. At the end of a 3-2-1 countdown, you pull your own rip cord (yikes!) and plummet toward the earth. After a 130-foot free fall, the pendulum action takes over and gently swings you across the pond at speeds up to 80 miles per hour, depending on the weight of the passengers. The more weight, the faster the speed and therefore more back-and-forth trips, though 10 is considered the max. To disembark, you must grab a pole and stop yourself over the wooden platform.

TOURING TIPS Because SkyCoaster can handle only about 20 people an hour, the wait can be excruciating. We recommend coming during the middle of the day when crowds are fewer. The price is steep, but the three-person deal is not a bad call because increasing the mass of a pendulum increases its speed. If the ride were $15, we would ride it twice, but at $40 for a single rider for less than 1 minute of ride time, you'll need a disposable income. Remember, $40 is almost half the price of an entire day at Disney.

Surf's Up ★★

| APPEAL BY AGE | PRESCHOOL — | GRADE SCHOOL ★★★ | TEENS ★★★ |
| YOUNG ADULTS ★★★ | | OVER 30 ★★ | SENIORS ★½ |

What it is Surfing without the surf. **Scope and scale** Minor attraction. **Special comment** 42″ minimum height requirement to ride alone. **Authors' rating** ★★. **Duration of ride** 1½ minutes. **Cost** $3.

DESCRIPTION AND COMMENTS Riders stand atop a giant surfboard that, in much the same manner as a barroom electric bull, pitches up and down and goes in circles. *Note:* You are not in water.

TOURING TIPS It's kind of fun to try balancing, but roller board ninjas may find this tame.

Tilt A Whirl ★★

| APPEAL BY AGE | PRESCHOOL — | GRADE SCHOOL ★★★ | TEENS ★★★ |
| YOUNG ADULTS ★★½ | | OVER 30 ★★ | SENIORS ★½ |

What it is The same ride you've seen at every county fair. **Scope and scale** Minor attraction. **Special comment** 46″ minimum height requirement. **Authors' rating** ★★. **Duration of ride** 1½ minutes. **Cost** $3.

DESCRIPTION AND COMMENTS Riders sit in a car that is anchored in the middle so that it can whirl, and the platform on which the several cars ride then rotates around a central hub, while also rising and dropping.

TOURING TIPS We're not sure whether it's better to have something in your stomach or nothing because the centrifugal force can toss you side to side, even as you're going up and down.

Yo-Yo ★★★½

| APPEAL BY AGE | PRESCHOOL — | GRADE SCHOOL ★★★½ | TEENS ★★★½ |
| YOUNG ADULTS ★★★½ | | OVER 30 ★★★½ | SENIORS ★★★ |

What it is Swings that rise to 40 feet. **Scope and scale** Major attraction. **Special comment** 42″ minimum height requirement. **Authors' rating** ★★★½. **Duration of ride** 1½ minutes. **Cost** $3.

DESCRIPTION AND COMMENTS Riders are belted into swings attached to a pole that rises 40 feet, and then the swings twirl about.

TOURING TIPS If you don't care for heights, this isn't for you. If you'd rather not get a bird's-eye view of urban blight, it's not for you either.

PART TWELVE

INTERNATIONAL DRIVE

AT ITS INCEPTION, International Drive, also known as I-Drive, was nothing but a small road off I-4 serving local area hotels. After Disney came to town in 1971, developers were soon to follow. Now servicing Universal; SeaWorld; two smaller amusement parks; a host of roadside attractions; multitudes of hotels, eateries, bars, and malls; and the Orlando Convention Center, International Drive has become its own attraction—but not necessarily one that's easy to enjoy.

Many attractions found on International Drive are covered in other parts of this book (SeaWorld, Universal, Water Parks, Miniature Golf, and the like), but there are still more attractions that are worthwhile and noteworthy. The two amusement parks, Fun Spot America and Magical Midway, offer thrill rides, go-cart tracks, and top-notch arcades. WonderWorks, Ripley's Believe It or Not!, and Titanic: The Experience can be categorized as museums. Though all three cater to entertainment instead of learning, WonderWorks is ostensibly a science museum, Ripley's a museum of natural history, and Titanic a museum of living history. And iFly offers thrills you won't find at any of the parks. After years of being overshadowed by additions to the area's major attractions, I-Drive has begun booming recently with the completion of major new projects such as I-Drive 360 (home to the Orlando Eye observation wheel and other Merlin Entertainment exhibits) and the announcement of several more. Construction is expected to begin by late 2015 on Skyplex, a $300 million indoor entertainment and retail complex at the northeast corner of International Drive and Sand Lake Road, slated to open in 2017. The 1.5-million-square-foot Skyplex will be anchored by the world's largest Perkins Restaurant and the 570-foot-tall Skyscraper Polercoaster—which should set a new record as the world's tallest roller coaster—along with a 450-foot-high SkyFall drop tower and numerous indoor rides and games. Across the street, the "World's Largest Entertainment McDonald's" is being supersized to 19,000 square feet, and there are plans to upgrade street landscaping, add mass transit lanes, and possibly install a pedestrian overpass in the area.

There are so many options along International Drive that you may want to set aside more than a day just to explore this strip. Because International Drive contains an amalgamation of sideshow entertainments, each too large to fit into a major theme park but too small to occupy a full or even half day of touring, picking three to four attractions is both a pleasant and paced way to experience what's roadside.

PLAN AHEAD

IN CONTRAST TO OTHER FAMOUS ROADS, such as the Strip in Las Vegas, you won't want to spend your vacation time cruising up and down this 7-mile drag. Because International Drive is just four lanes wide (only occasionally six), the influx of tourists clogs the road, creating waits that can exceed 2 hours. Because the wait time, especially 8–10 a.m. and 4–8 p.m., is excessive, you should plan what sites you want to visit and what times you would like to visit them. Even if you plan your visits to avoid the rush hours, remember that traffic lights, pedestrians, and U-turning vehicles can make International Drive a hectic passage at anytime. Trying to turn left into the parking lot of your destination can be more than a little trying, especially as your day wears on. One solution: Check online maps to plot your destinations, and then map your route so that you only have to cross the oncoming lanes once.

But don't let the traffic dissuade you from visiting the attractions of your choice. If you stay in a hotel in the area, you should be able to become one of those pedestrians slowing down the cars. The I-Ride Trolley is also an option for short hops. The fee is nominal—$2 for a single ride, 25¢ for those over age 65, $1 for children ages 3–9 riding with a paying adult, free for children under age 3, a one-day pass for $5, and a three-day pass for $7. Schedules are available at **iridetrolley.com.**

Because many of the attractions on International Drive are open until midnight or later, visitors can spend their days at the major parks and, with any leftover energy, step out at night. Attractions will be more crowded in the evening than during midday, so you will need to schedule more time at night to experience them.

Most of the attractions along International Drive are enclosed, so when large thunderstorms threaten, many visitors choose to hop around International Drive instead of hoofing around major theme parks in the rain. Because crowds build during rainy days, make sure to arrive at least 30 minutes earlier than normal to any attraction you want to visit. Touring first thing in the morning is also advantageous and will keep both you and your umbrella dry.

GETTING THERE

INTERNATIONAL DRIVE extends from the Central Florida Parkway to a cul-de-sac at Orlando International Premium Outlets. You can reach International Drive from any exit between Exit 71 and Exit 75A off I-4. For attractions on the south half of International Drive (between Sand Lake Road and the convention center), Universal Boulevard parallels I-Drive and provides hassle-free access to venues on the road's east side, including I-Drive 360.

▮ ATTRACTIONS

Chocolate Kingdom ★★★½

APPEAL BY AGE PRESCHOOL ★★★★ GRADE SCHOOL ★★★★½ TEENS ★★★½
YOUNG ADULTS ★★★½ OVER 30 ★★★½ SENIOR ★★★

9901 Hawaiian Ct., Orlando; 2858 Florida Plaza Blvd., Kissimmee;
☎ 407-705-3475; **chocolatekingdom.com**

Hours Daily, 10:30 a.m.–6 p.m. Tours begin hourly at 11 a.m.; last tour is at 5 p.m. **Cost** $16.95 + tax for adults; $12.95 + tax for children ages 4–12; free for children age 3 and under. $10 Groupon tickets are often available.

DESCRIPTION AND COMMENTS Chocolate Kingdom is an hour-long guided walking tour through the rich past and delicious present of that most delectable of bittersweet treats. The museum-style exhibit traces the cocoa bean's path from sacred fruit (ancient Mesoamericans used it as money) and drink of kings (Spain's Princess Anne d'Autriche insisted that it be imported to France before she married King Louis XIII) to the candy bars we enjoy today. Colorful, well-lit displays, similar to what you might see in a children's science museum, illustrate each stage of the story, starting with primitive but effective methods still employed in the rain forests of Ecuador to harvest and ferment the raw cocoa, through the era of European conquest and the accompanying explosion of chocolate's popularity among the elite, and concluding with the tools used to process cocoa into the sweets we currently enjoy. The displays aren't too elaborate, but they do the job, and you'll probably be unable to read all the descriptive text before your guide moves on. If you've visited Hershey's Chocolate World in Pennsylvania, this is much more modest in scale (no dark rides with singing cows) and presents a more balanced perspective on the material; Milton Hershey is mentioned in passing as "not the first or the best, but fast and affordable."

At several points along your path, the guide plays video clips featuring Prince George the Good and his friendly dragon sidekick Meechu, who are on their way to present a pair of chocolate shoes to Princess Chocolina for her birthday. Meechu accidentally melts the shoes (which are displayed in a glass case near the tour's start), so our whole voyage is framed as helping George learn how to make a replacement pair. The computer animation in these clips is awful, with zombie-eyed unsynchronized lips, but the kids in our group seemed fairly entertained, and our tour guide maintained good humor during her awkward interactions with the canned dialogue. Toward the end of the tour, there's a diorama of the princess's castle (including a flowing river of liquid chocolate) made entirely from candy and a cheesy but diverting carnival game where guests catapult marshmallows into a plastic dragon's mouth.

Of course, it would be cruel for them to show you all this chocolate without getting to taste any. Luckily, the tour starts with a sample candied cocoa bean, followed by a Mayan-style dark cocoa with chili, which tastes like

Mexican mole sauce. Next, you get a chocolate-dipped marshmallow before entering the demonstration factory. There, you'll sample each stage of the chocolate-making process, from freshly cracked cocoa nibs to the unsweetened chocolate liqueur (sorry, it isn't actually alcoholic). For the grand finale, guests are given three chocolate shoes—each a little larger than a fun-size candy bar—in white, milk, and dark chocolate. If you spend an extra $6, they'll make a custom half-pound chocolate bar right in front of you, mixing items such as pretzels, nuts, coffee, or bacon into the base of your choice; give your creation 5 minutes or so to cool before you chow down.

The lobby gift shop sells a selection of individually priced sweets, along with edible oddities such as chocolate wine and Cocoa Cola; you don't need a tour ticket to buy a treat and see the cocoa trees growing inside a room-size terrarium. Chocolate Kingdom was created by the Schaked family, German-Argentinean immigrants who founded the worldwide chain of Schakolad gourmet chocolatiers, so you know the house-made products here are first class. There are two Chocolate Kingdom locations, one in Kissimmee next to Fun Spot and the other off International Drive across from the Orange County Convention Center. The I-Drive location is slightly larger, but the content and experience are essentially the same at both.

CoCo Key Water Resort ★★★½

APPEAL BY AGE	PRESCHOOL ★★★★	GRADE SCHOOL ★★★★	TEENS ★★★½
YOUNG ADULTS ★★★	OVER 30 ★★½	SENIORS ★½	

7400 International Dr., Orlando; ☎ 406-351-2626 or 877-875-4681; **cocokeyorlando.com**

Hours During peak summer and fall months, generally 11 a.m.–9 p.m.; winter, 11 a.m.–5 p.m., with occasional closures or longer hours. Check the website for exact times on the day of your visit. **Cost** Monday–Thursday, $25.95 + tax; $21.95 + tax for Florida residents. Friday–Sunday, $26.95 + tax for all. Free for children under 36″.

DESCRIPTION AND COMMENTS This attraction is an unusual hybrid. The current owners bought a nondescript two-story motel that had a small pool, and in 2010, on the land behind this existing space, they opened a miniature water park available to non-hotel guests. Day guests stop at the reception desk in the lobby, buy a wristband good for admission to the water park, and set off to paddle about two free-form pools or choose from an assortment of slides and aquatic playthings.

Minnows Lagoon is aimed at the littlest visitors and has a walk-in entry at one end and three short, straight slides and one gently curving slide at the other end. The "deep" end here is just 3 feet. As with all of the water park pools—but not the plain pool just behind the lobby—there are plenty of watchful lifeguards. This pool is under a canopy, so kids and parents can enjoy the warm air but not the harsh sun. It's also fenced off from the other pools, so tots won't wander off.

The next pool is just a few feet away, in the **Coral Reef Cove** area. Part of it is under the same canopy as Minnows Lagoon, while the other part is open to the sun. The pool has a couple of water cannons for squirting fun and the **Cyclone** body slide, an enclosed corkscrew affair. The minimum height for the slide is 48 inches; pool depth is up to 5 feet.

The final area, **Parrot's Perch,** holds the exotic thrill slides. First are three large corkscrew slides: Two are fully open, while one is enclosed until the exit.

To access the entrances to these slides, guests must climb about 15–20 feet up a fancy multistory structure. This area also features a couple of mini-slides for more-timid users, some water cannons, and areas to duck in and out of on the open-sided perch. All of the slides, water cannons, and aquatic toys are enclosed in a water-play area topped by a giant bucket that dumps up to 400 gallons of water every 5 minutes on those below. The big slides have minimum height requirements of 36–40 inches.

The final elements at CoCo are three *very* impressive slides that are positioned side by side. On the **Boomerango,** one or two people ride a raft through an open tube that sends the raft back up a broad, steep, open wall—sort of like the half-pipe courses that skateboarders and snowboarders ride. Then gravity sends the raft back down and into the straight exit chute. The experience lasts about 25 seconds. It takes much longer to haul the raft back to the launch platform, about 45 feet high. Boomerango has a 48-inch minimum height requirement. Leaving from the same platform are riders in the one- and two-person inner tubes on the **Surfer Splash** slide. They go through a full 360-degree turn in the enclosed slide and then complete another 180 degrees before coming to the exit straightaway. The ride, which lasts about 30 seconds, has a 42-inch minimum height requirement. The tallest slide here is **Over the Falls.** Leaving from a platform about 60 feet up, single body-sliders head through an enclosed tube that has a corkscrew and other turns before exiting. This slide takes about 35 seconds and has a 40-inch minimum height requirement.

The water park area has numerous tables and chairs for adults who want to watch the little ones splash about or need to rest from their own exertions. There's also a full bar, a Pizza Hut, a burger-style grill, and an arcade.

CSI: The Experience ★★★½

APPEAL BY AGE	PRESCHOOL	–	GRADE SCHOOL ★★	TEENS ★★★½
YOUNG ADULTS ★★★★	OVER 30 ★★★★½		SENIORS ★★★★	

7220 International Dr., Orlando; ☎ 407-226-7220; **csiexhibit.com**

Hours Monday–Thursday, 10 a.m.–6 p.m.; Friday–Saturday, 10 a.m.–9 p.m.; Sunday, 10 a.m.–8 p.m. Last admission is 1 hour before closing. **Cost** $19.99 + tax for adults; $12.99 + tax for children ages 6–11. Add $5 to play a second crime scene and $7.50 more to play all three.

DESCRIPTION AND COMMENTS This is a clever high-tech mystery game based on the wildly popular *CSI* TV series, which, at its peak, pulled in 73.8 million viewers worldwide (and spawned a plethora of spin-offs).

You are a rookie investigator assigned to study one of three murder scenes. Arriving at a diorama of realistic items, you mark your observations on the printed form you've been given. Then you head off to six specialty labs—blood, fingerprints, DNA, and so on—and the morgue, learning to what and whom your evidence leads. Five suspects are presented for each murder. The lab stations are spread about the exhibit space, and some include videos of actors from the original series explaining how various evidence is studied.

The deck is stacked in your favor: As you sit in front of a touch screen at each lab, you are asked to choose among options of a scenario involving your crime scene. If you guess incorrectly, a message on the screen gently suggests that you touch the BACK button and try again.

Finally, you go to a touch screen showing a video of William Petersen, the actor who portrayed original *CSI* lab boss Gil Grissom (did you know that the pilot aired in October 2000?). Here you present the findings you made when you selected choices at the labs. He'll let you know if you are correct. Then you can type in the special agent ID number at the top of your printed form, and (for an additional $3 fee) print out a CSI completion certificate or souvenir photo.

This is a clever gimmick, but there are a couple of matters that interfere with the fun. Though the attraction attendants, who are quick to help you once you start your case, do try to space out the arrival of new players, it doesn't take much to cause you to wait for the next lab station called for on your printed form. In this case, you can find another lab, and then double back. And because the monitors force-feed you the right answer by sending you back if you pick incorrectly, that lessens the puzzle-solving aspect, which should be the best part of this game. It would be better if the touch screens perhaps corrected you only once in the case of a wrong selection on a lab screen. Even making a few wrong choices, most guests spend less than an hour completing their (cue The Who, please) Crime Scene Investigation. If you've already experienced CSI in Las Vegas, the Mall of America, or any of the many museums it's traveled to since 2007, there is nothing new or improved about this installation, and some wear and tear is evident on the sets and props (especially the outfits that guests are supposed to wear). Of the three scenarios, the consensus is that #2 ("Who Got Served?") is the most interesting, while #3 is the weakest. Sharing the building with CSI are a couple small exhibit spaces. On the same floor is a hall that hosts traveling museum-style displays, such as a collection of (mostly malfunctioning) model machines made from Leonardo DaVinci's designs. Upstairs is a room of so-called 3-D art, which are simply flat backdrops that look vaguely dimensional when you pose for a photo in front of one. Don't get suckered into paying anything extra for either, as they are not worth more than a few minutes of your time.

Fun Spot America ★★★★

APPEAL BY AGE PRESCHOOL ★★★ **GRADE SCHOOL** ★★★½ **TEENS** ★★★★½ **YOUNG   ADULTS** ★★★★ **OVER   30** ★★★★ **SENIORS** ★★★

555 Del Verde Way, Orlando; ☎ 407-363-3867; **fun-spot.com**

Hours Peak season: Daily, 10 a.m.–midnight. Off-season: Monday–Thursday, 2 p.m.–midnight; Friday–Sunday, 10 a.m.–midnight. **Cost** Single-Day Pass Over 54" Tall, $44.95 + tax; Single-Day Pass Under 54" Tall, $34.95 + tax; season pass (good until December 31), $75–$149 + tax, depending on time of year purchased.

DESCRIPTION AND COMMENTS Just off I-Drive and visible by its Ferris wheel and ginormous swing ride is Fun Spot America, an old-style amusement park with the best go-cart tracks in Orlando, carnival rides, and arcades. There is both free parking and free admission, so you can wander through the site and peruse the attractions before you purchase armbands. Rechargeable Fun Cards can also be used to pay for rides individually, ranging from $3 for carnival and kiddie rides to $9 for the coasters and go-carts. You get a bonus $4 for every $20 that you put on a card (which retains its value indefinitely), and credits can be used at Fun Spot's Orlando or Kissimmee (see page 309) locations. Discounted armbands may be purchased in advance at local Walgreens drugstores.

Fun Spot America was tripled in size, to about 15 acres, in the spring of 2013. Formerly known as Fun Spot Action Park, the enlarged venue added two roller coasters (one 64 feet tall; the other 80 feet), a double-decker carousel, and a 250-foot-tall **SkyCoaster** swing. Further plans call for a small water park on the site.

WHITE LIGHTNING Orlando's best (and only) wooden roller coaster has the familiar clack-clack-clack as the cars climb that first 80-foot-high hill. The six two-passenger cars of White Lightning take 25 seconds to climb the first hill, which builds your anticipation. The reward is quick and constant, over a track measuring 2,036 feet long. Traveling through about a half-dozen small drops, your butt will be off the seat—but restrained by both a seat belt and lap bar—for about 15 seconds. The coaster has no inversions but reaches speeds of about 44 miles per hour.

As with all of Central Florida's blockbuster rides, you'll want to head here when the park opens, or at least when you first arrive. One of the advantages of Fun Spot America is that the cadre of ride attendants will let riders remain in place for another spin on the coaster as long as those waiting to board can be accommodated. However, if you rode in the front car, you will be asked to move to another one to make room for those waiting. The coaster has a 46-inch minimum height requirement. With its unusual double-down/double-up track design, thrilling vertical turnaround, and relentless pacing until the final brakes, White Lightning is one of our favorite coasters in any Florida park and is a must-do for any thrill ride enthusiast.

FREEDOM FLYER This suspended roller coaster has a 48-inch minimum height requirement to ride alone; children 36–47 inches must be accompanied by an adult. Because you are seated with your feet dangling, there's the added thrill of worrying that your legs will smash into some of the supports—they won't.

This is a moderately exciting version of the suspended metal coaster, on which riders sit beneath an overhead railing but have no floor beneath their feet. There are no inversions but plenty of whipsawing turns to the right and then quickly back to the left. True to the ride's name, the comfortable safety restraints give your torso plenty of room to move around during your flight, while your bottom half stays securely seated.

Freedom Flyer reinforces the thrill ride truism: The view from the front seats is by far the best. Without that openness, you are constantly facing the backs of the chairs in front of you and lose the thrills that arise when you see what you are about to plunge or swerve to. However, riders in the back row pull pleasantly powerful g-forces during the finale helix.

GO-KARTS A prime draw at Fun Spot is the go-carts. Fun Spot has concrete tracks, which allow for both a faster and smoother ride. Those tracks also allow Fun Spot patrons to experience go-carts rain or shine. There are four tracks here, plus one for kiddies, and collectively they are better than any of the other area tracks.

The five tracks are the Quad Helix, Conquest, Commander, Thrasher, and Cadet, a short oval track located in the park's Kid Spot section. The **Cadet** requires kids to be at least 4 years old and 42 inches tall. All the other tracks are adjacent to one another and are color-coded to make their routes easier to distinguish. All tracks, except the Cadet, have 4-minute ride times.

The yellow **Quad Helix** is the longest track at 1,600 feet. As the name indicates, the three-story track comprises four corkscrews, or helixes. The lack of long straightaways or very sharp turns makes it difficult to pass other go-carts, but if you're not feeling very competitive, the banked turns and elevated layout are a good use of your ticket. As with all the tracks, the cars are virtually identical mechanically, meaning only the driver's skills can advance his cart past others. Riders on this and the other major tracks must be at least 54 inches tall to drive; kids under 54 inches can ride shotgun with an adult in a two-seater cart.

The tallest, steepest descent at Fun Spot is found at the climax of the blue **Conquest** track, which climbs a hill to 28 feet high, but with underpowered go-carts, height is not an advantage. The dawdling ascent through the long corkscrew is rewarded with a "Florida ski jump" as you crest the course's apex, followed by a fast but short downhill leg, and the rest of the track winds slowly back to the starting gate.

The **Commander** track, its borders painted green, was rebuilt during the park's expansion to be the highest track here, reaching 45 feet above the ground. Fun Spot calls Commander its most extreme track, and the unpredictable mix of road course–style hairpin turns and steep elevation changes makes it the most competitive of the park's multilevel courses.

The **Thrasher** track is red and, if you're competitive, the best racetrack in Orlando. The track is completely flat and packed with hairpin turns and short straightaways. The variety of angles in the course will both test your skill as a driver and allow you the opportunity to pass other carts. The cars used here are all single-rider (no riders under 54 inches permitted), with beefier engines than the other tracks; if you tap the brakes just right, you can pull off a power slide around the corners. Besides the intense ride, the unassuming flat track will have shorter lines because most guests will be drawn toward the multistoried Quad Helix and Conquest tracks.

SKYCOASTER Visible from a fair part of Orlando are the twin steel towers that form an inverted V—the guts of the **SkyCoaster.** One, two, or three persons at a time pay to be snugged into a sort of nylon bag secured by metal cables, while another cable lifts the bag(s) to the top of the towers—250 feet high. One rider pulls the release, and the securing cable lets the rider(s) swing down and forward, over a fountain in the middle of Fun Spot. The rise to the top takes about 45 seconds; the to-and-fro swinging after the free fall usually lasts 60–90 seconds, depending on the weight of the rider(s). SkyCoaster, which has a minimum height requirement of 42 inches, costs extra: $40 for a solo flyer, $35 per person for two people, and $30 per person for three people. If you already have an armband, the ride is discounted to $20 per rider. The moments waiting before you pull the ripcord, and the initial free fall until the cable goes taut, are sheer terror, but once you are swinging, you can admire the scenery while practicing your Superman pose. For us, it was a once—but only once—in-a-lifetime experience.

OTHER RIDES The older rides at Fun Spot are generic—you've seen them at carnival and state fair midways. These familiar rides usually spin you around a center axis for about 3 minutes but do not invert you. They are the **Scrambler, Tilt A Whirl, Enterprise** (two riders to an enclosed bucket first head in a circle until the center post rises straight up, so the circle also becomes an up-and-down ride), and the **Paratrooper** (riders sit in a bucket suspended from an overhead arm, and the ride goes forward and back, your car climbing and dipping and turning from side to side—it's rather unsettling, actually). **Space Invader,** a more recent addition, is the twin to Fun Spot Kissimmee's Hot Seat ride. The giant pendulum swings victims back and forth past 180 degrees, forcing them to alternate facing sky and earth until their lunch is liberated. **Screamer** is a modest-size drop tower that repeatedly lifts and releases riders, whose feet dangle free; think of it as a theme-free little sibling to Disney's Tower of Terror. The fastest of the carny rides is the **Rip Curl,** where a train of cars roars in a circle over a couple of hills as a DJ sounds a siren and an 18-wheeler's horn, shouts encouragement, and plays really loud rock music.

There are also bumper cars in a small arena, bumper boats in a small pool, a 21-bucket Ferris wheel named **Revolver,** a beautifully painted two-story carousel, and a 25-foot-high **Fun Slide,** on which riders sit atop burlap cloths to slide down the three chutes.

New in 2015, **Gator Spot** gives guests a bite-size sample of the Gatorland attraction (see Part 4) within the boundaries of Fun Spot for a modest $6 entry fee. This small expansion adds a number of small pools stocked with baby and adolescent alligators that you can feed for about $1 per turkey dog. There's also a couple full-size gators, including one who lived in the basement of a New York high school for three decades, along with a handful of exotic birds. The star attraction is Bouya Blan (Cajun Creole for "White Fog"), an exceedingly rare white—not albino—gator that is the largest of his kind in the world. He doesn't do much more than sit silently inside his glass enclosure and wait for his feeding, but when you're that big, that's all you need to do. Guided tours are held four times a day and are included with admission; you can get an up close encounter with a baby gator or blue-tongued skink. Gator Spot is just enough to satisfy most visitors' reptile itch, though it may spark some kids' desire to visit the full-size attraction.

KIDDIE RIDES Also included with armband purchases (or à la carte at $3 per ride) are about a dozen rides for very young children. Located in the **Kid Spot,** these rides are recommended for kids ages 2–5 and have minimum height requirements ranging from 24 inches tall (the **Super Trucks** ride, in which the vehicles go around on tracks, with no directional control by the young riders) to 42 inches. The tiny area contains a set of miniature teacups, a carousel, a kiddie swing, a kiddie train (five to seven loops around a central fence painted to resemble a building), and a few other minor rides. On Saturday nights, the Power2Improv comedy troupe performs a free family-friendly interactive show using Muppet-style puppets.

ARCADES Fun Spot also boasts two **arcades**. While the downstairs arcade houses newer arcade games, as well as Skee-Ball, football and mini-basketball tosses, and air hockey tables, the upstairs arcade is a collection of vintage games ranging from *The Simpsons* and *Tekken* to classics such as *Pac-Man, Defender,* and *Centipede.* Many of the games dispense virtual tickets stored on your park pass, redeemable for cheaply made prizes.

When the video games wear you out, you can pick up typical fast food at the snack bar downstairs: pizza, double-bacon cheeseburgers, soft drinks, and several brands of beer. Daily happy hours 8–9 p.m. and 10–11 p.m. offer $3 brews, and the $6 souvenir soda with unlimited refills is a good deal. You can also get Dole pineapple soft-serve here for a lot less than you can get it at Disney.

THEME PARK CONNECTION There's no emporium-style souvenir super-store at Fun Spot, nor do the go-carts exit through the gift shop, but there is one very unusual spending opportunity near the main entrance. **Theme Park Connection (☎ 407-284-1934; themeparkconnection.com)** stocks a selection of one-of-a-kind objects—including signs, props, costumes, and even furniture—that were salvaged from Orlando theme parks and actual movie sets. In addition to Disneyana, it also specializes in NAS-CAR collectibles. The Fun Spot location—which doubles as the studio for *Orlando Attractions Magazine: The Show* (**attractionsmagazine.com**), a weekly program about the area parks—holds only a small fraction of Theme Park Connection's vast inventory. True collectors will want to check out its warehouse at 2160 Premier Row in Orlando, which is open to the public Monday–Friday, 10 a.m.–5 p.m., and Saturday, 10 a.m.–3 p.m. You could come home with a piece of your favorite ride.

Hard Knocks ★★★★

APPEAL BY AGE	PRESCHOOL –	GRADE SCHOOL ★★★½	TEENS ★★★★½
YOUNG ADULTS ★★★★½	OVER 30 ★★★★	SENIORS ★★½	

9101 International Dr., Orlando; 5707 Dot Com Court, Ste. 1025, Oveido;
☎ 855-926-6228 or 407-359-9091; **indoorwar.com**

Hours Monday–Thursday, 2–11 p.m.; Friday, 2 p.m.–midnight; Saturday, noon–midnight; Sunday, noon–10 p.m. (Hours vary at Oveido location.) **Cost** With a 1-year membership ($6): 4 missions for $24; 8 missions for $34. Without membership: 3 missions for $25; 6 missions for $37.

DESCRIPTION AND COMMENTS Laser tag was all the rage 30 years ago, but franchises like Q-Zar and Photon have long since gone the way of Betamax tapes. Orlando still has a few arenas integrated into larger family-entertainment centers, such as the ones at WonderWorks and Whirly Dome, but two Hard Knocks locations are the town's largest facilities dedicated to blasting your buddies with harmless light beams.

Rather than a fantasy sci-fi setting, Hard Knocks battles take place in real-world environments modeled after industrial warehouses and office complexes, filled with stacked shipping crates and cubicle mazes. And you won't be running around with Buck Rogers ray guns; these infrared weapons accurately mimic shotguns, Mac-10s, M-16s, and other authentic firearms, down to the heft of metal in your hand and tactile click when you reload. Each weapon includes a digital display that tracks your ammo supply and shuts down temporarily when an opponent scores a hit on your sensor-studded vest.

Hard Knocks bills itself as a combat simulation rather than a game, and going in with guns blazing is usually the quickest way to get (virtually) killed. More than 75 different mission scenarios are available, each with its own aggressive name (such as Onslaught and Regulator), story line, and game-play objectives, which can include capturing the flag, defending your base, or simply annihilating the other team. Each mission lasts approximately 10 minutes. Strategize with your comrades-in-arms and choose your shots carefully to come out on top. (Players must be at least 8 years old or 50 inches tall.)

Whether you grew up with laser tag or are one of today's generation of first-person shooter fans, an hour of indoor combat should get your heart pumping and satisfy your primitive blood lust without actually spilling any. Hard Knocks isn't inexpensive, but it's the closest you'll come to starring in your own war movie without enlisting. There are two locations; the original is near the University of Central Florida and has free parking and slightly larger arenas but shorter operating hours. The newer one is on I-Drive at Pointe Orlando, where parking costs $3 for the first hour, up to $9 for a full day.

I-Drive 360 featuring The Orlando Eye ★★★★

APPEAL BY AGE PRESCHOOL ★★★ **GRADE SCHOOL** ★★★½ **TEENS** ★★★½
YOUNG ADULTS ★★★★ **OVER 30** ★★★★ **SENIORS** ★★★★
8445 International Dr., Orlando; **i-drive360.com, officialorlandoeye.com**

Hours The Orlando Eye: Monday–Thursday, noon–10 p.m.; Friday–Saturday, noon–midnight; Sunday, 10 a.m.–10 p.m. Hours for other attractions may vary. Complex: Daily, 10 a.m.–2 a.m. **Cost** One attraction (Orlando Eye, Madame Tussauds, or Sea Life Aquarium): $25 + tax for adults; $34 + tax for children ages 3–12. All three attractions: $49 + tax for adults; $44 + tax for children ages 3–12. All three plus one-day Legoland admission with transportation: $99 for adults; $94 for children ages 3–12. 25%–50% discounts available online and through AAA. Other attractions priced individually.

DESCRIPTION AND COMMENTS Rising from the ashes of the long-defunct Mercado shopping center as a new icon of Orlando's skyline, I-Drive 360—anchored by the unmissable 400-foot-tall Orlando Eye observation wheel—was the biggest thing to hit International Drive in a decade when it opened in 2015. The attractive new entertainment complex integrates three headlining attractions from Merlin Entertainment, with a handful of independently operated diversions, a diverse range of dining options, and (best of all) seven stories of free parking, all surrounded by inviting green space and active water features.

We've noticed a large number of international visitors enjoying the area with their families as if it were a public park, perhaps reflecting Merlin's popularity with European guests (it's the No. 2 attractions company in the world, behind Disney but ahead of Universal). If you take in all three Merlin offerings, along with another attraction and maybe a meal, you can easily fill an afternoon or evening here. And if you are planning to visit Legoland (another Merlin property), you can park here for free and take the daily scheduled bus for $5; see Part 3 for details.

ORLANDO EYE The star of the show here is the Orlando Eye, which towers above everything in its neighborhood and is easily visible to drivers on I-4 and the Beachline Expressway. The same team that built the iconic London Eye observation wheel is behind this one, and while the view of I-Drive isn't quite as inspiring as the Thames River, you can see clear to the coast if the clouds are in your favor.

The experience starts with waiting to pose in front of a backdrop for an extra-cost souvenir photo (a common theme at all three Merlin attractions). That's followed by a standing-room-only 3-D preshow (accompanied by obligatory water sprays and scents) featuring flyover footage of Central Florida sights such as Lake Eola, Gatorland, and even Universal Studios' Diagon Alley; some of the shots are sharp, but others suffers from shoddy stereo conversion.

Finally, you're ready to board the big wheel, which never ceases its slow rotation; you'll be given the cue when to briskly board as it glides past the loading platform. Inside you find some slender benches, but most passengers will press up as close to the floor-to-ceiling windows as they dare for the best possible picture taking. Once you're away, soothing music is played, and a pleasant voice narrates the sights as you rise above the surrounding structures. The ride itself takes less than 20 minutes, with only about half that spent near the apex of the 400-foot wheel. From the top, you can make out Spaceship Earth from Epcot and Hogwarts Castle in Islands of Adventure, but the view is mostly of I-Drive strip malls and undeveloped land around the Orange County Convention Center.

The capsules are air-conditioned, weatherproof, and fully ADA compliant. Companion animals and wheelchairs up to 36 inches wide are allowed, as are oxygen tanks, with advance notice, but this obviously isn't advised for those with a fear of heights or enclosed spaces. Be aware that the Eye shuts down whenever lightning approaches, which is pretty much daily during summer afternoons. If it's closed for weather during your visit, you'll get a rain check good for 30 days. Call ☎ 407-270-8644 for the wheel's current operational status.

MADAME TUSSAUDS By now, it seems that every major city has a Madame Tussauds wax museum, and now Orlando has joined other world-class cities such as Las Vegas and Bangkok with its own collection of creepily lifelike celebrity statues. If you haven't visited a Tussauds exhibit recently, the 150-plus-year tradition of presenting realistic replicas of notable figures behind velvet ropes has given way to a hands-on experience, in which guests are encouraged to not only look but also fondle the faux famous folks.

The museum begins with a nod to Florida's past, featuring Ponce de Leon, and then proceeds through a grab bag of historical greats, from Abraham Lincoln and Martin Luther King Jr. to Andy Warhol and Albert Einstein (marvel at the masses of individually applied hairs!). Many of these icons appear at other Tussauds locations, but there is an exclusive Walt Disney figure, who was strangely sculpted with Nicholas Cage–style crazy eyes.

About a third of the way through, you'll find a gallery giving background on Tussauds origins (accompanied by a mostly inaudible expository video, a common feature throughout the exhibits), along with a counter where you can have your hand cast in hot wax for $15.

After this point, the exhibit abandons history for a hit parade of pop-culture celebs. If you've ever wanted to see Shaq's armpit hair or Miley Cyrus's ear tattoos from a millimeter away, here is your chance. Interactive touch screens and informational plaques abound, but the real appeal is snapping selfies with stars who would rather sic security on you in the real world. Orlando's Tussauds isn't as cramped as some other outposts, with plenty of breathing room between figures, but the sets are mostly simple printed backdrops, and misfocused lights leave some stars in shadow. Orlando's Tussauds also has no haunted dungeon or 4-D film like other locations, leaving the Hollywood A-List Party room to serve as a somewhat lackluster finale; on the plus side, there's nothing scary or objectionable that parents with young kids will want to skip. While you could rush through in 15 minutes, a thorough Tussauds tour will take nearly any hour, longer than the other two attractions here. We rate this Tussauds higher than its sister attraction at Vegas's Venetian, and slightly behind the one on New York City's 42nd Street.

SEA LIFE AQUARIUM The final Merlin attraction is a walk-through aquarium engineered with preteen ichthyologists in mind. The tour begins with an animated preshow of talking sea creatures projected onto a domed ceiling; unfortunately, poor acoustics and thick accents make it mostly unintelligible. The aquarium itself represents regions from around the world, with the Atlantic Ocean tank alone holding 192,000 gallons of salt water. There are no dolphins or orcas here, but there are plenty of tropical fish, sharks, sea turtles, giant octopuses, and a luminous wall full of jellyfish that glow with guest-controlled colored lights. Guest pathways wind through underwater caves, ancient shipwrecks, and sunken cities. At numerous points, indentations or overhangs built into the aquariums allow intimate fish-eye views (if you're able to crouch down), while touch screens and trivia stations provide an element of interactive intellectual stimulation.

The highlight of Sea Life is a 360-degree underwater tunnel, where we watched giddy grown-ups get down on all fours to get a better view of the sharks swimming underfoot. After that, the touch-tank finale feels anticlimactic; the spiny sea urchins and starfish provided are unpleasant to pet, but the stingrays (popular in other aquariums' touch tanks) are kept out of reach.

Scenic theming is well executed with some nice faux rockwork and lighting effects, resembling a less elaborate version of Shark Reef at Las Vegas's Mandalay Bay, though unfinished ceilings and flat wall graphics indicate that it isn't quite Disney quality. If you want something slightly more educational than Epcot's Living Seas but are uncomfortable with attending SeaWorld, Sea Life is a mammal-free way to spend 30 minutes. For an even more in-depth experience, the 25-minute Behind the Scenes guided tour (additional $5 per person) will show you how Sea Life cares for and feeds its scaly staff; see the box office for tour departures, which are generally scheduled every 45 minutes 10:45 a.m.–6:15 p.m.

OTHER I-DRIVE 360 ATTRACTIONS The chief non-Merlin attraction at I-Drive 360 is **Skeletons: Animals Unveiled! (skeletonmuseum.com)**. This self-guided osteology exhibit—that's science talk for bone museum—features the mortal remains of more than 400 creatures from every genus and continent, reassembled in poses that would be lifelike, save for the absent skin. You may have seen similar displays at a natural history museum, but the atmosphere here is a bit less stuffy and more appealing to tweens, with explanatory signage written in accessible language. Most of the specimens on display are animals, and almost all are authentic, though a handful are marked as replicas, and some human remains—including those of an achondroplastic dwarf, and a victim of kyphosis (hunchback disease)—are tastefully presented. The museum isn't too large, but if you take your time reading the information (and watching the gruesome video demonstrating how bugs are used to clean flesh from fresh bones), you'll kill nearly an hour here. The gift shop is stocked with unusual jewelry and educational toys, many made from real bones, bugs, or other preserved critters. Hours are 10 a.m.–10 p.m. daily, last entry at 9 p.m. Admission is $19.99 + tax for adults, $12.99 + tax for kids ages 3–11, free for children 2 and under; discounts are available at the website and through Groupon.

Also at I-Drive 360, **Arcade City** boasts an up-to-date collection of video games and carnival-style redemption games, including the *Star Wars Battle Pod* and *Candy Crush Saga*. For a more adult form of entertainment, **Tin Roof** is a later-day juke joint with live music and a Southern-influenced menu, while

Cowgirls Rockbar is the home of Orlando's only mechanical bull and a bevy of sassy barmaids.

In 2016, a new **StarFlyer** swing ride is scheduled to be constructed next door to I-Drive 360 in the adjoining complex (recently rechristened **Vue at 360**) that currently houses the Kings Bowling alley and Sleuths mystery dinner theater. At 420 feet, it will be the tallest such attraction in the world (the one at Magical Midway is only 230 feet tall), putting 24 riders at a time at nearly eye level with the top of the Orlando Eye. A 3- to 4-minute ride should run about $10 per person.

iFLY Orlando ★★★½

APPEAL BY AGE PRESCHOOL ★★★★ GRADE SCHOOL ★★★★ TEENS ★★★½ YOUNG ADULTS ★★★ OVER 30 ★★★½ SENIORS ★★★

6805 Visitor Cir., Orlando; ☎ 407-903-1150 or ☎ 800-759-3861; **iflyorlando.com**

Hours Daily, 10 a.m.–10:30 p.m. **Cost** $59.95 + tax for visitors age 3 and up; $130.86 for 2 people; $271.89 + tax for up to 5 people.

DESCRIPTION AND COMMENTS iFLY Orlando is a high-velocity vertical wind tunnel that attempts to re-create the thrill of skydiving. The blue-and-red tunnel resembles a large spaceship. When not floating tourists, the tunnel is used for skydiving team-member training to coordinate stunts before they leap. Unlike jumping out of a plane, "skydiving" in the tunnel works by having five large fans at the top of the tunnel suck air upward. The balanced suction creates a wind tunnel for you to float around in, and though you won't experience the acceleration of free-falling from thousands of feet, you will be able to float around in relative safety. Though the price is steep, at $59.95 plus tax per person for only 2 minutes of actual flight time, it is still much cheaper than actually skydiving. Due to the nature of the activity, there are some strict restrictions for participants. You must weigh less than 230 pounds if you are under 6 feet tall, and less than 250 pounds if you are taller than 6 feet. If you are pregnant or have heart trouble, back issues, or a dislocated shoulder, this isn't for you. There is no set minimum age or height, but children under age 18 will need the signature of a parent or legal guardian on the waiver form to fly.

The flight chamber is enclosed in plexiglass, so if you arrive a few minutes early or are waiting for a member of your group to fly, you can watch other guests float around, and if you are lucky, you might see an instructor performing a few aerial stunts.

After you are suited up in the proper equipment, including a helmet, a flight suit, elbow and knee pads, earplugs, and proper footwear (if you forgot it), you proceed to the preflight briefing room and watch a video on basic body positioning and hand signals. After the video, the instructor gives every student a chance to practice the in-flight pose. Remember, once you're in the flight chamber, you have only 2 minutes of flight time, so optimize your flight time by memorizing the hand signals (necessary because the wind tunnel is too loud for speech) and asking any questions beforehand.

When entering the chamber, put your hands by your head—as if you're surrendering—and slowly lean forward until the air catches you. Your 2-minute flight time will be divided into 1-minute sections. While you wait for your next turn, you'll have time to reflect on what adjustments you'll need to make to improve your next flight.

Flying in the wind tunnel is very difficult. Unless your body posture is perfect, you will careen toward the glass or end up face-first in the netting on the bottom. Thankfully, the instructors are very helpful and hands-on, keeping you from running headlong into the glass. But don't worry; if you can't get the hang of flying in 2 minutes and fail to find the right position, the instructor can take hold of you and fly you both into the air.

Safety in the wind tunnel is important, so avoid sudden movements. You'll find that very subtle changes in your posture can affect how you are flying. You don't have to worry about flying too high in the tunnel; you will not get sucked up into any massive fan. Go as high as you want to—if you are able—and for the best flight, watch and follow the instructor's hand signals.

Before leaving, consider tipping your instructor. Tipping is not expected, but with an instructor in any sport, a "tip for tips" policy is generally a good practice. If you find your first taste of iFly addictive, experienced flyers can buy blocks of air times starting at $79.99 plus tax for 5 minutes, and up to $645 plus tax for a solid hour to share with a dozen friends.

Magical Midway ★★½

APPEAL BY AGE	PRESCHOOL ★★	GRADE SCHOOL ★★½	TEENS ★★½
YOUNG ADULTS ★★	OVER 30 ★½	SENIORS ★	

7001 International Dr.; ☎ 407-370-5353; **magicalmidway.com**

Hours Vary, but usually daily, noon–midnight. **Cost** $3 each for midway rides; $7 for go-carts and the Starflyer; $25 for the Sling Shot; $25 + tax for 3-hour armband, which includes 3 hours of unlimited go-carts and midway rides (but not the Sling Shot); $32 + tax for all-day armband, which includes all-day, unlimited access to the go-carts and midway rides (but not the Sling Shot). Coupons are available on the website.

DESCRIPTION AND COMMENTS Near the north end of I-Drive, well after WonderWorks but before iFLY, are the hard-to-miss signs for Magical Midway. The enormous towers of both the Sling Shot and Starflyer make it easy to find. Parking at the Midway is free but minimal. You can park across the street, but be wary of rubbernecking drivers while crossing I-Drive traffic. The I-Drive Trolley is also a sound option for arriving (**iridetrolley.com**).

Magical Midway's location, front and center on International Drive, draws many visitors, and their wear on the facility is apparent. The heavy traffic in the amusement park also makes riding the attractions during evening visits tedious at best.

Fortunately, the park offers free admission, so you can take a look around before you decide to purchase any wristbands or tickets.

GO-CARTS Magical Midway has three go-cart tracks: Avalanche, Alpine, and Fast Track. You must be at least 12 years old and 58 inches tall to drive the single-seat carts, while the two-seat carts require the driver to be at least 16 years old and 58 inches tall with a valid driver's license and the passenger to be at least 5 years old and 36 inches tall. The two-seat carts are available only on the Avalanche and the Alpine tracks.

On the multistory **Avalanche** and **Alpine** tracks, be prepared for a very bumpy ride. Instead of concrete, slats of wood are laid across the tracks. Though the Midway attempts to keep the slats as flat as possible, the design flaw not only slows the carts as they clank over the seams, but the raised ridges of wood will also leave your tailbone aching.

The Avalanche track is the largest track and the most popular. The track begins with a corkscrew and winds around in a figure eight as it descends. The conservative straightaways and slow bends did not impress us; neither did the long lines that build during the day and become unbearable at night.

The Alpine track is a shorter version of the Avalanche and contains all the same construction problems. After driving up a long and tedious corkscrew, you are given a brief burst of speed down a straightaway, but the banked turns quickly cease any major thrills. The track is less crowded than the Avalanche, but the ride is shorter. With a lack of sharp turns and speed, passing other drivers is difficult. Your best bet is to wait until someone slows down to ease the jostling caused by the wooden slats, or to move on to the Fast Track.

The **Fast Track** is the best track for racing. A single concrete oval, the track is small, but it's large enough to allow you to accelerate your cart to top speed before making the turns. Because you are allowed the same amount of time on this track as on either of the others (about 8 minutes), you will have time to practice the turns and pass and repass your friends. Because the track is simplistic and small, many patrons will skip it for the long lines and slow, bumpy ride on the other tracks; don't be so hasty.

OTHER ATTRACTIONS As with Fun Spot America, Magical Midway includes a small **bumper car arena,** with a height requirement of 48 inches for the driver and 36 inches for the passenger, and an even smaller **bumper boat pool,** with a height requirement of 42 inches for the driver and 36 inches for the passenger. However, Magical Midway's three rides— Space Blast, Starflyer, and Sling Shot—are all more extreme than any found at Fun Spot (save the SkyCoaster).

Space Blast has a 48-inch minimum height requirement and is similar to Doctor Doom's Fearfall at Universal's Islands of Adventure, without any of the theming or grandeur. You sit in a seat that is launched 180 feet into the air and then free-fall back to the ground. The ride is short, and the three g's of force are not dazzling.

The eye-catcher at Magical Midway is the **Starflyer,** with a height requirement of 44 inches. Towering over I-Drive, the Starflyer is a set of rotating swings that lifts riders up 230 feet and spins them at up to 54 miles per hour. To facilitate the thrill, the swing chains were built to be about 1 centimeter thick, forcing patrons to place their trust in Orlando's safety inspectors. Once you've overcome the vision of having your body flung onto I-Drive, you will have to resist the urge of having your stomach follow suit. Though the ride may induce motion sickness and mild terror, the view from the top of the Starflyer is one of the best in Orlando. The ride costs $7 and is *not* included with the purchase of any armband.

The **Sling Shot** is also not included in any armband admission and costs $25 per person; you must be at least 44 inches tall to ride. The Sling Shot is the same as the one at Old Town (the one at Magical Midway is actually taller by a foot or so, and only noticeable if you're bragging). The structure is a massive V-shape with flashing rainbow lights. Riders latch into a two-person cart at the base of the V, and a bungee cord system stretches down the legs of the V to the cart—like a slingshot. Once you're latched in, the cart is pulled below the boarding area, then released, flinging riders 365 feet into the air, spinning head over feet the entire time. Surprisingly, the ride is almost peaceful and less frightening than many of the major roller coasters in the area. After the initial launch, the elastic cable makes for a smooth rise and fall. Being more than 300 feet above the ground silences much surrounding noise, and the nighttime view is even better—for a few seconds at a time as you bob—than even the Starflyer's. As with most rides, the thrill is in the anticipation, not in the event. For $25, however, you're better off taking a helicopter for sightseeing or, for thrill junkies, paying out a few more bucks for the SkyCoaster at Fun Spot.

NASCAR I-Drive Indoor Kart Racing ★★★

APPEAL BY AGE PRESCHOOL – GRADE SCHOOL ★★★½ TEENS ★★★★
YOUNG ADULTS ★★★½ OVER 30 ★★★ SENIORS ★★

5228 Vanguard St., Orlando; ☎ 407-581-9644; **idrivenascar.com**

Hours Sunday–Thursday, noon–10 p.m.; Friday–Saturday, 11 a.m.–midnight. **Cost** $25 + tax for one adult race; $22 + tax for one junior race (age 15 and under, 55" minimum height requirement). Packages include racing, arcade credits, and food for $39–$129 + tax. Discounted races with annual membership for Florida residents.

DESCRIPTION AND COMMENTS Do you feel the need for speed, but not the need to be outside on the asphalt in the Orlando sun? You can indulge your *Days of Thunder* fantasies while still basking in air-conditioning at NASCAR I-Drive Indoor Kart Racing, a colorful blue-and-yellow warehouse that contains a single racetrack, along with a full-service restaurant/bar and arcade. With the name NASCAR, you might expect the track to be a single oval where you only turn left, but instead you'll find a fiendishly twisted road-style course riddled with a dozen hairpin turns. Drivers navigate said curves in Sodi RTX carts, which are also styled more like Formula 1 vehicles than stock cars; their all-electric engines avoid the noise and smoke of gas carts but can still achieve 45 miles per hour in a straightaway. (That top speed is remotely limited to about 25 miles per hour during junior races for under-16 drivers.) NASCAR I-Drive Indoor Kart Racing's flat course doesn't provide the roller coaster–style thrills of Fun Spot's banked curves and big dips, but for pure racing to test your technical driving skills, this is the stronger layout.

Safety barriers are installed along the track (which is isolated from nondrivers by floor-to-ceiling windows) and intentional bumping is illegal, but everyone must wear a provided full-face helmet just in case. Closed-toe shoes are also mandatory (you can rent a pair if you show up in flip-flops), and skirts are not allowed.

Those disinclined to tear up the track can instead relax in the Grandstand Bar & Grille—which has happy hour specials on liquor, beer, and appetizers 4–7 p.m., Monday–Friday—or play in the midsize arcade, whose distinguishing attraction is a scaled-down four-lane bowling alley.

Ripley's Believe It or Not! Orlando Odditorium ★★★½

APPEAL BY AGE PRESCHOOL ★★ GRADE SCHOOL ★★★½ TEENS ★★★½
YOUNG ADULTS ★★★½ OVER 30 ★★★ SENIORS ★★★½

8201 International Dr.; ☎ 407-345-0501; **ripleys.com/orlando**

Hours Daily, 9 a.m.–midnight, last entry at 11 p.m. **Cost** $19.99 + tax for adults; $12.99 + tax for children ages 4–12; free for children age 3 and under. Discounted tickets available on the website.

DESCRIPTION AND COMMENTS With one side of the building slipping into a sinkhole (on purpose, of course), Ripley's is another of the odder buildings on International Drive. Located just a few blocks from WonderWorks (the oddest building on I-Drive), Ripley's has free parking. To tour the exhibits, you should need only about an hour. Even with the quick turnaround of guests, the lines for Ripley's can be monstrous, with wait times outside exceeding an hour. On rainy days, be sure to arrive at least 20 minutes before opening, or come very late in the evening.

Ripley's consists of 16 galleries, each with a different twist. Each gallery hosts a menagerie of odds and ends from around the world that fit with each room's general theme. The collection consists mainly of optical illusions, anthropological oddities, genetic oddities, and some of the oddest objects built by man (including a portrait of Beyoncé made from candy, a 25-foot-tall mural of Jimi Hendrix made from more than 8,500 playing cards, a sculpture of a dog made from clothespins, and so on).

Once you enter, a hologram of Robert Ripley, one of the many optical illusions inside, greets you. Most of the other optical illusions are simple posters with questions such as, "Which line is longer: >—<, or <—>?" Others are on a grander scale, such as the billiards room, a room built to appear flat but that is actually listing to one side. The Inversion Tunnel is another large-scale illusion, and just like the WonderWorks version, the tunnel can make you believe that you are spinning sideways.

The anthropological and animal oddities also may set your head spinning. They include wax sculptures of deformities, Siamese piglets, ceremonial masks, and a shrunken human head. After these galleries, guests can walk through the man-made oddities, from the strange (an authentic vampire-slaying kit) to the stranger (a replica of a Rolls-Royce made from 1,016,711 matchsticks, or the portrait of Elvis constructed from 600 smaller portraits).

Because Ripley's is more of an amusement than a museum, many of the descriptive plaques in front of each item contain factoids instead of in-depth accounts. You won't find any lengthy analysis of items to educate you inside the Odditorium. You will, however, be privy to a fine collection of some fringe aspects of nature and humanity. The items displayed are changed occasionally—the warehouse that supplies the numerous Ripley's venues around the world is in the Orlando area—so if this stuff appeals to you but you haven't been to the Odditorium in a while, you might want to visit again.

Titanic: The Artifact Exhibition ★★★½

APPEAL BY AGE	PRESCHOOL ★	GRADE SCHOOL ★★	TEENS ★★½
YOUNG ADULTS ★★★	OVER 30 ★★★½	SENIORS ★★★★	

7324 International Dr., Orlando; ☎ 407-248-1166; **titanictheexperience.com**

Hours Peak season: Daily, 10 a.m.–8 or 9 p.m. Off-season: Daily, 10 a.m.–6 p.m.; last tour departs 1 hour before closing. Hours may vary, so check the website before leaving. **Cost** $21.95 + tax for adults; $19.75 + tax for adults age 65 and older; $15.95 + tax for children ages 5–11; free for children age 4 and younger. Discounts available on the website.

DESCRIPTION AND COMMENTS Titanic is not an amusement park; rather, it is a pricey museum filled with about 100 actual remnants from the ship, plus replicas of structures from the *Titanic* and period pieces from other ships. It is a fine museum: Artifacts range from a 2-ton slab of the hull to place settings, from a deck chair to a note, written in pencil by a steward and handed to one of his colleagues for her to present if she survived; as it turned out, both of them survived, though roughly three-fourths of the crew perished. Admission includes a guided tour, which lasts about an hour to an hour and a half, though you are free to return to read the signage or study the artifacts and period pieces. The tour guides, in costume, assume the identity of a passenger who was onboard the *Titanic*. Depending on your guide, his or her narration can either save or sink your experience.

When you arrive, you'll receive a ticket with a brief biography of an actual *Titanic* passenger; you'll find out at the end whether the person you were assigned survived or not, providing a personal connection. Your guide greets you at the entrance and ushers you into the first room, where you watch a video on the building of the *Titanic*. The museum is set up chronologically, so that after the video you are taken into rooms featuring ship schematics, details of the launch, and such. Your narrated tour begins in a room themed to look like the boarding dock in Southampton, England, complete with period luggage and ambient ship noise. Your guide arrives to escort you into the *Titanic*.

The theming is excellent, and the museum's full-scale replications of living quarters, hallways, and the famous grand staircase (quite attractive but surprisingly small) are all well crafted but can only be seen from behind velvet ropes. The last rooms contain low lighting to create a nighttime atmosphere, and the small replica of the ship's railing, with stars and cold air, makes you truly feel as if you are on board a ship.

Next, your guide walks you through the events preceding the accident and relates the circumstances of the tragedy. You learn that the suggested minimum number of lifeboats (64) was reduced to just 16 because the White Star Line executives wanted nothing as inconsequential as a lifeboat to interfere with passengers' views from the decks. You are also told that, similarly, a safety measure that would have extended below-deck walls to the ceiling of each compartment, thus helping to contain any flooding, was ignored because it would have interfered with the passage of first-class passengers to their dining room. Finally, you hear that while the *Titanic* carried two operators of the still-new Marconi radio device, the Marconi operators on the only ship close enough to reach the *Titanic* before it sank had gone to bed.

On the approach to the final gallery, the walls are covered by framed copies of more than a dozen actual newspapers and magazines from April 1912, reporting the tragedy. In the final gallery, a large block of ice set to the temperature of the water the night the *Titanic* sank is meant to transport you back in time. Video animations depict the ship hitting the iceberg and then its foundering and breaking in two. Your guide will offer tales of some passengers and will disclose whether his or her adopted persona survived.

Formerly known as Titanic: The Experience, this exhibit has been around Orlando for more than a decade at various locations; the current 20,000-square-foot installation includes a reconstruction of the vessel's bridge and an 8-foot model of the wreck. Ironically, when the attraction first opened, it didn't include any items actually salvaged from the *Titanic,* and most of the artifacts on display were reproductions or from other ships. Today, it is owned by Premiere Exhibitions, whose subsidiary RMS Titanic, Inc., holds exclusive salvage rights to the wreck. For the 100th anniversary of the sinking in 2012, the current owners renovated the museum, adding authentic items recovered from the vessel, including a fascinating display of currency and playing cards (discovered remarkably intact inside a leather bag), and a ragged 2-ton slice of the ship's starboard skin known as "Little Big Piece," the second-largest chunk of the *Titanic*'s hull ever retrieved from the ocean's depths. Similar attractions are found in Las Vegas, Buena Park, and other cities, with artifacts regularly rotated among locations.

Note that personal photography or video recording is prohibited inside the exhibit, though you can have your picture taken on the Grand Staircase for an additional fee.

For the serious *Titanic* fan, First Class Gala Dinner Events are held every Friday and Saturday night. The evening starts at 6:30 p.m. with a captain's cocktail party (cash bar), followed by a sit-down three-course meal of mixed greens, beef filet or chicken, and white-chocolate mousse (vegetarian and fish options available on request when booking). Throughout the evening, a dozen actors playing notable passengers and crew, such as Margaret "Unsinkable Molly" Brown and Captain Edward John Smith, interact with you; a willingness to play along makes the meal far more fun. The evening concludes with a dramatic reenactment of April 14's fateful events. Though there's no dress code, you may want to wear your Edwardian best, or at least something warm for the event's frigid finale. Dinner costs $69 + tax for adults, $42 + plus tax for children ages 5–11. Shows fill up, so be sure to book online in advance.

Whirly Dome ★★★

APPEAL BY AGE	PRESCHOOL	†	GRADE SCHOOL	★★†	TEENS	★★★½
YOUNG ADULTS	★★★★	OVER 30	★★★★	SENIORS	★★★	

6464 International Dr., Orlando; ☎ 407-212-3030; **whirlydome.com**

† Younger children are generally too short to ride.

Hours Tuesday–Thursday, 4–10 p.m.; Friday, 4 p.m.–midnight; Saturday, 11 a.m.–midnight; Sunday, 11 a.m.–10 p.m. **Cost** $3–$8 per game.

DESCRIPTION AND COMMENTS Located in a strip shopping center—is there anything else on I-Drive?—this indoor playground is for the 20-something-and-up crowd. It has a standard laser tag course under black light ($8 per person for one 10-minute game); Laser Frenzy, where a single person must maneuver *Mission: Impossible*–style through a hazy mirror maze without breaking the light beams ($3 per person for one game, $5 for two); a Formula 1 racing simulator ($8 per ride), where the rider sits in a cockpit and faces video monitors, but the parking lot outside is visible just beyond the simulator; and an electronic bowling hybrid in which you roll a real ball down a shortened alley at pins projected on a screen ($5 per game).

But the gimmick here, and the basis for the attraction's name, is a combination of bumper cars, polo, and basketball. Called Whirly Ball, this competition involves two teams of two to five players. Each player sits in a bumper car and carries a plastic scooping device that looks like the safety cover for a do-it-yourself utility light. With this, the player tries to chase and scoop a whiffle ball. When a player has the ball, he or she can pass it to a teammate or fling it toward a backboard with a sensor that sounds when it is hit. The game is $8 per person for 10 minutes of playing time; occasional specials are offered, such as unlimited playing time for $25 during certain hours. You can buy game packages—ranging from 5 games for $36 to 20 games for $135—and split them between multiple players to save about a buck per round. If you want to throw a Whirly Ball party, $250 will get you a court to yourselves for an hour. There are full-size Whirly Ball courts both on the ground floor and one level up. Players must be 54 inches tall.

A restaurant and bar, with liquor, wine, and 20 beers on tap, occupies one wing of the ground floor, and another bar is on the second level. The menu features gastropub food items, including a veggie burger, coconut shrimp, salads, soups, and sandwiches. Both the bar and play areas get busy after 5 p.m. on weekdays and shortly after lunch on weekends. While no food or drink is allowed in the play areas, you just know that some of those Whirly Ballers have fueled up their own tanks.

WonderWorks ★★★½

APPEAL BY AGE PRESCHOOL ★★★½ GRADE SCHOOL ★★★★ TEENS ★★★½
YOUNG   ADULTS   ★★★   OVER   30   ★★★   SENIORS   ★★

9067 International Dr., Orlando; ☎ 407-351-8800; **wonderworksonline
.com/orlando**

Hours Daily, 9 a.m.–midnight; last ticket sold at 10:30 p.m. **Cost** General admission to the exhibits, one 4-D motion ride, and one use of the ropes course: $26.99 + tax for adults; $20.99 + tax for seniors age 55 and older and for children ages 4–12; free for children age 3 and under; check the website for prices for numerous combo tickets and individual rides. Parking fee: $3 for the first 2 hours.

DESCRIPTION AND COMMENTS The unmistakable upside-down building is located on I-Drive in Orlando, between the Orange County Convention Center and Ripley's Believe It Or Not! The interior of WonderWorks is stacked with small displays, a cross between a science museum and an arcade. Kids will enjoy this place more than adults, but even the older crowd can find a few exhibits to interest them. When the learning is completed, a laser (here, spelled lazer) tag facility is upstairs.

To enter WonderWorks, you must first pass through the **Inversion Tunnel,** a very effective optical illusion that gives you the sensation of spinning upside down. If you begin to get queasy, or fear you'll be hurled over the left-hand railing, simply close your eyes and walk forward. Once you've successfully cleared the tunnel and are fully inverted, you can watch other visitors wobbling their way into the first of the four rooms at WonderWorks.

NATURAL DISASTERS ZONE The main attractions in the first room are the Hurricane Shack, the Earthquake Cafés, the Natural Disasters quiz center, global virtual reality, Tesla Coil, and the Anti-Gravity Chamber. The **Hurricane Shack** is a small box with four metal poles, such as you'd find in a subway car. Before the 71-mile-per-hour winds start blowing, you'll receive safety glasses and a brief tutorial on hurricanes (for example, the 71-mile-per-hour winds in the Hurricane Shack are slower than the requisite 74-mile-per-hour winds needed to call it a hurricane). The wind blows for less than a minute, and, to get the full impact of the attraction, the best place to stand is directly in front of the fan.

The **Earthquake Cafés** are two small, open-sided boxes next to the Hurricane Shack. Each box contains seating for four adults at a booth you would find at a diner. Once you are seated, the "earthquake" begins with a series of tremors and jolts, replicating the effects of an earthquake of 5.3 on the

Richter scale. The effect is equivalent to driving on a dirt road. (You must be 36 inches tall to ride the Earthquake Cafés.)

Next to the Earthquake Cafés is the **Natural Disasters** quiz center, where you can play tic-tac-toe on a series of computers. If you get the question right, you get the square. The quiz center is a good place to sit and wait your turn to play with the **Google Earth** kiosk. The familiar virtual globe software has been enlarged onto an array of three giant high-definition screens, tilted sideways in a vision-filling array. Nearly any spot on the entire planet can swiftly be rendered with 3-D terrain mapping and satellite scanning. You can scroll around to find your home or school, just like you do on your table at home, only writ large. Next, place your hand inside a steel mesh glove while a **Tesla Coil** sends 100,000 volts to the glove. A final illusion is located in the **Anti-Gravity Chamber,** where water appears to run toward the ceiling. Take a minute to figure out how the illusion is created before heading upstairs to the second room.

PHYSICAL CHALLENGE ZONE The second main room at WonderWorks contains the Bed of Nails, the Wonder Wall, Mindball, the Virtual Sports Velocity Tunnel, and Bubble Lab. The **Bed of Nails** sits in the center of the room and contains 3,497 nails. To keep your weight evenly distributed, you lie on a plastic plank and the nails rise from beneath you. Though lying on nails is uncomfortable, it makes a great photo op. Next to the Bed of Nails is the **Wonder Wall,** a human-size example of pin art. People press their hands or faces into a screen of flat-tipped pins, raising the pins on the other side to make a cast. The Wonder Wall is a scaled-up version of most pin art, with 40,000 pins in all.

If using your brain instead of your body to play interests you, **Mindball** is worth a try. Players sit across a table from each other, on opposite ends of a clear plastic tube, and don EEG biofeedback headbands that measure brain activity. The player with the calmer brainwaves will cause the small ball inside the tube to roll toward their opponent, so the more Zen you are, the better you'll do. If you can master your mental state, this will make you feel like a Jedi.

Another exhibit that highlights technology is the **Virtual Sports Velocity Tunnel,** where, after selecting a major-league batter—choices include Derek Jeter, Chipper Jones, and Barry Bonds—you throw actual baseballs at a slotted screen, giving you more respect for the real guys out on the mound.

If all the high-tech attractions are overcrowded or uninteresting to your children, there is always the **Bubble Lab,** an entire corner of the room dedicated to bubbles and bubble making. Just about every conceivable device for blowing bubbles is represented here, including the bubble screen and bubbles that you can fit inside.

LIGHT & SOUND ZONE The third room at WonderWorks features a couple of walls that can capture your image, freezing your shadow with a ghostly green glow (**Strike a Pose**) or manipulating your silhouette with a kaleidoscope of colors (**Recollections**). There is also a giant Simon Says–like arcade game called **Speed of Light,** where you have to slap an array of buttons as quickly as possible when they illuminate, and a **Giant Piano** where you step on the keys to play the notes.

SPACE DISCOVERY The fourth and final room in WonderWorks contains **Space Discovery,** a small space exhibit that imitates some of the experiences found at the Kennedy Space Center Visitor Complex, only with mock artifacts and on a much more modest scale. In here, kids can climb inside a replica NASA EVA **Space Suit,** squeeze themselves into a repro- duction of the **Mercury Capsule** (complete with fake control switches), or sit at a computer terminal and steer a simulated Mars rover on a **Mission to Mars** or **Land the Shuttle.**

The computer banks around the perimeter of the room also hold another flight simulator where you can fly an F-18 Hornet **Fighter Jet.** The three computer-screen displays that cover your main peripheral vision, coupled with the quality of the graphics, make this the best of the simulators.

If you still feel the need for speed, test your mettle with the **Astronaut Training Challenge.** Two victims at a time are strapped into this randomly rotating gyroscope, which resembles a human hamster ball being spun by a sadistic child. Consider yourself warned. For a final thrill in this room, strap into the **Wonder Coaster,** a close cousin of the CyberSpace Mountain sim- ulators in the soon-to-shutter DisneyQuest. First, you pick your combination of track elements to build your ideal thrill ride, and then the full-motion sim- ulator tosses you and a friend around in sync with your customized render- ing like a pair of socks in the dryer. It isn't quite as extreme as the Astronaut Training Challenge, but don't even think about it if you are susceptible to motion sickness, for the sake of your seatmate. (You must be 42 inches tall to ride the coaster.)

OTHER ATTRACTIONS For the littlest kids, the **Imagination Lab** will keep them distracted while older siblings explore elsewhere. There's an oversized Lite-Brite (**Wonder Brite**), touch screens for digital finger painting (**Fun Express**), and a motion-sensing video game where you squish aliens projected onto the floor (**Alien Stomper**).

WonderWorks boasts two other attractions, the **4D XD Motion The- ater** and an Indoor Ropes Course. The 12-seat theater alternately shows three films that combine 3-D film images with the synchronized motion of the special chairs in which you are belted. (Moviegoers must be at least 40 inches tall.)

In the third level of WonderWorks, known as the basement, is a three- story (36-foot) glow-in-the-dark **Indoor Ropes Course**—the first of its kind in Orlando. More than 20 different obstacles and activities await, including a tire traverse, suspension bridges, and swinging beams. Climbers must have closed-toe shoes and pants (no skirts or dresses), weigh less than 300 pounds, and be 48–80 inches tall; kids taller than 42 inches can participate with an adult, and everyone under 18 must have a parental waiver. On your way up to the "basement," you'll pass the **Far Out Art Gallery,** a collection of paintings and print illusions, including some by M. C. Escher.

LAZER-TAG Once you've exited through the turnstile at the far side of the fourth room, the learning aspect of WonderWorks is gone. The fifth area at WonderWorks is upstairs, where there is a small arcade and a large laser tag room that is black-lit for added effect. The arcade and the **Lazer-Tag** area are accessible without paying for WonderWorks (use the elevator in the lobby), a convenient alternative if you decide to return and play.

In Lazer-Tag, each player is given a laser gun to shoot other players and a vest that registers each shot, placing your scores on a large screen in the arcade. Once your vest has been activated, you may enter the room, where you can hide behind panels and shoot at other players. When you've been shot, your gun stops firing and your vest stops accepting hits for a few seconds and then restarts, allowing you time to run to another area of the room. Besides shooting other players, you can also shoot lights on the partitions for extra points. The key to winning is to keep moving and to aim well. (Players must be at least 40 inches tall.)

World of Chocolate ★★★

| APPEAL BY AGE | PRESCHOOL ★★★ | GRADE SCHOOL ★★★ | TEENS ★★★½ |
| YOUNG ADULTS ★★★½ | OVER 30 ★★★½ | SENIORS ★★★ |

11701 International Dr., Orlando; ☎ 407-778-4871; **wocorlando.com**

Hours Daily, noon–7 p.m. **Cost** $16.95 + tax per adult; $12.95 + tax for children ages 4–12, seniors, and military; kids age 3 and under are free. Discounts available on website and through Groupon.

DESCRIPTION AND COMMENTS World of Chocolate is an hour-long guided walking tour through the past and present of cocoa, tracing the bean's path from sacred fruit to the candy bars we enjoy today. If you're experiencing a sudden sense of déjà vu, don't panic; this attraction is almost identical in theme and concept to Chocolate Kingdom, reviewed on page 317. Both are museum-like exhibits that feature a live narrator who teaches you about the history of chocolate and helps you enjoy some tasty samples. World of Chocolate's displays are more dramatically lit than Chocolate Kingdom's, which helps conceal the fact that its artifacts are less impressive, and curatorial signage is entirely absent. Our guide was pleasant and personable but became vague and evasive any time she was pressed for additional information that wasn't scripted.

One major element World of Chocolate has that Chocolate Kingdom doesn't is its art gallery, featuring 25 famous world monuments—including the Eiffel Tower, Statue of Liberty, and Big Ben—made entirely out of baker's chocolate, with support dowels or wires like they use on TV confectionery competitions. There's also a collection of bas-relief pictures and life-size busts of famous figures, including President Barack Obama, also all made of cocoa. The room is kept between 67° and 70°F, but you can still see some cracks and warping on the sculptures.

Finally, though it does have a collection of classic chocolate-making machines, there is no working factory on-site. You still get your share of samples throughout the tour, starting with a mouth-puckering cold cacao drink. The tour's highlight is the tasting session toward the end, where thumbnail-size fragments are offered from 10 different commercially available chocolate bars, all of which can be purchased in the café afterward. The available brands vary from day to day but include both sweet and bitter varieties, some with exotic add-ins; we tried chocolate infused with orange, pear, mushroom, and even masala spices. As a farewell, you are handed a thimbleful of hot cocoa, which was disappointingly thin and redolent of burnt milk.

After your tour, the aforementioned café has an eye-catching array of truffles and macaroons, along with a full menu of hot and cold drinks and sandwiches. If you'd like some Cabernet with your chocolate, add-on wine tasting packages are available ($17.90 plus tax per person, $27.95 plus tax with tour, age 21 and up only). After experiencing both of Orlando's chocolate tours, we prefer Chocolate Kingdom overall, especially for families with children; for adults with a sweet tooth for the strange and unusual, World of Chocolate's exotic samples may give it a slight edge.

ESCAPE ROOM GAMES

ONE OF THE NEWEST ATTRACTION CRAZES to sweep Orlando, having already conquered Asia and other American cities, is the escape room, also known as a puzzle room or escape game. Part scavenger hunt, part live-action video game, and part pen-and-paper brainteaser, each of the area's escape rooms has its own themes (which rotate regularly) and pricing (often with deep online discounts), but all operate in about the same way.

Players select a scenario and are assigned a team (typically 3–10 people) with whom to cooperate in completing the tasks. The group is closed inside a room and given 60 minutes in which to uncover and solve the puzzles that will effect their egress. Typically, you start by ransacking the room, emptying furniture drawers, rifling through bookcases, and peeking behind picture frames to find your first clues. They'll lead you to unlock some object, which will contain further clues, and so forth; often, you'll unseal initially inaccessible areas, expanding the space you have to explore. A staff member monitors your progress, either in person or via video cameras, and provides hints when you get hopelessly stuck (usually at the expense of a time penalty). You'll probably find yourself banging your head against the wall in frustration at some point, but the satisfaction derived from cracking that final code with seconds to spare is unlike the pleasure of any theme park ride.

Despite their ominous-sounding names, you are not truly trapped inside an escape room, and you always have the option to quit early. Most of the scenarios are geared toward grown-ups, but many are accessible to school-age kids, who sometimes see things that the adults miss. You shouldn't need any specialized knowledge beyond basic literacy and arithmetic, but a familiarity with cryptography, crosswords, or Sudoku often comes in handy. The primary requirement is an eagerness to search thoroughly, read carefully, and think laterally.

Escape rooms are a fast-growing fad, and we expect several of these start-ups to flame out in this competitive market. Here are our favorites that we feel should still be around by the time you read this.

America's Escape Room ★★★★½

APPEAL BY AGE PRESCHOOL — GRADE SCHOOL ★★★½ TEENS ★★★★
YOUNG ADULTS ★★★★½ OVER 30 ★★★★½ SENIORS ★★★★

8723 International Dr., Ste. 115, Orlando; ☎ 407-412-5585;
americasescapegame.com

Hours Sunday, 11 a.m.–6 p.m.; Tuesday–Thursday, 1–9 p.m.; Friday–Saturday, 11 a.m.–1 a.m.
Cost $35 + tax per person.

DESCRIPTION AND COMMENTS Of all the escape games we've tried, this had the best balance of production values, plot, and puzzle difficulty. The playing area is among the largest in town, and the Oval Office scenario employed a clever mix of presidential trivia and technology-based challenges. Even though this was the first escape game we failed, it was among the most satisfying to attempt.

The Escape Game Orlando ★★★★

APPEAL BY AGE	PRESCHOOL —	GRADE SCHOOL ★★★	TEENS ★★★½
YOUNG ADULTS ★★★★	OVER 30 ★★★★		SENIORS ★★★½

8145 International Dr., Ste. 511, Orlando; ☎ 407-501-7222; **orlandoescapegame.com**

Hours Monday–Thursday, 1:30–10 p.m.; Friday, 11:30 a.m.–midnight; Saturday–Sunday, 10 a.m.–midnight. **Cost** $28 + tax per person.

DESCRIPTION AND COMMENTS Stop an international terrorist attack (choose this one if you're a newbie), break out of prison, or reveal an art thief at The Escape Game. Prison Break may be one of the most difficult escape rooms in Orlando. The well-themed rooms may include secret passageways or trap doors and show a great attention to detail.

Escapology ★★★★

APPEAL BY AGE	PRESCHOOL —	GRADE SCHOOL ★★★	TEENS ★★★½
YOUNG ADULTS ★★★★	OVER 30 ★★★★		SENIORS ★★★½

11951 International Dr., Unit C3, Orlando; ☎ 407-278-1515; **escapology.com/orlando**

Hours Monday–Thursday, 12:30–9:40 p.m.; Friday, 12:30–11 p.m.; Saturday, 10 a.m.–11 p.m.; Sunday, 10 a.m.–9:40 p.m. **Cost** $30 + tax for adults, $27 + tax for children under age 18, students, and seniors age 65 and over. 50% off for active or retired military with ID. $2 off per person for advance online bookings.

DESCRIPTION AND COMMENTS Another top pick, Escapology has the plushest facilities, with a comfy waiting lounge and professional video and sound tracks to accompany each scenario. Though the game rooms are a bit small, they conceal many secrets; we played the Cold War spy scenario with a former military intelligence officer, who declared it suitably authentic.

Great Escape Room ★★★

APPEAL BY AGE	PRESCHOOL —	GRADE SCHOOL ★★	TEENS ★★½
YOUNG ADULTS ★★★	OVER 30 ★★★		SENIORS ★★½

23½ S. Magnolia Ave., Orlando; ☎ 386-385-8860; **thegreatescaperoom.com**

Hours Wednesday, 6–9 p.m.; Thursday, 6–10 p.m.; Friday, noon–10 p.m.; Saturday, noon–midnight; Sunday, noon–6 p.m. **Cost** $28 + tax per person, Friday–Sunday; $23 + tax per person, Wednesday–Thursday.

DESCRIPTION AND COMMENTS Orlando's first escape room and its least impressive example of the genre. The decor is bland IKEA modern, and the puzzles bear no relationship to the supposed Sherlock Holmes story line. This is the only game where you must unscrew furniture to find the clues, and you'll need prior knowledge of subjects like astronomy to crack the codes. There's no free parking; use the nearby parking garage across from the Orlando Public Library.

It's A Trap! ★★★★

APPEAL BY AGE PRESCHOOL — GRADE SCHOOL ★★★ TEENS ★★★½
YOUNG ADULTS ★★★★ OVER 30 ★★★★ SENIORS ★★★½

6744 Aloma Ave, Winter Park; ☎ 407-960-3824; **itsatrapgame.com**

Hours Monday–Thursday, 7–8:45 p.m.; Friday, 7–10:15 p.m.; Saturday, 1–10:15 p.m.; Sunday, 1–5:45 p.m. **Cost** $23 + tax per person; $20 + tax per student, military, or theme park employee with ID; $28 + tax plus person to have only your party in the room.

DESCRIPTION AND COMMENTS The furthest escape room from the tourist corridor, but worth the drive for the live actors (and sometimes puppets) who serve your interactive hint system. The fantasy and superhero themes are more imaginative than most (and supported by fun special effects), and though the puzzles aren't too tough, they require creativity and group participation to solve, sometimes with hilarious side effects.

Mindquest Live ★★★★

APPEAL BY AGE PRESCHOOL — GRADE SCHOOL ★★★½ TEENS ★★★★
YOUNG ADULTS ★★★★ OVER 30 ★★★★ SENIORS ★★★½

9938 Universal Blvd., Orlando; ☎ 407-392-0885; **mindquestlive.com**

Hours Daily, 11 a.m.–10:30 p.m. **Cost** $26 + tax per person age 7 and older. No players under age 7; minimum 2 players per booking.

DESCRIPTION AND COMMENTS If you have tweens or teens in your group, go for The Bomb or Diamond Heist; these rooms have low lighting, so go elsewhere if your kids are scared of the dark. Cyber Crash and Mad Scientist are more challenging, with more-difficult puzzles that require your team to work together.

■ SHOPPING

INTERNATIONAL DRIVE AND ORLANDO in general offer a wealth of shopping opportunities to ensure you come home a little less wealthy. Central Florida's premier shopping experience is found just north of I-Drive at **The Mall at Millenia** (☎ 407-363-3555; **mallatmillenia.com**), anchored by Bloomingdale's, Macy's, and Neiman Marcus. It also has the closest Apple Store to Orlando's tourist attractions. Other stores include Anthropologie, Burberry, Cartier, Coach, Crate & Barrel, Gucci, Guess, J. Crew, Kate Spade, Louis Vuitton, Lululemon Athletica, Tiffany & Co., Tory Burch, Urban Outfitters, and Versace. Hours are Monday–Saturday, 10 a.m.–9 p.m.; Sunday, 11 a.m.–7 p.m.

A few minutes south of Millenia, on the north end of International Drive, is **Artegon Marketplace** (5250 International Dr.; ☎ 407-351-7718; **artegonorlando.com**; open Monday–Saturday, 10 a.m.–9 p.m.; Sunday, 11 a.m.–7 p.m.), an artsy bazaar à la Faneuil Hall or Chelsea Market; there are also some midrange restaurants, a SkyTrail indoor ropes course ($15–$20 per adult, $8 for kids under 48 inches), a trampoline gymnasium, and a nice movie theater attached. The mix of merchants is eclectic, to say the least—everything from local honey to cell phone cases—but a few are worth seeking out, such as Gods & Monsters (the nation's second-largest comic book and pop-culture collectible store) and International Hot Glass, where former Walt Disney World artisans will guide you through blowing your own ornament or other glass bauble, starting at about $45.

Like every major tourist destination in the United States, Central Florida has hundreds of factory outlet stores, most of them situated near major attractions. Having spent many hours checking prices and merchandise, we generally conclude that at most stores you'll save about 20% on desirable merchandise and up to 75% on last season (or older) stock. Some stores in the outlet malls are full retail or sell a few brands at a 20% discount and the rest at full price.

Orlando Premium Outlets–International Drive (4951 International Dr.; ☎ 407-352-9600; **premiumoutlets.com/orlando;** open Monday–Saturday, 10 a.m.–11 p.m.; Sunday, 10 a.m.–9 p.m.), across the street from Artegon, features 180 of the world's hottest designers and brand names, among them BCBG Max Azria, Hugo Boss Factory Store, Kenneth Cole, Michael Kors, Saks Fifth Avenue OFF 5TH, Sean John, St. John, Tommy Hilfiger, Under Armour, Victoria's Secret, and the only Neiman Marcus Last Call in Central Florida. There's even a Disney's Character Warehouse, where unsold Walt Disney World souvenirs go to die. You can reach the outlets by car, taxi, or I-Ride Trolley (it's stop #1).

On the south end of International Drive is **Pointe Orlando** (9101 International Dr.; ☎ 407-248-2838; **pointeorlando.com**), with a handful of stores. This complex gets a lot of its business from the Orange County Convention Center, less than a mile away, rather than from locals. It's home to the only real giant-screen IMAX cinema in town, as well as a B. B. King blues club and Improv comedy club. Hours are October–May, Monday–Saturday, noon–10 p.m., and Sunday, noon–8 p.m.; June–September, Sunday–Thursday, noon–8 p.m., and Friday–Saturday, noon–9 p.m. (Bars and restaurants stay open later.)

A few minutes east of southern I-Drive along the Beachline Expressway is **The Florida Mall** (8001 S. Orange Blossom Trl./US 441; ☎ 407-851-6255; **simon.com/mall/the-florida-mall;** open Monday–Friday, 10 a.m.–9 p.m.; Saturday, 10 a.m.–10 p.m.; Sunday, noon–8 p.m.), the biggest in the area with about 200 shops, including Coach, Gymboree, Macy's, MAC Cosmetics, M&M, Nordstrom, and Sephora. It is also home to the **Crayola Experience** (**crayolaexperience.com/orlando**), featuring 25 creative kid-friendly activity areas (including Modeling Madness, Scribble Square, and Doodle in the Dark) based on the all-American art supplies. The facility isn't an actual factory, but there are regular demonstrations of how hot wax is made into crayons. Younger kids could spend 3 or more hours playing here, while older ones are likely to be bored within an hour. Hours are 10 a.m.–8 p.m. daily. Admission is $19.99 plus tax for ages 2–64, $16.99 plus tax for seniors age 65 and up; children under age 2 are free. This mall is extremely popular, especially with South American visitors seeking bargains on clothing and electronics. Go early and park near one of the major stores you want to explore.

PART THIRTEEN

OUTDOOR RECREATION *and* MORE

DISNEY'S ANIMAL KINGDOM, SeaWorld, and Busch Gardens all have unique and spectacular animal exhibits, yet the massive scale of each of these parks prohibits some Orlando visitors from experiencing all three—or any—of the major animal attractions of Central Florida. Because each of these parks requires an entire day to visit, costs upward of $70 per person, and is ostensibly a man-made re-creation of the natural environment, many visitors will opt for a smaller, cheaper, and more grassroots operation to fulfill their wonder for wild creatures. Orlando offers fulfillment in many forms. Airboat tours of the local lakes, nearby zoos, conservation projects, and horseback tours are all amenable answers to allow for animals in your itinerary. The quality of the attractions does vary drastically, and though none—or very few—are on par with an open-back truck ride on the Serengeti at Busch Gardens, the Wild Africa Trek at Animal Kingdom, or a swim with the dolphins at Discovery Cove, they are all sound additions to a trip laden with animatronic creatures and miles of concrete.

AIRBOATS

AN AIRBOAT IS A FLAT-BOTTOM BOAT powered by a large fan. The versatile machine, which can travel on both water and flat land, allows vacationers to explore the wetlands of Central Florida. All the airboat tours near Orlando operate on lakes, so do not expect much of the swampy terrain common to the Everglades. You will see plenty of wildlife on these tours, and any ornithologists should have a field day. The two animals that awe most visitors are the bald eagle and the American alligator—you have a very good chance of seeing both on these tours, though neither animal is guaranteed. Some, but not all, bald eagles are migratory birds, flying north in the summer and returning in the winter. Migrating eagles do return to the same nest year after year, so clued-in tour guides will show you where their nests are located.

Bald eagles may be the animal icon of the United States, but the alligator is the animal icon of Florida (animated mice come in at a close second). You can see and feed baby alligators at Congo River minigolf, or marvel at the full-size gators at Gatorland. Wild alligators, on the other hand, are more difficult to spot, and you may see only their eyes and snout above the water. There are a few tricks to help you spot wild alligators. Alligators are ectothermic, or cold-blooded, which means that they have a minimal amount of inner body temperature regulation and must rely on outside sources of heat, such as air and water, to stay alive. Alligators are most active between 82°F and 92°F but seem to be easiest to spot when the air temperature outside is less than 84°F. During the winter, alligators stop feeding when the ambient temperature drops below 70°F, and become dormant, lying low in alligator holes, when the temperature drops below 55°F. Watch the weather during your visit, and try to pick a day when the water is cool and the air temperature is around 84°F. Even if you follow none of our advice, chances are that you will see at least one alligator.

At a distance, telling an alligator from a clump of floating mud can be difficult unless you can see the alligator's eyes or part of its tail. Some operators offer night tours with "gator shining." Like many nocturnal animals, alligators have a layer of cells behind their retinas that reflect light back into their photoreceptors, increasing night vision. When you shine a flashlight into a nocturnal animal's eyes at night, this layer of cells (called tapetum lucidum) creates an eerie red glow. You will see more alligators on night tours—but only their eyes, and waterfowl are scarce.

Airboat tours are a great way to get out on the water on a hot afternoon, blast around a lake, and see much of the local wildlife. They aren't amusement rides, and you should have at least a hint of curiosity about the natural world before you go. Most tours require reservations, so plan ahead. Many of the airboat tours take coupons that can be found online or in any of the free magazines around town.

AIRBOAT TOURS

Big Toho Airboat Rides ★★★

2017 Neptune Rd., Kissimmee; ☎ 321-624-2398; **bigtohoairboatrides.com**

Hours 10 a.m.–4 p.m. or by reservation. **Cost** Daytime airboat tour (minimum 2 paying guests), 1 hour: $40.65 for adults; $35.30 for children ages 3–10. 90 minutes: $51.35 for adults; $40.65 for children ages 3–10. Free for children age 2 and younger.

DESCRIPTION AND COMMENTS Big Toho does not have a permanent ticket booth location but launches from a public boat ramp on the north end of Lake Tohopekaliga (Lake Toho for short). The public boat ramp is easy enough to find, but be aware that a separate company called Big Toho Marina does have a permanent dock nearby; make sure to go to the public parking lot in front of the public dock.

The owner and operator, Brent, is a jovial character and happy to demonstrate the handiness of his airboat, popping over the reed beds and skimming through the lotus fields. The information on the tour is lackluster, but the boat's speed and handling should keep you entertained and makes this the most thrilling airboat ride available. Seating is theater style, with back rows higher than those in front.

Coupons are available in all the free local magazines and should be brought with you, but if you forget them, you should still be able to receive the stated prices above.

Boggy Creek Airboat Rides ★★★

2001 E. Southport Rd., Kissimmee, and 3702 Big Bass Rd., Kissimmee; ☎ 407-344-9550; **bcairboats.com**

Hours 9 a.m.–5:30 p.m. **Cost** Basic tours, 30 minutes: $26.95 + tax for adults; $20.95 + tax for children ages 3–10. 1 hour: $43.95 + tax for adults; $38.95 + tax for children ages 3–10. 45-minute swamp excursion (6-person maximum): $56.95 per person. 1-hour night or sunset tour (4-person minimum): $51.95 + tax for adults; $47.95 + tax for children ages 3–10. Free for children age 2 and younger.

DESCRIPTION AND COMMENTS Boggy Creek Airboat Rides operates from two locations: one on Lake Toho and the other, a 45-minute drive from Walt Disney World, on West Lake Toho, a separate lake. Both locations offer very similar tours. The airboats each fit 18 people and have bench seating instead of height-staggered seating, so you should attempt to sit in the front row for the best view.

The 30-minute airboat tour leaves every half hour beginning at 9 a.m. and takes you out onto the lake alongside open cow pastures. Herons, egrets, and a few other birds are visible here. Tours do not pass through reeds or much marsh but stick instead to the open water. Houses dot the landscape at both locations, but the development at both sites is not as pronounced as that found on tours operating from the north end of Lake Toho. The guides provide a moderate amount of information, including how to estimate an alligator's length (the number of inches between the eyes and the snout is equal to the alligator's length in feet). The ride is stop-and-go, pausing every time someone suspects a gator is present, and at only 30 minutes, it seems over before it has begun.

Boggy Creek is one of the most popular tours in the area due to its accessible locations and prolific advertising. It does not require reservations for the 30-minute airboat tours, though we strongly recommend making them. When you do make your reservation, find out if enough other guests have reserved spots for the boat to leave at the appointed time.

Wild Willy's Airboat Tours ★★★½

4715 Kissimmee Park Rd., St. Cloud; ☎ 407-891-7955; **airboatwilly.com**

Hours 9 a.m.–5 p.m. or by reservation. **Cost** Daytime airboat tours, 1 hour: $43.93 + tax for adults; $34.58 + tax for children ages 3–12; free for children age 2 and younger. Book online and save $4, or bring the coupon found in any of the free local advertising magazines. Seasonal 1-hour sunset tour (Sunday–Thursday, November–March): $65 + tax for 2–3 customers (all ages); $60 for 4–6 customers (all ages).

DESCRIPTION AND COMMENTS You can find Wild Willy's in a campground a few miles from Orlando. In the small office at the campground is a terrarium that is home to a few baby gators, and the staff will even let you hold the toothy critters. The staff's knowledge of local wildlife, from the receptionists to the tour guides, is above average. When it's time for the tour, you board a 6- or 14-passenger airboat and meander off onto the eastern end of Lake Toho. This end of the lake has fewer developments than the north end, allowing you to encounter a more pristine Florida.

On your tour, your guide may reveal a few eagle nests. The eagle pairs here leave during the summer, but lone immature eagles are found year-round. Other wildlife includes anhingas, spoonbills, and, of course, alligators. The guides at Wild Willy's carry a pair of binoculars, so you may observe the birds even if they are perched in a distant tree. These tours are peaceful and can involve a bit of drifting under the Florida sun. Wear sunscreen and sit back with one eye closed and the other open to look for gators.

Note: Call for directions if you do not have a Sunpass (most rental cars have them); the closest interstate exit is Sunpass only, no cash.

ADDITIONAL BOAT TOURS
Airboat Rides at Midway

28501 E. Colonial Dr., Christmas; ☎ 407-568-6790; **airboatridesatmidway.com**

Hours Daily, 9 a.m.–5 p.m.; evening tours by reservation. **Cost** 1-hour non-private daytime tour: $40 + tax for adults; $30 + tax for children ages 4–12. 1-hour private daytime tour: $300 + tax for up to 6 guests. 1-hour private night tour: $350 + tax for up to 6 guests. Free for children age 3 and under.

DESCRIPTION AND COMMENTS Unlike the many Kissimmee-area airboat outfits, this one cruises the scenic St. Johns River. It is located almost an hour east of Orlando and is closer to Cape Canaveral than Disney.

The Black Hammock

2316 Black Hammock Fish Camp Rd., Oviedo; ☎ 407-365-2201 or 407-365-1244; **theblackhammock.com**

Hours Daily, 9 a.m.–5:30 p.m.; evening tours by reservation. **Cost** 30-minute non-private daytime tour: $26.95 + tax for adults; $20.95 + tax for children age 10 and under. 1-hour non-private daytime tour: $43.95 + tax for adults; $38.95 + tax for children age 10 and under. 1-hour non-private night tour (4-person minimum): $55 + tax per person. 45-minute private tour (4-person minimum): $50.95 + tax per person; $20 extra per person for departures after 5:30 p.m.

DESCRIPTION AND COMMENTS The Black Hammock on Lake Jessup (about 30 minutes northeast of Orlando) is a waterfront restaurant and bar that offers airboat tours off of its dock. You can also rent a pontoon boat ($19.99 + tax per person for a 1-hour tour; $400 + tax per hour for a private ride) and have a party with 5–24 of your best buddies.

Kissimmee Swamp Tours

4500 Joe Overstreet Rd., Kenansville; ☎ 407-436-1059; **kissimmeeswamptours.com**

Hours Daily, 8 a.m.–5 p.m. **Cost** 1 hour: $49 + tax for adults; $35 + tax for children ages 3–12. 90 minutes: $64 + tax for adults; $44 + tax for children ages 3–12. Free for children age 2 and under. Show Florida ID or mention website discount to save $4 per person.

DESCRIPTION AND COMMENTS Tours of the undeveloped Lake Kissimmee wetlands in six-passenger airboats operate out of Middleton's Fish Camp, about 45 minutes southwest of Walt Disney World. Situated along the Great Florida Birding Trail, it advertises sightings of bald eagles, whooping cranes, and endangered birds.

Orlando Airboat Tours (Marsh Landing Adventures)

4275 Neptune Rd., St. Cloud; ☎ 407-572-3651; **orlandoairboattours.com**

Hours Monday–Saturday, 8 a.m.–10 p.m.; Sunday, 10 a.m.–10 p.m. **Cost** 1 hour: $49.95 + tax for adults; $44.95 + tax for children ages 3–10. 90 minutes: $65 + tax for adults; $60 + tax for children ages 3–10. 2 hours: $85 + tax for adults; $80 + tax for children ages 3–10. 1-hour sunset tour (October–April): $64.95 + tax for adults; $54.95 + tax for children ages 3–10. Free for children age 2 and under.

DESCRIPTION AND COMMENTS Six-passenger boats with shaded tops take guests on guided tours of Shingle Creek, the headwaters of the Florida Everglades.

Spirit of the Swamp Airboat Tours

2830 Neptune Rd., Kissimmee; ☎ 321-689-6893; **spiritoftheswamp.com**

Hours Monday–Saturday, 8 a.m.–5 p.m.; Sunday, noon–5 p.m. **Cost** 1 hour: $49.95 + tax for adults; $44.95 + tax for children age 10 and under. 90 minutes: $65 + tax for adults; $60 + tax for children age 10 and under. 2 hours: $85 + tax for adults; $80 + tax for children age 10 and under.

DESCRIPTION AND COMMENTS Boats are equipped with communication headsets for all guests and hold a maximum of six passengers; book at least four seats to guarantee a private tour. Like Big Toho, it launches into Lake Toho from a public dock.

Wild Florida Airboats and Wildlife

3301 Lake Cypress Rd., Kenansville; ☎ 407-957-3135 or 866-532-7167; **wildfloridairboats.com**

Hours Monday–Saturday, 9 a.m.–6 p.m.; evening tours by reservation. **Cost** 30-minute non-private daytime tour: $26.50 + tax for adults; $23 + tax for children ages 3–12. 1-hour non-private daytime tour: $47.50 + tax for adults; $37 + tax for children ages 3–12. 1-hour private daytime tour (4-person minimum): $63 + tax per person. 1-hour non-private night tour (4-person minimum): $63 + tax per person. 1-hour private night tour (4-person minimum): $73 + tax per person. Free for children age 2 and under.

DESCRIPTION AND COMMENTS This airboat tour departs from a private facility on Cypress Lake, south of Lake Toho. The tour price includes admission to a wildlife park with bobcats, wild boar, ring-tailed lemurs, and—of course—lots of gators; stand-alone park admission is $18 for adults, $15 for children ages 3–12. A barbecue restaurant is on-site, and ranch buggy tours leave from here for tours of a local cattle ranch ($25 for adults; $20 for children ages 3–12).

HELICOPTER TOURS

FOR A BIRD'S-EYE VIEW OF ORLANDO, consider a helicopter tour. Several companies offer short tours above the Orlando theme park areas. Rates start at $20 per person, often with a minimum requirement of two passengers (most helicopters can hold just three passengers). A $15–$20 flight lasts just 4–5 minutes and essentially circles only the attraction closest to the helicopter base. You can also pay $125–$230 or more per passenger for the grand tour, a 40-mile route that covers the big guys—Walt Disney World, Universal Orlando, and SeaWorld, a half hour trip—or up to $350 per passenger for an evening tour to see the fireworks from Epcot. Rates for children are typically $5–$35 less than the adult fare, depending on the length of the flight. Passengers usually are equipped with headsets and microphones to communicate with the pilot, who will identify the sites below.

The following companies offer sightseeing flights:

- **Air Florida Helicopters** 8990 International Dr., Orlando; ☎ 407-354-1400; **airfloridahelicopter.com**

- **Air Force Fun** 12211 Regency Village Dr., #13, Orlando; ☎ 407-842-1446; **airforcefun.com**

- **Hawkeye Heli-Tours** 5071 W. US 192, Kissimmee; ☎ 407-507-2682; **hawkeyehelitours.com**

- **Leading Edge Helicopters** 4623 W. US 192, Kissimmee; ☎ 407-341-1020; **leadingedgehelicopter.com**

- **Max Flight Helicopter Services** 4009 Fifth St., Kissimmee; ☎ 321-247-8043; **maxflightheli.com/sightseeing-tours.html**

- **Orlando Heli-Tours** 12651 International Dr., Orlando; ☎ 407-239-8687; 5519 W. US 192, Kissimmee; ☎ 407-397-0226; **orlandohelitours.com**

ANIMAL ATTRACTIONS

THERE IS A FINE ASSORTMENT OF OTHER CREATURES in the Orlando area that do not pose the threat of cleaving an arm. These attractions allow visitors to spend a half day away from the zoo of visitors on US 192 and I-Drive and to come in contact with a more natural side of Central Florida.

Audubon Center for Birds of Prey ★★★½

1101 Audubon Way, Maitland; ☎ 407-644-0190; **fl.audubon.org /audubon-center-birds-prey**

Hours Tuesday–Sunday, 10 a.m.–4 p.m. **Cost** $8 for adults and children age 13 and older; $5 for children ages 3–12; $7 for seniors; free for children age 2 and younger.

DESCRIPTION AND COMMENTS With a mission to "conserve, protect, and restore Florida's natural resources," the Center for Birds of Prey is an urban environmental nature center focused on the rescue, rehabilitation, and release of injured and orphaned birds of prey. More than 18,500 birds have been treated here since its inception in 1979. For such a small center, with barely 2½ acres of land, this is quite a feat. The center is also the leading North American caretaker of bald eagles, with more than 1,750 birds treated and more than 500 released back into the wild. Of the birds treated here, 40% are released back into the wild. Those that are unable to be rehabilitated are sent to zoological parks or nature centers.

The small grounds have quite a number of birds, including peregrine falcons, barred owls, burrowing owls, northern caracaras, red-tailed hawks, kestrels, and kites. You will not be allowed to hold any of the animals, but if you ask a keeper, he or she will give you an up close look of the eagles, hawks, or owls. Guided tours are available only to groups larger than 10 people, cost $100, and require reservations. The center offers a self-guided tour with guidebook, included with regular admission.

It is a great addendum to the nearby Orlando Science Center or the Central Florida Zoo, and the price is right if you can find the place. Here are the directions from I-4: Take Exit 88, head east on US 17/92, and immediately take a left onto Wymore Road. In less than 1 mile, turn right onto Kennedy Boulevard. Continue 0.2 mile to East Street, and turn left. The center is just ahead at the three-way stop on your left. Even with the directions, we were forced to call multiple times. If that doesn't get you anywhere, just ask the locals; people walking dogs and jogging tend to know where they are going.

The Central Florida Zoo & Botanical Gardens   ★★★½

3755 NW US 17/92, Sanford (off I-4 at Exit 104); ☎ 407-323-4450; **centralfloridazoo.org**

Hours Daily, 9 a.m.–5 p.m.; closed Thanksgiving and December 25. **Cost** $16.50 for adults; $13.95 for seniors (age 60+); $11.95 for children ages 3–12; free for children age 2 and younger.

DESCRIPTION AND COMMENTS To see the animals at Busch Gardens or at Disney's Animal Kingdom, you have to buy admission to the entire park. If you were not able to spend an entire day of your trip at either of these destinations or found their prices overbearing, the Central Florida Zoo is worth a visit. It may be a slight drive from Orlando, taking about 30 minutes, but it is closer than Busch Gardens and makes a great half-day trip.

The zoo was founded in 1923 as the Sanford Zoo, moved to its current location in 1975, and has been growing ever since. The variety of species is impressive for such a small zoo. Cheetahs, crocodiles, giraffes, lemurs, leopards, and zebus are some of the more interesting animals you will see as you traverse the boardwalks, etched with names of prior visitors. The zoo also offers a free audio tour using your cell phone.

Weekend visitors will be able to partake in the zoo's lectures and animal interactions. The current weekend schedule is as follows but is subject to change at any time, so call ahead before the day of your visit: Rhino at 10:30 a.m., Cheetah at 11 a.m., *Flying High!* at 11:30 a.m., *Venom!* at noon, *Wild Tales!* at 1:30 p.m., Giraffe at 2:30 p.m., Spider Monkey at 3 p.m., and Snake or Alligator/Crocodile Feeding at 3:30 p.m. A member of the zoo staff hosts each 15- to 30-minute exhibition and gives a short fact-laden lecture and answers any questions.

Because almost all the zoo's exhibits are outside, except for the Discovery Center with its 10-centimeter millipedes and Goliath tarantulas, you will need good weather. Sunscreen and water are also advisable, especially with the small aquatic play area called **Tropical Splash Ground** (bring swimsuits and towels). A snack bar is on the premises, but you are better off bringing your own food; picnic tables are located just outside the zoo entrance.

The zoo also features—but does not operate—an aerial-adventures attraction called **ZOOm Air**. With a pleasing nod to younger children, the Kids' Course is restricted to those 36–60 inches tall, but on this junior version of a zip line, the kids are never more than 4 feet above the ground—close enough that an adult could walk alongside for moral and physical support. There are some minimal obstacles to overcome and a brief zip line swing at the end. Cost is $19.75 plus tax. Estimated time to complete the Kids Course is 45–75 minutes.

More intense are the Rainforest and Upland courses, each with a 54-inch height minimum. Upland has four zip lines and more than two dozen elements to navigate, with a maximum height as you progress to 35 feet above the ground. Each participant is always hooked to a safety line. Among the various challenges is a series of bridges with differing "floors" to step on—narrow planks or wide planks that are regularly and irregularly spaced, poles, netting, angular planks, various alternating shapes such as a circle or a triangle, and even a single cable beneath you (you hold on to the overhead safety cable for balance). Options for height and difficulty allow each person to customize their experience. Cost for Upland is $30.95 plus tax. Estimated time to complete the course is 1½ hours.

The Rainforest course has five zip lines and more than two dozen similar challenges, and you are almost 50 feet aboveground. Rainforest can only be experienced after doing the Upland course; that joint ticket is $50.95 plus tax, and the estimated time for completing Rainforest is an additional hour.

Zoo admission is not included with ZOOm Air's prices but is also not required for ZOOm Air. Last admission for the Kids' Course is 4:30 p.m., and for the Upland/Rainforest courses, it's 4 p.m.

A word of caution: While there is instruction and a practice area for the zip lining, and the receiving platforms are padded, there is no one to catch you at these platforms. If you do not brake properly or are not arriving feet first, there is no professional aide to slow or turn you. This would not be a good introduction to zip lining.

Forever Florida ★ ★ ★ ★

4755 N. Kenansville Rd., St. Cloud; ☎ 407-957-9794; **foreverflorida.com**

Hours Daily, 9 a.m.–5 p.m.; reservations required for horseback rides and recommended for other attractions. **Cost** See individual attraction descriptions for prices.

DESCRIPTION AND COMMENTS A long drive from Walt Disney World at a little more than 1 hour, Forever Florida may fit into your plans if you are either headed to Miami or have just finished an airboat tour south of Kissimmee. Forever Florida is 4,700 acres of working cattle ranch, nature conservancy, and thrilling, zip line–oriented rides. It offers hiking trails, horseback safaris, eco-safaris, and several adventures using zip line and other treetop devices.

When you arrive, you should report to the main desk, located in the Cypress Lodge. The lodge is clean and modern and contains the Cypress Restaurant, whose menu consists of grass-fed beef raised on the ranch there, as well as barbecue pork, salads, and sandwiches.

The **horseback experiences** vary in length from 1½ hours to overnight excursions, and all require reservations, closed-toe shoes, and long pants. You will not see much on the 1½-hour Horseback Safari ($70 plus tax for each rider; departures at various times during the day) but scrub, dried-out pine trees, open fields, and streams. The Rawhide Roundup ($99 plus tax per person with a minimum of four participants) is a 2-hour experience that includes both horseback riding and lessons in being a ranch hand. The Overnight Horseback Safari ($199 plus tax per person with a minimum of four participants) includes riding, campsite meals, and overnight camping.

The **Wild Coach Adventure Tours** are 2 hours aboard a specially built vehicle with large tires that provides an elevated view of part of the cattle ranch, then travels past a small ditch with alligators, and then out into the conservation area. This trip begins with an explanation of the creation of Forever Florida and the dedication of the area to the son of the owners, a young man who was an environmentalist before his life was cut short by cancer. The tour is fully narrated, and though it won't captivate younger kids, it is one of the most educational attractions in Central Florida. After a ride through the open fields, you arrive at Bull Creek and walk around the promenade, and then return back to the lodge.

We support Forever Florida's commitment to preservation and think it has a fine product, but we would be remiss if we didn't emphasize the often-plain and somewhat uninspiring landscape. Besides Bull Creek, the open plains and mild woodlands are not very scenic. However, the zip line adventure tours increase the entertainment level for many guests.

These various adventures (the Peregrine Plunge, Panther Pounce, and Rattlesnake Zipline Roller Coaster) are grouped in a single admission called the **Thrill Pack** ($70 plus tax per person). The **Peregrine Plunge** is a 1,300-foot-long zip line straightaway. The rider starts at a platform 71 feet above the ground—be ready to climb seven stories to enjoy this ride—and reaches speeds up to 30 miles per hour, a pretty good clip when you can see the ground rushing below and the end platform racing toward you. For those *really* not afraid of heights, the **Panther Pounce** has you hooked to a cable as you step off a platform 68 feet above the ground. Pulleys work to slow your descent, but this is not a zip line–style glide: You are going down, not across. The **Rattlesnake Zipline Roller Coaster** is a new generation of canopy thrill rides, a solid rail under which the rider glides via the harness and safety lines. But unlike the standard zip line cable, the Rattlesnake railing curves, dips, and has small rises. Though the rider leaves from a 65-foot-high platform and the course is about 1,000 feet, the speed is not breathtaking, but the steep drop just before you come into a landing, and the sharp bounce at the bottom over gator-friendly waters, may well launch your lunch.

In addition to the Thrill Pack, the **Zipline Adventure** ($80 plus tax per person) lasts 2½ hours, but allow at least 4 hours for the entire experience. A special all-terrain coach transports you to the zip line area, where everyone is suited up in safety gear. The harness keeps you in a sitting position while zipping across the trees. The zip line tour and Thrill Pack are open to anyone age 8 and up who weighs 55–265 pounds, and both experiences require you to wear knee-length or longer clothing and closed-toe shoes.

During the course, your tour guides will help you cross seven zip lines and two footbridges. At the highest point you will be 68 feet in the air and can zoom up to 30 miles per hour down the zips. One tour guide will be the first to go across each zip and be on the other side ready to catch everyone. The tops of trees are the main scenery, but the fourth zip line features a small pond with one small alligator in it. The main thrill is gliding along the treetops.

Evening tours are offered and occur in complete darkness with no lights to illuminate your way up the ladders. The tours operate in the rain, cold, or extreme heat but not during high winds or lightning. Summer is the busy season and also extremely hot. To ensure a pleasurable experience, try to book in the winter or fall to avoid the summer heat.

Green Meadows Petting Farm ★★★½ / ★★★★

1368 S. Poinciana Blvd., Kissimmee; ☎ 407-846-0770; **greenmeadowsfarm.com**

Hours Tours operate continuously 9:30 a.m.–4 p.m. (Last tour begins at 2:30 p.m.) **Cost** $23 + tax for age 13 and up; $20 + tax for children ages 3–12; $21 + tax for Florida residents; $19 + tax for seniors and military; $5 + tax for children age 2. **Comments** ★★★★ for preschoolers and grade-schoolers; ★★★½ for anyone older.

DESCRIPTION AND COMMENTS Six miles down Poinciana Boulevard off US 192, you will find Green Meadows Petting Farm on the right side. The 40-acre "farm" features animal interactions. The animals include the standard barnyard fare of chickens and goats, pigs and cows, but also more exotic animals such as llamas and zorses. After you buy your tickets, the attendant at the booth will show you where you can meet up with the rest of the tour. A guide will take you on a 2-hour tour of the animals and rides. Each station features a different animal and takes 5–15 minutes to visit.

The farm is clean and well maintained. Though only a fence separates you from the highway, the traffic noise is slight, for the most part, and most of the attractions are set back from the road. Scattered tractors and other farm equipment add to the farm theme (no sharp equipment), and besides the smell of animals, the place is charming.

The animal interactions are as up close as you can imagine. At the chicken station, you can pick up and hold the baby chickens. You can pet and feed most of the other animals, including the sheep, goats, pigs, and alpacas, and everyone gets a turn to milk the cow and ride the pony. All of the animal feed is free, and hand-sanitizer locations are at every station. There are some larger animals here, and though you cannot pet all of them, they are worth seeing. These include ostriches, llamas, zebus, a zorse (a horse-and-zebra offspring), water buffalo, and the like.

Besides the animal exhibits, a small train takes guests around the perimeter of the park, and there is also a hayride. For in-park personal transportation, you can rent a small red wagon for $3 to pull diapers and tired children. Most children will love all of the animal interactions. Children will find this place much more interesting than adults will, and you may get a bit restless. Prying them away from the petting zoo, even if they've already seen everything, almost always results in tears, but these can be mended with the bribe of ice cream.

HORSEBACK RIDING
All Hitched Up

1141 Fort Hill Rd., St. Cloud; ☎ 407-908-8716; **allhitchedup.com**

Hours Monday–Saturday, 10 a.m.–6 p.m.; Sunday, 11 a.m.–6 p.m. **Cost** 45-minute beginner trail: $40 + tax per person. 1-hour intermediate trail: $50 + tax per person. 90-minute adventure trail: $70 + tax per person. 2-hour adventure trail with picnic: $95 + tax per person. 3- to 4-hour adventure trail: $125 + tax per person. 30-minute carriage ride (4-adult maximum): $60. 1-hour carriage ride (4-adult maximum): $100.

DESCRIPTION AND COMMENTS All Hitched Up offers horseback rides through St. Cloud's Lake Lizzie Nature Preserve for all different levels of equestrian expertise, from first-timer trails for kids as young as age 4, to multi-hour treks through lakes and marshes (you will get wet). You can also book carriage rides, take private lessons, or even get married here, if so inspired.

Al-Marah Arabian Horses

1105 Autumn Ln., Clermont; ☎ 407-301-0800; **al-marah.com**

Hours Daily, 9 a.m.–4 p.m. **Cost** Interactive Horse Experience: $195 + tax for first participant; $95 + tax for each additional participant, up to 6 people; free for observers. VIP barn tour: $20 + tax per person.

DESCRIPTION AND COMMENTS When the long-running *Arabian Nights* dinner show shut down, some feared for the fate of its equine stars, but owner Mark Miller has put his stable of horses out to pasture in a way that still lets equestrian enthusiasts enjoy these amazing creatures. Hard-core horse lovers can have a hands-on Interactive Horse Experience, where you'll meet and greet some of the 70-plus former performers, get a riding lesson tailored to your expertise level, learn secrets of mane braiding, and even create a real live horse of a different color. If that's a little too much horsing around for you, an hour-long guided tour of the barns is reasonably priced, as are à la carte 30- and 60-minute riding lessons; a 30-minute intro class is tailored toward children climbing on horseback for their first time. Reservations are by phone only; call to book at least two days in advance of your visit.

Rock Springs Run Trail Rides

31700 County Road 433, Sorrento; ☎ 352-266-9326; **rockspringsruntrailrides.com**

Hours By reservation. **Cost** 1-hour ride: $50 + tax per person. 90-minute ride: $60 + tax per person. 2-hour ride: $70 + tax per person. Discounts may be available through Groupon.

DESCRIPTION AND COMMENTS This gentle, family-oriented horseback ride takes you through a nature reserve with forests, meadows, and an old cemetery. It's located about 30 minutes northwest of Orlando near the Wekiwa Springs State Park (**floridastateparks.org/park/wekiwa-springs**), which offers primitive campsites and world-class paddling opportunities.

 *And* **MORE**

Machine Gun America   ★★★½

5825 W. Irlo Bronson Memorial Hwy., Kissimmee; ☎ 407-278-1800; **machinegunamerica.com**

Hours Daily, 10 a.m.–9 p.m. **Cost** Live shooting packages: $99.99–$799.99 + tax per person. Cadet package for children ages 10–12: $49.99 + tax. Virtual simulator: $30 for first 30 minutes; $20 for additional 30 minutes.

DESCRIPTION AND COMMENTS Machine Gun America is a fully enclosed facility, but because we don't usually think of firing fully automatic weapons as an indoor activity, we've decided to include it here. Conveniently located across the street from Old Town, Machine Gun America (MGA) allows you to exercise your Second Amendment rights—even if you have absolutely no prior gun experience—in a safe, air-conditioned environment. MGA was founded by a couple of people from Machine Gun Vegas, which is our pick for the best shooting range in Sin City. This Kissimmee counterpart isn't quite as plush, but it has a clean, brightly lit lobby where you can look into the firing ranges. To step into one, you'll need to select a weapons package, which will include use of between 2 and 11 firearms, ammunition for each, and a safety instructor (mostly ex-military or law enforcement) to guide you through the process. You even get to pick out your own paper target to aim at: zombie, terrorist, zombie terrorist, and so on. Weapon packages have themes such as Special Ops, 007, or Big Screen Legends, and they'll tell you what movies each gun was featured in. A semiautomatic rifle special just for tweens (with parental permission, of course) includes a blood-spurting undead target. Pony up for the ultimate Man Card package, and you'll have 345 rounds of ordnance to blast away with, including 10 shots with a Remington 700 sniper rifle. Some weapons can be added on to a package, and you can buy extra ammo; be careful, or you could blow a bigger hole in your wallet than on any bull's-eye.

After you've exhausted your ammo, you can fire virtual bullets in one of MGA's virtual combat simulation rooms, similar to those used to train cops and soldiers. The simulators feature realistic-looking laser rifles and wall-size projection screens; it's a bit like a grown-up version of the old Mad Dog McCree light-gun arcade games.

Orlando Balloon Rides ★ ★ ★ ★

44294 US 27, Davenport; ☎ 407-894-5040 (flight line status: ☎ 407-374-2622); **orlandoballoonrides.com**

Hours Daily; arrive approximately 30 minutes before sunrise. **Cost** Monday–Friday: $195 + tax per person. Saturday–Sunday: $225 + tax per person.

DESCRIPTION AND COMMENTS The sensation of being in a hot-air balloon is unlike any other form of flight: Serene and silent, you effortlessly float above the landscape and imagine what clouds must feel like. If that image appeals to you and you aren't afraid of heights, Orlando Balloon Rides operates some of the area's largest air-powered aircraft. This adventure requires sacrificing some sleep because you'll have to report before dawn to the departure field in Davenport, about 15 miles southwest of Walt Disney World. While you stand around yawning and signing paperwork, the flight crew will be busy blasting the afterburners to inflate your balloon, a fascinating process to watch.

Once your airship is erect, it's time to climb into the big basket; depending on how many are aboard, it can be a bit of a cozy fit, but the chest-high sides should ease any anxiety about accidentally tumbling overboard. Then it's up, up, and away, wherever the wind takes you; your FAA-certified pilot can control your altitude, but direction is largely up to Mother Nature. Depending on which way you wander, you may see Florida's unspoiled wilderness, carefully manicured golf courses, or even a glimpse of the attractions. After about an hour, you'll return to terra firma (the landing can be a bit of a thrill ride, depending on wind speed), and the chase crew will be there to take you back to where you started for a traditional Champagne toast.

A balloon flight should be on everyone's bucket list, but there is a big catch; they can only fly in favorable weather, and departures may be scratched on short notice for safety. Reserve your flight in advance, and be sure to call the flight line the night before to confirm your trip. Even if the weather looks clear, be sure to wear warm clothes (think layers) and flat shoes; it can get chilly at 500 feet. As Orlando attractions go, this is among the most expensive, but you can save around 30% with Groupon vouchers.

Orlando Tree Trek Adventure Park ★★★

7625 Sinclair Rd., Kissimmee; ☎ 407-390-9999; **orlandotreetrek.com**

Hours Daily, 8 a.m.–sunset. **Cost** Kids Course (ages 7–11): $29.95 + tax. Junior Course (ages 9–11): $38.95 + tax. Adult Course (age 12+): $49.95 + tax; $39.95 for seniors age 65 and older and active or retired military with ID. Climbing glove rental: $3.

DESCRIPTION AND COMMENTS Orlando Tree Trek offers an outdoor ropes course adventure similar to those found at Forever Florida (see page 350) and the Central Florida Zoo (see page 349), only without the abundance of animals or the hour-plus drive from Orlando. The obstacle course goes from 10 to 60 feet above the forest floor; multiple color-coded routes accommodate different heights and skill levels. The Kids Course is designed for parents to watch (and snap photos) while their children climb, while the Junior and Adult Courses both climax in a 425-foot-long giant zip line. The full circuit takes up to 3 hours to complete, including your safety briefing and equipment fitting. Visit the website to learn specific size requirements for each course, and download a waiver to save time when you arrive.

PART FOURTEEN

MUSEUMS *and* CULTURAL ATTRACTIONS

MANY VISITORS TO ORLANDO LIMIT THEIR VISITS to a few major theme parks, bypassing the local community. There is often no time allotted for days outside the major parks, and with a run-til-you-drop vacation mentality, many people will find themselves worn out, in need of the proverbial vacation from their vacation.

Because the ride-to-ride shuffle of the major parks becomes monotonous after a few days, and that distinguishing line between individual attractions begins to blur, it becomes important to spark your brain before atrophy sets in. The museums and cultural attractions of Central Florida all offer convenient ways to reactivate your mind, and most are very interesting. From Orlando Science Center's exhibits on astronomy and dinosaurs to the Morse Museum's collections of Tiffany glassware, Central Florida contains museums and cultural attractions for all ages and tastes. The prices for many of the exhibits are also more affordable than their touristy competition, and crowds and lines are almost always less.

Thanks to the steady employment offered by the attractions, Orlando is home to a surprisingly large number of fine and performing artists who lend their after-hours talents to local cultural institutions. And with the development of state-of-the-art venues downtown, including the **Amway Center** (**amwaycenter.com**) and **Dr. Phillips Center for the Performing Arts** (**drphillipscenter.org**), Orlando is regularly hosting top-name touring concerts and Broadway shows, which supplement a rich year-round calendar of homegrown festivals and arts events. To keep up with the latest in Central Florida's vibrant arts scene, visit **orlando weekly.com, orlandosentinel.com,** and **orlandoatplay.com.**

KIDS *and* MUSEUMS

MENTION TO MANY ADULTS that you are planning a trip to a museum, and you may receive the requisite groans of disgust. But children have a natural curiosity about the arts, science, and the world around them; if the adults in their lives evidence enthusiastic reactions to museums, gardens, and other cultural attractions, kids are likely to adopt similar attitudes.

Of course, it may be challenging to convince your family to take time away from the major theme parks, with their cartoon-character mascots and patina of utter happiness, especially if you have only a few days in the area. However, if you are a repeat visitor to Orlando, or are here on an extended holiday, it's worth your while to take a break from manufactured fantasy and explore a different type of park.

Because many of the following institutions are within blocks of Loch Haven Cultural Park on the north side of Orlando (take I-4 East to Exit 85 and make a right onto Princeton Street), you could easily make a day out of the attractions clustered there—including the Orlando

Museum of Art, Mennello Museum, and Orlando Science Center— along with the Cornell Fine Arts Museum and Harry P. Leu Gardens a short distance away. Enjoy a meal in the hip Mills 50 district (home to the best Vietnamese restaurants outside of Ho Chi Minh City), and then return to Loch Haven in the evening for a play.

However you plan your itinerary, stay attuned to the likes and dislikes of your group. If you can find something at one of these venues that sparks your child's interest in a new subject, you could come home with a lasting souvenir far more valuable than plastic mouse ears.

▮ ATTRACTIONS

Bok Tower Gardens ★★★

APPEAL BY AGE	PRESCHOOL ★★	GRADE SCHOOL ★★½	TEENS ★
YOUNG ADULTS ★★★	OVER 30 ★★★½		SENIORS ★★★★

1151 Tower Blvd., Lake Wales; ☎ 863-676-1408; **boktowergardens.org**

Hours *Gardens:* Daily, 8 a.m.–6 p.m. *Visitor Center:* Daily, 9 a.m.–5 p.m., with limited hours on holidays. *Pinewood Estate:* Monday-Saturday, 11 a.m.–3 p.m.; Sunday, noon–3 p.m. **Cost** *Gardens:* $12 for adults; $3 for children ages 5-12. *Estate* (includes gardens): $18 for adults; $8 for children ages 5-12; free for children age 4 and under.

DESCRIPTION AND COMMENTS A long, 55-mile drive away from the maelstrom of Orlando entertainment (but just 10 miles from Legoland), Bok Tower Gardens is a stately place for those seeking solace. Built on the top of Iron Mountain, the gardens offer some spectacular views of the plains 298 feet below—quite an altitude shift in Central Florida. The chief attractions are the gardens, the tower, and Pinewood Estate—though it is quite a trek on the hiking trails. The visitor center features a cutout of the Singing Tower's biggest bell, which is more than 6 feet tall and weighs almost 12 tons, along with displays about the endangered plants and animals that survive on the sand dunes of the nearby Lake Wales Ridge. Another guest favorite is the Window by the Pond, a small cabin with a serene view of the water.

The gardens were designed by the world-famous landscape architect Frederick Law Olmsted Jr., who, among other achievements, also designed landscaping for Washington's National Mall and the grounds of the White House. The gardens sprawl over the entire hilltop, and a mixture of concrete and wood-chip walking paths allow you to see most of the landscaping. The design of the gardens is exceptional, but many of the flowers are seasonal, so plan your visit accordingly. There are few plaques to tell you what the plants are, so take a free hour-long tour (Monday–Saturday, noon and 2 p.m.; Sunday, 2 p.m.) with one of the knowledgeable volunteer garden guides.

The Singing Tower at Bok is the literal centerpiece of the gardens. Built on top of the mountain, this neo-Gothic colossus dominates the landscape, made even more virile by the reflecting pool at its base. You cannot enter the tower or even cross the moat that surrounds it unless you donate at least $1,200 for a Tower Club membership, so don't plan on getting the view from the top. Daily carillon concerts are played at 1 and 3 p.m. from the bells at the top of the tower, and though some prolonged tones can be discordant, many patrons seem to enjoy the music.

Away from the tower, Pinewood Estate, on the far side of the hill from the visitor center, joined Bok Tower Gardens in 1970. Docents are prepared to answer your questions as you tour this Mediterranean Revivalist mansion.

At press time, Bok Tower Gardens was in the midst of a $12 million expansion project, announced on the park's 85th anniversary. Improvements include a new entryway that will make it easier to navigate the gardens (especially for those with mobility issues), a new 2.7-acre children's garden with an interactive playground, an outdoor kitchen for farm-to-table cooking demonstrations, and additional green space for special events. Construction should wrap up in 2016, with some areas of the gardens temporarily off-limits until then.

TOURING TIPS If your kids aren't into botany, they may become a bit bored and restless here. To prevent that, ask for a free family-adventure guide and loaner Discovery Backpack at the visitor center information desk. Inside you'll find nature books, binoculars, bubbles, and other educational baubles to keep the babes busy; just be sure to bring it back by 5 p.m.

Bok Tower Gardens is a silent place, and time passes very slowly on the mountain. Self-reflection and quietude are the two chief results of a visit, so prepare your head before you come. Much of the serenity propagated at the visitor center seems forced, but if you are ready for a bit of solitude and don't want to shell out for a mud spa, this is a high-quality alternative.

The Charles Hosmer Morse Museum of American Art
★★★★

APPEAL BY AGE	PRESCHOOL ★	GRADE SCHOOL ★★	TEENS ★★★
YOUNG ADULTS ★★★½	OVER 30 ★★★★		SENIORS ★★★★

445 N. Park Ave., Winter Park; ☎ 407-645-5311; **morsemuseum.org**

Hours Tuesday–Saturday, 9:30 a.m.–4 p.m.; Sunday, 1–4 p.m. (open until 8 p.m. on Friday, November–April); closed major holidays. **Cost** $5 for adults; $4 for seniors; $1 for students; free for children under age 12; free for everyone on Friday, 4–8 p.m., November–April.

DESCRIPTION AND COMMENTS After watching the introductory video, make your way through one of the world's most extensive and astounding collections of works by Louis Comfort Tiffany. The collection includes his jewelry, but the real gems—pun intended—are found in his glasswork. Vases, jars, lamps, and stained glass windows are all testament to his skill as a renowned craftsman.

The 6,000-square-foot Laurelton Hall displays some objects that belonged to the Morse collection—it owned 250 pieces salvaged from Tiffany's Long Island home before it was razed—but had not been displayed (except in an exhibit at New York's Metropolitan Museum of Art) due to a lack of space here until this wing was added in 2011. These fascinating pieces include a 13½-foot-tall marble mantelpiece, the stunning Daffodil Terrace with its iridescent glass skylight, and the *Tree of Life,* one of the last stained glass windows that Tiffany designed.

Also at the Morse Museum is the Tiffany Chapel. Built in 1893 for the World's Fair Columbian Exposition in Chicago, the chapel was almost destroyed multiple times before arriving in Florida in the mid-20th century. The porticos and stained glass are remarkable, but the chandelier, in the shape of a hypercube cross, will drop your jaw.

TOURING TIPS The one-story museum contains 19 small galleries, in addition to the 10 Laurelton Hall displays. The museum is kept at a cool 68°, so bring a light sweater if you wish. The layout is clean, and every item is well marked. Docent tours, which do not include Laurelton Hall, are often available daily; ask at the visitor information desk. Curator tours, which *do* include Laurelton Hall, are available at 11 a.m. and 2:30 p.m., Tuesday and Thursday, on a first-come, first-serve basis. After walking through the galleries, stop by the gift shop. It does not contain any authentic Tiffany but does sell some fine glasswork. After your visit to the Morse, take a stroll south past the ritzy shops along Park Avenue, or relax in Central Park and the nearby rose gardens, which are the site of monthly outdoor movies and other free family events; see **experienceparkavenue.com** for details.

Cornell Fine Arts Museum ★★★★

APPEAL BY AGE	PRESCHOOL ★★	GRADE SCHOOL ★½	TEENS ★★½
YOUNG ADULTS ★★★	OVER 30 ★★★½		SENIORS ★★★

1000 Holt Ave., Winter Park; ☎ 407-646-2526; **rollins.edu/cfam**

Hours Tuesday–Friday, 10 a.m.–4 p.m.; Saturday–Sunday, noon–5 p.m. **Cost** Free.

DESCRIPTION AND COMMENTS Unlike many small museums, the six-gallery Cornell, located on the Rollins College campus, owns works by very substantial artists, including Winslow Homer, Henri Matisse, Pablo Picasso, Gilbert Stuart, and Tintoretto. The free admission, free parking, and lakeside location aren't bad visitor bait either.

TOURING TIPS Though the facility is large at 9,000 square feet, the museum still cannot display all 5,000 of its works at once. The collection rotates every few months, and two of the galleries regularly feature traveling exhibits. Despite its small size, the Cornell boasts one of the best fine art collections in Central Florida, and Rollins College itself is an architectural treasure that was named "America's Most Beautiful Campus" by Princeton Review. Pair a visit here with a trip to the Morse Museum, less than a mile away.

Harry P. Leu Gardens ★★★½

1920 N. Forest Ave., Orlando; ☎ 407-246-2620; **leugardens.org**

Hours Daily, 9 a.m.–5 p.m.; last admission is 4:30 p.m.; closed December 25. **Cost** $10 + tax for adults; $3 + tax for children attending kindergarten–12th grade; free for children age 4 and younger.

DESCRIPTION AND COMMENTS Less isolated than Bok Tower Gardens, the Harry P. Leu Gardens are situated in downtown Orlando, only a few blocks from the Orlando Science Center and the Orlando Museum of Art. Besides the location, the gardens' free parking and low admission prices are also appealing to visitors.

There are 50 acres' worth of smaller gardens situated within the Harry P. Leu Gardens. You enter through the Tropical Stream Garden, home to a variety of exotic equatorial plants. Continuing clockwise, you'll pass through the Idea Gardens, where you may pick up tips for landscaping your own yard. Next you will reach the Vegetable Garden and then the Butterfly Garden.

In the bottom corner of the gardens is the Arid Garden (cacti and the like) and multitudes of camellias. As you continue along the paths, you will pass more flowers at the Rose Garden and Floral Clock before reaching the forest area. Here, you will find bamboo, pines, live oaks, cycads, and an array of deciduous and coniferous trees. The forest area also borders Lake Rowena. Stop at the small overlook before you make your way back to the entrance.

The Leu Museum House is located at the gardens and belonged to the benefactor Harry P. Leu before he donated the land to the city of Orlando in 1961. Tours of this refurbished house are available daily every half hour 10 a.m.–3:30 p.m., but please note, the house is generally closed in July.

TOURING TIPS Children may become a bit bored here, but adults over age 30 and seniors with a green thumb should find more than a few good ideas for their gardens at home. The palm trees and bamboo groves in the back of the gardens make a great place for a picnic, as does the lakefront deck. Admission is free for all on the first Monday of each month (September–January), with story time for the kids at 10 a.m.

The Mennello Museum of American Art ★★★

900 E. Princeton St., Orlando; ☎ 407-246-4278; **mennellomuseum.com**

Hours Tuesday–Saturday, 10:30 a.m.–4:30 p.m.; Sunday, noon–4:30 p.m.; closed major holidays. **Cost** $5 + tax for adults; $4 + tax for seniors age 60 and older; $1 + tax for students with ID and children ages 6–18; free for children under age 6 and active military with ID.

DESCRIPTION AND COMMENTS When you walk in, your first question will be, "Where is the rest of the museum?" We're not sure, but the four rooms do hold a fine, if compact, collection of local and national artists. About half of the artworks on display are by Earl Cunningham, a St. Augustine resident and folk artist. The majority of his works are oil paintings on fiberboard. Most depict landscapes dotted with ships and houses, images ingrained from his upbringing in Edgecomb, Maine, and his travels up and down the East Coast. His use of vivid colors is unique, and his ability to flatten three-dimensional shape is reminiscent of Fauvism.

Though tiny, the Mennello Museum is actually a Smithsonian affiliate, so the remaining galleries are regularly rotated with well-curated traveling exhibits. The Mennello, which has been honored by *Playground* magazine and *USA Today* as a top family-friendly cultural attraction, hosts Family Day on the second Sunday of every month, with free art activities for children. The museum is also home to an Indie Folkfest Music Festival (**orlandofolkfestival.word press.com**) in February and the annual Kids' Fringe Festival (**orlandofringe .org/what/kids-fringe**) in late May. Finally, it's worth strolling the grounds of the museum to view the sculpture garden and The Mayor, an enormous tree that, at more than 350 years old, is among the oldest oaks in the area.

TOURING TIPS Check out an Earl Cunningham painting before arriving to see if it suits your taste. Some works may be seen online at **mennello museum.com.** Behind the museum is a large grassy area on the side of Lake Formosa, a good place for a picnic.

Orange County Regional History Center ★★★

APPEAL BY AGE	PRESCHOOL ★★	GRADE SCHOOL ★★★½	TEENS ★★
YOUNG ADULTS ★★★	OVER 30 ★★★½		SENIORS ★★★½

65 E. Central Blvd., Orlando; ☎ 407-836-8500 or ☎ 800-965-2030; **thehistorycenter.org**

Hours Monday–Saturday, 10 a.m.–5 p.m.; Sunday, noon–5 p.m.; closed major holidays. Cost $8 for adults; $7 for children ages 5–12; free for children age 4 and younger.

DESCRIPTION AND COMMENTS With an apropos location in the heart of downtown Orlando, the history center documents the growth of the Orlando area. Besides the myriad of facts and artifacts, the museum's layout and theming rival those found in other major metro areas. Instead of placing each artifact in a glass case with a small explanatory plaque, the museum has integrated many of them into re-creations, or has placed them in unorthodox positions, such as hanging from the ceiling.

Visitors start their chronological tour on the fourth floor with the American Indian and pioneer exhibits. The Timucuan were the original inhabitants of the area, and the museum goes a long way to bring them back to life by displaying original canoes, wax sculptures of the people, and the remains of a massive shell pile. Skipping across the hall transports you a few hundred years into the future to a room dedicated to the first homesteaders. Re-creations of their lives and documents of their hardships fill this room. A replica of a cabin, complete with period tools, is the centerpiece of the exhibit.

Descending to the third floor, visitors will find a restored 1927 criminal court, which is worth a peek if meetings are not being held. Across from this is the exhibit on the area between 1900 and 1971, when Disney came to town. The second floor is home to modern regional history, ranging from the civil rights movement to the influence of Disney on the community. The positive economic impact of Disney is balanced against the displays highlighting the rise in crime and expansion of urban sprawl. In addition to the permanent galleries, the History Center often presents traveling exhibits with a pop-culture connection; displays in recent years have highlighted Jim Henson's Muppets, Warner Brothers cartoon art, and costumes from *Gone With the Wind.*

TOURING TIPS Though the theming is top-notch, the history lessons of Orange County may be more compelling to local residents than guests from other states, though the Disney material has broader appeal. For a chronological tour, begin on the top floor and work your way down. Street parking is difficult to find, though plenty of parking garages are in the neighborhood. If you do find street parking, the 2-hour time restraint should allow you enough time to peruse the museum and make it back to your car before you receive a ticket.

Orlando Museum of Art ★★★½

APPEAL BY AGE	PRESCHOOL ★★½	GRADE SCHOOL ★½	TEENS ★
YOUNG ADULTS ★★★	OVER 30 ★★★★	SENIORS ★★★★	

2416 N. Mills Ave., Orlando; ☎ 407-896-4231; **omart.org**

Hours Tuesday–Friday, 10 a.m.–4 p.m.; Saturday–Sunday, noon–4 p.m.; closed major holidays. **Cost** $10 for adults; $7 for seniors age 65 and older; $5 for children ages 4–17, military, and college students with ID; free for children age 3 and younger.

DESCRIPTION AND COMMENTS The collection of the largest art museum in the area is arrayed around a towering glass sculpture by Dale Chihuly (it looks a little like a giant psychedelic sea anemone) and includes a fine standing exhibit on the art of the ancient Americas (back to 2000 BC). More interesting for some will be the works of American artists such as John Singer Sargent, Thomas Moran, George Inness, Georgia O'Keeffe, and Ansel Adams highlighting the exhibition. A separate display includes some of the museum's signed and numbered original etchings and lithographs by such masters of the late 20th century as Andy Warhol and Robert Rauschenberg. Despite its small size, a dedicated donor base has allowed it to grow its permanent collection and bring world-class traveling works to Orlando, including a 2015 installation by Vietnam Veterans Memorial designer Maya Lin. Recently installed director Glen Gentele has reinvigorated the institution with a renewed focus on contemporary art, and OMA's monthly First Thursday art party is a trendy meeting spot for young culturistas.

TOURING TIPS Call ahead to see what exhibit the museum is hosting. Free parking is available in front of the impressive building, and the museum is located within walking distance of both the Mennello Museum and the Orlando Science Center.

kids Orlando Science Center ★★★★

APPEAL BY AGE	PRESCHOOL ★★★★	GRADE SCHOOL ★★★★½	TEENS ★★★½
YOUNG ADULTS ★★★½	OVER 30 ★★★½	SENIORS ★★★½	

777 E. Princeton St., Orlando; ☎ 407-514-2000 or ☎ 888-OSC-4FUN (672-4386); **osc.org**

Hours Daily, 10 a.m.–5 p.m.; closed Easter, Thanksgiving, and December 24–25. **Cost** $27 + tax for adults; $24 + tax for seniors age 55 and older and students with ID; $18 + tax for children ages 3–11; free for children age 2 and under. Prices vary for traveling exhibits.

DESCRIPTION AND COMMENTS When the thrill rides and shows have pounded your frontal lobe into slack-jawed submission, you may be ready for something more educational. In this case, a trip to the Science Center is a good idea, and more entertaining than you might expect. Like WonderWorks (see page 335), the Science Center contains a menagerie of scientific exhibits geared toward kids, a mixture of playtime and learning. Unlike WonderWorks, the Science Center provides more than a series of factoids that give a gist of the mechanics on hand. Almost every exhibit at the center contains an in-depth analysis of the history and physics behind the items on display. Most of the attractions found at Wonder-Works are found at the Orlando Science Center—but with exponentially more attractions, a much larger complex, a giant-screen dome theater, and shorter lines, the Orlando Science Center is the superior choice.

The first floor, located below the main entrance, contains the cafeteria, **NatureWorks, KidsTown,** and the **CineDome** theater. Animals such as baby alligators, sea turtles, stingrays, and fish can be found at NatureWorks at the base of the elevator. Check the daily schedule for feeding times.

Next to these natural exhibits is KidsTown, which at press time was in the process of being relocated to the second floor in a $5 million expansion. You must be less than 48 inches tall to enter, or be accompanying your child. Some high points of KidsTown are the tree house, the orange-picking simulator (we couldn't make that up), and the Water Table, where kids can build dams and channels.

The real draw on the first floor is the CineDome. The eight-story screen acts as both a theater and a planetarium. Tickets are included in your entrance fee; however, you will need to stop by the main ticket counter on the second floor before each show—we recommend 45 minutes before—to claim a seat. The quality of the movies varies, but the towering screen makes even the dullest documentary tolerable, and the interesting shows spellbinding. Remember, as with any theater attraction, adults with babies and children given to crying should sit in the back of the theater near the aisle. In addition to the CineDome, the Digital Adventure Theater has a conventionally shaped screen with cutting-edge 4K 3-D projectors. Science documentaries (similar to those on the CineDome but with an extra dimension) screen during the afternoon, and a second-run Hollywood film starts when the rest of the facility closes on Thursday–Sunday. The films are included in admission; tickets to the mainstream movies can also be purchased à la carte.

The other three floors of the museum contain nine massive halls with exhibits, science stations, and live programs that change seasonally. Permanent exhibit halls at OSC include **Our Planet, Our Universe** (with a Mars rover simulator and giant interactive globe), **Dino Digs** (where kids can uncover faux fossils), and **Science Park,** where you can race matchbox cars or pilot a flight simulator. The center also brings in top-notch traveling exhibits, such as a gallery of props and costumes from the Star Wars saga, and a collection of authentic Egyptian mummies and other preserved human remains. Admission prices may fluctuate depending on what blockbuster exhibit is installed; call ahead or check the museum's website to see what shows are occurring during your visit.

The cafeteria, located on the first floor, is now a Subway outlet. The recently enlarged gift shop, located on the second floor near the new front desk, is cheaper than many Florida attractions and features many educational toys. Puzzles, space shuttle models, books, glow-in-the-dark stars to decorate your ceiling, and construction helmets with lanterns are all on sale here.

TOURING TIPS This museum is a fantastic mixture of learning and play. The building is laid out around an open and circular center, with a glass elevator in the middle. There are four floors in the Science Center, and you may see them in any order, though starting on the second floor and working up, saving the first floor for last, is our preferred method. Maps are available at the front desk/ticket window. The Orlando Science Center is rarely crowded on days when school is in session but can be overwhelmed on rainy weekends and holidays. During the year, OSC hosts periodic special events like Science Night Live, where adult amateur astronomers can take a peek through the Crosby Observatory's telescope, and the annual Otronicon (**otronicon.com**) video game and simulation technology fair. And if your child has an autism spectrum disorder, OSC holds Sensory Mornings on select Sundays with sensory-friendly light and sound levels; see the website for a schedule.

Orlando Shakespeare Theater at the Lowndes Shakespeare Center ★★★★½

APPEAL BY AGE	PRESCHOOL ★★	GRADE SCHOOL ★★½	TEENS ★★★
YOUNG ADULTS ★★★★	OVER 30 ★★★★★		SENIORS ★★★★★

812 E. Rollins St., Orlando; ☎ 407-447-1700; **orlandoshakes.org**

Hours Performance schedule varies. *Box office:* Tuesday–Friday, noon–5 p.m.; Saturday–Sunday, 1 hour before showtime. **Cost** Varies by show. General admission to main stage shows: $21–$60. Children's series shows: $15 for adults; $12 for children. Military discounts and student rush tickets are available.

DESCRIPTION AND COMMENTS Located across the Loch Haven Cultural Park parking lot from Orlando Museum of Art, the Orlando Shakespeare Theater at the Lowndes Shakespeare Center—or the Orlando Shakes, as its known to local theatergoers—is like a multiplex cinema for the legitimate stage. Inside, you'll find no fewer than five performance spaces, ranging from the 324-seat arena-style Margeson Theater to the intimate 69-seat Santos Dantin Studio. All are fully equipped with modern lighting and sound technology, and on any given weekend you might find three or more plays being performed simultaneously.

Orlando Shakes's resident company has received accolades from *The Wall Street Journal* and other national critics for its engaging interpretations of the Bard's classics (it performs two in rotating repertory each spring), as well as its mountings of modern works; its 27th season included recent Broadway hits *Peter and the Starcatcher* and *Vanya and Sonia and Masha and Spike*. Shakes also sponsors an annual PlayFest, where the National New Play Network premieres original scripts and creates an original children's series with comical twists on familiar fairy tales.

Hidden in the back corner of Shakes's courtyard, the Orlando Fire Museum (☎ 407-246-3128; **cityoforlando.net/fire/community**) showcases antique fire engines and other equipment used by the Orlando Fire Department, which dates to 1885. The two-story brick firehouse is open Friday, 9 a.m.–3 p.m., and Saturday, 9 a.m.–4 p.m.

In addition to the shows presented by Orlando Shakes, the stages are rented out to local "gypsy" theater companies, both community and professional. Many of these productions, listed in the *Orlando Weekly* and *Orlando Sentinel*'s arts calendars, are very polished, and ticket prices are usually less than $25. If in town during the Halloween season, keep an eye out for Phantasmagoria (**phantasmagoriaorlando.com**), a Victorian steampunk storytelling troupe that happens to be coproduced by one of this book's coauthors.

Orlando Shakes is also ground zero for the Orlando International Fringe Theatre Festival (**orlandofringe.org**), the oldest such performing arts festival in the country and one of the largest outside the original in Edinburgh, Scotland. During the 13 days each May leading up to Memorial Day, more than 100 different productions from all over the world are staged at the Shakes and in surrounding venues, representing every genre and style of show imaginable, from one-man monologues to cast-of-thousands musicals. All tickets are priced at $12 or less (after purchasing a $9 festival admission button), and there are plenty of free performances and fair foods on the festival lawn. Not all shows are family-friendly (some are downright family-hostile), but the Kids' Fringe activities on weekends balance them out, providing something for every age and taste (or lack thereof).

If you are interested in Orlando's theater scene, other area stages worth checking out include the Orlando Repertory Theater (**orlandorep.com**), a professional children's theater located across Loch Haven Cultural Park from the Shakes; The Venue (**thevenueorlando.com**) in nearby Ivanhoe Village, a cabaret-style black box that specializes in burlesque and contemporary dance; and Mad Cow Theatre (**madcowtheatre.com**) on downtown's Church Street, with two handsome houses presenting professional casts in challenging contemporary classics.

Scenic Boat Tour ★★★½

APPEAL BY AGE	PRESCHOOL ★★	GRADE SCHOOL ★★½	TEENS ★½
YOUNG ADULTS ★★★	OVER 30 ★★★½		SENIORS ★★★★

312 E. Morse Blvd., Winter Park; ☎ 407-644-4056; **scenicboattours.com**

Hours Daily, 10 a.m.–4 p.m.; tours depart on the hour; closed December 25. **Cost** $12 for adults; $6 for children ages 2–11; free for children age 1 and under; cash or checks only. **Duration of tour** 1 hour.

DESCRIPTION AND COMMENTS Scenic Boat Tour is located on Lake Osceola in Maitland, north of Orlando, a few miles from the Orlando Science Center and the Orlando Museum of Art, and near the Rollins College campus. The 1-hour tours begin on Lake Osceola.

The fully narrated tours take place on 18-passenger pontoon boats and review the history of Maitland County. After passing the summerhouse of oil tycoon Harry Sinclair, you squeeze through a thin canal into 223-acre Lake Virginia. Modern mansions adorn the east side of the lake, while Rollins College, and the home of the late Mr. Rogers of children's TV fame, are to the west. Passing back through the canal and to the other side of Lake Osceola, you head through a longer and thinner canal into Lake Maitland. Here you will see more mansions, including one previously owned by basketball star Horace Grant. The tour is similar to being in the backyard of the very affluent, but aside from the stargazing, you'll get a glimpse into an Old Florida that is rapidly fading into history. And depending on how high the lake's water level is, you may get a head-chopping thrill as your captain navigates below low bridges.

TOURING TIPS The boat is a fine way to break up your day while touring museums, and the narration is very informative, though the guides are hesitant about revealing the present owners of the houses you pass by. The boats have no bathrooms and the seats are not covered, so be sure to use the facilities dockside and bring sunscreen and sunglasses.

PART FIFTEEN

AFTER DARK

DINNER SHOWS

CENTRAL FLORIDA PROBABLY HAS MORE dinner attractions than anywhere else on Earth. The name *dinner attraction* is something of a misnomer because dinner is rarely the attraction. These are audience-participation shows or events with food served along the way. They range from extravagant productions where guests sit in arenas at long tables, to intimate settings at individual tables. Don't expect terrific food, but if you're looking for something entertaining outside of Walt Disney World, consider one of these.

If you decide to try a non-Disney dinner show, scavenge local tourist magazines from brochure racks and hotel desks outside Disney World. These free publications usually have discount coupons.

Capone's Dinner & Show

APPEAL BY AGE	PRESCHOOL ★	GRADE SCHOOL ★★★½	TEENS ★★★½
YOUNG ADULTS ★★★	OVER 30 ★★★		SENIORS ★★★½

4740 W. US 192, Kissimmee; ☎ 407-397-2378 or 800-220-8428;
alcapones.com

Showtimes Mid-August–mid-June: nightly, 7:30 p.m. Mid-June–mid-August: nightly, 8 p.m. Additional shows and matinees may be added; see website for calendar. **Reservations** Make reservations several days in advance. **Cost** $65.98 + tax for adults; $41.98 + tax for children ages 4–12 (does not include tip). **Discounts** Book online or mention the Internet special when calling for a 50% discount; also discounts for Florida residents, AAA, seniors, military, and hospitality workers. **Type of seating** Long tables with large groupings facing an elevated stage; some smaller tables for parties of 2–6, or arrive 30–75 minutes early and request Al's Secret Hideaway Bar for balcony seating and preferred time at the buffet. **Menu** Buffet with lasagna, baked ziti, spaghetti, Italian sausage, chicken nuggets, roast turkey, steak, pork tenderloin, mashed potatoes, mac and cheese, pizza, salad bar, and brownies. **Vegetarian alternative** Spaghetti, ziti, cheese pizza, or pasta salad. **Beverages** Unlimited beer, wine, tea, coffee, and soft drinks. Rum Runners, rum and Coke, and vodka and cranberry juice are also available.

DESCRIPTION AND COMMENTS The audience, attending a celebration for mobster Al Capone at a 1930s speakeasy in Chicago, enters through a secret door using a password. The show is a musical of sorts, with most songs from other sources sung by cast members to recorded accompaniment. The story revolves around two female leads. There is Miss Jewel—the speakeasy's hostess, who is enamored of Detective Marvel, the only cop in Chicago whom Capone can't buy—and Bunny-June, one of Capone's favorite squeezes. Others have speaking roles, and there is a shoot-out, of course. (Can you say *Guys and Dolls?*)

The audience parades through the buffet line before the show; seconds are invited. The food, which had been passable in the past, should now just be passed up. Perhaps to compensate for the poor food quality, Capone's pours generous quantities of alcohol; the Rum Runners are probably the most potent bottomless drinks you'll find at any area dinner show.

For a musical, this show employs a lot of non-singers. Even the dancing is second-rate. The waiters—who speak with tough-guy accents and kid around with guests—did more to entertain the children than at any other show. Still, the theme is a bit too adult for families.

Two lines form before the show. You must go to the line on the left, directly into the box office, to pick up or purchase your tickets before joining the long line of guests leaning against the building. If you don't want to loiter outside, you can buy one drink per person and sit in the lounge upstairs.

kids Medieval Times Dinner and Tournament

APPEAL BY AGE	PRESCHOOL ★★★½	GRADE SCHOOL ★★★½	TEENS ★★★½
YOUNG ADULTS ★★★		OVER 30 ★★½	SENIORS ★★

4510 W. Vine St., Kissimmee; ☎ 866-543-9637; **medievaltimes.com /orlando.aspx**

Showtimes Vary according to season and nights. **Reservations** Best to make reservations a week ahead. **Cost** $62.95 + tax and processing fee for adults; $36.95 + tax and processing fee for children ages 3–12; free for children age 2 and younger who sit in adult's lap; tips not included. For $20 more, get first- or second-row seating, a photo of your group, and a behind-the-scenes DVD; inquire about other packages for added fees. **Discounts** Florida residents and seasonal discounts; call or check the website for current offers. **Type of seating** Arena style, in rows that face the riding floor. **Menu** Garlic bread, tomato bisque, roasted chicken, herb-basted potatoes, and apple pastry. Everything is eaten by hand. **Vegetarian alternative** Three-bean stew, raw veggies with hummus, and fresh fruit. **Beverages** Nonalcoholic beverages included; also a cash bar.

DESCRIPTION AND COMMENTS A tournament set 900 years in the past pits six knights against one another. Audience members are seated in areas corresponding to the color of the knights' pennants and are encouraged to cheer for their knight and boo his opponents. Part of the tournament is actual competition. The knights perform stunts, including hitting a target with a lance or collecting rings on a lance while riding on horseback. After each event, successful knights receive carnations from the queen to toss to young ladies in their sections.

After a while, the tournament takes on a choreographed feel—and with good reason. It comes down to a fight to the finish until only one knight is left standing. Cheating knights pull others off their horses and have hand-to-hand combat with maces, battle-axes, and swords. The winning knight selects a fair maiden from the audience to be his princess.

In all, the show is predictable fun, but the knights give 100% (the bruises they must get!). The sword fights are so realistic that sparks fly off the metal blades, but the kicking and punching choreography is worse than that found in professional wrestling. Even so, audience participation reaches a fevered pitch, with each section cheering for its knight and calling for the death of the dastardly opponents.

With all the horses, jousting, and fighting, children shouldn't be bored (though it does get repetitive), but parents of very young children might be concerned about the violence.

The food is remarkable only in that you eat it with your hands, including a quarter chicken you must pull apart. The chicken is good, but the soup tastes canned, and the ribs have been 86'ed off the menu. Arrive a little early and explore the Medieval Village just outside the castle. This cluster of authentic-looking cottages contains a free walk-through museum of daily life in the Dark Ages—including a blacksmith's forge and a gallery of gruesome torture devices—and houses some authentic antiques dating back 800 years.

Outta Control Magic Comedy Dinner Show at WonderWorks

APPEAL BY AGE	PRESCHOOL ★½	GRADE SCHOOL ★★★★	TEENS ★★★★
YOUNG ADULTS ★★★½		OVER 30 ★★★½	SENIORS ★★★

9067 International Dr., Orlando; ☎ 407-351-8800; **wonderworksonline.com**

Showtimes Nightly, 6 p.m. and 8 p.m. **Reservations** Can be made up to day of show. **Cost** $29.99 + tax for adults; $19.99 + tax for seniors and children ages 4–12 (does not include tip). **Discounts** Florida residents, AAA, AARP, and military. **Type of seating** Communal tables. **Menu** Unlimited pepperoni and cheese pizza, popcorn, salad, and cake. **Vegetarian alternative** Cheese pizza. **Beverages** Unlimited beer, wine, and soft drinks.

DESCRIPTION AND COMMENTS For younger children, this is the funniest dinner show in Orlando. A magician performs sleight of hand magic tricks coupled with a constant barrage of puns and sophomoric humor. A sound effects board with a series of push buttons allows the magician to add a version of morning radio show humor to his repertoire of jokes, all the while keeping the audience guessing, "What's in the box?!" Tony Brent is the regular headliner here, and he's a true talent who could easily get a gig in Vegas. The substitutes on his off nights (usually Sunday and Monday) are competent, but try to book based on Brent's performance calendar if you can.

Though legerdemain and a few other illusions will awe young children, adults may find the tricks ordinary and will be unimpressed with the magician's ability to make a sponge ball disappear. However, the magician's repartee with the audience keeps the show alive and entertaining. Almost every group of people who attends will have a member hauled up onto the stage. If you're brought up, the safest thing to do is just play along. You may get teased and hassled, but only a fraction as much as you will be for refusing to come on stage.

The show is enjoyable and the food service is good, but the pizza is just so-so, and you may have to share the popcorn bowls and pizza pies with other people's children. Make sure that your kids wash their hands before the show. Other than the communal consumption, the biggest issue is Outta Control's maddeningly inefficient check-in procedure. Even if you arrive 30 minutes before showtime as instructed, you'll still stand around aimlessly for a while. Try to pick up your tickets the day before, and show up extra early if you want to sit front and center. Otherwise, wait until the last minute to arrive and settle for a table in the back.

Pirate's Dinner Adventure

APPEAL BY AGE	PRESCHOOL ★★★½	GRADE SCHOOL ★★★★	TEENS ★★★
YOUNG ADULTS ★★½		OVER 30 ★★½	SENIORS ★★★

6400 Carrier Dr., Orlando; ☎ 407-206-5102 or 800-866-2469; **piratesdinneradventure.com/orlando**

Showtimes Sunday–Thursday, 7:30 p.m.; Friday–Saturday, 8:30 p.m. Additional shows may be added during busy seasons. **Reservations** Can be made up to day of show. **Cost** $65.95 + tax for adults; $39.45 + tax for children ages 3–12 (does not include tip). Upgrades to preferred seating, other food items, and more are available for $15–$30 per person; $5 parking fee. See the website for details. **Discounts** Online-only family packages are $35 + tax per person, with a minimum of four in the party; $38 each for a party of three; or $40 each for two. Seasonal offers on the website change frequently and can sometimes go as low as $29.99 per person. **Type of seating** Arena style. **Menu** Salad, soup, beef sirloin kabobs or half roasted chicken, rice and steamed vegetables, and fudge brownie à la mode; children's alternative is chicken nuggets and mac and cheese. **Vegetarian alternative** Lasagna. **Beverages** One mug of beer or two mugs of soda during the show; cash bar outside the performance arena.

DESCRIPTION AND COMMENTS Audience members are told to arrive long before the doors open to the auditorium. In the meantime, guests mill about and look over maritime memorabilia and the gift shop. If they've bought a ticket upgrade, they might be noshing on a buffet of appetizers and sipping adult beverages in a separate VIP room. As showtime approaches, a "host pirate" leads the audience members in song and dance. After a bit more preshow—everyone gets a paper pirate's hat—guests are ushered into the dining area, which features a large pirate-ship set, surrounded by water.

The set is impressive, and throughout the evening, energetic and even acrobatic pirates swoop from overhead, race around the ship in small boats, toss balls into nets with the help of audience volunteers, and bounce on a trampoline that's part of the ship's deck. What's mystifying is that there doesn't seem to be a reason for any of this. The script still doesn't make much sense even after the addition of a "Rise of the Sea Dragons" story line, and the climactic creatures look pretty cheesy, though the Cirque-style aerial acts are quite pretty. Special seasonal shows are cycled in for Halloween and Christmas. The sound system is poor, and it was difficult to tell what was going on and why. The audience sits in color-coded sections, and guests are encouraged to cheer for pirates wearing their colors as they compete against each other. There's plenty to interest kids. Adults might be interested, too, if the story were easier to follow.

Sleuths Mystery Dinner Shows

APPEAL BY AGE	PRESCHOOL ★	GRADE SCHOOL ★★★	TEENS ★★★½
YOUNG ADULTS ★★★★		OVER 30 ★★★★	SENIORS ★★★★

8267 International Dr., Orlando; ☎ 407-363-1985; **sleuths.com**

Showtimes Vary by season. Typically Saturday–Wednesday, 7:30 p.m.; Thursday–Friday, 6 p.m. and 7:30 p.m. Occasional matinees at noon. **Reservations** Can be made up to day of show. **Cost** $59.95 + tax for adults; $28.95 + tax for children ages 3–11 (does not include tip). **Discounts** Coupons for per-ticket discounts are available online; also discounts for Florida residents, AAA, and others; call the box office to find your best deal. **Type of seating** Large round tables that seat 8–10; some smaller tables. **Menu** Hot and cold hors d'oeuvres; tossed salad; cheese spread; choice of Cornish hen, prime rib (at an extra $6 + tax), or four-cheese lasagna; veggies and a potato; and mystery dessert. **Vegetarian alternative** Lasagna. **Beverages** Unlimited beer, wine, soft drinks, coffee, or tea.

DESCRIPTION AND COMMENTS Sleuths enact a repertoire of murder mysteries that the audience must solve. Guests are part of the show from the moment they enter the theater. Actors in character direct seating and try to drop clues as to who and what their parts are in the play. Though they work from a script, much of the show is ad-libbed. Fortunately, the cast tends to be very talented and capable of ad-libbing well. After the audience is seated, the first act occurs and someone is murdered. During intermission, each table must choose a spokesman and prepare a question to ask during the second act, when the collective audience interrogates the actors in an attempt (foolhardy as it seems, due to the actors' elusive responses) to solve the murder. Know that unless you come with a group of eight people, you will probably find yourself interacting with the strangers at your table.

Sleuths celebrated its 25th anniversary in 2015, and we've consistently found it to be our favorite of the area's entertainment eateries. You'll probably have more fun if you go with a large group and occupy your own table. Older children might find the show interesting, but younger ones may be bored and may disturb the other guests who are trying to follow the show. There are usually a half dozen or so mysteries rotating in the schedule.

The food at Sleuths is probably the best of any Orlando dinner show. The prime rib can be a bit tough, but it's often better than what you'd get at Outback, and the Cornish hen is always excellent.

After the show, stick around on Friday nights for *Mama's Comedy Show* (the funniest uncensored improv act in town) and on Saturdays for stand-up. Entry to *Mama's* is $5 with your Sleuths ticket or $10 for stand-alone admission; the stand-up is free with the purchase of a drink from Sleuths's full-service bar.

The Three Musketeers: Voyage Home

APPEAL BY AGE	PRESCHOOL ★★★½	GRADE SCHOOL ★★★½	TEENS ★★★
YOUNG ADULTS ★★★		OVER 30 ★★★	SENIORS ★★★

6400 Carrier Dr., Orlando; ☎ 407-206-5102; **3musketeersorlando.com**

Showtimes Friday–Saturday, 6 p.m.; Sunday, 3 p.m. **Reservations** Can be made up to day of show. **Cost** $65.95 + tax for adults; $39.45 + tax for children ages 3–12 (does not include tip); free for children age 2 and under. Upgrades to preferred seating, other food items, and more are available for $10–$20 per person; $5 parking fee. See the website for details. **Discounts** Tickets as low as $19 are frequently offered through the website and Groupon. **Menu** Salad; beef sirloin kabobs, half roasted chicken, or salmon with rice and steamed vegetables; and apple cobbler with ice cream. Children's alternative is chicken nuggets and mac and cheese. **Vegetarian alternative** Lasagna. **Beverages** Two rounds of beer, Pepsi products, or water. Cash bar available.

DESCRIPTION AND COMMENTS What do Alexander Dumas's 17th-century swashbucklers, 18th-century pirates, and 20th-century pop music have in common? Absolutely nothing! But that hasn't stopped the producers of Pirate's Dinner Adventure from installing a new show starring Athos, Aramis, Porthos, and D'Artagnan (yes, there are four for those of you keeping count) in their pirate-ship arena, to play on weekend afternoons before the scurvy stars perform their evening show. The setup is much the same, with the story line—wannabe Musketeer stows away on Queen Anne's France-bound boat to thwart an assassin and woo Her Majesty's handmaiden—set up in the preshow and played out in the main theater through acrobatics, audience-participation competitions, and anachronistic musical numbers.

The titular heroes take a backseat to the singing ingenues and Scooby-Doo-worthy villains (one of whom performs some memorable aerial contortions), and only one even attempts an accent, but the script is a master class in clarity compared to Pirate's incoherence, and the pace is pretty lively. As at Pirate's, volunteers from each color-coded seating section assist with American Gladiator–style games (ring tossing, cannon firing, and the like), but instead of dragging on interminably, these games are compressed into 15 minutes during dinner service. Speaking of dinner, the inedibly tough beef skewers are the same ones served at Pirate's, as is the liberally seasoned chicken. The salmon isn't bad and is included here but costs extra at the other show; the vegetarian lasagna may be the smartest choice.

The climactic cutlass-clashing fight sequences are knowingly filled with classic movie-combat clichés and are energetically executed, but they're undermined by cartoonish amplified sound effects that are out of sync with the swordplay. The sound system also undermines the singers, who have some talent but are turned to mush by the microphones. Though the lushly orchestrated pop songs (The Beatles, Styx, Madonna, and A-Ha are all in the mix) and melodramatic plot come across like a fever-dream community-theater production of *Moulin Rouge,* the personable cast just about makes it work with a fourth wall–breaking wink. If the idea of Cardinal Richelieu reciting preshow safety announcements makes you giggle, this might be just absurd enough for you. Though not among the top dinner shows in town, we think Three Musketeers is a better bet than its bigger brother, especially if you can get tickets for half-price or cheaper.

Guests are instructed to arrive a full hour before showtime, but if you arrive just 15 minutes prior, you won't miss anything besides some unexciting appetizers (bread and rice) and the opportunity to spend more money on photos, drinks, and annoying light-up toy swords.

Treasure Tavern Dinner Theatre

APPEAL BY AGE	PRESCHOOL —	GRADE SCHOOL —	TEENS ★
YOUNG ADULTS ★★	OVER 30 ★★★		SENIORS ★★★

6400 Carrier Dr., Orlando; ☎ 407-206-5102; **treasuretavern.com**

Showtimes Tuesday–Saturday, 8 p.m. **Reservations** Necessary but can be made up to day of show. **Cost** $65.95 + tax; $34.95 + tax for college students (does not include tip). **Discounts** Sliding discount for parties of 2, 3, 4, or 6; group pricing for 10 or more; $5 parking fee. **Type of seating** Tables seating up to 10 face an elevated stage; some smaller tables for parties of 2–6. **Menu** Four courses with soup; green salad; choice of beef tenderloin, chicken, or lasagna; and cake. Upgrade to prime rib or salmon for additional cost. Appetizers such as shrimp, chicken kabob, and ahi tuna available for purchase. **Vegetarian alternative** Vegetable lasagna. **Beverages** Unlimited soft drinks; full cash bar.

DESCRIPTION AND COMMENTS Miss Gretta Von Kegel is your outlandish hostess for 2½ hours of mildly bawdy entertainment recommended for age 18 and older (though teens 15 and older can attend with an adult), with some impressive acts throughout the evening—a woman who lithely Hula-Hoops with dozens of lighted hoops, a quick-change artist from Russia who defies logic, and astounding acrobatics by a flexible young couple from Eastern Europe. Throughout the night the risqué jokes flow, but nothing so improper as to make diners do anything more than laugh as they sip pricey cocktails and make their way through four courses of so-so food in a dimly lit room that could use a little fixing up. There's the requisite audience interaction, but not much more than attempts to embarrass a few men with off-color quips.

Tables are tended by the Jewels, young, well-stacked burlesque dancers who also participate in song-and-dance numbers on stage. Along with Miss Gretta, the show's comic relief comes from three sidekicks who spend a little too much time on the stage. "It's nice not to have kids running around," commented our tablemates, so that's a plus for grown-ups. Doors open at 7, and the earlier you get there, the better your seat. Some of the most talented members of the show's original cast have moved on, and the live musicians are replaced with prerecorded tracks, taking a little of the luster off this treasure.

In 2015, Treasure Tavern debuted the family-friendly Cirque Magique (**thecirquemagique.com**), which takes over the theater Tuesday–Saturday at 6 p.m., and Sunday at 3:30 p.m. The vaudeville variety-act format is essentially the same, but all the double-D cleavage and double entendres are swapped for 90 minutes of dancing dogs, joking jugglers, and slapstick clowning. Prices are lower for the magic show ($45.95 + tax for adults; $32.45 + tax for children ages 3–12), but the menu is strictly kid-centric: cheeseburgers, chicken sandwiches, hot dogs, and ice cream sundaes.

FAMILY-FRIENDLY COMEDY SHOW

SAK Improv Comedy

APPEAL BY AGE	PRESCHOOL ★½	GRADE SCHOOL ★★½	TEENS ★★★★
YOUNG ADULTS ★★★★½		OVER 30 ★★★★½	SENIORS ★★★½

29 S. Orange Ave., Orlando (downtown, off Exit 82 from I-4);
☎ 407-648-0001; **sak.com**

Showtimes Varies; *Duel of Fools,* Thursday–Saturday at 7:30 p.m., with periodic performances of this or other shows at 9:30 p.m. and at 11:30 p.m. on the weekend. Reservations strongly encouraged. **Cost** $15 per person; $12 for Florida residents.

DESCRIPTION AND COMMENTS SAK is an improv comedy troupe whose graduates include daytime talk show host Wayne Brady and writers for shows such as *SNL, Mad TV,* and *Everybody Loves Raymond.*

SAK offers a variety of shows, which in the past has included an improv opera, but its baseline show is the long-running *Duel of Fools.* The show features two teams competing in a series of improv sketches, very much like the

TV show *Whose Line Is It Anyway?* (which also featured Wayne Brady). Because shows besides the *Duel of Fools* change frequently, call or check the website for a list of other available shows.

Duel of Fools is a clean show with no cursing, and the humor relies on absurd situations. The types of improv sketches vary throughout the evening, from on-the-spot songs based on audience suggestions to raw pantomime. Each sketch is about 5 minutes, so any that are mundane are over quickly, while the funnier ones continue until the scenario becomes too absurd to comprehend. Because there is no script, the performance varies each show, but the quality of actors remains the same, and their ability to integrate any suggestions into a humorous scene is outstanding.

Parking for SAK is available on the street for free or in the nearby Plaza Cinema Garage. The theater performs in a 200-seat venue with a concession and lounge area. SAK is located on the second floor of the CityArts gallery complex, which is headquarters for downtown Orlando's free monthly Third Thursday (**3rdthu.com**) cultural events.

UNIVERSAL ORLANDO CITYWALK

CITYWALK IS A SHOPPING, DINING, AND ENTERTAINMENT venue that doubles as the entrance plaza for the Universal Studios and Islands of Adventure theme parks. Situated between the parking complex and the theme parks, CityWalk is heavily trafficked all day but truly comes alive at night.

CityWalk offers a number of nightclubs to sample, many of which depend on well-known brand names. At CityWalk you'll find a **Hard Rock Café** and concert hall; **Jimmy Buffett's Margaritaville; Emeril's Restaurant;** a **Bubba Gump Shrimp Co.;** an **NBC Sports Grill & Brew;** a branch of New Orleans's famous **Pat O'Brien's** club; and a reggae club that celebrates the life and music of **Bob Marley.** Places that operate without big-name tie-ins include **The Red Coconut Club,** a lounge and nightclub; **the groove,** a high-tech disco; and **CityWalk's Rising Star,** a karaoke club with a live backup band.

Another CityWalk distinction is that most of the clubs are also restaurants, or alternatively, most of the restaurants are also clubs. Restaurants and nightclubs are different animals. Sight lines, room configuration, acoustics, intimacy, and atmosphere—important considerations in a nightclub—are not at all the same in a venue designed to serve meals. Though it's nice to have all that good food available, the club experience is somewhat dulled. Working through the lineup, Pat O'Brien's, the groove, and Rising Star are more nightclub than restaurant, whereas Margaritaville is more restaurant than club. Bob Marley's is about half and half. The Hard Rock Cafe, Emeril's, and NBC Sports Grill are restaurants. Strictly a performance space is the venue for the Blue Man Group, though a full bar and fast food are available.

Continued on page 376

Universal Orlando CityWalk

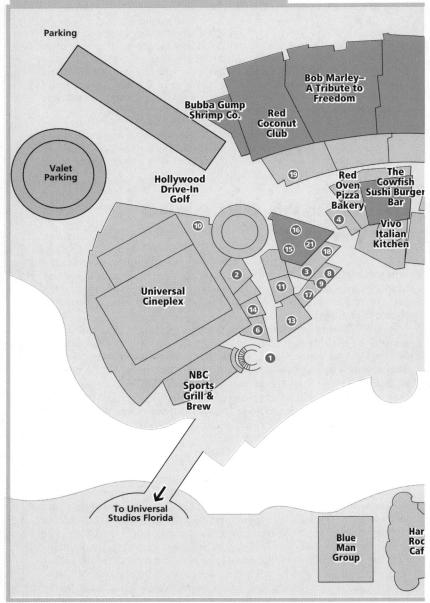

Parking

Valet Parking

Bubba Gump Shrimp Co.

Red Coconut Club

Bob Marley– A Tribute to Freedom

Hollywood Drive-In Golf

19

Red Oven Pizza Bakery

The Cowfish Sushi Burger Bar

4

Vivo Italian Kitchen

10

16

15 21 18

Universal Cineplex

2

11 3 8
9
17

14

6 13

1

NBC Sports Grill & Brew

To Universal Studios Florida

Blue Man Group

Har Roc Caf

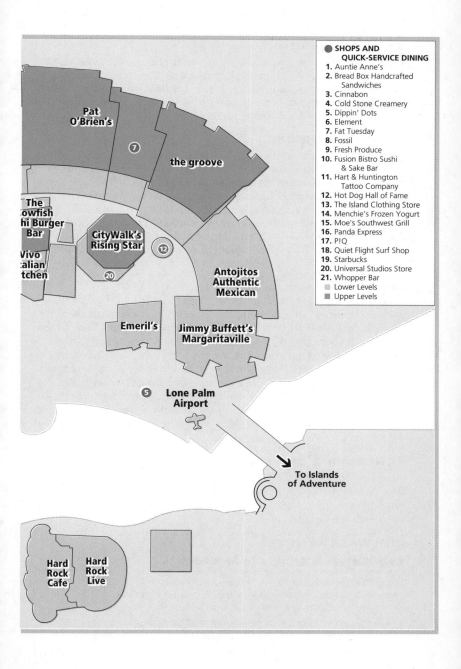

Pat
O'Brien's

⑦

the groove

The
owfish
hi Burger
Bar

Vivo
alian
tchen

CityWalk's
Rising Star

⑫

⑳

Antojitos
Authentic
Mexican

Emeril's

Jimmy Buffett's
Margaritaville

❺ Lone Palm
Airport

To Islands
of Adventure

Hard
Rock
Cafe

Hard
Rock
Live

● SHOPS AND
   QUICK-SERVICE DINING
1. Auntie Anne's
2. Bread Box Handcrafted
   Sandwiches
3. Cinnabon
4. Cold Stone Creamery
5. Dippin' Dots
6. Element
7. Fat Tuesday
8. Fossil
9. Fresh Produce
10. Fusion Bistro Sushi
    & Sake Bar
11. Hart & Huntington
    Tattoo Company
12. Hot Dog Hall of Fame
13. The Island Clothing Store
14. Menchie's Frozen Yogurt
15. Moe's Southwest Grill
16. Panda Express
17. P!Q
18. Quiet Flight Surf Shop
19. Starbucks
20. Universal Studios Store
21. Whopper Bar
▨ Lower Levels
■ Upper Levels

Continued from page 373

GETTING THERE

THE UNIVERSAL FLORIDA COMPLEX can be accessed via Kirkman Road from I-4, Exit 75B. Driving from the Walt Disney World area, take I-4 Exit 74A onto Sand Lake Road heading north (away from International Drive) and turn right onto Turkey Lake Road. Follow the signs to the Turkey Lake Road entrance.

ADMISSION PRICES

CITYWALK'S PARTY PASS ALL-CLUB ACCESS is $11.99, which gets you into all the clubs (you can also pay $15.98 and add a movie). The Party Pass is complimentary with the purchase of any multiday theme park admission. Otherwise, you can pay individual cover charges, about $7 apiece, at each club. Getting the all-access pass makes the most sense unless you intend to visit just one club. Not into the club scene? The Meal and Movie Deal is $21.95 and includes—what else?—dinner at one of the CityWalk restaurants (you choose from a special menu) and a movie.

ARRIVING

ONCE WITHIN THE UNIVERSAL COMPLEX, you'll be directed to park in one of two multitiered parking garages. Parking runs $20 for cars and $22 for RVs. Be sure to take a photo with your phone of the location of your car—the evening will end on a considerably brighter note if you can avoid searching for the rental car. An alternative: If you're out for a special occasion or just want to have everything taken care of, Universal also offers valet parking (2 hours) for $15; $35 for more than 2 hours ($30 if you arrive after 6 p.m.). After 6 p.m. the price for self-parking drops to $5 (except on special-event nights) and after 10 p.m. it's free. From the garages, moving sidewalks transport you directly to CityWalk.

CONTACTING CITYWALK

CONTACT CITYWALK GUEST SERVICES at ☎ 407-224-2691, or visit its website at **citywalk.com.** CityWalk personnel may not be up on individual club doings, so contact the specific clubs directly when you reach the Orlando area.

CITYWALK CLUBS
Bob Marley—A Tribute to Freedom

What it is Reggae restaurant and club. **Hours** Daily, 4 p.m.–2 a.m. **Cuisine** Jamaican-influenced appetizers and main courses. **Entertainment** Reggae bands in the outdoor gazebo every night. **Cover** $7 after 9 p.m. nightly (more for special acts).

COMMENTS This club is a re-creation of Marley's home in Kingston, Jamaica, and contains a lot of interesting Marley memorabilia. The courtyard is the center of action. Must be age 21 or older after 9 p.m.

CityWalk's Rising Star

What it is Karaoke club with live band and backup singers Tuesday–Saturday (Sunday–Monday, sing to recorded tracks with live backup singers). **Hours** Nightly, 8 p.m.–2 a.m. **Cuisine** Red Oven Pizza delivery. **Entertainment** Karaoke. **Cover** $7.

COMMENTS With a live band backing you up, you can pretend that you've hit the big time at this karaoke club.

the groove

What it is High-tech disco. **Hours** Nightly, 9 p.m.–2 a.m. **Cuisine** No food. **Entertainment** DJ plays dance tunes. Sometimes there are live bands. **Cover** $7.

COMMENTS Guests must be age 21 or older to enter this très chic club, designed to look like an old theater in the midst of restoration. Seven bars and several themed cubbyholes allow you to get away from the thundering sound system. Dancers are barraged with strobes and lasers.

Hard Rock Live

What it is Live music concert hall and club. **Hours** Vary with live shows; performances usually begin 7–9:30 p.m. **Cuisine** Concession stand. **Entertainment** Musical acts, both nationally known and up-and-coming, as well as stand-up comedians. **Cover** Varies depending on act, $24–$163.

COMMENTS Great acoustics, comfortable seating (for 3,000), and good sight lines make this the best concert venue in town.

Jimmy Buffett's Margaritaville

What it is Key West–themed restaurant and club. **Hours** Daily, 11 a.m.–2 a.m. **Cuisine** Caribbean, Florida fusion, and American. **Entertainment** Live rock and island-style music after 10 p.m. **Cover** $7 after 10 p.m.

COMMENTS Jimmy's is a big place with three bars that turns into a nightclub after 10 p.m. If you eat dinner here, you'll probably want to find another vantage point when the band cranks up.

Pat O'Brien's Orlando

What it is Dueling pianos sing-along club and restaurant. **Hours** Daily, 4 p.m.–2 a.m. **Cuisine** Cajun. **Entertainment** Dueling pianos and sing-alongs. **Cover** $7 + tax after 9 p.m. for piano bar only.

COMMENTS A clone of the famous New Orleans club of the same name. You can dine in the courtyard or on the terrace without paying a cover. You must be age 21 or older to hang out here after 9 p.m.

The Red Coconut Club

What it is Modern lounge and nightclub. **Hours** Monday–Saturday, 7 p.m.–2 a.m.; Sunday, 8 p.m.–2 a.m. **Cuisine** Expensive appetizers. **Entertainment** Lounging and dancing. **Cover** $7 after 9 p.m.

COMMENTS Billed as an ultra-lounge, advertising talk for "hip place to be seen," this nightclub has an eclectic mix of decor—part 1950s, part tiki. It has three bars on two levels serving signature martinis plus a dance floor.

DOWNTOWN ORLANDO/ CHURCH STREET STATION AREA

VISITORS IN THEIR 20S AND EARLY 30S may find the experience at Universal CityWalk a bit contrived. Indeed, any nighttime entertainment that attempts to bring in families and individuals between the ages of 18 and 80 will have a hard time indulging the "hip" demographic. When you attempt to offer a select amount of evening entertainment over large age and taste ranges, you compromise your selections of music, theming, and prices, usually settling for the most generic solutions possible. For people in their 20s, downtown Orlando makes no compromises in taste. This is a hip urban center, and though it is not New York or Miami, the nearby University of Central Florida provides plenty of other young people to party with over a whole swath of different bars and dance clubs.

Once you're there, remember that bars in the Orlando area close at 2 a.m. The bars below represent a cross section of what is available, but there are many more bars on and around Church Street. You must be age 21 and older (and have a valid photo ID) to enter any of the bars. Some nightclubs may let you in if you are between 18 and 21 years old, but you will not be allowed to drink. Call ahead for details.

GETTING THERE

FROM DISNEY OR UNIVERSAL, take I-4 East to South Street (Exit 82B) and continue straight on Garland Avenue. You may find metered parking on your left underneath I-4, or turn right on Central Boulevard and park in the municipal garage across from the fire station for a flat fee. Free street parking can sometimes be found a few blocks east along Rosalind Avenue, but spots are quickly snatched up on the weekends. If you do not have a designated driver, you must take a taxi. A cab ride one-way to Universal costs around $25, while a trip to Disney will cost around $55. There are no good reasons to drive drunk, and Orlando police set up frequent sobriety checkpoints to catch inebriated drivers (if you think we are just being cautious, take a sober drive around downtown or along I-4 at night). When taking a cab, try to go with a group of people—if you're not with one, check your hotel lobby—to spread the cost.

BARS AND CLUBS

23

What it is Cocktail lounge. **Hours** Wednesday–Saturday, 9 p.m.–2 a.m. **Entertainment** DJ with dance floor. **Cover** $10. **Location** 23 W. Church St. **Contact** ☎ 407-420-1111; **23orlando.com.**

COMMENTS A second-floor establishment with a touch of class—if wood floors, a curving bar, and exposed brick walls count. There are specialty martinis and a couple of separate rooms to get away from the recorded music.

Chillers/Big Belly Brewery/Latitudes

What it is Nightclub. **Hours** Daily, 4:30 p.m.–2:30 a.m. **Entertainment** Small dance floor. **Cover** $6 on Wednesdays. **Location** 33 W. Church St. **Contact** ☎ 407-649-4270; **churchstreetbars.com.**

COMMENTS Chillers is a frat boy's fantasy—and some women's too, since it advertises itself as great for bachelorette parties. This compact bar is rather dirty, with the unmistakable scent of stale beer. Young adults in collared shirts make use of the myriad frozen daiquiri machines that line the wall behind the bar. Upstairs is a small balcony with booth seating. College students will appreciate the $1 well drinks on Wednesday, two- and even three-for-one drinks at various times, and Ladies' Night on Fridays. DJs and an emcee keep it hopping, with music and games.

On the second floor above Chillers, Big Belly Brewery serves a solid selection of craft beers (though it doesn't actually brew its own) and cocktails in a 1920s speakeasy environment. Trivia competitions on Wednesday nights are popular, as are the three-for-one happy hour specials on Fridays.

Finally, the building is crowned by Latitudes, which boasts that it's Orlando's largest rooftop bar. The tiki-flavored terrace makes for an inviting tropical oasis for chilling out when things get too steamy in the bars below.

Cleo's Lounge

What it is Lounge with pool tables. **Hours** Monday–Friday, 5 p.m.–2 a.m.; Saturday and Sunday, 8 p.m.–2 a.m. **Entertainment** Pool tables; occasionally live DJs; great atmosphere. **Cover** None. **Location** 11 S. Court Ave. **Contact** ☎ 407-841-4545.

COMMENTS Cleo's is near the Wall Street bars at the corner of Court Street and Pine Street. This is one of our favorite hangouts. Live DJs often spin underground records and old hip-hop, but the music is not so loud as to drown out conversation. The place is cozy, and the decor is kitschy/man cave-ish. Domestic bottles can cost just $3.50, and it has a large collection of wines. Cleo's is not to be confused with the other Cleo's, a gentlemen's club on Orange Blossom Drive.

EVE Orlando

What it is High-end nightclub and event space. **Hours** Thursday, 10 p.m.–2 a.m.; Friday–Saturday, 10 p.m.–2:30 a.m.; Sunday, 8 p.m.–midnight. **Entertainment** DJs and dancing; variety acts during special events. **Cover** $10. **Location** 110 S. Orange Ave. **Contact** ☎ 407-602-7462; **eveorlando.com.**

COMMENTS Formerly known as Vanity, EVE Orlando is a cross between a high-end nightclub like you might find in Vegas or Miami—complete with cutting-edge lighting system and earsplitting amplification—and an event space that can be rented out for corporate meetings or private parties. The club features a 5,000-square-foot main floor with multiple bars, balconies, and a bevy of perks for high rollers who pay for VIP treatment. We never feel like we're quite fashionable enough to fit into places like this, but if you are looking for the party people who possess glamour and wealth (or at least those who want you to think they have it), this is the place.

The Lodge

What it is Bar made to look like a ski lodge. **Hours** Monday–Friday, 4 p.m.–2 a.m.; Saturday, 7 p.m.–2 a.m.; Sunday, 8 p.m.–2 a.m. **Entertainment** Beer and talk. **Cover** None. **Location** 49 N. Orange Ave. **Contact** ☎ 407-650-8786; **facebook.com/lodgeorlando.**

COMMENTS Located a short walk up Orange Avenue, The Lodge is where people in their late 20s and early 30s congregate. The bar has a ski-lodge vibe, including wooden-log walls, deer heads, and stuffed fish on the walls, and for the whole month of July, it celebrates Christmas in July, decorating the interior with snowmen, Christmas lights, and candy canes. The music is generally 1980s rock ballads. On the second story above The Lodge you'll find The Woods (**thewoodsorlando.com**), a boutique bar specializing in craft cocktails using house-made mixers.

The Social

What it is Music venue. **Hours** Vary according to show, usually 3 p.m.–2 a.m. **Entertainment** Bands and DJs playing reggae, pop, salsa, alternative, and electronica. **Cover** $7–$50, depending on show. **Location** 54 N. Orange Ave. **Contact** ☎ 407-246-1419; **thesocial.org.**

COMMENTS The ideal spot in Orlando to see mid-level touring acts, The Social is not at all pretentious and offers a more intimate experience than the nearby House of Blues or Hard Rock Live. Many shows are all ages, though some are 18-plus and require a valid photo ID. A full-service bar lines the back wall of the club, with plenty of room for standing and watching the stage. Stairs on either side lead to an enclosed pit area for those who seek a more up close, personal, and sweaty experience. The sound quality is always spot-on, and the intimacy of the club makes it easy to wait around and meet the artists before or after their set. The Social is squeezed in between and connected to (via interior doors that may be unlocked during special events) The Beacham, a vintage movie house that has been converted into a dance club/concert hall, and Olde 64, a hipster-friendly hangout with a rockabilly theme. Also next door is Independent Bar (**facebook .com/independentbarorlando**), the best dance destination for fans of 1980s new wave and 1990s alternative; if you used to wear black and bang your head to New Order and The Cure, this is the club for you.

Wall Street Plaza Bars

What it is 7 bars together. **Hours** Vary, but as long as 11 a.m.–2 a.m. **Entertainment** Some dancing; normal bar activities. **Cover** None, except during special events like Halloween and New Year's Eve. **Contact** ☎ 407-849-0471; **wallstplaza.net.**

COMMENTS These bars are the hub of weekend nightlife in downtown Orlando. The bars that put on the weekly block party are Hooch, the Wall Street Cantina, WaiTiki, Shine, Slideshow, the Hen House, and the Monkey Bar. (A tip: Bar names, motifs, and operators come and go, so it might serve you best to simply wander through these venues rather than checking the slow website to make your choice.) Most of the bars have outside seating; guests can carry drinks from one bar to another. Some serve food into the evening. Shine has a dance floor, but there are better dance clubs to visit on Church Street and Orange Avenue. This area really takes off around 10:30 p.m.—our pick for the place to go on the weekends.

PART SIXTEEN

DINING

UNOFFICIAL GUIDE RESEARCHERS LOVE GOOD FOOD and invest a fair amount of time scouting new places to eat. Alas, Orlando is not exactly a culinary nirvana. If you thrive on fast food and the fare at chain restaurants (Denny's, T.G.I. Friday's, Olive Garden, and the like), you'll be as happy as an alligator at a chicken farm. Among specialty restaurants, location and price will determine your choice. For instance, Orlando has some decent Italian restaurants—which one you select depends on how much money you want to spend and how convenient the place is to reach. Our recommendations for specialty and ethnic fare are summarized in the table that starts on page 382.

BUFFETS *and* MEAL DEALS *in* ORLANDO

BUFFETS, RESTAURANT SPECIALS, and discount dining abound in Orlando, especially on US 192 (known locally as Irlo Bronson Memorial Highway) and along International Drive. The local visitor magazines, distributed free at non-Disney hotels, among other places, are packed with advertisements and discount coupons for a host of buffets and other specials.

For a family trying to economize, some of the come-ons are mighty sweet. But are these places any good? Is the food fresh, tasty, and appealing? Are the restaurants clean and inviting? Armed with little more than a roll of Tums, the *Unofficial* research team tried all the eateries that advertise heavily in the free tourist magazines. Here's what we discovered.

CHINESE SUPER BUFFETS

WHOA! TALK ABOUT AN OXYMORON. If you've ever tried preparing Chinese food, especially a stir-fry, you know that split-second timing

Continued on page 384

WHERE TO EAT IN ORLANDO

AMERICAN

• **JOHNNIE'S HIDEAWAY** 12551 FL 535, Orlando; ☎ 407-827-1111; **johnnies hideaway.com;** moderate–expensive. Seafood and steaks, with an emphasis on Florida cuisine.

• **THE RAVENOUS PIG*** 1234 N. Orange Ave., Winter Park; ☎ 407-628-2333; **theravenouspig.com;** moderate–expensive. New American cuisine. Award-winning menu changes frequently depending on seasonal ingredients. Check out its nearby sister restaurant at **thecaskandlarder.com.**

• **SEASONS 52** 7700 W. Sand Lake Rd., Orlando; ☎ 407-354-5212; **seasons 52.com;** moderate–expensive. Delicious, creative New American food that's low in fat and calories. Extensive wine list.

BARBECUE

• **BUBBALOU'S BODACIOUS BAR-B-QUE** 5818 Conroy Rd., Orlando (near Universal Orlando); ☎ 407-295-1212; **bubbalous.com;** inexpensive. Tender, smoky barbecue; tomato-based Killer Sauce.

• **4 RIVERS SMOKEHOUSE** 11764 University Blvd., Orlando; ☎ 844-474-8377; **4rsmokehouse.com;** inexpensive. Award-winning beef brisket; fried pickles, cheese grits, fried okra, and collard greens.

• **PIG FLOYD'S URBAN BARBAKOA*** 1326 N. Mills Ave., Orlando; ☎ 407-203-0866; **pigfloyds.com;** inexpensive. Southern comfort with a Southwest twist; try the Big Floyd sandwich or pork belly tacos with a side of fried yucca and Fancy Sauce.

CARIBBEAN

• **BAHAMA BREEZE** 8849 International Dr., Orlando; ☎ 407-248-2499; **bahamabreeze.com;** moderate. A creative and tasty version of Caribbean cuisine from the owners of the Olive Garden and Red Lobster chains.

CHINESE

• **MING COURT** 9188 International Dr., Orlando; ☎ 407-898-9672; **ming-court .com;** inexpensive. Dim sum, crispy roast pork, and roast duck.

CUBAN/SPANISH

• **CAFE TU TU TANGO** 8625 International Dr., Orlando; ☎ 407-248-2222; **cafetututango.com;** inexpensive-moderate. Eclectic tapas (small plates) and tasty sangrias served alongside live artists, dancers, and Tarot readers.

• **COLUMBIA** 649 Front St., Celebration; ☎ 407-566-1505; **columbia restaurant.com;** moderate. Authentic Cuban and Spanish creations, including paella and the famous 1905 Salad.

ETHIOPIAN

• **NILE ETHIOPIAN RESTAURANT** 7040 International Dr., Orlando; ☎ 407-354-0026; **nile07.com;** inexpensive-moderate. Authentic stews and delicious vegetarian dishes. Bob's favorite Orlando-area restaurant.

FRENCH

• **LE COQ AU VIN*** 4800 S. Orange Ave., Orlando; ☎ 407-851-6980; **lecoq auvinrestaurant.com;** moderate–expensive. Country French cuisine in a relaxed atmosphere. Reservations suggested.

*20 minutes or more from Walt Disney World

INDIAN

• **MEMORIES OF INDIA** 8204 Crystal Clear Ln., Ste. 1600, Orlando; ☎ 407-370-3277; **memoriesofindiacuisine.com;** inexpensive–moderate. Tandoori dishes, samosas, tikka masala, Sunday Champagne brunch with buffet.

ITALIAN

• **ANTHONY'S COAL-FIRED PIZZA** 8031 Turkey Lake Rd., Orlando; ☎ 407-363-9466; **acfp.com;** inexpensive. Pizzas, eggplant, pastas, beer and wine.

• **BICE ORLANDO RISTORANTE** Loews Portofino Bay Hotel, Universal Orlando Resort, 5601 Universal Blvd., Orlando; ☎ 407-503-1415; **orlando.bice group.com;** expensive. Authentic Italian; great wines.

JAPANESE/SUSHI

• **AMURA** 7786 W. Sand Lake Rd., Orlando; ☎ 407-370-0007; **amura.com;** moderate. A favorite sushi bar for locals. The tempura is popular too.

• **HANAMIZUKI** 8255 International Dr., Orlando; ☎ 407-363-7200; **hanamizuki .us;** moderate–expensive. Pricey but very authentic.

• **KABOOKI SUSHI*** 3122 E. Colonial Dr., Orlando; ☎ 407-228-3839; **kabooki sushi.com;** moderate-expensive. Exquisite traditional sashimi and *nigiri,* plus innovative fusion creations using Wagyu beef, foie gras, and black truffles. Seth's favorite Orlando restaurant.

• **NAGOYA SUSHI** 7600 Dr. Phillips Blvd., Ste. 66, in the very rear of The Marketplace at Dr. Phillips; ☎ 407-248-8558; **nagoyasushi.com;** moderate. A small, intimate restaurant with great sushi and an extensive menu.

MEXICAN

• **CHEVYS FRESH MEX** 12547 FL 535, Lake Buena Vista; ☎ 407-827-1052 or 407-827-1119; **chevys.com;** inexpensive–moderate. Conveniently located across from the FL 535 entrance to WDW.

• **EL PATRON** 12167 S. Apopka–Vineland Rd., Orlando; ☎ 407-238-5300; **elpatronorlando.com;** inexpensive. Family-owned restaurant serving freshly prepared Mexican dishes. Full bar.

• **MOE'S SOUTHWEST GRILL** 7541-D W. Sand Lake Rd., Orlando; ☎ 407-264-9903; **moes.com;** inexpensive. Cheap, dependable Southwestern fare.

• **TAQUITOS JALISCO*** 1041 S. Dillard St., Winter Garden; ☎ 407-654-0363; inexpensive. Low-key atmosphere; flautas, chicken mole, fajitas, hearty burritos, good vegetarian.

NEW WORLD

• **NORMAN'S** 4012 Central Florida Pkwy., in the Ritz-Carlton Orlando; ☎ 407-393-4333; **normans.com;** expensive. Norman Van Aken, dean of New World cuisine, offers a menu that changes often—but you'll always find his sinfully delicious conch chowder. World-class wine menu.

SEAFOOD

• **BONEFISH GRILL** 7830 W. Sand Lake Rd., Orlando; ☎ 407-355-7707; **bone fishgrill.com;** moderate. Casual setting along busy Restaurant Row. Choose your fish and a favorite sauce to accompany. Also steaks and chicken.

• **CELEBRATION TOWN TAVERN** 721 Front St., Celebration; ☎ 407-566-2526; **thecelebrationtowntavern.com;** moderate. Popular hangout for locals, with New England–style seafood. Clam chowder is a big hit.

WHERE TO EAT IN ORLANDO *(continued)*

SEAFOOD *(continued)*

- **LEE & RICK'S OYSTER BAR*** 5621 Old Winter Garden Rd., Orlando; ☎ 407-293-3587; **leeandricksoysterbar.com;** inexpensive–moderate. An Orlando institution since 1950, this unpretentious dive bar (shaped like a sinking ship) serves up cold beer, country music, and live or steamed shucked shellfish by the bucketful.

- **OCEAN PRIME** 7339 W. Sand Lake Rd., Orlando; ☎ 407-781-4880; **ocean -prime.com;** expensive. Elegant supper club ambience; classic fare focusing on fresh seafood, perfectly cooked meats. Outdoor dining and piano bar.

STEAK/PRIME RIB

- **BULL & BEAR** Waldorf Astoria Orlando, 14200 Bonnet Creek Resort Ln., Orlando; ☎ 407-597-5500; **waldorfastoriaorlando.com/dining/bull-and-bear;** expensive. Classic steak house with a clubby ambience. Steaks, seafood, lamb chops, and more.

- **THE CAPITAL GRILLE** Point Orlando, 9101 International Dr., Orlando; ☎ 407-370-4392; **thecapitalgrille.com;** expensive. Dry-aged steaks, good wine list, and classic decor.

- **DEL FRISCO'S DOUBLE EAGLE STEAKHOUSE** 9150 International Dr., Orlando; ☎ 407-351-5074; **delfriscos.com;** expensive. This purveyor of prime meats and massive lobster tails relocated in 2015 to upscale new digs on I-Drive. The original location still operates at 729 Lee Rd. in north Orlando under the new name **Christner's Prime Steak & Lobster** (☎ 407-645-4443; **christner sprimesteakandlobster.com**).

- **TEXAS DE BRAZIL** 5259 International Dr., Orlando; ☎ 407-355-0355; **texas debrazil.com;** expensive. All-you-care-to-eat in an upscale Brazilian-style *churrascaria*. Filet mignon, sausage, pork ribs, chicken, lamb, and more. Kids age 6 and under free, ages 7–12 half-price. Salad bar with 40+ options.

- **VITO'S CHOP HOUSE** 8633 International Dr., Orlando; ☎ 407-354-2467; **vitoschophouse.com;** moderate. Surprisingly upscale meat house with a taste of Tuscany.

THAI

- **THAI SILK** 6803 S. Kirkman Rd. at International Drive, Orlando; ☎ 407-226-8997; **thaisilkorlando.com;** moderate. Housed in an unassuming strip mall location and acclaimed by Orlando dining critics for its authentic Thai dishes. Delicious vegetarian options; impressive wine list. Try the distinctly non-Thai fried cheesecake for dessert.

- **THAI THANI** 11025 International Dr., Orlando; ☎ 407-239-9733; 600 Market St., Celebration, ☎ 407-566-9444; **thaithani.net;** moderate. Specializes in Thai duck preparations. Some Chinese stir-fry.

**20 minutes or more from Walt Disney World*

Continued from page 381

is required to avoid overcooking. So it should come as no big surprise that Chinese dishes languishing on a buffet lose their freshness, texture, and flavor in a hurry.

For the past few editions of this guide, we were able to find several Chinese buffets that were better than the rest and that we felt comfortable recommending; unfortunately, we would return the next year only to discover that their quality had slipped precipitously. We then searched for new buffets to replace the ones we deleted from the book, and we can tell you that wasn't fun work. At the end of the day, **Dragon Court Chinese Buffet & Sushi Bar** (12384 S. Apopka–Vineland Road, just after FL 535 turns 90 degrees to the west; ☎ 407-238-9996; **dragoncourtbuffet.com**), **Ichiban Buffet** (5269 W. Irlo Bronson Memorial Hwy., ☎ 407-396-6668; 5529 International Dr., ☎ 407-930-8889; **ibuffetorlando.com**), and **Kim Wu** (4904 S. Kirkman Road; ☎ 407-293-0752) are the only Asian buffets that we've elected to list. Dragon Court is friendly and low-key, with a good selection of mainly Chinese dishes. Ichiban is our pick, with Japanese hibachi and sushi, plus traditional Chinese and Americanized dishes, including steamed snow crab legs (for an extra charge), raw oysters, and grilled head-on shrimp. The Irlo Bronson location was our favorite, but quality has declined of late; its new I-Drive restaurant has picked up the banner, at least for now. Kim Wu is another locals' favorite and is convenient to Universal Orlando, but the buffet is only available Monday–Friday during lunch.

INDIAN BUFFETS

INDIAN FOOD WORKS BETTER on a buffet than Chinese food; in fact, it actually improves as the flavors marry. In the Disney World area, most Indian restaurants offer a buffet at lunch only—not too convenient if you're spending your day at the theme parks. If you're out shopping or taking a day off, these Indian buffets are worth trying:

AASHIRWAD INDIAN CUISINE 5748 International Dr., at the corner of International Drive and Kirkman Road; ☎ 407-370-9830

AHMED HALAL INDIAN RESTAURANT 11301 S. Orange Blossom Trl., #104; ☎ 407-856-5970; **ahmedindianrestaurant.com**

WOODLANDS PURE VEGETARIAN INDIAN CUISINE 6040 S. Orange Blossom Trl.; ☎ 407-854-3330; **woodlandsusa.com**

CHURRASCARIAS

A NUMBER OF THESE SOUTH AMERICAN–STYLE meat emporiums have sprung up along International Drive. Our picks are **Café Mineiro** (6432 International Dr., ☎ 407-248-2932; 9204 Crystal Clear Ln. #1700 near Florida Mall, ☎ 407-730-9800; **cafemineirosteakhouse.com**), a Brazilian steak house north of Sand Lake Road, and **BoiBrazil Churrascaria** (5668 International Dr.; ☎ 407-354-0260; **boibrazil.com**). Both offer good value. More expensive are the Argentinean churrasco specialties at **The Knife** (12501 FL 535; ☎ 786-866-3999; **thekniferestaurant.com**); be sure to try the sweetbreads, an Argentine specialty rarely found in the United States. If you prefer chain restaurants, the pricey **Texas de Brazil** and **Fogo de Chão** also have locations in Orlando.

SEAFOOD AND LOBSTER BUFFETS

THESE AFFAIRS DON'T EXACTLY fall under the category of inexpensive dining. The main draw (no pun intended) is all the lobster you can eat. The problem is that lobsters, like Chinese food, don't wear well on a steam table. After a few minutes on the buffet line, they make better tennis balls than dinner, so try to grab your lobster immediately after a fresh batch has been brought out.

Two lobster buffets are on International Drive, and another is on US 192. Though all three do a reasonable job, we prefer **Boston Lobster Feast** (6071 W. Irlo Bronson Memorial Hwy., ☎ 407-396-2606; 8731 International Dr., five blocks north of the Orange County Convention Center, ☎ 407-248-8606; **bostonlobsterfeast.com**). Both locations are distinguished by a vast variety of seafood in addition to the lobster. The International Drive location is cavernous and noisy, which is why we prefer the Irlo Bronson location, where you can actually have a conversation over dinner. The International Drive location has ample parking, while the Irlo Bronson restaurant does not. At about $40 for early birds (4–6 p.m.) and $45 after 6 p.m., dining is expensive at both locations.

SALAD BUFFETS

THE MOST POPULAR OF THESE IN THE ORLANDO AREA is **Sweet Tomatoes** (6877 S. Kirkman Rd., ☎ 407-363-1616; 12561 S. Apopka–Vineland Rd., ☎ 407-938-9461; 3236 Rolling Oaks Blvd., off US 192 near the FL 429 western entrance to Walt Disney World, ☎ 407-966-4664; **souplantation.com**). During lunch and dinner, you can expect a line out the door, but fortunately one that moves fast. The buffet features prepared salads and an extensive array of ingredients for building your own. In addition to salads, Sweet Tomatoes offers a variety of soups, a modest pasta bar, a baked-potato bar, an assortment of fresh fruit, and ice cream sundaes. Dinner runs $11.79 for adults, $6 for children ages 6–12, and $4 for children ages 3–5. Lunch is $9.79 for adults and the same prices as dinner for children.

BREAKFAST AND ENTRÉE BUFFETS

MOST CHAIN STEAK HOUSES IN THE AREA, including **Ponderosa, Sizzler,** and **Golden Corral,** offer entrée buffets. Among them, they have 16 locations in the Orlando area. All serve breakfast, lunch, and dinner. At lunch and dinner, you get the buffet when you buy an entrée, usually a steak; breakfast service is a straightforward buffet (that is, you don't have to buy an entrée). As for the food, it's chain-restaurant quality but decent all the same. Prices are a bargain, and you can get in and out at lightning speed—important at breakfast when you're trying to get to the theme parks early. Some locations offer lunch and dinner buffets at a set price without your having to buy an entrée.

Though you can argue about which chain serves the best steak, Golden Corral wins the buffet contest hands-down, with at least twice as many offerings as its competitors. While buffets at Golden Corral and Ponderosa are pretty consistent from location to location, the buffets at the different Sizzlers vary a good deal. Our pick of the Sizzlers is the one at 7602 W. Irlo Bronson Memorial Hwy. (☎ 407-397-0997). In addition to the steak houses, area **Shoney's** also offer breakfast, lunch, and dinner buffets. Local freebie visitor magazines are full of discount coupons for all of the previous restaurants.

MEAL DEALS

DISCOUNT COUPONS ARE AVAILABLE for a wide range of restaurants, including some wonderful upscale-ethnic places such as **Ming Court** (Chinese; 9188 International Dr., Orlando; ☎ 407-351-9988; **ming -court.com**).

A meat eater's delight is the Feast for Four at **Sonny's Real Pit Bar-B-Q.** For $44 per family of four, you get sliced pork and beef plus chicken, ribs, your choice of three sides (choose from beans, slaw, fries, among others), garlic bread or corn bread, and soft drinks or tea, all served family-style. The closest Sonny's location to Walt Disney World and Universal is at 7423 S. Orange Blossom Trl. in Orlando (☎ 407-859-7197; **sonnysbbq.com**). No coupons are available (or needed) for Sonny's, but they're available for the other "meateries."

COUPONS

FIND DISCOUNTS AND TWO-FOR-ONE COUPONS for many of the restaurants mentioned in freebie visitor guides available at most non-Disney hotels. The **Visit Orlando Official Visitors Center** (8723 International Dr.; ☎ 407-363-5872; open daily, 8:30 a.m.–6:30 p.m., except December 25) offers a treasure trove of coupons and free visitor magazines. In Kissimmee, visit the **Osceola County Welcome Center and History Museum** (4155 W. Vine St.; ☎ 407-396-8644; **osceolahistory.org**). In addition to visitor information and restaurant coupons, the center also houses an excellent free museum tracing the colorful history of Central Florida. On the Internet, check out **couponsalacarte.com** and **orlandocoupons.com** for printable coupons. **Groupon.com** and **livingsocial.com** are also great sources for dining and entertainment deals, and you can redeem discounts directly on your smartphone (no need for a printer).

THE GREAT ORLANDO PIZZA SCAM

PLENTY OF REPUTABLE LOCAL PIZZA JOINTS deliver to hotels in and around the theme parks; many Disney and Universal resorts offer pizza delivery as well. But for a few years now, con artists have been distributing flyers advertising delivery to hotel guests—they ask for your credit card number over the phone, but the pizza never arrives. Disregard any such flyers you find.

FAST FOOD *in the* THEME PARKS

BECAUSE MOST MEALS DURING VACATION are consumed on the run while touring, we'll tackle counter-service and vendor foods first. Plentiful in all theme parks are hot dogs, hamburgers, chicken sandwiches, salads, and pizza. They're augmented by special items that relate to the park's theme or the part of the park you're touring. Counter-service prices are fairly consistent from park to park. Expect to pay the same for your coffee or hot dog at Busch Gardens as at SeaWorld.

Getting your act together in regard to counter-service restaurants in the parks is more a matter of courtesy than necessity. Rude guests rank fifth among reader complaints. A mother from Fort Wayne, Indiana, points out that indecision can be as maddening as outright discourtesy, especially when you're hungry:

> *Every fast-food restaurant has menu signs the size of billboards, but do you think anybody reads them? People waiting in line spend enough time in front of these signs to memorize them and still don't have a clue what they want when they finally get to the counter. If by some miracle they've managed to choose between the hot dog and the hamburger, they then fiddle around another 10 minutes deciding what size Coke to order. Folks, PULEEEZ get your orders together ahead of time!*

Beyond Counter Service: Tips for Saving Time and Money

Even if you confine your meals to quick-service fare, you lose a lot of time getting food in the theme parks. Here are some ways to minimize the time you spend hunting and gathering:

1. Eat breakfast before you arrive. Restaurants outside the parks offer some outstanding breakfast specials. Plus, some hotels furnish small refrigerators in their guest rooms, or you can rent a fridge or bring a cooler. If you can get by on cold cereal, rolls, fruit, and juice, this will save a ton of time.

2. After a good breakfast, buy snacks from vendors in the parks as you tour, or stuff some snacks in a fanny pack.

3. All theme park restaurants are busiest between 11:30 a.m. and 2:15 p.m. for lunch and between 6 and 9 p.m. for dinner. For shorter lines and faster service, don't eat during these hours, especially 12:30–1:30 p.m.

4. Many counter-service restaurants sell cold sandwiches. Buy a cold lunch minus drinks before 11:30 a.m., and carry it in small plastic bags until you're ready to eat (within an hour or so of purchase). Ditto for dinner. Buy drinks at the appropriate time from any convenient vendor.

5. Most fast-food eateries have more than one service window. Regardless of the time of day, check the lines at all windows before queuing. Sometimes a window that's staffed but out of the way will have a much shorter line or none at all. Note, however, that some windows may offer only certain items.

6. If you're short on time and the park closes early, stay until closing and eat dinner outside the park before returning to your hotel. If the park stays open late, eat dinner about 4 or 4:30 p.m. at the restaurant of your choice. You should sneak in just ahead of the dinner crowd.

Our readers use variations on these tips with great success. A Missouri mom writes:

We arrived with our steel cooler well stocked with milk and sandwich fixings. I froze a block of ice in a milk bottle, and we replenished it daily with ice from the resort ice machine. I also froze small packages of deli-type meats for later in the week. We ate cereal, milk, and fruit each morning, with boxed juices.

Each child had a belt bag of his own, which he filled from a special box of goodies each day with things like packages of crackers and cheese, packets of peanuts and raisins, candy, or gum. Each child also had a small, rectangular plastic water bottle that could hang on the belt. We filled these at water fountains before getting into lines.

We left the park before noon; ate sandwiches, chips, and soda in the room; and napped. We purchased our evening meal in the park at a counter-service eatery. We budgeted for both morning and evening snacks from a vendor but often didn't need them.

A Whiteland, Indiana, mom suggests:

If you're traveling with younger kids, bring a supply of small paper or plastic cups to split drinks, which are both huge and expensive.

DINING *at* UNIVERSAL ORLANDO

ONE OF OUR CONSTANT GRIPES about theme parks is the food. To many guests hustling through the parks, dining is a low priority—they don't mind the typically substandard fare and high prices because their first objective is to see the

unofficial **TIP**
You may be pleasantly surprised by the quality of the food at the Universal Orlando Resort.

sights and ride the rides. This is certainly understandable, but *The Unofficial Guide* team is made up of big fans of big eating. We feel that there's no reason not to expect high-quality food and service when theme parks invest so much elsewhere in design, production, and development.

The good news is that, today, food in Universal is almost always on par with, or a step ahead of, what you can find at Walt Disney World and other parks. Thanks largely to the efforts of the resort's award-winning executive chef Steven Jayson, more variety, better preparations, and more current trends are generally the rule at Universal. And best of all, a first-class meal at Universal will almost always leave less of a dent in your credit card than the equivalent repast would at Mickey's table.

Quick-service (or counter-service, as it is called at Disney) offerings are largely comparable to Disney, both in quality and cost, with the newest additions—Harry Potter's **Leaky Cauldron** and **Three Broomsticks,** and The Simpsons' **Fast Food Boulevard**—setting a new bar for theme park fast food.

USF's two full-service restaurants are **Finnegan's Bar and Grill** in New York and **Lombard's Seafood Grille** in San Francisco. Finnegan's serves typical bar food—burgers and wings—as well as fresh fish-and-chips and other takes on Irish cuisine. Lombard's is the better restaurant, but it's not in the same stratosphere as Disney's Hollywood Brown Derby (in quality or price).

IOA has two sit-down restaurants: **Confisco Grille** in Port of Entry and **Mythos Restaurant** in The Lost Continent. Confisco is fine for pizza and drinks. Despite its Hellenic-sounding name, Mythos isn't a Greek restaurant; rather it serves something-for-everyone fusion fare, including Italian risotto, Asian noodles, and Mexican fish tacos, plus steaks and burgers. Diners with dietary restrictions will be happy to see that Mythos has more options for vegetarian, vegan, and gluten-free diners than almost any other in-park Universal restaurant.

For even better eating options, exit the parks into **CityWalk,** Universal's dining, shopping, and entertainment district (think a more-compact counterpart to Disney Springs). CityWalk saw some welcome upgrades to its restaurant lineup in 2014 with the addition of **Vivo Italian Kitchen** and **Antojitos Authentic Mexican Food,** along with **The Cowfish's** much-better-than-it-sounds burger/sushi bar. The best choice for a white-linen experience at CityWalk is **Emeril's Restaurant Orlando.** We also like **Bob Marley** and **Pat O'Brien's** for drinks and music.

Many of the older CityWalk restaurants' menus are similar to Applebee's or Chili's. Given the average entrée from **Hard Rock Cafe** or **Jimmy Buffett's Margaritaville,** it would be difficult for a blindfolded diner to be certain from which restaurant it came. That blindfolded diner would probably guess that any plate with shrimp on it had a decent chance of coming from the **Bubba Gump Shrimp Co.,** but there's little else of note on its menu.

Some of Universal's best sit-down restaurants are found at the resort hotels. **The Palm Restaurant,** an upscale steak house in the Hard Rock Hotel, serves Grade A meat at prices to match. If you're in the mood for Italian, try **Bice** (expensive) or **Mama Della's Ristorante** (moderate), both at the Portofino. Asian food is the specialty at Universal's Royal Pacific, where **Emeril Lagasse's Tchoup Chop** is the top destination. Probably because they handle a lot of convention traffic, menu prices at Universal's deluxe resorts tend to be higher than you might expect, though they are still easier to swallow than the bill at Disney's top tables.

DRESS

DRESS IS INFORMAL at all theme park restaurants and in CityWalk's restaurants. At upscale resort restaurants such as Hard Rock's Palm

Restaurant or Emeril's Tchoup Chop, men are not permitted to wear sleeveless shirts, and resort casual wear is appropriate (but not required) for dinner: khakis, dress slacks, jeans, or dress shorts with a collared shirt for men and Capris, skirts, dresses, jeans, or dress shorts for women.

FOOD ALLERGIES AND SPECIAL REQUESTS

FOR SIT-DOWN MEALS, if you have food allergies or observe a specific diet such as eating kosher, make your needs known when you make your dining reservation and again when your waiter introduces himself at your table. The waitstaff or chef will be able to tell you the kinds of accommodations the kitchen is prepared to make for your meal.

Accommodating dietary needs is more difficult at fast-food places because the staff may not be as familiar with the menu's ingredients or preparation. Ask to see the allergen information book, which should be kept behind the counter at every quick-service location; it lists the menu items that can be made or modified for various diets. When our vegetarians and vegans have doubts about menu descriptions, their strategy is usually to default to the simplest, most-likely-to-be-acceptable item.

CHARACTER MEALS

UNIVERSAL CHARACTERS SHOW UP for dinner at the resort hotels on select nights each week. The cast of characters changes frequently, and it's possible to see the same characters in different restaurants during the same week. It's common to see the Minions from *Despicable Me,* Scooby-Doo and Shaggy from the Scooby-Doo cartoons, Shrek, Woody Woodpecker, or characters from *The Simpsons* at these evening meals.

You'll find characters at the Portofino Bay Hotel's Trattoria del Porto on Friday, 6:30–9:30 p.m. Characters also make appearances at The Kitchen at Hard Rock Hotel on Wednesday and Saturday, 6–9 p.m., and at the Islands Dining Room at the Royal Pacific Resort on Monday, Wednesday, and Thursday, 6:30–9:30 p.m.

Character breakfasts are held at Cafe LaBamba inside Universal Studios on Thursday–Sunday and select Mondays, 9–11 a.m.; at The Kitchen on Tuesday, 8–11 a.m.; and at Jake's in the Royal Pacific on Sunday, 7 a.m.–noon. A holiday breakfast with the Grinch is held inside Islands of Adventure on select dates in December.

DINING AT UNIVERSAL CITYWALK

DINING AND SHOPPING ARE THE FOCUS at CityWalk, whose restaurants tend to cater more to adult tastes than the theme park restaurants do. Probably the best of the bunch is **Emeril's Orlando,** but each restaurant has a couple of decent options if you know what to look for. One thing all of them have in common is noise: Your fussy toddler will have to fight to be heard in some of these places. Some of the restaurants use **OpenTable** (**opentable.com**) for online reservations, and you can make reservations to the other venues from **universalorlando.com** via **NexTable,** making it easy to get seats before you go park-hopping.

UNIVERSAL ORLANDO RESTAURANT PROFILES

BELOW ARE PROFILES for full-service restaurants found in Universal Studios, Islands of Adventure, CityWalk, and the Universal hotels.

Antojitos Authentic Mexican Food ★★★½

MEXICAN MODERATE QUALITY ★★★½ VALUE ★★★½

CityWalk; ☎ 407-224-3663

Customers Locals and tourists. **Reservations** Accepted via NexTable. **When to go** Dinner. **Entrée range** $14–$27. **Service rating** ★★★. **Friendliness rating** ★★★★. **Parking** Universal Orlando garage. **Bar** Full service. **Wine selection** Good. **Dress** Casual; *luchador* masks and sombreros optional. **Disabled access** Good. **Hours** Sunday–Thursday, 4–11 p.m.; Friday–Saturday, 4 p.m.–midnight.

SETTING AND ATMOSPHERE This festive postmodern tribute to Mexican street culture features a large open kitchen framed by graffiti graphics and eye-catching neon, with the central bar and surrounding booths fashioned from reclaimed wood and metal. The downstairs can get very noisy, so if you want a quieter meal, ask for one of the private rooms upstairs. Or grab a seat on the patio or balcony to watch the CityWalk crowds go by.

HOUSE SPECIALTIES Guacamole prepared table-side, empanadas, roasted corn *esquites,* quesadillas, enchiladas, tacos, fajitas, pan-roasted mahi, seafood stew, roast pork loin, churrasco steak, and *cajeta de leche* cake with sour cream ice cream.

ENTERTAINMENT AND AMENITIES A modern mariachi ensemble plays outside and inside the restaurant Wednesday–Sunday.

SUMMARY AND COMMENTS The colorful Antojitos offers unique and craveable tapas-style Mexican food, featuring handcrafted tortillas and fresh sauces for a taste of Mexico City without the high crime rate.

Antojitos has Orlando's best tequila selection this side of Epcot's La Cava. Order from the four-sided bar on the ground floor or from the converted Volkswagen bus outside the entrance. Try a signature drink such as the Handsome George (made with George Clooney's own brand) or The Horse You Rode In On (garnished with an expensive Amarena black cherry).

While it's pricier than your local taco joint, Antojitos prepares familiar plates with exceptionally fresh ingredients. The table-side guacamole is a must-have that will convert the most hardened avocado-hater, and the *esquites asados* (roasted corn with *queso fresco* and jalapeño mayo) is almost a meal in itself. The portion sizes of the enchiladas and tacos aren't enormous, but you'll probably be full after the free chips and house-made salsa and the excellent rice and black beans accompanying most entrées. The *comidas de la casa* include churrasco steak and pork loin, which are both wonderfully seasoned, though the pork can be a bit dry. The sour cream ice cream served with the molten *cajeta de leche* cake will make you shout, "*Ay, caramba!*"

Bice ★★★★½

ITALIAN EXPENSIVE QUALITY ★★★★½ VALUE ★★★★

Portofino Bay Hotel; ☎ 407-503-1415

Customers Locals and tourists. **Reservations** Recommended via Open Table. **When to go** Dinner. **Entrée range** $19–$49. **Service rating** ★★★★★. **Friendliness**

rating ★★★★. **Parking** $5 valet or free self-parking at hotel with validation. **Bar** Full service. **Wine selection** Very good. **Dress** Resort dressy. **Disabled access** Good. **Hours** Daily, 5:30–10 p.m.

SETTING AND ATMOSPHERE Cedarwood and marble floors, crisp white linens, opulent flower arrangements, and waiters in black suits give Bice ("beach-ay") the feeling of a formal restaurant, but there is nothing stiff or fussy about the space or the staff. It is beautifully lit and relatively quiet even when it's crowded. Outdoor seating overlooks the bay.

HOUSE SPECIALTIES Menu changes seasonally; selections may include prosciutto with fresh melon and baby greens; homemade braised beef spareribs ravioli with spinach in mushroom-Marsala sauce; veal Milanese with a Roma tomato and Kalamata olive Tuscan salad; or risotto of the day.

ENTERTAINMENT AND AMENITIES Piano in bar.

SUMMARY AND COMMENTS The food is incredibly fresh, well prepared, and elegant, and the service is top-notch. But be prepared: Even a modest meal will put a dent in your wallet, and even though the food and service are definitely worth it, it may be too expensive for many vacationers. If you want to try a variety of things on the menu, split a salad, appetizer, or pasta dish between two people for a starter; portions are large enough for sharing.

Our favorite appetizers are the mussels with lemon butter sauce, and the Mediterranean seafood salad, which is served inside a large, scooped-out tomato. The other appetizers, mostly salads and antipasti of meats and cheeses, aren't bad, but you've probably had something similar already.

The best entrée is the roasted duck breast, topped with a truffle-oil glaze and accompanied by a small cheese soufflé. Also good is the breaded veal, pounded so thin that it takes up almost the entire plate. It's served with a small salad on top, and the salad's dressing serves to keep the veal juicy. The penne *all' arrabbiatta* is even spicier than advertised.

We rate Bice as one of the best restaurants in all of Universal Orlando Resort, and it compares favorably to any of the similar restaurants at Walt Disney World. Because the Portofino gets a lot of business-convention traffic, it's probably easier to get a reservation at 5:30 p.m. than 7:30 p.m.

Bob Marley—A Tribute to Freedom ★★½

JAMAICAN/CARIBBEAN MODERATE QUALITY ★★★ VALUE ★★★

CityWalk; ☎ 407-224-3663

Customers Locals and tourists. **Reservations** Accepted via NexTable. **When to go** Early evening. **Entrée range** $9–$17. **Service rating** ★★. **Friendliness rating** ★★★. **Parking** Universal Orlando garage. **Bar** Full service. **Wine selection** Poor. **Dress** Casual; dreadlocks if you have them. **Disabled access** Good. **Hours** Sunday–Thursday, 4–10 p.m.; Friday–Saturday, 4–11 p.m.

SETTING AND ATMOSPHERE Set in a replica of reggae singer Bob Marley's Jamaican home, the building is filled with memorabilia and photos showcasing his career and life. Lots of lions, the colors of the Jamaican flag, and other Rastafarian influences pay tribute to the musician's career. Most of the area is open to the elements, and there's no air-conditioning, though there are shelters from the occasional rainstorm.

HOUSE SPECIALTIES Jerk-marinated chicken breast; smoky white–Cheddar cheese fondue; Jamaican vegetable or beef patties; yucca fries; oxtail stew.

ENTERTAINMENT AND AMENITIES Live reggae band and DJ in courtyard nightly; cover charge after 9 p.m.

SUMMARY AND COMMENTS None of the food is spectacular or particularly adventurous, but it's worth it for the laid-back atmosphere. Sure, you're allowed to get up and dance.

The Bubba Gump Shrimp Co. Restaurant & Market
★★½

SOUTHERN/SEAFOOD   MODERATE   QUALITY ★★★   VALUE ★★

CityWalk; ☎ 407-903-0044

Customers Tourists. **Reservations** Not accepted. **When to go** Anytime. **Entrée range** $10–$23. **Service rating** ★★★. **Friendliness rating** ★★★★. **Parking** Universal Orlando garage. **Bar** Full service. **Wine selection** Minimal. **Dress** Casual. **Disabled access** Good. **Hours** Daily, 11 a.m.–midnight.

SETTING AND ATMOSPHERE The movie that inspired the chain, *Forrest Gump*, plays on TVs throughout, but without sound, just subtitles. Movie memorabilia decorates the wooden walls of this seafood shanty. License plates that say RUN FORREST RUN on one side and STOP FORREST STOP on another help signal a waiter when you need service, and the waiters will ask you trivia questions from the movie.

HOUSE SPECIALTIES Fried, stuffed, or grilled shrimp (and shrimp cooked almost every other way); burgers; salads; grilled salmon; fried chicken; baby back ribs. A gluten-free menu is also offered.

SUMMARY AND COMMENTS The theme may seem a little cheesy, but this is a fun and festive atmosphere to bring the kids. The food is no worse than your average seafood chain (think Red Lobster without cheese biscuits).

Confisco Grille   ★★★

AMERICAN   MODERATE   QUALITY ★★★   VALUE ★★★

Islands of Adventure/Port of Entry; ☎ 407-224-4012

Customers Park guests. **Reservations** Accepted via NexTable. **When to go** Anytime. **Entrée range** $9–$17. **Service rating** ★★★. **Friendliness rating** ★★★★. **Parking** Universal Orlando garage. **Bar** Full service. **Wine selection** Moderate. **Dress** Casual. **Disabled access** Good. **Hours** Daily, 11 a.m.–park closing.

SETTING AND ATMOSPHERE A way station on the road to Morocco, perhaps? Actually, it's meant to look like a customs house. Look for "smuggled goods," representing the park's various islands, decorating the lobby's upper level. You'll see giant dinosaur skeletons from Jurassic Park, golden urns from Lost Continent, and even a wand from The Wizarding World of Harry Potter if you look hard enough.

HOUSE SPECIALTIES Wood-grilled pizzas; hummus served with a puffy lavash bread larger than most human heads; selection of salads; beef and chicken fajitas; grilled sandwiches and burgers; pad Thai.

SUMMARY AND COMMENTS Confisco isn't fine dining, but it does fine when you just can't stand in another line. Because of its varied menu of Mediterranean, Italian, Mexican, and Asian dishes, most people should find something to please them at Confisco Grille. Wood-grilled pizzas have a pleasing crust—check with your server to find out the daily special pies. Several options on the menu can be made vegetarian and vegan friendly.

The adjoining Backwater Bar has happy hour 4–7 p.m. daily, with $3.75 draft Buds and red sangria and $4.25 well cocktails.

The Cowfish ★★★★

AMERICAN/SUSHI   MODERATE   QUALITY ★★★★   VALUE ★★★½

CityWalk; ☎ 407-224-2275

Customers Locals and park guests. **Reservations** Not accepted. **When to go** Early afternoon or late evening. **Entrée range** $12–$27. **Service rating ★★½. Friendliness rating ★★★★. Parking** Universal Orlando garage. **Bar** Full service. **Wine selection** Good. **Dress** Resort casual. **Disabled access** Good. **Hours** Sunday–Thursday, 11 a.m.–11 p.m.; Friday–Saturday, 11 a.m.–midnight.

SETTING AND ATMOSPHERE A photo op of this restaurant's mascot—a giant bug-eyed fish with a riding saddle on its back—should clue you in that this isn't the spot for stuffy food snobs. The Cowfish takes irreverent postmodernism and cranks it up to 11 with colorful Pop Art, larger-than-life displays (including Universal icon King Kong and a noodle-filled fish-bowl), and silly signage—be sure to check out the restrooms. Guests enter through the small lobby on the ground floor or the patio bar on the upper level; all seating—both indoors and outdoors—is on the second and third floor, offering spectacular views over CityWalk. Cowfish also has multiple bars.

Young children enjoy the touch screen games and a make-your-own-fish app, which you can then watch swim in a virtual aquarium.

HOUSE SPECIALTIES Crab Rangoon dip, blackened tuna nachos, half-pound burgers, sushi and sashimi combos, fusion and "burgushi" rolls and bento boxes, hand-spun milk shakes, specialty cocktails, and spiked shakes.

SUMMARY AND COMMENTS A one-of-a-kind dining concept that melds pan-Asian cuisine with the good ol' American burger, Cowfish brings something completely unique to the table. We were initially nervous about the fusion of a burger joint and a sushi place, but like peanut butter and chocolate, The Cowfish's burgers and sushi both taste great, and taste great together.

The voluminous menu starts with familiar-sounding appetizers, such as Parmesan truffle fries and tuna nachos, expertly prepared and presented in generous portions (a recurring theme). Next comes an extensive list of half-pound hormone-free hamburgers, with names such as the Jalapeño Popper Show-Stopper, Big Squeal, and Rise & Swine. Veggie and turkey burgers are also available, and all are served with seasoned fries, which can be substituted with seaweed salad, bacon coleslaw, or edamame. The Boursin Bacon Burger, with garlic-herb cheese and sautéed mushrooms, is a standout. Traditional sushi selections range from chef combos of sashimi and *nigiri*; classic makimono rolls; and fusion specialties stuffed with tuna, coconut shrimp, shiitake mushrooms, or crabmeat. The premium tuna and salmon on Jen's Fresh Find roll was particularly flavorful.

Finally, we arrive at the creative center of Cowfish's menu: the burgushi. You can try a sushi roll made with lobster and filet mignon (The Prime Time), bison and fried green tomatoes (BuffalOOOO-shi), or pulled pork and barbecue sauce (High Class Hillbilly). On the flip side, "pick-ups" feature steak and pastrami or rare tuna, sandwiched between spring roll wrapper "buns" filled with sushi rice and *kani* (fake crab). Doug's Filet roll (with ginger dipping sauce for the steak) is a safe bet. If you are still apprehensive, try a bento box, which brings a slider mini-burger, sushi roll, and several side dishes together on a Japanese TV dinner tray.

Its extensive craft cocktail list includes a bourbon and candied bacon concoction, and old-fashioned "mules" made with ginger beer. Hand-spun milk shakes (nonalcoholic or spiked) headline the dessert menu, which also features sushi-shaped pastries exclusive to the Orlando location.

We love the atmosphere, but the time it takes for a meal to come out can be inexplicably long. The wait can be long on a busy weekend, but the host will text you when your table is ready. In addition, a free app for Apple and Android phones lets you join the wait list from anywhere within 0.5 mile of the restaurant; use it to check in while exiting a ride, but be sure to check in once you arrive because the app isn't prompt at letting you know your table is ready.

Emeril's Restaurant Orlando ★★★★

SOUTHERN EXPENSIVE QUALITY ★★★★ VALUE ★★★½

CityWalk; ☎ 407-224-2424

Customers Locals and park guests. **Reservations** Required via Open Table. **When to go** Lunch; early or late evening. **Entrée range** $21–$45. **Service rating ★★★★**. **Friendliness rating ★★★★**. **Parking** Universal Orlando garage; check with restaurant about validation for valet during lunch. **Bar** Full service. **Wine selection** Very good. **Dress** Casual to dressy. **Disabled access** Good. **Hours** Sunday–Thursday, 11:30 a.m.–3 p.m. and 5–10 p.m.; Friday–Saturday, 11:30 a.m.–3 p.m. and 5–10:30 p.m.

SETTING AND ATMOSPHERE Not to be confused with Emeril's Asian-inspired Tchoup Chop at the nearby Royal Pacific Resort, Emeril's Orlando, the Florida outpost of Emeril Lagasse's New Orleans restaurant, has probably the best food and best wine list within CityWalk. The food is Louisiana-style with creative flair. The main dining room is two stories high and features hardwood floors, wooden beams, and stone walls, all of which act as sounding boards for the noisy dining room. Sliding glass doors lead to the kitchen, where Emeril probably won't be cooking. Part of the kitchen is open, and there are eight seats at a food bar—some of the best seats in the house.

HOUSE SPECIALTIES The menu changes frequently. The smoked wild and exotic mushroom appetizer is one of the menu highlights. The banana cream pie will renew your faith in humanity. Items that might be available include gumbo, slow-braised lamb shank, and andouille-crusted redfish.

SUMMARY AND COMMENTS Owner Emeril Lagasse also has restaurants in New Orleans and Las Vegas, so it's unlikely that he'll be on the premises, though he does visit sometimes. But even when he's not there, you're in for some good eating.

If you want a taste of Emeril's "bam" without the big bill, the lunch menu offers entrées such as shrimp and grits or mussels and *frites* for a more digestible $14–$19. Specials frequently offer a free appetizer or dessert with any entrée purchase for valid park-admission holders (including Annual Pass holders), and a daily happy hour at the bar 4–8 p.m., with half-priced drinks and affordable small plates, can also soften the sting.

Note: Last-minute reservations may be hard to get during peak season or major conventions. To get a table on the same day as your visit, check Open Table or call the restaurant at 3:15 p.m. and inquire about cancellations.

Emeril's Tchoup Chop ★★★★

PAN-ASIAN EXPENSIVE QUALITY ★★★★ VALUE ★★★★

Royal Pacific Resort; ☎ 407-224-2467

Customers Locals and hotel guests. **Reservations** Required via Open Table. **When to go** Lunch or dinner. **Entrée range** $24–$34. **Service rating ★★★★. Friendliness rating ★★★★. Parking** Free valet parking at Royal Pacific's convention entrance (don't pull up to the front lobby). **Bar** Full service. **Wine selection** Very good. **Dress** Smart casual to dressy; no sleeveless men's shirts. **Disabled access** Good. **Hours** Sunday–Thursday, 11:30 a.m.–2:30 p.m. and 5–10 p.m.; Friday–Saturday, 11:30 a.m.–2:30 p.m. and 5–10 p.m.

SETTING AND ATMOSPHERE A cavernous space on the bottom floor of the Royal Pacific, with painted concrete floors and tall ceilings. Tchoup Chop features an open kitchen with seating where you can watch your food being made. A glass and wood partition separates the bar from the main dining room, and there's an outdoor bar just a few feet from Tchoup Chop's entrance too.

HOUSE SPECIALTIES The menu changes frequently. Lunch offerings include rice and noodle bowls, large salads, and sandwiches. Dinner features *robata*-grilled vegetables, sushi (*nigiri* and maki), Korean fried chicken, smoked duck, and blackened fish.

SUMMARY AND COMMENTS Long a dark horse favorite among local foodies, Tchoup Chop's new chef de cuisine Ryan Vargas reinvigorated the restaurant in 2014, renovating its kitchen with an expanded sushi bar—rolling creatively overstuffed maki such as the Red Dragon (tuna, panko shrimp, and habanero mayo) or Surf & Turf (blue crab, hibachi steak, and truffle oil)—and one of Central Florida's only *robata* grills, capable of searing small morsels (such as pork belly *tocino* or randomly spicy *shishito* peppers) at a scorching 1,000°F.

The best appetizer is still the deliciously messy kiawe-smoked baby back ribs, which are often discounted during the bar's daily (5–8 p.m.) happy hour and are Royal Pacific's best-kept culinary secret.

The beef and duck entrées stand out more than the seafood or vegetarian dishes, which is a bit surprising for a restaurant that bills itself as Asian/Polynesian fusion. The roasted duck breast was the hit of the meal. For seafood, the cedar-wrapped salmon or sesame tuna is your best bet.

The bartenders seem to have a slightly better grasp of the wine list than some of the waitstaff. Don't be shy about asking one of the bar staff for a wine recommendation.

Finnegan's Bar & Grill ★★½

IRISH MODERATE QUALITY ★★★ VALUE ★★½

Universal Studios/New York; ☎ 407-363-8757

Customers Park guests. **Reservations** Accepted via NexTable. **When to go** Anytime. **Entrée range** $11–$22. **Service rating ★★★. Friendliness rating ★★★★. Parking** Universal Orlando garage. **Bar** Full service. **Wine selection** Limited. Ireland is not really known for its wines; good beer selection, though. **Dress** Casual. **Disabled access** Good. **Hours** Daily, 11 a.m.–park closing.

SETTING AND ATMOSPHERE Fashioned after an Irish bar in New York City, albeit one built as a movie set. Along with the requisite publike accoutrements—such as the tin ceiling and belt-driven paddle fans—are movie lights and half walls that suggest the back of scenery flats. Obligatory references to Guinness beer and New York City abound. The bar area is a popular gathering spot for locals and gets insanely busy during special events like Halloween.

HOUSE SPECIALTIES Shepherd's pie; fish-and-chips; Guinness beef stew; bangers and mash; Dingle seafood pie; Irish coffee.

ENTERTAINMENT AND AMENITIES Singer/guitarist in the bar.

SUMMARY AND COMMENTS The food is modest, but the entertainment is fun and the beer is cold; brew fans can happily explore a five-sample flight of international ales as they rest from the park. Add to that the fact that this is one of only two full-service spots in Universal Studios Florida, and the average pub fare starts to look a bit more attractive.

The fish-and-chips, which come wrapped in "newspaper," are about the same as those served in The Wizarding World. The Scotch egg was a dry disappointment, and the shepherd's pie was bland, but the potato-leek soup is good, and the fried potato/onion "web" is addictive. For entrées, burgers, sandwiches, salads, and Guinness stew are safe choices.

Galaxy Bowl ★★

AMERICAN INEXPENSIVE QUALITY ★★½ VALUE ★★½

Cabana Bay Beach Resort; ☎ 407-503-4000

Customers Park guests. **Reservations** Accepted via Open Table. **When to go** Early afternoon or late evening. **Entrée range** $6–$10. **Service rating ★★**. **Friendliness rating ★★★**. **Parking** $20 for self-parking at hotel. **Bar** Full service. **Wine selection** Limited. **Dress** Casual. **Disabled access** Good. **Hours** Daily, 11 a.m.–10 p.m.

SETTING AND ATMOSPHERE Galaxy Bowl, located on the second floor of the main Cabana Bay building directly above Starbucks, is the only full-service dining option inside the hotel. The 10-lane bowling alley is inspired by the Hollywood Star Lanes bowling alley, made famous in the film *The Big Lebowski*. The lanes are illuminated in trippy colors at night, and large projection screens broadcast sporting events.

HOUSE SPECIALTIES Chicken quesadillas, chicken wings, salads, sandwiches, hot dogs, burgers, and pizza.

ENTERTAINMENT AND AMENITIES Bowling costs $15 for adults, $9 for kids age 12 and under. Parties of one to three people get 1 hour of lane time; four to eight people get 90 minutes.

SUMMARY AND COMMENTS Galaxy Bowl has several tables where you can enjoy a meal, but you can also order snacks and drinks while taking in a game of bowling. When the wait for a lane grows long (as it often does on rainy days), ask for a table, and order drinks and appetizers until your turn arrives.

The limited menu offers fast-food selections similar to items served downstairs in the Bayliner Diner, and quality is about on par for greasy bowling-alley grub. Draft beer is served in pitchers, and the list of specialty drinks is nearly as long as the food menu. The 300, a 32-ounce mega-margarita made with blood oranges, probably won't help your score much, but it will numb the embarrassment of those gutter balls. There are two Coke Freestyle machines at Galaxy Bowl for your Sonic Fill mugs.

Hard Rock Café ★★★

AMERICAN   MODERATE   QUALITY ★★★   VALUE ★★★

CityWalk; ☎ 407-351-7625

Customers Tourists. **Reservations** Priority seating. **When to go** Afternoon or evening. **Entrée range** $10–$35. **Service rating** ★★★. **Friendliness rating** ★★. **Parking** Universal Orlando garage. **Bar** Full service. **Wine selection** Moderate. **Dress** Casual. **Disabled access** Good. **Hours** Daily, 11 a.m.–midnight.

SETTING AND ATMOSPHERE This is the biggest Hard Rock Cafe in the world (or in the Universe, as they like to say in this part of town). Shaped like the Coliseum, the two-story dining room is a massive museum of rock art memorabilia. The circular center bar features a full-size pink 1959 Cadillac spinning overhead. If you need to be told that this is a noisy restaurant, you've never been to a Hard Rock Cafe before.

HOUSE SPECIALTIES Barbecue pork sandwich, charbroiled burgers, barbecued ribs, fajitas, New York strip steak, hot fudge brownie, and milk shakes.

ENTERTAINMENT AND AMENITIES Rock-and-roll records and memorabilia, the biggest such collection on display anywhere in the Hard Rock chain. Ask at the check-in podium about free guided tours of the restaurant; if you're lucky, you may get a glimpse of the VIP-only John Lennon room upstairs.

SUMMARY AND COMMENTS The best meals we've had here are when we order only appetizers or only desserts, plus drinks. The entrées are average, and you'd be hard-pressed to differentiate them from anything you'd get at, say, Margaritaville.

Hard Rock Cafe offers a 15% discount on food for Preferred and Premier Annual Pass holders before 5 p.m.; AAA and military discounts apply all day. Admission to the adjoining Hard Rock Live concert hall is separate from the restaurant, though you can sometimes order food from the venue's bar.

Islands Dining Room ★★★

PAN-ASIAN   MODERATE   QUALITY ★★★½   VALUE ★★★

Royal Pacific Resort; ☎ 407-503-DINE (3463)

Customers Hotel guests. **Reservations** Suggested for character dining and during holidays via Open Table. **When to go** Breakfast or character dinners. **Entrée range** Breakfast, $12–$17; dinner, $16–$30. **Service rating** ★★★. **Friendliness rating** ★★★. **Parking** Free self-parking at hotel with validation. **Bar** Full service. **Wine selection** Average. **Dress** Casual. **Disabled access** Good. **Hours** Monday–Friday, 7–11 a.m. and 5–10 p.m.; Saturday–Sunday, 7 a.m.–noon and 5–10 p.m.

SETTING AND ATMOSPHERE Pretty standard hotel dining room; big and open, and always spotless.

HOUSE SPECIALTIES Breakfast features waffles with mixed berries, Tahitian French toast *à l'orange,* and Hawaiian pancakes. Dinner options include family-style stir-fry, chicken wonton soup, seafood noodle pot, and Asian spice–rubbed rib eye.

ENTERTAINMENT AND AMENITIES Character dining is available on Monday, Wednesday, and Thursday, 6:30–9:30 p.m.

SUMMARY AND COMMENTS Breakfast here is a treat—the specialties are all tasty and (surprisingly) moderately priced. Dinner is good too, but with all the other restaurants around, especially if you're spending the day in the parks, we suggest having a hearty breakfast here and an evening meal elsewhere. The exception is if you have kids who want to dine with the characters, who appear here three nights a week at no extra charge; children also get their own special dining area with downsized tables and a finger food buffet.

Jake's American Bar ★★★

AMERICAN MODERATE QUALITY ★★★ VALUE ★★½

Royal Pacific Resort; ☎ 407-503-3200

Customers Hotel guests. **Reservations** Accepted via Open Table. **When to go** Early or late evening. **Entrée range** $13–$35. **Service rating** ★★★. **Friendliness rating** ★★★. **Parking** Free self-parking at hotel with validation. **Bar** Full service. **Wine selection** Average. **Dress** Resort casual. **Disabled access** Good. **Hours** Daily, 11 a.m.–1:30 a.m.

SETTING AND ATMOSPHERE Run-of-the-mill hotel bar and restaurant with a vaguely 1930s Rick's Cafe feel. The menu explains the backstory of Captain Jake McNalley and his association with Royal Pacific Airways, continuing the overall theme of the resort, which centers on the golden age of travel.

HOUSE SPECIALTIES Homemade pretzel rods, charcuterie, kale salad, flatbreads, pork osso buco, rib eye and *frites,* grilled salmon, and grilled tomato-and-mozzarella sandwich.

ENTERTAINMENT AND AMENITIES Live music or karaoke Thursday–Sunday; character breakfast on Sunday.

SUMMARY AND COMMENTS This is a viable option if you're staying in the hotel, but as far as special meals go, this place doesn't deliver—and really isn't meant to. Jake's hosts the hotels' only weekly character breakfast every Sunday morning; see "Character Meals" on page 391 for details.

Beer lovers will want to check out the four-sample flights, as well as the four-course pairing parties held on select nights. Jake's serves a limited late-night menu 10 p.m.–1:30 a.m. and is usually the only restaurant at the resort serving hot food after midnight.

Jimmy Buffett's Margaritaville ★★★

CARIBBEAN/AMERICAN MODERATE QUALITY ★★★ VALUE ★★★

CityWalk; ☎ 407-224-2155

Customers Local and tourist Parrotheads. **Reservations** Accepted via Open Table. **When to go** Early evening. **Entrée range** $13–$24. **Service rating** ★★★. **Friendliness rating** ★★★★. **Parking** Universal Orlando garage. **Bar** Full service. **Wine selection** Minimal. **Dress** Flowered shirts and flip-flops. **Disabled access** Good. **Hours** Sunday–Thursday, 11 a.m.–1 a.m.; Friday–Saturday, 11 a.m.–2 a.m.

SETTING AND ATMOSPHERE A boisterous tribute to the chief Parrothead, this two-story dining space has many large-screen TVs playing Jimmy Buffett music videos and scenes from his live performances. The focal point is a volcano that erupts occasionally, spewing margarita mix instead of lava.

HOUSE SPECIALTIES Cheeseburgers and margaritas, of course; fish tacos; jambalaya; coconut shrimp; Key lime pie.

ENTERTAINMENT AND AMENITIES Live music on the porch early; band on inside stage late evening.

SUMMARY AND COMMENTS This is a relaxing, festive place, but it's not always worth the wait (especially if it's 2 hours, which it has been known to be). This place is wildly popular with Jimmy Buffett fans. The atmosphere, though, is like a taste of the beach without having to travel to the coast.

The food is a mix of Floridian and Caribbean, so expect lots of seafood and Jamaican seasoning. The food is good, but not good enough for non-Buffett fans to make a special trip. If the line for a table is outrageous, see if you can sidle up to the bar for a margarita and appetizers, which is just as much—if not more—fun than actually having a full meal. None of the entrées, including the cheeseburger, will make you think that you're in paradise, but fans don't seem to care.

The Kitchen ★★★½

AMERICAN   MODERATE   QUALITY ★★★   VALUE ★★★

Hard Rock Hotel; ☎ 407-503-DINE (3463)

Customers Tourists. **Reservations** Recommended via Open Table. **When to go** Breakfast or dinner. **Entrée range** $15–$37. **Service rating ★★**. **Friendliness rating ★★★★. Parking** $5 valet or free self-parking at hotel with validation. **Bar** Full service. **Wine selection** Good. **Dress** Casual. **Disabled access** Good. **Hours** Daily, 7 a.m.–11 p.m.

SETTING AND ATMOSPHERE With the appearance of a spacious kitchen in a rock megastar's mansion, The Kitchen's walls are adorned with culinary-themed memorabilia from the Hard Rock Hotel's many celebrity guests. A colorful "kids' crib" adorned with beanbag chairs and TVs allows the adults to eat in peace.

HOUSE SPECIALTIES Breakfast choices include eggs Benedict, spinach-and-sausage frittata, and custom omelets. The lunch menu has salads, burgers, flatbreads, three-cheese mac and cheese, and chicken pot pie. At dinner, seared ahi tuna, crab cakes, shrimp tacos, and boneless short ribs are served. A gluten-free menu is available.

ENTERTAINMENT AND AMENITIES Visiting rock stars often perform cooking demonstrations of their favorite dishes at the Chef's Table, so call ahead to see if any rock stars will be in the kitchen—you may find yourself having dinner with Joan Jett or Bob Seger. Character dining is offered Saturday, 6–9 p.m., and a magician performs table-side on Friday, 6–9 p.m. On Tuesday and Thursday, Kids Can Cook lets kids make their own pizzas or quesadillas 5–7 p.m. For adults, Re-Wine on Monday and Wednesday offers $35 flights and discounted bottles.

SUMMARY AND COMMENTS Though expensive, the food is actually quite good, and the setting is pretty fun. The 10-ounce Angus beef Kitchen Burger will set you back about $18, but the regular version is just as tasty and less expensive. Brave and/or crazy souls can take part in the Kitchen Sink Challenge, which consists of eating The Kitchen burger, a side of fries, a fried pickle, and the humongous Kitchen Sink cake within a 30-minute time limit. If dinner is a little out of your price range but you still want the experience, visit at lunchtime or go for the $19.50 breakfast buffet ($10 for kids), which includes a host of fresh, yummy selections and an omelet station; for $31.50, adults can upgrade to unlimited Bloody Marys and mimosas, always a smart choice before walking around a hot theme park all day.

Leaky Cauldron ★★★½

BRITISH **INEXPENSIVE** **QUALITY ★★★½** **VALUE ★★★★**

Universal Studios/The Wizarding World of Harry Potter–Diagon Alley;
☎ 407-224-4012

Customers Park guests. **Reservations** Breakfast only. **When to go** Early or late.
Entrée range $9–$20. **Service rating ★★★. Friendliness rating ★★★★. Parking**
Universal Orlando garage. **Bar** Beer and wine. **Wine selection** Limited. **Dress** Casual.
Disabled access Good. **Hours** Daily, park opening–10:30 a.m. and 11 a.m.–park closing.

SETTING AND ATMOSPHERE Modeled after the Leaky Cauldron in the Harry
Potter books and films, this table-service restaurant is the flagship diner of
Diagon Alley. A haunt of wizards, Leaky Cauldron is located outside The
Wizarding World on Charing Cross Road in the novels and movies, but in
the Universal Studios version it is located inside Diagon Alley. (You can find
a non-opening replica of the pub door from the original film just outside
Diagon Alley, tucked between the bookstore and record shop.) Meals are
ordered and drinks received at a counter; then you are seated with a candle, which helps servers deliver food directly to your table.

HOUSE SPECIALTIES Breakfast specialties include English bacon, black
pudding, baked beans, and grilled tomato; pancakes with bacon; and an
egg, leek, and mushroom pasty with breakfast potatoes. Lunch and dinner
selections feature bangers and mash, cottage pie, toad-in-the-hole, Guinness stew, fish-and-chips, shepherd's pie, and a ploughman's platter for
two of Scotch eggs and imported cheeses.

SUMMARY AND COMMENTS The Leaky Cauldron serves hearty British pub
fare similar to that of the Three Broomsticks but with even more authentically Anglo favorites. You can reserve breakfast by booking through
your travel agent or the ticket desk at your Universal resort hotel; walk-
ins for day guests are also usually available. The morning menu costs $16
for adults ($12.39 for kids) with a small drink and has a similar mix of
American and British breakfast foods to Three Broomsticks. The breakfast is fair at best; the blood sausage and beans aren't bad if you have a
taste for them, but the scrambled eggs are awful, and the oatmeal outrageously overpriced, making the quichelike mushroom pasty your best
bet. Before you ask, yes, you can have hot or cold Butterbeer for breakfast. If you want to eat breakfast here, do it as late in the morning as possible; your early-entry time is better spent riding Harry Potter and the
Escape from Gringotts.

The star of the lunch and dinner menu is the ploughman's platter for two,
with an array of gloriously stinky imported cheeses. The bangers are also
bang on, whether ordered with mash, in a sandwich, or (best of all) baked
into a toad-in-the-hole with Yorkshire pudding. The fish-and-chips are the
same as those served in Hogsmeade, as is the soup and salad (which isn't
vegan). The fisherman's pie is extremely salty, as is the Guinness stew, which
comes served in a nearly inedible bread bowl. Top off your meal with chocolate potted cream or sticky toffee pudding for dessert. Children's menu
items include macaroni and cheese, fish-and-chips, and mini meat pies (for
your budding *Sweeney Todd* enthusiast).

Leaky Cauldron can be overwhelmed by Diagon Alley crowds. To avoid
long waits, eat early or late.

Lombard's Seafood Grille ★★★

SEAFOOD   MODERATE   QUALITY ★★★½   VALUE ★★★

Universal Studios/San Francisco; ☎ 407-224-6401

Customers Park guests. **Reservations** Recommended via NexTable. **When to go** Anytime. **Entrée range** $13–$20. **Service rating** ★★★. **Friendliness rating** ★★★. **Parking** Universal Orlando garage. **Bar** Full service. **Wine selection** Good. **Dress** Casual. **Disabled access** Good. **Hours** Daily, 11:30 a.m.–2 hours before park closing or park closing, depending on park attendance. Call to verify hours; there is no set schedule.

SETTING AND ATMOSPHERE Situated on the park's main lagoon, Lombard's looks like a converted wharf-side warehouse. The centerpiece of the brick-walled room is a huge aquarium with bubble glass windows. A fish-sculpture fountain greets guests, and private dining rooms upstairs have balconies that overlook the park.

HOUSE SPECIALTIES Stuffed portobello mushrooms, crab-cake sandwich, shrimp mac and cheese, lobster roll, fried shrimp, beef medallions, and fresh fish selections.

SUMMARY AND COMMENTS Universal Studios Florida's San Francisco–inspired seafood restaurant, where the emphasis is on deep-fried favorites and daily fresh fish specials. There are arguably better food options in the park, but as one of only two full-service restaurants inside USF, it's your best choice for a quiet meal off your feet.

On nights when *Universal's Cinematic Spectacular* is being shown (see page 219), prix fixe dinner packages are available at Lombard's for $45 adults, $13 kids (tax and gratuity included; park admission required). Diners choose an appetizer and entrée from a limited menu (no crab or lobster, but you can get mahimahi) and later attend a dessert reception on the deck behind the restaurant with an up close view of the *Cinematic Spectacular*—sometimes drenchingly so, depending on which way the wind blows. Dinner seating starts at 4 p.m., and the dessert party starts 1 hour prior to showtime. After you purchase your dinner package online at **universalorlando.com,** you must call ☎ 407-224-7554 at least 24 hours before arrival to confirm your reservation.

With two floors of seating, it's generally easy to get a table, even during the busier times.

Mama Della's ★★★★

ITALIAN   EXPENSIVE   QUALITY ★★★★   VALUE ★★★½

Portofino Bay Hotel; ☎ 407-503-DINE (3463)

Customers Hotel guests. **Reservations** Recommended via Open Table. **When to go** Dinner. **Entrée range** $21–$38. **Service rating** ★★★★. **Friendliness rating** ★★★★. **Parking** $5 valet or free self-parking at hotel with validation. **Bar** Full service. **Wine selection** Good. **Dress** Nice casual. **Disabled access** Good. **Hours** Daily, 5:30–10 p.m.

SETTING AND ATMOSPHERE Just like being in the dining room of a Tuscan home, with hardwood floors, provincial wallpaper, and wooden furniture. Check out the collection of chicken-themed tchotchkes adorning the walls.

HOUSE SPECIALTIES Veal saltimbocca, pan-seared sea bass, grilled lamb chops with rigatoni, and lasagna.

ENTERTAINMENT AND AMENITIES Strolling musicians perform Italian American standards on select nights.

SUMMARY AND COMMENTS This restaurant falls on the fancy scale somewhere between Bice and Trattoria del Porto. Traditional Italian food is served in a comfortable atmosphere conducive to a special meal but not quite as extravagant as its lavish neighbor, Bice. If you want food (almost) as tasty but for (a bit) less dough, Mama Della's is a great choice.

Mythos ★★★½

STEAK/SEAFOOD   MODERATE   QUALITY ★★★½   VALUE ★★★★

Islands of Adventure/The Lost Continent; ☎ 407-224-4012

Customers Park guests. **Reservations** Recommended via NexTable. **When to go** Early evening. **Entrée range** $11–$20. **Service rating ★★★. Friendliness rating ★★★. Parking** Universal Orlando garage. **Bar** Full service. **Wine selection** Good. **Dress** Casual. **Disabled access** Good. **Hours** Daily, 11:30 a.m.–3 p.m. or park closing; call ahead for closing time.

SETTING AND ATMOSPHERE A grottolike atmosphere suggests that you're eating in a cave. Large picture windows, framed by water cascading down from waterfalls on top of the restaurant, look out over the central lagoon to The Incredible Hulk Coaster. You can time your meal by coaster launchings.

HOUSE SPECIALTIES Tempura shrimp sushi, roast-beef panini, crab-cake sliders, blackened fish tacos, Mediterranean chicken-salad wrap, meat loaf, seared salmon or mahimahi, pad Thai, and risotto of the day.

SUMMARY AND COMMENTS Outside the restaurant is a sign proclaiming that Mythos was voted BEST THEME PARK RESTAURANT. Read the fine print and you'll notice that the voting happened more than five years ago. This was originally the park's one stab at fine dining, but things are now more casual, much to the chagrin of those who remember the whole roasted lobster, chicken Oscar, and blueberry pork chop.

Nothing stands out as either great or terrible. The food is well above average for theme park eats, and the setting provides a pleasant retreat. Your best bets among the entrées are the mushroom meat loaf, seared mahimahi, or daily risotto. Our usual advice in a situation such as this is to stick to appetizers (the tempura sushi is a cult favorite) and drinks, a less expensive option than a full meal with entrée. Regarding price, Mythos is generally less expensive than most Disney theme park sit-down restaurants. Make your reservation early if you want to dine here on a busy day.

During the off-season, Mythos may close before dinnertime, as this reader discovered:

We were disappointed to find out that Mythos closed at 5 when the park closed at 7 p.m.

NBC Sports Grill & Brew ★★

AMERICAN   MODERATE   QUALITY ★★★   VALUE ★★

CityWalk; ☎ 407-224-2353

Customers Sports fans. **Reservations** Not accepted. **When to go** Anytime. **Entrée range** $12.99–$44.99. **Service rating ★★. Friendliness rating ★★. Parking** Universal Orlando garage. **Bar** Full service; more than 100 beers. **Wine selection** Modest. **Dress** Casual. **Disabled access** Good. **Hours** Daily, noon–1 a.m.

SETTING AND ATMOSPHERE NBC Sports Grill & Brew opened in October 2015 on the site of the former NASCAR Sports Grille. The new venue features 90 big-screen high-definition TVs and more than 100 beers—including two special drafts available only here. The open design echoes a luxury skybox in a sports stadium (only on an enormous scale), and the central show kitchen sports a signature open-flame kettle grill. The exterior is distinguished by supersize video screens that broadcast games to all of CityWalk, as well as an outdoor beer garden in which to relax.

HOUSE SPECIALTIES Burgers, steaks, and crab Scotch eggs.

SUMMARY AND COMMENTS With the exception of the beer list, the restaurant is similar to its predecessor, NASCAR Sports Grille, with a more modern feel and diverse focus.

Orchid Court Lounge & Sushi Bar ★★★

AMERICAN/SUSHI   MODERATE   QUALITY ★★★   VALUE ★★

Royal Pacific Resort; ☎ 407-503-3000

Customers Hotel guests. **Reservations** Not accepted. **When to go** Early or late evening. **Entrée range** $12–$57. **Service rating ★★★**. **Friendliness rating ★★★**. **Parking** Free self-parking at hotel with validation. **Bar** Full service. **Wine selection** Average, but an excellent sake selection. **Dress** Resort casual. **Disabled access** Good. **Hours** Monday–Friday, 6–11 a.m.; Saturday–Sunday, 6 a.m.–noon. Lounge: Daily, noon–midnight. Sushi: 5–11 p.m.

SETTING AND ATMOSPHERE Located on the lobby level of the Royal Pacific Resort with gorgeous views of the pool and central reflecting fountain, the Orchid Court Lounge is decorated with inviting hand-carved Balinese furniture and flowering orchids. At one end of the lounge, you'll find a bar with coffee and liquor; at the other end, a traditional sushi bar with see-through seafood cases. In between, clusters of couches and armchairs separated by wooden screens form intimate seating areas.

HOUSE SPECIALTIES For breakfast, Starbucks coffee, cinnamon buns, pastries, cereal, and yogurt. The lounge menu has burgers, Asian chicken salad, a tomato-mozzarella sandwich, spring rolls, Thai lettuce wraps, and tuna tartare. The sushi bar offers miso soup, seaweed salad, edamame, tuna *tataki, nigiri,* sashimi, maki rolls, and cold and warm sake.

SUMMARY AND COMMENTS The Orchid Court Lounge almost exclusively caters to guests staying at the Royal Pacific Resort. In the morning, it's a quick-service stop for Starbucks coffee and Continental breakfast pastries. From noon to midnight, it's a bar and lounge with free Wi-Fi and a brief "bytes" menu that incongruously features bacon cheeseburgers and grilled mozzarella sandwiches alongside orange-ginger chicken and rice paper rolls. Finally, in the evenings, the sushi chefs arrive, preparing fishy fare that falls (in terms of quality and creativity) somewhere between The Cowfish and Fusion Bistro at CityWalk. Most of their rolls are adequate executions of Japanese American standards—California, spicy tuna, spider, and volcano—though a couple, such as the Tropical, use more unusual ingredients such as kiwi and mango. This is the only place on Universal property to order some expert items such as Uni (sea urchin), but be warned: They are formerly frozen and outrageously expensive. Ordering à la carte can quickly add up, but the combinations aren't cheap either: A

25-piece sashimi combo will set you back more than $50, and a Tahitian longboat for four is more than $100.

The Palm ★★★★

STEAK VERY EXPENSIVE QUALITY ★★★★ VALUE ★★

Hard Rock Hotel; ☎ 407-503-7256

Customers Tourists. **Reservations** Recommended via Open Table. **When to go** Dinner. **Entrée range** $22.50–$79. **Service rating** ★★★. **Friendliness rating** ★★★. **Parking** Free valet at hotel with validation. **Bar** Full service. **Wine selection** Very good. **Dress** Resort, business casual, smart casual; no sleeveless men's shirts. **Disabled access** Good. **Hours** Sunday–Monday, 5–9 p.m.; Tuesday–Saturday, 5–10 p.m.

SETTING AND ATMOSPHERE Despite the celebrity caricatures drawn on the wall, the restaurant exudes sophistication due to the dark woods and white tablecloths. The chain's flagship location is in New York, and the decor reflects this. Waiters wear long, white aprons.

HOUSE SPECIALTIES New York strip, porterhouse, veal parmigiana, whole live lobster, Chilean sea bass with corn relish, Atlantic salmon, and iceberg lettuce wedge salad.

SUMMARY AND COMMENTS The crowd here can get noisy, so The Palm may not be the best place for a romantic night out. However, if you're looking to celebrate with friends or family, this is a good, if very expensive, choice. Stick with the signature dishes: The steaks are done well, and the ginormous lobsters are impeccably prepared, while some of the other dishes could be better. The side dishes are meant for sharing, and the creamed spinach and Brussels sprouts are justly famous. If you want a taste of The Palm on a hamburger budget, drop by the bar during PrimeTime (Sunday–Friday, 5–7 p.m.) for half-priced appetizers like steak sliders and lobster tempura.

Pat O'Brien's Orlando ★★★

CAJUN INEXPENSIVE QUALITY ★★★½ VALUE ★★★½

CityWalk; ☎ 407-224-2106

Customers Tourists. **Reservations** Accepted via NexTable. **When to go** Anytime. **Entrée range** $10–$18. **Service rating** ★★. **Friendliness rating** ★★★. **Parking** Universal Orlando garage. **Bar** Full service. **Wine selection** Modest. **Dress** Casual. **Disabled access** Good. **Hours** Sunday–Thursday, 3–10 p.m.; Friday–Saturday, 3–11 p.m.; bar open until 2 a.m. nightly.

SETTING AND ATMOSPHERE A fairly faithful rendition of the original Pat O'Brien's in New Orleans, from the redbrick facade to the fire-and-water fountain in the courtyard. The outdoor dining area is the most pleasant place to eat. Inside areas include a noisy "locals" bar and a dueling piano bar, featuring some of Orlando's most talented musicians 5 p.m.–2 a.m. nightly. A cover charge is levied after 9 p.m.

HOUSE SPECIALTIES Shrimp gumbo, jambalaya, muffuletta, and red beans and rice.

SUMMARY AND COMMENTS The food is surprisingly good and surprisingly affordable. Be careful about ordering a Hurricane, the restaurant's signature drink. Not only is it deceptively potent, but you are also automatically charged for the souvenir glass, and if you don't want it, you must turn it in at the bar for a refund.

Red Oven Pizza Bakery ★★★½

ITALIAN   INEXPENSIVE   QUALITY ★★★½   VALUE ★★★★½

CityWalk; ☎ 407-224-4233

Customers Tourists. **Reservations** Not accepted. **When to go** Anytime. **Entrée range** $9–$14. **Service rating** ★★. **Friendliness rating** ★★★. **Parking** Universal Orlando garage. **Bar** Wine and beer only. **Wine selection** Limited. **Dress** Casual. **Disabled access** Good. **Hours** Daily, 11 a.m.–2 a.m.

SETTING AND ATMOSPHERE Hardwood beams, colorful tile, and gleaming countertops make Red Oven look unexpectedly upscale for an open-air pizza joint. You can pose for photos on the red scooter parked out front.

HOUSE SPECIALTIES White and red pizza with gourmet toppings, salads, and imported beer and wine.

SUMMARY AND COMMENTS Only whole pies, not slices, can be ordered at Red Oven. However, with a reasonable price of only $12–$14 per pizza, two people can eat very cheaply. The five white and five red Neapolitan-style artisan pies are made with San Marzano tomatoes, organic extra-virgin olive oil, buffalo mozzarella, fine-ground "00" flour, and filtered water, and then baked in a 900°F oven while you watch. Salads and a limited selection of beer and wine are available, with free refills on soda.

After placing your food order and receiving your drinks, a server will seat you and bring your order once it's ready. Plenty of covered outdoor seating is available, which is a welcome relief from the Florida sun (and rain). Because of its location in the main hub of CityWalk, Red Oven is a great place to get a bite to eat and people-watch. Red Oven Pizza can also be delivered to the freestanding bars along the CityWalk waterfront.

Three Broomsticks ★★★

BRITISH   MODERATE   QUALITY ★★★½   VALUE ★★★

Islands of Adventure/The Wizarding World of Harry Potter–Hogsmeade; ☎ 407-224-4012

Customers Park guests. **Reservations** Breakfast only. **When to go** Early or late. **Entrée range** $8–$14. **Service rating** ★★★. **Friendliness rating** ★★★. **Parking** Universal Orlando garage. **Bar** Beer and wine only. **Wine selection** Limited. **Dress** Casual. **Disabled access** Good. **Hours** Daily, park opening–10:30 a.m. and 11 a.m.–park closing.

SETTING AND ATMOSPHERE Modeled after the Three Broomsticks inn in the Harry Potter books and films, this "buffeteria" is the most visually interesting eatery at Islands of Adventure, with open beams, dark furniture, and the contiguous Hog's Head pub. The detail inside is amazing, and it's one of the best-themed restaurants we've seen. Alfresco dining is behind the restaurant.

HOUSE SPECIALTIES Breakfast items include English bacon, black pudding, baked beans, and grilled tomato; pancakes with bacon; and porridge with fruit. Lunch and dinner offerings are fish-and-chips, rotisserie chicken, smoked spareribs, shepherd's pie, Cornish pasty, turkey legs, and nonalcoholic Butterbeer. Children's menu items include chicken, macaroni and cheese, fish-and-chips, and chicken fingers.

SUMMARY AND COMMENTS Because it was converted from a larger restaurant during The Wizarding World development, quite a number of seats were sacrificed to achieve the desired look. The menu is very similar to Thunder Falls Terrace in Jurassic Park, with which it shares the title of best counter-service restaurant in Islands of Adventure. The ribs or chicken, or the combo plate, are your best bets, though the tartar sauce is a tasty side to the fish-and-chips (made from fresh cod). As the only dining option in Hogsmeade, the Three Broomsticks stays busy all day. Like the Leaky Cauldron, you can reserve breakfast at Three Broomsticks by booking through your travel agent or the ticket desk at your Universal resort hotel, and walk-ins for day guests are also usually available, but there are probably better uses of your morning touring time.

Trattoria del Porto ★★★

ITALIAN MODERATE QUALITY ★★★ VALUE ★★

Portofino Bay Hotel; ☎ 407-503-DINE (3463)

Customers Hotel guests. **Reservations** Suggested for dinner via Open Table. **When to go** Breakfast or dinner. **Entrée range** Breakfast, $12–$17; dinner, $18–$34. **Service rating ★★★. Friendliness rating ★★★. Parking** $5 valet or free self-parking at hotel with validation. **Bar** Full service. **Wine selection** Average. **Dress** Resort casual. **Disabled access** Good. **Hours** Tuesday–Wednesday, 7–11 a.m.; Thursday–Monday, 7–11 a.m. and 5:30–10:30 p.m.

SETTING AND ATMOSPHERE Like a boisterous down-home Italian kitchen. A play area lets kids watch cartoons while the grown-ups eat.

HOUSE SPECIALTIES Charred calamari, a 12-ounce New York strip, 10-ounce churrasco, shrimp and clam scampi, bone-in salmon steak, and pancetta-wrapped meat loaf.

ENTERTAINMENT AND AMENITIES Character dining is on Friday, 6:30–9:30 p.m.; face painter and balloon artists entertain on Thursday and Saturday, 6:30–9:30 p.m.

SUMMARY AND COMMENTS Where Mama Della's succeeds in not feeling like a hotel restaurant, Trattoria del Porto does not. The food is perfectly fine and moderately priced (relatively speaking). Fridays and Saturdays are interactive Pasta Cucina nights, where you can create your own entrée from a variety of noodles and sauces ($26 adults, $12 kids). Omelets at breakfast can set you back more than $14, so opt instead for the buffet offered most mornings.

Vivo Italian Kitchen ★★★★

ITALIAN MODERATE QUALITY ★★★★ VALUE ★★★★½

CityWalk; ☎ 407-224-2318

Customers Locals and tourists. **Reservations** Accepted via NexTable. **When to go** Lunch or dinner. **Entrée range** $10–$27. **Service rating ★★★. Friendliness rating ★★★. Parking** Universal Orlando garage. **Bar** Full service. **Wine selection** Good. **Dress** Casual. **Disabled access** Good. **Hours** Daily, 11 a.m.–11 p.m.

SETTING AND ATMOSPHERE Sleek and contemporary without being stuffy, Vivo brings a touch of casual class to CityWalk's central crossroads. There are outdoor tables (with embedded chessboards) and a well-lit bar, along with plush semicircular booths surrounded by sinuous steel cages. But the real action is around the open kitchen; see if you can snag a seat at the food bar in front of the "tree" where fresh pasta is hung.

HOUSE SPECIALTIES Freshly made pasta, homemade mozzarella, pizza, salads, lasagna, chicken Marsala, and risotto.

SUMMARY AND COMMENTS Vivo's menu is filled with comfortingly familiar dishes—such as chicken piccata, veal parmigiana, spinach cannelloni, and linguine and clams—presented without unnecessary postmodern flourishes, just classic recipes prepared à la minute with the freshest ingredients. Best of all, you can dine here for half the price of Bice, Mama Della's, or one of Disney's Signature restaurants.

Start by ordering an enormous house-made meatball, hand-pulled mozzarella, or beet-and-Gorgonzola salad. Standout entrées include linguine (when razor clams are in season), black squid ink pasta with seafood, risotto with short ribs, and pear-stuffed *fiocchetti* in brown butter. Save room for warm orange-walnut cake; the recipe came directly from chef Steven Jayson's grandmother. On a cost/quality basis, this may be the best table-service meal you'll have on Universal property.

Wantilan Luau ★★★½

HAWAIIAN MODERATE QUALITY ★★★ VALUE ★★★

Royal Pacific Resort; ☎ 407-503-DINE (3463)

Customers Tourists. **Reservations** Required via Open Table. **When to go** Dinner only. **Entrée range** Buffet: $63 adults, $35 children ages 3–11. (Prices include gratuity for everyone, and mai tais, wine, and beer for guests age 21 and older.) **Service rating** ★★★. **Friendliness rating** ★★★★. **Parking** Free valet or free self-parking at hotel with validation. **Bar** Mai tais, wine, and beer available. **Wine selection** Limited. **Dress** Flowered shirts, beachy casual. **Disabled access** Average. **Hours** Saturday night, year-round; Tuesday night, seasonally; seating begins at 6 p.m., with registration starting 30 minutes before.

SETTING AND ATMOSPHERE Typical luau setting with tiki torches and wooden tables.

HOUSE SPECIALTIES Buffet includes pit-roasted suckling pig with spiced rum–soaked pineapple purée; Pacific catch of the day; Hawaiian chicken teriyaki; fire-grilled beef with mushrooms; and chicken fingers, mac and cheese, PB&J, and pizza for kids. Dessert buffet has johnnycakes and pineapple upside-down cake.

ENTERTAINMENT AND AMENITIES Polynesian dancing, storytelling, hula dancers, and live music.

SUMMARY AND COMMENTS This is a fun diversion and a change of scenery from the other restaurants on Universal property. Though dinner is a bit expensive, it's the best food of any luau show in the area, and the entertainment is more energetic than *Disney's Spirit of Aloha Dinner Show.* Priority Seating reserves you a table near the front for an extra $7 per adult ($5 per kid), but either way the check-in process can take a while.

INDEX

Unofficial Guide Reader's Survey

If you'd like to express your opinion about traveling in Central Florida or this guidebook, complete the following survey and mail it to:

> Unofficial Guide Reader's Survey
> 2204 First Ave. S, Ste. 102
> Birmingham, AL 35233

Inclusive dates of your visit: _____

Members of your party:

	Person 1	Person 2	Person 3	Person 4	Person 5
Gender:	M F	M F	M F	M F	M F

Age: _____

How many times have you been to Central Florida? _____
On your most recent trip, where did you stay?   _____

Concerning your accommodations, on a scale of 100 as best and 0 as worst, how would you rate:

The quality of your room? _____   The value of your room? _____

The quietness of your room? _____   Check-in/checkout efficiency? _____

Shuttle service to the airport? _____   Swimming pool facilities? _____

Did you rent a car? _____   From whom? _____

Concerning your rental car, on a scale of 100 as best and 0 as worst, how would you rate:

Pickup-processing efficiency?____   Return processing efficiency?___

Condition of the car?_____   Cleanliness of the car?_____

Airport shuttle efficiency?_____

Concerning your dining experiences:

Estimate your meals in restaurants per day?   _____
Approximately how much did your party spend on meals per day?
_____

Favorite restaurants in Central Florida: _____
_____

Did you buy this guide before leaving? ____While on your trip?____

How did you hear about this guide? (check all that apply)

❑ Loaned or recommended by a friend   ❑ Radio or TV
❑ Newspaper or magazine   ❑ Bookstore salesperson
❑ Just picked it out on my own   ❑ Library
❑ Internet

What other guidebooks did you use on this trip? _____

_____

_____

On a scale of 100 as best and 0 as worst, how would you rate them?

_____

_____

Using the same scale, how would you rate the *Unofficial Guide*(s)?

_____

Are Unofficial Guides readily available at bookstores in your area? _____

Have you used other Unofficial Guides? _____

Which one(s)? _____

_____

Comments about your Central Florida trip or The Unofficial Guide(s):

_____

_____

_____

_____

_____

_____

_____

_____

_____

_____

_____

_____

_____

_____

_____

_____

_____

_____

_____